A/4   (1992)   30

                                        20

                                    9532

                                        P

                                        &

Journeyman in Jerusalem

Self portrait, Jerusalem, 1939.

Journeyman in Jerusalem

Memories and Letters, 1933–1947

Raphael Patai

University of Utah Press
Salt Lake City

∞This symbol indicates books printed on paper that meets the minimum requirements of American National Standard for Information Services—Permanence of Paper for Printed Library Materials, ANSI A39.38–1984.

Library of Congress Cataloging-in-Publication Data

Patai, Raphael, 1910–
  Journeyman in Jerusalem: memories and letters, 1933–1947 /
Raphael Patai.
    p.   cm.
  Includes index.
  ISBN 0-87480-383-7
  1. Patai, Raphael, 1910–   2. Jews—Jerusalem—Biography.
3. Jewish scholars—Jerusalem—Biography.   4. Folklorists—
Jerusalem—Biography.   5. Jerusalem—Biography.   6. Patai, Raphael,
1910–   —Correspondence.   I. Title.
DS109.86.P39A3   1992
956.94'4204'092—dc20   91-51095
                                                                    CIP

To my daughters
Ofra and Daphne
the dearest gifts
I brought out of
Jerusalem

Contents

Preface

November 22, 1985

Today is my seventy-fifth birthday. To have lived this long in good physical and mental health is a privilege not granted to many even in this age of great medical achievements. It was certainly not allotted to any of my ancestors in the paternal line of whom I know, but it seems to have been an heirloom passed on to me by my mother, who lived to be ninety, whose sister lived to be eighty-six, and whose parents were both in their eighties when they perished in the Budapest ghetto into which the German and Hungarian Nazis crowded the city's Jews in 1944.

My seventy-fifth birthday is, I feel, an appropriate moment to begin writing the second volume of my reminiscences which, as I decided while working on the first, will deal with the fifteen years I spent in Jerusalem, from 1933 to 1947, from the age of twenty-two to thirty-seven. Those years were, I believe, more formative for me than any other period in my life. My first twenty-two years, in Budapest, I consider years of apprenticeship, laying the foundations of everything I was to do and to become thereafter, down to this very day. But it was during the subsequent fifteen years, in Jerusalem, that my life structure took shape.

In the new Jerusalem, of which I rapidly became part after my arrival there in the spring of 1933, I was no longer an apprentice, I was "Dr. Patai," a promising young scholar. While I neither felt that I was a master in my chosen fields of specialization nor was considered such by those who came to know me, I certainly occupied an intermediary place between apprenticeship and mastership. I was a journeyman, who still had much to learn, but who already had a modest store of knowledge on which he could draw.

As I begin to think back on my Jerusalem years, memories come flooding in waves, overlapping and crisscrossing, chasing and replacing one another, in a confused and confusing disarray. The ordering principle of temporal sequence is entirely lacking in these memory fragments: even before putting pen to paper I know that I shall have quite a job in deciding what came first and what later in trying to organize the scenes, incidents, and events that sweep for a moment into conscious memory. Yet I feel that such an organization is important if I want—as I do—to have these memory fragments serve as a basis for tracing the development I believe I underwent in those crucial years of my late youth and early manhood. But I suspect I shall not be able to unroll everything in strict chronological order and shall instead have to allow topical presentation to disrupt the sequential story of that formative phase of my life that began more than half a century ago, within thy gates, O Jerusalem!

November 22, 1991

The writing of this volume took considerably more time than I expected when, six years ago, I embarked upon it. The delay was due mostly to all kinds of other literary projects that were more urgent or more attractive; the present book was often shoved onto the back burner and had to await its turn to be pulled forward again. But, at long last, it is completed.

The story of the fifteen years of my life told in this volume is inseparable from that of the *yishuv*, the Jewish community of Palestine, in one of its most turbulent eras, and from that of European Jewry in the most tragic period of its history. It was during those fifteen years that the tiny quasi-utopian society that the Jews of Palestine constituted in 1933 developed into the still small but strong and self-reliant nation-in-the-making it was in 1947, ready to take up arms for its independence in the face of overwhelming odds. And it was during the same fifteen years that the culturally rich millennial history of European Jewry, which to that point had constituted the center of the entire Jewish diaspora, came to an unbelievably horrible end. Nevertheless, in telling the story of my own life in those years, I have made only minimal use of external historical sources and have tried instead to tell what I myself, living in the very midst of the rushing events, knew about them and to present evidence contained in the hundreds of letters exchanged among members of my family in those years. Hence, the rise of Nazism, the Armageddon of World War II, the Holocaust, the British whittling down of the Palestine Mandate, the obscene indifference of the Allied powers to the fate of the Jews, and the intensifying struggle of the *yishuv* for its survival—all events that cast their shadow over us and touched our lives more than we knew, yet seemed to remain curiously peripheral in relation to our personal problems and endeavors—play only a minor part in the story told in this book.

This story is based primarily on two types of private sources very disparate in nature: one is the voluminous correspondence among members of my family, the other—my memory. As soon as I started working on the book, it became clear that these two types of sources were not only disparate but also incongruous. In fact, they presented me with two entirely different pictures of that period in my life.

As far as the letters are concerned, my years in Jerusalem from my arrival in May 1933 to my parents' immigration in the fall of 1939 are the most fully documented period in my life. Whenever my parents and I did not live in the same city—and most of that time we did not—I wrote them long letters twice a week on the average, and they wrote to me with the same frequency. In addition, my sister and brother and I exchanged letters. The correspondence was polyglot. I wrote to my father mostly in Hebrew, and he answered in Hebrew. To Mother and Évi and Guszti I wrote either in Hungarian or in German, and they answered in the same languages, although my brother wrote to me occasionally in Hebrew. From 1939 to 1947, when our whole family was "ingathered" in Palestine, letters were fewer; hence, regarding that period in my life I must rely mostly on my memory alone.

Contemporary documents, such as letters or diary entries, are both a help and a hindrance for the memoirist. They help, because they contain a contemporary record of events, acts, plans, feelings, hopes, fears, reactions— the stuff that memoirs are made of. In my case, the family letters amount to a detailed chronicle of the life of the family as a whole, and, beyond it, give a picture of the environment in Hungary and Palestine of which our disjointed family was part. The record is almost continuous, and the flow of correspondence is interrupted only for the duration of the relatively few months when all the five of us lived in Jerusalem, when intensive mutual visits made letters unnecessary. On the other hand, letters can be an impediment if the purpose of the memoirist is not to reconstruct things as they can be pieced together from contemporary documents, but rather to present what he remembers from the past, because he feels that the important things in life are those that he retained in memory, and their importance lies precisely in the manner in which he retained them.

The contemporary letters show members of a family group, separated by circumstance and dispersed during the first half of those fifteen years in Palestine, Hungary, France, and Switzerland, but united by a deep mutual concern about one another's well-being, physical safety, health, diet, sources of livelihood, career, and emotional attachments, as well as constant anxiety about what was happening in the *yishuv* and was about to happen to the Jews of Europe. Had I no other source but these letters upon which to base a reconstruction of my life in Jerusalem in those years, I would have to conclude that they were, by and large, tense, worrisome, unhappy years for me, times of struggle for a position, of financial stringency, of danger of Arab attacks on the roads and even in the city streets, of jealousy and machinations on the part of colleagues, of efforts to help my parents get out of Budapest in time before the spreading war trapped them in Hungary, followed by exertions to help my father find a job in Palestine that would provide him with at least a minimal livelihood, of fighting against debtors who did not pay what they owed to the press of which I was part-owner and against creditors the press was not able to satisfy, of the tragedy of the fatal illness of my sister's first husband, of antagonism on the part of my parents-in-law, of nagging worry about my father's deteriorating health, and more—in a word, a time of sustained stress and strain, with only a sprinkling of satisfaction provided by my scholarly work, public lecturing, the publication of my writings, love affairs, and my marriage and children.

If, on the other hand, I had only my memory to rely on, I would have reconstructed an entirely different picture, even one diametrically opposed to the former. The memories I have retained of those fifteen years in Jerusalem are of a period of happy achievement, of challenges successfully met, of the gratification I felt in becoming a member of the intellectual circles of the *yishuv*, of having made a contribution to the budding Palestinian Jewish scholarship, of having been able to make a living, albeit a modest one, almost exclusively with the literary and scholarly work I loved, of having been part of the great adventure of building the Jewish homeland and founding a nation in Palestine, and, on a more personal level, of having won and enjoyed the friendship of several women (each of whom meant a lot to me even if only temporarily), and then of marrying the girl I loved, who gave me two wonderful and adorable daughters, and with whom I lived happily until the very moment when I left Jerusalem for—as planned at the time—a year's stay in New York.

In the first volume of these memoirs I have given some of my thoughts on the nature and character of memory and on the puzzles with which it presents us—or me, at any rate—with its unaccountable selectivity. In contemplating the discrepancies sketched above between the contemporary evidence of letters written and received in the very midst of the unrolling events and the memories retained, not of the same events but of the period as a whole, I am again puzzled and prompted to reflect on how memory works and why it works as it does. It cannot be doubted that the letters present a true picture of what I did in those years and how I felt about the events that shaped or at least influenced my life, and of how my parents, my sister and brother, and (from 1940 on) my wife viewed and perceived those events. And yet, the different picture retained by my memory forces me to ask whether the essential truth of a situation is what one sees while one is in the midst of it, caught up by the daily flux of ups and downs, advances and setbacks, and worries about "what will the day bear?" as Job expressed it thousands of years ago—or whether the truth lies in the images one retains, often unawares, of one's past life, images that live on for decades somewhere on the threshold between the subconscious and the conscious, and then, when the time comes to put pen to paper, burst forth and proclaim: this is the way it was and this is the way you were.

Perhaps the answer to this troublesome query is that both pictures are true, but on different levels: the first on the actual, factual, temporal level, and the second on the deeper level of meaning, of the lasting significance that those same events, reactions, and emotions are destined to retain for the total span of one's life.

I wish to thank Dr. Joseph Schweitzer, head of the Budapest Rabbinical Seminary, for supplying vital statistics on Hungarian Jewish personalities mentioned in the letters that I was unable to find in printed sources; my brother Saul Patai, professor emeritus of the Hebrew University of Jerusalem, for having rendered me the same service in connection with individuals who lived in Palestine in the years covered by the letters; the Lucius N. Littauer Foundation and its president, William Lee Frost, for their generous support of the publication of this book; Professor Harris Lenowitz of the University of Utah for his active interest and help in the publication of this and two previous books by the University of Utah Press; and Ms. Nana Anderson, director of the University of Utah Press, and her courteous and highly competent staff.

A word is in order on the transliteration of the many Hebrew (and a few Arabic) names and words. In the original letters these names and words were spelled in many different ways. In order to facilitate identification I substituted for those variants the accurate spelling, which I also used in my own annotations to the letters. Thus, for "Chile" of the letters I substituted "Hile"; for "sejk" or "sheik" I put "shaykh," etc.

1

First Year in Jerusalem

Arrival

Two or three days after I passed my doctoral orals at Budapest University I took the train to Trieste and there boarded the S.S. *Vulcania*, a 24,000-ton luxury liner of the Lloyd Triestino. After a smooth voyage of five or six days we sailed into Haifa Bay.

I was the nominal leader of a group of Hungarian Jewish tourists who had signed up in response to announcements published in my father's monthly, *Mult és Jövő* (Past and Future), purchased the required round-trip tickets, and joined the tour, several of them with the unstated but nevertheless tacitly understood purpose of remaining in Palestine as "illegal" immigrants. If that indeed was in their minds, neither the Lloyd Triestino nor I knew anything about it officially; once we landed in Haifa and the British port authorities admitted them as tourists—the return ticket was considered sufficient proof of their intention to return—neither the Lloyd nor I had any further responsibility for them.

As group leader I was given a second-class cabin free of charge, while all the members of the group traveled third class, and I remember that an experienced official of the Lloyd cautioned me in a friendly way not to let the people see my "luxurious" accommodations lest they become dissatisfied with the poorer quarters allocated to them. I have retained no memory of the group or of the voyage. But I remember the first glimpse I caught of Mount Carmel, a moment of emotional impact: the first sight of the land that for so many years I had longed to see, where I wanted to spend the rest of my life.

I also recall that Father was at the port to meet me and my charges and that most members of our group were likewise met by friends or relatives who took them under their wings and spirited them away from the port area. After Father and I were free, he led me to a taxi that took us up to the top of Mount Carmel to the Hotel Teltsch where he was staying, which overlooked Haifa Bay.

The next thing I remember is sitting with Father, after dinner, on the terrace of the hotel. By that time night had fallen, but the streetlights that radiated in all directions below gave some indication of the lay of the city, as did the far fewer lights along the sweep of the bay that stretched toward the north in a large right-hand arc to the city of Akko. There, in the middle of the bay, surrounded by the pitch-black water, the *Vulcania* was anchored, its lights outlining the deck and its smokestack and endowing it with a fairyland quality.

Although I cannot remember what Father and I talked about on that balmy May night, I can assume that we discussed such practical questions as where my sister Évi (who had come to Palestine with Father some four weeks earlier) and I would live, what I should do about my studies, and how long Father intended to stay before returning to Hungary. We must have spent quite a long while sitting there on the terrace talking and planning, and most of the time my eyes were focused on the glittering outline of the *Vulcania* lying motionless in the bay. Suddenly, there were two long and deep blasts from the ship's siren (or is it foghorn?), and soon thereafter I noticed that its rows of light began to move toward the left, out from the bay, in the direction of the open sea. The progress of the ship seemed very slow, but nevertheless its lights soon grew smaller and dimmer, and before long it disappeared altogether, swallowed up by the night.

As the *Vulcania* vanished from sight, I was overtaken by a vague sense of desolation. I was sitting on the well-appointed terrace of what was at the time the finest hotel in Haifa; I was with my father, whose presence had always inspired me with a sense of safety; I was just about to embark on the greatest adventure of my life, to which I had looked forward with impatience and yearning for many years—yet I felt like a mutinous seaman put ashore on a desert island, watching as his ship, the one link with civilization, sailed away and left him marooned in a strange and frightening place. Even today, after more than half a century, I can still remember with uncanny clarity the feeling that gripped me at the sight of that departing ship, while I was sitting there on the sheltered terrace high above the bay and the city. It was not a feeling of terror or fright. It was certainly not a fear of what was to come and what I was expected to accomplish. I had the youthful arrogance of believing I would be able to achieve whatever I wanted. Perhaps it was the realization that I was, from that moment on, cut off from the home in which I had spent all my life, from the city in which my loved ones and my friends lived, which up to that time was the undisputed center of my universe despite my Zionist longings to go to Palestine, and from the life that had been mine until then and that, I knew, I could never again recapture. Perhaps it was also the feeling of inscrutable sadness that overtakes one when one's most fervent wish, nurtured for years, at long last begins to be realized. To tell the truth, to this day I don't know why I felt what I felt at that moment, but I can still remember the tightness that constricted my chest, the sense of desolation, of—I must repeat—being left marooned in a strange place by the departing ship.

How lucky I was that Father was there with me! Of course, I said not a word to him about how I felt—that would have been entirely impossible given the powerful restraints that governed the loving relationship between us—but I did find reassurance in his presence. Here he was, a man full of energy (he was fifty at the time), secure in his achievements in two worlds, that of Hungarian Jewry and that of the *yishuv* of Palestine, recognized in both as a Jewish leader and an important literary figure, yet also, and for me primarily, *my* father, committed entirely to me, ready to support me in more senses than one, to help and direct me to achieve goals that were as dear to him as to me. As we continued to converse, the feeling of anxiety passed. I breathed freely, felt better, and again got caught up in planning what we would do tomorrow and the day after. Soon we went to our rooms and I slept soundly through the night.

The next morning Father and I took the bus to Jerusalem. Again, peculiarly and puzzlingly, I remember nothing at all of that bus trip, which afforded me my first glimpse of the landscape of Palestine, although I *know* that I must have observed with eager interest the gently undulating barren hills dotted with Arab villages, and at greater intervals with a few Jewish settlements, and the Arab towns of central Palestine through which the road led.

My next memory from those first days in Palestine brings me to the morning after our arrival in Jerusalem: I see myself standing on a small balcony in front of my second-story hotel room and looking down on a small but busy square, formed by two streets opposite the hotel that pointed toward the square at sharp angles and a third one that passed along the front of the hotel to the right and the left. This, as I was to learn on that very day, was Zion Square, the center and hub of the new city, of Jewish Jerusalem. The streets that radiated from it were the sloping and short Ben-Yehuda Street and a very narrow alley called, I believe, Nahlat Shiv'ah (Patrimony of the Seven), while the street on which the hotel fronted was Jaffa Road, the most important thoroughfare in the city, which led from the Jaffa Gate of the Old City to the east, toward the highway that started at the western outskirts of the new city and wound its way toward Jaffa and Tel Aviv on the seashore, a distance of some forty miles.

Accustomed as I was to the generously laid out and beautifully proportioned squares of Budapest flanked by palatial buildings, the modest dimensions of Zion Square could not and did not impress me at all. It was irregularly triangular in shape, perhaps 150 feet across, surrounded by rather old-fashioned buildings, none of which was more than two stories high and all of which had simple stone facades with small windows. Opposite me and somewhat to the left as I stood there on the balcony was the Cinema Tziyon (Zion Cinema), at the time the only motion-picture theater in Jerusalem, whose Saturday-night program I soon learned to attend as a quasi-civic duty, and in whose Sabbath-morning Bet ha'Am (People's House) lectures I subsequently appeared quite frequently. Facing the movie house and somewhat to the right of my balcony was a big office building whose ground floor was occupied by a combination of cafe and restaurant, while its second floor, as I learned later, contained offices of lawyers and business firms. A few more buildings in the streets issuing from Zion Square were visible from my balcony, but I don't remember having found anything noteworthy about them.

Much more interesting than the buildings were the people who, in the hustle and bustle of the morning hour, moved across my field of vision. Most of them were evidently Jews, dressed in European garb, no different in any substantial manner from what one could observe on a Budapest street. Here, however, in contrast to the Hungarian capital, the street scene was sprinkled with Arab townsmen dressed in European suits but with a red *tarbush* (fez) on their heads; Arab townswomen with long black robes and black veils covering their faces; Arab villagers and Bedouins in their traditional flowing *thawbs* (cloaks) and *kufiyyas* (headcloths) held in place with the black *'iqāl* (headband), some of them driving heavily laden donkeys and even a few camels; and here and there a couple of British soldiers with their khaki uniforms and topees (pith helmets); a few Orthodox Jews in their long black or striped kaftans; and Greek or Russian priests likewise robed in black and sporting equally long and unkempt beards.

The sights and sounds that most vividly etched themselves into my memory were those of the Arab street hawkers who passed slowly beneath the hotel with big, highly decorative brass urns lashed to their backs. In one hand such a peddler would carry a drinking glass, while in the other he would hold two brass saucers that he rhythmically beat together, creating a din that easily topped the other street noises. From time to time he would cry out, in a peculiar singsong, a few words (which I could not understand); when a customer stopped before him to buy a glass of his beverage, the peddler would bend from the hip so that the long, carved spout of his pitcher that protruded above his shoulder tipped forward and a thin jet of dark brown liquid spurted forth. He would deftly catch the liquid in the glass, held at a distance of perhaps two to three feet beneath the spout, without spilling a drop, and then hand the filled glass to his customer. All this I could see clearly from my perch, but only later did I learn the words he would utter again and again: *tamr hindi* (Arabic for tamarind, literally meaning Indian date, but used as the designation for a fruit drink made of date juice and water).

The hotel where we stayed was called Tel Aviv Hotel, but everybody referred to it as the Warshawsky Hotel, after its owner, Mr. T. Warshawsky. It was an Arab-style building, of two stories, faced with the omnipresent pink Jerusalem stone. The street floor was occupied by some four or five stores, the second floor by five rooms facing Jaffa Road and several more opening to two side streets. All the windows had semicircular tops, and each of the rooms had two beds in it, with common bathroom and toilet facilities down the corridor. My sister, my father, and I put up at Mr. Warshawsky's establishment for several days, and Father introduced us to some of the many friends he had in Jerusalem. Of all those visits I remember only one: he took me to meet Professor Samuel Klein, who was to become my teacher and mentor at the Hebrew University (I shall have much more to say about him later).

I also remember a very different kind of visit on which Évi and I accompanied Father. Ever since our grandfather Moshe Klein died in Jerusalem, Father would, on the occasions of his visits to the Holy Land, fulfill the traditional filial duty of making the pilgrimage to *qever avot* (the tomb of the fathers). Grandfather Klein was an extremely pious Hasidic Jew, who spent the last four years of his life in Jerusalem. When he died in 1928, his two sons, my uncles Yehiel (Hile) and Yom-Tov (Yantev), who lived next door to him in the Meah Shearim quarter of Jerusalem, made sure that the great wish of pious Jews to be buried on the Mount of Olives should be fulfilled for him.

We took a taxi from the hotel to the cemetery. Father had no difficulty in finding grandfather's tomb among the many, all of which looked exactly alike: a mound about two feet in height enclosed with stones and covered by a horizontal slab, the actual tombstone, which had the shape of one of the two traditional tablets of the law as shown in all synagogues, an oblong with a rounded top end. In accordance with strict Orthodox custom, grandfather's tombstone had no decorations, no symbols, and no words of praise for the deceased, but only this brief sentence: "Here lies Moshe son of Hayyim David and Leah, buried on the 20th of Av, 688 [1928]. TNZB"H." I still have the photograph I took of the tomb at that time. The concluding abbreviation is the acrostic of the traditional Hebrew blessing, "May his soul be wrapped in the bundle of life."

Father recited the *El male rahamim* (God full of mercy) prayer appropriate for the occasion, which asks God to grant the deceased repose under the wings of the Shekhina (I was surprised that he knew it by heart), wiped a furtive tear from his eye, then picked up a pebble from the foot of the tomb and placed it on the tombstone—another traditional gesture whose original meaning, to enlarge the monument and thereby secure its permanence, has long been forgotten. Évi and I followed suit and placed our pebbles carefully beside Father's. That was the only time I saw my grandfather's tomb. During my fifteen Jerusalem years I was busy with the present and the future and had no interest in visiting any cemetery. In 1948, in the course of Israel's War of Liberation, the Jordanian army destroyed grandfather's tomb together with almost all the others on the Mount of Olives.

I do not know whether in taking us along to the ancestral tomb Father had another purpose in mind, in addition to filial duty: to make us aware that in settling in Eretz Israel we not only had a future for which we were supposed to work, but also a personal past, family roots, symbolized by grandfather's tomb, which imposed upon us the obligation to continue, to some extent at least, the traditions he represented. I still remember the feeling I had standing there before the grave that I was not merely a newcomer, but a third-generation resident of Eretz Israel, over and above being a remote descendant of the nation that had lived there in antiquity.

As we made our way down the rocky slope to the road where the taxi waited, I caught a glimpse, on the hill facing us, of the Dome of the Rock, whose gracious lines presented a strange contrast to the stark area of gray stone slabs that was the Jewish cemetery. We had to watch our steps as we picked our way down the rocky slope, so I was unable to let my eyes rest on the dome's refined beauty, but I vowed to myself that I would have a close look at it as soon as possible.

A few days later Father took the Lloyd Triestino ship back to Trieste and returned to Budapest. Évi and I struck out to make our way in the country that Theodor Herzl called the "Old-New Land," of which we knew very little.

Jerusalem: First Impressions

One of the first things my sister and I had to do after my arrival in Jerusalem was to find lodgings since we could not stay in the relatively expensive Warshawsky Hotel for any length of time. Before long we did find a furnished room, a sublet in an old Arab-style house located in a street that sloped down from Jaffa Road, opposite the Russian Compound, toward the eastern corner of the old Arab Mamillah cemetery. While Jaffa Road, as well as Ben-Yehuda Street, had paved roadbeds and sidewalks, our street, although it boasted the impressive name of Princess Mary Avenue, had only its roadway paved. Its sidewalks were unpaved, and I remember distinctly the whitish-gray dust that covered them. One did not have to take more than a few steps before enough of the dust clung to one's shoes to make them indistinguishable in color from the street itself. The lack of paving on the sidewalks was one reason why Jerusalemites in those days preferred to walk in the roadway rather than on the sidewalks; since wheeled traffic was as yet quite sparse, that habit did not entail serious hazards to life and limb. The other reason, as I was to find out a few months later when the rainy season began, was that the very first rain turned the dust of the sidewalks into a layer of sticky mud.

Some 300 meters from Jaffa Road Princess Mary Avenue ended. Its continuation, now sloping upward, was called St. Julian's Way and led to two of the most impressive edifices of the new city of Jerusalem in the early 1930s—the King David Hotel and, facing it, the YMCA building with its huge tower, which was in the course of completion about that time.

The people from whom we rented the room were a young couple whose name I have long forgotten, but I remember that the woman was the sister of the wife of engineer Andrew Koch, who served as director of the Jerusalem Municipal Waterworks. Mr. Koch was of Hungarian origin and hence of course knew Father, and I think that it was through him that we were referred to Mrs. Koch's sister. In any case, we rented the room, which was quite spacious, located on the ground floor of the house (it was a one-story building containing only one apartment), which boasted two windows opening toward the street but set a few yards back. The (iron?) shutters of the windows were closed when we arrived, and our landlady advised us to leave them as they were to keep the room cool and the glances of the passersby out. The room was very sparsely furnished, the main items being two twin bedsteads along two opposite walls, a wooden wardrobe, a table, and two chairs. The facilities opened from the same central corridor that we had to pass to reach our room. I remember one curious detail about the bathroom: its ceiling had a hole in the middle from which a piece of string hung down, with a blue bead tied to the end. Our landlady explained that the top end of the string was tied to a piece of wood floating in a water tank resting on the ceiling; all the water in the house came from that tank. The string went over the edge of the tank, so that when the level of the water was high much of the string hung down below the ceiling. As the water diminished, the wooden float sank lower with it, and the visible part of the string became shorter. Since the Municipal Waterworks allowed water to flow into the tank only once a week, it was imperative, she told us, to observe the string: the shorter it was the more sparingly one had to use water. I no longer remember whether there was any provision for heating water for a bath or a shower.

The minor inconvenience presented by my sister and I sleeping in the same room was easily solved. If we happened to go to bed at the same time, I turned my back while she was undressing and getting into bed, and she did the same while I went to bed. In the morning we observed the same ritual.

Our landlady was not a particularly pretty woman, but her sister, Mrs. Koch, was one of the celebrated beauties of Jerusalem. She made quite an impression on me on the occasions when I was invited to the Koch home. She was a woman of medium height, with an hourglass figure, a rich black head of hair, light olive skin, flashing brown eyes with heavy lashes (this was long before artificial eyelashes were introduced), a small upturned nose, and a generous mouth. She was vivacious and determined; when she addressed you, you felt that she knew precisely what she wanted and was used to having her way. At the same time I felt a certain animal magnetism radiating from her. Later, when my sister and I began to move in what was considered "society" in Jerusalem, we heard rumors to the effect that Mrs. Koch was the "girlfriend" of Ragheb Bey Nashāshībī, the Arab mayor of Jerusalem—and that engineer Koch could thank this "connection" for his high position in the municipal administration.

When I became a member of the executive committee of the Hitahdut 'Ole Hungaria (Association of Hungarian Immigrants) in Jerusalem, of which Mr. Koch was also a member, I met him regularly. Some years later when, for reasons I no longer recall, Koch was fired from his position in control of the Jerusalem waterworks, I wrote a spirited note in his defense that was published in a Jerusalem daily. I can no longer locate it, but I remember I said that, as a result of the absence of the experienced guiding hand of Mr. Koch, we could expect serious disruptions in the water supply that was the lifeline of Jerusalem.

With my first visit to the campus of the Hebrew University on Mount Scopus, the routine that I was to follow for about a year commenced. The bus to the university—it was actually one single rickety bus with two creaky benches upholstered in cracked leather along its sides—started out from Zion Square and followed a winding, mostly uphill, road to its destination in front of the big, fortresslike library building of the university. On its way the bus passed the old Sha'are Tzedeq (Gates of Righteousness) hospital, crossed the Geula (Redemption) Quarter, skirted the Meah Shearim (Hundred Gates) Quarter, where the ultra-Orthodox Hasidic Jews lived (among them two of my father's brothers and one sister and their families), wound its way along the Arab Shaykh Jarrāh Quarter, then climbed up to Mount Scopus (passing in front of the British military cemetery, where soldiers who had died in World War I in the course of the British conquest of Palestine were buried under monotonous rows of identical cross-shaped tombstones), and, finally, rolling along the top of the otherwise empty hill, arrived at its destination at the foot of the library.

The driver-owner of the bus, who must have held a franchise monopoly for the route from both the municipality and the university, was a certain Mr. Schwarz, a Polish or perhaps Russian Jew, small of stature, rotund, with olive skin, piercing greenish-blue eyes, and the demeanor of a pocket Napoleon. When his bus began to fill up, he would get up from his driver's seat and march down the middle of his vehicle, sternly ordering the professors and sundry other passengers to crowd more closely together to squeeze in one or two additional passengers on the narrow benches on each side— only then did he admit a few more standees. The trip itself took about fifteen minutes each way, so that one had to wait half an hour before it arrived back and turned around for its next trip. A year or perhaps two after I arrived in Jerusalem the traffic to and from the university grew. Mr. Schwarz had to purchase a second bus and employ an assistant driver, Menashe by name, and the waiting time was cut in half, to fifteen minutes instead of thirty. Later the number of buses increased further, with Mr. Schwarz still in charge of all of them.

Only the truly tough-minded students disdained Mr. Schwarz's vehicles and walked instead from the city to the campus. They did not follow the paved highway but cut straight across the American Colony, down through the open terrain into the Wādī al-Jōz, then up again on the slope of Mount Scopus. From 1936 on the Arab attacks made it hazardous to walk across Arab-inhabited or uninhabited areas, and the relatively greater safety of the bus was sought by nearly everybody.

In 1933 the university campus on Mount Scopus consisted of only a very few buildings. There was, first of all, the library, by far the largest and most impressive structure with its fortresslike walls faced with a special variety of the omnipresent Jerusalem stone. In one corner of its flat roof there was a low dome-capped room that served as the office of the university chancellor (later president), Dr. Judah L. Magnes, one of the founders and builders of the university. Facing the library, on the eastern side of the road, there were some three or four additional buildings, much smaller, housing classrooms, offices, and laboratories. And then there was the crowning glory of the campus, the amphitheater, in which the opening ceremonies of the university had taken place in 1925. It was built into the slope of the mountain facing east, toward the Judean desert with its hills rolling downward like huge frozen waves, and with a corner of the Dead Sea shimmering far below. The backdrop to this fantastic landscape was formed by the Transjordanian mountains, appearing in the distance pale yet clearly visible across the haze that always covered that deepest rift on earth.

On that first occasion, and each time thereafter when I had the time to stop and look, I did not know where I should let my eyes linger: on the view to the east or to the west. The austere natural magnificence of the desert to the east was certainly matched by the unique artistic beauty that pulled the wandering eye to the west, toward the incomparable panorama of Jerusalem. There, at surprising proximity, was the ancient wall of the Old City, and behind it, but still astoundingly near, stood the lead-gray dome, rising on its octagonal base, of the Mosque of Omar or, more correctly, the Qubbat al-Sakhra, the Dome of the Rock, one of the finest examples of early Arab architecture. (After the 1948 Arab-Jewish war, when King Abdullah's Arab Legion captured the Old City, the dome was made garish by ambitious Jordanian overrestoration that included covering the age-mellowed gray husk of the dome itself with a skin of shiny gold-colored anodized aluminum.)

Long before I stood there for the first time and looked down across the narrow valley toward the Dome of the Rock, the spacious platform of open space surrounding it, and the Aqsā (Farthest) Mosque to its right, I had seen photographs and paintings of that compound, in fact I even caught a glimpse of it from the cemetery on the Mount of Olives, so I was well prepared for what I saw and my eyes greeted the sight as something long familiar. And yet, when I saw it that first time from Mount Scopus, with the morning sunlight falling on it from behind me, with the air slightly shimmering and trembling around it, my breath was taken away, and I was captivated by the spell of Jerusalem, which neither fifteen years of familiarity nor many visits after 1947 could break or even weaken. Today, after more than half a century, I still carry within me that enthralling moment when I first laid eyes on the palpable reality of Jerusalem, whose ideal image had formed part of my consciousness ever since childhood.

Of all this I had, of course, no inkling on that sunny spring day when I stood there in front of the library and drank in the beauty of the Haram (Sanctuary) area and the city behind it, not only the Old City with its tightly packed old houses and many churches and synagogues, towers, and domes, but also the new city, which already in those days had spread out quite a distance beyond it, mainly toward the western horizon. When I had enough of gazing at the view, I turned around and sought the secretariat of the university in order to go through the formal registration as a graduate student or, as such a person was designated in those days, a *talmid mehqar* (research student).

The man into whose office I was ushered in was Ari Ibn-Zahav (1899–1971), academic secretary of the university, who was to become one of my best friends as long as I lived in Jerusalem. His name was originally Goldstein, which he Hebraized into Even-Zahav, and then changed Even (stone) into Ibn (Arabic: son of), as in the names of several great medieval Hebrew poets who lived in Spain, such as Ibn Ezra, Ibn Gabirol, etc. He was not the only one who made this double change in his name. Ibn-Zahav, as everybody called him (only his wife called him Ari), was born in Grajevo, Poland, studied for a while in Leipzig, Germany, and made his *'aliya* to Palestine in 1922, serving since 1924 as academic secretary of the university. He was a talented and ambitious writer; by 1933, when I first met him, he had to his credit several novels and volumes of poetry. He prided himself on the fact that all of his poems were devoted to Jerusalem.

Ibn-Zahav was a slightly built man of very small stature (he could not have been more than five feet tall), with a thin and prominent nose, light hair, and a controlled intensity in his eyes and in demeanor. He had the peculiar ability of some people of small stature of making every word they uttered sound as if it were a significant *pronunciamento*. He received me in a very friendly manner, complimented me on the fluency of my Hebrew, told me that Professor Klein had already spoken to him about me, and gave me some sort of mimeographed application form to fill out and sign—and therewith the formalities of my admission as a "research student" were complete.

In connection with my admission I remember one financial detail. The annual tuition fee research students were required to pay was one Palestinian pound, the equivalent of about 100 dollars today. The amount, I believe, was stated on the application form. However, in actuality, neither then nor at any time thereafter was I asked to pay this fee, and I registered as a research student for three consecutive years without ever paying a penny to the university. One pound constituted precisely one-sixth of my total monthly living expenses: to pay it would have made quite a dent in my tight budget, so I never volunteered to pay it.

Speaking of budgeting, I may as well mention here how I apportioned the monthly allowance of six pounds I got from my father during the first year of my sojourn in Jerusalem. Two to three pounds went for the rent of a furnished room; fifty mils daily, or one and a half pounds monthly, covered the cost of a full-course midday meal, the main meal of the day; the cost of the two other daily meals was about one pound a month; this left me between a half a pound (500 mils) and one and a half pounds for such incidentals as bus fare, newspapers, a weekly movie ticket, and, very occasionally, an article of clothing or a trip to Tel Aviv. Before long, however, I began to supplement this tight budget with some modest author's fees for articles and book reviews, as well as honoraria for occasional lectures. My budget was, and remained throughout my fifteen years in Palestine, rather meager, but I never suffered actual want.

As for the Hebrew University, of which I thus became a graduate student, it was in 1933 still a very small institution, teaching only a sprinkling of subjects. The central part of the land on which it was located, on the top of Mount Scopus (in Hebrew Har haTzofim, literally, Mountain of Lookouts), was purchased just before World War I from the estate of Sir John Gray-Hill by Yitzhaq Leib Goldberg (1860–1935), a wealthy orange-grove owner and Maecenas of Hebrew letters, whose granddaughter I was to marry in 1940. Goldberg in turn donated the land he had acquired to the Keren

Kayemet l'Yisrael (Jewish National Fund, usually referred to by the acronym KKL), one of the central national institutions of the *yishuv*, whose purpose was (and has remained to this day) to hold land in Israel in perpetuity on behalf of the nation. An agreement with the KKL enabled the planning committee of the university to proceed with plans to build the university campus on that site; in 1918, shortly after the British army liberated Palestine from the 400-year-old Turkish rule, the twelve foundation stones, representing the twelve tribes of Israel, were laid. After 1920 the KKL purchased the remaining grounds of the Gray-Hill estate, as well as additional adjoining land, and thus the university-to-be had ample space for its campus.

The erection of the first building proceeded apace, and by 1923 the committees in charge of the university were ready to make the first appointments. It so happened that the first three scholars to be appointed as professors were Hungarians. In 1923 Andor Fodor (b. Budapest, 1884, d. Jerusalem, 1968), at the time professor of biochemistry at the University of Halle, Germany, was appointed professor of chemistry and entrusted with building a department of chemistry at the projected university. In 1924 Dr. Samuel Klein (b. Szilasbalhás, Hungary, 1886, d. Jerusalem, 1940), at the time rabbi of Érsekujvár, was appointed lecturer at the Institute of Jewish Studies that was to open in December of that year. In the same year Dr. Michael Guttmann (b. Hungary, 1872, d. Budapest, 1942), at the time professor of Talmud and *Seminar-rabbiner* at the Jüdisch-theologisches Seminar in Breslau, Germany, was invited to serve as visiting professor of Talmud at the young university.

The formal inauguration of the university took place on April 1, 1925, in the half-finished amphitheater on Mount Scopus. It was a great cultural event not only for the small and young *yishuv*, but for world Jewry as a whole: for the first time in its long history, the Jewish people possessed a university whose plans called for both research and teaching in all fields of Jewish studies, the humanities, and the social and exact sciences. In the presence of the High Commissioner of Palestine, Sir (later Viscount) Herbert Samuel, the president of the World Zionist Organization, Dr. Chaim Weizmann, and many other top Jewish intellectual, rabbinical, and financial leaders, Lord Balfour, author of the historic Balfour Declaration, delivered the inaugural address. Dr. Judah L. Magnes was appointed chancellor of the university, a position later changed to president.

For the first three years the young university engaged only in research, while intensive discussion was carried on about whether the university was destined to be a research or a teaching institution. The problem still preoccupied the powers at the university when I arrived on the scene in 1933. In 1928 courses leading to the master's degree were introduced, and the first M.A. diplomas were awarded in 1931. From then on the university was clearly committed to both basic aims: to be a center of research and scholarship and at the same time to train academic personnel for the *yishuv*, and for the diaspora as well. Added to these two clear-cut purposes was a group of rather vaguely described goals: furthering the cause of human progress by widening the boundaries of knowledge, cooperating with other institutions of higher learning, and assisting developing nations all over the world.

The growth of the university was relatively slow, due in part to the absence of any governmental or major institutional sponsorship and in part to the relative ease with which Jewish teachers and researchers could find placement, and students gain admission, in the universities of the Western world. When the university opened, in 1925, it was comprised of only two institutes: the Institute of Chemistry and the Institute of Jewish Studies, to which the Institute of Microbiology was added soon thereafter. The total number of the faculty was 33; of the student body, 164. By 1933, when I arrived in Jerusalem, the student body had grown to 307, including 23 "research students" (I am indebted to my brother Saul for these figures).

However, precisely because it was such a small institution, the only university in Palestine, and the only Jewish university in the world, the university soon came to enjoy tremendous prestige. The faculty was composed of only two ranks: the professors at the top (titles such as full, associate, and assistant professor did not exist), and, on a lower level, assistants in the sciences and lecturer in the humanities. The entire academic staff of the university was looked upon as the intellectual elite of the *yishuv*, which itself was very small, counting not more than some 200,000 in 1933. This, then, was the institution in which I became a "research student" in May 1933, in fact the only research student with a Ph.D. from a European university in his pocket.

Learning Research: Professors Klein and Heller

Two scholars played an important role in guiding me in writing my Jerusalem thesis, which was my first serious scholarly undertaking: Professor Samuel Klein of the Hebrew University of Jerusalem and Professor Bernard Heller of the Rabbinical Seminary of Budapest.

Professor Klein and my Father were long-time friends, from the days when Klein was still a rabbi of an Orthodox Jewish congregation in a Hungarian country town, and so he was one of the first people to whom Father introduced me after my arrival. Either at that first meeting or at a subsequent one, Klein and I agreed that I would write my thesis, whose exact subject we were to decide later, under his sponsorship.

Samuel Klein became one of the first professors of the Hebrew University due to a fortuitous concatenation of circumstances. While still a rabbi in

Érsekujvár (after the Trianon Peace Treaty, Nove Zamky, Czechoslovakia) he specialized in the study of the historical geography of Palestine with special attention to what he, as well as other scholars, called *toldot hayishuv,* that is, the history of the Palestinian Jewish settlement or population throughout the ages. His published studies attracted the attention of Dr. Chaim Weizmann and the other Zionist leaders who were engaged in the preparatory work for the establishment of a university in Jerusalem. These men felt—not because of any particular scholarly interest in Klein's field, but rather because of political considerations—that a chair devoted to the study of the Jewish presence in Palestine throughout history and scholarly work aimed at demonstrating that the Jewish element has always been an important part of the population of the country could make a significant contribution to the Jewish political claims to Palestine. The man who best filled the bill was Samuel Klein, and in 1924, even before the official opening of the university, he was invited to serve as lecturer of Y'di'at haAretz (literally, the knowledge of the Land), as his chair was termed in Hebrew. In English it was called Palestinology. From 1932 to 1936 Klein served as dean of the Faculty of Humanities and in 1934–1935 was chairman of the Standing Committee of the University Senate.

In 1933, when I made his acquaintance, Professor Klein was forty-six years old. He was a short man of slight build, his head always covered by the traditional black *yarmulke,* the emblem of Jewish orthodoxy, his face sporting a long beard untouched by scissors or razor. He had an aquiline nose, thin, bony, and gently curved, and the habit of slightly contracting his left eye, which gave him a somewhat roguish expression. In fact he was a man of great sincerity, whose basically religious outlook was translated into a natural honesty and decency in all his dealings and into an uncompromisingly strict morality. I still remember with what contemptuous indignation he reacted when one of his colleagues at the Hebrew University divorced his wife of many years and married one of his students, while another also divorced his wife and married the divorced wife of the first. In Klein's eyes such goings-on were, as he once expressed himself to me, a veritable *middat S'dom,* (feature of Sodom).

Professor Klein's great sorrow was that he had no children. (Childlessness, peculiarly, was a widespread phenomenon among members of the Hebrew University faculty: I remember at least a dozen couples who had no children.) According to the *halakha,* the traditional Jewish law, a wife's failure to bear children within ten years of the marriage is considered grounds for divorce (see Babylonian Talmud, tractate Yeb. 64a), but Klein loved his wife dearly and in this respect did not follow the halakhic recommendation. Mrs. Klein was somewhat taller than her husband, rather corpulent, with a smiling round face. She did not wear the traditional wig of religious Hungarian Jewish women; instead, her head was always covered by a kerchief, which was preferred by the most Orthodox. Throughout the seven years of my contact with the Kleins she was almost always ailing, often seriously ill, and spent many a summer in Budapest in a sanatorium or hospital. The Patai family letters from those years contain frequent references to the failing health of "poor Mrs. Klein," and expressions of hope that she would soon be better. For Professor Klein, his wife's health was a constant worry. But on April 21, 1940, at the age of fifty-four, he suddenly and tragically died of a heart attack, and his wife survived him by some twenty years.

After my father's return to Budapest, I continued my visits with Professor Klein, and soon we agreed on the subject of my planned doctoral thesis. Within a few weeks I was able to report to my father:

[Undated; probably June 1933; in Hebrew]

Dear Father:

Yesterday I received the attestation from Professor Mahler. A few days earlier the certificate from the office of the dean of Budapest University reached me. Yesterday I went to Professor Klein's, and he translated the Hungarian certificates into Hebrew for me. Before the end of this week I shall submit my application to the secretariat of the Hebrew University.

Also, in consultation with Professor Klein I found an interesting subject for my doctoral thesis. The title: "Mountain, Plain, Valley, and Water: A Study in Palestinology and Palestinian Folklore in Biblical and Talmudic Times." This subject belongs to the study of both Palestine and the Bible and Talmud, and I hope that I shall succeed in producing a serious and valuable piece of work. Before submitting the application, which must contain not only the title of the study but also its outline, I shall talk again to Professor Klein in order to decide on the whole plan and the chapters of the study in proper order. I think that even if with this study I should not earn the Ph.D. degree, which after all I no longer need, the profit from it will be great.

Yesterday we visited the Ben-Dor family. We gave Father's book to Mrs. Ben-Dor, and she thanks you for it most sincerely. From the building contractors we have as yet received nothing. As soon as we shall get anything, I shall let you know.

One of my eyes is not yet quite well, but it has improved. I am still going to Dr. Ticho, and I hope that within a short time all redness will disappear.

With greeting of *shalom,* also to Mama and Saul,

Your loving son,
Raphael

A few explanations of references in this letter are needed. In order to be admitted as a research student at the Hebrew University I had to produce certificates attesting that I had completed my doctoral work at Budapest University. Professor Eduard Mahler, the outstanding expert in ancient Near Eastern chronology, about whom I have written in the first volume of these memoirs, was one of my teachers there. The Ben-Dor family consisted of an elderly widowed mother and her two sons, the architects Dan and Raphael Ben-Dor. My father had asked the Ben-Dor brothers to prepare architectural plans for a two-family house he and his friend Dr. Lajos Fodor, a lawyer from Hatvan, Hungary, intended to build on a plot of land they had bought in Shekhunat Boruchov, a suburb of Tel Aviv, a year or two earlier. Father had also contacted a firm of building contractors to get a cost estimate for the planned house. I had suffered from occasional eye inflammations for several years in Budapest prior to my *'aliya,* and after I moved to Jerusalem continued to be troubled for a few more years. I became a patient of Dr. Ticho's eye clinic, where I was administered eyedrops and was given instructions to apply warm camomile compresses twice a day.

As soon as I began to think seriously about my dissertation, whose title was a compromise between what I wanted and what Professor Klein wanted me to write about, I felt the need of a guiding hand. Since I was determined to devote most of the thesis to biblical and postbiblical Jewish folklore, I recognized that I could not count on too much help from Klein, whose interest and expertise, as mentioned, lay in the field of the history of the Jewish settlement in Palestine. Nor was there any other scholar at the Hebrew University, or in all of the *yishuv* for that matter, who specialized in Jewish historical folklore and could have been helpful.

In this situation I could think of only one man who had the expertise to help me find my way in these uncharted seas, to point the direction I should follow, to review my work, and to pass judgment on it: Professor Bernard Heller, the renowned scholar of Jewish and Arab folktales, who was my teacher of Bible and Jewish philosophy at the Rabbinical Seminary of Budapest and whose own work on the Hebrew and Arabic *Märchen* was to a great extent responsible for awakening in me the interest in folklore. (I wrote about him in the first volume of these memoirs.) He was the only one of all my teachers in Budapest whom I regretted leaving behind when I made my *'aliya* and with whom I maintained contact through correspondence for many years.

As soon as I became fully aware of the nature of the task before me, I therefore sat down and wrote to Professor Heller, informed him of the subject of my thesis, and asked for his advice and guidance. No copy of that letter has survived, but I did preserve Professor Heller's reply, because I valued it highly. He was always extremely cordial, conscientious, and even punctilious in his relationship with his students, past or present, and the letter he sent me was characteristic. It was a long, painstaking, and detailed epistle, contained many suggestions, and, what was most important for me at that juncture, was most encouraging. He wrote in Hungarian, in longhand, but his pages were studded with Hebrew expressions and quotations, which he jotted down, not in the cursive hand generally used by those who wrote in Hebrew, but in his own individual simplified version of the Hebrew printed alphabet, the so-called quadratic script. It was the same hand that I remembered so well from his jottings on the blackboard in his classes. (I have substituted a transliteration in Latin characters of the words he wrote in Hebrew letters and added their English translation in square brackets.)

Budapest, July 13, 1933

My Very Dear Doctor!

I greet you with affection and my best wishes on the occasion of the valuable recognition the University of Jerusalem gave you by raising you to the rank of *talmid mehqar* [research student]. I congratulate you on the distinction of the great scholarly task with which the University has entrusted you.

The task is colossal. It manifests the character of the farsighted conceptions of Professor Klein. *Har, biq'ah, 'emeq umayim* [Mountain, plain, valley, and water]. As I say, a colossal task. Perhaps even too great. One must take into consideration that you may not be able to work up the material to be gathered in its entirety. I can see several methods of narrowing it down. The thesis could be divided into two: the *har* [mountain] group could be worked up separately, and the *mayim* [water] group separately, since the latter too is an entire group in itself: *yammim, n'harot, n'halim, ma'ayanot* [seas, rivers, streams, springs]; indeed, I imagine that the *ma'ayanot* [springs], if we take the folk-belief attached to the hot springs, e.g., the *hame T'verya* [hot springs of Tiberias] and other springs, became prominently significant. And as for the *har* [mountain] group, I think also the *m'arot* [caves] belong to it, which, from the Machpela, the history of David, the period of the Maccabean wars, until the hiding of *RShbY* [Rabbi Shim'on ben Yohai] and his son, have a role of providing protection that was notable both historically and legendarily. The other method of narrowing down the material to be worked up would be to leave the last chapters of the work-plan for later, perhaps following chapter 6, *har umayim barituale* [mountain and water in ritual].

You ask me for guidance. But again we see realized the thesis of *Sifre, sheha Tora b'E"Y* [that the Tora is in the Land of Israel], and the

pride of *Ber. Rabba, she'en Tora k'Torat E"Y v'lo hokhma k'hokhmat E"Y*
[that there is no Tora like the Tora of the Land of Israel, and no wisdom like the wisdom of the Land of Israel]. Precisely the scholarly
work of Professor Klein fills me with ever increasing admiration. Nevertheless, I shall attempt a few indications, at the risk that I shall write
things that you are mindful of or that have long since been called to
your attention.

Let me interject here that the two titles *Sifre* and *Ber.* (that is, *Bereshit* or
Genesis) Rabba are those of two early Palestinian Midrashim, which, incidentally, we never studied at the Seminary. Professor Heller simply assumed
familiarity with them in a budding scholar. Following this introductory part
of his letter, he jotted down a long list of bibliographic references relating to
the individual chapters of my planned study, whose outline I evidently had
sent to him, including works by Louis Ginzberg, Hermann Gunkel, Oskar
Dähnhardt, James G. Frazer, P. Saintyves, Stith Thompson, the *Handwörter-
buch des deutschen Aberglaubens,* etc. He, of course, took it for granted that I
could read French, German, English, Hebrew, and Aramaic. Then he added
with his characteristic modesty:

> May I be permitted to refer also to my own article *Oqyanos*
> [Ocean] in the Hebrew *Eschkol Encyclopaedia.* That there is still *hinihu
> maqom l'hitgader* [room left to distinguish oneself] also becomes clear
> from the fact that the highly valuable collection of Michael Guttmann,
> *Eretz Yisrael baMidrash v'Talmud* [The Land of Israel in the Midrash
> and the Talmud] does not devote a separate chapter to *meme Eretz Yis-
> rael* [The waters of the Land of Israel], and that *Harim uG'va'ot
> sheb'E"Y* [Mountains and hills in the Land of Israel] (p. 24) takes up
> less than one page.

Before concluding his letter, Professor Heller touched upon some personal matters:

> On Sunday, at the wedding of Rózsi Ligeti (II, Zsigmond Street 49,
> Professor Edelstein officiated), I was together for quite a while with
> your dear parents. They both look fine. One can see that the blessing
> *bara m'zakke abba* [the son bestows merits on the father] has been real-
> ized for them. May it be realized also in the future for their hon. fam-
> ily.
>   I send my regards to Professor Klein with great respect. I have long
> ago prepared the article "E"Y baAggada" [The Land of Israel in the Ag-
> gada], but I am still continuing to polish it.

I greet you with my best heartfelt wishes for success in your work and career.

Bernard Heller

Within a few days of my receipt of this letter I replied (in Hungarian):

Deeply Respected Professor Heller:

Accept, please, my most grateful thanks for your letter and for its signal kindness, and for the most valuable advice and directions contained in it.

I shall without fail follow your suggestion as to narrowing down the material to be worked up, to wit, by treating first only a few chapters enumerated in the outline. Precisely which chapters these should be, I believe I have time to decide when, with the help of God, I am through with the lengthy work of gathering material and classifying it.

By mentioning caves, deeply respected Professor, you have named an entirely new group of subjects of which so far I have not thought at all. If my work should turn out to be successful, such a chapter will doubtless contribute to it to a great extent.

I myself have also thought of working up the Jewish folklore of springs. The fact that you too call my attention to this seems to me to substantiate and underline the significance of such a chapter.

Thank you very much for your bibliographical references. You mention several works that so far have escaped my attention. Besides the works of Frazer and Guttmann, it is precisely due to your kind advice that I had already been acquainted with the Genesis commentary of Gunkel and the *Essais* of Saintyves.

I thank you again for having gone into such detail and taken such trouble in writing out accurate literary references for me. I see a sign of your affection and goodwill in your entire letter, and your kindness will give me the courage not to hesitate to turn to you again when next I again need advice and direction.

With deep respect and grateful affection, your disciple,

Raphael Patai

Professor Heller's letter confirmed my intention to narrow down the subject matter of my dissertation to a treatment of water in ancient Jewish folklore and folk-life and to leave the other geographical features enumerated in the title to a book or books I hoped to write after having earned my Ph.D. at the Hebrew University.

While the precise subject of my thesis thus gradually crystallized, I was entirely on my own when it came to devising the method of work and the procedure for gathering material from the ancient Hebrew sources. When I embarked on that task, only one thing was clear to me: the gathering of material would have to proceed in chronological order, which, of course, meant that I would have to start with the Bible and only thereafter go on to the later Jewish literature—the Apocrypha, the New Testament, the Mishna, and the talmudic and midrashic sources. My first idea was to use Solomon Mandelkern's biblical *Concordance* and copy the passages listed in it under such key words as *mayim* (water), *nahar* (river), *yam* (sea), etc. However, I soon rejected this method, because, although it was fast and efficient, I came to the conclusion that by relying solely on Mandelkern's listing I would miss many passages important for my work but not containing any of the key words. I therefore decided on a much more laborious and time-consuming but also much more thorough method: I would read the entire Bible from beginning to end and copy out each passage I found relevant.

Storing the material thus extracted and having it readily available for organization according to subject matter caused me no problem. I purchased a ream of blank writing paper, cut up each sheet into eight pieces, and, behold, I had a stack of thousands of handy slips about 2 3/4" by 4 1/4" in size. Once this technical preparation was done, I sat down and began to read the Bible. How happy I was then that my private tutors, and later my teachers in high school and at the rabbinical seminaries of Budapest and Breslau, had so relentlessly drilled me for so many years in Hebrew in general and in the Hebrew Bible in particular—thanks to them, I could without any difficulty read the Bible in the original and had to use a dictionary only occasionally. So I began by copying out the second sentence of Genesis, which contains the word *t'hom* (abyss): "and darkness was upon the face of the abyss," adding the source reference: Gen. 1:2. Then, on a second slip, I copied the sequel to that verse: "and the spirit of God hovered upon the face of the water." This was the beginning of my work, which, as it progressed, resulted in the accumulation of thousands and thousands of slips.

These very first entries confirmed my resolve to read the entire Bible rather than rely on Mandelkern's *Concordance*. Had I done that, I might have overlooked the word *t'hom* (deep or abyss), because I might not have been aware of its "watery" connotation. Reading the whole verse, I could not miss the parallelism between *t'hom* and *mayim* (water), and I could not miss what it meant: that in the ancient Hebrew worldview, of which that verse was a reflection, the primeval, precreation abyss was of a watery nature. Of course, later in my work, this view was amply borne out by many other biblical passages, as well as by the ancient Babylonian parallels.

To read the whole of the Bible in this attentive manner and to extract information from what I read required keeping at it conscientiously for many hours every day for several weeks, and as soon as I was finished I had to do the same with the postbiblical ancient Jewish literature. Depending on the nature of the texts I read, this work was at times fascinating, at others boring, but it just had to be done, and I did it, day after day, often late into the night.

Summer was followed by autumn; as autumn drew to a close, the weather turned cooler, and then became really cold, so that I was forced to make a dent in my small budget by investing in a kerosene heater. It was a two-foot-tall black tin tube some eight or ten inches in diameter, at the bottom of which was a cylindrical fuel tank, out of which emerged a circular wick that had to be adjusted carefully so that its flame was blue or else it produced more stench than heat. When I bought this stove, which was used by almost everybody in Jerusalem—except the well-to-do Arabs, who used old-fashioned charcoal burners that gave off more heat and less smell but for some reason were never adopted by the Jews—I was advised to keep a kettle of water on top of it so that its steam should replace the humidity consumed by the fire. The kettle of boiling water, incidentally, enabled me to make myself a cup of tea whenever I felt like it. Once I lighted my *tanur neft* (kerosene stove), as it was called, even though it took quite a while before it began to warm up the room, I instantly felt warmer—I evidently associated the sight of the flame and the smell of kerosene, which immediately filled the room, with warmth. After a while the stove did, in fact, raise the temperature sufficiently to make sitting in the room in a sweater quite comfortable. However, the small ring of fire in the stove could not affect the temperature of the tile floor, which remained stubbornly cold. I tried various methods to keep my feet from freezing: I crossed my legs so as to raise first one foot then the other from the cold floor; I held up one foot at a time toward the stove; I even piled up a few books under my feet—but nothing helped. Icy feet and the smell of kerosene are the two things I remember most clearly from that little room in which I spent much of my first Jerusalem winter.

What else do I remember? I lived in that room alone, since my sister had married in the fall of 1933 (the story of her marriage is told in my book *Between Budapest and Jerusalem: The Patai Letters, 1933–1938*). It was in an old Arab house, rented by a young Jewish couple who made a living by providing room and board to some eight or ten people, mostly young men like myself. My room was furnished with the usual iron bedstead with a mattress, a wardrobe, a small table that served as my desk, and a chair, as well as a small bookshelf, which I filled within a few days after my arrival with books borrowed from the university library. The room was so small that more pieces of furniture could not have been placed in it. Had it been bigger, my kerosene stove would have been even less effective.

As the days and weeks passed, the stack of small slips with my notes grew steadily, at what I considered a satisfactory pace. I did not, I should add, spend all my working hours reading the sources and making notes of what I found in them. I was aware that, despite the quite passable familiarity with the scholarly literature on biblical folklore I had acquired during my student years in Budapest and Breslau, there was much more I would have to get acquainted with. Hence, each time I went up to the university to attend the classes of Professor Klein or other teachers, I also stopped by at the university library to look for and borrow books relevant to my work. I took home and kept in my room for many months—the rules of the library were at the time very lax—the three volumes of Frazer's *Folk Lore in the Old Testament,* as well as all twelve volumes of his *Golden Bough.* Even after I had become quite familiar with these classics, I was interested enough to browse in them again and again, often after going to bed and covering myself with a warm blanket. Among the other books I reread during that year were P. Saintyves's *Essais du Folklore Biblique* (although its French caused me some difficulty), and Oskar Dähnhardt's *Natursagen*—both basic books to which Professor Heller had first called my attention. But the opus that impressed me most was that of Frazer, under whose spell I was to remain for several years.

Professor Klein was a great admirer of the German *Palästinaforscher* (Palestine investigator) Gustaf Dalman and suggested that I read his multi-volume classic *Arbeit and Sitte in Palästina* (Work and Customs in Palestine). I did so and found it to be a magisterial encyclopedic study comparing everyday life in Palestine in ancient days with life in modern times as it could be observed among the Arabs of the country. (Many years later I was to write a book along those lines, entitled *Sex and Family in the Bible and the Middle East.*) It was the reading of Dalman and other similar works (such as Hilma Granqvist's studies of the village of Artas) that, together with my growing personal contact with Arabs and Oriental Jews in Jerusalem, awakened my interest in the folklore and anthropology of the contemporary population of the country and of the Middle East in general.

But to get back to those early months, when the stack of slips grew to a height where it threatened to collapse, I felt that I had better begin to break it up into smaller heaps according to subject matter. This procedure, done entirely empirically, yielded the first approximation of chapter subjects in my planned book. I found, for instance, that many of the references I culled from the Bible and the Talmud pertained to the role of water in religious rituals: purificatory rites consisting of ablutions and immersions, the washing of hands, laundering of clothes, rinsing dishes, etc. Other references contained intriguing allusions to legends in which water played a crucial role: miracles God performed with water (the deluge, the parting of the Red Sea, the water from the rock). I also found fascinating but always fragmentary statements about water in the mythical structure of the universe in which the abyss and the sea, and mythical monsters populating it, played important roles. Then again, many biblical and talmudic passages contained technical terms for hydrographic features; others spoke of the actual hydrography of Palestine, its seas, rivers, lakes, wells, sources, etc.; while still others were place-names containing a hydrographic element, such as Beer Sheva' (Well of Oath), 'Eyn haQore (The Source of the Partridge), and the like.

By the time I completed this work of excerpting the water material from the Bible and later literature, my interest in the folkloristic aspect of water in ancient Israel had become overwhelming. I was determined to concentrate on following up the legends, myths, customs, and rites in which water played a role and to present as complete a picture as possible of the role of water in the daily life, the religious life, and the imagination of the Hebrews in biblical times and of their heirs, the Jews, in postexile days. In connection with the latter period, I soon became convinced that the cutoff point must be the time of the conclusion of the Mishna, that is, ca. 200 C.E. The length of time it took me to gather the biblical material alone made it clear to me that I would have to spend years on excerpting material from the sources if I were to take the completion of the Talmud (ca. 500 C.E.) as the *terminus ad quem.*

At the same time I began to feel with great certainty that it would be impossible to include in the volume I planned a treatment of the geographic elements other than water listed in the initial formulation of the title of my dissertation. It was clear that to do justice also to "mountain, valley, and plain" would require an opus of several volumes that would go far beyond even the most stringent requirements for a doctoral thesis. When I next visited Professor Klein to present him with an oral progress report (he never asked me for a written one), I gave him a detailed account of what I had been doing, what chapters I envisaged at that stage, and what I saw as the probable length of my treatment of water alone. Then I humbly asked his consent to consider this subject in itself as the topic of my dissertation, with the understanding that at a later date I would follow it up with a sequel covering the land features he had originally suggested. It was evident that he was not happy with this change in my thesis outline, but, being a friendly and a considerate man and sensing my commitment to the work as I envisaged it, he agreed. Thus, my way to writing about water, and water alone, was clear, and I could put mountains, valleys, and plains out of my mind. In the event, I did return—if not to mountains, valleys, and plains—to the telluric counterpart of water, that is, the role of the earth in ancient Jewish custom, belief, and legend, although the two volumes I published on that subject turned out to be very different from what Professor Klein had originally envisaged. Unfortunately, he died while I was still at the very beginning of work on that study and thus missed the satisfaction he might have derived seeing his erstwhile student strike out in new directions.

In January or February 1934 I felt that my work of collecting and classifying the source material had advanced sufficiently to justify an attempt at working up a chapter. The subject I chose was a purely folkloristic one, dealing with the biblical stories about and references to the marvels God performed with the waters, including the deluge, the water out of the rock, the water turned into blood, hailstones, rain, clouds, storms over the sea, and the like. I titled the chapter, rather daringly, I felt, "Mishaq Elohim baMayim" (God's Play with the Waters), typed it carefully (I had by that time acquired a Hebrew typewriter), and mailed it to Professor Heller. The copy of the cover letter I sent with it has long been lost, but I did preserve Heller's reply, a long handwritten letter on five folio-sized pages, full of Hebrew quotes and detailed critical remarks. I give here some excerpts of the less technical parts in my literal translation from his Hungarian:

Budapest, March 12, 1934

My Very Dear Doctor Gyuri:

I read the chapter of your study entitled "Mishaq Elohim ba-Mayim" with sympathetic attention. I shall first attach my comments on the contents as the whole, then on the details.

The presentation differs basically from the original plan I have in my hands. According to it, the first chapter was to be "Hare E"Y uMemeha 'al pi haTNa"Kh v'haMishna" [The Mountains and Waters of the Land of Israel according to the Bible and the Mishna]. I myself gave the advice that *mayim* [water] should be separated from *harim* [mountains]; indeed, that the treatment of one will be abundantly rich contents for a study. Naturally, I agree with this change. But I notice that you deviate from the original plan in another essential respect: in your first plan the titles of chapters 2 and 3 were "Har uMayim b'Shirat haTna"kh v'haMishna" [Mountain and Water in the Poetry of the Bible and the Mishna], and "Har uMayim baAggada" [Mountain and Water in the Aggada]. But the actual presentation barely pays attention to the Mishna and the Aggada, whereas the Aggada strongly needs to be included in the *mayim* [water] chapter.

After adducing a number of quotations from the Aggada that he felt would organically belong in my chapter, Heller continued: "In the tone of your work the impetus of youth can strongly, too strongly, be felt; often we hear not the discourse of the researcher but the exuberant rhetor." He then offered detailed comments on practically every one of the forty-one pages of the chapter I sent him. The nature of his comments can be illustrated by one single example:

> On p. 11, in the summary, you state that the difference between the biblical and the mythical view of water is that the myth always explains a local phenomenon, connected with the Nile, the Euphrates, the Tigris, or some spring, while the Bible views the eternal, the universal. This contraposition is not entirely just: Indian, Iranian, Greek, and Babylonian myth, even the myth of peoples with much lower culture, also tries to understand the whole earth, the whole sea. Cf. e.g., the American legends, Dähnhardt, *Natursagen,* I:74–60.

The conclusion of this letter was typical of his modesty: "I would be glad if you could make some little use of my comments. I wish that by following the expert instructions of your teachers, and especially of Professor Klein, you might perfect your study so that it should redound to the honor of the university and yourself. *V'ase hayil . . . uq'ra shem.*" The concluding Hebrew words are an abridged quote from Ruth 4:11, where the people say to Boaz, ". . . and do thou worthily in Ephrath, and be famous in Bethlehem."

I have no recollection of how I reacted to Professor Heller's comments, nor has my response been preserved. But I know that his constructive criticisms were the most useful directives I received from anyone in shaping my first attempt at a serious historical-folkloristic study, and I took careful account of his strictures. Incidentally, I also changed the title of the chapter to "God's Miracles with Water."

What I said above about my first year in Jerusalem is apt to create the impression that all I remember is that I spent all day and every day in my cell-like room working on the first phase of my thesis. That remembrance and that impression, however, require a corrective that is supplied by other memory flashes in whose light I see myself engaged in other activities as well during that same year. There were, of course, the classes of Professor Klein and of other teachers that I attended at the university. There were occasional get-togethers with friends and fellow-students, movies, lectures, trips, and meetings. And there were, above all, courtships and friendships with girls that provided—how shall I put it?—the diversion, relaxation, stimulation, color, challenge, excitement, adventure, and I don't know what else, of which I had need.

Still, the fact remains that being engaged in and committed to such an utterly private enterprise as writing a scholarly thesis based on ancient literary sources inevitably meant spending most of my day in confining solitude, which, in turn, often became oppressive loneliness. Although I was never, or at least never for long, without a girlfriend, my friendships with girls were of the attenuated sort that meant meetings not more often than once or twice a week. Five or six evenings a week I sat in my cell, as I came to think of my room, and worked on my thesis until I got tired and went to bed. Occasionally the loneliness of the evening became so unbearable that it made me put down the pen and go out for a walk, as if under compulsion. Since my rooms were always near the very center of modern Jerusalem, that is, near Zion Square, my walks usually meant plying that neighborhood and making the rounds, or rather the triangle, of Ben-Yehuda Street, King George Avenue, and Jaffa Road. There was nothing particularly attractive in those streets, even though they were the most urbanized area of the city. The small shops lining them were, of course, closed in the evening, the Egged bus terminal on Jaffa Road was deserted, the last performance at the Zion Cinema had long been over, and the coffeehouse opposite it as well as the small Atara Café higher up in Ben-Yehuda Street were also closed. Still, those streets were the nearest approximation to city life Jewish Jerusalem had to offer at night (only in the Arab part of the Old City, and only in the month of Ramadān, was there what could be called nightlife). While sauntering along the barely lighted streets of that city triangle, my thoughts would wander back to the splendid, bright boulevards of Budapest with their gay evening crowds, where I also used to take such short night walks. I have a very dim recollection as if, in making those rounds, I may have been moved by the vague and irrational fantasy that, perhaps, perhaps, I could encounter a beautiful, fascinating, charming woman, and we would instantly recognize each other as kindred spirits. After an hour or so, tired out and disappointed, I would return to my cell and go to sleep.

2

A Palestinian
Portrait Gallery

Much of the social life of the families that were, or had pretensions to
be, part of the top layer of Palestinian Jewish society consisted of being "at
home" at a given hour once a week. At such "at homes" any friend or acquaintance could drop in without special invitation: he would be greeted in
a most friendly manner by the host and hostess, be served a cup of tea and
something to eat, chat with them and the other assembled guests, and an
hour or so later take his leave when told politely, "Come again!"

In the course of my early years in Jerusalem (and also during my one-
year stay in Haifa) I frequently attended such gatherings. Most of the homes
I visited in this manner I have long forgotten, but I do remember those of
the ophthalmologist Dr. Arye Feigenbaum; the painter Abel Pann; the
deputy-mayor (and, after the independence of Israel, mayor) of Jerusalem,
Daniel Auster; the head of the Palestine Broadcasting Service, the Hon. (later
Viscount) Edwin Samuel, Professor Harry Torczyner (later Tur-Sinai) of the
Hebrew University; the head of the Jewish National Fund, M. M. Ussishkin—all these in Jerusalem. Also, in Tel Aviv, those of the unofficial poet
laureate of the *yishuv*, Hayyim Nahman Bialik (who died in 1934); the
owner of the Omanuth Publishing House, Mrs. Shoshana Persitz; the celebrated painter Reuven Rubin and his beautiful Hungarian-born wife; the orange-grove owner and Maecenas Yitzhaq Leib Goldberg and his wife Rachel;
and their daughter Hanna and her husband Samuel Tolkowsky, whose
younger daughter Naomi I was to marry in 1940. During my year in Haifa
(1942–1943) I was occasionally a guest at the "at homes" of the graphic
artist Hermann Struck; the antiquities collector S. Foguelson; the industrialist Arno Hochfeld and his wife Sulamith, who was a younger sister of Mrs.

Hanna Tolkowsky; and the family in whose villa I rented a room on Mount Carmel, whose name I have long since forgotten.

I first learned of the existence of such a social ritual in the home of the Tolkowskys. It must have been during the three weeks or so that passed between my arrival in Palestine in May 1933 and the departure of my father on June 7 to return to Budapest, because I remember distinctly that it was he who took me along. The Tolkowskys' "at homes" were observed as long as I lived in Palestine and probably thereafter as well, on Friday afternoon between five and seven. Since they were not religious, the onset of the Sabbath in the course of those two hours on winter Fridays did not bother them at all. They lived at 111 Allenby Road, not far from its intersection with Rothschild Boulevard, in a big two-story house that stood in its own grounds, with a colonnaded portico facing the street and a big garden behind it. The Tolkowskys lived on the ground floor, the Goldbergs on the second. By the time I left Palestine the Tolkowskys and Mrs. Goldberg had moved out of the house, which was sold, demolished, and replaced by an office-building complex with a shopping arcade on street level that ran the whole length of the lot.

As I first entered the Tolkowskys' apartment that Friday afternoon, I was struck by its spaciousness, quite unusual in those modest times of the still largely proletarian *yishuv*. Especially impressive was the generous size of the combination living room/study in which the guests were received. Its walls were lined with books—on that first visit I was impolite enough to spend a lot of time looking at the books rather than conversing with the other visitors—arranged on fine mahogany shelves. Before the windows stood a large double desk of the type that, as I later learned, is called a "partners' desk," because two partners can work at it facing each other. In front of the bookshelves stood two large and well-worn leather club chairs, while several smaller chairs and tables were scattered in various parts of the room. In front of the side of the desk that faced the room stood a small table, on which was laid out a silver tea set, china cups and saucers, and silverware. Behind this small and rather low table, on a high-backed chair, sat the hostess, Mrs. Tolkowsky, serving tea. She sat ramrod straight, her generous but tightly corseted figure held in a stiff vertical position, her brown wavy hair kept closely shingled, her round, full face slightly shiny, her eyes barely visible behind heavy glasses, and her mouth, broad and thin-lipped, kept in a constant frozen smile.

As guest after guest entered and greeted her, she poured some of the almost black tea essence from a small pot into a cup, added the proper amount of hot water from a larger pot, and asked, "Lemon or cream?" Then she raised the cup and saucer gently to a height where the person standing in front of her could easily take them from her hand, and, for a moment, broadened her smile somewhat. Near the door hovered a uniformed maid in black dress and white apron, and from time to time Mrs. Tolkowsky would indicate to her with a slight movement of her head that she needed replenishment of the paraphernalia behind which she sat enthroned: tea, hot water, lemon, sugar, and cream. Everything went utterly smoothly—one could feel that a long-established and well-practiced routine was being acted out. After the guests got their tea, they stood around or found a seat, chatted for a while, and then, after having tarried for the proper length of time, for a second time made their obeisance to Mrs. Tolkowsky, thanking her and saying good-bye, whereupon they were accompanied to the door by Mr. Tolkowsky and quietly ushered out. Mrs. Tolkowsky, as far as I can remember, did not get up from her seat even once.

Subsequently I attended these formal informal gatherings at the Tolkowskys' many times. When I became a member of the family and they spoke before me with less than their usual restraint, I learned (not so much from what they said as from their no less expressive mien and tone) that if at least one or two high officials of the British Mandatory Government of Palestine dropped by they considered the "at home" a success; if not, if only Jewish "notables" turned up, the afternoon was an indifferent one as far as they were concerned. Evidently, the real elite of the country in their eyes were the British, the Mandatory masters of Palestine.

Samuel Tolkowsky was a small, stocky man, with a big head, blue eyes, and a prominent nose. At the time I first met him he was forty-seven years old. He was born in Antwerp, Belgium, of Polish-Jewish parents who had settled in Antwerp some years prior to his birth. His father, if I remember correctly, was a diamond dealer. Samuel Tolkowsky himself settled in Palestine in 1911. In 1915 he married Hanna, a daughter of Yitzhaq Leib Goldberg. The Tolkowskys lived in England during World War I, and their younger daughter Naomi was born in Manchester on December 8, 1917. From 1916 to 1918 Samuel Tolkowsky served under Chaim Weizmann as a member of the Zionist Political Committee in London and in 1918–1919 was secretary of the Zionist Delegation to the Versailles Peace Conference. After the end of the war, in October 1919, he returned to Palestine, where his parents-in-law also settled in the same year. I have no information about what he did in the interwar years, but after World War II broke out he was entrusted by the British Mandatory Government of Palestine with an extremely responsible position as general secretary of the Citrus Control and Marketing Board, a body set up by the government to oversee the total Jewish and Arab citrus fruit production of the country and its sale abroad. I still remember how, upon his appointment to this post, Mr. Tolkowsky told Naomi and me about it with excited pride, not omitting to mention the rather high salary that went with the job.

Of Naomi, who was fifteen in 1933, I don't remember much from those early fleeting encounters at her parents' "at homes." She was shy, reticent, and taciturn—this much I did retain in my memory—and I don't believe we exchanged more than a formal *shalom*. I certainly had no idea that seven years later—during which time, in contrast to our ancestor Jacob, I did everything but serve my future father-in-law—she and I would marry.

In the Khālidī Home and Library

One of the first things I did after having found my bearings around the campus of the Hebrew University was to pay a visit to its Institute of Oriental Studies, as the department devoted to Arabic and other Semitic languages and literatures, Persian, and Middle Eastern archaeology and history was called. The senior member of the Institute was Professor Leo Arye Mayer (1895–1959), a man of most impressive appearance: tall, with a flowing black beard, regular, finely chiseled features, and penetrating black eyes. Born in Stanislav, Galicia, Mayer studied at the University of Vienna, specializing in the history of Middle Eastern art. In 1921 he emigrated to Palestine, started to work for the Department of Antiquities of the Government, and, when the Hebrew University opened in 1925, was appointed lecturer in the art and archaeology of the Near East. He became a professor in 1932 and served as rector of the university from 1943 to 1945. He never married, and in the years during which I knew him he was something of a recluse. Once, I remember, I spoke to him about my plan to study the folklore and anthropology of the Arabs of Palestine; he said that those were important subjects indeed and advised me to study Arabic as intensively as I was able to, since a knowledge of Arabic was a prerequisite for work in those fields. This, of course, was nothing new to me, as an avid reader of Edward Westermarck's great *Ritual and Belief in Morocco*. Although by inclination an art historian, Mayer also worked in archaeological explorations and participated in the excavations of the "Third Wall" of Jerusalem and of the Eshtemoa synagogue. His reputation, however, rested primarily on his book *Saracenic Heraldry*, published in 1933, just when I arrived in Jerusalem.

The next ranking member of the Oriental Institute was Professor Shlomo Dov (Fritz) Goitein. Of Hungarian rabbinical descent, Goitein was born in Burgkunstadt, Bavaria, studied in Berlin and Frankfurt, and emigrated to Palestine in 1923. At first he taught at the Reali high school in Haifa and some years later became instructor in Islamic history at the Hebrew University. At the same time he also worked as school inspector for the Department of Education of the British Mandatory Government. Finally, in 1947, he was promoted to the rank of professor at the university. In 1948–1949 Goitein served as visiting professor at Dropsie College in Philadelphia, in which capacity he was my colleague at that institution. In 1957 he accepted the invitation of the University of Pennsylvania in Philadelphia to serve as professor of Arabic. His decision to leave the Hebrew University was strongly criticized by his colleagues, who felt that this step, taken by somebody who had reached the top rung on the academic ladder and was a respected leader of Islamic studies in Jerusalem, was something akin to desertion.

One of the major scholarly undertakings directed by Goitein at the Hebrew University was the preparation for publication in a scholarly edition of volume 5 of the *Ansāb al-Ashrāf* (Lineage of Eminent Men) of Ahmad ibn Yahyā al-Balādhurī, the ninth-century Arab historian. Three or four researchers who served under Goitein did the actual work. One of them was none other than Dr. Meir M. Bravmann, who had been my friend in Breslau when we both were students at the Rabbinical Seminary and at the university, where our teacher was the great Carl Brockelmann. Bravmann and I greeted each other as long-lost brothers, recounted our experiences in the three years since we last had seen each other, and remained friends not only until I left Jerusalem in 1947, but also in New York, when, at my recommendation, he was appointed professor of Arabic at Dropsie College.

Another Arabist who worked on Balādhurī was Dr. Noah Braun. Braun was several years older than Bravmann and I, a man of thin frame and medium height, with a few strands of scant fuzz on his chin, and a withered right hand. He and Bravmann must have become close friends, or perhaps Braun simply had the need to tell somebody intimate details of his marital life, for on one occasion Bravmann reported to me that Braun had told him that he and his wife used to read erotic literature in bed in the evening. Bravmann himself never married and despite our long friendship never opened up as far as his relations with women were concerned, but somehow I always suspected that he never had any experience with the opposite sex.

Sometime after I made Goitein's acquaintance, he suggested that I join him and Dr. Braun in an evening visit to the house of Shaykh Khalīl al-Khālidī, the chief *qādī* (judge) of the Muslim Sharī'a court of Jerusalem. I described that visit, which took place after the onset of the winter rains, in a short article and sent it to Father, who published it in the February 1934 issue of his monthly, *Mult és Jövő*. It was my first visit to an Arab home. Shaykh Khālidī lived on the second floor of an old house in the Old City; although he must have occupied the whole of the floor, we, of course, saw only the reception room, which was spacious and furnished in a mixture of traditional Arab and nineteenth-century European styles. When we arrived we found there, in addition to our host, three old Arab shaykhs, each with a flowing white beard and garbed in the traditional long black kaftan, with a white turban wound around the red fez. After lengthy formalized greetings and welcomes, all of us were seated, the four shaykhs along one wall of the room on a low bench covered with long and narrow hard mattresses, we Jewish visitors opposite them on comfortable old-fashioned easy chairs. As I described the scene at the time:

> Our host left his low-cut shoes on the floor and folded his legs on the seat. Before him, on a big red-copper bowl (the descendant of the biblical *ah*) glowed a heap of charcoal, spreading pleasant warmth in the whole room. The discussion took place in Arabic, partly in the literary language and partly in the colloquial, which I understood well.
>
> By way of introduction, old Shaykh Khalīl addressed a few polite questions to the company and then began to tell about his travels and his studies, which revealed him to me to be a man of great culture and broad knowledge (for the others this was nothing new). He had visited all the important scenes of Islamic history, from India to Spain, which latter country he knew as well as he did Jerusalem. The eighty-year-old shaykh gave a demonstration of his memory as he enumerated the historical cities of Arab Spain, citing both their Arabic and Spanish names. Then he went on to speak of the places where there were famous libraries in which were preserved the manuscripts of ancient Arab poets, philosophers, and historians, and this in turn led him to talk of Arab historiography and literary history. . . . And, as an aside, perhaps even somewhat disdainfully, he mentioned that "in recent times some Europeans too have begun to study the literature of Islam, e.g., Goldziher, Brockelmann, and Schacht." When speaking of this he slowly stroked his not yet totally white beard, and smiled indulgently. . . .
>
> Sitting there in that milieu, suffused with culture, imbued with poetry, I could not visualize that outside, in the sober light of reality, there were opposing interests that did not allow the Jew and the Arab, these two sons of Shem, to realize that there was a close relationship between them. . . .
>
> There, in that milieu, I understood that there was a deep-rooted kinship between those two peoples. And, at the same time, I also understood that it was not possible simply to dispossess this Arab people, it was not possible to argue that there was enough room for the Arabs in Happy Arabia—the Arabs have struck roots in this country with their millennial culture, and for us, the people of the Bible, the people of the book, no other possibility was left but to seek the road of understanding and cooperation with them. I do believe that this is possible, and I see that there is no other way.

This is how I felt then, late in 1933, when I wrote that article. Three years later, when the Arab riots started in Palestine, my feelings on the issue of Arab-Jewish relations were forced to undergo a change. As a matter of fact, even in that 1933 article I was less than completely frank in describing my visit in Shaykh Khālidī's house. In my initial enthusiastic and romantic reaction to that first encounter with the latter-day heirs of the great old Arab culture I overlooked and left unmentioned something of which I had remained unaware until Dr. Braun called my attention to it. After we left the Khālidī house, while walking along the narrow alleys of the Old City toward the Jaffa Gate, Dr. Braun burst out indignantly: "We were treated most shabbily by the shaykh. He did not address as much as a single question to any of us!"

The Khālidīs, as I was to find out subsequently, were a well-known Palestinian family of scholars, the most famous among whom was Shaykh Khalīl's cousin Rūhī al-Khālidī (1864–1913), the author of the first modern Arabic work on comparative literature and of several political and science studies, including one on chemistry among the Arabs published posthumously in Cairo in 1953.

One of the guests present that evening in Shaykh Khalīl's house was Shaykh Amīn al-Ansārī, keeper of the Khālidiyya Library in the Old City, a small but most valuable collection of Arabic works established by the Khālidī family. Before we left, Shaykh Amīn invited me to visit him in the library, which, he said, would certainly interest a young European *tālib* (seeker, i.e., student). A few days later I followed up the invitation and together with my new friend Ahmed (of whom more anon) I sought out the library, which was located just a few steps off the street that led from the Jaffa Gate to the Western Wall. From the narrow alley a heavy, metal-studded old wooden door led into a small courtyard, from which a similar door opened into the library itself. Inside there was just one large room, with the usual thick walls of old Arab buildings, broken by tall, narrow windows with heavy iron bars across them. What struck me more than the size of the room was its height. All the walls, from floor to ceiling, were lined with shelves, holding Arabic books, mostly old, and quite a number of manuscripts. A ladder, which could be pushed in front of the shelves, provided access to the upper shelves.

Shaykh Amīn was unquestionably the most beautiful man I have ever seen. He was of medium height, rather slim, his smooth olive skin tightly stretched across the bones of his face, with deep black eyes and a narrow, somewhat aquiline nose. His face was framed by a tall white turban above and a rich white beard below. His reception of us was most friendly—by that time I was sufficiently sensitized to Arab manners to be aware of the difference between Shaykh Khalīl's formal politeness and Shaykh Amīn's true warmth—and as soon as we entered he rapped on the window opening into the street, whereupon a young boy who was sitting below it got up, and the shaykh told him to fetch coffee.

In the course of our conversation the shaykh told me that the library was founded by the father of Shaykh Khalīl some hundred years earlier (that is, about 1834) and that it was the most complete library of Muslim religious literature and jurisprudence in all of Palestine. Especially valuable was, he said, its *Hadīth* collection, which included several extremely rare printed books and manuscripts. To illustrate what he meant, Shaykh Amīn pulled over the ladder and with surprisingly youthful agility climbed its rungs until he could reach the top shelf from which he took down a large folio volume, blew on it vigorously to remove the layer of dust that covered it, and put it on the table in front of us.

"Look," he said, "this is a very rare manuscript of Bukhārī's *Sahīh!*"

At the time I did not have too clear an idea about who Bukhārī was, and when Shaykh Amīn noticed my hesitancy he explained that Bukhārī had lived about a thousand years ago, that he was the most outstanding *muhaddith* (traditionalist), and that his *Sahīh* (Authentic) was the most reliable collection of traditions going back to the Prophet Muhammad.

Shaykh Amīn showed us some more of the treasures of his library, mounting the ladder again and again. I expressed my admiration at his strength and agility and asked him, somewhat hesitatingly, how old he was. "I am eighty," he answered, whereupon I expressed the wish that he live a hundred and twenty years in good health—I simply assumed that this traditional Jewish wish must be part of the Arab folkways as well. After we left, Ahmed said to me with a smile: "He told you he was eighty, but actually he is only sixty years old." Coming as I did from a culture in which everybody tried to appear younger—this certainly was the tendency in Hungary even in the 1930s—I found it remarkable that in Arab culture old age should be considered of such value that a person should pretend to be twenty years older than he really was. Subsequently, until the Arab disturbances made visits to the Old City hazardous, I went to see Shaykh Amīn several times, on occasion accompanied by members of my family.

In 1967, after Israel had conquered and opened up the Old City of Jerusalem, I again stopped by the Khālidī Library on my way to the Western Wall. The gate leading from the street into the little courtyard was open, the courtyard itself strewn with rubbish. The door to the library building was locked, but returning to the street I could look through the iron bars of the window, which had no glass panes left. The room was empty.

My Friend Ahmed

It was through Dr. Noah Braun that I got acquainted with Shaykh Ahmed Fakhraddīn al-Kinānī within a few weeks of my arrival in Jerusalem. My first meeting with Ahmed must have taken place in the summer of 1933; it led to a friendship that stood the test of time, including periods of great stress when the Arab attacks pitched Arab and Jew against each other all over Palestine.

Ahmed was about twelve years my senior, a man of average stature and slender build, with black hair that he wore cropped short, light olive skin, black eyes (one of which was turned slightly outward without making him pronouncedly wall-eyed), a straight and narrow nose, generous lips that enclosed a set of sizable white teeth, and a strong chin. He always wore European suits—dark in the winter, light in the summer—at least on the occasions when he and I met. At first he wore the traditional red fez of the Palestinian (and Syrian, Egyptian, etc.) effendi. A snapshot taken of us in the summer of 1933 at the entrance of the mosque built around the tombs of the patriarchs in Hebron still shows Ahmed with his fez and me with my topee, but soon thereafter he gave up his fez and I my topee, and we both walked about bareheaded. When going out, Ahmed would invariably carry a thick wad of Arabic newspapers in the left outer pocket of his jacket—all the outdoor photographs I have show him with such papers sticking out, reaching well above his left elbow.

Ahmed was a member of one of the oldest families in Jerusalem. As he carefully pointed out to me early in our friendship, the Kinānīs, better known as the *khatīb* (preacher) family because they held the hereditary position of the *khatīb* in the Aqsā Mosque, could trace back their history in Jerusalem for no less than eight centuries, while the two other great Arab families that outshone them in influence, the Nashāshībīs and the Husaynīs—the former the family of the mayor of Jerusalem, and the latter that of the mufti—went back a mere four hundred years. I never bothered to verify this claim, but once or twice I did meet through Ahmed his cousin (I forget his first name) who actually was the *khatīb* of the Aqsā Mosque at the time, and he quite spontaneously supplied me with the same information. Other old families that constituted the *a'yān* (literally, eyes, that is, the notables) of Muslim Arab Jerusalem were the Khālidīs, Ansārīs, Dajjānīs, and 'Ālamīs.

Ahmed himself was a teacher (*ustādh*) in an Arab boys' school in Jerusalem. He was considered eminently qualified for that position since he was a graduate of the famous al-Azhar, the Cairene Muslim school of higher learning, with the title *shaykh*. Come to think of it, in all the years of my friendship with Ahmed, while I was frequently a guest in his house, I never once visited his school.

Politics was a subject that Ahmed and I did not often touch in our conversations, but I was soon to find out that between the two major rival family-parties of Arab Palestine, the Nashāshībīs and the Husaynīs, all the Kinānīs' sympathies lay with the former. In fact, one of Ahmed's best friends was Ribhī Nashāshībī, a cousin of the mayor of Jerusalem. As for Arab-Jewish relations, that was a subject we discussed but rarely. Since Ahmed sympathized with the Nashāshībīs, his attitude toward the Jews was more liberal or friendly than was that of the Husaynīs, who, led by Hājj Amīn al-Husaynī, the mufti of Jerusalem, organized attacks on the Jews from 1936 on. As for Ahmed and me personally, we heartily agreed that, as he put it succinctly, *al-'Arab wal-Yahūd ikhwān* (the Arabs and the Jews are brothers); as for the undeniable political differences between them, we took refuge in blaming the English, that is, the British Mandatory Government of Palestine, which, we agreed, incited the two brother-peoples against each other in order to make the prolongation or perpetuation of their control over the country appear necessary. In 1936, when the mufti-incited Arab rioting began and security of life and limb for both Jews and Arabs diminished (the Arab terrorists killed more Arabs who disagreed with them or failed to support them than Jews), Ahmed and I solemnly vowed that if either one of us should be in danger, the other would take him in, give him shelter, and protect him.

Fortunately it never came to that. But tension between the Arabs and the Jews not only made visits to the Old City hazardous for me, but also rendered it difficult for Ahmed to come to the Jewish part of the city where I lived and for me to visit him in his house in the Arab quarter of Shaykh Jarrāh. Although the Arab attacks lasted through 1936 and 1937, the tension was not constant, ebbing and flowing; whenever it abated to an appreciable extent, we felt that we could again take up visiting each other. About this time Ahmed acquired the habit of coming to my house bare-headed—in the absence of any Arab headgear, such as the red fez he previously used to wear, and dressed as he always was in a conservatively cut European-style suit, he could not easily be recognized as an Arab. For me, likewise hatless—I had abandoned my topee, the pith helmet that had been the first piece of accoutrement I acquired after my arrival in Jerusalem—it was somewhat more difficult to make my way through the Arab quarter to Ahmed's house, but I still made it, albeit less frequently.

As far as religious observance was concerned, Ahmed's position toward Islam closely paralleled mine toward Judaism. We both felt that we could safely disregard the ritual prescriptions of our respective religions, while at the same time remaining faithful, and even enthusiastic, upholders of its values, its ethical doctrines, and its cultural orientation. Since in these areas there are great similarities between Judaism and Islam, we felt that we did share a common cultural heritage that made us brethren far more than did the tradition of our joint Abrahamic descent. As a graduate of al-Azhar, the great and venerable central institution of Islamic learning in Cairo, Ahmed was as well grounded in the Muslim *'ulūm al-dīn* (sciences of religion) as I was in those of Judaism, thanks to my studies in the equally venerable, although much younger, Rabbinical Seminary of Budapest. Thus, what I learned from him was not only Arabic, but also something of the rich Muslim scholarship al-Azhar imparted to its students; similarly, Ahmed not only learned Hebrew from me, but also acquired an understanding of the various branches of traditional Jewish learning. We noted the correspondences between the Jewish and the Muslim Scriptures, between the Jewish *halakha* (tradition) as developed and laid down in the talmudic and later rabbinic literature and the Muslim *hadīth* (tradition) as developed and laid down in the great collections of Muslim, Bukhārī, and others, and likewise between the

Jewish *minhag* and the Muslim *sunna*—both terms meaning "custom" and having an obligatory connotation—and went on to note the differences between the historical development of the two religions, with Islam split at an early age by sectarian divergences, and Judaism experiencing branchings-off only from the eighteenth century on.

Because Ahmed was a nonobservant Muslim, he did not feel bound to follow the Muslim religious custom with regard to the position he assigned to his wife and the comportment he expected of her. Ahmed married quite late, about the same time I did, in 1940—neither of us was invited to the wedding of the other—but I was less than thirty at the time, while he had passed his fortieth year. As for polygamy, it was a foregone conclusion for him that he would marry only one wife and not make use of the Koranic permission to marry four wives at a time, which for Muslims was also legal according to the laws of British-ruled Palestine. With regard to the religious background of the women he considered eligible—we occasionally spoke about it—he said he would not mind marrying a Jewish woman if she would fit into his family as his brother's Baghdadi Jewish wife did. But when I asked him whether he would consider marrying a Christian Arab woman, his answer was a definite, even vehement, and final "no!" which, I felt, betrayed a strongly negative attitude on his part to Christian Arabs in general.

On one occasion when we talked about this, he told me that he considered the Christian Arabs renegades and betrayers of Islam and was unwilling to budge from this position even though I pointed out the obvious fact (which, of course, he had known anyway) that the Christian Arabs were not descendants of Muslim Arabs who had converted to Christianity, but the remnant of Christian populations that had lived in Palestine (and in other countries of the Near East) long before the days of Muhammad, who, after the Arab conquest, became Arabicized while remaining faithful to their old religion. His point was that, whatever their antecedents, the Christian Arabs were a sore on the body of Arabdom, which in his mind was inseparably identified with Islam, that they not only denied the prophethood of Muhammad—as of course the Jews did too—but, worse, were caught in the mire of *shirk,* the fallacy of attributing associates to God, which was akin to the grievous sin of idolatry. Once, when I went with him to one of the old Christian churches in Jerusalem—I think, but am not sure, that it was the Church of the Holy Sepulcher—he looked around at the two- and three-dimensional representations of Christ with a contempt that revealed to me the deep Muslim revulsion at the *asnām* (idols or images)—a revulsion that, I felt, was more vehement than that of the most religious Orthodox or Hasidic Jew, perhaps because in contrast to the latter it never had to be suppressed but was given free rein for thirteen centuries.

In any case, the woman Ahmed ultimately married was a Muslim, about twenty or twenty-five years his junior. She was a daughter of one of the leading Arab families in Jerusalem, a pretty woman with dark eyes always framed by thick black lines of kohl, a low and narrow forehead, regular features, beautiful white skin—highly prized by the Arabs—and a tendency to put on weight, which markedly increased after she began bearing children. I don't know whether Mrs. Ahmed (I have forgotten her first name) wore a veil when she went out shopping or visiting in the Arab quarters of the city, but whenever she came to visit us with Ahmed she was unveiled—her head was covered with a black kerchief, much in the manner of tradition-abiding Oriental Jewish women. Her dress was also black, of the length fashionable at the time, and over it, in winter, she wore a cardigan of some subdued color, but not black. When we, in turn, went to visit Ahmed's house, his wife would come in unveiled, serve us the inevitable black coffee and sweets, and sit down and chat with us exactly as any European woman would have done.

The Ahmeds had several children who arrived in rapid succession. I remember the oldest, a son whom they named Badr (Full Moon), who became an employee in the office of the Arab electric company of Jerusalem. I also remember, from one of my post-1967 visits, a daughter (her name escapes me), who had been slightly wounded during the Arab-Jewish fighting that resulted in the Jewish occupation of all Jerusalem and its unification as the capital of Israel. With the annexation of East Jerusalem after that war, Ahmed and his family became Israeli Arabs.

Throughout the years of my friendship with Ahmed until 1947, he had no phone in his house (neither did I—a home phone in those days was a rare privilege), so that, unless we made an appointment in advance, whenever I went to visit him I had to chance not finding him at home. If he was at home, he usually opened the door himself, wearing pajamas (irrespective of the hour), as was the custom among townspeople when at home. He would usher me (or us, as the case might be) into the salon, then ask our pardon, disappear, and a few minutes later return, dressed in a suit, with vest and tie. Another two or three minutes later there would be a knock on the door, and the inevitable coffee and sweets would be handed to him by a person who remained invisible or brought in by his wife.

The coffee and sweets would be followed by the narghile, the tall, ornate water-pipe, consisting of a slender vaselike glass body of some two feet in height; at least two always stood around in the corners of Ahmed's *qāʿa* (sitting room). Just as it was a custom of Arab courtesy to pick out a cigarette from a box or a pack and hand it to the guest, so it was a much older custom to prepare a narghile for him. Ahmed began by calling out, *Yā ʿAbed!* whereupon a little black boy appeared at the door, and Ahmed told him to bring in charcoal from the kitchen. When I heard the boy's name and saw that he was black, I was, of course, intrigued by his presence in Ahmed's house. At the time there were rumors afloat in Jewish Palestine that in some parts of the Arab world (especially in areas remote from contact with the West) household slavery, including concubinage, still existed. I would have liked to find out what precisely was the status of the little black boy in the Kināni family. I knew that the Arabic word *'abed* (in literary Arabic *'abd*) meant primarily black or slave and that it was also used in the sense of servant, but usually only in such constructions as *'Abd Allah* (Servant of God). One of the things that had already fascinated me about Arabic in Germany when I sat at the feet of the great Brockelmann was the infinite variety of plural forms, which contrasted sharply with the stark simplicity of the one single masculine (-*im*) and one single feminine (-*ot*) plural in Hebrew. Thus, I happened to know that Arabic differentiates the plural forms of this one word *'abd* according to its meanings: *'abīd, 'ubdān, 'ibdān* and many other forms mean slaves or blacks, while *'ibād* means servants of God.

But I was embarrassed to put a direct question and instead only asked Ahmed whether *'Abed* was the name of the black boy. In response he explained that it was the abbreviation of *'Abd ul-Rahmān* (Servant of the Merciful), a famous old Arabic name, which however was too long to use in summoning the boy or addressing him. Since Ahmed volunteered no information about the identity of the boy or his position in the household, I felt that a second question about him would have been out of place.

'Abed brought in the glowing charcoal and Ahmed placed it into the metal cup that topped the narghile, covered it with roughly cut chunks of tobacco, and began to suck vigorously at the mouthpiece (*narbij* or *narbish*), from which came the long flexible tube whose other end reached into the body of the narghile, but ended well above the level of the water. By sucking at the *narbij*, air was pulled out from the small chamber of air above the water level, which in turn forced the outside air to go through the burning tobacco and charcoal into the water and take down the smoke by means of a rigid tube that reached down into the water almost to the bottom of the vase. From there the smoky air rose in bubbles through the water and, properly cooled, went from the air-chamber into the flexible tube, and from there into Ahmed's lungs. Because the smoke thus goes through the water, the Arabic expression when offering a narghile to a guest is *b'tishrab narghīle?* (Will you drink a narghile?). When, after several energetic pulls, Ahmed got the narghile going, he wiped the *narbij* dry, sterilized it by lighting a match, wiped off whatever soot might have discolored the ivory mouthpiece, and finally offered it to me. I went at it, and although I did not particularly like the sensation of the cold smoke, I expressed my due appreciation of his fine tobacco.

In relation to the "drinking" of the narghile, I am reminded of another Arab custom, which, when I first encountered it, caused me much suppressed amusement. When drinking the inevitable small cup of strong, black coffee, the customary polite way of showing one's appreciation of the beverage, and of the host's hospitality in offering it, was to take small but noisy sips, letting out an emphatic "ahhh" after every sip—these noises were supposed to demonstrate that one truly enjoyed the coffee. Once one finished the cup, taking care to stop slurping the syrupy liquid just before one reached the mudlike sediment that accumulated at the bottom, one put down the cup, saying *dayman* (always), the abbreviated expression of the wish that the host should always be in the position to serve coffee to his guests.

I also remember the seemingly interminable polite formulaic greetings of welcome, the veritable question-and-answer period about each other's well-being, first in a cursory form while entering the house and the *qā'a* and then, after being seated, again in a more extensive and leisurely fashion. But I quickly got used to these formalized niceties and learned to enjoy them to the extent that the matter-of-fact brevity with which I was received when visiting a Jewish friend began to appear unsatisfactory, cold, and lacking refinement.

All in all, there was much that I liked in the Arab world with which I got acquainted after my arrival in Jerusalem. As I advanced in understanding the colloquial Arabic of the street, which I did despite the reluctance of my friend Ahmed to teach it to me, I began to appreciate the flavor of that idiom, the richness of the folklore that colored it, the many proverbs, sayings, and elaborate and pithy expressions that sprang to the lips of even the most uneducated, including small children, who seemed to absorb an extraordinary language ability with their mother's milk, as it were. I became fascinated by the burgeoning Arab folk life and supplemented the random information I gathered in the course of my excursions into the Arab world of Jerusalem and Palestine, in the company of Ahmed or alone, with books on this subject.

Occasionally, when an Egyptian theatrical troupe came to give guest-performances in Jerusalem, Ahmed would take me to see a play. I remember in particular one such play in which the hero was a cardinal whose brother was accused of having committed murder. The cardinal knew that his brother was innocent because the real murderer had confessed his crime to him, but he had done so under the secrecy of the confessional, which the cardinal was unable to violate. I have long since forgotten the name of the author and the title of the play, but I do remember its most dramatic scene and the solution of the cardinal's problem. I also remember that the play was given, not in the Egyptian colloquial, but in classical literary Arabic. I can still hear the great monologue of the cardinal in which, strutting up and down the stage, he describes, in sonorous classical Arabic cadences, the inner struggle between his desire to save his brother from execution and his inviolable commitment to the sanctity of the confessional. At one point, in utter desperation, he cries out, *walākin hatmun 'alā shafatayyī* (But there is a seal upon my lips!) Perhaps I remember precisely this phrase because I was struck by the close parallel between Arabic and Hebrew these words happen to illustrate: the same phrase in Hebrew would be *v'ulam hotam 'al s'fatay.*

When the murderer next came to see the cardinal, a witness hid behind a curtain in his study. In the course of the conversation with the murderer, the cardinal led him to make clear references to having committed the crime. The witness was not bound by the confessional secrecy and could testify to what he had heard. I was not sure, and still am not, whether Catholic canon law countenances this kind of entrapment of a criminal whose crime had become known to a priest under the confessional, but the point was the dramatic moment.

It was thanks to Ahmed that I got a taste of what Ramadān, the month of fasting, meant for the Muslims. I don't think that he himself observed the onerous fast that requires the believers to eat and drink nothing from sunup to sundown for a whole month, but he did like to participate in the entertainments that, during the nights, balanced and compensated for the rigors of the fast during the days. For the month of Ramadān several storytellers (sing. *qassās*) and so-called poets (sing. *shā'ir*), actually poetry-reciters, would come to the Old City to the more popular cafes, where they would entertain appreciative audiences throughout the nights. On many a Ramadān night I sat with Ahmed in one of those cafes, listening to these performers, who seemed to have an interminable repertoire of story and song that carried them through the month without ever repeating themselves. They also must have had prodigious memories, for I never saw one of them refer to written notes. It is even possible that they were illiterate—illiterate people are known to have a better memory than literate ones—but in any case their unaided delivery hour after hour was a marvel.

The audience sat on the very low backless stools typical of Arab coffeehouses, drinking cup after cup of coffee and in between smoking the narghile. I never attended any of these performances that the audience did not enjoy enormously and visibly, or rather audibly, to judge from the frequent interjections of brief exclamations expressive of appreciation. The performers, whether they sang or recited stories, in most cases had very hoarse voices, as could be expected after the first few nights of using, or rather abusing, their vocal cords for hours on end. The storytellers, who catered to uneducated (and in most cases illiterate) audiences, used the colloquial dialects, which meant that in Palestine only Egyptian or Syrian *qassāsīn* could perform; the dialects of storytellers from more remote Arab countries would not have been understood.

There was one more scene in the Old City of Jerusalem that I shall never forget. In one of the houses lining the *sūq* there was a small grain store, and behind it, in a semidark room, a camel going around in a tight circle, tied to a heavy wooden pole that turned a large millstone. The camel was blindfolded, its eyes covered by two cup-shaped pieces of wood that protruded from its forehead like two rudimentary horns; around and around it went, seemingly without any prodding by its driver. "What does it grind?" I asked the store-owner. "The wheat I am selling here," he answered. "Why is it blindfolded?" "Because if it could see it could not go around for hours and hours." I did not know, and don't know to this day, whether this piece of Arab folk animal psychology has a basis in reality, but I do know that the poor camel did in fact go around the mill all day long—I passed that store at varying hours and always saw it making its melancholy rounds. Inevitably, I was reminded of Samson, who, blinded by the Philistines, was forced to take the place of such a camel and "grind in the prison house."

As time passed and our friendship deepened, Ahmed began to tell me about his personal life, including, prior to his marriage, his relationships with women. As a teacher in an Arab boys' school in Jerusalem he had some contact with his pupils' families, which, of course, included women. Once, he told me, the sister of one of his pupils came to the school to consult with him about her brother, whose school performance was unsatisfactory. Since they were alone in the teachers' room—it was after school hours—she lifted her veil. One thing led to another, and thereafter she would come to see him in the school after the pupils and the teachers had left the premises, and they could make use of the couch in the teachers' room undisturbed.

Ahmed confided in me that he was well aware that he was not a nice-looking man, but, he said with a certain self-satisfaction, he had something that attracted women more, namely, *rujūliyye* (manliness). He had quite a number of Jewish acquaintances, and more than one Jewish girl (or woman) had, according to him, succumbed to his *rujūliyye,* even if he did not take the initiative. On one occasion, he told me, when he paid a visit to a German Jewish woman and sat next to her on a sofa chatting with her for quite a while but without making any other move, she brought her hand down on his knee, giving it a smart tap, and exclaimed, "What is it with you, Ahmed, don't you have any feelings?" I don't remember what, if anything, he told me about his reaction to this provocation.

Early in our friendship I introduced Ahmed to my sister and brother-in-law, and thereafter all four of us would meet from time to time, visit each other, and undertake joint walks around the city. On at least one occasion my parents also joined us, and all of us paid a visit to Shaykh Amīn al-Ansārī in his library in the Old City. I took some photographs of my family with Shaykh Amīn in the library courtyard; making use of the self-timer of my Leica, I was able to join them in the pictures. One of the pictures taken during that same visit to the Old City shows both Ahmed and me wearing the traditional red fez of the Arab effendi, but I cannot remember who was the second Arab from whom I borrowed the headgear.

At about that time Ahmed and his brother (who, as I mentioned, was married to a Jewish woman from Baghdad) planned to build a house for themselves and their widowed mother. They had a sizable building lot in the Shaykh Jarrāh Quarter, on the hillside not far from the road leading from Meah Shearim to the British military cemetery and on to the campus of the Hebrew University on Mount Scopus. Ahmed asked my brother-in-law to prepare architectural plans for the house. What he had in mind was a really big house in which there would be room for the whole extended al-Kinānī family. Leon prepared a beautiful plan for a one-story house, keeping in mind that it had to provide comfort and privacy for two or more married couples and numerous children. The front of the house had a central entrance, from which two sizable reception rooms opened to the left and right, each fronted by an impressive arched terrace. From the front to the back of the house ran an elongated central hall from which doors led on each side into a series of rooms. At the rear of the house were the kitchen, bathroom, and toilet. The lot was big enough to leave room for a garden that surrounded the entire house.

Since Ahmed was a friend, Leon never discussed his fee with him. When the plan was completed and delivered, Ahmed declared himself delighted with it; then, instead of asking Leon what he owed him, he simply handed him a check for an amount he evidently considered adequate—and perhaps by the Arab standards of those days it indeed was. But Leon, and all of us, thought it rather shabby. Not a word, of course, was said about it, and the friendship with Ahmed continued unimpaired.

In contrast to the Jewish trade custom that required the architect to supervise the construction of a house he had planned, the Arab custom seems to have been to give the architectural plans to a building contractor who translated the drawings into brick and mortar, without making any use of the architect's services. In any case, this is what Ahmed and his brother did, so that once Leon delivered his plans he had nothing more to do with the building. Only when the house was finished did Ahmed invite us, together with many of his Arab and Jewish friends, to a kind of housewarming, in which the women gathered in one of the two reception rooms, the men in the other. On that occasion, or perhaps on one of my subsequent visits to the house, I went to the lavatory and, to my surprise, found that it contained not a "European" toilet with a seat, but an "Arab" toilet (known in French as *toilette à la Turque*), consisting of a (ca. 3' by 3') molded white enamel floor-plate with a hole in its middle flanked by two somewhat elevated footrests, on which one had to balance oneself facing either backward or forward. I remember how surprised I was: Ahmed spent a large amount of money to build a beautiful and spacious house of some ten or more rooms and then saved a few pounds by installing such a primitive (not to mention uncomfortable) toilet.

For several years I met Ahmed almost once a week, either in his home or in mine, for the avowed purpose of exchanging language lessons. I taught him Hebrew; he taught me Arabic. With the Hebrew there was no problem, since there was only one Hebrew language in use, whether in books, newspapers, lectures, or everyday conversation, and that was the language I taught him. He had no particular aptitude for languages, and although (as he often told me) Hebrew seemed to him but a simplified variety of Arabic, which is certainly true as far as grammar is concerned, his pronunciation remained typically and heavily Arabic throughout. Interestingly, this was not the case with Ahmed's brother, who spoke Hebrew exactly as the language was pronounced by Jews from Arab countries, nor with our mutual friend Ribhī Nashāshībī, who had a women's dress shop on the lower Jaffa Road, not far from the Jaffa Gate, and who had an astounding ability to speak Hebrew and Yiddish precisely as these languages were spoken by Ashkenazi Jews.

However, with the Arabic that Ahmed taught me there was a problem. By the time I arrived in Jerusalem, having been drilled by Brockelmann and by my Hungarian professors, I had quite a good reading knowledge of Arabic. What I now wanted to learn was to *speak* the language, to be able to go to the bazaar in the Old City, to converse with the merchants, to haggle with them as I saw the Arab customers do. To this was soon added the scholarly desire to be able to gather folkloristic material among the Arabs of Palestine. Since the colloquial Arabic idiom in every Arab country was (and is) very different from the literary Arabic in which the books and newspapers were (and are) written, to familiarize myself with the Palestinian Arabic vernacular almost amounted to learning a new language.

This was the language I wanted Ahmed to teach me, but he balked. His attitude, like that of most educated Arabs at the time, was totally negative as far as colloquial Arabic was concerned. He had a strong contempt for the *basīta* (vulgar) Arabic and tried to convince me that, with the spread of education among the Arabs, a rapidly growing number of them could speak or at least understand the *fushā* (also called *nahwīyye*), the pure, grammatically correct Arabic language. The issue almost became a contest of wills between us; since his position was based on a deep conviction, while mine was simply a matter of practical utility—and I was not completely sure that he was not right—he prevailed, and we conversed in literary Arabic during the Arabic part of our study sessions. Nevertheless, as I listened to conversations in the street, I gradually picked up some of the *basīta*, and at our meetings I would always ask the meaning and derivation of a few expressions and phrases.

Ahmed's negative attitude to the *basīta* was only one manifestation of his disdain for the folkways of the simple, uneducated Arabs, a position shared by most of the educated Arabs, who made up what in those days was still called the "effendi class." Another expression of the same attitude was his unhappiness over my wearing a black-and-white knitted skullcap that was the traditional headdress of the Palestinian fellahin, which I purchased during one of my early visits to the Old City *sūq*. I tried to pooh-pooh his objections, but when I saw that he was actually embarrassed to show himself on the streets in the company of a man who wore such a head-covering, I gave in and thereafter we both walked about bareheaded.

It was Ahmed who, within a few weeks of my arrival in Jerusalem, took me for the first time to visit the Haram al-Sharīf (Noble Sanctuary), as the Temple area is called in Arabic. At the time, officially at least, the entire Muslim mosque-complex was out of bounds to non-Muslims, although in practice the guards did not scrutinize the visitors too closely to determine whether they were Muslims or not. So, when I was in the company of a well-known Arab effendi and *ustādh* (teacher), who for those occasions put on his red fez, I was never stopped or questioned. We went first into the Qubbat al-Sakhra (Dome of the Rock), popularly referred to as the Mosque of Omar. I can still vividly recall the awe with which I stood, at first in front of and then inside, that most magnificent example of early Arab architecture. This was a short time after I first laid eyes on the whole Haram area from Mount Scopus, but that first glimpse from a distance in no way prepared me for what I felt when I stood there in the door of the dome, took off my shoes, entered the building, and saw before me—and could approach and touch— that great primeval rock around which the dome was built.

Ahmed pointed out to me the small round indentation on the surface of the rock, considered by Arab tradition to be the hoofprint of al-Burāq, the legendary winged horse of Muhammad, which according to Arab tradition kicked itself up from this spot to take the Prophet into heaven for a nocturnal visit. Then we went down into the cave under the rock, and again Ahmed had something to tell me about it: when Muhammad flew heavenward on the back of al-Burāq, the rock wanted to follow him and started to rise, but the horse gave it a powerful kick with its hoof to keep it down. Thus, the rock remained hovering in midair, just a few feet above ground, and this is how the cave under it came into being.

Later I was to read much about the rock in Arabic and Jewish sources; in fact, for a time I toyed with the idea of writing a book about it since I found that the rock, called Even Sh'tiyya (Foundation Stone) in Hebrew, played an important role in Hebrew and Jewish history for almost two thousand years before the Muslim conquest of Palestine. I even started to collect material for such a book—I still have much of it in a bulky file—but somehow I never got around to writing it. Incidentally, the name Foundation Stone, which is the Talmudic designation of the rock, reflects the legend (or the legend reflects the name) that, when God decided to create the world,

He started by taking this stone from under his heavenly throne and casting it into the middle of the primeval abyss. Then He built up the dry land around it in concentric circles, just as the embryo develops—this was also believed by the ancient Hebrews—from and around its navel. Hence the Even Sh'tiyya was considered the navel of the earth, a claim duplicated by many *omphalos* myths attached to holy places of other peoples. To this day I regret that I did not take time from my other activities to write this study. Perhaps a young scholar, at whose disposal I would put my notes, will do it one of these days.

But, to return to that first visit to the Haram in 1933, after the Dome of the Rock the neighboring, much larger, Masjid al-Aqsā (Farthest Mosque) was a disappointment. It was originally constructed a hundred years after the Dome of the Rock, in the eighth century; although it is impressive in its huge oblong emptiness with the high pulpit on its southern wall, it lacks the exquisite beauty of the octagonal Dome of the Rock and, in particular, has nothing to match the raw power emanating from the primeval rock itself, which, if not actually the navel of the earth, is certainly the peak of the ancient and most holy Mount Moriah of legendary fame. I have long lost count of the number of times I visited the Haram both while I lived in Jerusalem and later when I was a frequent visitor to Israel, but the sense of awe I felt when I first saw it recurred again and again, each time I set foot in those hallowed precincts.

Although the dominant tone of the Old City was Arab and Muslim, it was equally sacred to the Christians and Jews. The chief Christian holy place was, of course, the Church of the Holy Sepulcher, which had for centuries attracted pilgrims from all over the world and induced some of them to settle around it and, in the case of the Ethiopian monks, to establish themselves on its very roof. The Jews had many synagogues in their quarter in the Old City, but only one really old and important shrine, the Western Wall, which was the retaining wall of the terrace built up by King Herod around the ancient Jewish Temple rebuilt by him. In the days I am trying to conjure up in these pages, there was only a narrow corridor in front of the wall, perhaps eight or ten feet wide, which ran along part of the length of the wall; the rest of it was blocked by small hovel-like buildings. Whenever I went to the Wall there was always a crowd of Jews praying in front of it, most of them from the ultra-Orthodox communities, dressed in kaftans and black velour hats, which on the Sabbath and holidays they exchanged for the fur-brimmed *shtraymel*. In those days the British Mandatory authorities did not permit the Jews to place even a single table or chair before the Wall, so that the Jews were unable to take a Tora scroll into the area and read out the weekly passage, which is an integral part of the Sabbath services. All they could do was to recite individual prayers and stick little slips of paper with pious requests scribbled on them into the crevices between the immense hewn-stone blocks of the Wall.

However, behind and above the Wall, in the spacious Haram area itself, memories of the biblical past of the Jews abounded. This fact was first pointed out to me by a relative of Ahmed whose office adjoined the Aqsā Mosque. I have long forgotten his name but I do remember that he too was a shaykh and wore on his head the red fez surrounded by a tightly wound white headcloth. He was a scholar and an expert on the history of the Haram and pointed out to us that, while the Haram area was rich in small monuments and structures traditionally associated with biblical Jewish historical figures, the hundreds of years of Christian occupation of the site had left no mark on it anywhere. To the south of the Dome of the Rock, he said, was the small Dome of Joseph; somewhat farther to the west, the Dome of Moses; in the northern corner of the central platform was the Dome of al-Khidr, that is, Elijah; close to the northern edge of the outer terrace was the Dome of Solomon; and, of course, right there to the east were the huge underground Solomonic stables, while in the north, hugging the eastern walls of the Haram, was the "Seat of Solomon." He also pointed out that Nabī Dawūd (the Prophet David), that is, King David, had his *mihrāb* (prayer-niche) here at the southern end of the Haram, while the Prophet Zechariah also had his own *mihrāb* right here in the Aqsā Mosque. At the opposite end of the area, in the north, there was the Minārat Isrā'īl (Minaret of Israel), and next to it, at the northeastern corner of the Haram, was the Bāb al-Asbāt (Gate of the Tribes), thus named after the tribes of Israel. "As you can see," the shaykh concluded, "the ancient history of the Banī Isrā'īl [Children of Israel] is well attested in our Muslim Haram, while of Christian history not a trace has been left." I should add that my ability to enumerate all these details is not an extraordinary feat of memory—as soon as the good shaykh began to list the biblical features in the "Noble Sanctuary," I whipped out my notebook and started to jot them down.

Later, in the course of my own investigations, I found that either inadvertently or for the sake of presenting a complete argument the shaykh omitted to mention that at least one Christian memento has, in fact, survived in the Haram: in its southeastern corner there was a small structure called the "Cradle of Jesus." It would be interesting to establish how and why Muslim tradition transplanted the cradle of Jesus from the manger in Bethlehem to the sanctuary in Jerusalem. For that matter, it would be equally interesting to trace how and why Joseph, Moses, David, Elijah, and the "tribes" came to be associated with particular spots in the Haram area that they certainly never visited.

My explorations of Palestine in the company of Ahmed were not confined to Jerusalem. They took in the environs of the city, the Kidron Valley with its ancient monuments, Bethlehem with its Christian holy places, and Hebron with its Muslim sanctuary erected over the traditional Tombs of the Patriarchs, of whom only the first, Abraham, is considered their common ancestor by both Jews and Arabs. The others—Abraham's wife Sarah, their son Isaac and his wife Rebecca, their son Jacob and his wife Leah, whose tombs are also shown there, in what is believed to be the original biblical Cave of Machpelah—were the ancestors only of the Children of Israel, but nevertheless they too are venerated by the Arabs as well. I described that first visit of mine to Hebron in a Hungarian article published in the September 1934 issue of Father's journal under the title "In the City of Abraham," and thus I don't have to strain my memory in recalling what I observed and experienced on that occasion.

The article says that our visit took place on a Friday, the Yawm al-Jum'a (Day of the Assembly) of the Muslims, when communal prayers were held in the mosque housed in the same building as the tombs of the patriarchs. As a non-Muslim, I was not allowed to enter. Ahmed, of course, could have gone in, but he did not want to leave me alone outside. So we went only a few steps up the broad stairs leading from the street level to the entrance of the building; there, using my self-timer, I took a picture of the two of us standing side by side, both in white (or very light-colored) suits, Ahmed with his fez on his head and I with my topee. When I gave vent to my indignation over not being allowed to enter and pay homage to my ancestors, Ahmed flashed a somewhat embarrassed smile and said, "Abraham expelled Ishmael from his tent for the sake of Isaac, and now the sons of Ishmael don't allow the sons of Isaac to enter the tent of Abraham." Then he added, "My friend Shaykh Ibrāhīm, the governor of the Hebron district, is now away on vacation. When he returns, I shall get his permission to take you inside the Haram al-Khalīl." *Khalīl* (friend) is the Arabic name of Hebron, so called after Abraham who was the friend of Allah.

Other excursions Ahmed and I undertook, sometimes in the company of several of my Jewish friends, but never with any of his Arab friends, led to the environs of Jerusalem, to the north and to the east. I remember a walk we took to the Arab village of Anātha to the east of Jerusalem, whose name preserved the biblical name of Anathot, the birthplace of the Prophet Jeremiah, which, in turn, seems to have been so called after the Canaanite goddess Anath. From Anātha we descended into the nearby deep gorge, called Wādī Fāra, to the source contained in it, called 'Eyn Fāra, from which water was pumped up to Jerusalem. There was also a *tell* there, known as Tell Fāra. These names, incidentally, preserved an old biblical name: I checked and found that in the Book of Joshua, among the cities of Benjamin, is listed a place called Parah (Josh. 18:23), and that in the book of Jeremiah it reappears as Perath (Jer. 13:4 and 7). Since Arabic has no *p*, an *f* is regularly substituted for the Hebrew *p*.

Another time we visited the Mar Saba monastery, located near the eastern end of the Kidron Valley, just before it debouches into the plain of Jericho. The monastery is built into the steep hillside, and from it a magnificent view opens to the plain lying beneath it. I still have a photograph (taken, I believe, by Ahmed) showing me walking down just outside the southeastern corner belltower of the monastery, with the plain of Jericho in the distance.

Other snapshots I still have, all dating from 1933 or 1934, show Ahmed and me or only him (if I took the picture) in the company of Hanna Kroch, Piri Breuer, and some other girls or with members of my family in various parts of the country, in the open, in front of buildings, or in the Judean Desert. He is happily smiling in all of them, and it was evident to me even at that time that he derived considerable pleasure from these outings, as, of course, did I. What I enjoyed most was to explore parts of the country I could not have reached without his guidance and thus to get a glimpse of Arab Palestine at a time when the Arabs formed the overwhelming majority of the population. For him, all the places he took me to were, of course, long familiar, but he enjoyed showing them to me and letting me see the respect people everywhere paid him. In addition, I suspect, he was intrigued by walking about in public in the company of women, something it would have been impossible for him to do within the confines of Arab society.

It was with the help of Ahmed that my sister and brother-in-law found lodgings in Jericho when the Public Works Department for which Leon worked sent him there to supervise several building projects. Ahmed contacted relatives in Jericho—he seemed to have relatives everywhere—who were willing to let Leon and Évi rent a house they owned not far from the ancient *tell* of Jericho. During the months Leon and Évi lived there (the winter and spring of 1936) I visited them several times, occasionally in the company of Ahmed, and thus I had the opportunity to get acquainted with that unique Palestinian town.

In January 1937, when I returned to Jerusalem after a sojourn of half a year in Hungary, I found conditions in the country greatly deteriorated. The Arab riots were in full swing, and the frequent attacks on Jews made one feel, to say the least, rather uncomfortable as soon as one set foot outside the solidly Jewish quarters of the city. I shall describe later what effect all this had on my life, but here I want to mention that one of the outcomes was to introduce a subtle change into the relationship between Ahmed and me. The frequency of our meetings decreased, and when we did meet we felt a strain. Not that our friendship was impaired, but we both felt that there was an incompatibility between the unquestionable loyalty each of us had to his own people and the devoted friendship we had for each other. Both of us deplored the activities of the murderous Arab gangs, which Ahmed opposed bitterly for the simple reason that the targets of their attacks were more frequently Arabs than Jews. By 1938 the internecine Arab strife had intensified;

when the Nashāshībīs withdrew from the Arab Higher Committee, which had instigated and organized the Arab revolt, several members of the Nashāshībī family and party were murdered by henchmen of their Arab opponents. Since Ahmed's family was allied with the Nashāshībīs, it was natural for him to be opposed to the Husaynī-dominated Arab Higher Committee and to condemn the murderous acts it engaged in.

I on my part was just as vehemently opposed to the violence committed by the Irgun and later by the so-called Stern Group (actually called Lohme Herut Yisrael, that is, Fighters for the Freedom of Israel, abbreviated Lehi), the two Jewish bodies that carried out armed reprisals against the Arabs as well as the British. I was convinced that the Havlaga (Restraint) policy adopted by the Jewish Agency and the Hagana, the official but underground Jewish self-defense organization sponsored by it, was the right stance to take.

Apart from the struggle to make ends meet, I was at the time totally immersed in three major tasks. One was the fascinating search into the world of the customs and beliefs, way of life, and way of thinking of the Jews in biblical and talmudic times. The second, to try to learn as much as I could of the folk-life of the Oriental Jews and of the Arabs who surrounded me in contemporary Palestine. And the third, which, I felt, was a historic mission I was called upon to carry out, was to create public interest in saving Jewish folklore from oblivion. Any one of these tasks would have been enough to demand my total commitment; the three together made it quite impossible for me to take more than a fleeting interest in the current politics of the *yishuv* and the ideological clashes between it and both the Arabs and the British. This, of course, did not mean that I shirked my patriotic duty of participating in the semiofficial self-defense formations of the Jewish community, about which I shall tell in a later chapter.

As for Ahmed, I had no way of knowing whether in his heart of hearts he was as apolitical as I was, but that certainly was the impression he conveyed throughout the years of our friendship. What I remember quite distinctly is that we never discussed either the Arab aspirations to shake off the British Mandatory rule and achieve an independent Arab Palestine or the parallel Jewish efforts, which gradually intensified in that period, of realizing Herzl's dream of a Jewish state on the same little piece of real estate. We frequently deplored the violence committed by either camp and agree on blaming the British for the tension between the Arabs and the Jews, to whom we continued to refer in a wistfully romantic way as *ikhwān*—brothers.

In the last few years of my Jerusalem period I saw Ahmed less frequently than before. He was busy with his teaching, his growing family, and difficulties brought about by the intensifying intra-Arab strife. I too had a wife and two small daughters to take care of and, in addition to the scholarly work that took up most of my time, was busy with the institute I founded, the journal I launched, and the series of books I edited—all with very little help from anyone other than my wife.

In the fall of 1947, when the day of my departure for America was set, I went to say good-bye to Ahmed and his family. We vowed to remain in touch, a vow that, in the event, neither of us kept. Certainly I never imagined at that juncture that twenty years would pass before we would meet again. Although I was a frequent visitor to Jerusalem—now the capital of the young state of Israel—the Shaykh Jarrāh Quarter in which Ahmed lived was on the other side of the border, under Jordanian occupation, in "enemy" territory, so that a meeting was out of the question. Once, and if I remember correctly only once, I wrote a letter to him from New York. To avoid embarrassing him with a Hebrew letter—I did not know to what extent letters received by Arab inhabitants of East Jerusalem were subject to Jordanian censorship—I wrote him in Arabic. In order to make sure that no errors slipped in and that my Arabic style was up to standard, I gave a draft of it to my friend Meir Bravmann to look over. I don't know whether my letter ever reached Ahmed, but I do not remember having received an answer from him.

Then came the Six-Day War of 1967, which brought all of the former Mandatory Palestine west of the Jordan River under Israeli rule and opened up the Old City and all the Arab sections of Jerusalem to Israeli visitors. A few weeks later, when I was on my annual prilgrimage to Israel (staying with my brother Saul in Jerusalem), I looked into the telephone directory of Arab East Jerusalem. When I found no al-Kinānī or al-Khatīb listed in the Shaykh Jarrāh Quarter, I picked another phone number in that quarter at random and called it. What happened next I described in the preface of my 1973 book *The Arab Mind:*

> A woman answered. "Do you know the *ustādh* Ahmed al-Khatīb? How is he?" I asked her. "I know him. He is well, and so is his family," she answered. I asked her to send over somebody to tell Ahmed that his old friend Rafa'il Bata'i would come to see him next morning. She promised to do so, and next morning I stood in front of Ahmed's house. I knocked. Ahmed's wife opened the door and bade me welcome. I sat down in the living room, and a moment later Ahmed entered. I had not seen him for twenty years. He was now well over seventy. As we embraced and cried, I was reminded of Jacob and Esau who, too, met after a separation of twenty years and fell on each other's necks and wept.

Rereading this description of my friendship with Ahmed and of the steps I took to get acquainted with Arab life in Palestine, I am again, as so many times in the past, seized with regret that I never took time off from my other work to write a study about traditional Arab Palestine, about that colorful, precious complex of folkways preserved faithfully for centuries, which began to disintegrate with the first Arab-Jewish war in 1948. I possessed, I believe, the prerequisites for undertaking such a study: a knowledge of the language and of the folkloristic *Arbeitsmethode*, contacts that would have enabled me to do fieldwork, and, above all, an interest in—and, more than that, an affinity with—the people about whom I would have written.

But there were always overriding factors that prevented me from realizing such a plan. During the first three years of my sojourn in Jerusalem I was committed to writing my doctoral thesis, which left me no time to undertake other major research projects. During the next three years (1936–1939) the Arab riots that engulfed the country made fieldwork in the Arab countryside and even in Arab Jerusalem, if not entirely impossible, certainly rather hazardous. After 1939, when security conditions in the country improved with the outbreak of World War II, I was deeply involved in courting Naomi, whom I married in 1940, in working on my book *Man and Earth in Hebrew Custom, Belief, and Legend* (two volumes of which were published in 1942 and 1943, respectively), in serving for a year (1942–1943) as academic secretary of the Technion in Haifa, and in bringing up my two daughters. From 1944 on I spent much time with the Palestine Institute of Folklore and Ethnology, whose work was directed primarily to the study of the various Jewish communities, editing its journal and its book series with very little outside help and studying the Jadīd al-Islām, the Marrano Jewish community of Meshhed, Iran, represented by a sizable contingent in Jerusalem. At the same time I worked on my first English book, *Man and Temple in Ancient Jewish Myth and Ritual,* which was published in 1947 in Edinburgh. Thus, my interest in Arab folklife was always pushed into the background, and once I left Jerusalem I lost the opportunity to do fieldwork among the Arabs and to write the book that I had long dreamt about.

Academic Acquaintances

Having recounted what I can remember of several of my Arab friends and acquaintances, I want now to speak of the faculty members of the Hebrew University whom I met and who befriended me soon after I started working on my thesis under Professor Klein. I shall mention only those with whom I had the closest contact; otherwise, I would end up with an almost complete listing of the Hebrew University faculty, which, in the early 1930s, counted no more than a few dozen members. I can no longer recall the circumstances of my meeting them, but I am positive that as soon as the 1933–1934 academic year began—after the Jewish High Holy Days—I got acquainted with practically all of them, including not only those who were in the humanities, but also those in the sciences, such as biology, chemistry, physics, and mathematics. I shall have more to say of several of them later, but here I want to speak primarily of those who helped me with my doctoral work and postgraduate studies.

Professor Samuel Klein

I remember quite a few things about Professor Klein himself that complement what I told about him in chapter 1. In addition to meeting his students in class, Klein would occasionally lead them in excursions to various parts of the country. In that manner he used the whole of Palestine as a big outdoor laboratory in which he could acquaint his students with the present-day status of the ancient Jewish places of settlement, whose very existence he was the first to establish. The group of fifteen to twenty students would take a bus to a kibbutz (communal settlement), *moshav* (cooperative settlement), or *moshava* (village of privately owned farms) and from there set out on foot to an elevated vantage point with a wide view of the surrounding area. Professor Klein would point out here and there a *tell*, a low mound with the characteristic flat top indicating that an ancient settlement lay buried below, giving us its ancient Hebrew name, its modern Arabic name, and the linguistic derivation of the latter from the former. He would then proceed to summarize the history of the ancient Jewish village or town that stood on that spot in biblical and talmudic times. If such a *tell* was not too far away, he would lead the group of students right up to it, and we would climb up its slope and look for telltale potsherds, which could be hundreds or even thousands of years old. Each time I stood on top of such a *tell* I had the feeling of being an heir to history, a descendant of those ancient people who lived right at that spot, some of whom may have been the very ones with whose names I was familiar from my readings of the Bible, the Talmud, and other works of ancient Jewish literature. If Klein's purpose was to make us aware of our deep roots in the land, he could not have chosen a better method to achieve it.

Professor Klein was not a great sportsman, and walking was not one of his strong points. When we would alight from the bus at the village of our destination, he would inquire whether the people there could let him have a horse for a few hours. He must have had friends in many of those places, because in most cases a horse was produced forthwith. We would set out together to explore the neighborhood, he riding in the midst of us, one of us leading the horse by the halter, and the others surrounding the solitary rider. Once, I remember, when we arrived at a spot about which Klein had much to tell us, he got off the horse, and I made use of the opportunity to mount the animal and asked one of my friends to take a picture of me as a horseman. I have long forgotten what I had in mind—possibly I remembered a line from a Hungarian poem I learned in high school many years earlier, which spoke of *a férfieszmény, a lovas vitéz*, of which I can give only a feeble translation as "the man-ideal, the mounted warrior."

On several of these excursions Dr. Benjamin Meisler (later Mazar) joined us. Benjamin, a budding archaeologist, was at the time twenty-seven or twenty-eight years old and worked as secretary of the Palestine Jewish Exploration Society, of which Klein was president. I don't know whether he was married by that time or married later, but I do remember that his wife was the younger sister of Yitzhaq Ben-Zvi, at the time chairman of the Va'ad Leumi (National Council of the Jews of Palestine), the precursor of the Israeli government. In 1952 Ben-Zvi became the second president of Israel. As for Benjamin, although he was a fine scholar, he had to wait until 1943 for an appointment at the Hebrew University, and until 1951 (when he was forty-five), to become professor of Israeli archaeology. Thereafter, his rise in the university hierarchy was meteoric. Within a year he became rector—academic head—of the university and in 1953 also its president, holding both positions until 1961. His excavations outside the southern and western sections of the ancient Temple enclosure in Jerusalem, and in many other places in Israel, secured him a lasting place in Israeli archaeology.

In 1933 Benjamin was a struggling young scholar and, like several other young scholars, was frustrated in his aspirations to be admitted among the "immortals" of the Hebrew University. He suffered from a physical frailty, a lateral curvature of the upper spine, that caused him considerable discomfort, but he was nevertheless a man of jolly disposition. I remember that on one occasion, on our way back to Jerusalem aboard a chartered bus, Professor Klein got off at a Jewish settlement where he was scheduled to give a lecture that evening, whereupon Benjamin turned to us and called out, "Well now, *hevre* [fellows], the professor is gone, let's have a good time!" and intoned a popular song of rather light character that began,

> *Doda, hagidi lanu ken, ken*
> *Anu rotzim l'hithaten, -ten . . .*
> (Auntie, tell us yes, yes,
> We want to get married, -ried . . .)

and all of us, of course, joined in with gusto.

One of the advantages of being a research student was that I was free to attend whatever classes I chose, either regularly or sporadically, without any formality of admission, except asking the instructor's permission. After further consultation with Professor Klein, and following his suggestion, I decided to attend all the courses he taught and did so conscientiously for two terms. That was the time when he was working on his important books on the historical geography of Jewish Palestine. His book *History of the Jewish Population of Palestine* (in Hebrew) was published in 1935 and was followed by other studies on related subjects. His courses dealt with the same field, and in them (as in the books he was writing) he used and quoted all the available historical sources, including the Bible, the talmudic literature, Hellenistic authors, the church fathers, etc. He was a master of extracting, even from the most unlikely contexts, items of information about Palestinian towns and villages in which Jews lived in various historical periods and thus of piecing together a picture of the *toldot hayishuv*, the history of the Jewish settlement in the country. It is the great merit of Professor Klein to have demonstrated that, after the destruction of the second Jewish commonwealth by the Romans in 70 C.E., the country continued to be populated by a sizable *yishuv*, despite the historical vicissitudes that brought it successively under Byzantine, Persian, Arab, Mameluk, Crusader, and finally Turkish rule. He showed how ancient Hebrew biblical or talmudic place-names survived, in clearly recognizable forms, in the current Arabic names of villages and of ruins, as well as of mountains, valleys, rivers, and other geographical features. What Klein's researches achieved can best be summed up by saying that they proved the historical continuity of the *yishuv* from biblical and talmudic times down to the modern age.

Because of the many variant forms in which place-names and geographical terms appear in the Talmud and Midrash, Professor Klein often had to resort to textual emendations in order to make the reference understandable. As I mentioned before, he was a very religious Jew, and the Talmud for him was a holy book albeit not quite as holy as the Bible, which, for him, stood at the acme of inviolate holiness. Thus, while he did not hesitate to emend readings of words in the Talmud when he concluded that it was necessary in order to make them yield good sense, he absolutely refused even to consider the possibility of doing the same in a biblical passage and was, in fact, a sworn enemy of all biblical criticism. Working as I was under his guidance and tutelage, I had to defer to his convictions, but I still could not help occasionally giving expression to an idea that he was unable to agree with. A few times, while working on my thesis, I felt that a textual emendation of a biblical expression was necessary, but he roundly vetoed it. I tried to argue, of course always with considerable restraint, that since he himself proposed such emendations in the talmudic text, he should not oppose the same procedure when applied to the Bible, a much older text than the Talmud and hence more likely to contain occasional textual corruptions. He remained adamant, and since it was up to him to approve or disapprove of my thesis, I had no choice but to give in.

I remember one particular instance of such a scholarly-religious disagreement between us. I had known that Immanuel Löw, one of the truly great Jewish scholars, whom I had met personally at his see in Szeged in 1936, had suggested a rather ingenious emendation of a passage in Ps. 74:14

that reads in the Massoretic text: "Thou didst crush the heads of Leviathan, gavest him as *food to folk, to wilderness-dwellers.*" The words in italics read in the Hebrew Massoretic text, *ma'akhal l'am l'tziyyim.* Several considerations render this reading suspect. The expression is strained and clumsy; it is out of context with the rest of the passage, which deals with God's great creative acts upon the primeval waters and in which mention is made of the sea, sea-monsters, Leviathan, fountain, brook, and rivers—how did the carcass of Leviathan, whom God killed in the sea in the great days of Creation, turn up thousands of years later in the wilderness of Sinai to serve as food for the tribes of Israel? Löw suggested that the words *l'am l'tziyyim* be emended to read *l'aml'tze yam,* that is, "to the sharks of the sea." This can be done without changing a single letter (except for the less important vowel signs) in the Massoretic text and makes excellent sense. True, the noun *'amlatz* does not appear elsewhere in the biblical text, but it is attested in Arabic, in which, as I knew from checking Adolf Wahrmund's old Arabic dictionary, the root *'amlas* means "to hurry," and from it is derived *'amallas,* meaning "inex-haustible" and "wolf." If the same word existed in biblical Hebrew, *'aml'tze yam* meant "sea wolf," that is, shark, which fits in perfectly with sea-monsters and Leviathan.

When Professor Klein saw the paragraph I wrote on this point, he ve-toed it in no uncertain terms, and I had no choice but to rewrite it, going along with the traditional explanation. In a footnote I added that Felix Per-les and Löw suggested the reading of *'aml'tze yam* and also referred to Köh-ler and Gunkel, who accepted this emendation. When Löw reviewed my dis-sertation (see chapter 5), he remarked caustically, "As against נמלצי ים Ps. 74:14 he tries to save the Massoretic version."

As this incident shows, my relationship with Professor Klein was not without occasional tensions and difficulties. Still, I learned a lot from him, although not in the field of folklore—he was certainly no folklorist and never claimed to be one—but in the area of meticulous research. I have re-mained indebted to him for demonstrating and teaching me—in his pub-lished writings, lectures, and private conversations with me—how to subject ancient sources to painstaking scrutiny and extract from them data useful for research purposes. Although my dissertation turned out to be a study quite removed from his own interests and specialization, he was always ready to see me and to give me the benefit of his scholarship whenever I encountered any problem in my work. This was especially important for me in the first years of my sojourn in Jerusalem when I missed the guiding hand of my father and of Professor Heller. If Professor Klein had any complaint against me it was that I did not visit him and consult with him often enough, especially after that first year. In expression of my gratitude I dedicated my second book, on Jewish seafaring in ancient times, published in Jerusalem in 1938, "To my teacher and master, Professor S. Klein, on his fiftieth birthday."

In addition to being my teacher, Professor Klein was also my friend, always ready to advise me in whatever nonacademic problem I encountered, and, most importantly, to help me in connection with my efforts to find a job. Rereading the letters I wrote to my parents from 1937 to the time of Klein's death in 1940, I see that I repeatedly expressed unhappiness about his failure to recommend me—the only student who took his doctorate under him—for a position at the university, even if only for one on the lowest rungs of the academic ladder. Especially after I had published my seafaring book as well as several scholarly papers in Hebrew, Hungarian, and English, I felt a certain resentment that Klein never as much as hinted that there might be a remote chance for me to get a position as his assistant, as an instructor, or in some other capacity at the university. Although I never mentioned this in my letters, I remember clearly that I had the feeling that, while Klein was willing to help me in my search for a job in other places, he carefully avoided even alluding to any possibility for me on Mount Scopus and that the reason for this was simple: one of his students (a few years my junior) was Judah Hershkovitch, his wife's brother, who lived with the Kleins, and Professor Klein planned to take him as his assistant once Judah finished his studies. Whether or not there was any basis for this suspicion I could not tell, for, in the event, Klein died before Judah earned his doctorate.

Today, looking back at those remote days across many decades, I think I judged Professor Klein too harshly in those letters. As a longtime member of the university faculty, he knew only too well what was and what was not possible within the narrow framework of what was at the time a very small institution. Besides, my main interest was not Palestinology, Klein's subject, but Jewish and Middle Eastern folklore, and Klein must have known that there was no chance for a teaching appointment in a field that was not part either of the actual curriculum of the university or of its planned future offerings. What I regret in retrospect is that I never had the courage to raise the issue with him—whatever he would have told me about my chances would at least have cleared up the situation for me. Speaking of this issue I am reminded that in my much closer and more comradely contact with Ari Ibn-Zahav, who was influential as the academic secretary of the university and was a really close friend of mine, I also never raised the question of what he thought about my chances of penetrating the academic bastion of Mount Scopus.

Long before I first met him Professor Klein had been a friend and admirer of my father. Whenever Father visited Palestine he went to see the Kleins, and when they were in Budapest (during several summers) they and my parents were often together. When Father first started to be interested in working for the Palestinian Friends of the Hebrew University, Klein was among his most fervent supporters: in one of his letters to me Father mentioned that Klein had told him that he went to bat for him in a confrontation with the almighty Salman Schocken.

I remember, lastly, that after Professor Klein died, Father and I went to pay a visit of condolence to his widow. She was, it turned out, not well enough to see us, but we talked to her brother Judah. We sat around the big dining room table in the Kleins' apartment. At one point, while Father spoke about Klein, what a dear and rare man he was, how his untimely death made one want to storm heaven, he broke into tears. This was the only occasion on which I ever saw Father cry.

Professor Joseph Klausner

Professor Klausner and Professor Torczyner were the two minor advisors entrusted, next to Professor Klein, with the responsibility of supervising my thesis work.

Joseph Klausner (1874–1958) was an eminent literary and general historian who grew up in Odessa and immigrated to Jerusalem in 1919. By the time the Hebrew University was established Klausner was world famous due primarily to his celebrated biography of Jesus, which was published in Hebrew in 1922 (and in an English translation by H. Danby in 1925). Klausner's *Jesus of Nazareth* was the first study to utilize all the available Jewish sources, and especially the talmudic literature, in portraying Jesus as he lived, a Jew among his Jewish contemporaries. While still in Odessa, Klausner had published a book based on lectures he had given on the history of Israel from the conquest of Canaan to the Maccabean period. These two books, as well as numerous other studies, unquestionably rendered him a most highly qualified candidate for the chair of Jewish history at the newly opened university in 1925. But, as the 1972 *Encyclopaedia Judaica* put it in Klausner's biography, "to his disappointment he was not appointed to the chair of Jewish history, as his views were considered too secular."

Another factor that militated against that appointment was that Klausner was a Zionist-Revisionist, that is, a follower of Zeev (Vladimir) Jabotinsky's brand of right-wing ultranationalistic Zionism, while most of the influential leaders involved in the preparatory work for the university stood at or near the opposite end of the Zionist political spectrum. Years later (in 1948), the right-wing nationalists put forward Klausner's name as their candidate for first president of Israel, in opposition to Chaim Weizmann, who, of course, was elected.

Fortunately for Klausner's academic career and for his ability to earn a living in Jerusalem, he had a strong second string to his bow—his book on the history of modern Hebrew literature (published in Russian in 1900 and in a Hebrew reworking in 1920). On that basis he was appointed to the chair of modern Hebrew literature, which remained the only subject he was allowed to teach at the university for some twenty years. Only in 1944, at the age of seventy, was he finally appointed to a chair of the History of the Second Temple, the period and subject to which he had devoted most of his work. That appointment was made possible by his friends and longtime admirers, who endowed a chair for him.

When I first met Professor Klausner, in the spring of 1933, I found him a most unprepossessing, in fact a somewhat naive, person, whose friendliness and heartiness made me immediately feel drawn to him as I never felt drawn to Professor Klein. Klausner was a friend of my father, and it was Father who took me along that first time to visit him. Klausner and his wife (they had no children) lived in a modest one-family house in Talpioth, a suburb south of Jerusalem, with a magnificent view eastward across the Judean Desert as far as the Mountains of Moab on the Transjordanian side. At the time extremely few people had telephones in their homes. It was not possible to make an advance appointment, so one simply went and hoped to find the person at home. We took a bus from the center of Jerusalem to Talpioth and did, in fact, find Klausner at home. He received us with a friendliness so effusive that, groping for an explanation, I attributed it to what I believed was Russian heartiness.

I remember his study: a medium-sized room with a large curtainless window (later I found that the windows in the houses or apartments of Russian Jews rarely had curtains), the walls all around lined with shelves that were bent, and seemed to groan, under the weight of the books. In front of the window stood a simple desk behind which, with his back to the window, sat Klausner. As Father and I sat down facing him, I was able to catch a glimpse through the window of that great desert panorama.

What I remember most vividly of Klausner's appearance is his friendly smile and the twinkle in his eyes behind his round glasses. His hair was white and sparse on top of his head, and under it a kind of flaky rash could be seen. On his chin sprouted a small goatee, also white, but his friendly, warm demeanor lent him a youthful appearance. He encouraged me to come to see him whenever I felt like it, and I regret to this day that I rarely made use of his kind invitation. But it so happened that in the course of that first visit it became clear to me that Klausner, in contrast to Professor Klein, would have little to contribute to the particular kind of research I was about to embark upon; thus, on the few occasions when I did visit him, our conversation was general and did not touch upon the technical problems with which I was struggling in writing my thesis. Yet two years later, when I submitted to him a completed typed copy of my dissertation, he went over its 400 pages line by line and word by word, and many times on every page he corrected my Hebrew style, making it conform to the Mishnaic Hebrew he favored. In 1934, on the occasion of his sixtieth birthday, I wrote an article about him entitled "Klausner—the Hebrew Man," which Father published in his Budapest monthly, *Mult és Jövő.*

Throughout my Jerusalem years Klausner always proved himself a true friend of the Patai family in general and of mine in particular. When Zvi Wohlmut and I edited our anthology of modern Palestinian Hebrew short stories, Klausner most readily agreed to write a preface for it. He also wrote, warmly and appreciatively, introductions to one or two books by Father, whom he admired and whose literary work he valued. In 1938 he was one of those who urged Father to make his *'aliya,* as I reported to my parents in a letter dated August 28, 1938: "a few days ago I went out to see Klausner. Both he and [his wife] Fanitchka asked wonderingly how can it be that the Patai family is still in Budapest, when the trend in the development of the situation is completely clear, and shows a marked identity with that of the late Austria. Well, well! . . ."

Professor Harry Torczyner

My other minor advisor, Professor Harry Torczyner (later Naphtali Herz Tur-Sinai, 1886–1973), was a very different person. From 1919 to 1933 he had taught Bible and Semitic philology at the Berlin Hochschule für die Wissenschaft des Judentums (College for the Science of Judaism), which was the rabbinical seminary of German Reform Jewry. The rumor had it that when Hitler came to power Torczyner sent desperate cables to his friends in Jerusalem entreating them to procure for him *any* teaching position in order to enable him to leave Germany. In fact he arrived in Jerusalem in the first half of 1933, aged forty-seven, and became affiliated with the Hebrew University; the next year, after Bialik died, a chair was established in his name, and Torczyner was appointed "Bialik Professor of Hebrew."

Torczyner's situation at the Hebrew University to some extent paralleled that of Professor Klausner in its restrictions. His major field of scholarly work was biblical research. In 1920 he published a volume in German on the Book of Job and in 1922 a study (also in German) on the Ark of the Covenant and the beginnings of the religion of Israel. But because of his radical views—he maintained, for instance, that the Book of Job was originally written in Aramaic, and that the Hebrew translation preserved in the biblical canon was made by somebody who did not have a sufficient mastery of that language—his ambition to be appointed professor of Bible was never realized; like Klausner, he had to be satisfied with teaching what for him was a secondary scholarly field—Hebrew language.

Before I met Torczyner I had been somewhat prejudiced against him be-cause I remembered the short shrift my Breslau professor, Carl Brockelmann, gave him when he once referred to a linguistic suggestion made by Torczyner only to dismiss it summarily. I still remember the occasion clearly. After re-spectfully quoting the opinions of several scholars on a linguistic point, Brockelmann added in a contemptuous tone: *Und ein gewisser Herr Tor-czyner, mit ce zet, meint* . . . (And a certain Mr. Torczyner, with *ce zet*, is of the opinion . . .). Yet when I went to see Torczyner I found him not only friendly and helpful, but a man with profound knowledge of both the Bible and the Hebrew language.

Since my planned book on water was to include a section devoted to Hebrew hydrographic terminology, which fell directly into the area of his ex-pertise, I consulted Torczyner concerning that aspect of my work, and he de-clared himself willing to go over whatever material I cared to show him. His manner was somewhat peculiar: the words he uttered were interspersed with snorts and accompanied by shrugs, and he gave the impression of a man constantly on the alert for attacks and belittlings. His face had a pronounced asymmetry, with one side of it shorter than the other, which made his entire stature seem lopsided. As for his many daring textual emendations in the Bible, needless to say, Professor Klein found them utterly unacceptable. This fundamental difference in approach led to mutually negative opinions held by the two men.

Mrs. Torczyner, Mrs. Klausner, and Mrs. Klein had one thing in com-mon: none of them had more than a most rudimentary knowledge of He-brew. This was characteristic of many of the wives of middle-class European immigrants in Palestine: they acquired just enough Hebrew to be able to give instructions in that language to their maids, who were in most cases women or young girls from the Oriental Jewish communities. They never managed, and probably rarely tried, to go beyond the stage that was referred to as *oz-eret Hebräisch* (maid Hebrew).

On one occasion—it was after 1936—I remember having visited the Torczyners. There were quite a few guests there. When Mrs. Torczyner in-troduced me, she wanted to inform them that I was the first Ph.D. holder of the Hebrew University, but could not formulate even a simple Hebrew sentence: all she managed to say was *Dr. Patai doktor rishon* (Dr. Patai, first doctor).

Professor Martin Buber

A third professor of the Hebrew University who was not enabled to teach the subject in which he had acquired prime prominence, but was in-stead given a chair in a field definitely secondary for him, was none other than Martin Buber (1878–1965), the most famous of the three. By 1938, when Buber, aged sixty, settled in Jerusalem, he was known and respected the world over (including pre-Nazi Germany) as the great expounder of Jewish philosophy, of Jewish messianic belief, of Hasidism, and of what he termed "Hebrew humanism." Even the briefest presentation of Buber's religious thought and teaching would require much more space than could be justified within the framework of these personal memoirs, but one thing can and must be said about them: they were Jewish through and through—Judaism was at their very center, and they dealt with the Jews as the human group that invested the concept of God and man, and the relationship between them, with a unique spiritual force. If Buber was the one modern Jewish philosopher who had the greatest influence on Catholic and Protestant thinkers, this was unquestionably due to the intrinsic Jewishness of his teachings. And yet, when his friends and admirers finally succeeded in establishing a chair for him at the Hebrew University—the pattern should by now be familiar—the subject he was permitted to teach was not the one to which the sixty-year-old master had devoted a lifetime, not any aspect of Jewish religious philosophy in which he was by that time a "beacon to the nations," but "social philosophy," an innocuous (and from the Jewish point of view neutral) field.

Throughout the years of my personal contact with Buber—from his arrival in Jerusalem in 1938 to my departure in 1947—this restriction placed upon him by the university was a source of irritation and aggravation for him, even though he managed to keep these feelings at a philosophical arm's length. I had numerous meetings with him, especially from 1940 on when I was working on my Hebrew book *Man and Earth*, for which I needed books not available in the only major library in the Palestine of those days, that of the Hebrew University. I knew that Buber had a rich library—he had the reputation of being a man of independent means, and it was also rumored that his wife, a Gentile, was a countess by birth—containing many anthropological works, and I went frequently to his house to ask him whether he could lend me a book not found in the university library.

Buber lived in an old, but beautifully restored, Arab house, in the Abū Tūr Quarter of Jerusalem, to the south of the Old City, not far from the Jerusalem railway station. It was located on a hillside and, I seem to remember, had a view of the Old City and the Haram area. In most cases, this I remember distinctly, Buber did have the books I needed and willingly lent them to me. He went from his study to a neighboring room that held his library and with unerring speed reached for the books and handed them to me. Then he asked me to enter the titles of the books and my name into a small black notebook, evidently in order to be able to keep track of the books he lent out.

It was on one of these occasions that I spoke to Buber about my desire to serve not merely as a Hebrew language instructor at the university but as a teacher of Jewish folklore and anthropology, the fields in which I had several publications to my credit by that time. He listened with sympathy and said with his characteristic lopsided smile, largely but not completely hidden by his Nietzschean moustache: "You know, don't you, what the Romans said, *Senatores boni viri, senatus mala bestia"* [The senators are good men, but the senate is an evil beast]. I felt that with this sentence he summarized his own experiences with the university.

Buber, as I remember him from those days, was short, slight of build, with a big forehead topped by a white shock of hair combed sideways and a white moustache and beard that he evidently never cut, which left only a small area of his face around the eyes and nose unmasked. He always wore a loose informal jacket and flat rubber-soled shoes. He had an impressive presence, and yet a friendly mien, and whenever I arrived at his house (unannounced, as was the custom in Jerusalem in those days) he always received me right away and always took time from whatever he was doing to chat with me.

In 1941, when I completed the manuscript of my book *Man and Earth* and submitted it for publication to the Hebrew University Press (later called the Magnes Press), they asked Buber to be one of the readers (the other was Professor Klausner). On one of my visits shortly thereafter Buber told me that he liked my book very much and had recommended its acceptance by the Press. Professor Klausner gave a similarly positive review of it, and on that basis the book was accepted for publication by the press and two volumes of it were actually published in 1942 and 1943, respectively.

(While I was working on the present memoirs, I became curious to know what precisely Buber and Klausner wrote about *Man and Earth*. I wrote a note to the Press asking for copies of those recommendations that now, fifty years later, were of purely historical interest. The director referred my request to the rector of the university, who in due course informed me that the Press was committed to preserving the confidentiality of the reviews and that therefore they were unable to fulfill my request. It amused me to see that the university authorities considered the confidentiality of favorable readers' reports more stringent and of greater longevity than that of sensitive political documents, routinely made available to the general public in democratic states, not after fifty, but after a mere thirty years.)

There were also other examples of partisan views and petty jealousies at the university of which I became aware during my Jerusalem years, but of the three cases mentioned above I knew firsthand, from occasional conversations with the men involved, who made no bones about their unhappiness with the situation. For some thirty-five years the Hebrew University was the only academic institution of its kind in Palestine-Israel, and this situation made for the development of a certain elitism and exclusivism. As Professor Fodor, with whom I often sat side by side in the rickety bus going up to the university campus, once remarked to me in a somewhat different but still related context, "The university is like a full bus; those outside try to push in, those inside try to keep them out."

Dr. Joseph J. Rivlin

Before concluding these sketchy portraits of the men with whom I had close contact at the Hebrew University, I must mention one more man on its faculty to whom I became greatly indebted, although he had nothing to do with my doctoral thesis. Dr. Joseph J. Rivlin (1889–1971), whose Koran classes I attended during my first year in Jerusalem, was a native of Jerusalem and a scion of a distinguished and sizable family. In fact, his family was so large that they used to say that there were three kinds of Jews in Jerusalem: Ashkenazim, Sephardim, and Rivlinim.

Dr. Rivlin had had quite an adventurous youth. In 1917 he was arrested by the Turks and kept in prison, first in Jerusalem and then in Damascus. After being set free he taught in the Damascus Hebrew schools for a while, returned to Palestine in 1922, and then went to Germany to study Arabic and Islamics. Returning to Jerusalem in 1927, he was appointed to the Institute of Oriental Studies of the Hebrew University and some twenty-five years later was promoted to professor. From 1930 to 1941 he was chairman of the Hebrew Teachers Organization. He was also one of the founders of B'nai B'rith in Palestine.

Among Rivlin's earlier published works the most popular were his translations into Hebrew of the Koran and the *Thousand and One Nights*. By the time I approached him with the suggestion that he serve as my co-editor of *Edoth*, he had been involved in collecting the oral literature of the Kurdish Jews—the type of research that was to be in the very center of the journal's interest. To its first issue (October 1945) he contributed an article discussing and giving the text of a Kurdish-Jewish folk-epic on "Moses and Batya, the Daughter of Pharaoh." He published this poem in his Hebrew translation as well as in the original Neo-Aramaic (Targum) language of the Kurdish Jews—not an easy task, considering that the Neo-Aramaic colloquial of the Kurdish Jews had no written form, so that Rivlin had to listen carefully to the oral delivery and write it down phonetically in Hebrew characters. Subsequently he included that epic in a volume he published on *Shirat Y'hude haTargum* (The Poetry of the Targum Jews) in Jerusalem in 1959.

Dr. Rivlin was the only one among all my former teachers with whom I was able to establish a really close, friendly, and collegial relationship, despite the more than twenty years' age difference between us. Once he agreed to be co-editor of *Edoth* and a member of the executive committee of the

Palestine Institute of Folklore and Ethnology, although he did not take an active part in the work of either, his presence in the background was extremely important for me both psychologically and practically, for it meant having the support of a man highly respected in the academic circles of the *yishuv*, whom I could consult and on whose help I could count. When I conceived the idea of launching *Edoth* I knew that I would be able to realize it only if I got institutional support. Looking back on my early efforts to obtain funding, I can see clearly that, had it not been for the co-editorship of Dr. Rivlin, I would not have been able to secure subsidies for the journal. Dr. Rivlin did not intervene actively in supporting the applications I submitted, but the very fact that I could apply in his name as well as in mine was, I believe, an important factor in the positive responses I elicited.

The last time I saw Dr. Rivlin was in New York in the 1960s. He had been invited by New York University to serve as visiting professor and got in touch with me soon after his arrival. He stayed with his wife in an apartment on lower Fifth Avenue, not far from the Washington Square campus of NYU. I went to see him, and we had what amounted to a real sentimental reunion. He was by that time an old man—in his seventies—but his memory was perfect, and we spent quite some time recalling the "good old days." In fact, he was able to tell me of some of the steps he undertook in the winter of 1947–1948, after my departure for New York, trying to secure the continuation of *Edoth* and the work of the Institute. That he did not succeed was due to the general conditions in the country, and we both agreed, sadly, that the journal and the Institute were victims of the War of Independence that resulted in the establishment of the state of Israel.

Dr. Max Eitingon

Let me append here my reminiscences of a man who, although not a member of the Hebrew University faculty, played an important role in the academic life of Jerusalem in the 1930s as well as in the Patai family history: the psychoanalyst Dr. Max Eitingon (1881–1943).

A scion of a wealthy Russian-Jewish family of fur-traders, Eitingon became a student and later friend of Freud in Vienna, founded the Berlin Psychoanalytic Polyclinic (later the Berlin Institute of Psychoanalysis) in 1920, and soon after his arrival in Jerusalem founded the Palestine Psychoanalytic Society and the Palestine Psychoanalytic Institute (in 1933 and 1934, respectively).

In the family letters Eitingon's name appears first in a Hebrew letter Father sent me in August 1934 in which he asked me to supply his journal with all kinds of small items. In that context he asked, "Have you also met Dr. Eitingon? Perhaps it would be worthwhile to interview him too (with a photo) about Freud and Freudianism, his plans in the country, psychoanalysis, Judaism, etc." I don't remember whether I followed up this suggestion, but I believe I first met Eitingon through the parents of my brother-in-law, who had known him from the time both families lived in Berlin.

What has remained in my memory from my first visit to Eitingon's apartment in Rehavia was not my impression of the man himself but of the luxurious lodgings. I remember in particular one feature that I had never seen anywhere before: the bookshelves in his extensive library were lined with soft beige leather all around so that no wood was visible. This struck me at the time as the acme of wasteful luxury and self-indulgence. Eitingon himself was a small man with a bald head, a black moustache, and a sharp glance from behind round glasses that contrasted peculiarly with his modest, almost self-effacing demeanor.

My contact with Eitingon was limited. He was a very busy middle-aged psychoanalyst, I an aspiring young folklorist. What impressed me more than anything about him was not that he was modest and soft-spoken, but that he possessed to an extraordinary degree the psychoanalysts' knack of listening intensively to what his interlocutor was telling him.

One of our earliest meetings took place fortuitously in the home of my brother-in-law's parents in Tel Aviv. When he told me that he was returning from there directly to Jerusalem, and knowing that he always traveled in chauffeur-driven rented cars (there were no limousines at the time in Palestine), I asked him whether he could give me a lift. This enabled me to chat with him for the duration of the one-hour trip between Tel Aviv and Jerusalem. I don't remember Eitingon telling me anything about himself during that hour, but I do recall that he asked me what I was working on, whereupon I described in some detail the major study on the role of tradition in culture I was planning to embark upon. I remember explaining to him—in German, of course—that I wanted to show, with examples taken from many periods and many different cultures the world over, what a powerful force tradition was in human culture and how tradition battled for supremacy each time innovative forces tried to reshape or transform a culture. I remember that throughout he listened with the peculiar intensity that I subsequently found was his hallmark. Although I knew by that time that Eitingon had been a close associate of Freud, his manifest interest in what I was saying kept me going to such an extent that I totally missed the opportunity to ask him to tell me something about the master, whose *Totem and Tabu* I at that time still considered one of the greatest masterpieces, presenting a breathtakingly broad panoramic picture of all human psychological processes and their influence on cultural development. When we reached the intersection of Jaffa Road and King George Avenue, I asked Eitingon to drop me off. I thanked him for the lift, and he said he would be glad to see me again. Incidentally, I never wrote the study on tradition and culture.

It was some two or three years later that I had closer contact with Eitingon. My sister's daughter Tirzah was born on March 3, 1937. Within a few months thereafter my brother-in-law Leon fell ill, and before long it became clear that it was no longer possible for Évi to live with him. After much hesitation and soul-searching she decided to seek asylum in the home of our parents in Budapest. In October 1937 I took her and her baby daughter to Haifa and helped her board the Italian ship that was to take her home. I have told the tragic story of Leon's mental breakdown and the disintegration of my sister's marriage in another book and hence can be spared the painful task of retelling it here. I shall mention only that in connection with Leon's illness I had several consultations with Eitingon, who was one of the physicians treating him.

My next series of contacts with Dr. Eitingon dates from about a year later, when I was working on the Jerusalem Academy project (about which I shall report in due course). In all my meetings with Eitingon I always found him to be a kind and helpful man. It was therefore with great surprise that fifty years later I read two articles in the *New York Times* (January 24, 1988, and January 5, 1989) that attributed to Eitingon an active role in helping the Russian Communist authorities in their efforts to entrap and apprehend Russian émigrés and in setting up the assassination of Trotsky in Mexico. Having known Eitingon as the soft-spoken, concerned healer he was in the 1930s, I just could not give credence to stories that "unmasked" him as an underhanded helper of killers.

3

Women in My Life

The relative brevity of this chapter within the total length of the present book should by no means be taken as indicating that my relationships with women had a correspondingly minor significance in the totality of my life during the seven years that passed between my arrival in Jerusalem and my marriage to Naomi—quite the contrary. The fact is that, although I was a diligent, serious, and industrious young man and spent almost all my time working on whatever research projects I was engaged in, I had inherited from my ancestor Jacob the trait attributed to him by the Midrash when it says that he was always in need of the company of women. I was—to switch from Midrash to folktale—like the king in the well-known story about the three daughters, who could not enjoy any food without salt. Likewise, I found life drab and lackluster unless there was within my horizon a woman I loved or, at least, was eager to see very frequently. There were, to be sure, other things too that I enjoyed in life, but none of them did I enjoy as much as female company. And when I say I enjoyed female company I do not necessarily mean sex—although that too, of course, came into play in several of my relationships with women—but rather being together with a woman to whom I was attracted, going places and seeing things, engaging in an exchange of views and observations, discussing the events in the country and in the world in which all of us in Palestine were always keenly interested, and the like. If sex could be part of such a relationship so much the better—it certainly made it more intense and more satisfactory for me; if not, no matter—the intellectual and emotional aspects of the friendship were sufficient to make it the salt that gave taste to every other activity I was engaged in.

Yet, while women played such an important role in my life, there was no organic continuity between my relationship with them and all the other activities that filled my day. My life was divided into two sharply delineated

compartments: work, which included earning a living by teaching and lecturing, studying, reading, doing research, editing, working on books, articles, and reviews, writing letters, doing translations, and frequent work-re-
lated meetings with scholars, writers, editors, publishers, heads of foundations, and the like; and relaxation, amusement, entertainment, "enjoying
life," in all of which, always and inevitably, women, or rather a woman,
played the central role. I still remember very clearly what an amount of time
and attention I devoted to planning to meet her, going places, or merely
being together, chatting and, in the case of some, having sex.

Occasionally at least I would tell a woman I was courting or with whom
I was friendly about the work I was engaged in, but this in no way changed
the fact that work and women constituted two disparate halves of my life
and that I pursued each as if the other did not exist. In addition, there was
a great difference in the character of the two: the work-half of my life was
continuous and developmental, while my relationships to women, whatever
their duration, were episodic, repetitious, and cyclical.

In my work, while dealing with one subject, I would become aware of
others related to it and would thus be led, by my own widening interests,
from one theme to the next. My work on water in ancient Palestinian life
and lore led me to ancient Jewish seafaring. From the watery element I
stepped to the shore, studying the role of the land, the earth, in ancient Jewish life. The next step, almost inevitably, was to study the rituals that aimed
at securing the fertility of the land and the beliefs that centered on the leaders of the people—kings, priests, pious men, and the like—whose acts and
comportment were believed to be responsible for the fertility of the earth
and thus for the well-being of the people. The step that led me from the
study of ancient Jewish folk-life, folk custom, folk belief, and folk religion to
that of their modern equivalents among their heirs, the Middle Eastern Jewish communities, was a greater one, but was still well within the logical pro-
gression from one theme to a related one, as was my branching out into a
study of the Arab and non-Arab Muslim Middle East of which the Oriental
Jews were a part.

As against this developmental continuity, my relations to women were
of an episodic nature that I always felt was disconcerting. I would meet a
woman, be attracted to her, embark on efforts to establish a relationship,
find reciprocation on her part, and then, after a longer or shorter period of
happy harmony, the relationship would come to an end for one of a number of possible reasons. When that happened, as it inevitably did, I was left
in a position where I was driven to engage in a new search, until I would
again meet a woman, be attracted to her, etc. The nature of my relationship
to the women in question varied greatly, even though, by and large, it alter-
nated between what is customarily termed Platonic and non-Platonic. Al-

though sex always played an important role in my life, it nevertheless happened more than once that I extricated myself from a sexual relationship with a woman, not because I met another woman to whom I was more attracted and who was sexually available, but because I got acquainted with someone with whom a purely Platonic relationship developed. The common feature between my Platonic and non-Platonic loves was that they would come to an end and that my lady-loves would be responsible for their termination as often as I was.

Because my relationships with women constituted a separate aspect of my life and were, with one or two exceptions, not touched upon in my correspondence with my family, it would be difficult for me to establish where they belonged in the chronology of the first half of my fifteen years in Jerusalem. I can recall clearly many of even the smallest incidents in those friendships, but I do not remember when, within those years 1933–1939, the relationships themselves took place. For this reason, and also because of the recurring pattern those friendships seem to evince when seen from the historical perspective of many intervening decades, I have grouped several of them together in this chapter rather than trying to assign them to what I could only guess were their places in the sequence of events.

Thinking back on those seven years, my definite impression is that I knew many more girls in whom I was interested—the interest ranging from mild to intense, and from short to long in duration—without even thinking of having sex with them than girls with whom I did have sexual relations. My experiences in Hungary and Germany still influenced my outlook on the other sex. Young members of it fell, in my view, into two sharply differentiated categories. One consisted of girls who lived with their parents or were under their aegis and who, in addition, usually happened to be a few years younger than I. For me they were just that: girls, whom I instinctively assumed to be virgins, inviolate in my code, so that my attraction never assumed the form of hoping, let alone trying, to have sex with them. Into the other category fell young women who lived alone, whose reaction to me made me feel that they were available and open to sexual adventure. It so happened that, more often than not, these women were one or two years older than I.

Although I was always on the alert for the possibility of having sex with a woman, I was never interested in casual encounters. For me, sexual intimacy always had to be preceded by a getting-acquainted process, even if a brief one, and sexual relations meant a situation of a certain duration, never a single, nonrecurrent event. In fact, I never had such an experience—with one single memorable exception, in which I was not the initiator but rather the object of the woman's choice.

What happened was that I got acquainted with a young girl who was the daughter of a respected Middle Eastern Jewish family in Jerusalem, whom, of course, I unhesitatingly assigned in my mind to the category of inviolate virgins. She may have been eighteen or twenty, was tall, shapely, with the serious dark beauty only women from Mediterranean countries have, was vivacious, and spoke the beautiful, "pure" Sephardic Hebrew that I always found extremely attractive. I went out with her a few times; once, I remember, we attended a big charity ball at the King David Hotel (it was one of the few occasions on which I wore my tuxedo), but I never dreamt that I could be as audacious as to try even to kiss her—after all, she was not only a girl guarded by her parents, but in addition an Oriental Jewish girl in whose world, as was well known, untouchability was almost as strictly observed as among the Arabs.

One day, to my great surprise, she asked me where I lived and what kind of lodgings I had. When I asked her whether she would like to see my rooms, she said yes, and we made an appointment for the next evening. I took her to my rooms, and from then on we did what came naturally. While we were making love, at one point she said, "I wanted to show you that we Sephardi girls can also be like the Ashkenazi girls." Thereafter we continued to meet occasionally, but she never again agreed to come to my place.

Apart from the important variable of the sexual ingredient, there was one more difference in my relationships with the two types of women. If the friendship did involve sex, then, for its duration, I was faithful. This was not a conscious decision that cost me an effort to adhere to, but rather an automatic attitude that I assumed, a natural stance like that of the compass needle, which cannot waver from pointing in the direction of the force that attracts it. On the other hand, I felt no such commitment to exclusivity in my Platonic relationships: in many cases they did not entail frequent meetings, nor did they mean emotional involvements so intense as to preclude the burgeoning of interest in other directions as well.

Lena

I no longer remember how I got acquainted with Lena, who became my first girlfriend in Jerusalem. She had come to Palestine from Vienna with her widowed mother, was two years older than me, had a Ph.D. in chemistry from the University of Vienna, and worked in the laboratories of the Health Department of the British Mandatory Government of Palestine, located in a large old Arab house on Jaffa Road not far from the Mahane Yehuda Quarter.

She was of medium height, slim but amply built, with light brown hair that she wore so short as to seem almost boyish (unusual in those days), blue eyes, a beauty-spot on the left side of her chin, a straight and short but somewhat fleshy nose, and a slight prognathism, which, I believe, was the basis for a mutual acquaintance to remark once, rather unpleasantly, that she had "a lion face." She was a charming, vivacious young woman, intelligent, easygoing, well-read, and capable in her profession. Our relationship, which lasted through the summer of 1933, was a happy one. She was an avid tennis player, and when I first accompanied her to the courts and watched her play, I recognized at once that she was a very competent player, far above the extremely limited hitting the ball back and forth that was tennis for me on the few occasions I had played in Budapest. For this reason, although Lena urged me repeatedly to play, I never did, nor have I played tennis ever since.

Lena had a studio apartment in an old Arab house in the Musrara Quarter of Jerusalem, consisting of one spacious room, a small kitchen, and a bathroom. I used to visit her in the evenings, after she had returned from work, stay with her until late at night, and then walk back to my own room. Occasionally, on Saturdays, when she did not go to work, we would take walks in and around Jerusalem. But I don't remember ever having gone out together with her to eat or ever having had dinner at her place. Food and the circumstances of eating seem to have been of such peripheral interest for me at the time, and for many years thereafter, that I remember almost nothing in connection with them. However, unless my memory entirely misleads me, I think that in those days eating meals together was rarely part of friendly outings.

In the fall of 1933, practically simultaneously, both Lena and I found other interests. She made the acquaintance of a young doctor from Germany (later my friend Ibn-Zahav was to become his patient and sang his praises to me), whose name I have long since forgotten. I did meet him once or twice. One evening, as I was walking along Jaffa Road in front of the Egged bus terminal, I saw Lena and her doctor friend get off a bus that had just arrived from the Dead Sea, where, evidently, they had spent the day. We greeted each other in a friendly but reserved manner, and I knew that my relationship with Lena had ended.

I never saw Lena again. Later I heard that she married her doctor, and many years thereafter, on the occasion of one of my visits from America to Israel, I learned that both she and her husband had died of illnesses.

It was through Lena that I got acquainted with the Feigenbaums. Dr. Arye Feigenbaum (1885–1981) had immigrated from Vienna to Jerusalem in 1913 as a young M.D. and soon became the leader of the fight against trachoma in the country. In 1920 he founded and thereafter edited the Hebrew medical journal *HaRefuah* and in 1922 became head of the Ophthalmology department of the Hadassah hospital in Jerusalem.

The Feigenbaums lived in an old Arab house in the center of the new city, and I still recall how taken I was with their comfortable living room, whose windows opened onto leafy trees—a rare sight in those days. Mrs. Feigenbaum, although no longer young, was one of the most beautiful women I ever saw. She was the daughter of Yosef Baran Meyuhas (1868–1942), the Sephardi folklorist, educator, and community leader, with whom I was to become friendly a few years later, after he asked my permission to include in a volume of his an Oriental Jewish folktale I had originally printed in the Hebrew daily *HaBoqer*. Mr. Meyuhas was a scion of one of the oldest and noblest Sephardi families in Jerusalem (the very name Meyuhas means "of noble lineage"), one of whose members was the chief rabbi in the eighteenth century, with the proud title of the Sephardi chief rabbis of Palestine Rishon l'Tziyon (First in Zion). Yosef Meyuhas was one of the first to follow Eliezer Ben-Yehuda in speaking Hebrew in his house. He married a daughter of the Russian-Jewish writer and leader of the *yishuv* Yehiel Mikhal Pines (1843–1913), who had settled in Palestine in 1877. Such a Sephardi-Ashkenazi intermarriage was at the time a daring deviation from the old Sephardi tradition that held such a union a degrading misalliance. When I looked at Mrs. Feigenbaum I thought, if this is the result of Ashkenazi-Sephardi miscegenation, we should energetically advocate it.

The Feigenbaums' daughter Hemda inherited much of her mother's beauty and, more importantly for her career, she spoke Hebrew with just the right amount of Sephardic traces in her pronunciation, which brought her employment as an announcer and reader of news in the Hebrew program of the Palestine Broadcasting Service (PBS) established by the government in 1936. I think I should explain that, even though the spoken language adopted by the *yishuv* under the prodding of Ben-Yehuda was "Sephardic" Hebrew, it was actually far from the authentic Sephardic pronunciation of the language as could be heard issuing from the mouths of Jews who hailed from Arab countries. That idiom comprised phonemes that the Ashkenazi Jews, most of whom had come from a Yiddish-speaking background, were unable to pronounce and simply ignored. The guttural *'ayin* fell by the way, the aspirated *het* was pronounced indistinguishably from the fricative *khaf* (both were given the sound of the German *ch*, as in *ach und krach*, as we used to say), the *tzade* was pronounced as the German *z*, and of such refinements as the more subtle differences between *tav* and *tet*, or between *kaf* and *qof*, there was not even an awareness. Eliezer Lubrani, who was in charge of the Hebrew program, felt that this amounted to an impoverishment of spoken Hebrew and tried to remedy the situation by introducing an improved, "purer" Hebrew into the Hebrew hour. In this endeavor Hemda Feigenbaum was a veritable find. Due to her mixed Ashkenazi-Sephardi descent, or rather upbringing, she retained just enough of the Sephardic pronunciation to give her speech the slight Sephardic flavor Lubrani thought ideal. This consisted actually of nothing more than the aspirated *het* (instead

of the Ashkenazi fricative version) and some slight guttural coloring of the
'*ayin*. I myself liked this way of pronouncing Hebrew and made efforts to
incorporate these two distinctive Sephardic phonemes into my speech, with
only indifferent and intermittent success. I could never get rid of my Hungarian accent and in daily conversation I could not pay attention to the *het*
and '*ayin*; only in public speaking did I try to remember to produce these
sounds *à la* Hemda Feigenbaum.

Rita

Another beauty employed by the PBS as announcer in its Hebrew program was Rita Persitz, who, although of Russian-Jewish descent, had mas-
tered the semi-Sephardic flavor of PBS-Hebrew to an astonishing extent.
Rita's father had established the Omanuth Publishing House in Moscow in
1917 and transferred it to Frankfurt in 1920. After his early death his wife,
Shoshana, brought Omanuth to Tel Aviv (in 1925), where it became a leading publishing house; she herself, widely known as G'veret Persitz (Mrs. Persitz), became a civic leader. When I got acquainted with her, in the early
1930s, she was the head of the education department of the Tel Aviv municipality, and I remember having a few times sought her out in her office
when I was trying to find a position as a high school teacher in Tel Aviv. She
was a huge woman, and I remember her seated behind her big desk in her
office like a frowning female Buddha. I had more contact with her from
1936 on, after Omanuth published my father's Herzl biography in Hebrew
and German translations, and even more from 1938 on when Omanuth had
several of its books printed by the press of which I was a part-owner for a
couple of years. At that time Omanuth was in serious financial difficulties
and was unable to meet its IOUs, which in turn almost caused my small
printing establishment to go bankrupt.

But to return to Rita Persitz, she was one of four Persitz children, one
son and three daughters. The son was an up-and-coming young lawyer in
Jerusalem; the eldest daughter, Sula, was the wife of Gustav Schocken, for
whom his wealthy father Salman had bought the Tel Aviv daily *HaAretz*,
putting him in as editor-in-chief in place of the veteran journalist Moshe
Gluecksohn; the second daughter was Rita; the youngest daughter was
Yemima, who became an actress at the Teatron Kameri (Chamber Theater)
in Tel Aviv. Rita was a strikingly beautiful girl, tall, with a mane of dark
bronze hair, and a bearing that conveyed the impression of great self-assurance, or, as those who were less than admiringly inclined toward her put it,
of great *hutzpa*. I saw her on and off, both before and after she got married.
One late evening, I remember, she and her husband took me and a few

other friends for a spin in their car—it was a convertible. Her husband drove, with a friend sitting next to him, while Rita and I and two other young men who were with us squeezed into the back seat, which was barely wide enough for three. Rita chose to sit on my lap, and as we drove around in the dark she settled back and leaned her cheek against mine.

Hanna

Speaking of the radio and its Sephardism led me ahead of myself, and I must return to my first year in Jerusalem.

The girl who replaced Lena in my affection was Hanna Kroch, a student at the Hebrew University, who also studied at the Law College run by the government of Palestine. Her father was the vice-headmaster of the Reali school in Haifa, which, together with the Gimnasiya Herzliya in Tel Aviv, represented the best the *yishuv* had to offer in secondary education. When I got acquainted with Hanna she lived in an old Arab house next to Zion Square, on its second floor, in a furnished room she and two of her former classmates from Haifa shared in the apartment of the painter Moshe Mokady. Her roommates were Piri Breuer, who later was killed by a bomb in Haifa, and Ruth Brandstetter, who later married the geographer David Amiran and became a well-known archaeologist.

Hanna, of Polish-Russian parentage, had black hair, a tawny complexion, large dark-brown eyes, and regular if somewhat heavy features. She was of medium height, slender but well built. What attracted me to her in the first place was her obvious intelligence, her well-rounded education in Jewish literature and history, and her rootedness in the soil of Palestine. She was a Sabra, a native of the country, and for me she represented the essence of what attracted me to the *yishuv*, a matter-of-fact, no-nonsense attitude, a natural, self-evident belonging to the Jewish society that was engaged in building its homeland. Hanna was the first Sabra who spoke to me with youthful enthusiasm about the Hebrew authors whom she had studied at the Reali, and above all about the writings of Ahad Ha'Am. It was she who insisted that I read that famous Hebrew author's essay on Moses and also his critique of the *yishuv* and who encouraged me to spend some time in a kibbutz, arranging with her friends in Giv'at Brenner that they accept me as a guest-worker for a few weeks in the spring of 1934. Once or twice she and I visited her city, Haifa, and on those occasions Hanna arranged for me to be put up for the night in the home of a friendly family. I also remember once interviewing her father and inquiring about the possibility of a teaching position at the Reali school—with negative results.

Much as I strain my memory I can remember neither the reasons nor the circumstances that brought about the end of my friendship with Hanna. All I know is that in the spring of 1934 we were still friends, and that by the fall of that year, when I began my work as a teacher at the Talpioth school, contact between us had broken off. I was never to see Hanna again, but years later I heard that she had become a successful lawyer in Haifa.

Ruth

One of the less Platonic, and less satisfactory, early friendships I had in Jerusalem was with Ruth Stein (not her real name). She was an elegant and self-assured young woman in her early twenties, who lived with her widowed mother and her sister Dorothy on the ground floor of the same house on whose second floor, only a few months earlier, Hanna Kroch and her two Haifa friends had lived. Mrs. Stein was a tall, striking-looking woman of about fifty, who had come with her daughters from Germany and must have been able to bring out, in those early months of Nazi rule, a substantial fortune, for the ladies lived quite lavishly, or so it struck me at the time. The apartment they rented was large and furnished with fine Biedermeier and other antique pieces of furniture, mother and daughters were always elegantly dressed, none of them was engaged in any income-producing activity, and the older daughter, Ruth, ran around in a fine convertible two-seater.

The younger daughter, Dorothy, was rather plump and good-natured and dabbled in amateur photography. She kept company with Raphael Dacosta, a young journalist from Vienna, who worked for the *Palestine Post* and was rather proud of his Sephardi name and descent. He was married and the father of a child, but kept his family well hidden somewhere in a suburb of Jerusalem—I never got to meet them. As far as Dorothy was concerned, he behaved and related to her exactly as if he had been a merry bachelor. Raphael and I often had light supper with Mrs. Stein and the two girls, and he and I became quite friendly. On one occasion—it must have been soon after the beginning of my friendship with Ruth—male solidarity got the upper hand over discretion, and he warned me that Ruth was a bitch—his very word—which I somewhat resented and totally disregarded.

My friendship with Ruth Stein fell in the period when I was teaching at the Talpioth school, that is, in the academic year of 1934–1935. I shall tell more about my experiences in that school in chapter 5. I mention it here only because I remember that Ruth would often drive up to the school in her car to take me back to the city after my classes—a distance of perhaps three miles—which was a pleasant change from my usual travel in the slow and overcrowded bus.

I lived at the time in a separate garden pavilion in the Schatz House in Bezalel Street, in which my sister and brother-in-law rented their apartment.

Ruth would come to visit me, and no one would see her either coming or going. It was an ideal arrangement for an adventurous bachelor. But my relationship with Ruth was far from ideal; in fact, it lasted only a few months and was unsatisfactory to both of us. To me—because Ruth refused to meet with me as frequently as I wanted and needed her company, and to her—because she found me an inadequate lover. I was at the time still so inexperienced that I did not know there was such a thing as giving satisfaction to a woman. For me, to make love to a woman was an entirely self-centered act. Once or twice Ruth did say to me, *Du kannst dich nicht beherrschen*, but she was too embarrassed to be more explicit, and I simply did not understand what she was talking about. Thus, our encounters were brief indeed.

Since I could not get Ruth to meet me as often as I wanted, I suspected that she had other lovers as well. But we were never friendly and open enough to talk about it, and once I concluded that my suspicions were well founded I felt that the situation was intolerable for me. So I simply stopped calling on her. Several days later I was walking on King George Avenue when Ruth overtook me in her car. When she noticed me, she put on the brakes, and her car stopped a few yards ahead of me. She remained seated in the car and waited for me to catch up. But I was at the time so resentful that I did not want to see her; as soon as I noticed that she had passed and was slowing down, I turned around and walked away from her. That same evening there was a knock on my door. It was Ruth, "Why did you turn away when I stopped to pick you up?" she asked. Instead of trying to explain how I felt, I reached for her. It was the last time we were together—the last time I saw her.

"Memorandum to Ilka"

While I remember the "Ruth fiasco" as having been largely due to my inexperience, clumsiness, and bungling, the next intimate encounter that proved to me anew the truth of the Goethean words *das Ewig-weibliche zieht uns hinan* should have taught me that too much restraint and too much understanding can be just as fatal in man-woman relations.

It was shortly after the breakup with Ruth that I met Ilka Rotband (not her real name), through my brother-in-law's parents, who had known the Rotbands from the time when both families lived in Berlin. Mr. Rotband was a wealthy industrialist who had left Germany early enough to be able to bring out all, or a major part, of his fortune, including his collection of German paintings. I do not know whether, after he settled in Tel Aviv, he engaged in any income-producing occupation, but, in any case, the Rotband parents and their son and daughter lived in a large luxury apartment on the Tel Aviv seashore, on a high floor. From their rooms there was a wonderful view of the sea as far as the Jaffa promontory in the south, and the way of life they led impressed me as opulent in the extreme. Évi's parents-in-law, too, must have considered the Rotbands well off, for financial status was in their eyes the decisive criterion of a girl's eligibility, and they thought that Ilka Rotband would make a suitable match for me. They told me they wanted me to get acquainted with the Rotbands and took me along on their next visit. Ilka, of course, happened to be at home.

She was eighteen at the time, of medium height and slender figure, with white skin, black hair, a *retroussé* nose that lent her face an impish charm, a smile on her delicately curved lips, and a look in her black eyes that seemed to be caught in a perpetual wonder at what they saw in the world.

If I today still know more of the short-lived relationship—and a most puritanically Platonic one—that thereupon developed between Ilka and me than of any of the other associations with women I had in my Palestine years, this is due not to having retained more in my memory, but to the simple fact that in the course of that relationship, which lasted in all not more than eight weeks, I composed a lengthy piece of writing entitled "Memorandum to Ilka" addressed to her, and all sixty handwritten pages somehow survived. I wrote it in German, the language in which we conversed, and when I sat down to write I started by putting the date on top of the page and, likewise, dated each subsequent entry. Hence, I know that the meetings between Ilka and me began a few days before January 24, 1935, and ended on, or soon after, March 22 of the same year. In the course of those eight weeks we saw each other frequently, even though each time I had to take the bus to Tel Aviv to meet her. While these meetings took place I added piecemeal entries to my memorandum, discoursing on what had transpired between us, what feelings and thoughts our discussions aroused, and what reflections they produced in me, as well as confessing all sorts of things about myself. I also branched off into psychological and even philosophical considerations on a large number of issues that preoccupied me, such as my relationships with men and women, my past and my future, the scholarly versus the intuitive grasp of the world, the role of poetic expression as a healing process for the wounded soul, and more of the like.

Rereading the sixty pages of that memorandum today I can see that I was much more interested in what I felt, thought, and wanted than in understanding what went on in the psyche of that young girl. In those pages I told very little about her, except for brief references to the unfortunate love affair in which she was involved, as I found out to my grief. Still, I can reconstruct what transpired between us by using that memorandum as the basis and by supplementing its record with a few details not mentioned in it.

When I got acquainted with Ilka I took it for granted that she was an innocent young girl who had grown up protected and sheltered by her parents and elder brother; consequently, I unhesitatingly assigned her to that clearly defined category of girls with whom only a Platonic relationship was possible. It was on the basis of that tacit and apparently self-evident assumption that I fell in love with her and tried to impress her with my mind, my esprit, my intellect. After all, what better way was there to impress a young girl with the great values I was ready to lay at her feet than to address her in a memorandum containing my innermost thoughts? At the age of twenty-four I could, of course, not think of marriage, but I could and did imagine that I would build a strong and lasting friendship between us, and that, after the passage of an appropriate number of years, at a more advanced stage of my career, that friendship could possibly lead to matrimony.

Then, as we became closer—and I repeat, the closeness was purely emotional, I never even once kissed her—Ilka began to confide in me and confessed that she had a boyfriend. After that meeting I entered in my memorandum under the date of March 4, 1935:

> What I learned from you in the course of our last conversation has shaken me, crushed me, much more than you would imagine.
>
> When I found out your secret, when you finally decided to confess to me everything—and you decided it, didn't you, because you simply could not do otherwise—my first impulse was to jump up and run away, to escape from you, away from your dark eyes whose uncanny depths I had now penetrated. But I was incapable of doing it, I was once again too weak, I could not treat myself so cruelly, I dreaded that thereafter I would again be so lonely, so terribly alone, so alone.
>
> You too surely know how terrible, how frightful it is to be alone, to be surrounded by an icy emptiness whose cold breath freezes one's whole being. And—can it be that something one has built up with so much joy, with so much confidence, should so suddenly collapse? Can the certainty of a thing about which one had forebodings and which one feared suddenly destroy everything?
>
> For I did have forebodings. When I was in Tel Aviv a few weeks ago, and that blond young man got out of the car to say hello to you, a fear gripped my heart. I had the foreboding that from this side great harm awaits me. But at that time everything was still new and undeveloped between us, my feelings toward you were still unclear and vague.
>
> Then, a few days later, when we were chatting at the Café Sapphire, and you resisted with such determination touching upon an experience in your life, speaking about it, I suspected what that secret experience must have been; but, peculiarly, it did not occur to me to connect it with that blond young fellow.
>
> On that occasion I pressed you in vain—you remained closed up, and only became a little sad.
>
> Now, when I went down again to Tel Aviv, I was determined to get the whole story out of you. That is why I insisted that we continue in the evening the conversation we had started in the afternoon. That is why I got rid of my

brother-in-law in front of your house, why I was so impatient when your relatives dropped in, and why, when they finally left, I steered the talk to the subject of my view about girls' premarital sexual relations. I told you that by now I no longer felt that girls must enter matrimony in an untouched state (the fact is, now I can admit it, that this is not at all my view), because in this manner I wanted to make it easier for you to confess, to make you believe that even if I should learn such a thing about you it would not mean that all was finished between us.

As you see, I was prepared for your confession, I even led you purposely into it. And yet, when I heard your mouth utter the words, "I am not the pure girl you think," when I had the certainty that everything I suspected, I feared, was true, I was shaken and bruised all over as never before in all my life.

I am still totally confused and perplexed. I don't know what to do. My ideal and dream have always been to form a union with a pure young girl who would become my companion in life and the mother of my children.

And then, when I learned that all those things happened at a time when I already knew you, that is to say, it would have been in my power to prevent them if only I had recognized you earlier and had drawn you to me, I was seized with a blind rage at myself, racked by a cruel pain. Can this be possible? Can the Great Guide over us be so blind, so blind, that he lets our ships pass each other, precisely at the moment when yours is about to be dashed to pieces on a reef?

It is terrible how feeble people are! Why, why did you do it? I don't know whether I could ever forgive you, whether I could ever again feel you my equal, whether I would not always have the nagging feeling that I took pity on you, that I raised you up to me because of compassion.

Since that hour in which you told me everything I am haunted by two visions that chase each other. I see you lying naked and shameless in the arms of that blond youth. And I see you lean your head crying against my shoulder.

March 5, 1935

What did you want of me is what I asked you, if you loved that blond fellow? You had hoped, you said, that I could take you away from him, would wrest you from him. You felt that you were tied to him as if against your will, that you would like to get away from him but could not. Meaning, that on your own you can not, it is beyond your strength. And that is why you hoped I would help you. You even said you wished I would abduct you, kidnap you by force, and shut you up somewhere for weeks, for months, so that you should be able to contemplate that entire experience from a distance, because when you see him, when he stands in front of you and looks at you, you melt and cannot resist him. Yes, but why precisely do you want to resist him? . . . And can it in truth be the case that you had given yourself to him—and not even given yourself completely, but only almost so, not crossing the ostensible physical boundaries—solely because you wanted to help him, because you saw how he suffered, how he tormented himself? Is it justified to take such a step, such a fatal, irrevocable step, only out of compassion, or out of the will to help? No, it is not justified! It was sinful and childish at the same time, it meant throwing yourself away, it was foolish irresponsibility, an act that undermined your future and placed it in jeopardy. And—have you not considered what a brutal egoist must be the man who demands such a thing of the girl he pretends to love?

I have told you and must repeat it now: one can forgive a person everything, everything, if he acts under the compulsion of a great, irresistible passion. No reasonable, feeling person will blame a girl if she gives herself to her beloved in the soaring intoxication of love. After all, when all is said and done, we are not masters of our feelings, we are only ships tossed to and fro on the stormy sea of feelings.

But there were two moments that made your act almost unforgivable. One was that you gave yourself to him, not driven by an inner compulsion, not because you simply could not act otherwise, but out of good will, with the intention of helping him. But that, don't you see, is a crazy notion, a terrible, absurd delusion, something totally unreal: to be able to help somebody through a physical relationship. And what sort of a man is he who demands this kind of help of a girl he allegedly loves? Can he be a man if he is helped through the momentary pleasure of physical union?

The other unforgivable moment was that once you decided to offer this "sacrifice," and to give yourself to him, you were still, even to the last moment, so conscious of yourself that you were able to guard the frontier, that you could, joylessly and passively, submit to everything except that you never ceased to bear in mind the preservation of the physical signs of your virginity. That is, you kept in mind the possibility that in the future you would belong to another man, in which case you would eventually need that physical evidence.

But here, as it turned out, nature played a trick on you. Accidentally you learned from your physician that you did not at all possess those signs, that some years earlier you must have lost them in the course of gymnastics or games.

This shook you. And—instead of setting out joyfully on the open path, you were suddenly seized by remorse and resolved never again to belong to any man except your future husband. And even to him only after he had married you.

Thus ended your brief excursion into the field of sexual love. You returned with muddied feet and a wounded heart. And now you want to free yourself completely from that blond fellow. But in your feelings you are still tied to him. And here you hoped for my help.

When you finished your confession and replied to all my inquisitorial questions, you were convinced that I would want to have nothing more to do with you. Hence, you asked me that on my next visit to Tel Aviv, in two weeks, on the occasion of the Purim feast, I should come to see you at least once more. Earlier you had told me repeatedly that you did not care at all about people's opinion and that you often consciously offended external appearances. And now—this request that could only have come for the sake of external appearances. Still, it touched me. I felt in it the voice of a great sadness. It touched me much more than your tearful confession that only a short time before you had thought of suicide.

But I just could not simply walk away. I was attached to you much too much. Your story shook me up terribly, but could not destroy everything I felt for you.

So I got up and said that you alone must fight out the matter with yourself and that thereafter I should expect a letter from you to inform me when you would come to visit me in Jerusalem.

When you heard this, you started to cry. You quickly went out to the terrace. I followed you, and when I heard your redeeming sobs I felt a warm wave engulf my heart. I became weak, I pulled your head to my shoulder, and touched your dark hair with a caressing hand.

Yes, you must fight your fight alone to the end. Nobody can help you, not even I, or, rather, least of all I. You must be able to break away from him, you alone must do it. I cannot abduct you, I can't even promise you that I shall receive you with open arms. No, you here on the spot must fight it to the end, right here in the magic atmosphere of his proximity. You must be able to tear yourself away from that atmosphere, where his whistle-call can penetrate the open window of your room, you must shut your window and your heart to him and be able to forget the whistle together with the mouth from which it issues.

March 22, 1935

Much has changed since I wrote the preceding lines. I was again in Tel Aviv, this time for four days, and we were together on each of them . . .

Here my "Memorandum to Ilka" ends or, rather, breaks off. But I do remember what happened next. When I went down again to Tel Aviv, on the occasion of the Purim holiday, Ilka and I again spent considerable time together. We walked along the seashore, watched the Adloyada parade down Allenby Road, enjoyed the carnival atmosphere, the bands, the floats, the banners, sat around in the fashionable Tel Aviv cafes or in the living room of the Rotband apartment, and talked and talked and talked. In the course of what turned out to be our last conversation Ilka told me of the latest consequence of her relationship with that blond fellow: she had become pregnant. That left her no choice but to tell her mother about it. An abortion was arranged, legally, of course, since their family doctor diagnosed that to carry the child to term would seriously endanger Ilka's health.

I still remember that when I went down to Tel Aviv I was more or less ready to "forgive her" and to go on with the relationship between us. But when I heard of these latest happenings in her life, I felt that they were more than I could take. Even the mere fact that she had a lover strained my sufferance to the utmost, conditioned as I was by the environment in which I had grown up and by all the formative influences I had absorbed up to that time to believe sincerely that premarital sex was permissible to men, and even expected of them, but was strictly taboo for the class of women among whom a man of my social background was supposed to find a wife. Still, the attraction Ilka exerted on me, her charm, and her evident remorseful self-condemnation, coupled with the initial breezes of modernism that had just begun to waft through the nascent Jewish polity of Palestine, made it possible for me to overlook the deplorable fact that Ilka had become a "fallen woman" and to assume the role of the noble rescuer and redeemer. But to have been impregnated by her lover and to have undergone an abortion—these were occurrences that placed Ilka unalterably beyond the pale for me. I was, to use a phrase from my memorandum, "shaken and bruised," but at that stage of my entrenched male chauvinism nothing could change the fact that she had become an outcast as far as I was concerned.

I don't remember whether there was any formal good-bye between us, tearful or otherwise, but I know that thereafter I never saw Ilka again.

Oh yes, one more thing: I never sent her or gave her my memorandum to read, nor did I ever tell her that I had written one.

Among all the women whom I knew in Palestine—"knew" either in the biblical sense of the word or, as was mostly the case, in its ordinary colloquial meaning—there were two who wanted me to marry them. And since I was both unable and unwilling to fulfill that wish, it became the rock on which both of those relationships foundered. Apart from that identical ending there was nothing similar in the two affairs. The first one was only of a few weeks' duration and is today memorable for me mainly because its inception brought me, for the first time in my life, a brief seizure of euphoria. The second, which lasted almost two years, was my only love affair prior to my marriage that made me seriously consider the possibility of marriage.

Lyuba

Twice in my life, and only twice, have I experienced a moment of euphoria. On both occasions it came quickly and passed just as quickly, but was powerful enough for me to remember it to this day from a distance of many decades. The sensations were, in themselves, not of an earthshaking character, nor did they come as sudden seizures, but were rather like warm waves that bore me quickly aloft, infused me with an indescribable mixture of happiness and pleasure, and then gently deposited me again into the physical environment in which I happened to be at the moment.

The first time this happened to me I was walking back to my rooms from the apartment of Lyuba, the young Polish woman with whom I had just spent our first night of love. The second time, perhaps twenty years later, my euphoric seizure came on a sunny afternoon, in the midst of a rare glorious fall day, while I was driving north in Central Park on my way to the class I taught at Columbia University. The sensations in both cases were similar, even though the circumstances were very different, and the second is more difficult to understand because, in contrast to the first, which may have been triggered by the proud intoxication and exhilaration a youth is apt to feel after having spent an intensely pleasurable first night with a beautiful woman, the second occurrence was not brought about by any such event: it seized me while driving to a class as I did week after week, and I am quite certain that nothing exciting or in any manner unusual happened to me either during or prior to that moment. The sun shone brightly, the winding road through the park was almost devoid of traffic, I had enough time to drive at a leisurely pace, I was looking forward to meeting my class but not more than usually—nor was the subject I was going to discuss with my students of greater interest to me than were the other subjects in my course outline. If I were mystically inclined I would say that a god or a goddess smiled upon me for a moment, for a reason known only to him or her, and this in itself would, of course, have been a sufficient cause for me to react with euphoria. Not being so inclined, all I can say is that this second euphoric seizure of mine must have been produced by some fermentation deep down in my subconscious of which I was totally unaware at the time and which to this day has remained hidden from me.

My first experience of euphoria, from the perspective of fifty years, is more easily understandable. Lyuba, this I remember quite clearly, was the first woman in my life who not only gave me pleasure—that I found in many women to whom I made love—but who also, manifestly and uninhibitedly, enjoyed making love with me. My unaccountably selective memory has retained nothing of the encounters I must have had with Lyuba prior to that memorable night, but as to her person, her appearance, her bearing, her way of looking, talking, and moving, and of course, her superb, abandoned lovemaking—all this is etched indelibly in my memory, as is her soft Polish-accented German—German was the only common language we had. She was a woman of somewhat more than medium height and must have been some two or three years older—I was about twenty-five at the time. She had an oval face with prominent cheekbones, a nose of the type often called "Jewish," a generous mouth, pale skin, violet-blue eyes, a narrow forehead, and a mop of unruly gold-blonde hair that she tried to gather in a bun on top of her head. Her body was slender, with a graceful neck, delicate shoulders, strong breasts, narrow waist, broad hips, and shapely legs.

Lyuba lived together with her mother, whom I saw occasionally, although I never exchanged with her more than a hello or *shalom*. Mother and daughter bore a certain resemblance to each other, but the mother was smaller, darker, and more "Jewish looking." She always kept in the background; her countenance was enveloped in a reproachful sadness, which, on the rare occasions when I caught a fleeting glimpse of her, I found strangely disturbing.

Lyuba's flat was on the ground floor of a three-story apartment house in the central part of Jerusalem between Ben-Yehuda Street and the Mamillah Cemetery, a kind of no-man's-land or buffer zone between the Jewish and the Arab sectors of the city. The cemetery was no longer used and was dotted only sparsely with a few old Muslim tombstones. It was gently sloping from Jewish Jerusalem down toward what was at the time an Arab-inhabited part of the city. Its distant lower end contained an old pool in which there was some water during the rainy season. The immediate vicinity of Lyuba's house was not yet built up, and the unpaved street that passed in front of it ran mostly between empty lots covered with the assortment of aromatic shrubs that grow wild all over the Judean hills.

Lyuba's bedroom, as I noticed when I gained entry into that inner sanctum, had a glass-paneled French window opening onto a small terrace from which one could step out directly into a strip of a garden and then, through an iron gate, gain the street. This feature had considerable advantages, for it enabled Lyuba's visitors to come and go without running the risk of an embarrassing nocturnal encounter with her mother.

That first night I spent in Lyuba's bedroom was stormy and exhausting. Although I had some experience with women of various backgrounds by the time I met Lyuba, I had never before encountered the ardor and the passion with which she responded. She was an entirely uninhibited woman and took a leading role in our lovemaking as a matter of course. She knew how to combine submission with direction, how to be pliant and yet let me know what she wanted of me. She was magnificent, frank, and overwhelming in her unashamed give and take. And, although she led and directed, she made me experience something I had never known before: what it felt to be a conquering, triumphant male.

When we both felt that it was time to call it a night, I got dressed in the semidarkness of the room—translucent curtains filtered out only part of the moonlight—kissed Lyuba on the left breast by way of saying good-bye, stepped out through the French window, crossed the terrace and the garden, and reached the street. The fragrant night air, balmy and yet fresh, carrying the spicy smells of the wild shrubs, of the furze and other aromatic growths of the "everlasting hills" that surround Jerusalem, was intoxicating, coming as it did on top of an intoxication of quite different kind. What I felt in those moments, walking under the incredibly bright moon of nocturnal Jerusalem, drinking in the fragrant atmosphere, listening to the silence broken only now and then by the faint eerie cry of a jackal coming from somewhere out there in the hills, was an indescribable sensation of well-being raised to the nth degree of intensity that one could not sustain for any length of time and live.

For the first time in my life I felt utter happiness—I don't think I was ever again to have the same feeling with such overwhelming power. That brief seizure of euphoria, more than the hours with Lyuba that preceded it, exhausted me so much that upon reaching my rooms I collapsed on my bed and fell asleep without undressing. When I again opened my eyes it was almost noon.

My subsequent encounters with Lyuba were tame in comparison. We continued to find great enjoyment in each other, but, for her at least, it was not the greatest she had known. Once, after we made love, she broke into tears, and when I insisted on knowing what was the matter, she confessed that she still had an irrepressible yearning for her divorced husband, who had remained back in Poland. A few weeks later she fell ill and had to go to a hospital or sanatorium; it took me several visits until I found her mother at home and got the address of the place. I remember visiting Lyuba in that sanatorium: it was an old Arab building of the luxurious type, with a large center hall—it made a great impression on me and I thought I would like to live in such a house. I don't remember whether I saw any traces of her illness in her face. After she returned home she told me that she wanted me to marry her, which for me—a student in his mid-twenties, supported wholly or partly by his father—seemed entirely impossible. Lyuba and I still met a number of times, but she became more and more distant and unwilling. Once, I remember, we actually wrestled while sitting on her sofa-bed, until I gave up and made ready to leave. When I smoothed my hair with my hand, I noticed that there was a trickle of blood over my left eyebrow—either she or I had scratched the spot in the hassle. There was no formal break between us—we simply drifted apart.

My friend the poet Dov Chomsky (1913–1976), who had come from Poland to Palestine in 1936, later complained to me in the course of one of our many conversations while we were strolling in the streets of Jerusalem that, as far as charm and warmth and passion and all the other feminine qualities he appreciated were concerned, the girls he met in Palestine could not hold a candle to the girls he had known back in Poland. And he embarked upon singing the praises of the Polish Jewish girls he had known and loved, who still made him yearn to go back to Poland. As he spoke, and then paused sunk in thought, I was on the verge of telling him about Lyuba, but I just could not break through the wall of restraint that had prevented me all my life from ever confiding to a man friend about a woman friend.

Margot

Soon after I moved into my rooms in Dr. Aescoly's house located off Ben-Yehuda Street, next door to the Orion Cinema (both structures have long since been replaced by large apartment buildings), one afternoon, on my way home from the bus that brought me from the university, I encountered a young woman whose appearance and very gait instantly attracted me. She was tall and slim, with a statuesque body and a noble head she carried tilted somewhat backward. Her black hair, parted in the middle and pulled back severely over her ears into a bun at the nape of her neck, shone as it caught the rays of the setting sun. She had large, dark brown, somewhat almond-shaped eyes, an aquiline nose, a broad mouth, arched lips on which played just a trace of a smile, and a generously rounded oblong face. As I looked at her, my mind's eye saw a picture of Judith, the warlike Jewish heroine as painted by Lesser Ury and long before him by the great Italian masters. Neither of us stopped or even slowed down.

A few days later we again passed each other in the same alley that, beyond Dr. Aescoly's home, led to only one or two other houses and then ended abruptly at the upper perimeter of the Mamillah Cemetery. This time I had the impression that she returned my glance for a moment, which made me slow down and hesitate for a brief instant before I went on. Thereafter, each time I passed that street in either direction, I watched in the hope of seeing her again. As the days passed without gratifying my wish, I resolved that—should I be lucky enough to encounter her a third time—I would stop, talk to her, and ask her whether she would allow me to accompany her. Although I was aware that in doing so I would reenact such famous literary encounters as that of Faust and Gretchen, the dire consequences of that fateful meeting did not discourage me, nor did I cast us into those classic roles: for one thing, I was only twenty-six years old, and she was the opposite of a German Gretchen type.

Before long the opportunity presented itself. Again I was on my way home. I saw her coming toward me, her head tilted slightly up, walking with unswinging hips, rhythmically moving her long, slender legs, putting one foot in front of the other with deliberate speed—an image, I felt, of the quintessentially feminine. My courage almost failed me. But just before she passed me it seemed to me that there was in her eyes not only a spark of recognition but also a slightly friendly expression—or, in any case, nothing like the forbidding mien one would expect of a Judith—and this gave me courage. I turned to her and said something like *G'virti, tarshi li l'lavvot otakh* (Madam, allow me to accompany you). *G'virti* (literally, my lady) was the most formal expression in Hebrew with which one respectfully addressed a woman.

To my relief, she stopped, smiled, and replied in English, "I am sorry, I don't speak Hebrew." I, of course, immediately switched to English, which I spoke with passable fluency, and fell in at her side. We proceeded to the house in which she lived, which turned out to be quite near my own rooms. Before we parted I introduced myself formally, and she told me her name— I shall call her Margot—and also told me that she had been visiting the family of Judge Valero, who lived in that neighborhood, to whom she was teaching English conversation. We made an appointment for the next day. I went home with a song in my heart.

This was the beginning of a long and ardent friendship, in fact, the longest, the most satisfying, and also the most painful friendship I had during the seven years that passed between my arrival in Palestine and my marriage. Margot and I loved each other deeply and steadily, so much so that for the first time in my life I considered the possibility of marriage. In the end, there were two factors that made it impossible for me to come to a positive decision: one was that she was two or three years older, and in my imagination I always saw myself, in that distant future in which the time would arrive for me to marry, choosing a girl—a virgin of course—who was several years my junior, as was the established custom in my family. The other factor was that I still had nothing more than a minimal and precarious income, barely enough for me alone to live on and, worst of all, no tangible prospects. To marry in such circumstances, I felt—I was convinced—would be utter folly, utter irresponsibility, and could only lead to problems, trouble, disaster. And yet, as I look back on the young man that I was, in love with a beautiful young woman who fully returned his feelings, I believe that had there been only one of these two factors present—had Margot been a few years younger or had I had a better and more reliable basis of livelihood—I would have married her, and, I fondly imagine, we would have lived happily ever after. As it was, we discussed the possibility of marriage more than once, and Margot even consulted her father, who lived in Canada and was the owner of a furniture factory, and he declared himself willing to help. But all this developed later.

After a few more meetings one evening Margot came to my rooms, and we passionately consummated our unofficial commitment to each other. Thereafter, as long as our friendship lasted—almost two years—neither the sexual attraction between us nor our pleasure in one another diminished in the least. This was the most powerful magnet that pulled us together and kept us together, although there were other attractions in our relationship. We liked to do things together, enjoyed each other's company, visited friends' houses, attended films on Saturday nights (it was almost a social or even civic obligation to do so), went to concerts (the Philharmonic Orchestra founded by Bronislaw Huberman already existed and played in Jerusalem several times a year), attended gatherings in the amphitheater of the Hebrew University on Mount Scopus, and the like. The only places I went without Margot's company were performances of the Habimah and Haohel theaters and Hebrew lectures, meetings, and conferences, since she never learned Hebrew well enough for that.

Margot had what is customarily referred to as a sunny disposition, an even temper, a rare kindness and softness, and an ability to entertain me with chitchat and stories about life in Canada and with reports of what she had seen and done since we last met. What, in fact, did she do while I was busy with my work? I really don't know, except that she had two or three adult pupils to whom she gave English lessons. Of course, she and I always spoke English, and my knowledge of that language improved considerably thanks to her.

As for Margot's ignorance of Hebrew, what bothered me about it was not that I was unable to converse with her in that language, but that it rendered my entire field of scholarly interest a closed book for her. She knew nothing about the millennial Hebrew literature that was the source material on which I based the books and studies I was working on, nor about the modern Palestinian Hebrew literature from which my friend Zvi Wohlmut and I selected the pieces to be included in our anthology. What therefore developed was a kind of dichotomy in my life. On the one hand, there was my scholarly and literary work through which, I felt, I was part and parcel of the Hebrew intellectual development of the *yishuv.* This work filled my entire being or, at least, almost all of my day; it was the work I knew I was destined to do, to which my father had steered me ever since my adolescence, which I myself had sought out, consciously and consistently, since the age of eighteen, and for which I had trained myself in four countries and six institutions of higher learning. On the other hand, there was the woman I loved, who made me happy, with whom I spent all my time not devoted to work, who wanted to marry me and become my life companion, but who neither understood nor indeed was interested in the work, the task, the world that meant so much for me. It appeared to me that my life thus consisted of two separate and unconnected halves, and I was bothered by this dichotomy. I found myself thinking occasionally with regret of my former flame, Hanna Kroch, who as a graduate of the Haifa Reali school had a thorough grounding in Hebrew and Jewish studies and as a student of the Jerusalem University could well appreciate the scholarly work I had just embarked upon when our friendship began.

Several times Margot and I discussed whether and how we could make ends meet in case we were to marry. She was supported by her father, and she told me that he had declared himself willing to increase her allowance if she should marry, so that we would have no financial worries. I may have been tempted by what seemed to be a generous offer. But there was something in me that made me feel that I simply could not accept such an arrangement. To be dependent on one's wife for one's livelihood, or a major part of it, would be bad enough; to be dependent on one's wife's father seemed totally impossible. The more we talked about it, the stronger became my conviction that I would marry only if I had a position at least relatively secure and an income, even if modest, on which I could depend. I made no bones about this, and the relationship between Margot and me continued unchanged.

Margot herself lived in a furnished room on the roof of a small three-story apartment house near Ben-Yehuda Street. From the top of the stairway a door led directly into her room, from which another door led out onto the flat roof of the house surrounded by a low stone parapet. It was a pleasant, light room, with a view over the rooftops of Jerusalem. Its advantage was that it afforded complete privacy; its disadvantage, that the bathroom and lavatory were located on the floor below it, inside the apartment of which the room formed a part. Margot did not find this inconvenient, but it meant that if I stayed overnight I had to go out to the roof if I had to urinate.

Later—I no longer remember when or why—Margot gave up that room and took another in the same apartment in which I had rented a furnished room after Dr. Aescoly's lease was not renewed by his Arab landlord, and I too had to move out. My new room was on the third floor of a sizable apartment house on lower King George Avenue, between Jaffa Road and Ben-Yehuda Street. It was a good-sized room, with a balcony overlooking the street. Margot's room had no balcony, but its window overlooked the same street. Our rooms were separated by one or two intervening rooms, all opening from the same corridor. Still, we lived in the same apartment, and for a while we enjoyed the situation. However, some months (or perhaps only weeks) later Margot must have felt that we lived together almost as if we were man and wife without actually being married and decided that, after all, this just would not do. So one day she told me that she was moving out, and soon thereafter she actually did so, over my objections. That my relationship with Margot was more serious than with any of my other girlfriends is attested—apart from my clear reminiscences—by the fact that she was the only one among many about whom I spoke, and even wrote, to my mother and sister. That they both discouraged me from marrying her may have strengthened me in my position not to take such a step.

As early as January 1938 Margot began to insist that I marry her. I would not remember the date of this development, but I have in my files a letter I wrote to my sister on January 16, 1938, that contains this brief sentence: "In recent times I am having troubles with Margot, for she wants at all cost that I marry her." I assume that I must have been evasive, and she could not bring herself to break with me. My memory is vague on the details, but the evidence of letters shows that things went on between us much as before for another seven or eight months. Then, in the fall of 1938, Margot finally "gave up on me" and informed me that she had decided to move to London. This came as a serious blow to me and I tried to dissuade her, but was unable to say the one thing that would have made her stay: that I was willing to marry her. So she left in November 1938, and I remained alone, feeling deprived and abandoned. On January 23, 1939, I wrote to my mother, who was still in Budapest at that time (in Hungarian):

Apart from all this, you want to hear something personal about me. Well, if I want to be really indiscreet, I have to admit that the desolate end of the Margot affair wounded me more than I could have imagined. It is now more than two months since she left for London; in the meantime more than one charming lady has come my way who would have liked to beat a merrier rhythm for the sad throbbing of my tired heart, and yet . . . I am beginning to await rather impatiently the onset of the proverbial healing effect of time. Her letters testify to a similar state of mind in her as well.

Curiously, I still remember the name of the London street in which Margot lived, and to which I addressed my letters—Maida Vale—although I have long since forgotten the name of her street in Jerusalem and, for that matter, even the name of the alley in which I myself lived in Jerusalem at the time.

Late in January 1939 my father, who at the time still lived in Budapest, paid a visit to Paris and London in the hope of obtaining help there to find a position in Palestine that would enable him and Mother to get out of Hungary. When he wrote to me that he was planning to go to London, I suggested that Margot might be able to help him get around in the big city. Father could read between the lines, and although he did not need her services as a guide, he did visit her and in one of his letters informed me that he had seen her.

The letters Margot and I exchanged while she was in London, to my regret, are all lost. However, one letter, in which I reported to my sister (who at the time was in Paris) that Margot had returned to Jerusalem, is extant:

April 20, 1939 [in Hungarian]

Dear Évikém:

I was deeply touched by your letter of the 13th, in which you commiserate with me at length. Not, of course, because you happened to hit the nail on the head concerning my internal and external situation, but rather because I see from it that you are concerned about me and think of me very much, I could even say, in excess.

I see from your letter that Mama, unbeknownst to me, has informed you of this and that and, in the manner customary among the female members of our family, piled up huge exaggerations in that information. Hence I feel impelled to give you a brief account of the true situation that will undoubtedly reassure you considerably.

Well, first of all, the fact is that Margot returned to Palestine. After she went to London, in November, the contact between us was not disrupted, and since I missed her very much I asked her to return. She replied that she would come back only if I married her. Thereupon I repeatedly expounded that that has to be counted out. Her first response was that in that case she no longer wants to know me. But, in the end, she too was unable to resist that inexplicable magnetic force that, as is well known, is more powerful from a distance than from proximity, and, forgoing all conditions, she came back.

Since then we have exchanged not a word about marriage, although she has been here now for about four weeks. And my decision not to marry her is as firm as a rock. In addition, you know what a dog's nature human beings have (according to the women, especially the males): as long as Margot was far away, I was unable even to look at another woman, but since she has returned—well, I am able to. In this respect, therefore, you can be quite reassured. On the other hand, you must not envisage her in such dark colors as it would appear from your letter. You know well that a person's well-being, tranquility, and equilibrium have certain physio-psychological preconditions, I could even say bases, and these she provides for me in all respects. It is mainly due to this that in the past few weeks I have been able to become absorbed in a very serious piece of work, which, once finished, will be of "passably epoch-making" significance. It is a new study that probably will grow into a hefty volume in the course of my work on it: I shall present a historical overview and a psychological analysis of the relationship of religion on the one hand and science and the freedom of thought on the other. In the course of this study the superiority of the Jewish religion will become unassailably evident, as will be its magnificent liberalism when compared to Christianity and Islam, which, together with Judaism, constitute the Mediterranean *Kulturkreis* [culture circle].

As long as one is busy with such themes, one does not feel that (as you put it) this is a small *Fleck* [spot] to which one is glued continuously and for too long, but rather sees, as did the ancients, that Jerusalem is the middle of the world, its center, its navel, and, more precisely, not Jerusalem as a whole, but I myself, with my fertile brain in which a whole world is concentrated, and whose creative work, penetrating and demonstrating historical connections, is the noblest joy.

Of course, this "exalted" feeling is not constant, there are times when, e.g., one reads of preparations for war, and involuntarily asks oneself, what sense does it make in the world of today to busy oneself with things of a higher order, when all such things are not timely, and the whole world is in travail trying to solve vital problems? But then one is again caught up in the work, and forgotten are all the disturbing circumstances, war, bombs, murders, and attacks.

Nevertheless, one's interests cannot be entirely filled with work. The six weekly hours of university instruction, the fight about the salary increase, taking care of sundry daily affairs, the last waves of settling the debts of the printing press, the situation of the family—all this introduces variety with the good effect of making me feel that the hours I can spend at my desk working are truly festive hours. [. . .]

Your faithful brother,
Raphael

I want to append one important elucidation to this letter as well as a few minor comments. Reading it today, it appears to me that I was not totally frank in describing my relationship with Margot. I wrote what I wrote because I wanted to reassure Évi that I was in control of the situation and that there was no "danger" that I would marry Margot or that, if we parted, it would plunge me into an emotional crisis. In our family letters this was an inviolate rule: whenever it seemed necessary to bend the truth in order to reassure the letter's recipient, we did not hesitate to do so. The fact was, as I remember with unquestionable clarity, that I was in love with Margot, and both before and after her London sojourn I was for a long time on the verge of marrying her. That in the end I did not, and rather endured the loss of her, was due to a combination of factors, among which my mother's and sister's opposition undoubtedly played an important role. Finally, some three months after her return, Margot had enough of my procrastination and reluctance, gave me up definitively, and broke with me irrevocably. I carefully hid from my family that I was heartbroken, but heartbroken I was, and it took me quite a while to recover sufficiently to be able once again to take any interest in a woman.

Now for a few minor comments. The phrase "passably epoch-making," which I put in quotes in my letter, was an expression both my sister and I remembered from our Budapest days as having been often used (in Hungarian: *meglehetősen korszakalkotó*) by an acquaintance of ours, Mr. Medvei by name, who was a functionary in a Zionist youth movement and had an unusual propensity for malapropish combinations of noun and adjective. As for the grand project of a historical overview of the relationship between science and religion—I never wrote it; it remained one of my many unrealized projects. My reference to *Kulturkreis* indicates that I had come at the time under the influence of the German-Viennese anthropological school known by this name, of which the only other adherent in Palestine was Dr. Erich Brauer, about whom I shall have more to say later. I am also aware, reading this letter, that I was at that time, at the age of twenty-eight, a selfish brat and that my behavior toward Margot left much to be desired.

Some weeks after her return from London Margot moved to Tel Aviv, where I still saw her once or twice on the occasions of my visits to that city. The last time I saw her, she told me that she had met a British scientist who was a liaison officer in the army stationed in Palestine and that he was seriously interested in her. Shortly thereafter I left for Paris and never saw Margot again.

Twenty years later, to my great surprise, I got a letter from her, mailed from London, in which she told me that she was married to a professor of chemistry in London and that they had twin sons. We exchanged a few letters. Then, one day—it must have been about 1960—one of the twins visited me in my office in New York. He was, he said, on a brief visit to America. He was a fine, handsome, intelligent young man of perhaps nineteen. While he sat facing me across my desk I discovered in his features a definite resemblance to the Margot I had known, loved, and lost many, many years earlier.

Grandfather Moshe Klein's tomb on the Mount of Olives. It was destroyed after the 1948 war.

At the Jerusalem Citadel, 1934. *Front:* Raphael, Hanna Krock, Ruth Brandstetter. *Behind:* Mrs. Kroch, Piri Breuer.

Raphael and Ahmed al Kinānī in Hebron, 1934.

Hanna Kroch, Raphael, Ahmed, and an unidentified friend, Jerusalem, 1934.

Raphael, Professor Klein, Joseph Patai, and Edith Patai, June 10, 1936, the day of Raphael's doctoral graduation, Hebrew University campus.

Joseph Patai, Edith Patai, and Raphael at the Shiber house, Jerusalem, 1938.

Naomi Tolkowsky, Jerusalem, 1940.

Raphael and Saul Patai at the Shiber house, Jerusalem, 1938.

Raphael, Jerusalem, 1942.

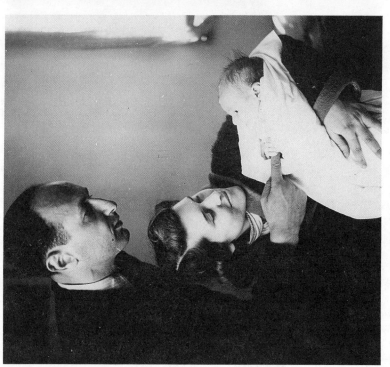

Raphael, Naomi, and Ofra, Jerusalem, 1942.

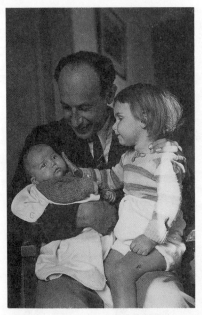

Raphael with his daughters Daphne and Ofra, Jerusalem, 1943.

Ofra and Raphael, Jerusalem, 1944.

The opening of the Jerusalem tutorial classes, 1945, by J. V. W. Shaw, Chief Secretary of the British Mandatory government of Palestine. On his left is Edwin Samuel. Raphael is second from left.

Daphne and Ofra Patai, Jerusalem, 1946.

Raphael, Jerusalem, 1946.

Raphael and Colin Malamet, Mount Carmel, 1947.

Mount Scopus with the Hebrew University Library. Watercolor by Raphael, 1933.

4

Life in
the Yishuv

Giv'at Brenner

In the spring of 1934, having weathered my first winter in Jerusalem, I felt like following up the suggestion of my friend Hanna Kroch and spending some time in a kibbutz in order to gain firsthand acquaintance with the social formation of which she and many of my new friends at the university spoke highly. Even before leaving Budapest I had, of course, known something of the kibbutz or *kvutza*, of which the entire Zionist movement was immensely proud, for there was much talk about it in every Zionist youth group, including the ones to which I belonged. I knew that it was an idealistic society, adhering the principle of "from each according to his ability, to each according to his need," and that all property in it, including even the clothes the members wore, were owned by the commune as a whole, which, to put it negatively, meant that no member owned anything individually. I also knew that everything the members earned with their work, whether in the kibbutz or outside it, belonged to the community and that all the expenses of every individual and of the group as a whole were covered from the common purse, that they all ate in a communal dining hall called in Hebrew *hadar okhel* (literally, food room), and that all members had equal voices in matters pertaining to plans for the future and in all other decisions, including the admission of new members.

The little I knew about the kibbutz was augmented by information supplied by my new friends among the students of the university. What I learned made me want to see a kibbutz for myself, and the spring vacation seemed just the right season to do it. I talked the matter over with Hanna, who was an enthusiastic admirer of the kibbutz, although she herself had never lived in one. She suggested Giv'at Brenner, where she had some friends, and offered to write to them to make sure they would accept me as a guest-member for an unspecified length of time. In the event, I spent two weeks there.

Giv'at Brenner (Brenner's Hill) was named after the Hebrew writer and pioneer of the Palestinian Jewish labor movement Yosef Hayyim Brenner (1881–1921), who was killed in 1921 in Jaffa in the course of the Arab riots that broke out at that time. Located a few miles south of Tel Aviv, near the town of Rehovot, Giv'at Brenner was founded in 1928 by pioneers from Lithuania and Italy and soon thereafter absorbed a considerable number of immigrants from Germany and other countries. It was affiliated with Ha-Kibbutz haM'uhad (the United Kibbutz), one of the three major country-wide kibbutz organizations, founded just a year earlier, whose principles included the admission of unlimited numbers of members to each kibbutz, openness to all comers, and engaging in all forms of production, both agricultural and industrial. As a result of these principles and policies HaKibbutz haM'uhad played an effective role in the absorption of immigrants, and Giv'at Brenner, for one, was to develop not only into a major agricultural producer, but also into an important industrial establishment, manufacturing textiles, furniture, sprinklers, baby food, ceramics, canned fruit and vegetables, etc. By 1968 its membership was to reach 1,520, making it the largest collective settlement in the country.

In the spring of 1934, when I took the bus from Jerusalem to Tel Aviv and then another one from there to Giv'at Brenner, all that, of course, lay far in the future. Nor, when I arrived in Giv'at Brenner, did I know anything of its history or of the principles it embraced. The bus put me down at some distance from the kibbutz, which was situated a few hundred yards from the highway, and I had to lug my valise—fortunately it was not heavy—along a dirt road until I arrived at a group of buildings, or rather cluster of barracks, surrounded by a large number of tents that comprised Giv'at Brenner at the time. Its total number of members, as I soon found out, was less than 300, most of whom were housed in those conical tents.

I sought out the *mazkirut* (secretariat), which proved to be located in a small room in a larger barrack, and introduced myself to the young girl who worked there. She informed me that on the basis of Hanna's recommendation they had decided to accept me as a guest-worker. Then, without any ado, she took me to one of the tents, pointed to one of the three beds in it—there would have been no room for a fourth—and said, "This will be your place." I asked timidly, "Who sleeps in the other two beds?" and in reply she gave me two women's names. I was too surprised to say anything, but later, at dinner, I found out that since it occasionally happened that young Arabs from nearby villages sneaked into the kibbutz, primarily to steal something, it had been decided some months earlier as a security precaution not to let women sleep alone in a tent but always to have a man share the tent with them. I no longer remember whether this information produced any lustful thoughts in me, but I do recall that the work I was assigned to exhausted me so completely that all I was able to do after finishing it was to crawl into bed, where I promptly fell asleep. For several days I went to sleep in an empty tent, and when I woke up the tent was again empty. Then, one night, I was awakened by some noise and movement, and when I opened my eyes I saw in the dim light of a kerosene lamp that two girls were getting ready to go to bed. I was too tired and drowsy to say even a single word, and before I knew it I was asleep again. Thus, throughout my stay in the kibbutz I never had a chance to exchange even a few words with my two female tentmates.

The various types of work that had to be performed to keep the kibbutz going were divided into two categories: income-producing work and service and maintenance occupations. The former carried much more prestige than the latter and was performed almost exclusively by men. It was mainly, as far as I can remember, work in the extensive orange groves of the kibbutz and in its dairy farm. The nonincome-producing service jobs were many, and most of them were done by women. Women cooked in the large communal kitchen, served the meals, washed the dishes, did the laundry for the entire kibbutz, mended the torn linens, underwear, and work clothes, and took care of the babies and the children in the child-care center. Since the whole kibbutz was only six years old at the time, there were as yet no children of school age. Later this sexist division of labor was to be changed, but in 1934 there were only the faintest rumblings of dissatisfaction with these arrangements among the women members.

Some of the members had permanent work assignments, others were shifted from one job to another at irregular intervals. The trained specialists, such as the mechanics, I was told, worked in the same job year in, year out. Their responsibility was to repair and maintain the vehicles, the tractors, and the other agricultural machines. The work-committee of the kibbutz, re-elected periodically by all the members, made the decision at its daily late-evening meetings as to the places that were to be filled by those members who had no special expertise in any particular field. The job allocations were listed on the bulletin board in the dining room, and the members consulted it every morning to know where to go and what to do that day.

The slogan "to each according to his need" was taken very seriously in Giv'at Brenner. Those who were smokers, for instance, got a weekly allotment of cigarettes. Those who did not smoke were given neither cash nor any other compensation representing the savings accruing to the kibbutz due to their being nonsmokers. As for alcohol consumption, that simply did not exist in the kibbutz—neither wine nor hard liquor was available. On the other hand—and I found this both amusing and touching—eau de cologne was allocated to those three or four young men who worked in the cowshed, in order to mask the odor of dung that stuck to them despite the thoroughest ablutions at the close of their working day.

During the two weeks I spent in Giv'at Brenner I was given the simplest of simple assignments: to work in the *pardes* (orange grove). Spring is the time when the orange trees are in blossom, and their fragrance permeated the whole place. But keeping the trees in shape required back-breaking labor. Each of the trees stood in the middle of a large, flat, saucerlike hollow surrounded by a low circular ridge of earth, so designed that the precious water used for irrigating the trees should remain around them and soak into the ground, without flowing off in any direction. To this day I don't know why, but the unquestioned tenet of keeping the trees in top condition was to make sure that no grasses or any other wild fescue, heather, or whatever grew within the saucers surrounding the trees. This meant that the rapidly sprouting growths that resulted from the ample irrigation had to be removed every few days or weeks. This work kept several members of the kibbutz busy for I don't remember how many months throughout the year.

The removal of the wild growth was done with an implement called *turiyya,* a hoe with a short handle to which a blade was attached at right angles. In order to hack away the unwanted herbage one had to bend forward from the hip and thus, with the upper body in an almost horizontal position, bring the *turiyya* down at the tufts of growth, dislodge them by cutting into the soil under them, and then pull the *turiyya* up, turn the roots upward, and fling them outside of the saucer, where the water did not reach them and they dried up and died within a day. Of course, once the trees were again irrigated (that is, the saucers around them were filled with water) new growth sprang up, and the hacking away had to be done again.

This was the work to which I was assigned. Early in the morning, after a quick breakfast, I took my place in the midst of a row of six men lined up at one end of a section of the *pardes,* and we started to work. One of the unwritten laws was that none of the workers was supposed either to forge ahead of or lag behind the others, but the whole line had to, or in any case did, advance abreast from tree to tree. Since I was the only inexperienced *turiyya* wielder in the line, I had to exert myself considerably in order not to slow down the others. The result can be imagined. Within an hour or so I had developed blisters on my fingers and palms, my arms felt heavy, and, worst of all, my lower back began to hurt from the unaccustomed position of bending forward and swinging the *turiyya,* which seemed to grow heavier by the minute.

Still, I managed to hold out. At noon, after some five hours of work, just when I thought I could go on no longer, we took our lunch break. Most of the members assembled in the dining hall, the girls who served put large aluminum pots full of steaming food on the tables, and we all helped ourselves. That I was very hungry goes without saying, and it is easily understandable that I remember nothing of the food we were given. But I have retained a general impression of the cheap aluminum utensils used, of the chipped heavy china plates, of the linoleum tablecloths, and of the noise that filled the big barrack, composed in equal shares of table talk and the clatter of the tableware. By 12:30 lunch, which was the main meal of the day, was over, and from then until 2:30 P.M.—the hottest part of the day—we had a rest. I hastily retired to my tent, which I found empty—I didn't know and didn't care what my two tentmates were doing during their lunch break. I lay down on my cot and enjoyed the luxury of stretching out and resting. I could not fall asleep, because I was not used to taking a nap after lunch and also because it was too hot in the tent, although the hottest time of the year was still several weeks away. But just to lie and do nothing was sweeter than I had ever imagined it could be.

While lying there I used the occasion to have a good look around the tent. It was cone shaped, held up by a single pole in the middle and made of light-gray heavy canvas. What surprised me most was that it was double-layered, as if two tents of identical shape, one somewhat smaller than the other, were stretched on top of each other. When I inquired about this someone explained to me that this kind of double-skinned tent was much superior to a single-layered one: it was better for keeping out the cold in the winter and the heat in the summer. I shuddered to think how hot a single-skin tent would be and at the same time recognized how badly this type of tent, whether double- or single-skinned, was adapted to the hot climate of lowland Palestine. It was closed all around, except for a flap that served as access. It was like a hothouse, inside which the temperature climbed much higher than it was outside. And I remembered the Bedouin tents I had visited with my friend Ahmed shortly before, which were broad and wide, with a tent-cloth stretched more or less horizontally on top of several tent-poles and—most importantly—with the sides open all around, so that in effect such a tent was a sun-roof, an awning, under which it was relatively cool because it allowed the air to circulate freely through it while providing shade.

Later I understood that not using Bedouin-type tents was but one example of the rejection by Jewish newcomers of features of the Arab material culture of Palestine, even if they were well adapted to the local climate. Another was the building style of houses. The typical Arab house had very thick walls and small windows, so that it was relatively cool in the summer and warm in the winter. The Jews built houses with thin concrete walls and large windows, so that they quickly absorbed the outside temperature: they were cold in the winter and hot in the summer. Several years later I discussed in a study (published first in Hebrew in *Edoth,* then in English as one of the Memoirs of the American Anthropological Association) the differences between the adoption of Jewish cultural features by the Arabs of Palestine and of Arab features by the Jews. To this day I believe that the rejection by the

Jews, upon their arrival in Palestine, of locally established cultural features was a lamentable manifestation of their conviction that their own modern European-Jewish culture was in every respect superior to the "stagnant" Arab culture of Palestine.

In any case, to come back to Giv'at Brenner of 1934, any suggestion that it could adopt with advantage the Bedouin-style tent for its own use would have met with scorn—not that I was tempted to make such a suggestion. I was much too shy, too uncertain of myself, and too conscious of my position of a guest graciously and temporarily admitted into an apparently well-functioning society.

After the midday break, at 2:30 P.M., I had to force myself to get back to work despite aching all over. Had I not been young and strong, and, most importantly, had I not been determined to be a credit to my friend Hanna, I would not have mustered the energy to get up and go back to work. But back I went, and continued to work for two and a half hours more, until, at 5 P.M., the workday came to an end. I could barely drag myself to the communal shower, and never before or after did I enjoy as much the refreshing force of cold water splashing over my body as I did then and there.

Dinner was a less substantial meal than lunch, but taken in a more leisurely fashion. When it was over the members of the kibbutz were free to engage in whatever activity they preferred. Those who had children would spend a pleasurable hour with them outdoors, in the nursery, or in their own rooms or tents; those who were members of some committee got together to discuss problems and plans affecting the kibbutz as a whole; those who liked music (some of the German members loved *Lieder* and other serious music) got together in a corner of the dining hall and listened to the kibbutz phonograph. Some just sat around and engaged in conversation either outdoors or in each other's lodgings. I might have joined any of these groups, but after dinner I was so tired that all I could do was return to my tent, undress, and go to sleep.

The young men who worked in the *pardes,* of whose slowly advancing front line I was a temporary member, frequently entertained themselves during the long hours of tedious work by conversing. In the first few days I was so absorbed in the effort to keep pace with them and so preoccupied with my aches and pains that I could pay no attention to what they were talking about. In my second week, however, after a day of Sabbath rest—which I spent doing absolutely nothing except for writing one letter to Hanna and one to my parents in Budapest—I felt better and was able to listen to what my immediate neighbors in the line to my right and left were saying. They were friends and they spoke to each other over my head—I don't know to this day why one of them did not suggest that I change places with him— and what they discussed gave me an insight not only into the working of the kibbutz but also into the mentality of its devoted members. That same evening I started taking notes and after I returned to Jerusalem I worked them up into an article (in Hungarian) that I sent to Father, who published it in the June 1934 issue of his monthly. I titled the article *Vita a mezőn* (Debate in the Field) and not "Debate in the Orange Grove," which would have been more accurate, because I felt that the former sounded better and reminded those who were in the know of the debates in the fields engaged in by the sages of old and recorded in the Talmud. To justify my title I began the article by saying (with a certain poetic license):

> Most people, when they hear the word "orange-grove," imagine a forestlike grove of tightly packed trees, orange tree next to orange tree, with their branches laden with heavy golden fruit caressing one another. In reality, however, the term "orange field" would be much more fitting than "orange grove." An orange grove is actually a field, in which the trees stand at quite a distance, some six to eight meters apart.

Then I went on to describe the work that had to be done in the *pardes* and finally got down to the main subject, the debate conducted by my two neighbors in the field. The name of one was Zelig, of the other Sitchuk. One was German, the other Lithuanian. One had a wife and child, the other was a bachelor. One of them was a member of the *mo'etza* (council) of the kibbutz whose task was to decide on the work assignments and the major economic policy questions. Both, as I wrote in my flowery Hungarian style, "were lovers of the kibbutz and the soil, obsessed by upbuilding, with all their thoughts, all their feelings belonging to the community, its progress, its development, its construction." Still, I added, there were differences between them that supplied seemingly inexhaustible subjects for weighty ideological discussions. One day the man who was a member of the council said: "The next meeting of the *mo'etza* must decide whether or not to admit fifty new members. Fifty boys and girls from Germany have applied. My opinion is that we must admit them. The kibbutz must grow."

The man on my other side replied: "This all too rapid growth cannot lead to anything good. A year ago we were a hundred and twenty. Today— three hundred, together with the children three hundred and fifty. And even though more than half a year has passed since we admitted the last group, we still hear more German spoken than Hebrew. The process of Hebraization is going too slowly. The Germans still speak German among themselves, and only those who have children learn Hebrew rapidly. The children force the parents to learn Hebrew, but, alas, there are too few children . . ."

"True," rejoined my other neighbor. "But we cannot as yet permit ourselves the luxury that children represent for the kibbutz. Although, looking at it from a distance, the child is not a luxury but a vital necessity. It is the most vital necessity of the kibbutz, and, beyond it, of the whole of Eretz Israel . . ."

The next day Zelig and Sitchuk discussed other plans of the kibbutz. Again the member of the council broached it, and again the view of the other differed.

"We expect serious differences of opinion at the next meeting of the council," the first one announced. "This week we shall close the accounts for the year, and it seems we shall have a sizable surplus. That means that we shall have to decide what to do with it. Shall we make new investments, such as adding another hundred dunams to our orange groves, or shall we improve our food, or perhaps build living quarters . . . ?"

My other neighbor cut in impatiently: "It goes without saying that we must use all surplus for expanding our economy, our farm. We can quite well continue to live in tents and barracks for another few years. And as for food, it is quite sufficient to have meat twice a week. But we *must* increase our economy, as fast as possible. Our land is excellent for oranges, there is much demand for our produce. Another hundred dunams of oranges will mean a doubling of our income in five years. *Then* can come the turn of houses, of meat . . ."

But the first discussant did not give in: "Yes, if there won't be *then* such ardent builders as you are. But there will always be such people. This fever spreads from year to year, and, as we can see in the children of the old kibbutzim, it is inherited from generation to generation . . . But if we go on like this, heaping five years upon five years, in the meantime we shall be ruined, we shall not be able to keep up this feverish pace, this life full of privation, of hardship, in which the only joy is the joy of work . . . Hasn't the time come to spare ourselves a little, to devote some thought also to the present instead of thinking only of the future? For five years, ever since we hammered the first tent-stake into the ground and planted the first orange sapling, we have always reassured ourselves that the first crops would make it possible for us to have a little ease, a little satisfaction . . . For five years we have been only machines, only drudges, the slaves of our own tomorrow . . . And now, when the long-awaited tomorrow is within our grasp, when finally the first golden apples have been harvested, you again want to extend the time of waiting, the time of bearing up, for another five years?"

Incidental problems of the kibbutz also came to my notice through the simple device of listening to my two neighbors' conversations. I learned that just recently a young man, a member, had returned from a lengthy stay in a Swiss sanatorium, completely cured of his tuberculosis, and I gathered that months before, when the council voted on the monetary allocation needed to send him to Switzerland, the approval was preceded by a bitter debate because it was difficult to take the money from the basic necessities for many members and give it for the restoration of the health of a single one. As I listened to the recital of that case I felt glad that I did not sit on that council and did not have to participate in what must have been an extremely difficult choice.

I learned about a case in which "private money" was found in the possession of a member—a serious breach not only of the statutes but also of the mores of the kibbutz. The decision of the council: confiscation of the money and a warning to the culprit that, if it happened again, he would be summarily expelled. I heard about another case in which a couple with two small children had asked for admission; after the six-month probationary period was over the council found only the woman suited for permanent membership, which she happily accepted, while the husband had to move out, and thus the marriage of the couple was disrupted. Was it right for the council to pass a resolution that, in effect, destroyed what had been, perhaps, a good marriage?

Much of the discussion revolved around the kitchen, with which not all members were satisfied. How to improve the food by making it more varied and tastier was an oft-recurring topic. Attention was repeatedly devoted to the question of whether it was right to sell all the milk and butter produced by the kibbutz to Tenuva, the countrywide dairy-products cooperative of the Histadrut, and to purchase butter imported from Lithuania and Australia for consumption by the kibbutz itself. True, the price of Tenuva butter was exactly the double that of the imported product, so that this arrangement appreciably increased the cash receipts of the kibbutz, but how could one publicize Tenuva butter by saying that it was the patriotic duty of all to buy *totzeret haAretz* (product of the land) butter, if, paradoxically, the producers themselves did not fulfill this duty but instead bought foreign butter?

These subjects and many similar ones were discussed interminably by Sitchuk and Zelig; as I listened to them, both the technical and the emotional mechanisms that drove the kibbutz gradually became clearer to me. I got a glimpse, or perhaps a little more than that, of what motivated these young men and women who had come from all corners of Europe and decided that the kibbutz, the commune, would be the frame in which they wanted to live, to which they would subordinate all personal ambition and interest. And it now strikes me that, although I spent many hours daily in the company of those two men, I learned nothing about their personal lives. Neither of them, in the course of those long hours of work and talk, said a word about himself. They spoke only about the kibbutz, its problems and plans, about the council that managed the community, and its agenda. This fact—that the topic which kept them preoccupied was the kibbutz and not their own individual lives—was, I believe, the most eloquent testimony to the emotional and cerebral engrossment of the individual in the affairs of the community, and, indirectly, to the power of the kibbutz to bring about this individual self-identification with the commune.

To return for one more moment to my 1934 article about Giv'at Brenner, I regret today that I devoted much of it to reflections on what some item in the life of the kibbutz meant and to comparisons between what I observed in the kibbutz and what I knew from my studies about similar discussions that had taken place seventeen or eighteen centuries earlier among talmudic sages who lived right here, in the vicinity of Giv'at Brenner and were members of the talmudic academy of Yavneh. Today I wish I had left much of that unsaid and had used the space for quoting more from the debates I overheard and reporting more of the firsthand observations I made in Giv'at Brenner. I regret even more that I did not possess (in fact, did not even know of the existence of) a recording machine, with the help of which I could have taken down hours of conversation between members of the kibbutz and could have even interviewed them. On that basis I could have produced a serious study of the kibbutz, or at least of one kibbutz, years before any other student of the *yishuv* discovered that it was indeed a "hot" subject. But since I was at the time totally involved in studying the role of water in ancient Jewish belief, custom, and legend, I did not consider the kibbutz a subject for scholarly inquiry and could barely wait to return to Jerusalem to my books, notes, and water studies.

Two weeks after my arrival in Giv'at Brenner I said good-bye to the few people with whom I had become acquainted and took the bus back to Tel Aviv and from there to Jerusalem. During the bus trip I went over in my mind what I had learned in the kibbutz. I no longer remember what résumé I gave myself at the time, but looking back at my eventless kibbutz-adventure from the present distance of more than fifty years, I feel that no amount of reading about the kibbutz or of listening to oral accounts could have given me as full and as immediate a grasp of the realities of that unique and original Palestinian Jewish social life-form as I gained by being part of it even if only for a very brief period. I felt somewhat like the ancient biblical spies in the Land of Canaan, except that my purpose was not parallel to that of Joshua, Kaleb, and their company, but to find a way to penetrate the mind of the kibbutzniks, to understand them, to get to view them as they viewed themselves, and to learn the secret of the influence those few communal villages had on the *yishuv*, quite out of proportion to the number of people living in them.

First of all, I understood a thing that had greatly puzzled me before: how young Jews, members of a highly individualistic and achievement-oriented people, could give up all ambitions for personal advancement and career and transfer to, and vest into, the collective all those drives to succeed that in the course of long centuries had become almost instinctual correlatives of Jewish intelligence. When I say I understood it, I don't mean that my participant observation (to use an anthropological term I learned much

later) laid bare to me in concrete detail the psychological mechanisms or processes of the transfer of ambitions from the individual ego to the commune.
But I did get a demonstration of the actual end results of those processes: I
could observe people in their daily lives, at work and at leisure, and when engaged in exchanging ideas, all of which showed the identification of the individual with the community and the giving of preference, albeit to varying degrees, to the commonweal over self-interest. Although the debates between
Zelig and Sitchuk demonstrated strong differences of opinion with reference
to the *degree* to which individual gratification should be subordinated to planning and working for a better future, neither of the discussants expressed any
doubt as to the primacy of the common welfare, and the question was only
about the balance to be struck between it and the irrepressible human desire
to enjoy at least a modicum of creature comfort. Although I kept my eyes and
ears open, never in the course of my stay in the kibbutz did I hear a word—
or even an indirect, veiled indication—of dissatisfaction with the basic principle of "to each according to his needs," which in practice meant that the
kibbutz treasury had to make quite unequal disbursements to cover the differing living expenses and requirements of its individual members.

At the time of my kibbutz jaunt I already had some familiarity with the
structure and functioning of the traditional Middle Eastern family (in later
years I was to write about it). Thus, I knew about the identification of members of a family with its joint interests, which in practice meant that the individuals belonging to it were conditioned from earliest childhood to subordinate their personal wishes, desires, and ambitions to those of their extended family as represented by the patriarch. While I was at Giv'at Brenner
I recognized something similar in the kibbutz: an effective shift from the all-
human desire to achieve individual satisfaction to a gratification derived
from extending efforts aimed at serving the community as a whole. That the
kibbutz succeeded in bringing about this shift in individuals who joined it
in adulthood, after a childhood and adolescence dominated by the desire to
satisfy personal wants, is something quite remarkable—I recognized this
then, and I have not changed my opinion since.

I had known, even before going to Giv'at Brenner, that Zionist youth
movements, which aimed at preparing their members to join a kibbutz,
could inculcate in them the conviction that the communal life as exempli-
fied in the kibbutz was *the* ideal form of society; but during my short days
in the kibbutz I learned that there was more than that to the full identification of the individual with the community I found there. There was, I
sensed rather than cognitively learned, something in the physical plant of the
kibbutz—in the tents, barracks, workshops, storehouses, barns, sheds, and
stalls, surrounded by the fields and groves—that, beyond the concrete factors of mutual dependence upon the conscientious performance by each

member of the assigned tasks, produced a spirit of commonality, an enchanted and enchanting atmosphere, a microcosm of probing and searching and struggling for betterment, all the while serene in its unshakable conviction of having found the right path.

At the same time I also understood that all this did not mean, of course, that there were no cases of individuals who found, after having lived in a kibbutz for varying lenghts of time, that it was not the society in which they wanted to spend the rest of their lives. Such cases, when they did occur, were painful for both the kibbutz and the person concerned. But they never injected even as much as a shadow of a doubt into the mind of the membership as a whole about the rightness of kibbutz life. All they did was to produce a commiseration with the person who decided to leave or who was excluded by the will of the community, not unlike the feeling one has for a family member or a friend who becomes sick, suffers an accident, or commits a crime.

Contemplating the similarity between the psychological hold on the individual exercised by the extended family and by the kibbutz, I was also aware of the significant differences between the structure and the functioning of the two, beyond the patent fact that one is born into the family so that membership in it is a given, a circumstance that preexists prior to the individual's mental development, while one joins the kibbutz as a result of a conscious and considered decision. The extended family is large only relative to the nuclear family; typically, it has ten, fifteen, twenty members, rarely more; the kibbutz, although it too can start with as few as twenty or so participants, in most cases includes a number upward of a hundred. Equally significant is the difference in management. The extended family is ruled by the patriarch, whose will is law, who is considered the undoubted representative and embodiment of the interests of the family, whose decision cannot be questioned but only obeyed, and who is the sole legal owner of all the property, whether land, buildings, or livestock.

In the kibbutz the principles of communality are scrupulously observed: not only is ownership of everything (even personal items such as clothing) vested in all the members jointly, but they together as a group decide by majority vote who should manage their various affairs. Hence, while relationships in the kibbutz are much more complex than in the extended family, they are also more equitable, because the dependence on one single powerful individual, characteristic of the extended family, is absent. Also absent in the kibbutz is the generational crisis to which the extended family is exposed when the patriarch dies. His death triggers, in most cases, a splitting-up of the unit into as many new units as the number of sons he leaves behind, with all the attendant locational, social, and property adjustments. In the kibbutz, the organizational guidelines provide for a continuity of membership, of ownership, of social structure, even though the old generation is gradually being replaced by a younger one. In 1934 this process was just beginning in the oldest kibbutzim (the first one, Degania, was founded precisely twenty-five years earlier, in 1909), but subsequently it became a routine matter, and the kibbutz as such survived, undergoing, not periodical crises, but gradual development.

Inevitably I also asked myself the question of whether kibbutz life was something I would consider for myself. I don't know anymore whether I gave myself an answer at that juncture, but I do have documentary evidence that the question continued, if not to preoccupy me, at least to remain somewhere in the back of my mind for several months thereafter. The evidence is a letter I wrote in the fall of 1935 to my brother Guszti, who was seventeen at the time and was faced with the problem of choosing a career or, rather, of deciding what studies he should pursue a year later when he would be the proud possessor of a high school diploma. I wrote to him in Hungarian, using the Hungarian typewriter I had brought along from Budapest, which had keys for the Hungarian vowels *á, é, í, ö, ő, ü, ű*. A carbon copy has survived in my files, one of the very few letters from those early years. Today, more than half a century later, that letter is almost a historical document—it affords me an insight into how I felt and what I thought at the age of twenty-five about a number of issues I considered important at the time. The first part of the letter deals with the difficulties Guszti faced in having to choose a profession, and the second contains my thoughts about the kibbutz.

Jerusalem, October 15, 1935

Dear Gusztikám:

I haven't written you for quite a while, although the truth is that neither have you made any effort, but still, now that I have finished my work and thus have more time, I am writing to you, the more so since remarks Mama drops in her letters let me conclude that our parents are not a hundred percent satisfied with you. Of course, in every letter you are "the little sweetie," or, rather, by now, "the big sweetie," but apart from these infantilisms I see that especially about the choice of a career you show yourself sullen and refractory, in which I, of course, see only one thing: that you yourself don't know what you want. I am not at all surprised at this. I remember well—it was, after all, not so long ago—that when I was a high school senior I did not know either what I should choose. Even after the *matura* [high school exam] I still did not know, and then, suddenly, merely because I could draw well, I decided to become an architect. Then, persuaded by poor Uncle Berti, I entered the mechanical engineering department [at the

Technical University of Budapest]. But when I did not find my place there, I gave in to Papa's persuasion and embarked upon rabbinical studies, at the same time also taking German and English language and literature at the university. However, I abandoned these subjects too even before the end of the first semester and instead took Semitic philology. After passing my doctoral exam I came out here with the intention of spending a year here and then returning, to sit for the rabbinical exam and become a rabbi somewhere in Büdösszentdisznód. Then, having become acquainted with the Land and fallen in love with it, I no longer wanted to return but decided instead to become a teacher here, which I actually was for one year. However, in the course of that year I discovered the taste and savor of scholarly work, and at the same time recognized that the teaching profession did not suit me either. Therefore, I arranged things so that I agreed to go back home, which I plan to do soon, because in that manner I shall gain one more year during which I shall not have to earn a living but can live for research. What shall become of me or happen to me, when, after next spring, I come back here, only God knows. But if He knows, the matter is in good hands, and there is no reason to worry.

Why am I telling you all this? So that you should see that one cannot figure out or direct in advance the course of one's life. There is therefore no reason at all for you to be disquieted by this matter; time will show, and whatever will be, will be good. One must trust. For the rest, when I come home we shall talk about it in greater detail.

Now I would like to touch upon another matter. Mama writes in her last letter that you insist on becoming a farmer. I assume that what you have in mind is to join a kibbutz, for otherwise how could you, owning no land, become a tiller of the soil?

Well, I grant you, to live in a kibbutz is a magnificent thing. Just the other day Nóci Léderer (now called Yehoshua) paid me a visit. He is sunburned and full of energy, in the best of spirits, level-headed. Although the fact is that their life is rather difficult there in Bet Zera', on the banks of the Jordan, some three kilometers south of Degania, about two hundred meters below the level of the Mediterranean. Four months a year the temperature tops 40° (centigrade) [104° F]; almost all of them went through some light malaria, his wife just recently, in the eighth month of her pregnancy. But they stand the climate, stand the work, and are happy. The same evening another two members of the same kibbutz visited us, and I truly enjoyed their company. These people radiate some kind of quiet, natural self-assurance, which, it would seem, only the soil can give. I admit frankly I liked these people very much, and from what they told me of life in the kibbutz I also liked the kibbutz as a whole. Truly, I felt like going there, joining them, and becoming part of that hard life and at the same time of that security that it can give. And, I thought, "If I don't succeed in finding a place at the university, I shall go to the kibbutz."

And, interestingly, the same idea came to me when I read in the papers about the Abyssinian war, and when I heard people speak of the possibility of a European conflict. If that comes to pass, I thought, and if it does it would mean a catastrophe for Palestine as well, I shall escape into the kibbutz.

Perhaps I am not mistaken when I say that it is precisely here wherein lies the wonderful power of attraction of this country: in this possibility that, in all probability, is before the eyes of everybody—here there is no shipwreck, if nothing else succeeds there is the kibbutz, asylum, refuge, and more than that: a home that harbors you.

But this same possibility, this consideration that endows this country with such an enormous superiority in the eyes of the young people compared to any fabulous America, this selfsame thing also reduces the value of the kibbutz in my eyes, and, I believe, not only in mine but in the eyes of every talented person who can create or at least wants to create. Yes, the kibbutz is home, where the prodigal son is received lovingly, but, first, before he returns home to the kibbutz, the son must become prodigal. The kibbutz is the home port, always there to receive the ships plying the stormy seas. But if the ship can face the storm it can reach the harbor that is its goal and doesn't have to turn back to the home haven.

You understand, don't you, what I want to say with all these lame similes? A talented young man does not start out by going into a kibbutz, but may end up with it. That is, he keeps it before his eyes as a possibility. But the mark of real talent and fitness is that this possibility remains an unexploited possibility to the end of his life.

Of course, everything I set forth here is valid only for a certain group of people, but we belong precisely to that group. The others, who are not predestined to individual creative work, can quite well find their places in the kibbutz from the very first. If you or I were to retire into a kibbutz before we put ourselves to the test in free competition, I would consider that a cowardly flight.

I believe that a man must strive to engage in a type of work that only he and nobody else is capable of performing. This scholarly work that I have just now finished could only be written by me. Likewise, you too must find the work that only you can do, for which you are the most suitable.

In conclusion I beg you to write me, write in detail what you think of all this. Take time, sit down, and put in writing in all seriousness what you think, and don't just jot down two lines and then add, "I have no time now, more next time." You must outgrow this childish foolishness. As you see, I also took the trouble, and spent all my afternoon typing this letter.

Now for a few concrete matters. Hirsch senior complains that he has not received the jubilee issue of *Mult és Jövő*. His address is: Balfour Str. 55, Tel Aviv.

I recently sent Papa a note asking him to initiate inquiries as to what steps must be undertaken so that I officially cease to be a Hungarian citizen. This is quite important, so please remind him, or perhaps you yourself could go to the police and inquire, you are big enough by now.

I asked you several times to look up in a historical dictionary the origin of the word *szivárvány* [rainbow]. Please, do this finally, urgently. You should find such a dictionary in the teachers' library at school.

After and despite all this I send you many kisses,

Your loving brother,
Raphael (formerly Gyuri)

A few references in the above letter require elucidation. Büdösszentdisnód is a name I made up for a Hungarian village or small town. Literally, it means "Stinking Saint Pigtown." My intention was to satirize Hungarian place-names of similar construction. Ignác (Nóci) Léderer was an acquaintance of our family who had served as secretary of a Zionist youth organization in Budapest prior to his immigration to Palestine, where he became a member of the kibbutz Bet Zera'. The Abyssinian war began in the fall of 1935 with the Italian invasion of Ethiopia. Hirsch senior was Emil Hirsch, the father of my sister's husband, Leon. In 1935 I obtained Palestinian citizenship. But I wanted, in addition, to be officially released from my Hungarian citizenship so as to be able to visit Hungary without any problem and then go back to Palestine. The reason I wanted to know the derivation of the Hungarian word *szivárvány* (rainbow) was that I was working at the time on an essay on the rainbow in folklore. It was published in 1937 (in Hebrew) in the *Samuel Krauss Jubilee Volume* in Jerusalem. I do not remember whether my brother answered this letter. If he did, his answer has not survived the years.

But to return to the spring of 1934, as the first anniversary of my arrival in Jerusalem approached, I felt that having spent a year studying at the Hebrew University I was ready to sit for the rabbinical exams at my Budapest alma mater. To be able to do so I had to obtain a leave of absence from the Jerusalem university, to be granted by Professor Klein in his capacity as both my major professor and the dean (actually chairman) of the Faculty of Humanities (called in Hebrew Faculty of *Madda'e haRuah*, that is, Sciences of the Spirit). Thus, when I submitted to him a chapter (the first chapter completed?) of my thesis for review I simultaneously asked him to grant me the leave and to inform the secretariat of the university.

After reading my chapter, Professor Klein wrote me a letter—one of the very few from his pen that survived my intercontinental moves. It shows the problems caused by the differences between his overriding interest in the historical geography of Palestine and my commitment to the study of Jewish historical folklore.

29. Siwan 5794 [June 12, 1934. In Hebrew]

Dear Dr. Patai:

I read with great attention and interest the chapter you gave me to read, as shown by the brief comments on the margins. But, despite my interest and my pleasure at a few fine results of your research, I must confess that I have not yet found in your presentation the central point, which is research pertaining to the *study of the Land of Israel.* After all, you titled your work "A Study in the Knowledge of the Land and the Folklore, etc."! Therefore, I think that you should shorten the general folkloristic matters and get down to the central issue: the value of water, etc., etc., in the study of the Land of Israel. I don't recall at the moment what the subsequent chapters are, but still I advise you to complete at least one or two chapters related more closely to Eretz Israel before you leave the country, so that I should be able to evaluate the method of your research concerning the study of Eretz Israel, and so that I should perhaps be able to show you the way in this matter.

I shall be glad to talk to you about all these things in the next few days (I am at home every day in the mornings), and only after that conversation shall I give my response to the secretariat concerning the leave of absence and the continuation of the work during your absence or sojourn abroad.

You have used the word *hasagah* several times—evidently in the sense of *Auffassung, Anschauung.* I think that this word in this sense is not fortunate, for *hasagah* has usually the meaning *Entgegnung* ("the *hasagah* of the RAV"D"). Therefore one must use another word, such as *hashqafah, de'ah.*

With best regards, yours,
S. Klein

In response to this letter I must have been able to reassure Professor Klein that my thesis would satisfy his scholarly expectations, for three weeks later he did give me a certificate, which evidently was intended for presentation to the Budapest Seminary. I needed such a document to make sure that my teachers at the Seminary would accept the work I did at the Hebrew University as the equivalent of the fifth (concluding) year of studies at the Seminary, a prerequisite for being allowed to sit for the rabbinical exam. I translate the document literally:

21 Tammuz 5694–July 1, 1934

Certificate

This is to certify that Mr. Dr. Raphael Patai participated in the 5694 academic year in the following lecture and exercise courses at the Hebrew University in Jerusalem:

Lecture Courses: 1. The Land of the Galilee from the Hasmonaic Times to the End of the Talmudic Period.

2. The History of the Jewish settlement in Eretz Israel from the Conclusion of the Talmud to the Hibbat Zion Movement.

3. The Hellenistic Cities in Eretz Israel.

Exercises: 1. The Book of Joshua.

2. Sources for Lecture Courses 1 and 2.

Private Seminar: Lectures by Advanced Students.

He also worked as a Research Student [i.e., graduate student] throughout the year on a scholarly subject for earning the Ph.D. degree at our university.

Respectfully,
Prof. S. Klein
Chairman of the Faculty of Humanities

As it turned out, I did not return to Hungary that summer, but did so only in the summer of 1936, after I earned my Ph.D. at the Hebrew University.

Jewishness versus Hebrewness

Looking back, from a distance of some seven decades, on my childhood and youth it is clear to me that I received from my parents and teachers two invaluable gifts. One was this: from my earliest years, without having ever been told anything about God or given as much as a hint that I was supposed to believe in Him, I yet absorbed in the atmosphere of the parental home an unquestioning belief in His presence. One of my earliest memories is that my grandmother would come to sit down next to me as soon as I was put to bed—I could not have been more than three years of age—and night after night, make me repeat after her the Hebrew words of the Sh'ma' prayer. I had not the slightest idea that what I was saying meant "Hear, O Israel, the Lord our God, the Lord is one," but her very demeanor was sufficient to impress me with the *tremendum* of what she said and what I had to repeat word by word. Before long, as I gradually learned the prayer by heart, the mere act of enunciating it gave me a wonderful feeling of well-being. Similarly, as I grew and was taught, primarily by example, the *mitzvot* (commandments) of Judaism, their performance filled me with a sense of having done my duty, having acted properly, and having earned the love and protection of God. This feeling, added as it was to the feeling of being loved by my father and mother, supplied me throughout my childhood with a consciousness of security, a sense of being protected, of living in a safe and good world.

The other gift I received from my father and teachers was a comprehensive and thorough Jewish education, which, as it turned out, was to become the basis of all the scholarly and intellectual work to which I have devoted my life. Among those who introduced me to Judaism were three or four private tutors who started to teach me to read and understand Hebrew even before I reached school age, and then several teachers in elementary and secondary school, and still later a dozen or so professors at the rabbinical seminaries of Budapest and Breslau and the universities of those two cities, and finally my masters at the Jerusalem university. In addition there was the instruction of my father, who in long Sabbath-afternoon sessions that continued for several years instilled in me not only an understanding of the Talmud, but also an appreciation amounting to love of that "great sea" of Jewish law and lore. While the first gift contributed immensely to the development of my personality, this second became a treasure trove from which I was able to draw throughout my life.

Yet, despite my saturation with Jewish knowledge, my intellectual horizon was never confined to the world of Judaism. In my high school, even though it was an institution sponsored by the Israelite Congregation of Pest in which six hours a week throughout eight years were devoted to Jewish studies, we had a general curriculum identical with that of all academic high schools in Budapest. Thus, I got a foundation in math, geometry, chemistry, physics, and art, as well as Hungarian and world history, and, in addition to Hebrew, also in Hungarian, Latin, German, and English language and literature. At the universities of Budapest and Breslau I studied ancient Oriental history and Semitic languages, concentrating on Arabic but also attending classes in English, German, psychology, and art history. After settling in Jerusalem at the age of twenty-two, I devoted most of my time to work in Jewish studies, but I also managed to acquire colloquial Arabic and to get acquainted with the life and lore of the Arabs of the country. As a result of this broader orientation I was always able to view Judaism within the context of a wider framework. I soon became fascinated by the similarities and differences between the cultures of the Jews and of the peoples among whom they lived at various stages of their long history and devoted increasing attention to the scholarly task of seeking out and analyzing these relationships. Similarly, my attention has always been divided between the past and the present, as manifested in the subjects of the papers and books I wrote in later years, several of which dealt with the religious and cultural history of the Jews and the Middle Eastern peoples, while others were devoted to the contemporary sociocultural scene of the *yishuv,* of non-Jewish Palestine, and of the surrounding countries.

One of the outcomes of this kind of scholarly orientation was that the significance I attributed to the strict formal observance of the practical commandments of Judaism gradually diminished. This process began, in fact, in my adolescence, when I started to think about God and to question whether it was possible that He should weigh the merits and demerits of individuals according to the degree to which they observed the numerous formalities required by Jewish tradition. In struggling with this problem—and struggle with it I did—the existence of God remained for me a pivotal and unassailable fact; all I did was to strive for a clearer understanding of what He wanted of us, of me. Still, while I lived with my parents it never occurred to me to "throw off the yoke of the Law," as the old Jewish expression has it; I continued to observe all the commandments that were the standards of behavior in our home. I prayed every morning, putting on the *tallith* (prayer shawl) and the *tefillin* (phylacteries), as had been done by Jews for many centuries. I ate only kosher food, which was, of course, the only food served in our house, and also did the same when I ate out. I observed the Sabbath laws (with one or two inadvertent lapses) by refraining from writing, working, touching money, and boarding a vehicle on that holy day of rest and went with my father to pray on Friday evenings and Sabbath mornings to the nearby synagogue or alone to the synagogue of my high school.

During my apprentice years in Budapest it never occurred to me that there might have been a hiatus in my Jewish education because neither my parents nor my teachers ever did tell me anything about God. God was taken for granted, and His presence—let me say this even though it may be a cliché—was like the air that we breathed, which enabled us to live, but which we never felt prompted to discuss. Theological questions were entirely beyond our horizon. God's presence was axiomatic, a given.

True, when I reached the Rabbinical Seminary of Budapest we did study *The Guide of the Perplexed* of the great Maimonides, but we studied it as a masterpiece of—not theology—but philosophy. Characteristically, we never studied the Thirteen Articles of Faith composed by the same Maimonides, which are contained in the daily prayerbook and the tenets of which were therefore considered as much axiomatic, and hence beyond scrutiny, as the basic Jewish credo expressed in the Sh'ma'. Both in Budapest and in Breslau we also studied several other works of Jewish religious philosophy, but the purpose of those studies, as made clear by our teachers, was to learn and understand what those medieval masters thought and taught about God, not to learn from them what we ourselves should think and believe about Him. Belief in God, I must repeat, was a given, and it occurred to nobody to make it a subject of discussion.

Although this may appear to be a negative evaluation, in fact it is not. The approach I was taught in the schools I attended has remained with me all my life, and I was directed by it in all my studies of both Jewish and non-Jewish cultural and religious history. In studying the sources—whether the Bible or the Koran, the Talmud or the *Hadīth*, the myths of the Hebrews or of the other ancient Near Eastern peoples—or focusing on the customs of the Jews and the Arabs and on the religious tenets and cultural orientations of the various population elements of the contemporary Middle East, the basic question that always intrigued me and kept me spellbound was not what can I learn from them about God, but what do they show about the beliefs, the thinking and feeling, the fears and hopes, the loves and hatreds, of the people. In other words, it was always the working of the human mind as manifested in its cultural products—primarily in literature, in folklore, in myths and legends, and in customs and beliefs—that interested me and kept me going book after book, study after study. To the extent that this is a valid, and valuable, approach, it is my early masters I have to thank for it.

As for my religious observance, the break came upon my arrival in Jerusalem, in the spring of 1933. All the students at the Hebrew University with whom I became acquainted, and with several of whom I became friendly, were ardent Zionists, proud to be members of the young generation of the *yishuv;* those of them who were Sabras, native-born, were very proud of that fact, but they were either indifferent to religion or were opposed to the observances it demanded. Whether they believed in God I don't know because, as far as I can recall, our discussions never touched that issue but were confined to the religious forms, which they condemned. I also remember quite clearly how impressed I was by their matter-of-fact manners, their rough and ready camaraderie, and their natural self-assurance. It was the first time in my life that I encountered a group of Jewish youths for whom being Jewish did not mean to be members of a minority trying to find its niche within the larger Gentile society, but to belong to the dominant element in the country, in fact, *to be* the dominant element.

I can recall how ardently I wished to be like them—to act like them, to speak Hebrew like them, and, yes, to share their attitudes and points of view. The most important change I underwent as a result of the attraction these young Hebrews exercised upon me was in the field of religious observance. Within a few weeks of my arrival I became aware that up to that point my

Jewishness had consisted primarily of religious observance and Zionist nostalgia for Palestine. The religious forms now lost their hold over me, and my Zionist yearnings, fulfilled with my *'aliya*, were replaced by the wish to become part of the *binyan haAretz* (upbuilding of the Land), as the constantly reiterated slogan had it.

But that was not all. There was something in the atmosphere of the country with the ubiquitous relics of its history spanning three millennia spread out right before my eyes that awakened in me an overwhelming desire to learn about its past and, beyond that, to find out things about it that were still unknown and that, I felt, I would be able to unearth. I am not quite sure to what extent I was conscious of this at the time, but in retrospect I can see that the surviving tangible remains of Palestine's past and the historical associations that dominated the landscape had as great a share in imbuing me with this ambition as the influence of my new teachers, primarily Professor Klein. In any case, I felt a powerful urge to delve into the religious-historical past of the land and the people of Israel and in particular to study the fields of Jewish belief and custom, law, and lore. Caught up as I was in what amounted to a veritable research fever, the observance of the *mitzvot* paled into insignificance. Soon I was so absorbed in my studies that there was simply no place in my life for rites and litanies.

As a result, for quite a while after my arrival in Jerusalem I took no interest at all in questions of religion in the *yishuv*. As far as my social environment was concerned, I was completely overwhelmed by its Hebrewness. My first reaction was that Hebrewness equaled Jewishness, and that was that. During the first few weeks after my arrival, as long as my father was still there, I dutifully accompanied him to the synagogue on Friday evenings and Sabbath mornings as I used to do in Budapest. We went mostly to the prayer-house in the center of Jewish Jerusalem, not far from Zion Square, where Chief Rabbi Kook was wont to attend and, very occasionally, to preach. But after my father returned to Budapest I discontinued going to synagogue, except as a tourist in the Old City, where several large synagogues were considered sights one must not miss. Thus, I visited the largest Ashkenazi synagogue in the Old City, called Hurva (Ruin) Synagogue because it was built on the ruins of the old House of Study of R. Yehuda heHasid, and the very tall Tiferet Yisrael (Splendor of Israel) Synagogue of the Sephardim, universally known as the Nisan Bek Synagogue, with its huge dome elevated high above the other structures of the Old City's Jewish Quarter. (Both these synagogues, as well as all the other public buildings in the Jewish Quarter, were destroyed in May 1948, when the Transjordanian Arab Legion occupied it.) However, within a few months thereafter, prompted by my awakening interest in the folk customs of the Middle Eastern Jewish communities, I began to attend services more or less regularly in the Yemenite, Persian, Bukharan, and other communities.

In Hungary I had learned to appreciate the truth of the oft-heard adage "In its language liveth the nation." Now, in Jerusalem, the omnipresence of Hebrew struck me as the most potent manifestation of the vitality of the new Jewish nation-in-the-making. The first impression was visual: merely sauntering along Jaffa Road or Ben-Yehuda Street, I saw everywhere Hebrew street signs, Hebrew posters covering the walls of houses, and large Hebrew billboards over the storefronts. To these sights were added the voices and noises: Hebrew cries, words, sentences, greetings, and calls, flowing from the lips of the passersby, men and women, adults and children, dressed in an astounding variety of Eastern and Western apparel. It was this chatter with which the street resounded that, together with the visual signs, impressed me first with the achieved reality of the new Jewish national existence in Palestine.

Also, immediately upon my arrival in Jerusalem I became aware of the completeness of the new Jewish social structure that presented itself to me in the city. Back in Budapest the Jews (who, incidentally, in 1933 still numbered more than the entire *yishuv*) constituted a narrowly circumscribed segment within the city's occupational structure: while in the academic fields and intellectual occupations there were many Jews, there were none, or almost none, in what we regarded as the lower ranges of occupations. About 1930 the 220,000 Jews of Budapest made up some twenty percent of the city's population; while two-thirds of all those engaged in commerce were Jews, as were almost half of those in academic or intellectual pursuits, there were no Jewish day laborers, no streetcar or bus conductors, no railroad employees, no taxi and carriage drivers, no soldiers, policemen, sanitation workers (who were still called "street sweepers" and "garbage collectors"), household employees, etc. In Jerusalem, as I could not help noticing from the very first minute I stepped out into Zion Square, there were Jews in all these occupations, as well as in several other specializations illustrating the eternal truth of "with the sweat of thy face shalt thou eat bread."

Then there were Jews engaged in types of work that did not exist at all in Budapest and therefore struck me as being "exotic": hawkers of soft drinks in the streets; porters carrying huge bales or boxes on their backs; carders who sat in doorways and used a one-stringed harplike implement to fluff up woolen mattresses flattened by long use; letter-writers who sat on low stools, holding a leaf of paper on the left palm and writing on it with their right hand to the dictation of evidently illiterate clients. Everywhere there seemed to be a considerable number of Jewish beggars who asked for alms with loud Hebrew utterances. As I soon found out, panhandling was considered a respectable profession: to ask for alms was seen as affording an opportunity to the well-to-do to fulfill the *mitzva* of practicing charity, an essential requirement in proper Jewish conduct. I remember in particular one elderly Jewish beggar whose nape was disfigured by a huge tumor that forced his head downward and forward; he would accost the passersby, and, since he was mute as well, would utter angry monosyllabic grunts and pat his deformed nape with one hand while thrusting the other hand, cupped to receive alms, right into the face of whomever he encountered. It was clear that he was not *asking* for alms but *demanding* what was due to him.

It was only several months later, after I got used to conversing in Hebrew with people belonging to all layers of society, that I began asking myself whether there was in the *yishuv,* beyond its obvious Hebrewness, a *Jewish* consciousness as well. In Hungary, with whose Jewish population I inevitably compared whatever I found in the Hebrew society of the *yishuv,* I had known many a Jew who was, as the hero of Galsworthy's play puts it, "proud to be a Jew," even if he knew no Hebrew and had little or no attachment to Jewish religion. Was there such a pride in, or at least an attachment to, Jewishness in the young Hebrews—especially the Palestinian-born among them, who proudly called themselves Sabras—I got to know in Jerusalem? Once this question arose in my mind I began to pay attention to the Jewishness of the life around me, and Jewishness in this context could, of course, mean only a consciousness of being part of that unique community that was marked off from all other peoples by its religion. Not that I made a study of the issue—I was much too preoccupied with staking out the area of my doctoral research—but I became sensitive to the religious aspect of the lives of the people with whom I had contact and of the Jewish society as a whole.

What I noticed first was the extent to which the Sabbath, the official day of rest of the *yishuv,* affected the lives of the religious and nonreligious alike. All the Jewish institutions and businesses were closed on the Sabbath, functioning instead on Sunday. The Muslims, I soon learned, did not observe Friday, their weekly *yawm al-jum'a* (day of assembly), in the same manner. Those who worked in institutions of the British Mandatory Government were free to take Friday off as their weekly day of rest, and many did so, but Arab businesses closed down only for an hour or two on Friday morning when the Muslims were supposed to attend services at the mosques. In the Jewish sector of Jerusalem, by contrast, all city buses came to a standstill Friday afternoon at dusk and began rolling again the next evening, after the Sabbath ended. The Jewish movie houses scheduled no performances on Friday evening and were supposed to open their box offices on Saturday only after sundown. Unofficially, and to the chagrin of the religious Jews, they opened somewhat earlier so as to be able to have an early and a late performance on Saturday evening, the time when many Jerusalemites attended movies.

The Jewish interurban bus lines (the most important of which were those running between the three major cities of Jerusalem, Tel Aviv, and

Haifa) also "rested" on Saturday, but those Jews who felt they had to travel could take jitneys owned and staffed by Jewish companies not subject to rabbinical regulations or the government-run railway. In Haifa, a city whose Jewish quarters occupied three "stories," one at the bayshore around the harbor, one on the slopes of Mount Carmel, and the third on top of the mountain, the Jewish-run city buses functioned on the Sabbath for the simple reason that the municipality was controlled by the nonreligious laborites. Sports activities were another bone of contention between the religious and the nonreligious sectors of the *yishuv.* Since the only weekly day of rest was Saturday, there was no other day on which events of spectator sports could be scheduled. The most popular were the soccer matches. Those between the two major teams, the Maccabi and HaPo'el, regularly took place on Saturdays, despite all the efforts of the rabbinate and the religious political parties to prevent what they considered a desecration of the Sabbath.

As for the utilities—the water supply, electrical works, and telephone services—a compromise was reached between the religious and nonreligious elements of the *yishuv.* These services were essential; in some places, such as hospitals, their suspension would have endangered human lives; therefore, it was agreed that they would have to go on functioning on the Sabbath, even though it required a goodly number of Jews to work.

All these phenomena I observed in the course of my everyday life. They practically forced themselves on my attention and led me to the conclusion that efforts were indeed being made by the *yishuv* to observe the Sabbath laws of rest—one of the most important groups of Jewish religious prescriptions—and to adjust them to an all-Jewish society in which, in contrast to conditions in the diaspora, there was no *Shabbes-goy* (Sabbath-Gentile) available to perform necessary tasks on the Sabbath from which Jews were barred by their religious laws and customs.

Nor could I fail to note, as I gradually became better acquainted with the Jewish society of Jerusalem, the same broad range of religious observance with which I had been familiar in Budapest. The great majority, I found, was nonobservant and tried to circumvent the restrictions imposed upon the *yishuv* by its Orthodox religious authorities. People traveled on the Sabbath using whatever private or public transportation was available, attended sports events rather than synagogue services, did not observe the dietary laws, and even indulged in having meals in Arab restaurants and purchasing nonkosher meat (ham!) in non-Jewish stores. If marriage, divorce, alimony, and confirmation of wills were within the exclusive jurisdiction of the rabbinical courts of the Jewish community, given legal standing by Mandatory regulations, the nonreligious Jews accepted it as a minor inconvenience. In fact, those rules did not materially impinge on the everyday lives of the nonreligious. There were those in the kibbutzim of the left-oriented HaShomer haTza'ir who on principle refused to make use of the services of rabbis and instead arranged for their own unofficial and rather informal approval of marriages among their members. In some kibbutzim all ceremony was dispensed with, and the two young people simply moved into a "family room," thereby becoming husband and wife. A very few free-thinkers (especially among the German Jews who arrived in increasing numbers from 1933 on) went so far in their demonstrative opposition to what they considered rabbinical despotism that—since in Palestine Jews could be married only by a rabbinical court—they went over to Cyprus and got married in a civil ceremony there. Most nonreligious Jews, however, felt that they could live with the religious laws imposed upon the *yishuv,* given the available choices of evasive action.

What I found more disturbing was that many nonreligious Jews looked upon the religious Jews with a kind of—not precisely contempt, that would be too strong a word, but—disdain, disparagement. Having solidly anchored their self-image in the newly won Hebrew nationalism, they felt that those Jews who adhered to traditional religiosity were somehow deficient, retarded, kept back on a lower stage of intellectual and emotional development, a stage that they themselves had succeeded in leaving behind. This attitude did not necessarily lead to overt antagonism or to a Voltairean demand of *écrasez l'infâme*—although that too did emerge occasionally—but it made friendly cooperation between the religious and the nonreligious rather difficult. Nor was the situation helped by the attitude of the religious, who, like religious people everywhere, considered their irreligious compatriots to be sinners and firmly believed that it was their religious duty to induce, or even coerce, those *posh'e Yisrael* (infidel Jews) to observe at least a modicum of the *halakha.*

In my own case, although under the influence of my young Hebrew peer group I moved away from formal religious observance, this process was paralleled, I could even say counterbalanced, by the increase and intensification of my scholarly interest in the history and development of Jewish religion. That this was indeed the case is amply attested by the books and studies I wrote in my fifteen years in Palestine, most of which dealt with the cultural history of the Jews, a subject by its very nature indistinguishable from the history of Jewish religion. (The same is true, incidentally, of my literary output in the years that have passed since I came to America.) If I never wrote anything about the role of religion in the life of the *yishuv* as a whole—I did write several papers on specific religious phenomena in the life of individual Oriental Jewish communities—this was not for lack of interest but because the other subjects to which I was committed demanded total concentration.

An added factor was that the role of religion in the life of the *yishuv* was an issue that was hotly debated in the press, in books, and in the public institutions of the country; given the ongoing struggle between the religious and nonreligious contingents, it had inevitably acquired sharp political overtones. But I had an innate disinclination to getting involved and taking a stand on political issues.

One of the observations I made on the relationship between the *yishuv* and religion pertained to a paradoxical phenomenon. In both the religious and nonreligious elements there was a keen interest in the Bible, while the much richer postbiblical Jewish literature produced in Palestine in the course of almost a thousand years after the conclusion of the Bible—the Apocrypha, the Mishna, the "Jerusalem" Talmud, and the Palestinian Midrashim—was totally disregarded by the nonreligious, and took a secondary place even among the religious. As for the postmedieval kabbalistic literature, produced in the little Galilean town of Safed in the sixteenth century, it was not only neglected but actually frowned upon even by Jewish scholarship until Gershom Scholem single-handedly rehabilitated it. Thus, a peculiar situation obtained: the majority of the *yishuv* appreciated the Bible—not as the holy book of Judaism but as the chronicle of ancient Hebrew history in Palestine, a kind of national charter of the Jews' rights to the land of their ancestors—but the same majority was ignorant of both the history and the literary output of the Jewish community of the country in the twenty-three centuries that followed the end of the biblical period. This is why the work to which Professor Klein dedicated his life—piecing together the documentation of the continuing Jewish presence in Palestine after the Romans put an end to the Jewish commonwealth in 70 C.E.—was of such paramount important not only from a scholarly but also from a Jewish national and political point of view.

I had known long before I first set foot in Jerusalem that the most important Jewish monument in all Palestine was (and of course still is) the Western Wall, also known as the Wailing Wall, but generally referred to by all the *yishuv* simply as HaKotel (the Wall). It is undoubtedly also the most dramatic single example of the inseparable intertwining of the national and religious aspects of the Jewish people's past in Palestine.

The Wall is part of the retaining structure of the Temple Place, built by Herod (ruled 37–4 B.C.E.) when he reconstructed the ancient Jewish Temple and enlarged the plaza surrounding it. When the Romans destroyed the Temple (in 70 C.E.), nothing of it survived except this outer wall, which supported the platform at its western end. When I first visited the Wall (in 1933) there was in front of it a narrow alley, some ten feet wide, where the Jews were allowed to pray, even though the Wall itself was considered the property of the Muslim religious authorities. The Jews had prayed at the Wall for centuries—it was for them the hallowed place for mourning over the destruction of the Temple and the exile of Israel. The Wall rose over the heads of those who prayed and wailed before it to a height of some sixty feet; it consisted at its bottom of several rows of immense hewn-stone blocks, some of them no less than forty feet in length. Over them were rows of smaller stones, the topmost of which were added in the Mamluk period. Beyond the Wall, invisible to those who stood beneath it, was the Temple Place itself, some forty feet higher than the Jewish praying area, centering on the Dome of the Rock, one of the most holy places of Islam. To be able to withstand the pressure of the land mass behind it, the Wall is built in a terraced manner: each successively higher row of stones is laid back a few inches in relation to the one beneath it, so that the Wall as a whole tilts somewhat away from the bottom and toward the platform at its top. The fact that the Wall, built without mortar, has remained intact for centuries, despite the periodic earthquakes that strike Jerusalem, testifies to the technical expertise of its ancient builders.

It is not easy for me to recall the feelings that gripped me when I first stood before the Wall and touched its ancient stones. At the time I did not know much of the moving legends contained in our ancient rabbinic sources about the Shekhina, the personified female Presence of God, who was said to mourn the fate of her children at the Wall. But I do remember that the sight of the Wall was for me too a wrenching emotional experience. It also was a concrete confirmation of something of which I had been aware only in a vague, abstract manner because the prayers I had recited daily referred to it: that there were unbreakable ties between the Jewish people and its lost land, the City of David, and the ruins of its Holy Temple. There, in front of the Wall, those ties suddenly were manifest: here was the Wall, and here were the children of those who built it—they could touch it with their hands and could lay their foreheads against it.

Subsequently I visited the Wall many times, and as I watched the crowds that were inevitably gathered there I felt that it was pointless to ask whether it was a national or a religious monument. The visitors to the Wall included more nonreligious young Jews, who appeared in the narrow alley in short-sleeved shirts, many of them bareheaded, than religious Jews of European and Middle Eastern extraction in their traditional garb, for whom uncovering the head anywhere, even for a minute, was a serious religious infraction. I doubt whether members of either group stopped to analyze the meaning the Wall had for them: very few of them could have had more than the vaguest idea of what the Wall was in its actual historical origin. What all of them were aware of was that here was a visible and tangible monument that harked back to the remote Jewish past, to times when Israel ruled the land and worshiped its God in the Temple that stood behind and high above the Wall, in the place where today Arabs prayed, and where they, the descendants of that ancient people, were not allowed even to set foot. To that prohibition the Orthodox Jews added their own: since it was not known where precisely the Holy of Holies of the Temple into which only the high priest was allowed to enter had stood, and since the sanctity of the place did not lapse with the Temple's destruction, they forbade, as a precautionary measure, entry into the whole Temple area.

The enormous significance the Wall had for both the religious and the nonreligious sectors of the *yishuv* was most eloquently demonstrated when the Israeli parachutists liberated it in the Six-Day War of June 1967. For nineteen years the Jordanians, in control of the Old City, had prevented the Jews from entering it, and the Wall remained out of bounds for them. When the Old City was conquered by the Israelis, they immediately demolished the dilapidated houses of the old Moghrabi Quarter facing the Wall, and on the very next day no less than a quarter of a million Jews flooded the place. The entire Jewish population of Jerusalem at the time was less than 200,000, of whom certainly not more than half were religious. Even if we assume that each and every religious and nonreligious Jewish Jerusalemite went to the Wall on that day, that still leaves 50,000 who must have come from outside the city, which meant using cars or buses. The day in question was the first day of the feast of Shavu'ot (Weeks or Pentecost), on which religious Jews are forbidden to travel, so that all the out-of-towners must have been nonobservant. That is to say, of the 250,000 Jews who sought out the Wall on that day some 150,000 must have been nonreligious. That a similar numerical relationship between the religious and nonreligious visitors to the Wall continued in subsequent years is indicated by a photograph in the *Encyclopaedia Judaica* of 1972 (9:1503–1504) which shows a crowd of young men in shirtsleeves dancing before the Wall on an anniversary of the reunification of Jerusalem.

Of the new religious developments that I was able to observe within a year or two of my arrival, the one I found most interesting was the production of updated versions of the Passover Haggada by several nonreligious kibbutzim. The traditional Haggada contains the story of the slavery of the Children of Israel in Egypt, their miraculous redemption by the mighty hand of God, and their conquest of Canaan. It has been recited, and the many lyrical pieces embellishing it sung, for many centuries all over the Jewish diaspora, in the family circle before and after the festive Passover meal on the Seder evening. For the historian of religion, the Haggada constitutes a prime example of the transformation of a series of historical events— whether they were actually historical or mythically considered so is irrelevant in this context—into a moving religious ritual *cum* recital in which the past is recalled and relived, and which has become a supreme instrument of religio-national instruction of the young generation. What several kibbutzim now did was to combine parts of this age-old traditional Haggada with newly written sections telling about recent events in Jewish history: the oppression of the Jews in Germany (which began in 1933), the Jewish exodus from Europe, and the return to the ancestral soil of Eretz Israel.

The work of revising, editing, and updating the Haggada was not without problems. The mood in those days in many kibbutzim, especially those belonging to the federation of HaShomer haTza'ir, was definitely antireligious, and consequently there was an insistence on excising all mentions of God and His miraculous intervention in redeeming the Children of Israel from Egypt, even though these references and the songs expressing the people's undying gratitude to Him form essential parts of the Haggada. Another problem was of a linguistic nature. The style of the newly introduced sections was often stilted, and the quality of their narrative fell far short of the charm and dignity of the traditional parts. However, what these new kibbutz Haggadot did achieve—although it was not their intention—was to repeat the old process of endowing historical events with a religious, or in any case a quasi-religious, significance and demonstrating the historical continuity between the first exodus from Egypt that led to the birth of the biblical Hebrew state and the latest one from Europe that resulted in the new Hebrew nation-in-the-making that the *yishuv* was in the 1930s. Although the authors of the new Haggadot and the kibbutz members who recited them at their Seder meals in the communal dining rooms would have objected to the imputation of any religious meaning to their revised Haggadot, psychologically the new kibbutz Haggadot unquestionably fulfilled the same function as the traditional religio-national Haggadot whose place they were designed to take.

It was a mere chance that first made me aware that something was afoot with the Passover Haggada in the kibbutzim. In 1934, when I spent a short time in Giv'at Brenner, the Passover fell on the eight days beginning with March 31. I arrived in the kibbutz a few weeks thereafter. One day, listening to the conversation of my neighbors in the communal dining room, I heard one of them say that it was wrong for them completely to disregard the Passover holiday that had just passed and that they should instead celebrate it in a suitable manner. A discussion ensued, the idea was thrown back and forth, and a consensus seemed to emerge to the effect that the Seder could, and should, be considered an opportunity to impress the kibbutz children, who would soon reach the age of understanding, with the historical background that led to the movement of return to Eretz Israel in general and the foundation of their kibbutz in particular. At the time I did not pay much attention to this subject—I was preoccupied with trying to understand the social and economic functioning of the kibbutz—and thus I did not even mention it in the article I wrote about my observations in Giv'at Brenner. However, about a year later a mimeographed pamphlet came into my hands—a modern, updated Haggada issued by Giv'at Brenner, one of the first of its kind.

From the second half of the 1930s the kibbutz Haggadot proliferated. Within a few years there were hundreds of them, and often new revised and updated versions were published year after year by the same kibbutz. As a rule, many of the historical parts of the classical Haggada were retained in them, augmented not only by accounts of or allusions to recent events, but also by quotations from modern Hebrew authors. In most of them references to God and His miracles were excised, but, as the years passed, some of them gradually reappeared.

Occasionally these kibbutz Haggadot contained a goodly measure of self-condemnation and breast-beating, of strongly negative appraisals of Jewish life in the diaspora, evidently intended to serve as the strongest possible foil to the glorious future for which the kibbutz worked. Thus, the 1937 Haggada of Bet haShitta (a kibbutz in the Jezreel Valley affiliated with Ha-Kibbutz haM'uhad and founded in 1935) has this passage: "Our people, we ourselves, have no present. Our people in the present is lacking all basis, is bereft of form, is assimilated among others. It is persecuted and banished, it is subject to destruction, subject to disasters, it wanders in ships, and its life is not human, not cultured—it is shattered down to its foundation. Our nation has no nature, no work, no homeland" (my translation from the Hebrew).

Or take the 1938 Haggada of Ma'oz Hayyim (a kibbutz in the Bet Sh'an Valley near the Jordan, also affiliated with HaKibbutz haM'uhad, founded in 1937), which quotes the following self-criticism from the pen of Micha Yosef Berdichewsky (Bin-Gorion, 1865–1921): "We serve God but forget the signs of creation, we have no emotional attachment to the mountains and hills, to the rivers and seas" (my translation).

The kibbutz authors who wrote the new parts of these Haggadot and the editors who compiled them were probably unaware that even in these self-recriminations they followed the example of the old biblical prophets who accused the people of Judah and Israel of the most heinous sins and crimes, always, of course, looking at the contemporary scene from a strictly religious, Yahwist point of view. That is to say, even in this respect the kibbutz Haggadot, quite inadvertently to be sure, nevertheless qualified as religious literature. While the annual recitation of these kibbutz Haggadot did not introduce religiosity into the kibbutzim, it created a link between the modern nonreligious, socialist kibbutzim and the Jewish past in which history and religion were inseparably interwoven. In the ensuing decade the production of kibbutz Haggadot continued and even intensified; by the time the fortieth anniversary of Israel rolled around the celebration of Passover with their recital had become an integral part of kibbutz life all over Israel.

While in the first flush of my eagerness to adjust to the new Hebrewness of modern Jerusalem I endeavored to liberate myself completely from what I considered the shackles of the *mitzvot ma'asiyyot* (practical commandments) and substituted scholarly observation for religious observance, there was one ancient Jewish religious injunction I never even thought of violating: the fasting on Yom Kippur, the Day of Atonement, the most solemn of all Jewish holy days. Why this should have been the case I can no longer recall. Perhaps I was still influenced by memories from my childhood and youth when I would stand awestruck next to my father and grandfather in the little synagogue of Father's uncle, R. Israel Braun, and saw them wholly absorbed in communion with an unseen power whose presence I too felt. Or it may have been due to what I had seen in the city of Budapest, where most Jews, even the least religious among them, observed this one "Day of Awe"—I knew that this was the case from my contact with people on all rungs of the assimilational ladder. Or again I may have felt that here was the ultimate, inviolable threshold of something I did not understand, something whose hold over me I never tried to shake off. In any case, even though I of course became interested in the ancient origins, subsequent development, and changing meaning of Yom Kippur, I never stopped observing it. In the course of my studies, to mention only one example, I found that in ancient times Yom Kippur was a joyous folk-festival, observed by dancing and merrymaking in the vineyards of Eretz Israel and that this form of celebrating it was retained down to modern times by several Oriental Jewish communities (I wrote about this in *Edoth*). But this knowledge did not impinge on my observing the day in the manner in which my father, grandfather, and all my ancestors for many generations had observed it. Well, to be accurate, I did not observe it *exactly* as they did: I fasted and spent the day in synagogue, but did not concentrate, as they did, on repentance and clearing accounts of conscience with God. Instead, on each Yom Kippur I went to the synagogue of one or another Oriental Jewish community in Jerusalem, prayed together with them all day long, and in the meantime observed as many details as I could of their customs, prayers, and comportment.

One of the first Yom Kippurs I spent thus fasting, praying, and observing was, I can still recall, in a Yemenite synagogue not far from the Schatz House in Bezalel Street where I lived at the time. I had made the acquaintance of its *mori* (rabbi) sometime earlier: he was a hearty, rotund, middle-aged man who specialized in writing *qame'ot* (amulets), who assured me that I would be more than welcome to spend the day in their synagogue. When I arrived I took off my shoes at the door as all of them did, sat down on the floor on a hard cushion, and joined them as best I could in chanting the prayers. From time to time I inhaled the fragrance of a green bunch of aromatic herbs my neighbors offered me (in Budapest, I remembered, we would inhale the smell of a big quince studded with cloves) and tried to follow their pronunciation of Hebrew, which was very different from the standard Sephardic as spoken in the *yishuv.*

On several Yom Kippurs in a row I went to the synagogue of the Jews of Meshhed, Iran, in whose study I was engaged in the early 1940s, and felt flattered when Mr. Farajullah Nasrullayoff, the head of the community, invited me to take one of the seats of honor next to him flanking the Holy Ark. In this manner I made the rounds in the course of the years of many Oriental Jewish synagogues in Jerusalem and learned how they observed that most holy day of the year; it was quite a natural thing that I should fast like the others, with whom I felt the brotherhood that grows out of a joint religious experience.

In retrospect I find it peculiar that in all my visitations of synagogues in Jerusalem—and they were not confined to those of the Oriental Jewish communities—I never once set foot in a synagogue of the Meah Shearim (Hundred Gates) Quarter, the stronghold of the ultra-Orthodox Hasidic Jews. It was in that quarter, in its complex known as Bote Ungarn (Hungarian Houses), that my paternal grandfather lived out the last years of his life (he died in 1928); during my own Jerusalem years two of his sons, my uncles Yehiel (Hile) and Yom-Tov (Yantev), still lived there with their large families. Aunt Rózsi and her husband, whose greatest sorrow was that they were childless, also lived in the same quarter. All of them were supported by the Hungarian Kolel, the religious charity organization that collected donations in the diaspora and distributed funds (hence the name *haluqqa,* distribution) to ultra-Orthodox Jews, who were also given modest apartments in the Hungarian Houses and were expected to devote all or most of their time to traditional talmudic study. Occasionally I did visit these three siblings of my father, but their religiosity was so intense that whenever I faced them I had the feeling that they belonged to quite a different species of the human race. We would exchange a few words of greeting: I would say, "How are you?" and they would answer *Borukh haShem* (Blessed be the Name, that is, God); after a few similar inquiries and responses there would be literally nothing we could talk about. We would lapse into silence, and soon I would feel compelled to take my leave.

It is quite likely that the barrier religion had erected between me and those closest relatives of mine was the factor that made me disinclined to visit the synagogues in which they prayed. Evidently I was unable to bring the same scholarly detachment to them and the ways they related to God with which I could approach the Oriental Jewish communities. Added to this may have been the resentment I felt—together with the overwhelming majority of the *yishuv*—against that small, self-secluded group of Jews, most of them Hungarians, who vehemently opposed, in fact hated, Zionism. Many of them were the disciples of R. Joel Teitelbaum, the Hasidic rabbi of

Satmar (from 1928 to 1944), who was saved from the Holocaust in 1944 by nonreligious Jews, sojourned for a while in Jerusalem, and settled in New York in 1947. Rabbi Teitelbaum and his followers not only opposed Zionism, the creation of the state of Israel, the secular use of Hebrew, and cooperation with Israeli communal institutions, but considered all this a sin, an unforgivable violation of Jewish tradition, which, they believed, prohibited all this and imposed upon the Jews the sacred duty of observing all the commandments scrupulously and praying and waiting for the Messiah, who, in God's own good time, would come and restore the kingdom of David in the land of Israel. They saw the Holocaust as a punishment for the sin of Zionism and the Jewish aspiration to statehood in Palestine as a transgression that delayed the coming of the divine redemption.

While I never entered a single synagogue in Meah Shearim, I visited it and the Bote Ungarn quite a number of times. The Bote Ungarn were founded by R. Hayyim Sonnenfeld (1849–1932), who had settled in Jerusalem in 1873, and was one of the founders of the Agudat Yisrael, an organization of ultra-religious Jews who nevertheless cooperated to a limited extent with the institutions of the Zionist movement. In 1935 R. Amram Blau broke with the Agudat Yisrael and founded the Neture Qarta (Guardians of the City), a small but vociferous extremely anti-Zionist organization. During World War II, when Agudat Yisrael drew nearer the *yishuv* and its official representation, the Jewish Agency for Palestine, the Neture Qarta stand became more rigid. This position was further intensified in 1953 when R. Joel Teitelbaum became its rabbi, even though he continued to live in Brooklyn as rabbi of the Satmar community. I remember, although I cannot at the moment find the historical documentation, that soon after the War of Independence the Neture Qarta sent a delegation (or perhaps wrote a letter) to King Abdullah of Transjordan asking him to take them under his protection so that they should not have to live under the rule of the godless Zionists. On a less serious note, I can also remember, even though I can no longer recall whether it was during my Jerusalem years or on the occasion of one of my later visits from America, seeing a large banner stretched across one of the alleys of Meah Shearim reading in Yiddish, "Jewish daughters! Have pity! Don't walk in *pritzes!*" the last word being the Yiddish adaptation of the Hebrew *p'ritzut*, meaning licentiousness or profligacy. The observance of a strict dress-code was one additional manifestation of the separateness of the world of Meah Shearim and its total rejection of the *yishuv*'s Hebrewness.

During my Jerusalem years, as I said earlier in this chapter, I never made a special study of religion in the *yishuv* or of the relationship between its Hebrewness and Jewishness. Hence, these notes are nothing more than random, incidental observations I made while living my own nonreligious life devoted to the study of the history of Jewish religion. Today, from the vantage point of the historical perspective of more than half a century, I can see that the *yishuv* in those years was engaged in a struggle to find a way to relate to the Jewish past in Palestine, for which the first prerequisite was a better grasp of that past, much of it still unexplored. Several scholars, studying the Jewish religio-historical past in Eretz Israel, contributed to a better understanding of the religious and cultural life of the people of Israel in their land, especially in the biblical and talmudic periods, and thus strenghtened the ties between the *yishuv* and its past. The important work done by Professor Klein has been mentioned. Equally, or perhaps even more, significant was the research of Professor Gershom Scholem, who, while a nonreligious nonobservant Jew, gave the *yishuv*, as well as the Jews of the diaspora and the Gentile scholarly world, an understanding of what the Kabbala meant for Judaism, the Jewish people, and Jewish history: a major new religious development that counterbalanced and supplemented the religio-juridical legalism expressed in the Jewish Codes, the last one of which, the Shulhan 'Arukh, happened to be written by Joseph Caro, the same sixteenth-century Safed rabbi who was also a leading figure of the Kabbala.

I would like to think that my own historical-religious studies, written in the fifteen years I spent in Jerusalem, on the roles played by water, by the earth, by the Temple, and by saintly men in the Jewish religion of the biblical and talmudic periods, also made a modest contribution to enabling the *yishuv* better to understand the religious life of its ancestors in Palestine and thereby to strengthen the ties between the present and the past, the people, and the Land, Hebrewness and Jewishness.

Movies and Theaters

Throughout my Jerusalem years I never had the feeling that the city did not provide enough entertainment and amusement. What the Arab sector of Jerusalem offered—theatrical performances, Ramadān storytellers, Egyptian films—I have touched upon briefly above. Jewish Jerusalem, the home base in which I was deeply anchored, was to my eyes so rich in artistic and social events that, spending most of my time in scholarly work, I often felt that I was missing out on things I would really have enjoyed. There were movies and lectures, concerts and political gatherings, sports events and social get-togethers, balls and flower shows and parties, and—above all—there were the performances of the Hebrew theaters, among which Habimah held the pride of place.

There were three motion picture theaters at the time in Jewish Jerusalem. There was Zion Cinema on Zion Square, the Edison Cinema in Yeshayahu Street, and the relatively new, hangarlike Orion Cinema, located in a nameless alley between Ben-Yehuda and Bezalel streets, next to which I lived for several years in the Shiber House.

For many of the younger generation of Jerusalemites to attend a movie performance every Saturday night was considered almost a civic duty, and I was one of those who rarely shirked it. The box offices of the movie houses opened at dusk on Saturday, much to the anger of the religious Jews, who considered it a sacrilege to handle money and to transact a purchase of any kind before the appearance of three stars indicating the end of the Sabbath. Even before they opened, lines began to form in front of them, with quite a bit of pushing and shoving, and cries of *Yesh tor!* (There is a line!) directed at those who in their eagerness to secure a good seat (there were no numbered seats) tried to get ahead of the rest.

There was usually a second performance too, but since Sunday was a regular workday, and most people had to get up very early in the morning—office hours were from 7:00 A.M. to 2:00 P.M.—the general preference was for the first performance, which started at a sundown and ended at a reasonable hour.

The majority of the Jewish population of Jerusalem was of Sephardi and Middle Eastern origin. They were referred to by some of the Ashkenazim, the Jews of European extraction, with the derogatory designation Frenkim (Frenks or Franks), a term that has a long history behind it, which, however, does not belong here. The compliment was reciprocated by the Frenkim by calling the Ashkenazim Vuzvuzim, a reference to their habit of saying *vuz, vuz?* (Yiddish for "What, what?"). Since the Frenkim had, on the average, twice as many children as the Vuzvuzim, the Frenk preponderance among the young generation was considerably greater than among their parents. This meant that most of those who filled the movie houses on Saturday evenings were young Sephardi and Oriental Jews, few of whom knew English well enough to be able to follow the English dialogue that blared forth, overamplified, from the screen. The useful art of dubbing in translated dialogue was not yet developed in those days or, at any rate, had not yet reached Palestine, so the movie theaters resorted to the simple expedient of installing two small screens to the right and left of the main screen, one of which showed the Hebrew, the other Arabic, translation of the English dialogue. The Arabic translation was offered for the sake of the relatively few Arabs who came over to Jewish Jerusalem to see American and European films, few of which were shown in the Arab cinemas of East Jerusalem. While the projection of the film proceeded on the large screen in the middle, the roughly handwritten lines of the translations moved up on the two small side screens. Occasionally the auxiliary screens did not keep pace with the film, so that if, for example, the film shown was a comedy, many in the audience burst out laughing at the wrong time, either before or after the characters in the film actually said something funny.

This arrangement had another result as far as the audience was concerned. Since many did not understand the spoken dialogue, but read in translation what the protagonists said in English, listening to the soundtrack was of no importance—hence, silence during the performance was neither required nor actually observed. Consequently, the hall constantly hummed with comments made *sotto voce* or aloud by hundreds of people, with the cumulative effect of producing quite a din. To this was added the constant cracking noise of biting open the roasted and salted pistachio nuts and other seeds without which the Sephardi and Oriental Jewish (and Arab) young people seemed unable to sit through a performance, which took the place of the popcorn consumed in American motion picture theaters. After the performance, when the audience left, the floor under the seats was littered with the yellow and brown shells spit out or dropped on the floor.

There are a few more things I recall from those Saturday nights at the movies. One is that prior to the main feature there was always an introductory part consisting, first, of a series of colored slides. These were usually not photographs, but commercial artists' drawings, which advertised merchandise available in local stores, such as shoes, clothing, furniture, women's accessories, chocolate products, and the like. Then came a newsreel, usually of British make, that gave us remote colonials an idea of what was happening in the great center of the world, namely England, especially London. It was thanks to these newsreels that we were quite familiar with the faces, movements, and voices of people who occupied center stage of world history. We saw and heard King Edward VIII and his American bride, Mrs. Simpson; Prime Minister Neville Chamberlain returning from Munich, triumphantly waving a piece of paper signed by Hitler and announcing "Peace in our time"; and, some months later, the bulldoglike figure of Winston Churchill with his big cigar and his defiantly flashed V-sign.

As for the films shown, they were mostly American with a few British-made thrown in now and then. I remember only a very few of them. I do recall *Mrs. Miniver* with Greer Garson in the title role and Walter Pidgeon as her sturdy husband, and, more vaguely, one or two of the Road pictures with Bing Crosby, Bob Hope, and Dorothy Lamour.

In general, the members of the audience were rather unruly and their attention often wandered. When something exciting took place on the screen, they watched attentively and reacted loudly with laughter or hissing or booing, as the occasion called for, as the inscription on the side screens informed them of the meaning of what was said. But when there was a lull in the action, the decibels of conversation instantly rose, and had it not been for the exceeding loudness of the soundtrack, it would have been totally drowned out.

After the performance, as the audience was on its way out, one could not help overhearing critical comments on the film. The evaluation usually fell into either of two extremes: the film was judged either very good or very bad. As my friend Dov Chomsky, the Hebrew poet, once remarked while we were exiting from the Zion Cinema: "You hear only one of two opinions. One will say, 'It was *nehedar* [wonderful]'; the other will respond, 'What? It was *zift*'" (*zift* is Arabic for pitch or asphalt and was used in the Hebrew colloquial of Palestine to designate something of the most inferior quality).

The audience at the performances of the Habimah Theater was of a different caliber altogether. It consisted largely of the more serious element of Jewish Jerusalem, or rather of those who knew Hebrew well enough to follow and enjoy a Hebrew theatrical performance. This meant that many of the German Jewish immigrants, whose professions did not require that they master Hebrew, and most of their wives, who got only as far as *ozeret Hebräisch*, were automatically excluded from attendance. Still, there were enough academic people associated with the Hebrew University, both teachers and students, as well as lawyers, doctors, and officials employed by the Jewish National Fund, the Palestine Foundation Fund, the Histadrut (General Federation of Jewish Labor in Palestine), the Jewish school system, and the like, to fill the Zion Cinema on those occasions when Habimah performed in it.

The behavior of this audience, as could be expected, was decorous. Although not evening attire but only street clothes were worn, there was still a festive air in the hall. The plays unrolling on the stage were followed in attentive silence. Comments and conversation, and the noise of pistachios cracking, were conspicuously absent. After every act there was much applause, and in the intermissions one could hear spirited arguments about the play, the staging, the actors—no shorthand terms like *nehedar* and *zift* here. People went to see a Habimah play with the intention of having an intellectual and emotional experience, and, by God, they had it.

In the 1930s Habimah was still dominated by the influence of the great Russian theater director Konstantin Stanislavsky, a founder of the famed Moscow Art Theater, and his disciple Yevgeny Vakhtangov, who directed Habimah's plays in Russia from 1922 on. Moving to Palestine in 1931, the company, organized as a cooperative, lived for years on the impetus it had received from Vakhtangov and other disciples of Stanislavsky—all of them, incidentally, non-Jewish.

Stanislavsky's technique of "method acting" demanded of the actors that they use not only their bodies and voices but also their minds, senses, and feelings and emphasize the characters' intentions or objectives and their "truth." This much we all knew because the subject was often discussed among admirers and opponents of Stanislavsky. Most vociferous among the opponents were the German Jewish admirers of Erwin Piscator, the celebrated director of the *Volksbühne* in Berlin, and of Bertolt Brecht, both of the "epic theater" fame. Bertolt Brecht and Kurt Weill's *Three Penny Opera* was performed in Palestine with great success in 1933 (I no longer remember by which company).

What I remember most clearly of those early Stanislavskyesque Habimah performances is that everything was done in a greatly exaggerated manner, from the paint applied to the faces of the actors, through the costumes they wore and the scenery before thich they moved, to their gestures and vocal intonation. Nothing was lifelike—everything was stylized, grossly overemphasized, with the palpable intention of endowing the characters, their words, movements, problems, reactions, with a larger-than-life dimension. Accustomed as I was to the refined and sophisticated performances of the Budapest theaters, I found Habimah crude, geared to external effect, and—I allowed myself the judgment to the consternation of many of my friends—lacking in true artistic value.

I remember in particular my reaction to *The Dybbuk* and *The Golem*, two of Habimah's oldest, most highly acclaimed, and most frequently performed plays. *The Dybbuk* was Habimah's first important production—it was written by S. An-Ski in Yiddish, translated into Hebrew by Hayyim Nahman Bialik, and first performed in Russia in 1922. Hanna Rovina (1892–1980), Habimah's most celebrated actress, played Leah, the rabbi's daughter, whose body is invaded and taken possession of by the spirit of her beloved Hanan after he dies, because he loved her and could not have her. The play was a very dramatic one indeed, culminating (if I remember correctly) in a scene of exorcism, in which the Dybbuk (that is, the spirit of Hanan) is forced to leave Leah's body, whereupon she collapses and dies.

The Dybbuk was considered for decades the crowning glory of Habimah's repertoire and was the grandest vehicle for Hanna Rovina's talents, which indeed were considerable. When I saw her in *The Dybbuk* she was in her forties, but she still played Leah with a youthful abandon and with all the theatrical exaggeration of movement, expression, and voice that the original Vakhtangov directives called for. When she suffered—and she suffered prodigiously—she did it so powerfully that it shook the whole stage and house. Her figure was quite a full one by that time, but its fullness was made statuesque by the long-sleeved, close-necked, floor-length white dress she wore, tight-fitting around bust and waist. More difficult to put up with was the masklike makeup she wore: her face was powdered or painted chalk-white, her black wig hugged her head and face, her eyes were framed with thick black lines, and the areas between her eyes and her thinly penciled-in black eyebrows, and even more so between the eyes and the ridge of her nose, were painted almost black. From the nape of her neck, pulled forward over her corseted ample bosom, hung a long and thick black braid of hair that reached down to her waist. The only color livening up this somber black-and-white appearance was her mouth, painted blood-red in the form of a narrow double bow that is familiar to those who still remember the heroines of the early silent Hollywood films.

The theatricality, the unabashed stylization, not only of the figure of Rovina, but of the whole troupe and of each and every one of the scenes, was, I felt, both overwhelming and disconcerting: nothing that was going on in the play, whether expressed or in the minds of the actors, was merely suggested or allowed to be felt; everything was hammered into the eyes and ears of the audience. And yet, such was the prestige of Habimah and the renown of its chief actors that—with the exception of the few German Jews who nostalgically remembered Piscator and Brecht and perhaps also Max Reinhardt—the audience, including myself, was enchanted and even mesmerized.

I have one more recollection of Rovina. On one occasion some celebration was held in the amphitheater of the Hebrew University—I have not the slightest idea what it was about—but I remember distinctly that Rovina appeared in the program. She recited the Song of Deborah (Judges 5)—one of the earliest poems that survived in the Bible, a rhapsodical text, several of whose passages are obscure to the point of defying precise interpretation. But the general import of the Song is clear: it celebrates, with dithyrambic abandon, the victory of Israel, led by Deborah and Barak and helped by the Lord God of Israel, over Sisera, captain of the hosts of Jabin king of Canaan, who had "mightily oppressed the Children of Israel" for twenty years.

Rovina did not let herself be deterred or inhibited by such minor details as inability to understand precisely the meaning of some of the passages she declaimed. There she stood on the stage of the amphitheater, with the magnificent landscape behind her, a truly regal figure, and belted out the ancient words at full force, emphasizing the more passionate passages with powerful sweeps of her arms—Vakhtangov would have been proud to see and hear her. When she cried out *Uri, uri, D'vora* (Awake, awake, O Deborah!) even the hills of the Judean Desert seemed to shake. While she declaimed the Song, all of us in the audience were spellbound, and I felt that if Deborah addressed with such passion the fighters of Israel *before* the battle, her fire must have been the secret weapon that ensured the Israelite victory over Sisera's 900 chariots of iron. When Rovina finished, there was thunderous applause.

The second most popular play of Habimah was *The Golem*. This play, written in 1921 by H. Leivick (1886–1962)—at the time the best-known

Yiddish poet and dramatist—was first produced by Habimah in Moscow in 1924 (in a Hebrew translation) and thereafter was revived and performed time and again for decades. The story of the Golem is a reworked and romanticized version of the ancient Prague legend that tells of the Golem, the huge homunculus made of clay by the famous Rabbi Judah Loew ben Bezalel, who lived ca. 1525–1609 and was in real life a talmudist, moralist, mathematician, kabbalist and alchemist, and the author of many books. According to the legend (which, incidentally, antedates Rabbi Loew by centuries), he creates the Golem in order to serve him, but is forced to return him to dust when the Golem runs amok and endangers human lives. In the later reworkings, Rabbi Loew creates the Golem by forming a human figure out of clay and placing under its tongue a parchment with the name of God written on it, for the purpose of saving the Jews of Prague from the attacks of the Gentile mob. The end of the Golem remains the same in the later versions: when he runs amok the rabbi removes the divine name from under his tongue, whereupon he becomes a lifeless heap of clay.

Using this legendary basis, Leivick endows his Golem with human feelings that inevitably bring about clashes between him and his master, the rabbi, especially when the Golem falls in love with—you guessed it—the rabbi's daughter. I don't remember who played the female lead in the play, but whoever it was she was totally overshadowed by the towering figure of the Golem played by Aaron Meskin (1898–1974), another founding member of Habimah and, since first playing the Golem in 1924, also a leading member of the company. Meskin was a tall man with a rough-hewn face and a deep, resonant voice, who also played Othello and Shylock with great authority. For the Golem he wore platform shoes and heavy shoulderpads that made him seem bigger and taller, and his face was painted with thick black lines running down his forehead, across his brows, and then again down his cheeks. When I, much later, first saw the biblical heads painted by Georges Rouault, I was instantly and strikingly reminded of Meskin's Golem.

As far as I can recall, *The Golem* was not quite as outlandishly stylized in its presentation as *The Dybbuk*. Or, perhaps, the towering figure of Meskin's Golem, with his superhuman height, lumbering gait, thunderous voice, and broad, unfocused, aimless movements that seemed to fit a Golem better than a human being, blocked out whatever else and whoever else was on the stage. In any case, the impression I got watching the Golem and took away with me for all time was that it was by far the most effective play performed by Habimah, at least among those I had a chance to see.

On my frequent visits to Tel Aviv—a 90-minute bus ride from Jerusalem—whenever I had to stay overnight to take care of my father's or my own affairs I tried to see a play performed by Habimah or by its rival Haohel Theater. The permanent home of Habimah, before it occupied its own more spacious premises on Rothschild Boulevard, was the Moghrabi Theater, at the intersection of Allenby Road and Ben-Yehuda Street near the seashore. The Moghrabi building had two halls, one on top of the other: one of them was a motion picture theater, the other the home of Habimah—I no longer remember which was on top and which on the bottom. The box offices of both had windows opening to the street, and I seem to recall that the one selling tickets for the movies as a rule had longer lines than the one for Habimah. In the fifteen years I spent in Palestine I got to see a good proportion of the plays performed by Habimah, both those written by Palestinian Hebrew playwrights and those authored by Europeans and Americans and translated into Hebrew.

The second ranking theater of the *yishuv* after Habimah, Haohel (The Tent), was known as the "workers' theater." It was founded in Palestine in 1925. The original intention of this company, still recalled in the 1930s with a certain amount of condescension, was to be a "socialist" theater, not only in the sense of performing plays with a socialist message, but also in consisting of actors who combined their work in the theater with agricultural or industrial labor. Needless to say, this concept soon proved unworkable, and Haohel became a theater of full-time actors, who, however, continued to remain members of the Histadrut (General Federation of Jewish Labor in Palestine) and to be identified with the "workers." Nor did Haohel adhere to its original program of presenting only plays with a socialist message; in fact, several of its most successful plays had nothing to do with socialism. Like Habimah, Haohel too made the rounds of the country at regular intervals, and it was especially well received in the kibbutzim and other rural settlements loyal to the Histadrut.

Of the plays I saw Haohel perform I remember only one. Its title was *Jacob and Rachel,* and all it did was retell the story of those two famous biblical characters in a dramatic form, adding many little embellishments, with what appeared to me (and to many of my friends who saw it) a slightly satirical bent. The acting was highly stylized—in this respect Haohel seems to have felt that it had to compete with Habimah—but also characterized by a certain comical twist. All the characters—Jacob, Rachel, Leah, Laban—spoke Hebrew with a peculiar accent that was a grossly exaggerated imitation of the Hebrew pronunciation of Yemenite Jews. They gesticulated and moved in a manner that, again, was a caricature of Yemenite Jewish mannerisms and added, for good measure, much handclapping, raising the hands skyward, and other sudden and abrupt gestures. Evidently, what the director believed and tried to convey by making the actors speak and act in this way was that the biblical ancestors of the Jews were some sort of primitive proto-Yemenite characters, of whom their descendants, the Yemenites of contemporary Palestine, were a refined and evolved version with an unmistakable residue of the more robust ancestral traits. Having read and been impressed by Thomas Mann's Joseph tetralogy only a few years earlier, I cannot say that I appreciated Haohel's version of my biblical ancestors.

There were other theater companies too in Palestine in those days, but I was not among their fans. I do remember, however, one performance of the Teatron Kameri (Chamber Theater), in which Yemima Persitz, the youngest of the three Persitz girls, played a leading role. I believe that she was married to the director of the Kameri theater. Of her acting I can recall only the extremely high-pitched voice she used.

I can also recall a cabaret performance I attended in Tel Aviv with my sister and brother-in-law, in which an actress dressed in a glittering light blue nylon dress that looked like a wetsuit sang a chanson whose first words were *Omrim yesh la mashehu* . . . (They say, she has something . . .). In another song a rather well-upholstered songstress declared repeatedly *Yesh li shadayim* (I have breasts). Yet another memory is of a sketch in which a man, digging in his Tel Aviv backyard, hits an oil pipeline and starts marketing the oil under the name of Hahevra Shel Kohen (the Company of Kohen), whereby he repeatedly emphasizes the word *Shel* (i.e., Shell), which in Hebrew means "of."

Isn't it remarkable, and puzzling, that of the hundreds of performances I must have seen in the course of my fifteen years in Palestine, I should remember so few—and that the few I do remember should include these entirely insignificant, in fact nonsensical, little items?

Report to Guli

Apart from the one letter I wrote in the summer of 1933 to Lizi Fischer—long since lost—the only letter I addressed to any of the Hungarian friends I had left behind in Budapest was the one I wrote in the fall of 1934 to Guli Friedmann. (The story of my friendship with Guli and Lizi is told in *Apprentice in Budapest*.) By a mere chance, a carbon copy of this letter has survived. Since it is the only comprehensive record of my thoughts, feelings, and plans in the second year after my arrival in Jerusalem, I give it here in full, in my literal translation. It reveals the markedly romantic attitude I seem to have had toward everything I encountered in Jerusalem in those days, when I was not yet twenty-four years of age.

Sept. 20, 1934 [in Hungarian]

Dear Guli:

Actually, I intended this letter to be my New Year's greetings, but then it grew late, and it has thus ultimately turned into a kind of report, a review sent by a friend—I hope a dear friend—who wandered off into foreign parts.

Foreign parts—I must stop for a moment right here. For the fact is that this designation is far from being correct. I do not feel at all that I am in a foreign country. Quite the contrary: although it may sound somewhat trite, the fact is that I feel at home here. Not because I came here loaded with preconceived notions. I came without any prejudice, almost like a stranger, just as I had gone earlier to Breslau: to learn, and then to return home. But here the dimensions shifted. Slowly I got to love this country. Then followed a stage in which I felt that I had already visited, at some time in the past, all the places that in fact I saw now for the first time. And then, finally, I came to feel, as I feel today, that I am totally at home. If possible, I could say, more at home than in Budapest.

I made friends with people. With Jews and Arabs. And it was as if in all places and at all times I could feel the common race. We are the sons of Shem. And we live here in the land of Shem. Your father, of course, felt nothing of this when as a tourist he was chauffeured the length and breadth of the country. To feel it one must go on foot, and even that is not enough, one must stay overnight, in kibbutzim, in the colonies, in Arab villages, in Bedouin tents. One must strike up conversations with people, and talk to them at length, in order to become conscious of their being not only men but brothers.

From the beginning I felt drawn especially to the Sephardi Jews. I felt that they were my relatives. Then I began to study the traditions of my ancestors and found that my great-grandfather, my father's father's father, lived in South Hungary. My grandfather, who is now buried here on the Mount of Olives, was born there, somewhere along the banks of the lower Tisza River. And it is known that the Jews of South Hungary had come up from the Balkans. They were Sephardim. Lo and behold, the blood bubbles up.

But this is only one point. Many others line up next to it. First of all, the complete and unconditional freedom. The human and Jewish freedom. Here we are only Jews, freely and unconfinedly, and nothing else. Not Hungarian Jews, not German Jews, not *deutsche Staatsbürger jüdischen Glaubens* [German citizens of the Jewish faith]. Some sort of peculiar joy is produced by this unconfined outcropping of ethnicity. Internally: if the events of daily politics come up in conversation, if we judge the budget of the state housekeeping, we talk about *our* state; if the city builds a water supply, it is *our* city that gets the water. And outwardly: if I discuss the Arab-Jewish question with my Arab friends, in the background there is always the thought, the sense, of the common interests we must jointly represent vis-à-vis the higher authorities; if I visit a Bedouin camp, the shaykh receives me as the son of a related tribe.

To all this is added the freedom from conventional ties. The young generation that has gathered here and has grown up here has broken with the conventions of the old homelands and sifted the flour of traditions through the sieve of a healthy outlook on life. In the kibbutz perhaps not all the people contract marriages hallowed by law and religion, but these rabbiless marriages are sacred and inviolable, a hundred times more so than the European marriages in which all formalities are observed but which in reality are often nothing but marriages in name only. Religion also acquires new content: the forms became fewer, the contents richer. The young people go to the synagogue on Rosh haShana and Yom Kippur, perhaps even in greater numbers than in Europe, not in order to cry and tremble before a threatening judgment, but to sing and to celebrate.

All this I gradually learned to see, to understand. And as my understanding grew I got to love the country more and more. And felt that my place is here.

All these are generalities. What represents, over and above all this, a special value for me is the university. A university in which I am at home. My university, our university. Because at the universities of Budapest and Breslau I never felt at home, just as I am sure that neither do you, Guli, feel at home at the university of Budapest. But the Jerusalem university, I feel, has an organic connection with its students, with me. I am glad when I can work in the spacious reading room of the library, when I find in the catalog cards listing my works, more modestly: my pamphlets, when I read that the university has received donations of funds that enable it to establish new chairs, and it is a special pleasure for me to look out from the windows of the library building at the eternal city shimmering in the sunlight. Next to all this, perhaps there lurks in the back of my mind the thought that the university will reward my work. I must only work, and I shall attain the aim I have set myself: the university will open its doors to me not only as a "research student."

In brief, I have decided to stay. First of all, I made myself independent of my parents. I accepted a position that provides me with a (not too finely cut) minimum of existence with the fewest working hours. I took a half-time position, that is, 15 hours a week, in the higher forms of a new high school in Jerusalem. I teach Arabic and Hebrew. Three mornings a week, five hours each time. This leaves me with enough time for my work. I already know Hebrew well enough to write scholarly and literary studies in it without any difficulty. So far, only some of my shorter articles have been published in the local daily and weekly papers, but just now two weightier studies of mine are in the press, one in *Moznayim*, the literary magazine of the Hebrew Writers' Association, the other in *Tarbitz*, the scholarly quarterly of the university. Therewith I have penetrated the most distinguished forums of Hebrew scholarship and literature. I have specialized in Jewish folklore. To date nothing has been published in this field in Hebrew. Hence, my work has met with considerable appreciation and approval everywhere in respectable circles.

My lodgings are located on the highest point of the city. More than 800 meters above sea level, a pleasant, detached, solidly built little stone pavilion, standing in a small garden. It consists of a sizable room, divided by a curtain running across its middle into a study and a bed-chamber. In front of the window a eucalyptus tree sighs. Beneath it—an assortment of cacti. A mosquito net. View to the Judean mountains. Opposite it, across the garden, live my sister and her husband. Mostly I take my meals with them. In this manner it is quite possible to vegetate until some unknown American Maecenas establishes a folklore chair at the university. When that happens, I shall move up to Mount Scopus.

I would be very glad, Guli, if I would hear from you soon. Please answer all the unasked questions. Many regards to your parents, siblings.

Your old friend,
Gyuri

For the sake of accuracy a few mistakes or misstatements in the above epistle should be corrected. At the time I wrote it I was not aware that the village of Eszeny, where my grandfather was born, was not in southern, but in northern Hungary, and that therefore my claim to Sephardi descent on this basis was not valid. However, considering the fact that my father and all of his six brothers and sisters had black hair and dark brown eyes, as well as a somewhat darkish skin, the phenotype of my paternal family definitely pointed south.

As for being received as a relative by Bedouin shaykhs—on the few occasions of my visits to Bedouin encampments in the Negev I was accompanied by my friend Ahmed. Hence I could not at all be sure whether the hospitable reception by the master of the tent was accorded me "as the son of a related tribe," or rather—and this is more likely—was extended to me because I came as a friend accompanying Shaykh Ahmed, who was an Arab "notable" of Jerusalem and thus, as a matter of course, *had* to be received in the most friendly manner possible, since by paying a visit he actually honored his host.

The two essays of which I wrote that they were accepted for publication by *Moznayim* and *Tarbitz* actually never appeared, and I no longer remember what they were about. I must have been notified by the editors that my papers had been accepted, and then, for one of many possible reasons, they were not published. This was the experience of many authors in Palestine.

In my description of my lodgings I took one deliberate liberty and made one mistake. I remember quite clearly that the only view from my windows was of the little garden and the house, some fifteen feet across it, in which my sister and her husband lived. There was no view of the Judean mountains there. And I was mistaken in writing that the tree in front of my window was a eucalyptus. Eucalyptus trees grow only in the lowlands, where there is ample water to keep them alive. Mostly they were planted in marshy areas to help dry them out.

However, apart from these few details, the letter does give a picture of what I did and how I felt some sixteen months after my arrival in Jerusalem. I was, evidently, enchanted with the atmosphere of the city, satisfied with the teaching position I obtained and with my scholarly and journalistic work, and hoped that before long the university would "open its doors" to me. I had a romantic view of life around me and a rosy picture of what it would bring me—in a word: I was young.

As far as I can recall Guli never answered my letter, nor did I again write to her.

5

Foothold in Academe

Teacher in Talpioth

After my return from Giv'at Brenner to Jerusalem, as the first year of my sojourn in Palestine was drawing to a close, I felt more and more uncomfortable with the situation of financial dependency on my father in which I found myself. I was nearing my twenty-fourth birthday, and although I had a doctorate from the Budapest University I was still a student and supported by my father. This, I increasingly felt, placed an undue burden on Father and should not be allowed to continue. In addition, I wanted to prove to him, and to myself, that I had reached the stage in my life in which I was able to earn a living and achieve not only economic self-sufficiency, but also emotional independence.

The only job I could think of was that of teacher. I had passed several intermediary exams at the Rabbinical Seminary of Budapest, I had my doctorate in Semitic languages and literatures from the Budapest University, I had started publishing articles, in the course of the year I had spent in Jerusalem I had acquired considerable fluency in speaking and writing Hebrew and had advanced in my knowledge of Arabic—on the basis of all this I felt I was qualified to teach Bible and other Hebrew subjects on any level and at least elementary Arabic. Consequently, without consulting either my father or Professor Klein, I started to look around for a teaching position and made inquiries first in the two foremost high schools of the *yishuv*, the Gimnasiya Herzliya in Tel Aviv, and the Reali school in Haifa.

I also tried to get a job in the school system of Mizrahi, the religious Zionist party. I asked the help of Professor Klein, who was a leading member of the Mizrahi. He wrote what must have been a very warm letter of recommendation to Rabbi Jacob Berman (b. 1878), the head of the Mizrahi section in the Department of Education of the Va'ad Leumi (National

Council of the Jews in Palestine). When Rabbi Berman answered, Klein gave me his letter, which was preserved in my files. I am giving a literal translation here as an example of the Hebrew officialese of those days:

27 Tammuz 5694—10.7.34

To His Honor
Mr. Prof. Dr. S. Klein
Here

My Very Honored Friend,

I received your letter concerning the candidacy of Dr. Patai. I would most willingly support the matter both because of paying attention to the request of my honored friend, and because of the very personality of the candidate, for I too esteem him very much, and I think that all the many praises told about him suit him very well, and perhaps he is even above them, but what can be done if even after the words of my honored friend I don't find Dr. Patai suited to work in the Mizrahi schools? He is very far from our worldview, and your honor, as one who worked in the committee of supervisors, knows our requirements.

I am transmitting your letter to Dr. Lurie, and I shall recommend with all my heart this candidacy for the general schools, and I think that also Dr. Patai himself should direct his endeavors in that direction.

With great respect and many regards, your friend,

Jacob Berman

I have no recollection whatsoever of this entire incident, but it seems evident that in the very small society of Jewish Jerusalem in 1934 Rabbi Berman got wind of my nonreligious attitude—the mere fact that I did not wear a *yarmulke* (skullcap) was enough to render me unsuitable for the Mizrahi schools. Nor do I remember whether I followed up Rabbi Berman's suggestion to get in touch with Dr. Joseph Lurie (1871–1937), who was the head of the Education Department of the Va'ad Leumi and who, as I do remember, was a member of the B'rith Shalom and an advocate of Arab-Jewish understanding.

None of these tentative approaches yielded any results. But in the spring of 1934 I learned that Mrs. Paula Nathan, a German-Jewish educator of fine reputation and good connections, had begun to organize a school that was to combine the best features of the German schools and of modern Hebrew education as it had developed in the *yishuv.* She and those who supported her plans may have had the Haifa Reali school before their eyes, which was founded by another German-Jewish educator, Dr. Arthur Biram, and under his principalship became the finest high school in Palestine. Mrs. Nathan planned a coeducational school, a combination of elementary and junior high schools offering classes to children ages six to fourteen.

Mrs. Nathan was an attractive middle-aged woman of impressive appearance, determined bearing, and considerable energy. She located a suitable building in Talpioth, a suburb to the south of Jerusalem, and went about recruiting students and faculty simultaneously. When Salman Schocken, owner of the Schocken Publishing House of Berlin and Jerusalem and head of the board of governors of the Hebrew University, agreed to send his thirteen-year-old daughter Eve, now called Hava, to Mrs. Nathan's school, the success of the new educational venture was practically ensured: the German-Jewish intelligentsia of Jerusalem felt that it was *the* school in which to enroll its children. The board of governors that was responsible for the teachers' salaries and the other expenses of the school consisted of well-to-do German Jews, many of the teachers employed by Mrs. Nathan were German-Jewish immigrants, and most of the pupils were children of German-Jewish immigrants.

I no longer remember whether I approached Mrs. Nathan or someone recommended me and she contacted me. However, once I became a candidate to teach Hebrew and Arabic, I wrote to my father in Budapest and asked him to obtain from the Rabbinical Seminary a certificate attesting that on the basis of an interim exam I was qualified to teach Hebrew and Jewish subjects. On July 31, 1934, Father informed me that Professor Michael Guttmann, the rector of the Seminary, was about to mail me such a certificate. As for Arabic, my Ph.D. in Semitic languages from the university of Budapest was, as far as I can recall, the basis of my acceptance by Mrs. Nathan as a teacher of that subject.

The negotiations with Mrs. Nathan were expeditious and revolved mainly around the question of salary. The position she offered me was a half-time one, which meant teaching 15 hours a week, and carried a salary of 4 1/2 pounds. I tried to hold out for more, but all she was willing or able to do was to give me an oral promise that within a few months after the beginning of the school year she would raise (or perhaps only that she would make every effort to raise) all the salaries by one-third: this would have meant 6 pounds for me.

Even before the negotiations were concluded I informed my parents about them and told my father that once I had the job he would no longer have to send me any money. My father, on his part, continued to remind me of the necessity of passing my final exams at the Rabbinical Seminary of Budapest.

Budapest, August 22, 1934 [in Hebrew]

My Beloved Dear Son,

I received your article "In the City of Abraham" and gave it to the printer for the September issue. The subject and the contents are interesting, and the form is also suitable and proper.

What you write about the job for which you are waiting does not surprise me. Our sages already had said that one's livelihood is as difficult as the parting of the Red Sea. Nevertheless "miracles" do occur for almost every person, and all find sustenance from the work of their hands. Also, "all beginnings are difficult." Your situation is among the happy ones since until now you were not forced to neglect your studies and earn a livelihood with the labor of your hands. Even now, I think, the most important thing is that you finish your studies to which you have devoted the best of your young life and stand ready and prepared for the rabbinical exam here in Budapest, and thereafter everything depends on luck . . . I think that also here in Hungary there are and will be opportunities, and in any case the rabbinical diploma that you get here will open for you the doors of all the congregations all over the world, and therefore it would be a criminal act if you would neglect this matter for the sake of other interests, just now prior to the completion of your studies and your ordination! Also, the doctoral degree is important for you, especially if you hope to be among the first ones to whom the Hebrew University in Jerusalem will award the doctorate.

I have heard that the exam under Professor Guttmann requires much preparation, and one cannot prepare for it in a few weeks. Therefore my advice is: if you don't now get a respectable job for which it is worth your while to bear the burden for a few years, it is better for you to return to Hungary and study here, rather than teach there. Also, for the coming High Holy Days you will surely get invitations to preach in public, and if not, it would be no misfortune either, here you have bed, chair, table, and quiet, can sit and study properly, and also set aside time for writing and for your scholarly work. After the exams and the ordinations at the Seminary and the university you can return to Jerusalem, or can wait here for a call from Jerusalem, or can return without any call. And in due time they will ordain you there too on the basis of your work, and then you can begin to seek a position and a livelihood in Eretz Israel (and in the meantime you could also work in the field of "secular pedagogy!"). But it would be a mistake to accept now some tiny job in Jerusalem that could harm you and your work. After all, who knows what the day will bear?—differences of opinion may arise in that tiny job, and they may criticize you unjustly, and instead of helping yourself you may cause yourself harm. Here too I would not agree that you should take a few hours in a low school, and give an opportunity to some "supervisor of sorts" to judge you and to voice his opinion before the heads of the congregation. It is better to wait awhile until you obtain a decent position with responsibility! In any case, the right thing to do is to see now "what is above and what is below" there in Jerusalem too.

In the following part of his letter Father reacted—rather lukewarmly—to a suggestion I made to the effect that he purchase some more land, either just a few dunams (1 dunam = 1/4 acre) in Jerusalem, near the university, or several hundred dunams in the vicinity of Beer Sheba or Gaza. Then he returned to my job problem:

> Today I met Dr. Naményi, the brother-in-law of "Government Chief Councillor" Izsó Székely. He asked me when you plan to return to Budapest, for they already have 150 members in the Reform congregation they call "Isaiah Society," and they hope that you will be their rabbi, and on the High Holy Days will preach to them. But I think that this is not a serious thing, "will not reach realization," and it is not worthwhile to join them.
>
> What did our friend Schwarz from America tell you about the rabbinate there? It is rumored here that young Dr. Hevesi will go to America, and Dr. Miklós Hajdu thinks that the Americans will grab him, and we shall remain orphans here, without a father! [. . .]
>
> No other news here under the sun, only the sun burns, perhaps even more than in Eretz Israel, but in our house and garden it is very pleasant.
>
> Your father who greets you all with great love,
> Yosef

I am unable to identify Dr. Naményi and Izsó Székely and have no further information about the "Isaiah Society." I can only state in general that no Reform congregation was able to establish itself in Hungray, where the most liberal congregation, that of Pest, officially called "Neolog," roughly corresponded in its religious position to that of the Conservative congregations in America. Dr. Samuel Schwarz was at the time a rabbi in America—in Yonkers I believe. He was a friend of Father from their yeshiva days. Dr. Ferenc Hevesi was the son of Dr. Simon Hevesi, "Leading Chief Rabbi" of the Israelite Congregation of Pest, where he too was a rabbi of the great Dohány Street synagogue. Subsequently he did move to America. Dr. Miklós

Hajdu (1879–1956) was a good friend of Father, an author and journalist, who also moved to Palestine just before the outbreak of World War II.

Despite the good fatherly advice contained in this letter, I decided to accept the Talpioth job. The letter in which I informed my parents of this has not survived, but Father referred to it in a letter he wrote to me late in August, most of which he devoted to the idea that I should write an article that would be a contribution to "oral Bialik." Hayyim Nahman Bialik had a special place in the heart and mind of the Jewish community of Palestine. For many years after he had moved to Tel Aviv he was considered the "national poet" of the Jewish renaissance and enjoyed love and respect bordering on adulation. When he died (on July 4, 1934) a movement arose in literary circles to collect what they called *Bialik sheb'al pe* (oral Bialik), meaning the gathering and publication of the stories, anecdotes, aphorisms, etc., that used to pour forth from the great poet's mouth in the course of the many public and private meetings in which he was listened to with awe. In 1930, after Father and I met Bialik in Karlsbad and Marienbad and had two long conversations with him, I wrote up in an article much of what Bialik had said, and Father published it in the September 1930 issue of his monthly, *Mult és Jövő*. Now, after the death of Bialik, Father returned to the subject and wrote:

[Budapest, undated, probably late August 1934; in Hebrew]

My Beloved Dear Son Raphael:

I mailed to you today the Sept. 1930 issue in which was published your article on Bialik in Karlsbad and Marienbad. I think it would be of interest to all the readers in the Land of Israel, and it would be worthwhile to translate it into Hebrew, or rather not to translate it but to use this material and write it anew, *as a chapter in "oral Bialik."* You have probably read that much is being written now about the "collection of oral Bialik," speeches and conversations, and what he told us in Karlsbad and Marienbad is worth being preserved for generations. You could write it "from your notebook," or possibly could also mention that at that time you followed us about like a disciple who listens and absorbs the words of the master and put it in writing so that the pearls of his words should not get lost (and also published an article on that conversation in the Hungarian monthly *Mult és Jövő)* and now you want to present it to the Hebrew readers and to those who write the life story of Bialik.

You could also mention Professor Guttman and Grünbaum, but, of course, only by the way, for the main thing is Bialik and what he said! Mention should also be made of his opinion of Hameiri, but only at the end of the article, and especially what Bialik said about the poetry of our Avigdor. Also what he said: that it is not the mission of the poet to work for the financial goals of the institutions, his mission is only to create enthusiasm in the public and arouse it from its indifference, and then let the clever people come and translate the enthusiasm into material help for the upbuilding of Eretz Israel. (Bialik himself once went this way, and therefore his words sounded as if he wanted to justify both himself and his lack of success financially, a matter of which Shmarya Levin also wrote in *HaAretz*.)

Everything he said subsequently about Hebrew poetry, about Samuel haNagid, etc., belongs to the history of literature and to literary criticism. The poem of Samuel haNagid that Bialik mentioned—you should look it up among his poems and quote it in its original form, and if you don't find it you can quote it in free prose. I think that Bialik too mentioned it in prose, only giving its contents. What he said about Hebrew poetry in the Middle Ages is very important, and what he said about the three aspects, or points of view, in the upbuilding of Eretz Israel—the will aspect, the economic aspect, and the political aspect—is also very interesting.

Also the anecdotes he told us about his visit to America should be published—Bayalik, Baylik, etc. And perhaps here one can pass on to the words about Hameiri, about the question of . . . and how he succeeded in Hungary. And also what he said in the name of Bloch who was then the mayor or deputy mayor. Gedaliah Bublick is a well-known Jewish publicist in America. And the finest thing was what he told us in Marienbad about the great tragedy of the spirit of Israel, and about the biblical verse, "and he [Jephthah] was buried in the cities of Gilead" [Judges 12:7]—that the limbs of Jephthah's body fell off one by one in the cities of his wanderings as a punishment for having sacrificed his daughter, etc.

I think that mention should be made also of what he said about Yitzhaq Leib Goldberg, that he is "unique in his generation," etc. Goldberg is one of the founders of *HaAretz*, his name is printed on the masthead of the paper, therefore I think that one should not pass in silence over the praise Bialik uttered about him. I shall send you also the photograph taken when we were together, perhaps they will want to publish also a picture on that occasion, or perhaps I shall send you the cut.

In the next part of his letter Father asked my help in obtaining illustrative material for the forthcoming issues of his monthly and suggested interviews I should conduct:

I read about the exhibition of a new painter in Eretz Israel, if you know about it (I forget his name), go to see whether it is worthwhile to publish his works in our monthly. In general, we now get no material from Eretz Israel. It is a pity that you did not arrange for an interview with Magnes. I think it is worthwhile to have an interview with Professor Klausner on the occasion of his sixtieth birthday, and also with institutional leaders in general, such as Ussishkin, Hantke, Ben-Zvi, etc., and with newspaper editors, Glicksohn, Katzenelson, etc., and with important professors, and with Budko on the renewal of Bezalel (he could also give you photos of his new pictures). And also with writers and poets, and school principals, Yellin, Mossinson, etc., and also on the construction of the water conduit with pictures—your brother-in-law will tell you whether now is the right time to publish it.

The first of September is approaching and we still don't know the results of your search for a job and teaching. Have you also met Dr. Eitingon? Perhaps it would be worthwhile to interview him too (with a photo) about Freud and Freudianism, his plans in the country, psychoanalysis, Judaism, etc.

In the meantime your letter arrived. It is difficult to give advice: there are good points also to being in Jerusalem (Talpioth), near the university and the library, and perhaps you could teach in another place there as well, or you could organize *a course in Bezalel for Hebrew and Arabic*, independently.

Today I received the tenth volume of the *Encyclopaedia* from Berlin: there are several articles by you in it. I think you should write them that you are in Jerusalem, and that they should send you the author's fee there, and that you are willing to send them articles from Jerusalem for the successive volumes.

Your father who greets you with love,
Yosef

What Father wrote in this letter about "oral Bialik" was actually a summation, with occasional elaborations, of the article I wrote about those conversations. Rereading that article today, after sixty years, I find that only two parts of it are still of interest. One is what Bialik said about Samuel haNagid (Ibn Nagrela, 993–1055/56). I translate from my 1930 article:

> Even now, here in Karlsbad (Bialik said), I am working on the publication of the unknown poems of Samuel haNagid. Whatever has been published so far of his poetry is trifling compared to what has come to light now. Only now was I able to get fully acquainted with him. It was he who introduced most of the

forms into Hebrew poetry. He was a trailblazer, and at once he blazed a highway. A thousand years ago! But he was not only a poet. He was a statesman like Disraeli, a thinker like Goethe. He was a scholar on a large scale, a great military leader who won twenty battles. Until now we did not know enough about his life, because the contemporary Arab historians kept silent about him as far as that was possible, and, if it was inevitable, they mentioned his name with a jealous gnashing of their teeth. But in the first place he was a lyricist whose like is not found in Hebrew poetry. How beautiful it is when he describes the thoughts aroused in him by the familiar sands of the desert: "I trod these sands as a barefooted child, and I vowed that I would rise high. Now I have reached my goal and walk here again as a victorious commander . . ."

And how picturesque is what he says about the battles: "When we raise our swords they flare aloft like torches; we lower them and extinguish their flame in the blood of the enemy . . ." Every image of his is magnificent, one can feel that each line is full of actual experiences. I must admit that there was a time when I gave the cold shoulder to this whole Spanish-Hebrew period, because I was not mature enough to fathom its beauties. Now I see what value it represents also from the point of view of world literature. Yet at the beginning I was disturbed by its flashy, complicated, carefully structured form. If we want truly to understand those poets, we must either clothe their thoughts in our modern forms or our present-day thoughts in their old forms. Then we shall make a wonderful discovery. We find whole lines of Pushkin or Goethe almost verbatim in the poems of haNagid or Moses Ibn Ezra. As if there existed a universal spirit of poetry that wandered ceaselessly about and alighted on the great poets . . .

The other item of interest is humorous. Recalling his experiences in America, Bialik said:

> In America, at the banquets, the chairman, who is as a rule a dollar-rich layman, usually introduces the guest of honor with grossly exaggerated encomiums. On one such occasion, the chairman rose, delivered a great speech, praised me to high heaven, heaped up superlatives, and said, "We are happy to welcome here the great benefactor of mankind, Mr.—" and at that point he bent down to me and asked, "What is your name"? "Bialik," I replied, and he continued with loud aplomb, "—Mr. Bialik!" But by the time he again came around to mentioning my name he had forgotten it, whereupon I wrote down my name on a piece of paper, which he read out in the American pronunciation, "Baylik." The next time he referred to me as "Dr. Baylik." "I am no doctor," I whispered to him. "Never mind," he replied in an aside, "for us you are a doctor." At the end I found out that I was "Professor Baylik." I again protested under my breath, but he rebuffed me: "No matter, here you are a professor."

Bialik told us about the confusion between Bialik and Bublick in the name of Mr. Bloch, the mayor of Tel Aviv:

> Bloch was showing a rich American around Tel Aviv, and when they passed my house he said, "This is the house of Bialik." "Who?" asked the American.

"Bialik? His name is Bublick . . ." "No, no, it is Bialik," said Bloch. "Don't tell me," said the American, "in America too it is the custom that immigrants change their names—Bublick came to Palestine and Hebraized his name to Bialik."

According to my 1930 article, at that two-stage symposium in Karlsbad and Marienbad also present were Professor Michael Guttmann of the Breslau Rabbinical Seminary, whose student I was to become that fall; Dr. Joseph Borsodi, who since 1922 had been chief rabbi of Kecskemét, Hungary; Jacob Isaac Niemirower, chief rabbi of Rumania and member of the Rumanian Senate; Yitzhaq Grünbaum, the Polish Zionist leader who at the time was a member of the Polish Sejm; Yitzhaq Leib Goldberg, the Russian Zionist leader and philanthropist who had settled in Palestine in 1919; Moses Schorr, rabbi and scholar, professor at the University of Warsaw and a founder of the Institute of Jewish Studies in that city; and Mrs. Károly Baracs, widow of the first president of the Pro Palestine Federation of Hungarian Jews. It was a truly international group of European Jewish intellectual and communal leaders, a get-together that was only possible in the interwar years. In his 1934 letter Father refers to several of them, as well as to Avigdor Hameiri, the Hebrew poet of Hungarian extraction, and to other intellectual and "institutional leaders" of the *yishuv*.

My brother-in-law, Alfred Leon Hirsch, was engaged at the time in a major public works project of the Palestine Mandatory Government: building a pipeline to bring water from Ras al-'Eyn near the seashore to Jerusalem, whose population was growing rapidly. Of Dr. Max Eitingon we have heard. Volume 10 of the *Encyclopaedia Judaica*, published in Berlin in 1934, contained several short biographical sketches of Hungarian Jewish personalities whose names began with the letter *K* written by me. It was the last volume to be published of that major German-language Jewish encyclopaedia, before the tightening Nazi rule made the continuation of the work of its publishers, the Eschkol Verlag, impossible.

A few days later Father wrote to me again:

[Budapest, undated, probably Sept. 3, 1934; in Hebrew]

My Beloved Dear Son Raphael:

I was half-glad reading your letter, for from it I see that the situation in the schools of Eretz Israel, as far as the salaries of teachers are concerned, is somewhat similar to our situation here. Four pounds a month is very little. Nevertheless, this too is good for the time being, and it is good that you get used to the language and to teaching, and ultimately the money and the honor will come. They will probably increase the amount somewhat in accordance with the demand of the teachers, and you can also earn a few pounds a month with literary work. The day will come when you will get a more respectable job, or that school itself will develop and will be able to pay more, and you will get a proper position there. In this possibly Dr. Rivlin is right.

I don't think it would be right to talk now to Professor Klein about your affairs. The time is not yet ripe, and there is no *concretum* that we could ask of him. First you must pass the doctoral exam there, and present your thesis, and also publish at least some important parts of it, and make your name known in the scholarly world. Then, after a short time, you can apply at first for a *privat-docentura* in Jewish folklore, and the rest will come by itself. In any case you must cleave to the teachers of the university and seek their friendship. Now that Professor Klein and Professor Fekete are about to become members of the Senate, they will surely facilitate your way, but you must work diligently in the scholarly field, and it is forbidden to force the issue, as the Holy One, blessed be he, adjured the Community of Israel. [. . .]

You must have received in the meantime the issue that contains your article on our conversation with Bialik. I think it would be good to give the article to *HaAretz*, and to begin it by saying that Mr. Glicksohn suggested that the "oral Bialik" should be gathered, etc., and it so chanced that you have this important chapter, our conversation with Bialik in Karlsbad and Marienbad, which you recorded at the time, with all the respect and awe of a disciple. I remembered in the meantime that what Bialik said about Jewish literature in foreign tongues he started by asking me about my Herzl biography that I had finished just then there in Marienbad. It was written in Hungarian, and, passing from one subject to another, he spoke about this whole great problem and concluded with the verse "and he was buried in the cities of Gilead," etc. And I also remember that he said, "Jephthah sacrificed his daughter and therefore was punished by losing the limbs of his body, and also the Jewish people was punished in this manner because it sacrificed the virgin daughter of Zion, the Shekhina and its soul, the Hebrew language, and attempted to assimilate to the nations . . . And, behold, members of its body fell off, etc. [. . .]

I think that tonight we shall again meet Professor Klein, and if your name comes up in our conversation, I shall hear what he has to say. In any case, he is fond of you as of a veteran student.

Your father who greets you with love,
Yosef

Of Dr. Rivlin we have already heard above. Michael Fekete (1886–1957) was professor of mathematics at the Hebrew University and a friend of the family. It so happened that in 1947 he was to play a crucial role in my move from Jerusalem to New York. *HaAretz* was the prestigious Tel Aviv daily, of which Dr. Moshe Glicksohn was editor-in-chief.

The story of Jephthah and his daughter, as told in Judges and embellished in the Midrash Gen. Rab. 34 (Theodor ed., p. 634), is rather complicated. Jephthah vowed that if victorious over the Children of Ammon, "whosoever cometh forth of the doors of my house to meet me . . . it shall be the Lord's, and I will offer it up for a burnt offering" (Judges 11:30). When he did return victorious, it was his only daughter who came out to meet him with timbrel and dances, "and when he saw her, he rent his clothes, and said: . . . 'I have opened my mouth unto the Lord, and I cannot go back' " (vv. 34–35). It is at this point that the Midrash takes up the story. Jephthah could have had his vow annulled had he gone to Pinhas the high priest. Pinhas said, "He needs me, let him come to me." "Not so," said Jephthah, "I am the head commander of Israel, I shall not go to Pinhas." As a result of this disagreement both of them became guilty of the blood of Jephthah's daughter. Jephthah was punished by his limbs falling off one by one as he made the rounds of the cities of Gilead, and they buried his limbs in each place (Judges 12:7). As for the high priest Pinhas, his punishment was that he was deprived of the Holy Spirit.

The very next day Father wrote me again:

> [Budapest, no date, probably Sept. 4, 1934; in Hebrew]
> Good inscription and sealing.

My Beloved Dear Son:
>   Yesterday we discussed your studies with Professor Klein, and he emphasized that he thought you must devote yourself in the coming months to the Talmud and the Decisors and their commentators, so as to be able to pass the exam with flying colors. I think he is right, since you have not studied these subjects for quite a while, and, as you have probably read in Bialik's article "Halakha and Aggada," there is also exaltation in the *halakha* and in Jewish history, and he who wants to delve into Jewish scholarship must direct his heart also to *halakha,* the Talmud, etc. Therefore, I think it is quite enough if you teach for the time being the number of hours you have undertaken in the school, but it is not worthwhile to burden yourself with the yoke of private pupils as well. As your sister writes, you will receive, or at least there is hope that you will receive, about six pounds a month, and two pounds we can send you from here (that is to say, you would send every month an article for our journal, and we shall figure one pound author's fee for the present, and one pound as advance against future author's fees).

I think you can get also something from the newspapers of Eretz Israel. And since it is important now that you should have a comfortable livelihood, and should not overdo working at night, devote your time only to those things that are necessary for the exam and for the research you are engaged in.

As I have already suggested, give your article on Bialik to *HaAretz*. I think I also mentioned that Bialik referred to Goldberg, who is the founder of *HaAretz*, and I remember that he also told a story about old Goldberg: one night, as he was walking on the street he heard two young men talk about the worries they had, that they had no implements for their work in the orange groves, and if they had implements they could get permanent and good jobs, etc. Goldberg followed them until he saw where they turned in, found out their names, went to the store and bought the implements they mentioned, and sent everything to them, anonymously. And Bialik also told wonderful things about Mrs. Goldberg!

By the way, in our talk Professor Klein mentioned the Society for History and Ethnography, and its monthly or quarterly *Zion*, of which he is one of the directors, and it so happened that just the day before I read in it his article "Three Good Gifts"—Tora, Eretz Israel, and the World to Come—which the Nations of the World covet, but which can be had only at the price of sufferings. In that article Professor Klein presented something new about which Bialik said, "How wonderful!" Hence I am sure that there was no [disparaging] tendency in his heart when he told you that you should submit your article to the journal of that society in which such an important article of his own was published.

> With best regards and much love, your father,
> Yosef

If a humoristic paper has been published, or will be published, for the High Holy Days, send it to me.

"Good inscription and sealing" is the traditional Jewish form of happy New Year wishes; it refers to the belief that on New Year's Day God inscribes into His great book the fate of every person for the coming year and that on Yom Kippur He seals it.

Some three weeks later Father sent off another letter to me:

> September 22, 1934 [in Hebrew]

My Dear Beloved Son Raphael:

Today Professor Klein and I were at the house of old Professor Blau (truly, he is a marvelous old man, remembers everything and knows everything), and when we left I told Professor Klein about your last letter, about the hydrography of Palestine, etc. He said you must not take on an additional job in Tel Aviv and spend your time in that manner; it is enough for you to teach in the Talpioth *gimnasia*, and the time you have left over you should devote to your studies. He said he would willingly, with love, give you Talmud lessons in his house, once, twice, or three times a week, so that you should learn fast all the material you need for your exam here. And as for the *Posqim*, he thinks it would be good for you to get together with a colleague, a Jerusalem scholar, and to study together with him the *halakhot* of the Yore De'a rapidly . . .

Ludwig Blau, retired rector of the Rabbinical Seminary of Budapest, was my teacher in my first year of studies there and one of the great Jewish scholars. *Gimnasia* is the Hebrew term Father used to refer to the Talpioth high school. *Posqim* is the Hebrew term for "Decisors" and refers to the medieval Jewish codes of law that constituted one of the subjects in which candidates had to show efficiency in their rabbinical examination. *Halakhot* are the laws, and Yore De'a is one of the four parts of the Shulhan 'Arukh, the sixteenth-century law code of Rabbi Joseph Caro.

But to come back to the Talpioth high school, it had quite a distinguished faculty. I remember among them Franz Ollendorf (1900–1961) who had been professor of electrical engineering at the Berlin Technische Hochschule until 1933 when he was dismissed. He taught in Talpioth for only one year, after which he returned to Germany to organize the transfer of Jewish children to Palestine within the framework of the Youth 'Aliya established in 1935. In 1937 he was expelled from Germany, returned to Palestine, and became professor at the Technion, the Hebrew Technical College in Haifa, where I again met him when I served as academic secretary of that institution in 1942–1943. Ollendorf was an outstanding scientist who received much international recognition. His scientific work was a closed book for me, but I always valued his kindness, friendliness, and helpfulness.

I remember well another of my colleagues at the Talpioth school, Karl Salomon (1897–1974), who had been active in Germany until 1933 as a conductor and singer. He was a giant of a man, blond and light-skinned. His wife, almost as big as he, had the same blonde and ruddy coloration. I remember him standing before his class teaching it to sing a choir piece— Bach's famous setting to Psalm 19, "The heavens tell the glory of God . . ." Although he did not actually jump up into the air as some of our modern conductors do, his whole body, topped by his shiny bald head, moved up and down in spasmodic rhythm as he tried to infuse an energetic beat into the rather sleepy voices of the children. Only later, when he became musical director of the newly established Palestine Broadcasting Service, did I find out that he was not only a singer and conductor, but also a composer of stature whose works were widely performed in Palestine.

Among my other fellow teachers at the Talpioth school I remember the pretty daughter of A. A. Kabak, at the time one of the most popular Hebrew novelists. In those early years in Palestine it was not yet easy for me to read Hebrew novels—not that I had any difficulty in understanding their language, but because of the difference in the alphabet I could not read Hebrew as rapidly as I could Hungarian, German, or English—but I remember having been sufficiently attracted by a Kabak novel, I believe it was his *BaMish 'ol haTzar* (In the Narrow Path), a novel about Jesus of Nazareth, to spend many hours with it. Miss Kabak bore a striking resemblance to her father and impressed me as being very young, very naive, and very innocent. She was in charge of one of the lower forms, and I had little contact with her.

Finally, I remember Dr. Menczel and his wife, Puah. He taught the upper forms, she the lower. Both were very friendly, warmhearted people and were the only ones among my colleagues with whom I occasionally met outside the school as well.

Of my work in Talpioth I remember little. This is probably due to the fact that, despite my satisfaction over having landed a job, my heart was not in teaching children. I considered my teaching merely a stopgap, and my ambition remained to be a scholar and a university professor. The highest form in the school was the seventh, attended by some twenty-five boys and girls aged thirteen to fourteen. This was the form I taught Hebrew and Arabic. Among my pupils was Hava Schocken, to whom a few years later I paid some desultory court. Still later she married an acquaintance of mine, Herzl Rom, who subsequently became editor of the New York branch of Schocken Books. Another of my students was Esther Herlitz, daughter of George Herlitz, the Zionist author and archivist, and editor of the *Jüdisches Lexikon*, to which I contributed a long article on the history of the Jews in Hungary in 1930. Esther went on to make quite a career in the Zionist movement and became Israel's ambassador to Denmark. Also in that form were children of several high officials of the Jerusalem headquarters of the Jewish Agency, but I can no longer recall their names.

With discipline, a sore point with many teachers in Palestine, I had no problem. When the children were alone in the school yard or in the classroom they were, of course, as noisy as children in large groups are apt to be everywhere, but as soon as I entered there was quiet, and I don't remember ever having had to reproach any of them for unruly behavior. To be able to keep order in class, I had learned many years earlier, was a gift some teachers had, others did not. Once, I remember, in the course of my job search I visited the Herzliya high school in Tel Aviv, one of the oldest and most prestigious schools of the *yishuv,* and its principal, Benzion Mossinson, invited me to attend his Bible class in the junior or senior grade. Dr. Mossinson was considered one of the foremost Hebrew educators in the country and was also a respected Zionist leader and editor. He looked quite a bit like Herzl, with the same broad forehead, deepset eyes, and square beard. I thought he had an impressive presence. In 1933 or 1934, when I went to see him, he had been principal of the school for over twenty years, but he still had difficulty in controlling his unruly pupils. When we entered the classroom, there was a terrible din that just did not subside until he started to shout to quiet it down. He noticed a girl doing or saying something that enraged him and yelled at her at the top of his voice *at hazir* (You pig!), which struck me as rather incongruous, since *at* (you) is the feminine form of the Hebrew second person pronoun, but the noun *hazir* (pig) is masculine in Hebrew. In any case, once Dr. Mossinson succeeded in establishing order in class, work proceeded without further serious disturbance. After his period Dr. Mossinson suggested that I attend a class in Talmud and introduced me to the teacher of the subject, a youngish man named Zak, Zhak, or Sachs. He had a thin face with a sharp nose and a pointed chin and wore thick glasses. When we approached the classroom, the same din greeted my ear that I had heard when I entered Dr. Mossinson's class with him, but now, the moment the students saw Mr. Zak enter, they fell instantly and absolutely quiet, and so they remained throughout the period, despite the fact that his subject, the Talmud, was of considerably less interest to Tel Aviv high school students than the Bible taught by Dr. Mossinson. Mr. Zak evidently had the gift of being able to dominate (or intimidate?) a class, just as I remembered Dr. Fuchs and my uncle Dr. Ernő Molnár having had it in my own high school days in Budapest, while Dr. Mossinson, though he was the principal, did not have it.

When I started to teach in Talpioth I remembered well what I had seen in Budapest and in Tel Aviv and knew how basic, nay vital, it was to keep order in a class, and I am glad to say that I was able to do so. There was, however, a time lag of perhaps two or three seconds between my appearance at the door and the subsiding of the normal noise generated by two to three dozen children assembled in a room without the inhibiting presence of a teacher. During those two to three seconds I occasionally heard a student yell *rosh po'ale Haifa* (head of the workers of Haifa). At first I did not understand why students should shout these words that had nothing to do with what was going on in class, but when I heard the same sentence a second or perhaps a third time, I got the suspicion that I was encountering an example of adolescent ingenuity: it dawned on me that the three words were cover words, substitutions for three other words starting with the same initials, and that when a student yelled *rosh po'ale Haifa* the class understood that what he was really saying was *Raphael Patai hamor* (R. P. is an ass).

Now I was in something of a quandary. I would have liked nothing more than to put a stop to this veiled insult, but saw no way of doing it. I could not call a student on the carpet for saying "head of the workers of Haifa," and tell him that I suspected what he meant by it, for he surely would have righteously denied any such intention, and I would have merely exposed myself to ridicule. So I decided to ignore the matter, and soon, when the culprits concluded that I did not grasp what they meant, they gave it up.

If I remember somewhat more clearly my Arabic than my Hebrew classes, it must be due to the fact that I was less sure of my Arabic than of my Hebrew and had to prepare for every period. I can still visualize and would instantly recognize the Arabic textbook we used in accordance with the rulings of the Department of Education of the Va'ad Leumi (National Council of the Jews of Palestine). It was a thin paperback book with a dark green cover. It started with the Arabic alphabet, going on to words, grammatical forms, simple sentences, and finally short narrative pieces. The purpose of Arabic instruction at the time in all Jewish schools was to teach the pupils, not primarily to speak Arabic, but to be able to read and understand it. Some years later that textbook was replaced, at least in some schools, by a series of more progressive texts authored by Dr. Yohanan Kapliwaczky, which were printed by the printing press whose half-owner I was to become in 1937.

My problem with my Arabic classes lay not in teaching the language on the basis of the textbook adopted for class use, but in answering questions unrelated to the textbook asked by the more alert pupils, who, living in Jerusalem, could not fail to overhear Arabic expressions in the streets. There was, I felt, always the possibility that one of them would ask me the meaning of a phrase I happened not to know—especially since in 1934 I was as yet not very strong in the colloquial Arabic of Jerusalem, which, like the local Arabic idiom of any other place, differed greatly from the literary Arabic used in books and newspapers and taught in both the Arab and Jewish schools. As a matter of fact, as far as I can remember, I was never actually baffled by any of the questions put to me by my pupils, but I was always concerned about the possibility.

Several times during the year forms were taken on walking tours around Jerusalem. One of those tours I led remains in my memory because of the faint sense, not really of danger, but of *Unbehagen*, at the place we visited. I don't remember who decided where we should go, but I know that we went down to the Kidron Valley, to the east of the Old City of Jerusalem, that separates the city from the Mount of Olives. The most famous ancient monument in the Kidron Valley is the so-called Yad Avshalom or Pillar (literally, Hand) of Absalom, a tomb built in the first century C.E., at a distance of not more than some three hundred feet from the eastern wall of the Old City. The valley between this monument and the city wall was narrow and deep, far from all habitation, and totally deserted. Although 1934 was a calm period in the country, in the sense that there were no Arab attacks on Jews (the Arab rioting was to start only in 1936), I still had the uncomfortable feeling of being in an unsafe place, with a bunch of defenseless children for whom I was responsible. Nothing happened, we met nobody at all as we made our way along the ancient tombs, but I breathed freely only when we were out and again in a Jewish-inhabited quarter.

It so happened that during that one school year when I was a teacher in Talpioth I gained experience not only in teaching but also in negotiating with management. I mentioned above that when Mrs. Nathan hired the teachers she promised them that their salaries would be adjusted upward within a few months after the beginning of the school year. On that basis full-time teachers agreed to work for 9 pounds monthly instead of the prevailing rate of 12 pounds, and I as a half-time teacher got 4 1/2 pounds instead of six. As the first term drew to a close and no salary adjustment was forthcoming, the faculty became impatient; after fruitless discussions with Mrs. Nathan we notified her that we wanted to have a meeting with the school board.

We elected a negotiating committee from among the faculty—I was one member, Dr. Menczel another. The meeting duly took place in the Rehavia apartment of the board chairman, a well-to-do German-Jewish lawyer (his name escapes me), whose son was one of my students. Mrs. Nathan was also present, as were two or three other members of the board. Since the chairman and the members of the board did not know Hebrew, or did not know it sufficiently well, the negotiations were conducted in German, which was also the mother-tongue of most of the teachers present.

The arguments put forward by both sides were foreseeable. As the spokesman of the faculty I argued that the salaries were inadequate, insufficient even for bare subsistence, much lower than those paid by other comparable schools, and that we all had received a promise from Mrs. Nathan that this disparity would be remedied within a few months. The chairman of the board countered by stating that the teachers had signed contracts accepting the salaries paid to them, that the contracts were valid until the end of the school year, and that the board simply did not have the money to pay more. Occasionally the exchange became quite heated, and the possibility of a strike was intimated, but at the end the faculty had the impression that we had gained some ground. However, when the next salary checks were issued they were identical with those of the preceding months, whereupon the faculty held an emergency meeting and decided to set a strike deadline for February 12 at 6:00 P.M. This I reported in a letter to my sister, who at the time was on a visit to our parents in Budapest, but I have neither a recollection nor letters to help me remember how the matter was resolved. My next extant letter, dated from three months later, indicates that the salary adjustment was, after all, made, but by that time I was eager to find another job.

Return to Studies and Change of Citizenship

In the spring of 1935 Father came to Palestine with his usual group of tourists, and on that occasion he and I had serious talks about my plans. He reproached me for having neglected my doctoral work for several months and advised me not to continue teaching at the Talpioth school or to take any other similar job, but instead to devote all my time to finishing my thesis and preparing for the doctoral exam at the university. He insisted that he would resume giving me the same monthly allowance I had received from him during my first year in Jerusalem. As against that, he said, I could take care of his Boruchov property.

Having tried out teaching school for a year I was not at all enthusiastic about continuing that kind of work, which I had not found satisfactory. So it was easy for me to comply with Father's wishes and to accept his very generous offer. We agreed that I should, nevertheless, keep my eyes open for any opportunity—should anything suitable turn up, we would then reconsider my situation.

Thus, even before the school year ended, I returned to my books and resumed my visits to Professor Klein, presenting him with whatever parts of my thesis I completed. I reported on this to my parents, who in the meantime had returned to Budapest:

May 19, 1935 [in Hungarian]

Dear Mama and Papa:

This morning I received the letters from Mama and Guszti. I was very glad that my misgivings in connection with Duci proved to be without basis.

Friday morning I visited Professor Klein. He had read my chapter on hydrographic terminology and was very satisfied with it. Of course, he made a number of comments, which served only to document his professorial qualifications, rather than to touch upon the essence of the work. However, my own opinion is that this chapter is not worth much, for actually there is scarcely an *hiddush* [innovation] in it. It is really nothing more than a compilation, a collection of technical terms found scattered in various dictionaries and lexicons, of course not without checking the sources. In this manner one or two innovations too did turn up, among which the most interesting is the following:

In *Sifre Zutta*, section *Para*, edited by Epstein on the basis of an old manuscript found in St. Petersburg, among several hydrographic terms the expression *mabu'a haqoles* appears. Epstein did not know what this was and emended the second word to read *qolet*. That is, according to him, this term designates a source that gets its water from another source. Soon thereafter Klein wrote an article in *L'shonenu*, entitled "On Hydrographic Terms," in which he rejects Epstein's emendation, but admits that he does not know the explanation of the term.

I take Wahrmund's Arabic dictionary and find in it the verb root *qalasa*, which means "to let wine or water overflow." That is, the learned professors of our university, who also stick their noses into philology, don't know enough Arabic even to the extent of being able to consult a small dictionary, whereas this is the most elementary thing to do if one wants to find the meaning of an unknown Hebrew or Aramaic root. After I found the root in Arabic, I looked it up in the big Arabic encyclopedic dictionaries, and also in the old lexicons compiled by Arabs, and finally in Professor Bräunlich's very thorough study entitled "The Well in Ancient Arabia." On the basis of merely thumbing through these pages I established that the root *qalasa* occurs in ancient Arabic literature spelled either with an *s* or an *ṣ* (to both of which the *samekh* can correspond in Hebrew), and both mean "water collects, rises, breaks forth." Bräunlich even adduces a term *bi'r qalus*, meaning a well in which the water collects and rises. After some philological considerations the matter is totally clear: *mabu'a haqoles* means a well or source from which water flows out at times, but not constantly. This is why they did not include it under the generic concept of *mayim hayyim* [living water]. If Klein should find something like this, he would instantly make an article of it for *Y'di'ot*.

I spent about two hours with Klein, of which one and a half were devoted to discussing my thesis, and then, in the last half hour, I switched to speaking of personal matters. Summarizing it briefly, Klein said that if I had a better job he would not advise me to leave it for the sake of the rabbinical exam [in Budapest]. However, the kind of job I now have I shall probably also find a year from now, when I return here. Even if this job, he said, should develop into a full one, that is, thirty hours weekly with a monthly salary of twelve pounds, even that would not be good, for teaching is very tiring work, and if one has taught five hours from morning to noon, one is as a rule so exhausted that thereafter one is not able to engage in scholarly work. Therefore, he thinks, it would be more suitable for me to become the principal of an eight-year elementary school (I had heard this advice from him already last year), or, perhaps, it would be even better to give up the teaching career altogether and take some kind of secretarial job that would bring a higher pay and more respect. True, it would also mean more working hours, but, as against that, the work is easy, not tiring. (Frankly, I consider this advice an impertinence!) In any case, he said, the best thing for me to do is to try to finish my thesis this summer, sit for the doctoral exam early in the fall, and then, if I don't find a very suitable job in the meantime, go home and pass the rabbinical exam. However, he also said that the rabbinical exam has very little value practically (where is, in that case, that pending resolution to the effect that in the future only rabbis will be employed for teaching Hebrew subjects?).

Otherwise the latest news at the university is that Bergmann was fired from his position of director of the library, because he gave financial support to a Communist paper titled *HaOr*. On the other hand, he keeps his lectureship in philosophy. This certainly is peculiar. If, because of his Communist sentiments, he is unfit to be director of the library, how can he remain fit to teach philosophy? In his place a certain Professor Weil of Frankfurt became director of the library.

The literary editor of *Doar haYom*, Heftman, asked me to write political articles for his paper, overviews of the European situation, it would seem in the style of the *Neue Weltbühne* or *Das Neue Tagebuch*. For the time being I cannot get to it because of my scholarly work, but perhaps after I return from Pest, if I have no other income.

Yesterday, Saturday, in the evening I went to the Dead Sea. The Fräulein Steins I and II took me down in their car. It was a beautiful night with a full moon, there was dancing on the lakeshore; on the way back the moonshine was so bright that practically all the way we drove without lights, as if it were daytime.

This evening Shaykh Amīn is due to come here on a return visit. He will be given a festive reception.

In the past few weeks I have made it a habit to go every Saturday to the neighboring Yemenite quarter. Recently there was a *brit* [circumcision] there; the evening before there was a festivity in the house of the happy parents. *Nebbikh* [unfortunate] happy parents: the father, twenty-four years old, is seriously ill, has epilepsy or something like it, can barely talk, is destitute, and survives only on the charity of his racial brothers. This is his second child, the first is a year and a half old, also a boy, a wonderful, beautiful little fellow. Yesterday afternoon, together with my friend Dr. Bravmann, we visited the rabbi, who is a man of about forty, a lively, loquacious person. It is really worthwhile to get acquainted with these people, especially for a folklorist.

Many kisses to the whole family, your loving son,
Gyuri

Several points in this letter need elucidation. "Duci" refers to David Rappaport, who was a good friend of mine in Budapest. He was a member of the left-wing Zionist youth movement HaShomer HaTza'ir. After my departure for Palestine he seems to have had some influence on my brother Guszti, and I was apprehensive lest, as a result, Guszti join a kibbutz of that movement in Palestine. Later Duci himself did live in such a kibbutz, but a few years afterward he moved to America, where he became a well-known psychologist and authored several important books in psychotherapy.

Jacob Nahum Epstein (1878–1952) was professor of Talmud at the Hebrew University. He edited the university's Jewish studies quarterly *Tarbiz*, in which (in 1930) he published a large section of the *Sifre Zutta*, a halakhic midrash on the Book of Numbers. *L'shonenu* was the quarterly published by the Academy of the Hebrew Language. E. Bräunlich's exhaustive study on "The Well in Ancient Arabia" was published in installments in *Islamica* in 1924–1925. *Y'di'ot* was the journal of the Palestine Hebrew Exploration Society. Professor Hugo Bergmann (1883–1975) was director of the National and University Library until 1935, lecturer in philosophy at the university from 1928 to 1935, professor from 1935 until his retirement, and rector of the university from 1935 to 1938. *HaOr* (The Light) was a Trotskyite Communist periodical, published in Tel Aviv in 1925 and again from 1930 to 1939. Professor Gotthold E. Weil (1882–1960) was an Orientalist, who headed the library from 1935 to 1946 and served as professor of Turkish until 1952. Joseph H. Heftman was literary editor of the Jerusalem daily *Doar haYom*, and in the same year became editor-in-chief of the Tel Aviv daily *HaBoqer*. About the Stein girls and Shaykh Amīn al-Ansārī we have heard in earlier chapters.

The laws of Palestine, promulgated and administered by its British Mandatory Government, provided that two years after a person's arrival in the country as a legal immigrant he or she could apply for Palestinian citizenship and obtain a "Palestinian British Passport." Since May 1935 was the second anniversary of my *'aliya*, I decided that I would apply for Palestinian citizenship and informed Father that I was about to do so. The letter in which I told him about it has not survived, but from his reply it is evident that he had certain misgivings about the step I wanted to take.

[undated, probably late May 1935; in Hebrew]

My Beloved Son Raphael:

Recently we sat together with Rabbi Dr. Hoffer and several other rabbis and teachers of the Rabbinical Seminary, and among other things we spoke about your coming home and your exams here, and as I heard from them the thing will not be difficult, since you will be allowed to select those chapters and tractates [of the Talmud] that you are studying at present in Jerusalem. Also, it is their opinion that you can submit to them a chapter from your folkloristic study of the Talmud, and only the *Poseq* [Decisor] will be new material for you. But, as I have told you, also in the *Posqim* [Decisors] there are interesting things for life, and apart from that, they contain important exercises in the ancient Hebrew language, so that it is worthwhile to deal with them even if it were not for the exams.

And now some important questions in connection with your visit, and do answer me point by point.

The question of your naturalization. I don't know whether it is right to apply for it now before your return here. After all, together with the acquisition of citizenship in Palestine one must give up the rights of citizenship in Hungary, and I am not sure whether that won't impede the examinations and the ordination here. Or, would it be possible for you not to state here what kind of citizen you are? Perhaps it would be wiser not to give up the citizenship here, but to do it only after your return to Palestine. This, I think, is the way. Thus, there will be no doubt that you will get a passport here for your return, especially since you are a student of the university in Jerusalem, and you could bring along a certificate attesting that you are continuing your studies as a "research student" or "researcher" in the folklore of Palestine. Professor Klein himself can give you such a certificate. And even without any *quntzim* [tricks] they give passports here to everybody, including young people. [. . .]

I was far from convinced by Father's arguments and went ahead with my naturalization process. At the same time I went through the formalities required to change my name officially from Ervin György Patai to Raphael Patai, which was the Hebrew name I was given at birth. I informed my parents about these steps (the letter, again, is lost), and Father answered me on June 4, 1935 (in Hebrew):

[. . .] I think it is absolutely necessary that you come home and pass the exam and get ordained. This is clear to me for several reasons that I shall not specify now. My feeling is that you must not miss this opportunity that can be used within a few months and that can perhaps become very important in your future. And if you don't do it now, it may be a mistake that cannot be remedied. Although you are right, it may be possible to arrange things so that you should lose nothing, if you don't disclose anything to Mrs. Nathan now, but wait until September. Then, if you are offered a full position, you could postpone your visit home until November. I am sure that if you start the school year and work there as a teacher for the second year, and then request three months' leave of absence for the purpose of completing your studies, she will agree, and you can come here and return in February or March, possibly together with us. After all, it will redound to the honor of the school if they can boast a teacher who has a "double and redoubled" ordination. You could provide a substitute for three months, at your own expense. If so, it will be sufficient if you mention this matter only after the Holy Days. [. . .]

If you have already submitted your application concerning your naturalization, I wish you *mazal tov* [good luck]. May God grant you your heart's desire and fulfill all your wishes to the good. I don't know whether you must now already give up your Hungarian citizenship, or is this a matter for the future that can be postponed? One must inquire about this.

And, *mazal tov* also to your change of name—be it to your good health! Therewith you have cast off the last remnant of the memory of the assimilation of the happy times twenty-four years ago. I too wanted even then to give you only the name Raphael, officially as well, but the whole family, and especially Grandmother and Grandfather, moved heaven and earth: one must not spoil your future with a Hebrew name! (Even though I argued that there is a Count Raphael Zichy here, they answered, "For the Goyim it is permitted") Happy times, in which there were no other worries, and people thought that "the name influences [one's fate]." Today it is well known in the whole world that the Goyim have decided that "we go after the taste and not after the name," and the Jews have tasted all the tastes of *hammarot v'hamarot* [apostasies and griefs] in the world.

I was glad to read of your rapprochement with Professor Klein. I think this is very important. He invited you last year, through us, to study Talmud with him, but you did not respond, and perhaps he feels a justified resentment against you that you have neglected his offer and kept away from him. But surely the direct road to the university is for you to work together with him so as to qualify to become his assistant, to help him in some things and become attached to him as a disciple is to his master. This is the way of universities in every country: students endear themselves to their master, and he draws them near, so that they become for him like lovers "in the time of need," and he raises them on their ladders. And know that if the sages said, "A man can be jealous of everybody except his son and his disciple," they reached this conclusion not by Midrash but by experience. And especially an esteemed and righteous man like Professor Klein will only be glad if he sees you advancing, following his way, and can take pride in you as his disciple. You should ask his advice in everything, and try to work according to his will, and when you reach your goal you can then choose your own way as you wish. [. . .]

Yesterday I spoke to Dr. Fischer. He asked me when you will come home and also expressed his opinion that you should sit for your examination here, etc. He said, "One cannot know what will happen, and it is good to keep several irons in the fire."

When will your doctoral exam take place at the Jerusalem university?

Your father who greets you with love,
Yosef

Only the latter part of this letter requires some explanation. In it Father gave free rein to his inclination to utilize the old-fashioned "Musive" style, popular in the Hebrew literature down to and including the *Haskala* (Enlightenment) literature of the eighteenth and nineteenth centuries, in which ideas were preferably expressed by quoting, or referring to, biblical and talmudic passages and phrases. Father was, of course, well acquainted with the Latin adage *nomen est omen*, but when he wanted to make reference to that concept he used instead the talmudic expression *sh'ma garim* (B. Ber. 7b), which literally means "the name causes," but is given the sense that the name is decisive in judging the character of a thing. Likewise, when he wanted to characterize the new anti-Semitic attitude the Goyim displayed toward the Jews he did it with a brief reference to another talmudic passage (B. 'Avoda Zara 66a) that reports a discussion between Abbaye and Rava, two leading talmudic sages, one of whom ruled that in deciding the permissibility of a certain mixed dish "we go after the name" of the ingredients it contains, while the other opined that "we go after the taste" of the dish. His abbreviated quotation, of course, presupposed that I was sufficiently well versed in the Talmud to understand what he meant—and this made me quite proud. What he meant, of course, was that the anti-Semitic Gentiles disregarded the Magyarized names the Jews had adopted and based their judgment of the Jews on the "taste" they perceived in them, that is, on the character and identity—today we would say ethnicity—they attributed to the Jews. By the way, Count Raphael Zichy was a well-known Hungarian nobleman and statesman.

As for the fatherly advice contained in the letter, there was much wisdom in it, as I did not fail to recognize. But there were two factors that prevented me from following it. One was that Professor Klein's field of study and scholarly interest, *toldot hayishuv* (the history of the Jewish settlement in Palestine), had no attraction for me. By 1935 I was irrevocably committed to the study of Jewish folklore and folkways, which, I felt, dealt with much more important issues, and which, in addition, were sorely neglected fields of scholarship. I was simply unwilling and unable to give up my interest in them and engage instead in Professor Klein's type of research. In fact it was precisely in that year that I published my first folkoristic studies, including a programmatic article titled "HaFolqlor Mahu?" (What Is Folklore?), and a folktale about King Solomon and the winds, both in the daily *Doar haYom*.

The other factor was that, in contrast to father's complete trust in and reliance on Professor Klein, I felt that Klein's friendship for me had definite limitations. I resented in particular that he never expressed the slightest willingness to help me penetrate the proud citadel of the Hebrew University. In all my consultations with him about problems of my career he acted as if the university simply did not exist as far as I was concerned. All the advice he gave me directed me to other institutions, to jobs as school principal, as secretary to public bodies, and the like. This hurt me, as can be seen from my parenthetical remark in my letter of May 19, although "impertinence" was certainly too strong a word. I on my part would have dearly liked to ask him point blank, "What about becoming your assistant at the university?" but I was not bold enough to do so. Thus, throughout the seven years of my close contact with Professor Klein, in the latter part of which I already had an increasing number of scholarly publications to my credit, he never gave me as much as the slightest hint that he would be willing to help me should the possibility of an academic position at the university open up. Even when the instructorships in the preparatory Hebrew language classes of the university were considered (in 1938), the supporters of my candidacy were Dr. Magnes and Ibn-Zahav, rather than Professor Klein.

I gave expression to these feelings in a letter I wrote to my parents on July 23:

Jerusalem, Tammuz 22, 5295 [in Hebrew]

Dear Papa, Dear Mama:
On Saturday I again went to see Professor Klein. He told me that he had received a letter from you and informed me of its content, of

the financial matters in connection with the Krauss Jubilee Volume and the university. He also said that you have invited him to come to Budapest and expressed the opinion that, as he sees the situation, this would not be worthwhile. Then he told me that you asked him about opportunities for me other than teaching in which I would have to work 30 hours a week for a small salary. He said that he could not answer this question, but thought that I could get a job in a high school where one has to teach only 24 hours. He said that a new high school has just opened in Beth haKerem, and perhaps when you are here you could talk to its principal. And this was all. On the possibility of working in the university—not a word. True, the situation in the whole university is difficult at the moment, Magnes is about to resign. At the meeting of the Board of Governors in Lucerne, in August, they will discuss that problem too.

Among other things we spoke also about my family, and when I said that I, of course, would be most happy if you would come here, he said that, truly, there would be an important task for you here in the Institute of Hebrew Poetry, in connection with the publication of old Hebrew poems, and the writing of a history of Hebrew poetry, which nobody here could undertake because such a work requires a person who is not only a scholar but also a poet.

All this is nice and fine, but I heard not one positive word from his mouth. I don't expect great promises, I would be satisfied if he would say, or only give me to understand, that *if* I continue my work satisfactorily, then *possibly* he could take me into the university or recommend me.

But let's leave all this aside. What is more important is that my work is really advancing very nicely now. I work a lot, actually all day long, and one can see the results. I am working now on a comprehensive part dealing with water in the *halakha.* Several chapters are already finished, among them "Water in Secular Custom," "On the Nature of Purifying Water," "Ritual Submersion," "Washing," "Lustration," "The *Sota* [the woman accused of adultery]," "The *'Egla 'Arufa* [The Beheaded Heifer]," "The Water Libation," "The Control of Rain." In these chapters I succeeded in explaining many things, rituals, views, beliefs, and customs, whose meaning was doubtful until now. My work method in these chapters is the comparative one, both internal comparison, that is, e.g., the comparison of one Jewish custom with another— occasionally this in itself adds quite a bit—and external comparison, adducing parallels from other peoples with whose help one can, at times, throw light on [Jewish] customs such as the *Sota,* the Red Heifer, etc., concerning which even our sages admitted that they did not understand them.

I hope you received my article that I sent you for the jubilee issue. Please let me know what you think about it.

Many regards to you and to dear Mama, congratulation to my "big" brother on the occasion of his seventeenth birthday,

Your loving son,
Raphael

The Krauss Jubilee Volume, in honor of the seventieth birthday of the great Hungarian-Austrian talmudic scholar Professor Samuel Krauss, was published in late 1936 in Jerusalem. The Jubilee Committee consisted of Assaf, Epstein, Torczyner, Yellin, Sukenik, Klausner, and Klein, all university faculty members, and I served as secretary, in which capacity I conducted much of the correspondence with scholars invited to contribute articles, and saw the book through the press. Father obtained the money needed for publication in Budapest. Both Father and I also contributed articles: he on the poet Meshullam Dapiera, and I a study about the folklore of the rainbow. Father invited Professor Klein to Budapest for the purpose of carrying out a fund-raising campaign for the university. In the event Dr. Magnes did not resign, but his title was changed from chancellor to president of the university, with greatly reduced powers and responsibilities. The Institute for Hebrew Poetry was founded in Jerusalem shortly before by Salman Schocken, chairman of the Board of Governors of the Hebrew University. The article I sent Father for the twenty-fifth anniversary issue of his monthly (September–October 1935) was entitled "Imitatio Dei in Yemenite Folk Belief." It concentrated on one point I succeeded in elucidating in the course of my inquiries among the Yemenite Jews in Jerusalem: that the sky-blue color with which they framed their doors and windows as a prophylaxis against the evil eye was considered an imitation of the color of the sky.

Soon after I mailed this letter, Professor Klein, despite his initial doubts, did go to Budapest, and my parents referred to a conversation they had with him about me in letters they wrote to me a few days before the High Holy Days:

[no date, probably September 1935; in Hungarian]

Dear Gyurikám:

I am very glad that you are now writing more regularly, although it is difficult to satisfy my demands . . . Nevertheless, I am now generally informed about the situation there. You are doing the right thing in encouraging Évi to engage in new literary work, but one must not forget that it is at the moment very important for her to get more decorating work so that when her substitution assignments come to an end she should not remain without work. I think that would be even more unpleasant for her now than it was when she was not yet used to work. On the other hand, she is right in thinking that a well-known woman writer can more easily find other types of work as well. I hope that after the Zionist congress it will be possible to get something at the Sokhnut . . .

I am glad to hear that you are eating in a new and better restaurant. I hope you will remain faithful to it and will not become again as thin as you were when I saw you in the port and got frightened. But of course it is not enough to have a good lunch, you should without fail drink two glasses of milk every day; as for tea, that you have time to drink in the rainy season.

Professor Klein and Rector Guttmann spoke very highly of you, that you have acquired such great knowledge at such a young age. But let this not make you conceited! I am afraid you undertook too great a burden with the translation of Évi's novel, although, on the other hand, it is very reassuring that one does not have to spend money on it . . .

> Many hugs and kisses,
> Mama

[in Hebrew]

My Beloved Son Raphael:

As I see, Mama writes to you only about superficial things, but, to our regret, I must also let you know about all kinds of worries and troubles that have overtaken us in the last few weeks and that I don't want to specify. The things cost us money and much anguish. I don't want to write about all of them: the main thing is that we lost a lot, and our financial situation has worsened even more. For about two years we shall lose all income from Czechoslovakia and shall have to work there for nothing, because all the income from there will go to covering the expenses we have had now. In your letters don't refer to these matters and don't mention anything to Hava [Évi] and *to Leon*, it is better that there should be no correspondence about this. At the utmost you could tell them that we had losses. It is a pity that precisely now days of duress have come upon them too, and we cannot help them as we would wish. We have restricted our whole household, have banished butter from our table, and also meat most days of the week, have reduced what we have been giving until now to Grandfather and Grandmother, and we must content ourselves with little. If you could send us from there two or three pounds a month, that too would ease our situation. You have probably read my article in our journal against the Congregation, and from there too we shall lose what we had. But all this is no catastrophe, "eat bread with salt," we shall survive and lift up our heads!

But the situation of Hava and her husband depresses us. As I understand it, Hava earned this month 12 pounds, and if so, *it is necessary to supplement this amount with only about two and a half pounds* on our part. She writes that she will earn something next month too, and one must supplement it accordingly. *But even this will not be possible in the long term,* and there is absolutely no way of sending anything from here. Therefore one must consider that if their situation continues, they will have to tighten the expenses of their household to one-half of what they are today. Surely there are also in Jerusalem people who now live a more frugal life than they do. And Leon must get whatever work he can. I don't want you to be the intermediary in this matter, lest they say that you disturb the peace in their house; but write me immediately what you think of the whole matter, and how can we extricate ourselves from this situation?

The IMIT money I have not sent on to you because we need that amount, and you can deduct it from your debt, which you must begin to repay from September, as I remember. And I hope that good days will still come, and we shall hear good news from each other. We are expecting Professor Klein, and therefore I conclude with greetings of "a good inscription and sealing,"

> Your father who greets you with love,
> Yosef

The above two letters are undated, but the New Year wishes at the end of Father's letter indicates that they were written a few days before Rosh haShana, which fell on September 28–29 in 1935. About my sister Évi's novel and her work as a decorator of store-windows I am telling in *Between Budapest and Jerusalem.* In view of Father's letter it is surprising that Mother's contains not even a hint of the troubles they had. I have no knowledge of what happened, but my guess is that the agent who collected subscription fees from the readers of Father's monthly in Czechoslovakia (where *Mult és Jövő* had many subscribers among the Hungarian-speaking Jewish population of the area known as Slovensko) must have embezzled the money he took in. The usual arrangement, as far as I can remember, between Father and his agents was that each covered a certain territory, made the rounds of the Jewish communities for several weeks or months, collected the subscription fees, and then returned to Budapest, where he was supposed to hand to

Father's office chief, Uncle Virág, one-half of the money he collected, retaining the other half as his commission. If an agent absconded with the money, Father was still responsible to the subscribers and had to send them the journal for a year or whatever their subscription period was. It must be the loss of this revenue that Father refers to.

The article Father wrote about the Israelite Congregation of Pest was published a few weeks earlier in his monthly. It was sharply critical of the leadership of the Congregation, and now Father feared that in retaliation the Congregation would cut off the modest subsidy with which it supported his journal.

The quotation "eat bread with salt" comes from Mishna Avot 6:4. The whole passage reads as follows: "This is the right way of acquiring the Tora: eat bread with salt, drink a little water, sleep on the floor, live a life of deprivation, and devote yourself to the Tora. If you do this, you will be hale and well: hale in this world, and well in the World to Come." IMIT is the acronym of the Hungarian name of the Israelite Hungarian Literary Society to whose 1933 annual I contributed an article on the Hebrew University. This letter is highly exceptional among all the hundreds of letters Father wrote me: it is the only one in which he discusses his financial situation.

My Palestinian naturalization completed, I was still left with the question of release from my Hungarian citizenship. This meant that I had to obtain an official document from the Hungarian Ministry of the Interior attesting that I was no longer a Hungarian citizen or subject. As long as I did not plan to visit Hungary I paid no attention to this issue, but when the time drew near to return to Budapest in order to pass my rabbinical examination and to be handed my doctoral diploma by the university, the matter began to assume the dimensions of a problem. In the fall of 1935 I again raised the issue in letters to my father. He, still thinking that I might, after all, want to take a rabbinical position in Hungary, tried to convince me not to press for my "denaturalization," but to retain my Hungarian citizenship at least until after my planned visit. I again disagreed and wrote him and Mother:

Dec. 3, 1935 [in German]

Dear Mama and Papa:

Today there are again several matters to be touched upon.

1. The issue of my dismissal from the Hungarian state. I don't know what alleged rights or advantages I could lose by also being officially dismissed from Hungary. On the other hand, the situation with regard to the duties is this: as a student of the Rabbinical Seminary I got a student's deferment until the completion of my studies. If, after finishing my studies, I right away take a position as a rabbi in Hun-

gary, I shall be freed from military duty; if not, I must serve my eighteen months. The fact that I have in the meantime acquired a Palestinian passport will in no way help—on the contrary, it will only
blacken me in the eyes of the authorities.

Just now my friend Wulcz was here; he has the same problem, and
he was told that the petition for dismissal must be submitted to the
Hungarian consulate general in London. He also told me of the case of
a young Hungarian who had emigrated to the U.S.A. and was denied
the dismissal for eight years, so that for eight years he was not able to
visit Hungary. Wulcz told me that in Budapest Dr. Ungar handles such
problems. Therefore, please, get in touch with him without delay. If
necessary, I can send you by registered mail my Palestinian citizenship
certificate. I emphasize again, expressly, that until this matter is settled,
that is, until I have the official dismissal certificate in my hands (that
such a thing does exist I know from Professor Klein), I shall not go
home.

2. [Here follows the report about my talk with the painter Rubin,
quoted in chapter 6.]

3. In Tel Aviv I went to Omanuth. They had received Papa's telegram that the cuts are being mailed and expect their arrival in the
middle of this week. Thereafter the book should be ready in another
three to four weeks.

4. Personal. I used Saturday morning to getting somewhat friendly
with the little Persitz. Friday afternoon I cultivated my good relations
with the Tolkowsky house.

5. Concerning the book *Sefer haB'diha w'haHidud* [Book of Jokes
and Humor] by Druyanoff, I asked the author for a review copy.
[. . .]

6. Mr. Yosef Meyuhas, an old, noble Jerusalemite, former member
of the municipal council and of almost all Jewish leading bodies, and,
in addition, a well-known folklorist and collector of folktales, wrote
me, after having read my article about Solomon and the winds, and
asked my permission to include that story in the book that he is about
to publish shortly. I went to see him, and after graciously giving him
my permission, we continued to converse at length about scholarly,
etc., subjects. At the end we agreed that I would translate his book,
about to be published by Schocken, into German. I also promised him
to try to find in Budapest a publisher for a Hungarian translation. I am
now translating one tale into Hungarian and shall send it to Papa.

7. [I report on my visits to Professors Torczyner and Klausner; see
below.]

8. Papa inquired in the name of Professor Guttmann what Dr.

Rabin will do in Haifa. He will become principal of the Netzah Yisrael school, a conservative school with eight grades, corresponding to our middle schools.

9. I have not yet received an answer to my request that Papa should accept the monies that were promised from various sides, such as congregations, IMIT, and family, and inform me about them, so that it should be possible to start the printing of the Krauss *Festschrift*.

10. For lack of other subjects I conclude my letter. [. . .]

Your good old son,
Gyuri

P.S. I have just now received your letter concerning my dismissal from Hungarian citizenship. I have presented above my view about this matter. Believe me, it is not merely *mayre* [fear] on my part. I have spoken about it with Professor Klein, and most recently also with Tolkowsky, as well as with other people who are in the know, and all of them say that in times such as these one should not go to Europe at all, and if one goes, this matter must first be settled without fail. I cannot at all understand what kind of fictitious rights I would lose as a result of it, determined as I am never again in my life to have anything to do with Hungary, except, at the utmost, to pay an occasional visit as a "distinguished foreigner." I repeat, I shall not go home as long as I don't have that certificate in my hands.

Wulcz was a friend of mine in Jerusalem, of the same age, likewise of Hungarian origin. He was a student at the Hebrew University and was an accomplished cellist. For a while he tried to give me singing lessons, but my tone-deaf ear defeated his and my efforts.

The Omanuth publishers of Tel Aviv (owned by Mrs. Shoshana Persitz) was printing Hebrew and German translations of Father's Herzl biography, and Father was supposed to supply them with the cuts printed in the original Hungarian edition.

I published the folktale "King Solomon and the Winds" in the March 15, 1935, issue of the Hebrew daily *Doar haYom*. Mr. Meyuhas's book, in which it was reprinted, was published in 1938 by Dvir, Tel Aviv, under the title *Ma'asiyyot 'Am liV'ne Qedem* (Oriental Folktales). To the best of my knowledge it was never published in any other language. Dr. Israel Rabin was my teacher at the Breslau Jüdisch-theologisches Seminar in 1930–1931, where he was a lecturer of Bible.

Three weeks later I returned to the subject of my dismissal from Hungarian citizenship (in Hebrew):

[. . .] As for getting rid of the Hungarian citizenship, I know from my own experience, in contrast to what Hausbrunner [registrar of the Rabbinical Seminary] told you, that the students of the Rabbinical Seminary must stand muster for the army. I myself, after my return from Breslau, had to appear at the recruiting office and, after handing my registration book from the Rabbinical Seminary to the examiners, had to undress and stand before them stark naked, until finally they exempted me for they found that I had fallen arches. My friend Wulcz, who, by the way, is not a Rumanian but a Hungarian citizen, had to take an oath that he would enter the army whenever they called him. Apart from this, I have several other reasons as well for having resolved what I have, and I shall not budge from that resolve. Within a few days I shall get from the university the required attestation, and then I shall send it to Dr. Ungar, and shall ask him to settle everything according to my will and request. [. . .]

There is no further mention of the problem of my Hungarian citizenship in the extant family letters. I must assume that the matter was resolved to my satisfaction, because in the summer of 1936 I did visit Budapest, and I don't recall having encountered any problem either when entering or when leaving the country. However, I also remember that during the six months I spent in my native city at that time I was never completely at ease, and several times I dreamt that I was trying to get out of the city (or country) and was not able to.

Thesis, Exam, Graduation, Reviews

The Thesis

An important milestone in my life was the completion of my Ph.D. thesis under the guidance of Professor Klein, its publication, and the passing of my orals. Since, as it turned out, I was the first student at the Hebrew University to be awarded the Ph.D. degree, I felt that at the same time I was making a contribution to the history of the young Hebrew alma mater.

Once I was through with teaching at the Talpioth school I devoted myself entirely to finishing my thesis, on which, I believed, my whole future in Palestine would hinge—and the only future I foresaw for myself was in Palestine. However, the work that remained to be done was prodigious. Instead of merely putting finishing touches on the draft I had composed earlier, I had to tackle several new subjects that I had not envisaged at all. Even in the summer of 1935 I still thought that the thesis would not be longer than 200 pages. I wrote to my father (no date, in Hungarian), introducing what I wanted to say with a facetious Yiddish-Hebrew quotation:

Otherwise *bin ich mekayem di Mitzve "vehogiso bay yaymom voloylo"* [I am fulfilling the commandment "You shall pore over it day and night"), and, accordingly, my work approaches conclusion. One would not believe, when reading a completed part, how much work and effort hide behind every single line and every single detail. The list of works consulted will itself take up several pages. About sixty pages are already typed. On this basis I can estimate the size of the study more closely. I think it will be about 200 pages . . .

As a result of "poring over it day and night" I was actually able to finish my manuscript, type it, and before the end of 1935 submit it to my chief advisor, Professor Klein, and copies to the two secondary sponsors, Professor Klausner and Professor Torczyner. Klein did not have much to criticize since in the course of my work I had been in close touch with him, had shown him each chapter as it was completed in first draft, and then, taking into account his comments, had corrected it accordingly. Klausner, although he conscientiously read the entire 500-page typescript, did not have any substantive comment to make. What he did was to pencil in dozens of minute stylistic changes on each and every page. My Hebrew at the time was quite fluent—the editors of the papers to whom I submitted articles found practically nothing to improve in them—but Klausner was a sworn believer in Mishnaic Hebrew, to which he adhered consistently in all his books and took the trouble of introducing hundreds if not thousands of times such corrections as substituting the Mishnaic *she-* for the biblical *ha-* or *asher* (all three are variants of "that" or "which") that I used. I still have somewhere in my archives the copy of that typescript with all these corrections.

Professor Torczyner took a different approach to his duties as co-sponsor of my thesis. He told me, with his usual subdued puffing and snorting, that he had no time to read those parts of the book that dealt with subjects in which he was not an expert (these happened to constitute the bulk of the manuscript), but that he was willing to read the linguistic chapters and comment upon them. This he actually did, and if the etymologies and linguistic derivations of proper names and hydrographic terms contained in my thesis were acceptable, much of that was due to his careful perusal and criticism. In one of my letters to my parents I reported briefly on my contacts with these two co-sponsors of my thesis:

Dec. 3, 1935 [in German]

Yesterday I visited the two co-readers of my thesis, Professor Torczyner and Professor Klausner. Torczyner already is deep in reading the study: he said he had several things to correct in the philological part and was willing to go over this part carefully when the book reaches the printer. Otherwise he praised the thesis. Klausner has not yet begun to read it, but he promised to do it as quickly as possible. Both of them emphasized that the thesis must be published *in toto*, as a whole.

Klausner has received an offer from a certain Mr. Benamy from Budapest, in the name of the Kaldor Publishers or of the Epocha Publishers, to bring out his Jesus book in Hungarian. He asks Papa to let him know, through me, his opinion as to whether Benamy is a reliable person, *v'im yesh lismokh 'alehem* [and whether one can rely on them]? I myself have received a negative reply from the Tabor Publishers concerning Klausner's *Qitzur Toldot haSifrut ha'Ivrith haHadasha* [Short History of Modern Hebrew Literature], of which I informed Klausner. They wrote that they wanted to publish a general history of Jewish literature, and not only one of modern Hebrew literature . . .

Klausner's article about Papa was published in the Shavu'ot issue of *HaYarden*. I shall ask the editorial office for one or two additional copies.

HaYarden (The Jordan) was a Hebrew Revisionist-Zionist daily and monthly, published in Jerusalem and Tel Aviv from 1934 to 1941. Since Klausner was a leading member of the Revisionist party (after the independence of Israel they wanted to have him elected president of the state) he frequently contributed articles to their publications.

In none of my letters did I mention that I intended to dedicate my book to Father. I wanted it to be a surprise for him. The dedication only said *L'Avi Mori* (To My Father, My Teacher), but I was sure that Father would feel the intensity of my love and gratitude that stood behind those two words.

As soon as I completed the manuscript I turned my attention to its publication. Actually, I started to make efforts in that direction even before I completed the typing and reported them to my parents:

[undated, probably summer 1935; in Hungarian]

Dear Mama and Papa:

[. . .] I must constantly "animate" Klein to do something for the publication of my book. By chance I learned that the Hebrew Society for the Study of Palestine and Its Antiquities, of which Klein is one of the leaders and pillars, recently received a sizable amount from the Bialik Foundation for the purpose of publishing a series of scholarly studies. Of course *I* had to approach Klein with the question of whether it would be possible to publish my thesis in that series. His answer was: we shall see, when he returns from Europe, and perhaps a part of it.

This has, of course, in the first place financial significance for me. The exam will involve great expenses anyhow. The exam fee itself is ten pounds—this will eat up the ten pounds that I deposited at that time at the university. I shall myself type the thesis in six copies, so that I shall have only quite minimal expenses in connection with it—for paper and carbon paper. On the other hand, if I have to print the thesis at my own expense, this again would come to 25–30 pounds, which amount I could, again, naturally, obtain only from Papa, and this I would be loath to do. According to the rules the thesis must appear in print, and two hundred copies of it must be delivered to the university prior to the Ph.D. award ceremony. But if I really want to be the first doctor of the university, I must try to be graduated right away after the exam. This means that it would be necessary to have the thesis printed by the end of October, the more so since that would enable me to go immediately thereafter to Pest. So, even if we suppose, taking the best case, that after his return Klein actually prevails upon some society to print my thesis, it will take a long time until it is accomplished. Perhaps this could be facilitated if we would advance the printer the amount or part of it, which later would have to be returned by the said society into my hands.

Klein told me on Friday that he had written to Papa that he and Magnes are willing to go to Pest if Papa can assure them of some kind of serious participation on the part of the well-to-do people. In this letter he asked Papa to reply to him by cable, but by Friday no reply had come. I think that if Magnes appears there that will impress the Jews of Pest more than Klein who, after all, was a rabbi there in a small community and cannot be a prophet in his own country. If Magnes is there, perhaps Papa could also talk to him, should the occasion arise, about my insignificance. One cannot count too much on any positive intervention by Klein, but, on the other hand, we can take it for granted that he will not oppose my aspirations.

As can be seen, when I wrote this letter I did not feel that Professor Klein took a serious interest in furthering my scholarly career, especially after I had finished writing my thesis—in which, this I must again emphasize, he helped me unstintingly—when the question of how to find a suitable position loomed larger and larger on my horizon. At other times, however, I felt that he was really helpful:

Dec. 24, 1935 [in Hebrew]

Dear Papa:
    The Dvir Publishing House is interested in my book. On Thursday I shall go down to Tel Aviv and talk to its editor personally. I hope that

we shall have only minimal expenses in connection with the printing. Professor Klein is helping me as much as he can, with advice and deed. I also applied, through the Hebrew Society for the Study of Palestine and Its Antiquities, to the Bialik Foundation, and it is possible that they will allocate a subsidy to the Society so as to enable it to publish such a big book. And, if all this comes to nothing, Mr. Rubin Mass is willing to publish the book if I cover one-half of the expenses. This will be about 40 pounds, and there is all the hope that I shall get back this amount from the sales. [. . .]

The Dvir Publishing House in Tel Aviv was founded and partly owned by Hayyim Nahman Bialik, the great national poet of the *yishuv*. Bialik died in 1934, and soon thereafter the Jewish Agency for Palestine established a foundation in his memory for the publication of serious books in various fields of literature and Jewish scholarship. In the course of two or three visits to Dvir we settled the matter. We agreed that my *HaMayim* would be published under the imprint *HaHoqer 'Al Yad Dvir*, that is, the scholarly subsidiary called *HaHoqer* (The Researcher), which Dvir maintained for precisely such purposes; that Dvir and I would jointly cover the printing costs; that I would take care of the printing and binding and deliver to Dvir one thousand copies; and that Dvir would have the sole distribution rights, pay me ten percent royalties, and refund my half of the investment from the sales.

The next problem was to find a printer in Jerusalem. I got in touch with several of the printing establishments in the city (there were quite a few), but found their prices much too high. At that point my friend Dr. A. Z. Aescoly suggested that I go to see the D'fus haMa'arav (HaMa'arav Press) in the Mahane Yehuda Quarter of Jerusalem. D'fus haMa'arav turned out to be nothing more than a small typesetting workshop, located in a store-front room near the market, in which two young men worked standing before two boxes of fonts from which they selected the types and assembled them in their small hand-held trays. They were the two Abiqsis brothers, Moroccan Jews (hence the name HaMa'arav, West, for Morocco), who, as I later was to find out, preferred to transliterate their name in the French manner as Abecassis. In charge was the older one, Yitzhaq, whom I estimated to be my own age and who, as I noticed with folkloristic interest, had his right earlobe pierced as was the custom in tradition-abiding Moroccan Jewish families. Yitzhaq explained to me that once the typesetting of the book, or part of it, was completed in his workshop, they would transport the type to another printer who had a printing press. The last step would be to move over the printed signatures to a bookbinder, and he would take care of all that. He also showed me a number of books he had typeset.

After some haggling Yitzhaq and I agreed on an overall price, considerably lower than any I obtained from other printers. The fact that the production of the book was to be done in three different places did not give me pause, since my first doctoral dissertation in Budapest in 1933 had also been produced in a similar way, by one Hebrew and one Hungarian printer.

The printing was accomplished smoothly, though not without some delays that rather tried my patience. Difficulties were caused by the Arabic and Greek words in my text, which I insisted on being set in their original alphabets. HaMa'arav Press was not equipped with Arabic and Greek fonts, so that Yitzhaq had to purchase them for this explicit purpose. Some argument arose about the additional cost of this, but it was settled.

I was involved in the production of the book from beginning to end. I frequently visited the press to watch the progress of the typesetting. Much of it was done by Yitzhaq's brother (whose name I have forgotten), a young man of rosy complexion—quite unusual among Moroccan Jews—who worked with amazing speed. He could beat any Linotype, Yitzhaq told me, because the top of his right index finger was turned at a 45-degree angle, and that slight deformity enabled him to pick up the small lead type pieces from their dozens of small compartments much faster than anybody else. I read the proofs, selected the paper, watched the printing, designed the words that were to decorate the spine in gold letters, selected the cloth for the binding, and even stood by when the finished copies were loaded on a truck to be shipped to Tel Aviv and to the university.

I still vividly remember the excitement I felt when I held the first copy of the book in my hands. It was a hefty and handsome volume of 290 pages, in dark blue cloth binding. I felt veritable physical pleasure handling it, turning it around, and glancing at the title page. I personally took presentation copies to my teachers and to Dr. Magnes and mailed others to my father and Professor Heller in Budapest. At the same time I was keenly aware that the completion of the book signaled the end of the preparatory chapter in my life, and a new one, with greater responsibilities and more formidable tasks was about to begin. I was twenty-five years old.

The Exam

Since I was the first candidate to sit for the Ph.D. orals at the Hebrew University of Jerusalem, there were neither precedents nor established rules as to how such examinations should be conducted. When the appointed day and hour arrived—it was, I believe, in March 1936—I was ushered into a small study room in one of the few buildings the university campus on Mount Scopus boasted at the time and was motioned to take the vacant chair along a largish rectangular table. The other seats were occupied by my major teacher and sponsor, Professor Klein, the two others who had read and found my thesis satisfactory, Professor Torczyner and Professor Klausner, and several other faculty members. No students were present: the exam was not public, as was the case in European universities.

As for the proceedings themselves, they were not only informal but also formless. I was not asked to "defend" my thesis, that is, to give a précis of what it contained, what its main argument was, and what I wanted to prove or demonstrate in it. Instead, I was asked, by Klein and two or three of the others present, several questions that may or may not have had anything to do with my thesis. I have long forgotten the questions, except for one that I do remember because I could not answer it. Professor Klein asked me what, according to the talmudic sources, were the characteristics of mountains, valleys, and plains of Palestine. I did not know the answer, which should have consisted of referring to a saying of R. Shim'on ben Gamliel, according to which "the sign of the highlands is oak trees, of the lowlands date palms, of the valleys reeds, and of the plains sycamores" (the passage is found in Y. Shevi'it 38d bot., and B. Pesahim 53a).

The subject had nothing to do, even remotely, with my thesis, nor with the role of water in ancient Palestinian Jewish life, and hence I thought it was a somewhat unfair question. However, on the whole the proceedings tended to assume the character of a conversation between me and the examiners and lasted for about two hours. When the professors felt they had interrogated me long enough, I was asked to wait in the adjoining room until I was called back to be given the verdict. While I waited for the judgment I had a general feeling of, not anxiety, for I had no doubt that I passed, but of frustration that I was not given an opportunity to explain to those assembled senior members of the faculty that my thesis gave a glimpse into one chapter of the folklore and folk-life of our ancestors in biblical and talmudic Palestine—their beliefs and customs centering on water, the primal element on which the very life of the country had depended in the past as it did in the present. When I was called and told by a beaming Professor Klein that I was from that moment on the first doctor of the Hebrew University, it was something of an anticlimax, not least because for me it was my second doctorate.

Graduation

Some three months later, on June 10, 1936, the official award ceremony of my Ph.D. degree took place. My memory of that event is helped by contemporary sources: I still have in my possession two photographs and the text of the response I made to the address of the president of the university and its rector. One photo shows the president, Dr. Magnes, speaking and turning to me, sitting on his left side, with Rector Samuel Hugo Bergman (1883-1975) on his right. In front of us is a long, high counter used for chemical demonstrations—the ceremony took place in the chemistry lecture hall. There was evidently no other room that could have accommodated the 100 to 120 people who were expected to turn up and actually did.

The proceedings, again for lack of precedent and tradition, were informal. To the very last minute I did not know whether I would simply be handed my diploma or be given an opportunity to say a few words of thanks. In order to be prepared I composed a one-page address and kept it in my pocket. As for the whole ceremony, I can quote the account written by my father, who was present, took notes, and a few weeks later published a report on it in his monthly. I am translating from his Hungarian article as published in the July–August 1936 issue of *Mult és Jövő*:

THE FIRST DOCTORAL GRADUATION AT THE HEBREW UNIVERSITY

The first doctoral graduation of the Hebrew University of Jerusalem took place in a festive and warm atmosphere. Dr. J. L. Magnes, the chancellor, opened the proceedings with words imbued with the historical significance of the contemporary events. Present were professors of the university, headed by the deans, representatives of the scholarly institutions of Jerusalem, guests, and students. On the dais sat the chancellor, the rector, Professor Bergman, and Dr. Raphael Patai, the first doctor of the Jerusalem university. The audience listened attentively to the moving words of the chancellor that conveyed the significance of the extraordinary times:

"It is precisely in these fearful times," said the chancellor, "that we have reached this important and great feast day. We hand the first doctoral diploma to the first doctor of the Hebrew University, Dr. Raphael Patai. Those who are privileged to be present at this festivity will remember this historical event all their lives. We have introduced several customs from the times of the scholastics, among them the title doctor, as the highest academic degree. But we accepted only the essence of the matter. The external embellishments, the festive garb, the caps and gowns, the wide-sleeved robes, the flowing hoods, all the external pomp and circumstance, which in the course of time have lost their value, all that we have not adopted. It is with simplicity, putting aside all superfluity, with inwardness, and with all our hearts that we greet our friend and colleague, the first doctor of the highest academic institution of the Jewish people!

"We have also introduced the custom of making a scholarly thesis the basis of attaining the doctoral degree. Our first doctor, Raphael Patai, devoted his research to the historical and ethnographic relations of water. He found a well of living waters, overflowing, great waters, which he gathered into a rich, fertile pool. This material, although it deals with water, could have been somewhat dry; but he transformed it into abundant, flowing, sparkling springs that fertilize the soil. Whoever delves into his big book will find in it great pleasure, instruction, and research, directed toward learning the truth.

"Learning has various degrees and types, but unselfish, profound study for its own sake is the foundation of the ancient foundations of the Jewish people.

"We must emphasize this especially in these days. For what else has remained for us in the course of the years, of the centuries, but the proclamation of truth and study? It is difficult for me to visualize that great miracle: pieces of paper and parchment survived the millennia, while iron and stone disintegrated with time. Fire is set to fields, trees are murdered, souls are killed, horrifying traits become dominant in the human heart—and yet pieces of paper survive! Whence comes this miracle? From what well of living waters does it flow? Is it possible to extinguish the fire and save the paper, the letters? How could these letters fly through the flames of centuries? How is it possible that good is victorious over evil? Evil has weapons, means of destruction that one must fear, how then can it happen that the people of study, the powerless, the breadless, triumph, and they, they, become everlasting? How can it be that the Jewish people, despite all vicissitudes and sufferings, preserved their deep, living tradition? They could draw only from one single source, the Tora, into which they delved with a selfless, pure heart. They saw the eternal values of universal humankind in studying, in searching for truth and teaching it, and this became the preserver of the People of Israel.

"When we endow the first doctor of our university with this title, our aim is to augment, deepen, and glorify study. We want to continue the chain of sacred tradition, and to pass it on especially in these days in which dangers threaten but cannot intimidate us.

"Doctor Raphael Patai, go and teach, study and search, continue untiringly the tradition, 'The words of a man's mouth are as deep waters, a flowing brook, a fountain of wisdom.'"

The audience listened with bated breath to the chancellor's words inspired by biblical strength. After warm applause, the rector, Professor Bergman, rose to speak:

"In the history of the Hebrew University this day, which we celebrate *inter arma*, stands for a new chapter, a new way station. Until now we had but reached in our development the stage where we awarded our students only the *magister artium* and the *magister scientiarum* degrees that correspond to the doctorate of the universities on the European continent. The degree of magister signifies the conclusion of university studies. And, although there is no study without independent work, we still wished to make it possible, in the first place, for our students to acquire the necessary basic knowledge, the requisite material in the subject of their choice. Today we have reached the stage where our university for the first time honors one of its students with the doctoral degree that testifies to our university being qualified to train researchers engaging in independent work.

"For years there has been a discussion going on whether our university should be a research institute or an educational institution. Today precisely it has become clear how pointless this polemic was. It was dialectics lacking all foundation. Today the fact that we award the doctoral degree for scholarly research shows that the harmonious unity of the double aim contains the truth in itself. It was important for us to raise our standards as high as possible, and in this we were helped as much by the professors as by the students of the university . . ."

Then Rector Bergman took the diploma encased in a leather box, and turning to Dr. Raphael Patai, continued: "Providence has chosen you for the great honor of being the first in the chain that will continue through the generations for the glory of our people. I ask you to remain faithful to the Hebrew tongue in which you wrote your first great work, and to remain faithful to the Holy Land studying which you merited to become the first doctor of our university."

While the audience applauded warmly, Rector Bergman handed the first doctoral diploma to Dr. Raphael Patai, who, visibly moved, responded . . .

Instead of continuing here with my father's summary of what I said, I can translate from the original Hebrew text of my acceptance speech (a copy managed to survive my continental moves):

President Magnes, Rector Bergman, My Teachers and Masters!

Permit me to express my deeply felt thanks to the scholars who helped me in my work, and in the first place to my teacher and master Professor Samuel Klein.

Permit me to express my happiness at having merited to be the first recipient of the Doctor of Philosophy degree from the Hebrew University of Jerusalem.

Permit me to express my pride that it was granted to me to work and do research at this high institution in which the work continues in an orderly fashion despite the terrible events of the last few weeks, and despite the murderous hand that smote a soul even here in our very vicinity.

Perhaps there is in this a sign for the future: we continue and shall continue to study and to search, to work and to build also in times of troubles, untiringly. It is this perseverance that holds the promise of our success in the building of our country.

And there is also a sign in the fact that the first doctoral diploma of the Hebrew University is being awarded for a thesis in Palestinology and Palestinian folklore: these are subjects that are dealt with in the whole world only in our university, while they are totally neglected even in the scholarly institutions of diaspora Jewry, finding their deliverance only here, in the Hebrew University.

And may I be permitted this time to echo the words with which our honored President, Dr. Magnes, is wont to conclude our celebrations: Long live the Hebrew University!

The references Dr. Magnes and I made to fearful days, *inter arma*, and terrible events were occasioned by the Arab attacks that had taken place within the preceding few weeks and were the beginning of the three-year-long Arab riotings that subsided only with the outbreak of World War II.

As I spoke, I saw my mother's eyes fill with tears. She sat right in front of me in the first row, flanked by Father and Professor Klein. When the simple observances were over, we all went outside the building, and there a press photographer took a picture of the four of us, Father, Mother, Professor Klein, and I, standing abreast. This is the second photograph I still have of that memorable day.

My graduation as the first Ph.D. of the Hebrew University was reported in all the Hebrew dailies of Palestine, and later the news made the rounds of the Jewish press of Europe and America.

My doctoral thesis brought me one unexpected dividend: the Bialik Prize. In 1933, on the occasion of the sixtieth birthday of Bialik, who was a major cultural force in the life of Tel Aviv, the municipality established prizes in his name to be awarded annually to the authors of the most outstanding books published during the twelve preceding months in Hebrew literature and Jewish scholarship. The jury awarding the prizes was appointed by the Agudat haSofrim, the organization of Hebrew writers. Among the recipients in earlier years were the novelist S. Y. Agnon and the biblical scholar Yehezq'el Kaufmann. After my return from Budapest to Jerusalem in January 1937, when I first went to see Professor Klein, he suggested that I submit my book to the jury of that year, which consisted of the historian Ben-Zion Dinaburg (later Dinur, 1884–1973), Kaufmann, and Klein himself. Seven weeks later, to my great joy, I did get one of the prizes for 1936. The papers duly reported the awards on March 8, 1937, not failing to mention the amounts of money involved: the prize for Jewish scholarship was divided between Rabbi (later Professor) Moshe Zvi Segal of the Hebrew University, who received 30 pounds, and me. I received 20 pounds, which enabled me to repay my father most of the money he had laid out for printing my thesis.

Reviews

I no longer remember who sent out review copies of my thesis to the press (it may have been the Dvir Publishing House), but I recall how impatiently I awaited the reviews. When, within a few weeks, the reviews began to appear, they were all very laudatory. They were published in the Palestinian Hebrew daily press, and in the weeklies, monthlies, and the scholarly journals in Palestine, Egypt, Germany, Hungary, France, and the United States—more reviews may have been published in other countries as well, but they did not come to my attention. What made me especially proud was that three of the greatest Jewish scholars of the age, Bernard Heller, Samuel Krauss, and Immanuel Löw, wrote most appreciative reviews. It was an enormous satisfaction for me to be taken so seriously by the Jewish scholarly world, and to receive a note from Professor Samuel Krauss thanking me for the book and concluding with the words *vivat sequens!*

On a different level I was curiously gratified when, in the June 20, 1938, issue of the leading Tel Aviv daily *Davar*, the following joke appeared in its "With a Smile" column:

CONVERSATION
—Why are you so sad?
—I am afraid I shall remain an '*aguna.*
—But your husband is sitting in his room and reading!
—Right. But he is reading the book of P.
—Well?
—He sank into water that has no end.

For readers not sufficiently versed in Jewish traditional law, the last sentence was explained in a footnote: "If he fell into water that has no end, his wife is forbidden (Yebamoth 121.)" For the sake of those for whom even this explanation is insufficient, let me add that *'aguna* is the legal talmudic technical term for a woman whose husband has disappeared and who is not allowed to remarry until proof of his death is found. If the husband fell into a body of water whose shores were visible all around, and witnesses could observe that he did not swim ashore, he was considered dead, and his wife could remarry. But if he fell into "water that has no end," that is, whose shores were not visible all around (such as the sea), the wife became an *'aguna*, because of the possibility that the husband swam ashore somewhere, unseen by any observer. Although the joke poked fun at the length of my book, the very fact that it was the subject of a joke in a daily paper seemed to me to be a compliment.

Of the many scholarly reviews that discussed my book I want to quote only from those written by the three Jewish scholars I mentioned above.

Samuel Krauss wrote in the January 22, 1937, issue of the Tel Aviv daily *haAretz* that, while it was possible to understand the biblical rituals in which water plays a role also in and by themselves, "much greater is the task of research when it seeks parallels between the biblical commandments on the one hand, and the laws, and occasionally even the customs and legends, of the Gentiles on the other. Many such parallels are adduced in Dr. Patai's book, and this comparative method endows his study with a special power of attraction. . . . A most interesting chapter is the tenth, 'Water in Cosmogony.' . . . In it the author presents the ancient views of mankind about water in the creation of the world . . ."

Immanuel Löw in his review in the 1937 volume of the *Monatschrift für Geschichte und Wissenschaft des Judentums* (p. 252) termed the book "very well organized" and said that "the young author demonstrates great 'joy of work' [*Arbeitsfreudigkeit*] and multifaceted reading": "The method and results of the work, which is rich in content, show the school and influence of his teacher, Samuel Klein. . . . In the choice of his subject the author was fortunate. The accomplishment of his task is achieved with a success worthy of appreciation." He made an interesting comment for a scholar for whom Hebrew was not a living language: "The Palestine-Hebrew of the author is readable and clear."

By far the longest, most detailed, and most penetrating review of my book was the one written by Professor Heller, published in the July–December 1938 issue of the *Revue des Etudes Juives* of Paris. It extended over six pages, was in French (Heller wrote with equal facility in Hungarian, Hebrew, German, and French), and stated that my *ouvrage* "merited attention for its intrinsic value, and the *justesse* [correctness] of most of its ideas and judgments. M. Patai's thesis excels above all by its comparative method to which he subjects the rites, beliefs, and legends. The author has penetrated his material thoroughly. We are indebted to him for hundreds of pieces of information, for which we are grateful to him." Then, for several pages, Heller went on to point out what he considered new insights, as well as what he regarded as incorrect interpretations. In conclusion he wrote: "M. Patai's work is more than a promise. That which he has already realized merits the appreciation that he has fortunately encountered."

In the years that followed I kept in touch with Professor Heller, although, again, the letters we exchanged are lost. Since my thesis dealt only with water, I returned later to a study of the telluric elements in ancient Jewish folklore, although in a manner very different from Professor Klein's original conception. In 1941 I sent Heller, in Budapest, a copy of the typescript of the first volume of the book *Adam vaAdama* (Man and Earth) that grew out of that original plan for my doctoral dissertation and asked him to honor me by writing a preface to it. With his usual kindness and conscientiousness, he complied with my request and sent me a preface, which, however, because of the war conditions reached me in Jerusalem too late for inclusion. I still have in my possession his original Hebrew handwritten text, on whose title page I jotted down the date of its arrival: November 4, 1941. In his preface Heller briefly summarized what the book was about: the customs, beliefs, and legends connected with the earth as they could be extracted from the biblical and talmudic literature and interpreted in the light of parallels drawn from the literatures of other peoples and from the Jewish and Arab folklore of the twentieth century. Then he concluded by stating:

> I had the pleasure of witnessing Patai's first steps in the field of scholarship, of seeing his book on *The Water* while still in manuscript, as well as his studies on the *'Egla 'Arufa* and the Red Heifer. Now he has authored this book on *Man and Earth.* In him the saying of Rabbi [Yehuda the Prince] has become fulfilled: "The kids you had left behind have become powerful rams." Patai has become a disciple who teaches his masters. Would that he continue to learn and to teach, to study and to expound, and to throw light on the traditions, legends, customs, and beliefs of Israel.

Almost every phrase in this paragraph, as well as much in the preface as a whole, is a quotation from or allusion to ancient Jewish sources. When writing in Hebrew, Heller was one of the last practitioners (my father was another) of the scholarly Musive style that by then had become outmoded among the scholars of Jerusalem. I, of course, wrote a hearty thank-you note to Heller, but had no way of knowing whether he ever received it, since by the end of 1941 postal communication across the war-torn Mediterranean was either nonexistent or unreliable.

Professor Heller, as I found out after the war, died in 1943 after a short illness. He was spared the horrors of the Hungarian Holocaust. For me, his memory has remained an inspiration all my life, and I have never ceased to consider myself his pupil.

Return from Budapest

Within a few days after being awarded my Ph.D. degree from the Hebrew University, I set out to return to Budapest with my parents. My purpose in visiting my hometown was to pass the rabbinical examination at the Seminary and to be handed my Dr. Phil. diploma at the Budapest University, for which my personal presence was required. As it turned out, my visit lasted longer than I had planned. In addition to taking care of those academic affairs, I gave numerous lectures in Budapest and in the country towns on the Hebrew University, on Jerusalem and on life in the *yishuv,* and also established contacts with potential supporters of the university in many places. From one of them, a certain Mr. Breuer of Kiskunhalas, Father obtained a sizable gift to the university, officially earmarked to be used for the financing of a fellowship in Palestinian studies, which was unofficially understood to mean that I would be the recipient. All this is described in *Apprentice in Budapest,* in which I also tell briefly the story of the Hungarian Israelite Society for the Support of Holy Land and Other Settlements that was established in those days by the president of the Israelite Congregation of Pest, Court Councillor Samu Stern, and was headed by Chief Rabbi Simon Hevesi and Rabbi Joseph Katona. In the same chapter I also reported of the clash that took place between me and the Zionist leader Dr. Kurt Blumenfeld, brought about by my well-meant intention to seek cooperation between the Zionists and the anti-Zionist leadership of the Pest Congregation. I can supplement that sketchy account with a few family letters exchanged within the first weeks after my return to Jerusalem.

Jerusalem, Jan. 21, 1937 [in Hebrew]

Dear Papa,

I arrived in Jerusalem three days ago and already I feel as if I had never left our city. I found my sister in very good condition: she spends much time with the Muntner family, and on the days on which my brother-in-law is in Jericho she even stays overnight with them. Her apartment is really very small so that I cannot live with them permanently, since they let the third room for 2.50 pounds and I want to pay less for a room. Next week, when I have a little time, I shall look for a room, and, with God's help, shall find one.

Immediately after my arrival I visited Professor Klein, who received me with great friendship. We took care of the money matter, and forwarded, through the Mizrahi Bank, 60 pounds to the university. Klein said that I should submit my book to him and to Mr. Dinaburg and Dr. Yehezq'el Kaufmann, who are the judges for the Bialik Prize of the Tel Aviv municipality, and it is quite likely that I shall get the prize, which, if I am not mistaken, is 50 pounds. Klein poured out his heart to me about the university in general and Mr. Schocken in particular, with whom he had several sharp run-ins. Among other things he told me that it had become known to him that in Zurich Mr. Schocken was told that "Dr. Patai has no influence in Hungary, and therefore it is not worthwhile to become connected with them," and that this was one of the reasons why at first they did not want to award me the fellowship. Klein became greatly incensed at this and told him, "Would that we had two men like Dr. Patai (that is, the father) in Jerusalem!" It is somewhat saddening that the decision about the award of a research fellowship should be discussed from such a point of view, but, on the other hand, this little incident shows how wrong it is to carry out all the activities as it were in secret, as Papa does it, who is in effect the soul of the entire Zionist movement in Hungary, and on whose shoulders alone rests all this heavy burden—and nobody knows about it because out of excessive modesty he has so far rejected all public offices, praises, and *hallels*. And behold, now it has almost come to it that his good son has had to suffer because of this "sin of the fathers." Klein also objected at first to my undertaking work for the university in their propaganda department, but at the end he agreed. Consequently, I spoke to Mr. Berger, and he too agreed, and now the final decision depends on Mr. Schocken, and I shall know it on Sunday . . .

My brother-in-law will return from Jericho on Friday, so that for the time being I can tell you nothing about things in Boruchov. But, as I see from the words of my dear sister, they don't object to letting me take over its management.

In connection with the radio nothing can be done because Dr. Aescoly already reviews books once or twice monthly. He will review my book on the radio in the near future.

With Yitzhaq Abiqsis I have already spoken several times. At first he wanted to squeeze some money out of me, but when he saw that I have not a penny in my hands he resigned himself to this fact. He has not yet paid up all the IOUs we had signed jointly, and now we must find a way to pay up the old debts and develop the printing press with joint efforts. He has not yet received the big job of printing all the works of Rabbi Kook of blessed memory, but we both hope that we shall succeed in this matter.

Your loving son who is happy to be again in the Holy City and to speak and think in the Holy Tongue, and to breathe the Hebrew atmosphere,

Raphael

[in Hungarian]

Dear Mama,

Since I have reported above all the *realia* to Papa, let me now turn to the less important things, which will probably interest Mama just as much. Well, I don't even have to mention that I was received everywhere with the greatest joy and friendship, in university and nonuniversity circles alike. Many had heard my radio talk, even those who don't understand Hungarian have heard about it and value highly its noble essence. Klein said that it was a *Kiddush haShem* [sanctification of the name of God].

Évi really looks well and is very well. If one sees their situation at close range, one really cannot judge things so severely as from there, from the well-heated rooms of Nyúl Street. Leon I have not yet seen so I cannot know in what condition he is, but, as a characterization let it be enough to say that they have been living six weeks in the new apartment, that is, Leon has already spent six weekends here, and when I arrived the curtains were not yet hung, because, it seems, he was too tired to drive into the wall the nails that hold the curtains. So, despite the pressure of my affairs, I took care of it. Thus, it is a little easier to understand why he has not yet sent the account. Of course, this too is an indication that the right thing is for me to take over this task, even though I too shall be very busy. Apart from this, my impression is that Évi is now economizing to some extent: for instance, she told me that she would not take on new help for the expected child, only the present *ozeret* [maid] for the whole day, and possibly for the first two weeks a nurse who, as Évi says, would wean the child from crying at night. For the clinic, including a sojourn of ten days, they have earmarked ten pounds.

Évi would like me to stay with them; they want to give notice to the present roomer. But I, on the one hand, would not like to pay two and a half pounds, and, on the other, I prefer independence. So I am now looking for a suitable room that will cost, say, two pounds unfurnished; for four pounds I shall purchase the most necessary furniture, that is, a table, bed, and wardrobe. I do have three chairs, a beautiful sofa-cover, a rug, and a mat. In any case, we have not yet reached a final decision on this issue.

I met Rav Assaf: he invited me for Friday evening. I also met young

Krauss near his apartment, and when I went in with him I found that he lives next door to little Naomi Tolkowsky, so I knocked on her door too. She received me very pleasantly and right away began to complain about Krauss, what an unpleasant character he was, she did not talk to him at all. Me, it seems, she was glad to see, we chatted a long while. This evening I shall officially pay my respects to her. She is a pleasant, intelligent, etc., girl, but still, please, don't be worried!

The situation is at present generally quiet in the country. Last night I went with Abiqsis to the Edison Cinema where they showed a film (free of charge) about the development of the port of Tel Aviv, and then there were speeches by Rav Berlin, Ben-Zvi, Grünbaum, Auster, about the port. The purpose was to launch new shares. The whole affair was "passably" uplifting, only the Revisonists, whose HaSappan lighter company incomprehensibly receives no part in the work, repeatedly caused understandable disturbances. I must now go to visit my friend Abiqsis to discuss our war-plans for the development of the press.

Many kisses to the whole family, and a special one to the big fatty,

Raphael

We have already met most of the people mentioned in this letter. Alfred Berger (1890–1939) was director of public relations at the Hebrew University. Rav Simha Assaf (1889–1953), rabbinic and legal scholar, became professor at the university in 1936, was its rector from 1948 to 1950, and from 1948 was also member of Israel's newly established Supreme Court. Stephen Krauss, M.D., was son of the famous talmudic scholar Samuel Krauss. He moved to England and engaged in medical psychiatric practice there. Rav Meir Berlin (later Bar Ilan, 1880–1949) was a foremost leader of the Mizrahi movement, and from 1938 to his death the editor-in-chief of the Mizrahi daily *HaTzofe*, to which I contributed several articles on Jewish folklore. Bar Ilan University in Ramat Gan, Israel, is named after him. Yitzhaq Grünbaum (1879–1970) was a leader of the General Zionists, first in Poland and then (from 1933) in Palestine, where he became head of the Jewish Agency's Labor Department. From 1935 to 1948 he also headed the Bialik Foundation. He took personal interest in my book on Jewish seafaring (see below), which was published in 1938 with the help of the Bialik Foundation. Daniel Auster (1893–1962) was a lawyer, deputy mayor and acting mayor of Jerusalem under the British administration, and from 1948 to 1951 the first mayor of Jerusalem in independent Israel. He was a good friend of mine who several times advised me informally on legal problems. His wife was a member of the important Mani family of Iraqi origin, a daughter of Yitzhaq Malkiel Mani (1860–1933), who had been an enthusiastic supporter of

Herzl and served as district judge in Hebron. "The big fatty" was my humorous-affectionate name for my brother Guszti, eighteen years old at the time.

Three days after sending off the above letter I again wrote to my parents:

Jerusalem, Jan. 24, 1937 [in Hungarian]

Dear Mama and Papa:

This morning I reached an agreement with Berger to take over the direction of Hungarian propaganda of the university, devoting one day a week to it, with a salary of 3 pounds per month, plus five percent commission on all the amounts received. I shall start working this Thursday. My first task will be to prepare, by correspondence, Berger's Hungarian trip. To this end, we have decided, we shall first of all ask Papa—which I am doing herewith—to arrange with Stern and Eppler that when Berger arrives in Budapest, late in March or early in April, the new Society for the Support of the Holy Land, etc., should have a meeting in the Goldmark Hall. In that meeting Berger would sketch, in a captivating lecture, the significance of the university. The purpose of that lecture would only be to create the mood, and it would in no way commit the Congregation. So, please, let me know by return mail whether I should write directly to Stern and Eppler, should introduce Berger to them in that manner, and ask them to give him the opportunity to deliver his lecture under the auspices of the new society, or whether it is better that Papa should first talk to them personally. Berger would go in place of Dr. Grau, as it was planned earlier, since he will be in Vienna and Czechoslovakia anyhow. In general, we reached an understanding with Berger to the effect that before I begin to work in earnest we shall ask Papa for general directives.

Now for another matter. Two weeks ago the Jerusalem Hitahdut 'Ole Hungaria [Association of Hungarian Immigrants] sent congratulations by cable to the new Stern initiative. Thereupon Blumenfeld and Hantke sought an opportunity to convince the leaders of the Hit. 'Ole Hung. that it was a wrong move to welcome with congratulation an enterprise directed against Hungarian Zionism. The opportunity was given them yesterday afternoon, in the apartment of Dr. Szametz (who is of Hungarian origin), where the leaders of the Hit. 'Ole Hung. gathered—Koch, Tikva, Professor Fekete, Mimi Fried, etc. And after they discussed at length whether the step taken was right or wrong, they asked me to report about the Budapest situation, what Stern's goals are, and what the position of the Hungarian Zionists is. I presented in a lengthy account, in Hebrew, the point of view I consider the right one, which Papa too embraced on this issue—namely, that the Zionists must not take action against this new organization and thereby *a priori* alienate them, but, to the contrary, one must do one's best to lead them, with gentle words, onto the right path, etc.

After me someone else gave his reaction, and while he was speaking, Blumenfeld, who sat next to me, whispered in my ear, greatly enraged, his whole body shaking with excitement, roughly these words: *Ich kann Ihren Standpunkt nicht verstehen, ich koche von Zorn, das ist ja ein geistiger Verrat, ich schäme mich dass so ein Mensch unser erster Doktor ist, und ich werde Sie bekämpfen so lange ich lebe* [I cannot understand your position, I am boiling over with anger, this is a spiritual betrayal, I am ashamed that such a person is our first doctor, and I shall fight you as long as I live]. Then he took the floor and said that there have always been Zionists who supported the Palestine-work initiated by non-Zionists, these are the gravediggers of Zionism, and real Zionism arises only out of a fight against them.

When the meeting broke up I told him that I want to talk to him again about all this, so that we can clear up this whole matter. Thereupon he said, yes, he wants to talk to me before he leaves on his trip, he wants to give me a good talking-to, and wants to screw off my head, even without a head I would remain tall enough, etc. That is, he regretted his former vehemence and tried to turn it into a joke. At the end they decided to convene a public meeting in which a resolution would be passed to write a letter that would explain that the meaning of the cable was that they welcomed the constructive work the Congregation had initiated and hoped that it would harmonize with the Zionist program, etc. Therefore, please explain to Stern and Eppler that in this meeting I saved the situation by declaring myself in sympathy with them, etc. I don't want to write to them directly about this affair, because if it becomes known to the leadership here they will get seriously angry with me. However, the wrath of Blumenfeld should not be taken seriously, he makes the impression of a terribly nervous, almost crazy, person. [. . .]

Another thing. It would really be desirable to settle the Krauss *Festschrift* urgently. Here Professor Klein applied to old Mrs. Goldberg to get coverage for the shortage that will exist in any event. About the press I shall write next time. I have not yet found a room: it is almost impossible to look for one at present because the weather is very bad, cold, one is glad to reduce one's outings to the minimum necessary.

Please let me have your prompt answer concerning the Berger matter. Many kisses to the whole family, your son, the head of the Hungarian section of the Friends of the Hebrew University of Jerusalem,

Raphael

We have already met Samu Stern, the president of the Israelite Congregation of Pest, a sworn anti-Zionist, who set up the Society for the Support of the Holy Land and Other Settlements primarily in order to steal the thunder from the Zionists. Dr. Sándor Eppler was the secretary-general of the Congregation and right-hand man of Stern. Dr. Arthur Hantke (1874–1955) was managing director of the head office of the Keren Hayesod in Jerusalem. The leaders of the Society of Hungarian Immigrants, of whom I was one, were all men of Hungarian origin who held various positions in Jerusalem. Of the Krauss *Festschrift* and "old Mrs. Goldberg" I shall have more to say later. My work for the propaganda department of the Hebrew University lasted about a year, after which, since Mr. Berger was dissatisfied with the results, I was fired.

Five days later I sent off another letter to my parents:

Jerusalem, Jan. 29, 1937 [in Hungarian]

Dear Mama and Papa:

First of all, two official matters: 1. Yesterday I began working for the university propaganda, and in connection with this it is now time to open a bank account in Budapest, preferably at the Angol-Magyar [Anglo-Hungarian] Bank, into which it will be possible to deposit the monies that hopefully will come in from all the cities of the country. Would you, therefore, please take care of this, and send me, as printed matter, the credit slips, so that I can then attach them to the letters I shall write to the congregations? To make things simple, it would possibly be even better to open an account at the postal savings bank. Yesterday I worked at the university from half past eight to two, and during that time I wrote eight letters: two to Hatvan (Fodor and Blumenthal), and one each to Dénes Friedmann, Emil Roth, Zoltán Wallenstein, Dr. Lipót Löw, Sándor Prager (Kiskunhalas), and Pál Hirschler. To Samu [Stern] and Eppler I shall write only if I get an answer from Papa to my former letter, and know whether he spoke to them, and, in general, how one should approach the matter with them. I believe that they will agree that at first a meeting should be arranged at which Berger would speak about the university.

2. Ibn-Zahav sends this request: would Papa translate into Hungarian his cycle of poems entitled *B'tokhekhi Y'rushalayim* [In Thy Midst, O Jerusalem]? This consists of twelve poems, two of which have already been published in *Mult és Jövő*, so that only ten are left—they should be published in a separate booklet. He is willing to defray the expenses up to three pounds. If, for any reason, this should not be possible, he would like us to publish five or six stories from his *Zappatim* [The Pitch-Workers] in *MéJ*, and then they should be published in a

small booklet, whose expenses, up to 7-8 pounds, he could cover. I believe that in either case, if the type is preserved in the press, the expenses will not be greater. The *Zappatim*, by the way, has just appeared in a second edition.

Monday I shall go to Tel Aviv and Boruchov. I shall try my best to settle everything. I shall talk to that rascal Henig and appeal to his better self. I shall talk to Mrs. Persitz, the more so since the Herzl book has been published in the meantime in German as well. It is very beautifully produced, exactly like the Hungarian edition, in size, paper, etc. I shall make sure that they send Papa copies.

I am making great efforts to develop the press. We shall begin to pay the IOUs that were not covered during my absence, since we shall soon begin to work on several big orders. The old printing machine that we have used until now has completely broken down—we are now looking for a machine to rent since for the time being we have no money to buy one. My calculation is that by March I shall have some income from the press.

I am often together with Professor Klein. I submitted the application for the Bialik Prize, attaching three copies of my book, one for Klein, one for Dinaburg, and one for Yehezq'el Kaufmann. The review by Professor Krauss, as you probably saw, was published in *HaAretz* last Friday.

Yesterday afternoon we collectively visited Ahmed in his new house, Shaykh Amīn [al-Ansārī], with the long white beard, was there too; he sends his regards to Father.

This evening I am invited to the Kochs'. Tomorrow afternoon there is again a meeting of the Hitahdut 'Ole Hungaria at the home of Dr. Szametz. Sunday morning we shall sign a contract of Aescoly's about the printing of an Arabic-language primer. For next Saturday the Yellins invited me for lunch. The same day we shall go to the Ben-Zvis'. Suffice it to say, I already long very much for a little rest, to be able to begin my scholarly work. Soon the news will be in the papers that "a fellowship was established at the university for research in Palestinology and was awarded to Dr. Raphael Patai, the first doctor of the university." I know, because I saw the propaganda office prepare this "material."

> For lack of other subjects, many kisses to the whole family,
> Raphael

Most of the Hungarian names mentioned in this letter are those of rabbis of various congregations in country towns in Hungary. Yitzhaq Ben-Zvi (1883–1963) was at the time chairman of the Va'ad Leumi (National Council of the Jews of Palestine). In 1945 he accepted the honorary presidency of the Palestine Institute of Folklore and Ethnology I founded in that year in Jerusalem and in 1952 became the second president of the state of Israel.

My father's reply to my January 21 letter reached me early in February.

[undated, probably Jan. 28, 1937; in Hebrew]

My Beloved Dear Son Raphael:

I was very glad to read in your letter that you reached your heart's desire in safety. Would that there be peace in the whole country and you continue your work in quiet and tranquility!

What you write about the Bialik Prize is a good and important thing. May God grant that you succeed! This has importance not only from the monetary aspect, but also from the moral aspect and in terms of your future—therefore it is worthwhile to attend to it. Perhaps the right thing to do would be also to speak to Yitzhaq Grünbaum in this matter, he certainly has influence in this respect.

What you write about the conversation between the dear Professor Klein and Schocken was no surprise for me. The rich are haughty, whether in Budapest or in Jerusalem—there are, of course, exceptions—and belittle people who don't approach them with flattery. But I was saddened by what you write in the name of Professor Klein, "If there would be two men like me in Jerusalem," woe to us if Professor Klein, who certainly is one of the 36 saintly men upon whom the world stands, sees thus the situation in the holy city of Jerusalem—that there are no two men like me in it! If so, what is our hope and what our salvation?

About your affiliation with the university in the publicity work, be very, very careful, lest they suspect you of having undertaken the thing only in order to earn a few pounds, and your work bring no results!

In the matter of the architect I shall reply soon, now again I have been laid up for a few days with influenza, etc., and I am not allowed as yet to go out. The people in Kiskunhalas, etc., have sent nothing in connection with the article, although they had held out the hope "up to a thousand pengős." Now they say that they discharged their obligation with what they gave you, and I believe they are right.

Tell Professor Klein that I sent his sister, right after the receipt of his letter, 57 pengős and some pennies, and she has since acknowledged the receipt of the money. This was done from the account of the Society for Antiquities, etc., so that we have sent so far for that account 5 pounds, and you know what more there is.

How much is your debt in the printing press?

Today the Lloyd Triestino informed me that there will be some discount for the pre-Passover sailing, and at that time a group of Christian pilgrims will also go from Hungary, and I thought that it might be good to join with them and sail together, for this will impress the Jews not to be afraid of going as they are because of the news that, to our regret, comes even now. If so, it is possible that, if God wills, we shall celebrate the Passover in Jerusalem. In any case it would be good to inquire at the hotels as soon as possible, so that we know the prices, etc. Our plan is to leave on March 17 and arrive in Jerusalem on the eve of Passover. Of course, before the publication of the prospectus we must obtain permission from the National Bank, etc., and also we have not yet secured places on the ship. Hence everything is still uncertain. In a few days I shall write to you again about all this. But in the meantime make inquiries about the prices one can expect for the Passover days, etc.

And what you write about the praises and admiration, etc.—I shall not budge from my position in which I have become old and hoary. I rejected the idea of a gala evening the Zionists wanted to arrange in honor of my jubilee, together with the Congregation, "the admirers of Dr. Patai," so to speak. But I shall continue to do all I can for the up-building of Zion in the future as well. Now they want to "hang a mountain over me like a pail," that I should accept the presidency of the Pro Palestine Federation, since Professor Pfeiffer does not want to continue to carry this yoke, and the other directors say that they want to work as vice-presidents under my presidency. Sweet old Professor Donath gave a long speech about this, he too wants to be only a vice-president, and likewise Professor Török, etc., and Baron Hatvany and his friends. Your father who greets you with love,

Yosef

Father was the main initiator and organizer of the Pro Palestine Federation of Hungarian Jews in 1926. Its purpose was to serve as a platform for those Hungarian Jews who for political reasons did not want to become members of the Zionist Organization but were nevertheless interested in supporting the cultural and economic institutions of the *yishuv*. Ignác Pfeiffer, professor of chemical technology at the Technical University of Budapest, who served as president of the Federation, resigned at the age of seventy in 1937, and the other leaders of the Federation wanted Father, who until then was vice-president for cultural affairs, to become president. Bowing to their pressure, he accepted. Professor Julius Donath was vice-president for university affairs. Among the other vice-presidents were Professor Lajos

Török, M.D., and Baron Bertalan Hatvany, industrialist and author. A few more details about the Pro Palestine Federation can be found in my *Apprentice in Budapest.*

Even before I received the above letter from Father I wrote to my parents again, in Hungarian, as I was wont to do when I addressed a letter to both of them.

Jerusalem, Jan. 31, 1937

Dear Mama and Papa:

[. . .] The leadership of the Hitahdut 'Ole Hungaria [Association of Hungarian Immigrants] asked me to take into my hands the direction of its cultural affairs. I told them I was inclined to accept it, and thus, at the first meeting, which we shall have on February 18, and at which Professor Klein will lecture, I shall give the chairman's introduction. In addition, we are organizing evening Hebrew language classes for Hungarian immigrants from which, I think, I shall have some income. The Hitahdut is now planning the publication of Hameiri's works; they think they will be able to get together the necessary finances by subscriptions. I hope we shall get the printing of the series planned to comprise fifteen volumes. Hopefully, by the end of the week we shall have new premises for the press with a suitable machine, and then the work will go like clockwork. We have already got the printing of the Arabic-language primer. We ordered Arabic type—it is due to arrive in six weeks, and then we shall start the typesetting. Also the printing of Rav Kook's works was settled, due to my personal efforts. In a few days the contract for a thousand printed signatures will be in our hands! Of course, there still are minor difficulties, especially because the expenses must be defrayed this minute while the revenues only start to come in after we have printed several signatures, but, with the help of a loan of 20 pounds from the Mizrahi Bank we shall wade through this too. If now the political situation too will be good, then, with the help of God, everything will be all right! For the time being there is complete quiet in the country, and I really don't understand why the papers write so much *Greuelpropaganda* [atrocity propaganda] without any basis. Many kisses to the whole family,

Gyuri

Today I got 2 pounds from Professor Klein.

The first half of my next extant letter to my parents, dated February 5, 1937, contains a detailed account of my negotiations with our tenants in

Shekhunat Boruchov to induce them to pay the rent they owed. I also reported about my efforts to find a buyer for the oranges that were ripening on the trees of the grove surrounding the houses. Then I turned to literary-business affairs and gave an account of my meeting with Rita Gerstner (née Persitz) to get from Omanuth the money that they owed Father for his Herzl biography which they had published in Hebrew and German translations, and of the visit I paid to the Dvir Publishers, who published my doctoral dissertation. Finally I added a few miscellaneous items:

> Last night Dr. Aescoly spoke for about ten minutes on the Jerusalem radio about *HaMayim*, naturally in tones of highest appreciation. I also went to the Tolkowskys, who received me with their usual reserved courtesy. I also went to see Hameiri in Ramat Gan, he was, of course, not at home, only his wife, who instantly deluged me with a torrent of complaints.
>
> I have as yet received no reply concerning the university action in connection with the Budapest Congregation, although it is by now quite urgent, nor concerning the Krauss *Festschrift*, which is also urgent, nor concerning the architect V., which is perhaps the most urgent.
>
> As for the tour, in accordance with the later, air-mail letter, we are doing nothing for the time being. Still, I hope it will come to fruition. The latest case of murder, the driver who was shot in his car, it would seem, remains an isolated incident—in general there is quiet and order in the country.
>
> I spoke to Tolkowsky about the Bognár boy——he said one can do nothing at present, but he is sure that they will release him soon, if for no other reason than because the government wants to release several Arabs, and they counterbalance that by also releasing a few Jews.
>
> Since the holy Sabbath rest is approaching, I conclude my letter with best wishes to the whole family and *r'fu'a sh'lema* [full recovery] to Papa, your loving son,
>
> Gyuri
>
> Monday evening *HaAretz* and *Davar* contained news items about my having received the fellowship. In fact, I have already been paid the first ten pounds.

I cannot track down the circumstances of the arrest of "the Bognár boy"—evidently a Hungarian Jewish immigrant in Palestine, probably arrested for some political offense—but in my letter to Father dated February

14, 1937, I was able to report that I had spoken to the lawyer Mordecai Eliash, who "told me that young Bognár has already been pardoned and in the meantime has probably been set free."

Instructor of Hebrew

By 1937 the deterioration of the position of the Jews was well under way in Central and Eastern Europe as a result of Hitler's policies and in the Middle East as a consequence of the Arabs' and Muslims' growing solidarity with the Palestinian Arabs in opposition to the *yishuv*. In response to these developments more and more students from both world areas sought admission to the Hebrew University, which would enable them to leave their home countries and enter Palestine legally.

For the university the admission of these students constituted a challenge and a problem. The rules of admission at the time required each applicant to pass an entrance examination in the Hebrew language prior to being admitted. Hebrew was the language of tuition in all university offerings, and a knowledge of Hebrew was therefore essential for students to be able to attend classes and understand the lectures. However, the great majority of the new applicants knew no Hebrew, and to make their admission contingent on passing a Hebrew entrance examination was therefore the equivalent of outright rejection.

The university authorities worked out a plan so that students applying for admission from abroad were to be admitted unconditionally. They would still have to pass a Hebrew entrance examination, but only for the purpose of determining the level of their proficiency in Hebrew. I no longer remember what the exact arrangements were. What I do recall is that late in 1937 the university decided to organize Hebrew language classes for freshmen who were deficient in Hebrew and soon thereafter began a search for an instructor.

The committee appointed to make the selection consisted of Professors Fraenkel, Klein, Torczyner, and Yellin, and Dr. Sambursky. Ibn-Zahav was secretary. For me this seemed a unique opportunity to get a foothold in the university, and I was determined to do whatever I could to get the appointment. On January 16, 1938, I wrote to my sister Évi, who was in Budapest at the time, that within the next few days I would have to seek out each member of the committee, and, in addition, would have to talk to all those "individuals who have influence on them. Of course, all this is not simple, it takes time and energy. We are working on the strategy with Ibn-Zahav. Recently I finally managed to be admitted as a member of the Irgun haMusmakhim, the Organization of University Alumni. This was essential because they can rightly insist that one of their members should be given the fervently desired position."

Ibn-Zahav, who attended the meetings of the committee as its secretary, kept me informed of developments within and around it. About a week later I was able to report to my parents and Évi that "the first meeting of the committee will take place within the next few days. At that meeting, in all probability, they will not yet decide about the candidates, but will only lay down the general ground rules. I do have chances, but of course we can know nothing as yet, because there are many candidates, and each of them has his own patron and protector among the committee members."

The work of the committee proceeded slowly, and on February 10 I reported to my parents that "about the university position there is still no decision. The applications must be submitted by the end of the month, and then who knows how long the matter will drag out."

On February 18, at the suggestion of Ibn-Zahav, I wrote: "As I see, much also depends on Dr. Werner Senator. Would Papa therefore please send off a letter to him too? He is now secretary-general of the university. Alas, there is need of considerable pressure because the Irgun haMusmakhim insists on having the position, or positions, given to others of its members, and the opinion of the committee is wavering."

I wrote "position, or positions," because by that time the committee was considering dividing the instructor's position among three candidates. Although the number of weekly hours envisaged was not more than eighteen—less than the teaching load of a high school teacher—so that it could have been easily taken care of by one instructor, under the pressure of the supporters of several candidates the committee in the event decided to employ three instructors, each with one-third of a job.

Father immediately sprang into action and wrote not only to Dr. Senator, but to quite a number of his other friends. When I was informed of this, I became apprehensive that too much string-pulling could be counterproductive. On March 2, 1938, I wrote to Évi:

> I thank Papa very much for the recent letter assault in connection with my job. But I think this should not be overdone, for the committee in whose hands the decision rests may say, in view of the overly great pressure: *davke* [in spite!]. Therefore Papa should write nothing more about it. What I have done in the past few days was to submit my application officially and laconically, and then wrote a personal note to Ibn-Zahav, to which I attached a copy of the application and in which I set forth that so far I have received no material or even moral support from the university, etc. He will certainly know how to make good use of this letter. In any case, no decision can be expected before Passover—Torczyner, who is now on a propaganda tour in Poland and is the most important pillar of the committee, will return only then.

One of the people to whom Father wrote before I asked him to cease efforts on my behalf was Dr. Nahum Goldmann. Early in March 1938 Goldmann answered, and Évi sent me a copy of his letter (in German):

Dear Dr. Patai:

I have spoken to Dr. Weizmann about the candidacy of your son for the position in the Hebrew preparatory courses at the Jerusalem university. Dr. Weizmann is willing and ready to recommend him, and at his suggestion I wrote to Dr. Fraenkel, professor in Jerusalem, and asked him in the name of Dr. Weizmann to do his utmost to help your son. I think it would be useful if your son would get in touch with Professor Fraenkel. Late in March Dr. Weizmann will be in Palestine, where your son could possibly talk to him. To Professor Fraenkel I wrote Friday.

With many hearty regards, yours,
Nahum Goldmann

Évi added in Hungarian:

Papa asks whether it would not be possible also to talk to Fraenkel to the effect that they should not divide the job into three, but rather create one position, which would provide at least a minimum existence, such as a teacher's starting salary of nine pounds. If Weizmann gets to know you, that can only help. His support will carry much weight. We think that it was he who made a professor of little Farkas, who surely is no greater authority in his field than you are in yours. One must win over Weizmann . . . Of course one must be careful in joining the battle for one single position, for it can happen that they will create only one position but will give it to somebody else, and it will make you appear as if you had belittled and deprecated the four and a quarter pound job.

Dr. Chaim Weizmann (1874–1952) was at the time president of the World Zionist Organization. "Little Farkas" refers to Ladislaus Farkas (1904–1948), of Hungarian origin, professor of physical chemistry at the Hebrew University.

I replied to Évi on March 18, 1938 (in Hungarian): "I received your airmail letter in which you copied Goldmann's letter. I think no further steps should be taken in this matter. Really, the great *Aufwand* [expenditure] with which the *aylem* [world] was set in motion in the interest of this matter could have served a greater goal than a miserable four-pound job. But it will be an important achievement if in this way I get university status, within which I shall somehow work my way ahead and up."

Finally, on April 10, 1938, I was able to inform my parents that I indeed got the job. Since I addressed the letter to both of them, I wrote in Hungarian:

First of all I hurry to inform you, happily, that the committee and the management decided to appoint me to the Hebrew instructor's position at the University. On Friday afternoon Ibn-Zahav came to give me the news. He related in detail how hard he had worked to have the committee meet before he left on his trip. There were seven candidates for the three positions. They put me in first place, and only after me old and tried men. He even managed to arrange that no test-lessons will be given: the appointment goes into effect without any trial, for one year.

The same day he had the management approve the decision, and so the matter is settled definitively. For the time being I know nothing officially, and Ibn-Zahav asked me explicitly that, if I write home about it, I should add that you must definitely not mention it to anybody, nor write any letters of thanks or any other letter, either here or anywhere else. I got this position, he said, because I deserved it, on the basis of my knowledge, qualifications, etc., and not because the university is indebted to Papa. Therefore, no thanks are due. At the same time he mentioned again that I shall, in all probability, get also the secretarial job of the university press, which, with half-day work, will carry a salary of eight pounds. The instructor's job will pay 4.25 pounds, so that the two together will make a decent income.

Of the other two instructors I remember only Dr. Mordecai Margaliot, because in the course of our work we conferred several times. He got the second doctorate to be awarded by the Hebrew University—he made no secret of his disappointment that I beat him to the first—and taught rabbinical literature at the Hebrew University from 1950 to 1957. In 1958, despairing of advancement at the university, he accepted an invitation from the Jewish Theological Seminary of America in New York to become professor of midrashic and gaonic literature. The last time I met him in New York, in 1967 or 1968, he was stricken with cancer and knew that his days were numbered. He was visibly in pain, but said, with a sad smile, quoting an old Jewish saying, in Hebrew, of course, "I accept it with love." A few weeks later, greatly weakened, he flew back to Israel in order to die in Jerusalem.

The Hebrew language classes met, not on Mount Scopus, on the university campus, but in a school building in midtown Jerusalem, near Jaffa Road, in the late afternoon hours. This was very convenient for me, because it enabled me to spend practically the entire day working on my various scholarly studies. Each of the three instructors was assigned one class of beginners and one of advanced students. Attendance was compulsory, and the students had to enter the course they took in their "index" (registration booklet) together with all the other classes they attended.

In the second half of October 1938 I was busy for two weeks administering the exams that served as the basis for determining whether the students had to attend one of these Hebrew preparatory classes or knew enough Hebrew to be exempted from attendance. The academic year began in the first week of November, and on November 13 I reported to my sister, who by that time was in Paris: "I have started my teaching at the Hebrew classes of the university. For the time being I teach two groups with a total of 75 students, which means six hours weekly. But it is possible that, if need be, I will be given a third group as well, that is, another three hours weekly, without any increase in salary." For four academic years (1938–1942) these classes were my only steady job and only permanent source of income. If I remember correctly, in 1940, in view of the inflation, our salaries were increased from the monthly LP4.25 to LP8.00.

Of my classes I remember very little. They were big, between thirty and forty students in each, and the student body itself was like a miniature *kibbutz galuyot* (ingathering of exiles). Many of the students hailed from the countries threatened by Nazi Germany, others from Turkey and several Arab countries. Among the latter, I can recall, were two pretty Egyptian girls, one small and dark, the other tall and blonde. By that time I was well aware that among the Egyptian Jews, and especially those who lived in Alexandria, there were many of European extraction, but still I was surprised to see an almost "Nordic"-looking Jewish girl from Egypt.

There were also several Hungarian students in the group assigned to me. One of them, László Nánási, I met again fifty years later in New York at a meeting of the American section of the World Federation of Hungarian Jews. He reminded me of two things I had entirely forgotten. One was that among my students there were two young Nashāshībīs, members of one of the leading Arab families of Jerusalem, who, wishing to study at the Hebrew University, had to attend the Hebrew language classes, like all students who knew no Hebrew or whose Hebrew was insufficient. The other thing Leslie Nánási (as he called himself after settling in America) remembered was that on one occasion a group of some fifteen of my students, he among them, was invited to my home—he even remembered that I lived in the Bukharan Quarter—for a friendly get-together.

The teaching itself, I remember clearly, was not at all onerous. The students were eager to learn Hebrew, since they knew that their entire academic future depended on it. We received no guidelines whatsoever from the committee that appointed us, and, as for supervision, during the four years of my tenure only one of its members visited my course on one single occasion. He was Professor Torczyner, who, as professor of Hebrew at the university, must have felt that it was up to him to see that the work of the instructors was satisfactory. One evening, when I was about halfway through with my session, he came in, unannounced, and stayed until the end of the hour. After the class he told me he thought I was doing fine and then pressed into my hand a small slip of paper, remarking in his characteristic apologetic manner, "Here is a comment, nothing of importance." After he left I looked at the paper: there was a single Hebrew word on it complete with the vowel signs: *mo'etza*. During the session I had written on the blackboard the phrase *mo'atzat hapo'alim* (the workers' council) contained in the piece we were reading, and then, to show the students how the first word looked when it stood alone, I erased its final letter, the *tav*, and substituted a *he*, so that the word read *mo'atza*. What Torczyner indicated on his piece of paper was that the correct vocalization of the word was *mo'etza* and not *mo'atza*. Since a quirk of memory has made me remember this little incident after so many years, I got curious and looked up the word in the largest modern Israeli Hebrew dictionary, that of Reuben Alcalay (published in 1963). I found that Torczyner's view of the correct vocalization of the word was not accepted by Hebrew lexicographers: Alcalay's entry reads *mo'atza*.

In the summer of 1938, a few months after my appointment to the Hebrew instructorship went through, I received—I can no longer recall through what channels—an invitation to serve as principal of the newly established Jewish school in Khartoum, Sudan, with a salary of thirty pounds monthly. It was a financially attractive offer, and the job was a respectable one, which would secure for me a leading position in the Khartoum Jewish community. I discussed the matter with Ibn-Zahav, who functioned as chief strategic advisor of our family, and he felt I should accept the invitation. I told him I would think it over; a few days later, while I was in Tel Aviv, I wrote him a brief letter stating that I had decided to decline, because I did not want to leave Eretz Israel, especially in those difficult times.

My memory supplies another reason for my rejection of the Sudanese offer. I had to go down to Tel Aviv to take care of some business. It was a hot summer day; after the jitney I took reached the lowlands between the Judean hills and the seashore, the heat hit me and made me feel very uncomfortable. I started to think: do I want to live in such heat for years to come? Although I had no idea of the actual climatic conditions in Khartoum, knowing that the Sudan lay to the south of Egypt I assumed that it must have a torrid climate. Incidentally, the pleasures of air conditioning were at the time still unknown in Palestine.

A few days later, when I returned to Jerusalem, I met Ibn-Zahav at the funeral of Professor Alexander Eig, the botanist of the Hebrew University, who had died the day before of cancer, at the age of forty-three. On the way home we walked together and among other things discussed the Khartoum invitation. As I reported to my family in Budapest, in a letter dated July 31, 1938, Ibn-Zahav "said that my letter, which testified to my fervent patriotism . . . moved him to tears, and that he read parts of it to the chairman of the university alumni association, reproaching him that 'behold, you intrigued against *such* a man to deprive him of the university job!' "

By the summer of 1938 two years had passed since the inception of the Arab riots in Palestine. Although the attacks of the Arab gangs in the towns and on the roads took their toll and constituted an omnipresent danger, in the course of the two years the *yishuv* had learned to live with it and to consider it little more than a new variant of the road accidents that also were parts of everyday life. Added to this was the conviction that—were it not for the restraint imposed by the British on the *yishuv* and by the *yishuv* on itself—the Jews could make short shrift of the Arab gangs. Jewish confidence was also bolstered by the fact that in those two years much of the Arab violence had become internecine, that the number of Arabs killed by Arabs was greater than the number of Jews, and that all the riots and attacks had achieved nothing for the Palestinian Arab cause. The confidence of the young generation of the *yishuv*, myself included, vis-à-vis the Arab riots comes through eloquently in a letter I addressed to my parents on August 21, 1938 (in Hungarian):

> As far as the general situation is concerned, my impression is that the gangs are making their last desperate effort. Their sources of money from abroad have completely dried up, and they have announced that now they want to raise 25,000 pounds inside the country. This fundraising activity began with robbing the Nablus branch of Barclay's Bank of 5,000 pounds, and then, still in Nablus, of getting hold of a cashnote of 2,000 pounds. Thereupon the management of Barclay's decided to close its Nablus and Hebron branches. On the day following this decision the gangs "occupied" Hebron, and since the cash offices of both the Barclay's and the local post office were closed so that they were unable to get hold of any money, they set fire to both, abducted a few Arab policemen, and then took to flight to avoid the approaching British military contingent.
>
> Already a few days ago, following Papa's advice, I bought a strongbox (it cost one and a half pounds), and now I keep all our valuable papers in it. The strongbox is hidden in the depths of the wardrobe. It would seem that this is safer than the safe deposits of Barclay's. But to return to the gangs: all these acts are undoubtedly signs of the approaching end. Despite all the sluggishness of the British government, it is still not possible for the gangs to storm a town and occupy it by

force. They surely knew in advance that they could hold Hebron only for one or two hours at the utmost, and that the end of it would be a shameful rout and much loss of blood. That they nevertheless did it shows in what a desperate position they are. By the way, the publication and implementation of the new directions in the British government's policies on Palestine is now only a matter of a few months. As soon as it is decided, they will start to keep public order with a strong hand.

The Seafaring Book and Other Works

Late in 1937, or perhaps early in 1938, I rented an apartment in the Shiber House in Jerusalem together with my friends Israel Friedman and Moshe Gelberman (later Maggal). Located close to the center of the city, the Shiber House was a large and old two-story Arab-built structure, long and narrow, with a few steps leading from the street up to a wide terrace that ran along its whole length at a straight angle to the street. Under the terrace was an automobile repair shop that also used the yard onto which it opened. Several apartments in a row had their entrances directly on the terrace, and from it stairs led up to the second floor. In one of the first floor apartments lived two Sephardi girls of no uncertain reputation whose bleached hair contrasted sharply with their tawny skin inexpertly glazed over by shrieking makeup, on whose windows drunk or sober British soldiers would not infrequently knock, or rather bang, at all hours of day and night. Also on the first floor lived Molly Lyons, a very pleasant Canadian Jewish girl who worked as a journalist and published occasional articles on cooking and other domestic subjects in the *Palestine Post*. A few times I attended small parties she gave, and once, when I went to ask her to go over the English of one of the papers I wrote and found her alone, she bade me sit down next to her on a large floor cushion and playfully kissed me—I remember the fresh fragrance of her mouthwash—but I had no difficulty in resisting her advances. Some years later she married a Dutch Jew, Jaap Bar-David by name, and they established a literary agency.

Our own second floor apartment consisted of three rooms, a bathroom, and a kitchen. One of the rooms was shared by Israel and Moshe; my own room was large, with a vaulted ceiling, which I liked very much, and a window niche some three feet in depth, duplicating on a smaller scale the large arches of the ceiling. We rented out the third room, which was the smallest, to a seamstress, Hanna, a lapsed Orthodox Jewish girl from Meah Shearim, whose clients included some of the most elegant women of the city. It was in this apartment that I did most of the work on my book titled *Jewish Seafaring in Ancient Times*.

Many young authors, when they finish their first book, having invested all the ideas they had accumulated through the years up to that point, find themselves at a loss as to what to tackle next, what subject to put in the center of their second book. I, fortunately, was spared this predicament for the simple reason that while collecting material for my first book, my doctoral dissertation on the role of water in ancient Jewish life and lore, I had also assembled a profusion of data bearing on the related but separate subject of Jewish seafaring in ancient times. Hence, in January 1937, upon my return from Budapest to Jerusalem, I started to work on my second book right away.

The experience I gathered in working on my thesis stood me in good stead in writing the seafaring book. Because the work went more smoothly, it also gave me more satisfaction; in fact, I remember quite distinctly that I enjoyed working on it much more than I did writing *HaMayim*. Part of this was perhaps due to the fact that, in addition to subjects that paralleled those contained in *HaMayim* (such as folk customs, legends, terminology, etc.), the new book had also a story to tell: that of Jewish seafaring in ancient times. For instance, it included a chapter on naval battles in which I traced the role ships played in the wars of the Jews from biblical times to the destruction of the Second Temple of Jerusalem by the Romans in 70 C.E. Other chapters dealt with shipbuilding, the various types of ships (I found in the biblical and talmudic sources special terms designating no less than thirty different types of ships and boats), the crew, the voyage, maritime trade, the commercial and legal aspects of shipping (covering both religious and secular law), the port, terminology designating the parts of ships and the materials used in building them, as well as parables in which ships and seafaring figured and fantastic accounts of the experiences of Jewish sailors. In addition to all this, I felt that the book had a special timeliness, since it so happened that, while I was working on it, a port was being built in Tel Aviv—the first port to be under Jewish auspices in eighteen centuries. In fact, just a few weeks before my book was published, the port of Tel Aviv was actually opened. Accordingly, I decided to add to the title page of the book the words "On the Occasion of the Opening of a Gate to Zion in the Port of Tel Aviv." I still remember the elation I felt when I attended a big gathering in the largest hall of Tel Aviv in honor of the opening of the port; while speaker after speaker held forth about the economic, commercial, and political significance of the event, I felt that by writing my book I provided the historical background to it: I showed that the *yishuv* was following historical antecedents when it engaged in navigation, as its ancestors had in ancient times. Not unmindful of the debt I owed Professor Klein, I dedicated the book "To My Teacher and Master, Professor S. Klein, on His Fiftieth Birthday."

While working on the book I kept my parents informed of its progress. On July 26, 1937, I wrote to them (in Hungarian): "My work is advancing in big steps toward completion. Last week I wrote the chapter on naval battles, now, turning night into day, I am working on the chapter on the parts of ships. By the time Yitzhaq Grünbaum returns from the Congress, I want to receive him with the finished work."

The last sentence shows that long before I completed the manuscript I started to explore the possibilities of its publication. I knew Yitzhaq Grünbaum personally from several visits I paid him in 1933–1935, when he was head of the Jewish Agency's Immigration Department and many would-be immigrants from Hungary asked my intervention to secure immigration certificates for them. Now, in the spring of 1937, thanks mainly to the efforts of my father, the Israelite Congregation of Pest made a sizable donation in support of Jewish cultural activities in Palestine—34 pounds of it allocated to the Bialik Foundation, the rest to the Hebrew University. What I now discussed with Grünbaum was whether the Bialik Foundation could use this Hungarian grant for the publication of my seafaring book. I found him receptive to the idea. At his suggestion, I wrote to Dr. Sándor Eppler, secretary-general of the Pest Congregation, asking him to send an informal note to Grünbaum expressing the Congregation's interest in my book. Eppler duly dispatched the requested letter, but even after its receipt it took the Bialik Foundation another six to seven months before it finally and formally allocated the money for the publication of the book. Originally I had accepted Professor Klein's suggestion that the book should be published by the Hebrew Society for the Exploration of Palestine and Its Antiquities, of which he was president, but when it turned out that the Society had no money whatsoever with which to participate in the publishing costs of the book, I contacted Rubin Mass (who at just about that time had accepted the anthology of Palestinian short stories for publication), and he was willing to take it.

Studying Jewish seafaring in ancient times made me curious about contemporary ships—how they were built, how they looked, and how they functioned. About one such inquiry I reported to my parents on August 6, 1937 (in Hungarian):

While in Tel Aviv I paid a visit to the port in order to gather some live material for my book. I had to ask permission to enter the port from the office of the Otzar Mif'ale Yam (Maritime Enterprise Company). At first they did not want to give me permission because I had not arrived within the time fixed for visits, but then, when I introduced myself, one of the engineers immediately offered to escort me through the port and give me expert explanations. They are working

intensively in the port; especially interesting is the shipbuilding workshop in which they are building at present several keel-boats of 14 tons
each. In talmudic times the size of the average Jewish keel boat (called
s'fina roqedet [literally, dancing or jumping ship]) was ten tons. Of
course they don't as yet have the necessary technical terms, those will
have to be established by the Va'ad haLashon [Language Committee],
on the basis of the relevant chapter of my book.

The problem of terminology continued to interest me, and on August
15, 1937, I returned to it in a letter to my parents:

Despite all my busyness my work is proceeding with great tempo
toward completion. Last week I finished two important chapters, one
on the secular and religious laws connected with seafaring, the other on
the terminology. In this latter I collected close to 300 terms from ancient literature in Hebrew and Aramaic. This vocabulary will serve as
the basis for the establishment of a new seafaring terminology. Today
each field of activity is so clearly organized in my mind that they don't
interfere at all with one another. I return from a business trip, rest for
half an hour, after which I can completely immerse myself in my work,
as if nothing else existed for me. Or I sit at home and work, and suddenly Abiqsis appears—I must go with him right away here or there,
scholarship is instantly locked into a desk drawer, and the "businessman" rises to the surface.

Throughout the months of September 1937 to March 1938 each of my
letters to my parents contained references either to the progress of my work
on the seafaring book or to the progress of my negotiations with various institutions about its publication. In October I finished the manuscript, and
since there was still no definite word from the Bialik Foundation, I delivered
a copy of the manuscript to Joshua Hana Rawnitzki (1859–1944), the venerable editor of Dvir, the house that had published *HaMayim* in 1936. At
the same time I started to be interested in new research projects. One book
I planned to write was about the so-called Even Sh'tiyya (Foundation Stone),
the huge rock that had constituted the floor of the Holy of Holies in the
First and Second Temples of Jerusalem, and around which was built the
beautiful Dome of the Rock, popularly known as the Mosque of Omar. This
rock was considered in talmudic times the navel of the earth; innumerable
legends were woven around it by Jewish lore and, after the conquest of Palestine by the Muslims, also in Arab folklore. It was a fascinating subject, and
I even started to gather material for it, but then my politically minded
friends powerfully discouraged me by arguing that such a book could exac-

erbate the already tense relationship between the Arabs and Jews, since the Arabs would undoubtedly see in it a Jewish attempt to establish proprietary rights over that sacred spot. To this day I regret that first I listened to them and then later I was busy with other projects and never did return to the Even Sh'tiyya.

Another scholarly project that occupied me in those days and has remained unrealized was a study on "The Place of Judaism in the Development of World Views," which, as I wrote to my parents on October 28, 1937, was to "throw light, from a folkloristic point of view, on the relationship between man and his environment."

In March 1938 the Bialik Foundation finally gave its formal agreement to finance the publication of the book with the 34 pounds that the Israelite Congregation of Pest had donated to it, and I was able to begin its printing. At the time I was still part-owner of the HaMa'arav Press, which, of course, got the work. On March 28 I wrote my parents (in Hungarian):

> [. . .] the printing of the *Sapanut* [Seafaring] is going ahead at full steam—the book will have the effect of a real surprise. [. . .] In the last few weeks I have been working a lot. The printing of the *Sapanut* alone demands full-time work. Not only must the manuscript be checked over carefully again before sending each signature to the press and the first, second, and third proofs must be read, but I myself must prepare the drawings so that they should not cost extra money. I must take care of the paper, the binding, the dust jacket, and, in the meantime, conduct negotiations with the publishers about "who offers more?"

Finally, in May 1938, the printing of the book was finished. Its title page indicated that it was a book of the Jewish Palestine Exploration Society, published by "The Bialik Foundation" of the Jewish Agency for Palestine at the Rubin Mass Publ. House, Jerusalem. Mass widely advertised it in the Palestinian Hebrew daily press, and its critical reception, both in Palestine and abroad, was excellent.

In 1936 a committee was formed for the publication of a *Festschrift* in honor of the fiftieth birthday of Professor Klein. I was one of those invited to submit papers. I wrote an essay (in Hebrew, of course) titled "On the Beginnings of the History of Human Thought," in which I discussed the place of customs, rites, and beliefs in the early stages of human development. The preparation of the volume was repeatedly delayed, but finally, in the summer of 1938, I got my manuscript back with a note jotted on the top left corner of the first page: "We cannot publish your article. In the name of the editors, Zvi Harkavi. Jerusalem, 24 of Av 5698." Zvi Harkavi (b. 1908) was a religious teacher, writer, and editor; in retrospect, I can easily understand why he did not accept my article, which contained such statements as "To behave, to act, and to believe as did the fathers, the ancient generations— this was a general characteristic in the human psyche for thousands, or possibly tens of thousands, of years of its development." Since according to Jewish religious doctrine the world had been created precisely 5,698 years prior to that year, such a statement was unacceptable. I spoke in that essay repeatedly about the long "prelogical" stage of human development, research on the prehistoric period, the "abyss of the well of time," and the origins of sympathetic magic (I was strongly influenced at the time by Durkheim and Frazer) and discussed religion as a development out of primeval magic. All this was, of course, anathema to the religious Orthodox mind-set of the volume's editors. What I am puzzled about in retrospect is my thoughtlessness that made me select out of the several topics I was working on at the time precisely this one for submission to an editorial board composed of religious people whose reaction I should have easily anticipated. Perhaps I was in a rebellious mood and intended to demonstrate that I was not one to give in to religious censorship. As far as I can remember, the Klein *Festschrift* was never published.

The next scholarly tasks that engaged my attention included an investigation of rituals in the Second Temple of Jerusalem and a historical evaluation of the only Jewish historian of that period, Josephus Flavius. On October 2, 1938, I wrote to my parents (in Hungarian):

> I have been working a lot these last weeks. I finished an essay about the celebration of water-drawing at Sukkoth [Tabernacles], and sent it to *HaAretz* for its Sukkoth issue. In addition, since last year was the 1,900th anniversary of the birth of Josephus Flavius, I am working on a longer essay in which I shall sketch, in an interesting manner, the life and personality of Josephus. This too is largely ready. Besides those, of course, the study on Jewish fishing is also on the agenda. *Ha'Olam* sent me today 1.300 pounds for my book reviews it published. If one has peace and a minimum subsistence one can earn something additional with literary work.

My article titled "The Joy of the House of Water-Drawing" was published in the October 9, 1938, issue of *HaAretz*. However, the subject continued to interest me, and I devoted to it a major part of my first English book, *Man and Temple in Ancient Jewish Myth and Ritual,* published in 1947 by Thomas Nelson in Edinburgh.

A few weeks later I wrote to my parents rather dejectedly:

Oct. 30, 1938

[. . .] The Sokhnut [Jewish Agency] finally, after protracted negotiations, agreed to take, instead of the 200 copies they originally ordered, 75 copies of the *Sapanut*. This, more or less, is the standard here
in Palestine as far as keeping promises is concerned, and, I am afraid,
also with regard to the realization of hopes: forty percent. What is the
only antidote for this? One must increase very substantially both the
demands and the hopes.

About this time I felt that my knowledge of English had advanced sufficiently to enable me to write, or at least to try to write, scholarly papers in
that language, which was for me the fourth, after Hungarian, Hebrew, and
German. On December 22, 1938, I wrote to Father (in Hebrew):

[. . .] In the last few days I completed the reworking of my long
study on "Control of Rain," which will be published in the next volume of the *Hebrew Union College Annual*. In its new version the paper
comprises 50 pages, and I finished it in one week. I gave it to one of
my English friends to go over it and correct stylistic errors, but he
found almost nothing that required correction. I think that for this article I shall also get some author's fee. Also, my lecture on Josephus
Flavius was accepted by the radio, and soon they will schedule it. But
all this is but crumbs, scraps. One has no strength to concentrate on
serious scholarly work in these troubled days. The news about the
atrocities committed in the new border towns and the harsh edicts
about to be issued against the Jews rob us of our peace of mind. [. . .]

In my December 19, 1937, letter to my parents, quoted earlier, I mentioned my lecture at the Bet ha'Am (the People's House) on Jewish sea battles. In fact, I was a frequently scheduled speaker at the Bet ha'Am, the most
popular lecture forum in Jerusalem. Its matinees were held every Saturday
morning at 10:30, first at the Zion Cinema, and in later years at the Edison Cinema, the largest hall in Jerusalem, with a seating capacity of upward
of 2,000. Its executive board, which I was asked to join in 1938 (I believe),
consisted of several members, of whom only two, David Avisar and T. Ben
Hefetz, were active. In effect they *were* the executive and, with great skill
and devotion, kept the Bet ha'Am going on a shoestring budget. Admission
was free, and the audience consisted mostly of young people who represented a veritable cross section of the Jewish population of the city, about
evenly divided between Ashkenazim on the one hand and Sephardim and

Oriental Jews on the other. For many of those who filled the hall week after week attendance at the lectures was not only entertainment and an occasion to see and hear well-known personalities, but also a chance for a social get-together.

For me, to lecture at the Bet ha'Am was a fine opportunity to stand before a large and often restless public, to speak freely, to modify what I was about to say in accordance with the mood of the audience, to learn how to influence it, to project my voice (there was no microphone) to be clearly audible in the farthest reaches of the hall and of its balconies, and, in general, to hone my speaking ability. The general memory I have retained from those appearances is that I was a good and popular speaker, able to hold the attention of the audience and even to evoke enthusiastic response from it. I remember one occasion when the Bet ha'Am commemorated the death of Theodor Herzl, the founder of political Zionism, on the Saturday nearest to the 20th of Tammuz (in June or July), the day, according to the Hebrew calendar, on which Herzl died. Ben Hefetz asked me to give the commemorative address, and I, busy at the time with some pressing scholarly paper, suggested to him that after a few introductory remarks I would read out the last few pages from my father's Herzl biography in which he described the last days and the death of Herzl. The description is dramatic. I gave full range to my declamatory ability in reading it, and I remember how the audience listened with bated breath, in deadly silence, and how I myself became quite goose-pimply and shaken by the power I conjured up in bringing the printed pages alive.

On another occasion I had the opposite experience: the full house of the Bet ha'Am turned on me with hissing and booing and almost threw me down from the podium. The occasion for this rough treatment was the lecture I gave on Josephus Flavius to which I referred in my December 22 letter, which the Bet ha'Am asked me to give on the occasion of the 1,900th anniversary of his birth. While Jewish scholars value Josephus highly as a historian without whose works there would be an enormous gap in our knowledge of Jewish history in the postbiblical period, he himself remained a controversial figure due to the fact that, as he describes it in his autobiography, he behaved anything but heroically when under siege by the Romans. Josephus had been entrusted with the command of the Galilean fortress of Yodpat (Jotapata); from there he escaped, together with the remnant of his men, into a cave, where they all soon recognized that their position was hopeless. Josephus and his soldiers entered into a suicide pact. They agreed that they would draw lots: the one whose lot came up first would be killed by the one who drew the second lot, the second by the third, and so forth. Josephus tells that the chance of the lot (but could it have really been mere chance?) left him and a fellow soldier the last two to survive, whereupon he persuaded the other to walk out and surrender to the Romans. Brought in font of Vespasian, he prophesied to the Roman general that he would become emperor, which secured him favorable treatment. When this prophecy came true, Vespasian restored Josephus his freedom, and thereafter Josephus became something like the court historian of the Romans' Judaean campaign. He was taken by Titus, Vespasian's son, to Jerusalem and witnessed—from the relative safety of the Roman camp—the siege, conquest, and destruction of the city and its ancient holy temple by the Roman legions. Thereafter Josephus accompanied Titus to Rome and wrote his invaluable histories, *The Jewish War* and *The Jewish Antiquities*. As long as Josephus was alive, the Jews hated and despised him and did everything they could to harm him. Only much later did a less severe judgment of his conduct arise in knowledgeable circles. However, the atmosphere in the *yishuv* in 1938 was by no means favorable for a dispassionate reconsideration of the judgment passed on him by his embittered contemporaries. The *yishuv* was, for the third year, in the throes of Arab attacks and, in addition, felt utterly betrayed by Britain's abandonment of its obligations under the Balfour Declaration and the Mandate. Nationalistic fervor ran high and was accompanied by an impatient intolerance of anything less than adamant refusal of all compromise. I don't know how many of the young people who habitually attended the Bet ha'Am matinees knew who Josephus was and what he did, but those who had any familiarity with his life history were inevitably and vehemently predisposed against him.

When I accepted Ben Hefetz's invitation I knew that what I planned to say about Josephus was not what the people wanted to hear, but my experience made me confident that I would be able to sway them and have them accept my judgment of the commander, the historian, and the man. I could not have been more mistaken.

My view of Josephus, with whose life and work I had a more than passing acquaintance, was that he was, to begin with, a Pharisaic scholar—a scion of an aristocratic priestly family, related to the Hasmonean dynasty—who believed that the survival of the Jewish people required that they submit to the superior power of Rome, as did his contemporary, Rabban Yohanan ben Zakkai, who in 68 C.E. (within a year after Josephus's surrender) pretended to have died and bade his disciples smuggle his "corpse" out of besieged Jerusalem. Once safely outside the city, he threw himself at the mercy of Vespasian, prophesied to him that he would become the emperor of Rome (I did not plan to go into the problem of how the same story could be told of both Josephus and Yohanan ben Zakkai), and asked the Roman general to grant him "Jabneh and its sages," which request Vespasian fulfilled. In this manner, according to the talmudic account, Rabban Yohanan ben Zakkai, one of the most respected and most beloved teachers of the Mishna, was able to secure the continuation of Jewish law and lore, and thereby the survival of the Jewish people itself.

This was the approach to the controversial personality of Josephus I tried to put across in my lecture. I also drew a parallel between what Josephus did at Yodpat and what the prophet Jeremiah preached some 650 years earlier, when Jerusalem was besieged by Nebuchadnezzar, and the prophet tried to persuade the people to "fall to the Chaldeans that besiege you," so as to survive.

That Sabbath morning the Edison Cinema was fuller than usual, probably because the subject of my lecture, announced on posters all over the city, aroused more curiosity than the usual noncontroversial cultural issues that constituted the staple fare of the Bet ha'Am lectures. When I began my talk the members of the audience listened with the attention I was used to receiving, but as soon as they sensed the trend of my argument, a certain restlessness became noticeable, which swiftly developed into open antagonism, expressed in catcalls, whistling, and cries of disapproval. I tried to hold my own, but the noise increased to the point where I could no longer be heard, and the chairman of the meeting, David Avisar, felt impelled to intervene and try to quiet down the tumult. This is as much as I remember of the only occasion on which I was publicly booed, and, if my memory serves me right, had fists shaken at me. But, however I strain my memory, I cannot recall whether and in what manner I was able to conclude the lecture.

Later that year I gave a shorter talk on the same subject over the Jerusalem radio and also wrote it up in an essay that was published in Hebrew in the May 26, 1939, issue of *HaAretz* under the title "Josephus Flavius the Jew." That essay made the rounds of the Jewish press in Europe and America—I myself translated it into Hungarian and it was published in the March 1939 issue of *Mult és Jövő* under the title "The Historian—On the Occasion of the 1,900th Anniversary of the Birth of Josephus Flavius"; it appeared in French under the title "Traitor or Patriot" in the June 1, 1939, issue of the Paris bimonthly *La Terre Retrouvée*; in Spanish in the July 21, 1939, issue of the Argentinian bimonthly *La Luz*; and in English in the December 1939 issue of the *National Jewish Monthly* of New York.

Parallel with the foregoing activities, I was editing a volume of short stories by modern and contemporary Palestinian Hebrew authors in 1937. The idea of such an anthology was the brainchild of my friend Ari Ibn-Zahav, who at the time was smarting under the indignity of not being included in several poetry anthologies edited in those months by literary critics who were entrenched members of what counted as the *yishuv*'s literary establishment. Ibn-Zahav persuaded the Jerusalem publisher Rubin Mass to publish such a volume and then suggested to me, and to a young literary critic, Zvi Wohlmut by name, that we be its joint editors. All I remember about Zvi is that he was a few years younger, of Polish origin, and was a teacher in a Hebrew school in Jerusalem. After our collaboration on the volume I lost contact with him. That we would give proper place to Ibn-Zahav in the anthology was a foregone conclusion—not once in the course of our frequent consultations with him did we as much as touch upon the issue. However, we did include two stories of his—as we did of five other authors as well—for which we were taken to task by some reviewers.

Once we started working on the book we approached Professor Joseph Klausner and asked him to write an introduction to it. After we gave him the manuscript to look over he wrote an essay titled "The Ancient Nation in Its Renewal—in Place of an Introduction." In it he analyzed the features characteristic of the modern Hebrew short story from the point of view of how it reflected that renewal. The first edition of the book, published in 1938 under the title *Mivhar haSippur haArtziYisr'eli* (Anthology of Palestinian Short Stories, 336 pages), contained stories from 27 authors. The second, enlarged edition was published in 1944 in two volumes, ran to a total of 502 pages, and contained stories from 44 authors (among them only 4 women), the oldest of whom was born in 1848, the youngest in 1916. This time we included only one story from each author. The book was highly successful and was adopted by schools. The second edition was reprinted several times year after year. In contrast to its popular success, the critical reception of the anthology was mixed. Some of the negative reviews were, in turn, objected to by other critics; one review published by *Davar* Zvi and I felt to be so unfair that we sent a letter to the editor containing factual corrections. That letter in its turn was answered by one of the editorial staff members of *Davar*. In brief, our anthology stirred up quite a few ripples on the literary scene, which, as our publisher Rubin Mass assured us gleefully, was all to the good.

In 1938 I also lectured and chaired conferences at the Union of Hungarian Immigrants in Jerusalem, lectured over the Jerusalem radio on Jewish folklore, served as a member of the committee for the publication of the writings of Thomas G. Masaryk in Hebrew and as honorary secretary of B'rit 'Ivrit (World Hebrew Union), lectured at the Bet ha'Am on Yosef Meyuhas's book *The Fellahim*, wrote an introduction to my friend Israel Friedman's pamphlet on the social philosopher Joseph Popper-Lynkeus, and published an article in *HaAretz* urging the Jerusalemites to dig cisterns as insurance against the eventuality of the disruption of the water supply (this article was favorably commented upon by a "Reflection" in the *Palestine Post*). In the same year I published seven articles, six book reviews, and a translation into Hebrew of one of my father's Hasidic stories.

Two of the papers on which I worked in 1938, published in 1939, led to an unpleasant encounter between me and the rector of the university, Professor Abraham Fraenkel. Since I was an instructor of Hebrew in language classes offered by the Hebrew University, all my students matriculated there, and I was paid for this work by the university, I took it for granted that when I sent articles to be published in scholarly periodicals in America I could add the words "Hebrew University" after my name for the purpose of identification. Such mention of institutional affiliation was routine in all scholarly publications outside Palestine with which I was familiar. The articles in question were "The 'Control of Rain' in Ancient Palestine," published in volume 14 (1939) of the *Hebrew Union College Annual*, Cincinnati, Ohio, and "The 'Egla 'Arufa, or the Expiation of the Polluted Land," published in the same year in volume 30, no. 1, of the *Jewish Quarterly Review* in Philadelphia, the two most prestigious Jewish scholarly periodicals in the English language. When I saw my articles in them it gave me considerable satisfaction that they were the first contribution in both periodicals under whose author's name the words "Hebrew University" appeared.

Some time later I received a message from the office of the rector asking me to come to see him. When I went at the appointed hour, Professor Fraenkel told me that since I was not a member of the academic staff of the university—the Hebrew preparatory courses were not considered part of the academic offerings—I did not have the right to identify myself as being affiliated with the university. "Now," he said, "please write to both periodicals informing them of this and asking them to publish corrections to this effect."

I was more than taken aback. I felt that, quite apart from the injustice of the demand itself, were I to send off such letters that would put an end to any chances of publishing additional articles in those two foremost American Jewish journals, or in any English-language periodical for that matter. I don't remember how I responded to the rector's demand. I do not know who was my well-wisher who brought the matter to his attention—since he was a mathematician it was highly unlikely that he himself read American journals devoted to Jewish studies. Nor do I know whether his demand was based on his own personal view or was discussed and decided in some academic body. What I do recall is that I asked Dr. Magnes, the president of the university, to see me, on the assumption that, being an American, he would have a different view of the matter. When I told Magnes what the rector asked me to do, he smiled and said that the American usage was for individuals to identify themselves with the name of the academic institution to which they belonged, even if they were not faculty members but administrative officials or even students. "Leave it to me," he said, "and don't do anything."

I don't know what Magnes said to Fraenkel—I heard nothing further from either of them. However, when I subsequently published papers in American or other periodicals, I did not again use the name "Hebrew University," making sure not "to take in vain" the name of that august institution.

It must have been in the spring of 1939 that I spent a few hours in a prison in Jerusalem. This came about as follows: one of the students of the Hebrew University was caught by the British police in the commission of a criminal act (what it was I have long since forgotten) and was sentenced to a prison term or, possibly, was in pretrial detention. While in jail he petitioned the authorities for permission to sit for an examination he was due to take at the end of the academic year. When permission was granted, the university was notified that it could delegate a faculty member or official to bring the exam questions to the prison and supervise the prisoner-student while he worked on the test papers.

For some reason—possibly because I spoke English—I was asked to undertake the task. All I remember today is that, provided with the required identification papers, I went to the prison building, was locked into a room with the student, handed him the questions, and sat opposite him for probably three hours while he worked on them. I also remember that, after he finished, we chatted for a while. He told me about his offense, his sentence, and some things about his life, and I was so impressed that, after I got back home, I sat down and wrote an article about him and his exam in prison. I remember nothing at all of what he told me, of what I wrote, of the exam, or of what I did with the article. But my memory has retained the fact of the exam itself and the impression of the daunting atmosphere of the prison.

I remember a tiff I had in those days, with none other than Father's erstwhile disciple and lifelong friend Avigdor Hameiri (1890–1970). Hameiri, originally Feuerstein, was born in Hungary, served in World War I in the Austro-Hungarian army, and was captured by the Russians, but was released after the 1917 October Revolution. Early writings by Hameiri in Hungarian, under the pen name Albert Kova-Feuerstein, were published in Father's monthly. In 1921 Hameiri emigrated to Palestine, where he was to become a well-known Hebrew poet and writer, novelist, and translator. He founded and managed haQumqum (The Kettle), a satirical theater in Tel Aviv, most of whose material he himself wrote. Throughout my Jerusalem years I had occasional contact with Hameiri and more than once asked him to translate into Hebrew some of my sister's Hungarian poems, which he promised to do but never did.

It was in 1937, I believe, that a group of Hameiri's admirers, mostly of Hungarian origin, formed a committee for the publication of a jubilee edition of his writings. One of the books, *Massa' b'Europa haP'rait* (Voyage in

Wild Europe), I undertook to print at the haMa'arav Press, of which I was part-owner. For reasons I no longer remember, its production was delayed. In any case, when the delay grew longer than Hameiri could take, he wrote me a brief note, in Hebrew of course, every word of which I remember clearly to this day: "Raphael, you will pay dearly for this abuse of the holy of holies of my life, my unfortunate book. Only disgust keeps me from writing more to you. Hameiri."

I was, of course, taken aback by this outburst, and I remember that I answered not to him directly but to the committee in charge of the publication of his books. Of that letter of mine I can recall only the last sentence: "Since then I no longer know Hameiri."

The spat, however, proved only temporary, because I have in my files a copy of an invitation sent out by the Society of Composers and Authors to a meeting to be held on February 15, 1938, in the home of Professor Torczyner in Jerusalem to plan a jubilee celebration for Hameiri, which states that I would open the meeting with a brief talk about him.

That invitation also documents that Professor Torczyner was on friendly terms with Hameiri, and this explains how it came about that, undoubtedly at the suggestion of Hameiri, Torczyner invited him to give a talk to his class at the university. One of Hameiri's hobbies was what can only be termed dabbling in Hebrew folk-etymology, which took the form of suggesting fantastic derivations of Hebrew words from other, actually totally unrelated, Hebrew words. This was the subject on which Hameiri spoke to Torczyner's Hebrew linguistics class. I was present on the occasion, and what Hameiri said impressed me so much with its unabashed absurdities that some of it I remember to this day. He said, for instance, that *melekh* (king) was derived from the verb *molikh* (to lead), because the king is the person who leads the people. *Qir* (wall) was derived from *qar* (cold), because it protected from cold; *homa* (another word for wall) was derived from *ham* (warm), because it protected from, or provided, warmth. The verb *bana* (to build) was derived from *ben* (son), because a son built up his father's house. The noun *bayit* (house) was derived from *bat* (daughter), because a daughter was supposed to stay in the house, and so on and so forth. What I remember more clearly than these examples of Hameirisms is that I felt sincere admiration for Torczyner for his restraint and kindness in thanking Hameiri after the lecture for his original observations and explanations of Hebrew word origins, without uttering a single word of criticism, although with his superior knowledge of Semitic linguistics he could easily have demolished Hameiri and held him up to ridicule. On that occasion at least Torczyner was the perfect gentleman toward his guest. What he told his students when he next met them, without the presence of Hameiri, I of course do not know.

In 1942, when a series of Father's books was published in a Hebrew jubilee edition, one of those who contributed an appreciation of Father's poetry was Hameiri. He did it in the form of a long essay entitled "Joseph Patai the Poet," which was published in the beginning of the volume entitled *Poems: From the Rivers of Babylon to the Gates of Jerusalem.*

6

The Ingathering
of the Patais

Two Hebrew expressions are key terms in telling the story of the Jewish immigration to Palestine-Israel. One is *'aliya* (literally, upgoing), meaning the act of settling in the country. The other is *kibbutz galuyot* (ingathering of the exiles), denoting the process of the return to Eretz Israel of Jewish communities from all over the world.

The ingathering of the Patai family in Eretz Israel was a long and difficult process. Actually it began in 1924, when Father's father, R. Moshe Klein, settled in the Meah Shearim Quarter of Jerusalem, where two of his sons and one of his daughters also lived, and Father visited Palestine for the first time. It ended fifteen years later, in the fall of 1939, when my parents finally settled in Tel Aviv. In between Father came to Palestine almost every year, accompanied by Mother from 1934 on, staying in the country for longer and longer periods.

My sister Évi and I arrived in Jerusalem in the spring of 1933. In 1935 there were serious family discussions about the possibility of launching in Palestine a Hebrew-English counterpart to Father's Hungarian Jewish monthly, *Mult és Jövő*, which would have enabled Father and Mother to make their *'aliya*. In 1938 my brother Guszti (Saul) came and became a student at the Hebrew University. In the summer of 1939 Évi returned to Jerusalem from a two-year sojourn in Hungary, Switzerland, and France, with her little daughter Tirzah. And finally, in the fall of 1939, a few weeks after the outbreak of World War II, my parents too came to stay. Therewith all five members of the Patai family (or six, if we count little Tirzah) were ingathered in Eretz Israel.

Of the many relatives we had in Hungary on both Father's and Mother's side, only a very few survived the Holocaust. Some of the horrors done to members of my family in Hungary in 1944–1945 are related in my *Apprentice in Budapest*. Here I shall tell the story of my brother's and my parents' *'aliya*, as I was able to reconstruct it on the basis of memories, letters, and documents.

First Attempt

The *'aliya* of my parents from Hungary to Palestine was first suggested by me in 1935. As the situation of the German Jews deteriorated, both my sister and I became more and more preoccupied with the problem of how to persuade our parents to leave Budapest and settle in Palestine. The problem was not an easy one: from far off-Palestine, Germany and Hungary seemed awfully close, but in Hungary itself the Jews considered the German events nothing more than distant thunder, and the mentality of "it can't happen here" held them in its thrall. To this commonly shared feeling of being safe in Hungary were added Father's personal circumstances: his position was good and his journal continued to flourish, being acclaimed far and wide by both Jewish and non-Jewish literary and artistic circles precisely in the fall of 1935 on the occasion of its twenty-fifth anniversary. He himself was feted as the cultural leader of one million Hungarian-speaking Jews, his books continued to sell well—he himself published them in several successive editions under the imprint of *Mult és Jövő*—and he received more invitations to lecture all over Hungary and in the surrounding Hungarian-speaking Jewish communities of Czechoslovakia, Rumania, and Yugoslavia than he could handle. He was, without doubt, one of the most respected and beloved figures of Hungarian Jewry. The "big Pintér," as the multivolume standard history of Hungarian literature was commonly called (after its author Jenő Pintér), devoted several pages to a discussion of his poetry, writings, and literary influence, in a chapter titled "Joseph Patai and His Literary Circle." His home was the gathering place of young and not-so-young Jewish writers, poets, critics, essayists, scholars, and artists. As president of the Pro Palestine Federation of Hungarian Jews he represented for Hungarian Jewry everything that was valuable and attractive in the developing *yishuv* of Palestine and hence worthy of support by Hungarian Jews, while on his frequent visits to the Holy Land at the head of tourists' groups he stood for the best that Hungarian Jewry had to offer and was seen as a leader of that remarkable Jewish community, which had produced within the preceding half-century men such as Theodor Herzl, Max Nordau, Ignaz Goldziher, and Arminius Vámbéry, and a string of great poets, writers, artists, scholars, and scientists.

Knowing the position Father had in Hungary, I took it for granted that, despite his lifelong Zionist convictions, he would not be able to consider moving to Palestine unless an attractive field of activity were found for him there. I gave much thought to the problem and hit on the idea that if a Hebrew-English literary and artistic monthly, similar in scope and quality to his own *Mult és Jövő*, was launched in Palestine, Father could serve as its editor, thus continuing the kind of work in which he had been engaged for a quarter-century, and would find it attractive and challenging enough to leave behind what he had built up in Hungary. I must have spoken with him and written

to him about this idea repeatedly, but his extant letters do not touch upon
it. Only two of my letters contain references to this plan. In December 1935
I sent Mother and Father a lengthy epistle, most of which dealt with this
issue:

December 3, 1935 [in German]

[. . .] From Friday to Sunday I was in Tel Aviv. My friend Mischkinsky got married: Saturday evening he gave a small party, and he
counted on my presence without fail. On that occasion I visited the
painter Rubin and spoke to him at length about the possibility of
transplanting *Mult és Jövő* to Palestine, in Hebrew and English. Briefly
summarized, he opined as follows: the journal has an unquestionable
marketability in the country and would also arouse great interest
abroad, where today Palestine already counts as an intellectual center.
The journal should devote less space to *belles lettres*, and if so, only to
poems, while the main emphasis should be on criticism, society, arts,
music, theater, etc. The Hebrew and English parts should not be identical: the Hebrew part should, among other things, cover all intellectual
movements and phenomena of the Jewish world abroad and follow
them critically; while the English part should be devoted mainly to
Palestine. Kurt Blumenfeld has just become the head of public relations
at the Hebrew University: one should get in touch with him and devote
one or two pages in every issue to the affairs of the university, in both
English and Hebrew. This column alone would assure the journal a certain stature on the one hand and considerable distribution on the other.
   Now the problematical aspect: the financing. If it were possible to
interest Mr. Salman Schocken, the problem would be solved at one
blow. I don't know whether you consider it possible or proper to approach him directly, already now, in a letter, or perhaps in the form of
a precisely drawn-up exposé. If not, one should try to find some contact with him. Perhaps you have an idea in this regard: through whom
could one approach him? I myself would not be too shy to talk to him,
but I am afraid that I alone could achieve nothing with him. For him,
to have his publishing house put out such a journal would actually be
quite a small matter. But if he is not so inclined, one could seek other
ways, such as, e.g., to find, say, five interested persons who would be
ready to participate in the venture with 200 pounds each. One thousand pounds would cover all expenses for a year, including office employees. Still another possibility would be to interest Mrs. Persitz. You
could possibly suggest to her that you would invest the royalties due to
you for the Herzl book.

I beg you to consider and treat this whole matter with the greatest seriousness. As I hear, now even emigrants can no longer bring money out of Hungary, and it would be damned necessary to prepare the ground here in some way. I myself would, of course, put myself totally at the disposal of this project, just as already now, in these weeks that I shall still spend here in the country, I am gladly willing to do my best for it. In any case, I expect more precise instructions. [. . .]

At the end of my letter I returned once more to the subject:

[. . .] I want to emphasize that one must not drag out the matter. Just as a few months ago *Shulamith* was launched, which does not constitute serious competition for us since it is much too popular and magazinelike, in the very near future another, more serious, journal could start to appear, and that would once and for all cut off all chances for us. We must make use of these weeks while I am still here and am relatively free for such things. If I succeed in preparing the soil, we could perhaps bring out the first issue in the spring when I shall again be here together with you.

A few of the names mentioned and points touched upon in this letter seem to require some elucidation. Yitzhaq Mischkinsky worked at the time in the editorial offices of *Davar*, the Tel Aviv daily of the Labor Movement. Later he changed his name to 'Ivry, moved to New York, and became editor of the American Hebrew weekly *HaDoar*.

Reuven Rubin (1893–1974) was one of the most highly regarded painters in Palestine, whose moody landscapes fetched respectable prices by the 1930s. Articles about his art, illustrated with his pictures, were published in Father's monthly. Kurt Blumenfeld (1884–1963) was a German Zionist leader who settled in Palestine in 1933, where he became a member of the Keren Hayesod directorate and held other high positions in the Jewish establishment. He developed a Zionist ideology to appeal to Jews who were already assimilated and opposed Zionist cooperation with anti-Zionist Jews in the diaspora. On this latter issue I had a sharp clash with him in 1937, as described above and in *Apprentice in Budapest*. Salman Schocken we have already met in another context, likewise Mrs. Shoshana Persitz. Father's Herzl biography, originally written and published in Hungarian, appeared at that time in a Hebrew and a German translation at Omanuth Publishers, owned and headed by Mrs. Persitz. The journal *Shulamith* was a fortnightly women's magazine that survived for less than a year in 1935.

After mailing this letter I continued to be preoccupied with the plan sketched in it, and on the very next day I mailed my parents another letter about it:

After careful consideration and careful discussions in the narrower family circle, I wish to return to point 2 of my letter of yesterday. I think it would be best to try first to win Schocken for the plan, which could possibly be accomplished in the following manner:

Papa should write him a letter directly, in which he would set forth the matter in rough outline. The financial aspect should not be touched upon, only the proposal made that he should publish such a journal through his publishing house, to wit, not in Berlin where its present headquarters are, but in Jerusalem. Papa would put his collaboration as editor at its disposal for a year at no cost, and also otherwise would interest and attract the best contributors. From this proposal it would be apparent that Papa has absolute confidence in this undertaking. Practically it would mean that Papa, if the plan is realized, would spend a few months here, which he is used to doing in any case, and would personally take care of the publication of the first three or four issues. Thereafter he could, for a while, continue to supervise the journal from Budapest until his affairs there are wound down. One would have to explain to Schocken clearly the general direction of the journal, whereby the planned cooperation with the public relations department of the university, in which Schocken, as the university's minister of finances, will be interested, must not remain unmentioned. At the same time one could refer in a clause to the appearance of Papa's Herzl book in German and in Hebrew in the next few days, which will considerably augment his popularity in Palestine. All this can be written to Schocken in German, and in conclusion it should be mentioned that I, who was for several years Father's assistant and collaborator in the editorship as well as in the administration [of *Mult és Jövő*] and have for the past three years lived in Palestine, will visit him in the next few days in order to discuss the matter with him in greater detail and to present him with a few issues of *Mult és Jövő*. After such an introduction, I believe, my visit could not be taken as lacking seriousness or being undeserving of attention. In any case, I must simultaneously receive a carbon of the letter addressed to Schocken, perhaps accompanied by further instructions. I believe that such a letter, whose content is a proposal of this kind, can be addressed by Papa to Schocken even without knowing him personally.

At the same time I would also advise the following: Papa should write to Dr. Magnes, president of the university, and Professor Bergman, its rector, and possibly also to Kurt Blumenfeld, to each of them a letter of similar content, in which, however, the significance of such a journal for the university should be more strongly emphasized. The task of these gentlemen would be only to convince Schocken that the university would be glad to see the launching of such a journal, which would be published independently of the university and could be expected to achieve wide distribution within a short time (in English and in Hebrew), and by means of which a possibility would be created for the university to remain in permanent contact with the Jewries of the whole world. Similar letters could be sent also to Professors Klein and Klausner, who, on their part, should make their influence felt, whether on Magnes, Bergman, and Blumenfeld or directly on Schocken. Copies of all these letters should be sent to me. If Papa considers it advisable that I should also talk personally to the people concerned, this should be mentioned in the letters. Mr. Salman Schocken's address is: Ramban Street, Rehavia, Jerusalem. That of the others: Hebrew University, Jerusalem.

I believe that these are all the steps one can take at the moment. Should all of them fail, one can take the other steps mentioned in my letter of yesterday. Please tackle the matter right away.

Most respectfully,
Gyuri

No response from Father has been preserved in my files, but from my next letter it appears that his reaction to my suggestions was negative. Soon thereafter he fell ill (I don't know the nature of his illness), and all plans had to be kept in abeyance for the duration. Before the end of 1935 I wrote to him again, making use of the Hebrew typewriter I had acquired in the meantime.

Jerusalem, Dec. 24, 1935 [in Hebrew]

My Dear Papa:

The news about your illness saddened me greatly. May God heal you quickly and grant you full recovery, amen.

I can well understand that in this condition (which will surely improve quickly and will pass completely after a while) you are not in a mood to deal with new and remote plans such as the founding of a Hebrew-English journal in Palestine. I, of course, am ready to do everything I can and shall try to get in touch with Mr. Schocken through the public relations department of the Hebrew University, but without your help and consent I cannot do anything. You write in your letter that it is not consistent with your dignity to turn to people here and that when the time of your "redemption" comes you will come and make your 'aliya joyfully. Did you forget the wonderful and deep saying of Hillel the Elder, "If I am not for myself, who is for me, and if not now, when?" Especially in these days, now that after having finished the writing of my thesis I am working on the publication of the book, I see how important it is in every place and in every matter to engage in personal initiative and action. In response to your comment that it is not dignified for you to volunteer your services to all kinds of people, I want to mention to you two cases that took place recently.

One is that of Professor Torczyner, of whom it is known that when Hitler came to power in Germany he wrote to his friends in Palestine, entreating them, begging them, to provide him with any kind of position, be it the most modest, so as to be able to leave Germany and come to Palestine. Thereupon some people collected money for him and founded a chair for him at the university. The second is that of Dr. Rabin, who was a master and teacher at the Rabbinical Seminary of Breslau, and whose position there was not even in jeopardy for the time being—still he came to Palestine several times and searched until he found work as the principal of an elementary school in Haifa. Such cases have occurred not only once or twice, and I think that those people who acted in this manner were absolutely right, for it is better to seek new work and new livelihood in Palestine while one's basis of existence abroad is not yet shaken, and there is still a chance to save from there and transfer here whatever is possible and whatever one still has, rather than wait until the day of wrath and arrive here bereft of everything, as was done by most of the German Jews. Also from the point of view of dignity it is better to undertake steps and even exert efforts out of one's own free will and without external compulsion. This will not diminish the dignity of anybody.

However, I think that it is altogether wrong to approach this issue from the point of view of dignity. This concept cannot apply here at all. For isn't the immigration of every family a veritable small-scale redemption and a small ingathering of exiles? The question is merely how to diminish the birthpangs of this redemption. But let us not speak of this at length—all this has significance only in principle; from the practical point of view all I want is your consent to negotiate in your name, that is to say, to be permitted to tell those to whom I talk that if anything is settled here you are willing to undertake the editorship of such a journal. Only the editorship, and not the worries of budget and administration. [. . .]

Today was the meeting of the Krauss jubilee volume. Present were the members of the committee, professors, and bigwigs. I delivered a report on the results of the steps we had undertaken until now. Then Klein drew up a list of the scholars who will be invited to contribute articles to the jubilee volume and, of course, entered my name too.

From Hungary we shall invite the following scholars: Löw, Blau, Guttman, Heller, Yosef Patai. They all will receive a circular letter to be signed by members of the committee and its secretary, Raphael Patai.

Mail seems to be out of order recently: your last postcard, mailed from Budapest on Dec. 13, arrived only today, Dec. 24!

I assume that the press abroad will make a big thing out of the legislative council. Here we don't attach great importance to it, and all the Jewish parties agreed to boycott the council. In a talk with the High Commissioner they informed him of this.

Your son who longs to see you in the Land of Israel and greets you with love,

Raphael

Please collect the monies the Congregation and IMIT promised for the Krauss jubilee volume.

I do not remember whether we actually undertook any steps to realize the plan for the Hebrew-English journal discussed in the above letters, nor do the extant family letters contain any additional reference to it. I must assume that nothing else was done—in the first half of 1936 all my attention was concentrated on the printing of my doctoral thesis and preparing for the orals, as I have already reported.

Guszti's 'Aliya

The plan for my parents' immigration to Palestine lay dormant in the years 1936 to 1937, for reasons I no longer remember. It may have been due to the outbreak of the Arab riots, which discouraged many a would-be immigrant. Or perhaps there is simply no reference to it in those family letters that chanced to survive.

In any case, in the spring of 1936 my parents did come to Palestine on a visit and thus were present in June of that year at my Ph.D. award ceremony at the Hebrew University. Later that summer Évi and her husband Leon visited Hungary and stayed with our parents in Nyúl Street, and I myself spent July 1936 to January 1937 there.

As mentioned earlier, in March 1937 Évi's daughter Tirzah (or, as Évi spelled the name in her German letters: Thirsah) was born. Soon thereafter Leon succumbed to a psychiatric disorder—the delayed consequence of an accident. When it was no longer possible for Évi to live with him, she returned with the child to our parents' home in Budapest (in October 1937).

After several months of sojourn in Budapest she went on to Paris, where she worked in the offices of the World Jewish Congress for over a year.

The Arab riots started in the late spring of 1936 and did not subside until the outbreak of World War II. While they lasted—their intensity rose and fell in waves—they constituted a rumbling leitmotif in the background of which, whether it was loud or subdued, we were always conscious and which could not fail to influence the daily conduct of our lives as well as our plans for the future.

One of the demands of the Arab revolt was halting Jewish immigration. Giving in, the British Mandatory Government sharply reduced the number of the coveted immigration certificates allocated to Jews. The "illegal" immigration organized by various Jewish bodies succeeded in bringing to Palestine only about 15,000 refugees from July 1934 to September 1939, when the outbreak of the war put an end to it. Thus, the number of Jewish immigrants, which had reached 66,472 in 1935, dropped to 29,595 in 1936, to 10,629 in 1937, and to 14,675 in 1938, to rise to only 31,195 in 1939. It was evident that the Arab riots and the British response to them thus had a share in the responsibility—even if only indirectly—for the death at the hands of the Nazis of tens of thousands of Jews who would have managed to escape if the obstacles to immigration to Palestine had not been all but insurmountable. As for my parents, despite the Arab riots they continued with their traditional annual pilgrimage to the Holy Land—visiting evidently was one thing, settling permanently another—and each spring, even in the difficult years 1936 to 1939, they came for several weeks at the head of a group of tourists.

The next member of the Patai family after Évi and myself to settle in Palestine was our brother Guszti (later Saul). Guszti was almost eight years younger than I was (he was born on August 2, 1918), and by the time he finished high school (like me, he attended the high school of the Israelite Congregation of Pest) he was as eager to make his *'aliya* as I had been when I was that age. However, Father's position on Guszti's moving from Hungary to Palestine was the same as it had been when I finished my high school studies. In 1928, when I argued with him about my *'aliya*, he insisted that I go to Palestine only after having earned my Ph.D. from Budapest University. In 1936, when Guszti completed his high school studies, Father laid down the same rule for him as well, despite the marked deterioration of the position of the German Jews after 1933 that cast its shadow over all the Central European Jewish communities.

Accordingly, Guszti duly submitted his application to the Faculty of Philosophy of the Budapest University, was accepted (as in the case of my admission, Father's influence was strong enough to secure it), and in the fall of 1936 started his studies in chemistry. He was in his sophomore year when, on March 12, 1938, the German army entered Austria, and thereafter history inexorably proceeded to tilt the balance toward the position of the younger generation in our family, oriented toward immediate *'aliya* to Palestine, as against that of our parents, who endeavored to maintain the status quo as long as possible and considered Palestine only as a matter for the indefinite future.

The year and a half that followed the German occupation of Austria will always live in history as one of the most shameful periods in modern European statesmanship. The next day Hitler announced the *Anschluss* of Austria to the German *Reich*. On September 28 he issued his ultimatum: either the Allies agreed by October 1 that he take possession of the Sudetenland (part of Czechoslovakia) or he would go to war on that very day. On September 29–30 the infamous Munich conference took place, and the Sudetenland was thrown to the German wolf. But Hitler's appetite and daring grew: in March 1939 he occupied all of Czechoslovakia; on September 1 the Germany army invaded Poland. Thereupon, finally, a reluctant Britain and France were forced to declare war on Germany on September 3. Italy, although it did not enter the war at that time, was allied with Germany; this created a situation in which civilian shipping between Italian and British-controlled Mediterranean ports became, if not disrupted, irregular and uncertain.

Peculiarly—and characteristically—of all these great political upheavals that inexorably led the world into the greatest war it had ever seen, only faint echoes are found in my family's letters. References to the gathering storm are found mostly in Mother's letters, in frequent but vague exclamations such as "If only there were peace . . ." More rarely, Father too mentions world events in brief and sober tones. In a letter written from Budapest on March 14, 1938, the very day after the *Anschluss*, and signed by Mother, Father, and Évi, they discuss many small matters, such as the author's evening Father organized for the Hebrew poet Avigdor Hameiri, permission from the Hungarian National Bank to transfer 100 pounds monthly to the Jewish National Fund in Jerusalem, the busts of Évi and her daughter Tirzah being made by a talented young sculptor, etc. In between, as if they touched upon issues of the same order of magnitude, there are scattered questions such as "What do you say about world events?" and more pious wishes such as "Here in our house we live quite pleasantly, only, alas, one cannot pursue an ostrich policy for long. The general mood is very bad, but let us hope that it will be managed somehow."

A few days later, in another letter, again discussing dozens of minor literary matters, financial arrangements, and plans for the next Holy Land tour, Father refers in passing to "the Austrian events," which "disturbed everybody's equilibrium here to such an extent that the few people who have registered for the tour so far are now wavering, so that the whole tour is in doubt."

After the *Anschluss* the three Patai children in unison increased pressure on our parents to move to Palestine without additional delay, and, at the very least, to let Guszti go. I have no contemporary record of what Guszti himself did in Budapest to achieve his desire, but I have no doubt that he clamored for going with increasing urgency. I on my part supported him wholeheartedly and in my letters to our parents tried to bring them to the point of letting him go.

May 20, 1938 [in Hungarian]

Dear Mama and Papa:

[. . .] I can't understand why you don't write me more precisely about Guszti. If he really wants to come, steps have to be taken right away. The best thing is for him to send the requisite certificate directly to the university and to inform me simultaneously so that I can take the necessary urging and recommending steps. For, as Ibn-Zahav undoubtedly mentioned, they admit only a very limited number of students to chemistry; hence, the matter must be settled as soon as possible. As I indicated in my previous letter, I think it best that he should come here not just before the beginning of the fall term, but the sooner the better, so that he should have time before the beginning of university studies to familiarize himself somewhat with both the Hebrew language and life here. Chemistry keeps students busy from 8 in the morning to 6 in the evening, so that during the study period they barely have time and strength left for anything else.

If Guszti comes, I advise him to bring along all his clothes, including the winter suits and his dinner jacket (that miserable piece of clothing, alas, is here too to some extent the entrance ticket to good society), books, whatever he can. During the trip this is a burden, but as against that here it is very important that he should have whatever is necessary, otherwise every little thing means expenses . . . As far as Guszti's life here is concerned, of course I shall take care of him morally as well as materially to the best of my ability. [. . .]

While the preparations for Guszti's *'aliya* were moving ahead in Budapest, I felt that I had to reassure my parents, and especially Mother, that conditions in Palestine did not constitute an acute danger for me and, once Guszti arrived, for him. On July 8, 1938, I wrote to her (in Hungarian):

Dear Mama:

You have surely read in the papers about the events raging here in the country. Probably the press abroad reports everything with the usual exaggerations and embellishments. The fact is that here basically everybody is glad—some in secret, some openly—that the patience of the *yishuv*, or rather that of a certain sector, the Revisionists, has finally run out, and that at long last they have begun to respond, to give the proper and due response, to the "neighbors." Of course, nobody has clear knowledge of the incidents, only rumors are afloat: the police "investigate" as is their duty—but find nothing, as is their intention. Jewish patience and restraint have snapped as a result of the execution of Ben-Yosef. That gave a powerful impetus to the impatient embitterment. [. . .]

Recently I have prepared a lecture on "Jerusalem in the Past and Future." It was scheduled in the Bet ha'Am, but because of the unrest this is already the second Sabbath on which the Bet ha'Am has canceled its meetings. The reason: they are afraid that after the lecture, when the crowd of two thousand Jews spills out into the street, they may start some demonstration. This apprehension is especially justified in connection with my lecture, which will have a historical-political subject and a rousing tone.

Sh'lomo Ben-Yosef (1913–1938) was a member of Betar, the Revisionist-Zionist youth movement, who, together with two comrades, tried to attack an Arab bus in the Galilee in retaliation for the murder of Jews by Arab terrorists. Their attack failed, the three were arrested, and Ben-Yosef was sentenced to death and executed in Acre prison on June 29. He was the first Jew to be executed by the British in Palestine; on the day of his execution riots broke out in Tel Aviv, and the crowd clashed with the British police. Ben-Yosef became a hero of the Jewish resistance.

About the time I wrote the above letter Guszti undertook in Budapest the first two steps necessary to prepare his move to Jerusalem: he applied to the Hungarian authorities requesting the extension of his passport to enable him to leave the country and submitted his application to the Hebrew University for admission as a junior in the department of chemistry. Both applications were granted after some delays, and not without some personal efforts. I in Jerusalem did my best to make sure that the university approved his application without the usual procrastination. On August 21 I was able to inform our parents that a few days earlier Guszti's certificate of admission had been mailed by the university to the Palestine Office in Budapest and that on that basis he could apply to the British Consulate in Budapest for an immigration certificate to Palestine.

A week later I informed Guszti that the academic year in Jerusalem would start on November 8 and advised him to come earlier, to have time to take care of the registration formalities. I suggested that he take the ship leaving Trieste on September 28, which would enable him to spend the High Holy Days (the Jewish New Year fell on September 26 and 27) with our parents at home. I also advised him to bring along a *Loden* overcoat with a detachable lining, because "occasionally it is very cold here in the winter and there is a strong wind." I informed him that I had found out that there were no prescribed textbooks in the chemistry department and that English and German books were used in preparation for the exams. Still, I recommended some eight or ten texts, adding that the main thing was that they should be books published within the last ten years. On September 5, 1938, I asked Guszti to bring me a big Hungarian-German dictionary, as well as some eighteen to twenty of my old books, which I needed for my work.

As the day of Guszti's departure approached, Mother became more and more unhappy about being deprived of the presence of her youngest child, the last one still in the parental home. It so happened that a short while before Guszti was due to leave Évi actually left Budapest for Geneva and Paris, and on that day Mother wrote to me:

[undated, probably August 1938; in Hungarian]

Dear Gyurikám:

We have just now taken Évi to the train station. It surely would be good if the family would not have to be torn apart all the time. The parting from Guszti will be even more difficult—he goes farther away and into a more insecure place. The papers write all kinds of things, and one lives in constant tension . . . Guszti is making the rounds of offices in connection with his passport, Papa in connection with his citizenship. Both are promised, but not yet in hand. Today we expected the certificate, but it has not come. Guszti does not look well, his stomach is somewhat nervous—I beg you, look after him in Jerusalem, see that he eats regularly and not too heavy food. As a matter of fact he knows more about cooking than you and will surely prepare a warm supper or a breakfast occasionally.

Soon after her arrival in Paris my sister Évi, who had always felt that she was the one who had the best insight into the problems of the Patai family, wrote me a detailed letter telling of her concern about how Guszti—twenty at the time—and I would get along once we were alone together in Jerusalem, without the cushioning presence of the rest of the family. She wrote on September 1, 1938 (in Hungarian):

[. . .] If Guszti should go out, I have something to say concerning him. The kid is terribly nervous, due, I believe, to no small extent to the fact that for about a year he has been living the life of a monk be-cause of a girl. Apart from that, he is not like you or me, but is very ex-citable, vehement, and undisciplined. I beg you, take care of him, if you maintain your authority in his eyes, and have a heart-to-heart talk with him, the two of you will get along wonderfully, for he has never had a single real friend, but only the kind to whom he gave moral support, but who, because of their lower level, meant no support for him. He has now immersed himself in chemistry—this should be encouraged so that he should have no time to commit some madness by any chance, to join the Hagana, which has no significance at all now except of endan-gering one's life . . . I cannot even start to enumerate what other thou-sand reasons may cause him to be, alas, so nervous—in any case, do try to treat him properly. I, always with a maximum of patience, got along fine with him: I simply took no notice of his vehemence and sundry ex-aggerated things. With Papa he had squabbles more than once, but Papa never lost his patience with him, because we all saw that when he was nervous he was unaccountable. One has to treat him motheringly, that is the best way—I also must tell you that Mama, in her rundown condi-tion, was very frequently nervous and absolutely unjust toward him, so that he was justifiably embittered about it. I know you have enough worries in your own life, but I must at long last tell you: our parents were concerned the least about Guszti, and now Fate too is unjust to him, for while you and I had everything in our "critical" years, he, in the years of his puberty that are ending only now, saw only worries at home, a nervous atmosphere, tight finances, and heard, very frequently, "Guszti, leave us . . . Guszti, don't disturb us . . ." In the house, al-though he was the youngest, he has for many years always played the last fiddle, even though he was vehemently *zärtlichkeitsbedürftig* [in need of tenderness], just as I was. A thousand things press upon him, the conditions doubly so, for he feels that he should study and at the same time earn money—and with all that he has a lot of inhibitions: for work the doctor prescribed for him glasses of only one-half or perhaps one-quarter of a diopter, and you should have seen how beside himself he was in those days, and how often he said, as if inadvertently, "although I can't see through one eye . . ."

I know that if you two live together you will have to swallow plenty from him until an unconstrained *Kameradschaft* [comradeship] develops between you—but try to make out of him a harmonious, self-assured, quiet person, because today, alas, he is the opposite of all that. In addi-tion, he is distrustful and believes (or so I feel) that you look down upon him, don't think him an equal, etc., etc.

I hope you won't be angry that I burden you with all this, but vis-à-vis Guszti a task awaits you, you yourself will see this as soon as he arrives, and I wanted to throw some light on the difficulties. Guszti is inclined to be, without reason, reckless—one incorrectly interpreted word is enough to make him rush into danger. Alas, for the time being there is nothing in him of your disciplined sobriety. I don't even know after whom he takes. Also, often he is in a melancholy mood for days . . . in a word, his nerves are in a mess.

Gyurikám, just as you helped me through the most critical months of my life, so help him now during his first months in Palestine that will be critical for him. I have nothing else to say about this, but I had to pour out my heart to you concerning Guszti, this heart in which in any case enough "difficulties" remain.

I still remember how taken aback I was upon reading this letter that told me about things of which I had not the slightest inkling. Every point Évi touched upon was totally new to me, and I simply could not believe that what she wrote was based on actual observation and was not rather merely the product of her proclivity to exaggeration that I had long known was a basic trait in her personality. Nevertheless I responded with restraint and confined myself to the concrete arrangements I felt could be made. I replied on September 10, 1938 (in Hungarian):

I got your letter, and first of all I want to thank you for writing about Guszti. Although I cannot imagine that his nervous state should be as bad as you describe it, even if there is some exaggeration in your report I shall do everything possible to create a good and friendly relationship between him and me and shall be helpful to him in every respect. I think it will be best if we don't live in one room—that could be difficult for both of us. Instead, I shall give notice to the boys who live in the room next to mine and shall place the kid there, even though that will mean a slight financial burden, but in the long run it will be very salutary.

Let me add here that, as far as I can remember, from the very first moment after Guszti's arrival the relationship between us was brotherly and harmonious, and, in fact, we became very close to each other. It was the first time that I had an adult brother, and I remember the warm feeling I had when he and I engaged in long conversations to while away the hours when we had to keep night watch on the roof of a house as members of the Hagana—needless to say, despite my sister's and my mother's warnings Guszti and I joined the Jewish self-defense organization very soon after his arrival.

My long-planned lecture on "Jerusalem in the Past and Future" finally took place on September 10, 1938, in the Bet ha'Am. The same evening, in a long letter devoted mostly to Father's early efforts to find a position with the Palestinian Friends of the Hebrew University, I reported to my sister briefly (in Hungarian) about the audience's response:

> This morning I lectured at the Bet ha'Am in the Edison Cinema. The house was full, there was an audience of some 2,000, and they listened with concentrated attention to my lecture, or rather speech, about the impossibility of forming a Jewish state without Jerusalem as its capital. It was a political subject but I treated it from the historical point of view, and while doing so did not refrain from daring attacks on the British government. It was very successful: I was often interrupted by applause; after it many people came up to me saying they would like to talk to me, and one of them instantly suggested, in the name of some society or organization, having my talk printed. If it is published, I shall send you a copy.

The next day, in a letter to my parents, I added that I was applauded especially when I demanded that Jerusalem should have a Jewish mayor, and remarked rather caustically, "All this only goes to show that it is with subjects having 'topical timeliness' that one can achieve real success, which is very difficult to attain with serious work. But, of course, all this does not make me swerve from scholarship." Then I returned to the current situation:

> These days the Arab contingents of the police stations along the Jerusalem–Tel-Aviv highway are being successively replaced by Jewish ones. This is being done because it has happened several times that Arab policemen by the dozens simply went over to the gangs, taking along the whole arsenal of the police station. In this connection it is also rumored that all the Arab policemen, numbering some 2,000, will be dismissed, and that, as against that, the government plans to organize a 6,000-man-strong Jewish legion! What is true of this one cannot know as yet for sure, but, if realized, the security situation in the country will greatly improve.

A week later I was able to acknowledge receipt of information about the date of Guszti's departure. First, however, I discussed the general situation:

Jerusalem, Sept. 18, 1938, Sunday
Bezalel Str., Shiber House [in Hungarian]

Dear Mama and Papa:

I see from Mama's letter that she gets unnecessarily and excessively worried about the situation both here and in Europe in general. As far as the general situation is concerned, the impression is that, for the time being, at least in the next few weeks, no war will develop out of the present conflict. England is not yet sufficiently armed and wants to gain time. Of course, one cannot know what will happen in a few months or a few years. And as for the situation here, it appears that the government, after all, is slowly beginning to proceed more energetically against the gangs. Last week the troops killed some 150 bandits, quite easily, shooting them down with machine guns from airplanes. Of course, in the meantime the gangs continue their attacks. In the past week they killed, among others, Dr. David Mossinson, the only son of the headmaster of the Herzliya high school, with whom, I believe, Papa went from here to Trieste on the ship. However, the activities of the gangs result each time in such great losses on their part that even if there are thousands of them they cannot go on for long.

Having thus given my parents the informed view of the man on the spot, I continued by assuring them that I would take good care of Guszti and provided him with some brotherly advice:

I am glad that finally the date of Guszti's departure has been set for Oct. 12. This means that he should arrive in Tel Aviv on Oct. 17. I am planning to go down to Tel Aviv a few days earlier to take care of a number of things that have accumulated in the meantime (Boruchov, etc.), then we shall spend a few days there together, and then, choosing the vehicle and the time with due circumspection, we shall come back together to Jerusalem.

As for "keeping an eye to him," you can rest assured he will be in good brotherly hands with me. There is no need for him to bring me anything apart from the books I mentioned in my last letter. But as against that it occurs to me that he could bring along instruments needed for experiments, retorts, and so forth, and he could set up here in my kitchen a private laboratory so as to be able to work quietly at home in the evenings. If I remember correctly, Professor Farkas, when he visited Budapest, got all kinds of such pieces of laboratory equipment as donations for the university. Guszti too could perhaps get similar gifts, from the same or other sources, for the university, and, of course, it would not be necessary to hand over each item to the university, but he could retain for himself whatever he needed. By doing so he would achieve on the one hand that his own work would be facilitated and on the other that he would make the university duly indebted to him. The shipping costs could be covered by Papa out of the money the university now has there. And as for the materials necessary for the experiments, Guszti could obtain them here in the university laboratories.

In a letter no longer extant Mother must have told me of additional difficulties that had arisen in connection with Guszti's departure, for a few days later I wrote:

Sept. 22, 1938 [in Hungarian]

Dear Mama and Papa:
This morning, immediately upon receipt of your letter, I phoned Ibn-Zahav at the university. In the meantime he too received Papa's letter and told me that he would undertake all the steps in the matter. However, I was not satisfied with that, but stormed into the Sokhnut [Jewish Agency], and there, at the immigration department, I found out from Giller that in Poland, where the [British] consul caused similar difficulties because of the military duty, the problem was solved by stamping the visa [to Palestine] not in the passport, but on the [immigration] certificate itself. Of course, I don't know whether we can get the British consul in Budapest to do the same. In any case, Giller said that as soon as the university applied to them officially they would contact the Government Immigration Department, and he was sure that they would settle the matter. But it is also possible that the university will not even need to resort to the intervention of the Sokhnut, but will apply directly to the government, which, in such cases, on its own instructs the consul in question by cable. Tomorrow morning I shall again talk to Ibn-Zahav to find out what he did in the matter. If the matter should nevertheless drag on, and if by the time you receive this letter it should still not be settled, then have the Palestine Office of Pest send a telegram to the Department of Immigration of the Jewish Agency asking for their intervention and immediate disposition. The telegram must be sent in the name of the Palestine Office of Pest, because that is the official representative in Budapest of the Sokhnut's Department of Immigration, and at its request they will have to do everything possible. But I hope this step will not be necessary, because the problem will have been settled in the meantime. Moreover, I request that on the same day on which Guszti boards the ship you send

me a telegram so that I should know in time when he will arrive and have enough time to choose the day and the hour for going down to Tel Aviv to meet him.

My "storming into" the offices of the Sokhnut must have resulted in some action, but in the meantime another difficulty arose: the border between Hungary and Yugoslavia was closed, as Mother informed me in a letter that crossed mine:

[undated, probably Sept. 20, 1938, in Hungarian]

Dear Gyurikám:
It's no use for you to write in your last letter that I worry too much about the situation, I cannot help it. When there will be peace here and in Palestine, my spirits will calm down . . . About Guszti's affair you are surely informed: we are waiting for the promised telegram of the British government to the British Consulate [in Budapest], and, thereafter, that the borders here should be opened up again. Then he can go. As you see, life is quite complicated. But let us hope that ultimately everything will be in order. Otherwise, my opinion is that you should by no means go to meet Guszti. Wait for him in Jerusalem, and if the situation quiets down you can go together to Tel Aviv . . . We have provided Guszti with a complete outfit—he felt that this would do him no harm here either, he was quite out-at-the-elbows. But, of course, he would prefer to wear out his shoes on the cobblestones of Jerusalem . . .

A day or so after Mother wrote this letter Guszti was actually able to leave Budapest. His first stop was Zagreb, Yugoslavia, where he had to wait for several days until his ship sailed from Split to Haifa. While he was in Zagreb, and subsequently while he was on his way from Split to Haifa, my parents wrote to him frequently. Father called Dr. Sik on the phone, and both he and Mother did everything they could to forestall any problem he might encounter. In several of her letters Mother complained that Guszti did not write her frequently enough and in sufficient detail. While to me she wrote that I should take good care of Guszti, she asked him to try to improve my diet: "It is a pity that you did not learn to cook, so you won't be able to improve the diet substantially; but still, you know a little, and with goodwill you can still give it a lift. I beg you, take care in this respect of Raphael, who is capable of living, apart from the midday meal, on nothing but tea and bread and butter, although precisely with his constitution he should'nt do this." Then she went on to express her concern about the relationship between us two brothers: "Otherwise, too, I beg you to be patient with him, I am terrified by the spectacle that possibly you two won't get along. Think of our difficult position, psychologically and otherwise; it must not happen that in addition to the worries caused by fate and today's life there should be something else too . . ."

On top of all this, Mother was apprehensive lest Guszti join the Hagana. She wrote, "We did not discuss before you left that you *promise us not to join any military or defense formation*, but you know that we want this of you. I hope I can rely on this. You will serve the country as a chemist, and may God grant that it should be in peace and not in war! Take care of yourself on the way, and especially and naturally also in Jerusalem. According to Reb Hile Raphael does not live in a good neighborhood, it is not advisable to go out there in the evening . . . God bless you!"

Reb Hile was Father's brother Yehiel Klein, who lived in the Meah Shearim Quarter of Jerusalem, where he tried to supplement the allocation he received from the Hungarian Kolel (see above, chapter 4), by manufacturing black shoe polish. At the time of the above letter he was in Budapest to sell *ethrogim* (citrons) for the approaching Sukkoth holiday. Why he should have thought that I did not live in a good neighborhood is not clear to me. The Shiber House, in which I had my apartment, was located some 200 yards from Ben-Yehuda Street, the central shopping area of Jerusalem, and in the immediate neighborhood of the Orion Cinema, one of the largest movie theaters in the city. Throughout the years that I lived there I never had the slightest feeling of insecurity.

On October 4 (Yom Kippur eve) I sent a letter to Guszti, addressing it to the *Princess Olga* in Haifa harbor and giving him detailed instructions how to proceed from Haifa to Jerusalem. In the event, Guszti arrived in Jerusalem without any mishap on Friday, October 7, in the afternoon. I had not seen him since January 1937, when I had left Budapest and returned to Jerusalem after a sojourn of several months in the parental home. In the time that had passed since then he had developed from a boy into a young man, tall and strong, who knew what he was after, self-assured and eager to embark on his course of studies and find his place in Jerusalem.

Two days later (October 9) we both wrote to our parents. Guszti described his voyage and explained that if our parents had received no letters from him from Zagreb it was due to problems with the mail. I wrote:

> The kid has happily arrived, as we indicated in our telegram. It was really unnecessary for me to go to meet him in Haifa—he and his friend Peter found the way to Jerusalem. I can see that he feels well here, liberated somewhat from the atmospheric pressure. Professor Klein received both of us in a very friendly way, with the love I am

used to from him, likewise the Ibn-Zahavs. We also looked in at Reb David's store, where we greeted him and Yantev. Tuesday morning, after the holy day, I shall introduce the kid to the university. I received Mama's and Papa's letters, also the material for Papa's book. Please don't let me wait long for the rest so that the printer should have no excuse for postponing the work.

Ibn-Zahav asked me, first of all, to tell Papa to forgive him for not writing directly: he is very busy with writing his latest epoch-making work. He asks that you should advertise in *MéJ* the publication of his book (the *Zappatim*); perhaps it will be possible to sell a few copies. He does not lay claim on money, in case there should be some profit—which, of course, I think most unlikely in the present circumstances—he puts it at the publisher's disposal. In addition he has this request: he is working now on a new novel that will deal with the fate of those refugees from Burgenland who lingered for months on a barge on the Danube. He asks Papa to inform him of everything he knows about that incident; he thinks that several of them spent a few days in Pest. He is interested in knowing from whom they got help, clothing, food, to what extent the Isr. Congr. of Pest helped them, and what was the fate of those who got no immigration certificates. Please answer him as soon as possible: of course, it is unnecessary for Papa to enter into research in this connection, write to him only what you can find out easily. If Papa has no time, let Mama answer these questions in German.

I don't think it is necesary to emphasize that my brother Saul will be well looked after in my house in every respect. I shall take care of his development in the right direction both mentally and physically. This afternoon we used the hours of rest for having him read my latest article, which was published this morning in the leading position of the holiday issue of *HaAretz*. I am satisfied with his knowledge of Hebrew and shall try to make sure that, insofar as he will have time (left over by his scientific work) to lead a social life, this should take place as far as possible in English circles so that in this way he should improve his English through practice.

Considering the advanced hour and the approach of the holy day I conclude my letter with many kisses to Papa and Mama,

Your loving son,
Raphael

Reb David was David Ehrenfeld, whose mother was Father's sister. He was married to Malke, a daughter of Father's brother Reb Yehiel, and had a small grocery store in the Geula Quarter of Jerusalem. Yantev was Yom-Tov

Klein, Father's youngest brother, who, like all Father's family, was extremely religious and lived in the Meah Shearim Quarter, in the Bote Ungarn. The article to which I refer, published in the October 9, 1938, issue of *HaAretz*, was titled "Simhat Bet haShoeva" (The Joy of the House of Water-Drawing) and described the joyous festivities held in the Temple of Jerusalem in connection with the Feast of Sukkoth (Tabernacles), arguing that they were essentially rites aiming at securing the rainfall that was due to begin soon thereafter, the precondition of all material well-being in the country. A year later a greatly expanded version of that article was published in the *Hebrew Union College Annual* of Cincinnati, Ohio, under the title "The 'Control of Rain' in Ancient Palestine: A Study in Comparative Religion."

After the arrival of Saul (Shaul in Hebrew), as Guszti was called from then on, in Jerusalem most of the family letters centered on the problem of our parents' *'aliya*. On October 1 Guszti wrote to them (in Hungarian):

> I arrived here a week ago yesterday and already I feel as if I were a native Jerusalemite. The city has now been quiet for several days: only the constantly changing political situation disturbs the spirits. Today we got the news that Hungary and Czechoslovakia have mobilized. We don't know how much is true of these rumors, but in any case they fill us with anxiety about the future fate of European Jewry in general and the future fate of our family in particular. When I was here in Jerusalem a year and half ago, that was the first time in four years that all the five members of the Patai family were together. I see in that a promising sign and hope that very soon we shall all meet again in Jerusalem. *Bim'hera b'yamenu v'nomar amen* [Soon in our days and let us say amen]!

A week later Guszti concluded another letter (dated October 23) with:

> I think it is superfluous to write about how well I feel. But it is likewise superfluous for me to write that I shall never feel completely well as long as several members of the family are in the Galuth [Diaspora]. We are getting very bad news from Europe. It is high time that Papa and Mama should come out, not to mention Tirzah . . .

Again, in his October 30 letter Guszti wrote: "Yesterday we were at the movies with the Ibn-Zahavs. They were very pleasant, as usual, only they cannot understand, and neither can I, why our parents don't make more serious preparations for coming out. *Im lo 'akhsav ematay*" [If not now, when?].

While Father Abroad Seeks Support . . .

My parents' transplantation from Budapest to Palestine was much more difficult than that of my brother Guszti. What Father would have liked most was to be invited to the Hebrew University to teach medieval Hebrew poetry. For several years, on the occasion of his visits to Palestine, he used to be invited to give one or two guest lectures at the university on that subject, which he had researched many years earlier at the Bodleian Library in Oxford. Subsequently he published a large anthology of Hebrew poets, in several editions, in his own fine Hungarian translation, with historical introductions. Another subject on which he lectured was "The Bible in Hungarian Poetry." Now, in 1938, I arranged for the publication of a collection of these lectures and asked Professor Klausner to write a preface to them, which he did with his customary friendliness. The book was published in 1939 by Rubin Mass, in Jerusalem, under the title *MiS'fune haShira: Hartza'ot ba-Universita ha'Ivrit* (From the Treasures of Poetry: Lectures at the Hebrew University). The publication of such a book, I felt, should help our friends on the faculty and in the administration of the university to succeed in having Father invited to teach at that august institution.

Also in the fall of 1938 Father devoted one issue of his monthly to the Hebrew University on the occasion of the fifteenth anniversary of its foundation. In preparation for that issue I wrote to a number of Jewish political and cultural leaders, including British Chief Rabbi Joseph Hertz, Viscount Herbert Samuel (the former British High Commissioner of Palestine), Dr. Chaim Weizmann (president of the World Zionist Organization), Justice Gad Frumkin (member of the Supreme Court in Jerusalem), Chief Rabbi Judah Loeb Landau of Johannesburg, South Africa, and Mrs. I. M. Sieff (director of education in the Government of Palestine). I asked each of them to send a short contribution, possibly in the form of a "message." I wrote these letters on the stationery of the Hebrew University, and the university mailed them for me. Of all this I reported to Father in my letter of September 18, 1938. Several of the addressees responded positively, and their articles, translated into Hungarian by my brother Guszti and me, were actually published in the November 1938 issue of *Mult és Jövő* At Father's request, I also sent him photographs to illustrate the university issue on September 22, 1938.

Apart from this, Father in his capacity as unofficial cultural ambassador of the *yishuv* to Hungary was constantly busy with the affairs of the Hebrew University. He lectured about the university all over Hungary, helped the professional fund-raisers that the Department of Public Relations (called at the time less euphemistically Department of Publicity) dispatched to Hungary, arranged public appearances for them and introduced them to wealthy Jews, and advised students who planned to enroll and scholars who were invited to teach at the university or were merely interested in a position there. In September 1938 he wrote to me (in Hebrew): "I am very busy, especially with the university's affairs, for every student and his father and mother want to talk only to me, and they rob me of my time day and night." This had been going on for more than ten years. I remember in particular that in 1928 Professor Michael Fekete, when offered a chair in mathematics by the University, came to Father for consultation and accepted the invitation on his advice. Father also engaged in campaigns to get donations of books for the university library. In brief, in the ten years prior to the *Anschluss*, Father was the chief activist in Hungary in matters pertaining to the Hebrew University and the authoritative source of information for all those who, in whatever capacity, were interested in it.

With all this behind him, and the German menace threatening to engulf Hungary, where the pro-Nazi groups grew stronger and louder day by day, in 1938 Father was finally forced to consider that he and Mother would be well advised to leave Hungary. While he still did not envisage this as something imminent, he nevertheless began to feel that an offer of a teaching position at the Hebrew University would be a desirable thing to have, even if only in order to be freer to decide whether he should leave Hungary.

At the same time, in the late 1930s, Father began to encounter personal difficulties in Budapest. The first Hungarian "Jewish Law," severely restricting Jewish rights and economic activities, was passed in 1938, followed by the second in 1939, and by the third Jewish Law in 1941, all aimed at undermining Jewish rights, life, and livelihood. Among the rules and regulations issued by the Hungarian government was one that decreed that only members of the Chamber of Journalists could be editors or publishers of newspapers and periodicals. For Father, this meant that he had to submit an application to the chamber and then wait for its decision, which was due to be made public in October 1938. All applicants had to submit proof, not only of their own Hungarian citizenship, but also of that of their parents— a Hungarian birth certificate alone was not deemed sufficient. In order to obtain such documents, Father had to travel to Eszeny, where his grandfather had lived and his father was born. On August 18, 1938, he wrote to me (in Hungarian): "I am busy with efforts to gather the documents required for my citizenship certificate. Even the marriage certificate of my great-grandfather was required. By now everything is in order."

Next it was decreed that all periodicals must obtain new publication permits, and Father had to make efforts in that connection as well. The issuance of the permit was postponed again and again, causing my parents considerable anxiety. On November 13, 1938, Mother said in her letter, "We are still waiting for the permit of the journal and hope it will be given." Again, on November 29, Father wrote, "The permits for the Jewish periodicals have not yet been renewed. Perhaps we shall receive them as a gift for Hanukka!"

Under the influence of these and other such developments, and in view of the fact that all three Patai children had left the parental home—Évi was in Paris, Saul and I in Jerusalem—Father at long last was ready to consider leaving the city and the country where he had lived all his life and the Jewish community whose cultural leader he had been for a quarter of a century. On November 17, 1938 (five days before my twenty-eighth birthday, to which he made no reference—it was not customary in our family to celebrate or even to remember birthdays), he wrote to me (in Hebrew):

> I wrote to Ibn-Zahav that it is the desire of my heart to go up [i.e., to immigrate to Palestine], even if they give me but a small job in which I can fulfill [the saying] "Eat a piece of bread with salt"—but the job *should be offered* to me from there. Or, at least, they should somehow initiate negotiations about it. The saying of our sages "All beginnings are difficult" pertains to such matters as well, and therefore if you think or hear that there is a possibility, do inform me. And know that *I am ready to go up immediately upon receiving a call* of love from Jerusalem.

Since no academic invitation was forthcoming, or was even in the offing, Father had no choice. During his spring 1938 visit to Jerusalem he discussed with Mr. Schneursohn, the treasurer of the university, the possibility of taking charge of the fund-raising activities for the university that were being initiated or expanded at that time within the *yishuv*. What a comedown this must have meant for Father! A writer, a poet, an editor, a scholar, a cultural leader of a million Hungarian-speaking Jews, a lifelong volunteer helper and guide in every effort made in Hungary for the Hebrew University and other cultural institutions of the *yishuv*, now had to express his willingness—in fact, his desire—to accept a position as a paid fund-raiser for the university! Worse, he now felt that he was in a situation in which he was forced to ask his friends in Jerusalem to help him get such a job. In the same November 17 letter he wrote me: "Professor Klein writes in his latest letter that you did not mention to him anything about my conversation with Schneursohn. At your first opportunity tell him what we are discussing, and perhaps he too can support the matter. I really don't understand why Schneursohn has not written to me."

Three days later I had a long conversation with Ibn-Zahav in his office at the university. He showed me the letter Father wrote him about the job that was dangled before his eyes, and we discussed in detail what could be done in order to move the matter off dead center. Later the same day I wrote to Father:

Jerusalem, Nov. 20, 1938, Sunday [in Hebrew]

Dear Father:

Today we received your letter at home and also today, at the university, I saw the letter you wrote to Ibn-Zahav. Thereafter I had a long discussion with him, and we came to the conclusion that you must undertake, without delay, the following steps:

1. Write to Mr. Berger. Tell him about your talks with Schneursohn and about his offer that you take upon yourself the management of the Society of Friends of the University in Eretz Israel. That letter should deal with nothing else but this matter: you are ready to accept the offer and would like a quick decision, because of well-known reasons. Mention in the letter that you are sending a copy of it to Dr. Senator.

2. Send a copy to Dr. Werner Senator [the university administrator] (all this in German, of course), and also attach a letter addressed directly to him. In this letter it will be desirable to let some warmth and a personal note enter, and to insist in it as well on an immediate decision.

3. Send a similar letter to Dr. Moshe Glicksohn, who has just now been elected member of the Board of Trustees of the University, wherewith his influence in these matters has increased.

All three letters should emphasize that the idea originated with Mr. Schneursohn. This will commit Schneursohn to a certain extent. Even though the final decision is in the hands of Schocken, if Schneursohn, Berger, Glicksohn, and especially Senator recommend the matter, it will, no doubt, be accepted. From Ibn-Zahav, as I see it, one cannot expect additional help, for his influence does not reach up into such "heights." Of course, this must remain between us.

After these letters are received here, we shall see, together with Ibn-Zahav, what is the reaction, and if we see that the moment is opportune, perhaps it will be advisable for you to come here. It would be good to send copies of all these letters to Ibn-Zahav, and perhaps to me too, so that we should be *am Laufenden [au courant]*. Today Ibn-Zahav again told me that there is room for you here and also a definite need of a man like you, but there is no order here, no unified management, and this is why things go so slowly and sluggishly. It will be advisable to send all the letters by airmail and to send them right away. And perhaps it would be good also to write to Schneursohn (mark the envelop "Personal"), to inform him that you have written these letters, and to spur him on, since he was the initiator of the matter, to complete the *mitzva* he started.

On November 29 my father responded (in Hebrew): "In my own affair, I wrote to Senator (copy enclosed), and to the same effect also to Berger, and today I also wrote to Glicksohn and Schneursohn, as you advised me to do. I don't know whether Schneursohn has already returned to Eretz Israel . . ."

From this letter I learned that my sister Évi had also taken a hand in Father's efforts to find a job in Palestine:

Hava writes that a certain Abraham Katzenelson of Tel Aviv spoke to her about my affair, and that she will send him particulars about my life history. I think she confused the name, and that it was *Berl* Katzenelson. She writes that several people, Naiditsch, Baratz, will talk to Professor Weizmann, but I don't know what they will talk about, and whether they know what to ask in this matter. I too hope and expect that there will be room for me in Eretz Israel and that I shall be able to work in the university and for the university, but it is difficult for me to be an 'ox that gores.' I still don't know what exactly Schneursohn's plan is, but, in any case, now that I believe he is back in Jerusalem, I was able to write to him directly and ask him to respond as soon as possible.

The rest of Father's letter deals with problems of students and of Hungarian Jewish writers who wanted to move to Palestine, with Évi's novel, and with plans for the forthcoming issues of his monthly. Then he returns once more to the university:

It would be pleasant for me if I were now to receive an invitation from the university to lecture on some subject, but I don't know how to initiate this matter. Perhaps through Yellin, from whom I have just now received a letter with the book of [his wife] Mrs. Etta Yellin. We shall publish excerpts from it, with pictures of Avinoam and his parents. I expressed to him my thanks, but of course I did not touch upon the question of the lectures, and I don't know who decides now in such matters.

Let me interject here that my sister did not mistake Berl for Abraham. Abraham Katzenelson (1888–1956), who later changed his name to Nissan, was a Jewish labor leader, director of the Health Department of the Zionist Executive, and a member of the Va'ad Leumi from 1931 to 1948. Berl Katzenelson (1887–1944) was a central figure of the Second 'Aliya and one of the most important leaders of the Zionist labor movement, as well as editor of the Tel Aviv labor daily *Davar*. Isaac Asher Naiditsch (1868–1949) was a philanthropist and Zionist, a close friend of Chaim Weizmann, who had lived in France since 1917 and became one of the first directors of the Keren Hayesod. Yosef Baratz (1890–1968) was a founder of the collective settlement movement in Eretz Israel and of the first *k'vutza*, Degania, whose story he described in his book *A Village by the Jordan*. We have already met the Yellins above.

Even before I received this letter from Father I wrote to him again (on December 3, 1938, in Hungarian), telling him that I would talk to Senator, Glicksohn, Berger, etc., as soon as I heard that Father had written to them. Then I touched upon a new idea: "Perhaps Father could write to Chief Rabbi Hertz (his address is 4, St. James's Place, Aldgate, London, E. C. 3), who could do a lot, both as a very influential member of the Executive Committee ('Curatorium') of the university, and as chairman of the funds for aiding Middle-European Jewish scholars. It is with his help that two teachers of the Breslau Seminary, Professor Heinemann and Dr. Lewkowitz, will arrive here these days."

Professor Isaac Heinemann (1876–1957) and Dr. Albert Lewkowitz (1883–1954) were both my teachers in 1930–1931 at the Rabbinical Seminary of Breslau. Heinemann settled in 1939 in Jerusalem, where he continued his studies in Jewish philosophy. Lewkowitz found refuge in 1939 in Amsterdam, where he lectured at the Ashkenazi Rabbinical Seminary, but was interned in 1943 at the Westerbork Concentration Camp, transferred to Bergen-Belsen, and, having miraculously survived it, went to Palestine, where he became rabbi of the Ahavat Zion congregation in Haifa.

It was, I believe, this letter that planted the idea in Father's mind to go to London and try to get some support there. However, even before he informed me that he planned to do so, I wrote to him again on December 13 (in Hebrew), reporting on the most recent developments and problems that had arisen in connection with this job:

> I have spoken to Schneursohn. He said that the matter is now being discussed and that he hopes it will be in order. After that I spoke to Dr. Senator, who said that he was very surprised at your letter, for he had not known anything about this matter. His opinion is that you are not suited to this job, because you don't know the people in this country well enough. Of course, I objected energetically, and finally he said that in the next few days he would discuss the matter with Schneursohn. In the meantime Ibn-Zahav too spoke again to Schneursohn and Glicksohn, and both of them will do what they can. But I was not satisfied with this, and went personally to see Dr. Glicksohn, spoke to him at length, informed him of what Senator had said, and told him that the decision in this matter has by now become very urgent. He said that next week (the week of Hanukka) he will be in Tel Aviv, will call a meeting of the Society of Friends of the Hebrew University, and has not the slightest doubt that he will be able to influence

the people there to accept his motion, that is, the motion that you be appointed director of affairs. Then, once he has in his hands such a resolution by the center (Tel Aviv is the center of the Friends in the country), he will be able to, and actually will, talk to Chief Justice Frumkin, and if his consent is also obtained, then the administration of the university will be obliged to accept it. All these steps will, according to him, take about two weeks. Today I made an appointment with Mr. Daniel Auster, and I shall ask him that he too should put in a word with people of influence in this matter, such as Frumkin and members of the committee in Tel Aviv. Likewise I arranged a meeting between Dr. Glicksohn and Professor Klein, who is willing to do everything he can for the plan. I also dropped in at Ibn-Zahav's and told him what Senator had said, and he said that as soon as tomorrow he would talk to Senator. So, I think, that within a short time there will be a positive decision.

Father's response to this letter was matter-of-fact, although it contained references to further unpleasant developments in Budapest:

Budapest, the third day of Hanukka 5699 [Dec. 20, 1938; in Hebrew]

Dear Raphael:

Your letter about the steps you took arrived, and I am waiting for their results. In the meantime a decisive thing has happened: the Ministry [of Internal Affairs] has entrusted the matter of the permits of Jewish periodicals to the National Office [of Hungarian Jews], which is headed by Stern: they are to suggest a small number [of papers] to the government, and the Ministry will make its decision on the basis of that suggestion. This being the case, I am sure that the head of our Congregation [Stern] will not miss the opportunity to take revenge on me, especially since also at the last conference I came out against him with sharp criticism because of his ugly behavior toward Eretz Israel and its rebuilding. He has not changed his "position" even in these terrible days, and he is the source of the enormous opposition to Zionism, a power that has almost no significance at all in helping, but has the ability to harm and destroy, and *D"L*. In the matter of the anti-Jewish laws and decrees they [the government] did not ask their [the National Office's] advice, nor did they in the past give them any sign of their "love," nor did they ask their opinion about the ritual slaughtering that was outlawed, but the "slaughtering" of the newspapers they entrusted to them—let the Jews argue and quarrel among themselves! In brief, it is clear to me that they will quickly suppress our paper, and we must hasten the redemption and arrange whatever is possible in Jerusalem!

[. . .] Has my letter about the invitation to lecture on Hungarian literature reached you? On that basis I hope to receive permission to transfer my pension that comes to ca. 6 pounds monthly. Such an invitation has importance in general in all the arrangements here with the National Bank in connection with my emigration. As for the [immigration] certificate, of course it is more suitable for me to get it through the university, even without any commitment on its part.

Your father, who send his regards with love,
Yosef

D"L is the abbreviation of the Hebrew words *Day laMevin,* (this suffices to him who understands). Father received a pension even in 1938 for his ten years of service as a high school teacher at a Budapest municipal school from 1909 to 1919. It is surprising that they continued with this pension payment even after the promulgation of the anti-Jewish laws and, in fact, even approved my father's request to transfer the monthly payments to Palestine.

Mother added to the letter (in Hungarian): "I hope both of you are well. Recently there was again war news from Palestine; truly, we could do with a little quiet! The best joke of the week was that somebody wrote to Papa that he would like to have a 'quiet home'—he has no other wishes! Modest man! And could Papa help him to obtain this modest wish."

During all this time Évi's little daughter Tirzah was still with my parents in Budapest, but now that they started seriously to consider leaving Budapest, this meant that Évi would have to take the child to Paris. In a brief sentence in another letter Mother remarked (no date, in Hungarian), "There is talk about Évi taking Tirzah to Paris, and we may let our apartment—but all this is only a plan."

On December 22, 1938, I wrote Father another long letter (in Hebrew) that was almost entirely devoted to his 'aliya. I informed him that Professor Klein had spoken to the rector of the university, Professor Abraham Fraenkel, who would, in the next few days, send Father an invitation to lecture at the university on "Hungarian literature and its relations with Hebrew literature." The invitation would not state how many lectures Father would give, although they were thinking of only one or two. I added: "I think the right thing to do would be to come immediately after you receive this invitation." Then I went on to describe in detail the additional discussions I had with all the people who could influence the outcome of the plan to entrust Father with the position of the director of the Friends.

As for the administration of the university itself, to my regret I must inform you that I did not meet on their part with the understanding I had expected. Especially Mr. Berger is openly opposed to your appointment, arguing that you do not know the people here well enough, and that therefore you are not suitable for the job. Berger has influenced Senator, from whose mouth I heard the same opinion, accompanied by the promise that he would try to find you some other work in connection with the university. Of course all that is but empty talk. The *de facto* situation is that most of the income of the Friends, about seventy-five percent, is being spent on administrative expenses, and this is why the university administration is wary of all further commitment. Of course, we and our friends, such as Ibn-Zahav, argue that a total reorganization is needed, a reduction of the expenses across the whole front, wider publicity, etc. Dr. Glicksohn said that in January they want to embark upon an energetic publicity campaign for the university and that he hoped that by that time you would be here and manage everything. In any case, the situation is such that there are sides for and sides against, and therefore one cannot as yet see the end. So that you should be informed let me mention that I saw in the report submitted by Dr. Grau to Mr. Berger on his work in Hungary that you are not an "organizational power" and that therefore the affairs of the university in Hungary should not be entrusted to you. (This, of course, must be kept between us.) In the same report Grau also writes that the letters I am writing from here to Hungary are only harmful and not useful. Of course, all this is simply wickedness: he wants to show that he is the man who gets results! But it is possible that this nonsense did influence Berger, that this is why he fired me from the "important" job in the publicity department, and this is why he is opposed to your employment here. He is a man coarse of body and coarse of spirit. One must be careful in dealing with him.

I spoke here with Dr. Abraham Katzenelson (*not* Berl), he is a member of the Va'ad Leumi. He had spoken to Berger, and Berger's negative position became known to me through him. He thinks, and this is what others too think, that this matter cannot be settled from afar, and that you must come here even without an invitation, and under the pressure of your presence here the matter will be concluded, without any doubt.

After emphasizing that I too felt strongly that Father should come to Palestine immediately, even before the appointment to the Friends materialized, I added: "I found out today that a week or two ago the first Hungarian transport sailed in a ship full of people (several hundred) who had left

Hungary without a passport and without visas. According to a reliable source, the Hungarian Betar organized it, and each of the 'refugees' paid 700 pengős for being thus transported to Eretz Israel. Do you know anything about this?"

Dr. Grau, mentioned here for the first time, was a professional fund-raiser employed by the publicity department of the university and had spent some weeks in Budapest, where Father did everything possible to help his work. Betar (B'rit Trumpeldor) was an activist Zionist youth movement founded in 1923 in Latvia, became a main constituent of the Zionist-Revisionist Organization, and was involved in taking thousands of "illegal" immigrants to Palestine.

At the time this letter of mine reached my parents, my sister Évi was with them on a short visit. The World Jewish Congress had sent her to Prague and Brno to do some work there, and she was able to stop over on her way from Paris to visit our parents and her little daughter Tirzah, about twenty months old at the time, whom she had left in Mother's care when she went to work in Paris for the WJC. Since it now seemed that our parents would soon move to Palestine, a new arrangement had to be made for the child. Father was invited to attend a meeting of the WJC in Paris in January 1939, and he undertook to fly with Tirzah to Prague, meet Évi there, and then continue together with her and the child to Paris. There Évi planned to place Tirzah in a children's home not far from her own lodgings. Father touched upon these matters in his next letter to me, in which he also informed me that he was planning to go to London to try to find support there—a clear indication of his discouragement:

Budapest, Dec. 23, 1938 [in Hungarian]

Dear Raphael:

Today I got letters from the university: an invitation from the Rector Fraenkel to the effect of what we wrote, but I don't know whether this will be sufficient, because it states explicitly that I shall receive no "remuneration" for the lectures, and hence it is possible that here they will think that such an invitation is not really serious enough to be able to build upon it. On the other hand, without such a statement they may think that it is possible to make a living there from these lectures, and that there is no need of transferring money. We shall see what the day will bear.

The second letter is from Senator, who writes that in his opinion this position is not suitable for me, and that Schneursohn did not promise anything in this matter. He wishes with his whole heart that I should come to Eretz Israel as a veteran Zionist, etc. (Instead of sum-

marizing it, I am enclosing the letter.) In any case—the first disappointment. But perhaps it will really be possible to find another field of
activity in connection with the university, and I want to tell you that it
would be better and more pleasant not to work in publicity . . . and if
I could get 10 pounds monthly for scholarly work in the tent of the
Tora it would be more pleasant for me than to get 25 pounds for the
tribulations of publicity. Therefore I decided to go to London next
week; I shall anyway go on January 8 to Paris and shall take with me
the child, who cannot stay here. Hava will leave already on the 2nd for
Prague and Brünn, and from there for Paris. We shall meet in Prague
and go on together. I shall continue my trip to London and shall talk
there personally to Chief Rabbi Dr. Hertz. He has some kind of foundation for "refugee scholars," and now that they denied the permission
to continue our journal, for reasons I told you about, I too stand in
need of that foundation. If I can obtain something from him perhaps
there will be a chance in Jerusalem for real work. I shall mention you
too to him—perhaps he can provide some scholarship for you or can
invite you to lecture in London.

I shall also talk to Stephen Wise in Paris at the meeting of the
World Jewish Congress. After that meeting I shall go directly to Trieste
and from there, on Wednesday, January 17, I shall sail for Tel Aviv,
where I shall arrive with God's help on January 22. Mother will stay
here to take care of the liquidation. It is possible that the grandparents
and the Molnárs will come to live in our apartment in Nyúl Street, and
thus the problem of supporting the old people will be solved, for it is
difficult to sell the apartment now. Late in February Mother will come
to Tel Aviv with a group of tourists, in order not to forfeit the work
that we started. I got a discount of fifty percent for the ship, and she
will travel free of charge.

If you have any idea in connection with my visit with Rabbi Hertz,
write me immediately to Hava's address in Paris. Perhaps it would be
well to talk to David Yellin about this (in the December issue a picture
of Avinoam and of his parents was published, together with excerpts
from her [Etta Yellin's] book), *that he should express his opinion that it
would be desirable to have lectures in general on the poetry of the post-
Spanish age* with which I have dealt, etc., and if I should get only a few
pounds as a lecturer I shall be not only a *martze* [lecturer] but also
m'rutze [satisfied].

As for Dr. Grau's "report"—there is no justice and no judge! I cannot imagine, how could your letters have "harmed"? After all, you
wrote primarily to the country towns, which he did not visit at all, and
from which certainly not even a penny came in through him. And if he

is, as it were, the "organizational power," why did he achieve nothing here? I opened all the doors for him, arranged for him an opportunity to lecture to IMIT, the women's organization, and other groups, and even to the *m'shumadim* [renegade Jews] of the Casino—why was he not able to make use of these opportunities to raise money at least to cover his expenses? He was the one who turned to the "organizational powers" of the heads of the Congregation and got not even a penny! The ten pounds Grau did get were raised by my friend Dr. Kende, who wanted to hand the money to me, but I thought that perhaps it would be better to use this to stimulate Dr. Hofert to work—a pity that this organizational power of Dr. Grau has taken not a single step!

I was very glad to get your study on "The Control of Rain," may God grant that you bring down rains of blessing in plenty upon all of us! As you see, I am not depressed, for already the Shekhina of Eretz Israel has begun to rest upon me, and I receive her with joy in heart and soul!

Your father who greets you with love,
Yosef

Dr. Stephen S. Wise (1874–1949), of Hungarian birth, was a leading Reform rabbi in New York, an organizer of the American Jewish Congress, a founder and leader of the World Jewish Congress, a great orator, and a dominant figure in American Jewish life. The Molnárs were my mother's sister Dóra, her husband Dr. Ernő Molnár, and their daughter Judith (Juci). They shared an apartment with my mother's and Dóra's parents. We have already met IMIT above. The Hungarian National Casino was an elite social club in Budapest, many of whose members were converted Jews. I cannot identify Dr. Kende and Dr. Hofert (or Hoffert).

This letter was the first clear indication that Father had definitely decided to leave Budapest and to come to Palestine, even without the promise of a job. At the same time it also shows that—despite all the efforts he felt constrained to make to be appointed director of the Friends—he disliked the prospect of becoming a salaried fund-raiser. That feeling was never to leave him, even though he was, in the event, very successful in raising considerable amounts for the university among the well-to-do and middle class of the *yishuv*. I still remember that a few years later, in a bitter moment, when the news of the destruction of Hungarian Jewry finally reached Palestine, he said to me, "It would have been far better for me to continue my work in Hungary and perish with my brethren there than to be reduced to what I have become here in Palestine."

However, in January 1939, all that was still mercifully hidden in the future. The task at hand was to enable our parents to leave Hungary, and I felt that in order to make that possible no stone must be left unturned. As soon as I received Father's December 27 letter I got into action again and reported to him, addressing my letter to Paris, c/o Évi, with a copy to Mother in Budapest:

Jan. 6, 1939 [in Hungarian]

Dear Papa:

This morning I received your letter in which you inform me of your London trip. I went immediately to Professor Klein, and we went to Professor Yellin, who will write to Hertz today. Tomorrow I shall get from him a copy of his letter. As for Klein, he will move at the next meeting of the [university] Senate that you be entrusted with teaching the Hebrew poetry of the post-Spanish age. Yellin too will support the motion, and if there is financial support from London, there will be no obstacle to the acceptance here of the motion, which will also be supported by Professor Assaf. I shall talk with him after a response from Hertz arrives from London.

In the afternoon I went to see Kleinmann (editor of *Ha'Olam*), who immediately wrote very warm letters to Hertz and Brodetzky, addressing the latter to the Zionist Organization, 77 Great Russell Street. Kleinmann writes in the two letters that due to the circumstances you must leave [Hungary] and that here the university circles would be glad if you could be won for the academic staff of the university, but that there is no financial possibility of this. Hence, he asks Hertz and Brodetzky to provide financial support from the scholars' fund that exists in London. I also spoke to Ibn-Zahav, who gave the advice that you should also turn to Dr. Buechler in London (but one must know that the relationship between him and Hertz is not too good), and also to Duschinsky (who lives not far from Buechler). Also, possibly, to Leon Simon, who is the translator of Ahad Haam into English and fills some kind of chief directorship of posts, and to Cecil Roth. Moreover, I wrote to Dr. Rosenfeld, asking him to write in the name of the B'rit 'Ivrit [World Hebrew Union] to all those in London who can be helpful in this matter. On Sunday I shall try to talk to Magnes, who is sick at present: perhaps he too can achieve something through London.

In general, the right thing to do will be not to hurry away from London, but to remain there for one or even two weeks and follow up everything to the end. On that occasion you could try to arrange finally for the English edition of the Herzl book, although that does not belong directly to the issue now on the carpet.

In any case, please give your London address to the Zionist Organization, 77 Great Russell Str., in case I have something urgent to communicate.

If you need technical help, I am sure Miss Margot M. [. . .] will be glad to be at your disposal. I am writing to her today that you will be there, and she could possibly serve as a guide, which will mean saving a lot of time.

No other subject at present. Please let me have urgently information about the developments.

Your loving son,
Raphael

Moshe Kleinmann was editor of *Ha'Olam* since 1923. Selig Brodetzky (1888–1954) was professor of mathematics at the University of Leeds, England, from 1920 to 1949. He was also a member of the governing board of the Jewish Agency and head of its political department in London, president of the Board of Deputies of British Jews from 1939 to 1949, and president of the Hebrew University from 1949 to 1952. Dr. Adolf Buechler (1867–1939) was ordained rabbi at the Rabbinical Seminary of Budapest in 1892 and became principal of the Jews' College in London in 1907, serving in that capacity until his death. Charles (Jacob Koppel) Duschinsky (1878–1944) was a London businessman and historian. Sir Leon Simon (1881–1965) was an English Zionist leader and Hebrew writer, served the British General Post Office in various capacities (1904–1944), and was first chairman of the Hebrew University's executive council from 1946 to 1953 and then chairman of its Board of Governors. Cecil Roth (1899–1970) was reader in Jewish history at Oxford. Dr. Alexander Rosenfeld was director of the B'rit 'Ivrit 'Olamit (World Hebrew Union), the organization devoted to the propagation of Hebrew language and culture. Father's Herzl biography, written originally in Hungarian, had by then been published in German and Hebrew translations by Omanuth in Tel Aviv, but an English translation was not published until 1946. Margot M. and I were close friends in Jerusalem from 1937 to 1939, as described above.

The very next day, January 7, 1939, I sent off another letter to Father, again addressing it to Paris, and in the same envelope a letter to Évi. I enclosed a copy of the letter Professor Yellin wrote the day before to Chief Rabbi Hertz and again urged Father to stay in London as long as necessary to take care of everything. I also sent a copy of Yellin's letter to London to the address of the Zionist Organization, to make sure Father would receive it before talking to Hertz. I felt that this was so important that I wrote to Évi that, if she had any doubts whether Father would get in touch with the Zionist Organization immediately upon his arrival in London, she should wire him at his London address, advising him that a letter awaited him at the Zionist Organization. I added to both letters that our friends here in Jerusalem had the impression that Father's London visit would be successful. At the same time I also wrote to Dr. Rosenfeld, who was a good friend of our family, asking him to write to several people with whom he had contact in support of Father's efforts. Dr. Rosenfeld immediately did as requested and wrote to Évi:

Jan. 8, 1939 [in Hebrew]

Dear Mrs. Hirsch-Patai:

Many thanks for the detailed report on the situation of the schools in Carpatho-Russia which we received through the secretariat of the World Jewish Congress.

In accordance with the suggestion of your brother we sent a memorandum to the Hungarian consul in Jerusalem. However, the memorandum has not yet been submitted officially, because we heard rumors that the Hebrew school in Munkacs is about to be reopened, unless the most recent events prevent it.

We sent letters today to Mr. Arye [Leon] Simon, president of "Tarbuth," Rabbi J. K. Goldblum, chairman of the Zionist Center, and Dr. S. Brodetzky, in accordance with your brother's letter, which we received this morning. Please give Professor Y. Patai our best wishes. I am enclosing copies of the letters we sent by airmail.

I want to request you to make sure that the meetings of the national committee of the B'rit should take place in proper form, and that they should, at long last, embark upon systematic activity according to the plan that was adopted at the time of my visit.

I hope to hear soon from you about what is being done in France.

Yours sincerely,
Dr. A. Rosenfeld

The same day a letter came from Mother, addressed to Saul and me, and written just a day or two before Father left for Prague, Paris, and London:

[undated, probably Jan. 5, 1939; in Hungarian]

Dear Sons:

You probably know Papa's program. He will take Tirzah to Paris; from there he will go to London, where Chief Rabbi Hertz will receive him. Let us hope that his trip will be successful. We enclose Grau's letter, from which it is apparent how he clings and tries to please. You could show it in responsible quarters, but keep it in any case.

Évi is in Prague today, she wrote from Pozsony [Pressburg/Bratislava], the first stop on her way: she is well, her work goes well. I cannot understand why you don't write once a week in these difficult times, that would not be such a great effort.

Here a thousand plans are rambling about, partly influenced by *Mult és Jövő having received* the permit. It can continue to appear without any change. Of course, the joy over this is not undisturbed . . . The Congregation wanted to thwart it; Immanuel Löw came to Budapest and spoke to Stern, who, as Löw put it, "remained unbending." On the other hand, great Hungarians, distinguished ministerial leaders, took up the cudgel for *MéJ*, so that when Ernő Munkácsi, returning from the ministry, reported to the Congregation that *MéJ* was approved as the *only* personal enterprise (the three national bureaus received permission for one weekly each), "their jaw fell." This is what Munkácsi reported. Subsequently Csergő congratulated us with honeyed sweetness, but Papa told him that he knew that they did everything to strangle *MéJ*. In any case, for the time being it is good that the journal exists, and it is good that such a case won over the meanness. Now we shall see whether our truth will also win in Jerusalem over the cohorts of the Bergers. Although Papa has not much hope about that position that is now under discussion—in fact, he himself would prefer a more tranquil scholarly job. But how can one achieve that?

I am very troubled also by the situation of the grandparents, even though I recognize that one must not complicate things. The tour has attracted countless applicants—of course, how many of them will become participants depends on how many get visas. Visas are hard to come by, but still there will be some 20–30 people.

We are trying to send out the Herzl pictures, let's hope we shall succeed.

It depresses me very much that I don't hear enough from you. Guszti has for weeks barely written a few lines—terrible! Take good care of Papa; here at home he has totally exhausted himself, nor will he rest in Paris. Moreover, on the way he will have to take care of Tirzah, who is the sweetest child but still a lot of work.

A thousand kisses to both of you,
Mama

The background of Mother's references to the "Congregation" is this: in response to the anti-Zionist stand of the leadership of the Israelite Congregation of Pest, headed by President Samu Stern, Father repeatedly attacked it in meetings of the Congregation's Council, of which he was a member, and in *Mult és Jövő*. Because of this, when the question of the governmental license for the continued publication of the journal came up, the Congregation did its best to have the license denied. A strong supporter of Father in this struggle was Immanuel Löw (1854–1944), chief rabbi of Szeged since

1927 and a member of the Upper House of the Hungarian Parliament, where he represented the "Neolog" (non-Orthodox, conservative) Jewish communities of Hungary. He was also a member of the Jewish Agency for Palestine since 1929. About Dr. Löw's very friendly attitude to me in 1936–1937 I have reported briefly in *Apprentice in Budapest* and elsewhere in the present volume. In the end Father's reputation and the high quality of his monthly won out against the intrigues of the Congregation. Dr. Ernő Munkácsi (1896–1950) was counsel to the Congregation, a scholar and art historian, several of whose papers Father published in his monthly. Hugó Csergő (1877–1944) was an author and journalist and Jewish community official. He was deported from Budapest in 1944 and died shortly thereafter.

The "Herzl pictures" were three oil paintings (portraits of Theodor Herzl's mother and two grandparents) that Father had purchased years earlier from surviving members of the Herzl and Diamant families in Budapest. Father did get permission to take the pictures along to Palestine. Today they hang in the reconstructed study of Herzl on Mount Herzl in Jerusalem.

I replied to Mother:

Jerusalem, Jan. 17, 1939 [in Hungarian]

Dear Mama:

Since your Jan. 5 letter, which was written before Papa left Budapest, we have had no news either from Pest or from London or from Paris. I am especially worried because precisely on the day Papa left, or perhaps a day before, the Hungarian-Czech border incident took place, and to this day we don't know whether Papa did go or stayed home.

I sent off several letters to Papa and to Évi, after the letter whose copy I sent you (dated Jan. 6). I hope Papa received my letters and the enclosed copies of Yellin's, Dr. Rosenfeld's, etc., letters.

The news that *MéJ* received the permit was, to tell the truth, greeted with mixed feelings by Guszti and me. On the one hand we were, of course, glad, since it is a moral recognition, etc. But, on the other, we became apprehensive lest as a result of this our parents' outward-tending momentum again abate. Whereas, in our opinion—and this is the opinion of everybody here—that would be a fatal mistake!

I am getting lots of letters from my acquaintances in Pest and in the country, from former colleagues, and also from unknown people. Dénes Friedmann wrote concerning five unversity students from Ujpest, asking me to arrange that they should get immigration certificates from the university, immediately and out of turn. In sooth, when I wrote to him that he should influence his congregation to support the university, he made no special effort, and the Ujpest congregation allocated—a crying shame!—all of 20 pengő's to the university. Of course, the memory of that incident did not enthuse me in particular, but I forwarded his request to the secretariat, which, I believe, will respond with its usual regretful form letter. If people should ask Mama for my address, please tell everybody that I can do nothing and that they should write directly to the schools in question, while in university matters they should turn to the Palestine Office in Budapest. If I wanted to answer all the letters I get I would have to set up an entire office.

Guszti, as I see, feels very well here. He has already totally adjusted to university life and is already popular in student circles, something he visibly enjoys. He pursues his studies with great fervor and completes the exercises in half the time needed by his colleagues. He feels that it is his duty to excel.

I would like to know: when are you planning to effect the move over here? When does Mama intend to come? What will happen to the furniture and Papa's library? I have to know these things if for no other reason than to be able to take them into account in connection with renting an apartment that is due to be done in the next few weeks, at Muharram. [. . .]

Mama expresses indignation in her recent letters that we don't write enough. But it is now our parents' turn to write as far as the need of reassurance is concerned. After all, here nothing new happens, after three years even if attempts and murders do occur, one begins, alas, to feel that they are ingredients of normal life, and one already dares to talk about a consolidation of conditions. And as far as our private circle is concerned, nothing worth mentioning happens. The days pass with trifling little things and affairs, but when one sits down to write to one's beloved and honored parents, one finds nothing worth mentioning, for, after all, one cannot fill a letter with telling that yesterday I had cocoa for breakfast and today I shall have liver paté for dinner— this would really be a shame for a family of such an intellectual level as ours. And as for affairs of an even more private character than this— that is, than eating—those must be struggled through by everybody for himself. In those matters even those closest to one neither can nor dare give advice.

Accordingly, I conclude my letter to which Guszti cannot add because he is at present at the university, and I want to mail it so that it will go with the afternoon post, and the kid comes home only at about six.

> Many kisses, Mama, your loving son,
> Raphael

Dénes Friedmann (1903–1944), a cousin of mine on Mother's side, was chief rabbi of Ujpest, a suburb of Budapest. In 1944, after witnessing the murder of his son by the Hungarian Nazis, he was deported and never heard of again. As for his request that I help Hungarian Jewish students who wanted to escape to Palestine, such appeals were received daily by me in Jerusalem and by my parents in Budapest. Practically all the letters exchanged between us contain references to such cases. For instance, in January 1939 Mother wrote (in Hungarian) from Budapest to Father, who at that time was in Tel Aviv:

> People come to me every day with new requests. Today the conductor of the choir of the Municipal Theater came to see me in the company of Bence Szabolcsi. Eighty percent of the choir are Jewish, which means that they must leave. According to Szabolcsi the conductor is wonderful (he is László Káldi—he spoke to you before you left) and the members are wonderful. They would like to appear in the big cities with Jewish programs, for the benefit of the refugees, and then get out, to the Tel Aviv opera. Káldi put the plan in writing, gave it to Dr. Miklós (in which Eppler supported him), but he asked me emphatically that I send you a copy.
>
> The physician Endre Fischer was here too. He has everything to be able to go to America: he is a relative of Dr. Jenő Fuchs, who recommended him. His request is that if you know of some contact for him in New York give him a few lines of recommendation. His address is Dr. Endre Fischer, Kisvárda.
>
> Of Michover's visit I have already reported to you. He has somebody who can quickly obtain a British visa (supposedly). If the man is reliable, that would greatly facilitate the matter of the travelers . . .
>
> [. . .] I am enclosing copies of the letters of choir-director Káldi, with the attachments. They certainly deserve support—the question is whether it is possible and whether you have time for it.

Bence Szabolcsi (1899–1973), a foremost Hungarian musicologist, was the younger son of Miksa Szabolcsi, editor of the Hungarian Jewish weekly *Egyenlőség*, in whose office Father spent his early apprentice years. Dr. Gyula Miklós (1887–1940) was the president of the Hungarian Zionist Organization in 1939. I cannot identify the others mentioned.

Father's next letter reached Saul and me in the second half of January:

Paris, Sabbath Evening [Jan. 14, 1939; in Hebrew]

My Beloved Dear Sons Raphael and Saul:
I spent only three days in London, and upon my return to Paris I

found your letters here. In London I spoke to Chief Rabbi Hertz. He complained that he had taken a great burden upon himself when he requested entry permits for 172 rabbis from Germany, and now they are coming to him and asking: on what will we live? Hertz received me with kindness and honor and promised that his heart will always be with "the Patais" with warmth and love. You, Raphael, he values highly, and termed your book *HaMayim* "a book of genius." However, he cannot do anything now because of the above reasons. He told me that Schocken has just recently written to him concerning Professor [Umberto] Cassuto of Italy, whom Hertz recommended as a teacher of Bible for the Hebrew University, and now Schocken asks him to supply half of the amount needed for that chair, and he can do nothing because recently he has exhausted all the philanthropists in England. He also complained of them that they have no "feeling" for Hebrew culture and spoke about the Jews of England almost as we speak of the Jews of Hungary in general. Still, I think that the letters of Yellin and Kleinmann were not in vain—Hertz will remember the matter, and perhaps he will do something at an opportune time.

I went to Great Russell Street, but your letter was not yet there. I did not find Brodetzky. I mentioned to Hertz the invitation for you to lecture in London, and he answered that there is no opportunity for that now. I did not go to Buechler because I hurried back to Paris before the Sabbath, to the meeting of the World Jewish Congress from which I got the travel expenses, and I must participate conscientiously in its sessions. Therefore I flew from here to London immediately after the flight from Budapest with Tirzah, who was happy all the way. And on Friday afternoon I flew from London to Paris: one hour and twenty minutes. A really wonderful trip, people should be happy in heart and soul that the Lord of heavens permits them such a great thing—to fly in the air of the world like a bird that is free of all sin.

Possibly I shall still return to London and then I shall try to talk to all the people mentioned in your letter. In the meantime I shall talk to Goldmann and to those who came here from London, so that perhaps it will not be worthwhile to return there. One more thing: I think that the main thing is that the Senate of the university should suggest me for this task, to lecture on Hebrew poetry, as Yellin wrote, and I shall find the framework for my work there, and as far as remuneration is concerned I shall be satisfied with whatever I shall find. Perhaps one could also find supporters for this matter among the Jews of Hungary. In the meantime the idea sprouted here in the brains of the directors of the World Jewish Congress to organize a "summer university" in Jerusalem, to attract young people from abroad who could attend lectures only for one or two months in the summer, and I would get the task of conducting negotiations about this with the university. Such schools exist in various universities. [. . .]

Your father who greets you with love,
Yosef

After receiving this letter I gave an account of its contents to Mother (on January 23, 1939, in Hungarian) and urged her to let me know the family's plans. I asked her whether I should rent a four-room apartment (that is, three rooms and kitchen) "in view of the fact that soon four of us will live here, Papa, Mama, Saul, and Raphael." In response to a question in an earlier letter, I gave her a list of expenses a person had in Jerusalem at the time: the rental of such an apartment would come to five pounds monthly and in addition there would be the following outlays: electricity—40 piasters; laundry per person—ca. 20 piasters; food—2½–3 pounds; cleaning per room—each time 2½ piasters; other incidental expenses—ca. 1 pound; so that a total of 6–7 pounds per person per month would suffice. I mentioned that "Saul can make ends meet quite nicely with his monthly 4 pounds—of course, he pays no rent" and added:

if a *tüchtig* [efficient] housewife were to manage the household, the expenses could be considerably reduced. Food, for instance, if one bought it not in a grocery but in the market, would cost about one-fourth less. Laundry too would cost much less if taken care of at home. As for lunch [the main meal], it is not worthwhile to cook at home, since for 5 piasters one can get a first-class menu. I eat at the regular time, at midday, Saul at half past five when he comes down from the university.

We got three more letters from Father, mailed from Paris:

Paris, Jan. 20, 1939 [in Hebrew]

My Dear Beloved Sons Raphael and Saul:
As I wrote to you, I was in London only for a short time, and now for a week I have been here in Paris, and I think that I succeeded here in connection with the World Jewish Congress in finding an important idea that we shall be able to realize in Jerusalem. Since Goldmann and all the people of the Congress think that the initiative must issue from Eretz Israel, and since I see that in London it is difficult to reach a decision in anything, I decided to leave from here Sunday [Jan. 22] in the evening through Venice to Trieste, and on Wednesday I shall sail for Tel Aviv, and, if God wills, shall arrive there at the end of January. Don't come to meet me—I shall come by taxi directly to Jerusalem.

I had an opportunity in London and Paris to get acquainted with several of the great ones of Israel, if only they were greater in measure, weight, and quality! A small people like ours needs gigantic men, for a great nation even small "great ones" are sufficient! They told me here that the Chief Rabbi in London does not have the influence people think he has, and, in general, one cannot rely on his promises. As for Brodetzky, I shall find him also in Eretz Israel, and I can also get in touch with him in writing. Buechler is old and weak, and therefore I thought that it is not worthwhile to return again to London. It will be better to go to Jerusalem and be on the lookout there.

In general I see that our movement does not have enough men, and if I wanted to remain and work abroad I would find an opportunity to distinguish myself, but, after all, our whole family must go up [to Palestine]. Hava does good work here and already has a respectable status. But her desire too is to go up as soon as possible, perhaps together with the chosen one of her heart, whom she will meet in her new life. Mama writes that it is very difficult to get visas to Eretz Israel and that perhaps she will postpone her trip by one month. If you have material for the journal, send it directly to Budapest.

Yellin's letter to the Chief Rabbi is really friendly, and I am indebted to the dear old man. Would that we succeed in realizing the idea of the lectures and that we get the finances through the action of the World Jewish Congress that I shall explain to you personally. Mama writes that Mr. Berger was in Budapest and did not phone her—perhaps he heard that I am away, or perhaps he did not want to meet me. Senator wrote to Goldmann that he was confident that once I am in Jerusalem some idea will be found for me in connection with the university, but that it was difficult at this time to arrange something definite for somebody who dwells abroad. [. . .]

Your father who greets you with great love and hopes to see you soon,
Yosef

Two days later Father wrote me again (in Hebrew):

In the meantime a letter came from Mama: she thinks that one must make use of all the connections one has in Paris and London, and therefore I decided to go back tomorrow to London, where I shall go to see all the people whom you mentioned in your letter. I shall return here at the end of next week and shall postpone my departure for Eretz Israel until early February. I think the *Gerusalemme* sails again on the first of February, so that I shall arrive in Tel Aviv on the sixth. As I already wrote to you, don't meet me in Tel Aviv: I shall go the same day to Jerusalem, and if there is a delay I shall come next day in the morning, God willing. I shall write to you again from London.

This letter did not reach us in time, so that, thinking that Father would arrive on January 30, on that day Guszti and I took an early bus down to Tel Aviv, went to the port, and waited for him. When he was not among those who disembarked, it finally occurred to me at 2:30 that there was a list of passengers in the office of the shipping company. We went there and inspected the list and found that Father's name was not on it. We stayed overnight in Tel Aviv; the next day, upon returning to Jerusalem, we found Father's letter of January 22 waiting for us. I informed Mother of all this, reported on several business matters we had taken care of in Shekhunat Boruchov, and advised her to make arrangements to ship all their furniture to Palestine in a crate.

Father returned from Paris to London on January 23; when he was back in Paris he mailed me a letter he wrote in almost illegible pencil on a page of stationery captioned "Committee appointed to Honor the Memory of Sir Moses Montefiore, Bart., as the Anglo-Jewish Pioneer of the Resettlement in the Holy Land, on the occasion of the Fiftieth Anniversary of his death in July, 1935. President: Sir Francis Montefiore, Bart."

Paris, Jan. 27, 1939 [in Hebrew]

Dear Beloved Son Raphael:

I am writing on the way from London to Paris, and am using the stationery I took from Mr. Paul Goodman, who is chairman of the above committee. From it you can see what *quntzim* [tricks] are needed here in order to establish a chair in the name of Montefiore. The action began in 1935 and is not yet completed, they have not yet raised enough money, and there is as yet not even a suitable person whom they could send to Jerusalem to lecture on English literature, as they wish. Goodman told me the most peculiar things about the Jews of England, who give only to "charity." I heard similar complaints also from Epstein and Buechler; the latter told me that his seminary [the Jews' College] has been unable even to publish the "News of the Institute" for the last twelve years because they have no money, and that he has in manuscript several completed books that await redemption, and there is no money. He thinks that the culprit is Dr. Hertz, who had received ten thousand pounds for the publication of his books (which, according to Buechler, have no value whatsoever), and therefore they give him [Buechler] not even a penny, and that Hertz wrote a "report" about Buechler saying that he was old and should hide within the "four cubits of the *halakha*" instead of creating a "bad atmosphere" through the Jews' College, in which there is a "foreign spirit," etc. I was shocked to hear and see the Jews of the capital of great England in jealous rivalry of scholars, and quarrels *not* for the sake of heaven.

I also met Leon Simon, a very dear man, he invited me to lecture in London to a big gathering, but I did not want to stay on because of that. As for the "real thing," his hands too are weak, and so are the hands of Duschinsky, who also has only limited influence. They all said that there was need in London of a man like Patai, etc., this is how they see it from a distance, but essentially one can expect less than little from them. Simon "will confer" with Goodman, and Brodetzky with Bentwich, etc. They all received me most kindly, but without any concrete results. Nevertheless, I don't regret that I went to London a second time: I got acquainted with the place and the people, and perhaps something useful will come out of it for the future, through correspondence, after having established personal contact.

Simon thought that something could be done in connection with the press of the university, that it could be expanded considerably, and that the university could derive some income from it. Also, in his opinion, and that of many others, there are great possibilities for the "summer courses" in Jerusalem that could make it possible to invite the great ones of the Gentiles and the liberal youth to Eretz Israel and could constitute an international connection. For this purpose they promised me in Paris an amount that would cover all the expenses, and possibly also the expenses of my *Lehrauftrag* [teaching appointment] at the university to lecture on poetry, as Yellin mentioned in his letter. Bentwich also said that this was a good plan and an important task that will find supporters, but the initiative must come from the university, and I should be entrusted with making the arrangements orally and in writing. Of course, one must not talk about all this—when I am, God willing, in Jerusalem, we shall discuss it among ourselves first. Goodman said they want to establish a kind of Jews' College for Sephardim, and perhaps it will be possible to do something in that connection. All this is merely "Passover of the Future," *Zukunftsmusik* [music of the future] in the foreign language, in which there is as yet neither Haggada nor *kneydlekh* [dumplings].

On Sunday or Monday I shall go from Paris to Trieste, and on Feb. 1 shall sail for Tel Aviv, and, God willing, shall arrive there on the 6th. As I already wrote to you, don't come to meet me. I read again today about incidents on the road—I shall find my way to Jerusalem alone as well. So under no condition come to meet me!

I visited Miss Margot M., but I did not ask her to help me in technical matters. I managed to find everything by myself, and I did not want to spend time unnecessarily in her company. This morning, before leaving London, I called her on the phone, to say good-bye and expressed my regret that I could not see her again.

And now, my dear sons, I wish you all the best, and hope to see you soon. May God grant that I find you in peace, in peace of the city and in peace of the country.

Your father who greets you with love,
Yosef

Paul Goodman (1875–1949) was a British official of the Zionist Organization, editor of the *Zionist Review,* and author of books of Jewish historical interest. Isidore Epstein (1894–1962), an English rabbi and scholar, was a lecturer and librarian at the Jews' College in London in 1939. He supervised the English translation of the Babylonian Talmud, published by Soncino Press in 35 volumes. Norman Bentwich (1883–1971), an English Zionist, lawyer, and scholar, served from 1931 to 1951 as professor of international relations at the Hebrew University.

Soon after his arrival in Palestine Father wrote an article entitled "Notes from London," in which he gave an account of Jewish life in the British capital, which he mailed to Mother for publication in his journal. It appeared in the February 1937 issue. In it he divulged nothing of the negative impressions he got of British Jewry, of which he wrote in quite an unrestrained manner in these letters.

Despite all the kind words and half-promises Father received in Paris and London, the concrete results of his trips to the two cities and his conversations with a dozen or so Jewish leaders came to nothing. Understandably, the leaders of French and British Jewry in early 1939 concentrated their efforts on rescuing German Jews who were in acute danger, while Hungary at the time still seemed relatively safe. As far as Father was concerned, this meant that if he wanted to get out of Hungary, he had to seize the only possibility that was available to him, the position of director of the Palestinian Friends of the Hebrew University.

. . . Mother at Home Holds the Fort

While Father was traveling in Prague, Paris, London, Trieste, and Tel Aviv, Mother held the fort alone in Budapest. She took care of the liquidation of their home, the publication of the current issues of Father's monthly, and the arrangements for the group of tourists with whom she planned to go to Palestine. As a result of the rapidly deteriorating civic and political situation of the Jews in Hungary, the number of those who tried to get out of the country increased dramatically, but so did the difficulties of obtaining entry-visas to Palestine from the British consulate in Budapest. In one of her letters, which she wrote on the day she received a letter from Father from his second trip to London, Mother wrote:

[undated, probably Feb. 2, 1939; in Hungarian]

Dear Raphael:

It is terrible that I am constantly bombarded with requests I cannot fulfill. Everybody here wants to get out to Palestine—it is a veritable mass hysteria that takes no account of the obstacles. Nevertheless, the tour is still quite uncertain, or even worse. They don't issue visas, except on the basis of instructions from Palestine. The head of the Palestine Office [of the Jewish Agency in Budapest] said that he is forwarding the list [of tour participants] to the Agency [in Jerusalem], which will submit it to the government for approval. But, of course, they keep track of the list of names, and actually one must undertake a guarantee for them.

There is a distinguished lawyer, Dr. Moskovits, here who wants to go together with six others, but now his son has problems about getting an extension of his passport and a visa. My request is: could you obtain a certificate for this boy, his name is Dr. László Moskovits (by the way: he studied the confectioner's trade), from some school attesting that he was admitted there? That would facilitate the situation, that is, his leaving the country. He could go elsewhere, he has connections, but he wants to go to Palestine above all. Even if a school would only indicate that there is *a possibility of admitting him*, that in itself would be good. Do respond to this question without fail, even if you can do nothing about it, so that I should be able to show it to Dr. Moskovits.

Today I got a letter from Papa from London. He thought it would be useful to return to London, and so he postponed his departure by a week. If only there were some results! For the time being he writes nothing essential. I too think that I shall postpone my trip, *kommt Zeit kommt Rat* [with time comes a solution]. Mrs. Nadler too wants to go with her two sons.

The papers here write with great sympathy about the fall of Barcelona. Alas, the European situation has now again become critical. May God grant that everything should turn to the good. In any case, if something does happen, the provisioning of Palestine is not at all secured, so that one should lay by food. Starving would do no good either to Papa or to you. It surely would be a serious ordeal if one would have to live through a war again in such a situation of being cut off from one another. Now they foretell that there will be an explosion about Gibraltar, so that possibly here they will get mixed up in it—but, of course, all this is only talk, even though really enough explosive material has accumulated. [. . .]

I am very worried, Gyurikám, that recently you have been writing in such a depressed mood, although many here envy you, but people are inclined to see the lives of others as easy and wonderful. You don't write on what you are working now. I sent the requested important book to Guszti by mail, his friend Kertész asked for it, but in the midst of the heaps of things to do (in addition Öhlmacher had the flu) I could not send it off. [. . .]

Please send some article without fail! I was able to assemble this issue only with the greatest difficulty. There was simply no material, and those I asked did not send anything. Ask something of Ibn-Zahav also, let Guszti translate it, and send it to me. The printers told me only today that there are not enough manuscripts even for the January issue. I shall have to do some scissoring.

A thousand kisses, also to Guszti,

Mama

The fall of Barcelona took place on January 26, 1939, when the nationalist forces captured the city. That event marked the virtual end of the Spanish civil war.

A few days later Mother again wrote to Guszti and me about Father's affairs in a rather depressed mood, produced by Father's reports about his visits to London: "You, Gyurikám, stop running around in a direction that holds out no promise." She also informed us that the British consulate in Budapest had stopped issuing visas for Palestine; thus the entire planned tour seemed to be doomed, even though "there are countless registrants, among them very wealthy people, who would undoubtedly return [to Hungary], and who can produce all kinds of guarantees (land registry documents, tax receipts, etc.), but are not even given an opportunity to produce them."

Although Mother and Father themselves had by then obtained their visas for Palestine, she was thinking of the expenses they would have to incur if they traveled alone, instead of enjoying free or reduced fares as tour leaders. Hence, she wrote, they might postpone their departure and, instead of on February 21, would leave two weeks later. Then, as in practically every one of her letters, she asked me to take care of an individual case: "Raphael's colleague, Dr. László Schächter, would like to go out as a *talmid mehqar* [research student]. He has the travel expenses and the money for two years' tuition fees, but he has to show also that he has enough to live on for a year, which he does not have. Could you perhaps take care of this there? He is not a Hungarian citizen, and on March 1 they will deport him. If at all possible, do something." In the event I was able to "do something," although I no longer remember precisely what. Laci Schächter did arrive soon thereafter in Jerusalem, where sometime later he married a distant cousin of ours, Lili. Several years later Laci, Lili, and their daughter emigrated to America, where Laci became a teacher at a Hebrew school in Chicago.

At the same time Mother was also busy arranging the shipping of the entire contents of the apartment in Nyúl Street to Palestine. This was not easy, because for every item of the slightest value permission had to be obtained from the authorities. In February she wrote me about her efforts to get permission to export the Herzl pictures, which, she wrote, "are here nothing but mediocre daubs, while there they will undoubtedly have great *pretium affectionis* [sentimental value], and, beyond that, possibly also monetary value." She also informed me that Father did not want to ship out any furniture at all, while she herself would have liked to send out at least a few really nice pieces: the practically new pair of leather club chairs, several antique cabinets, Persian rugs, paintings, and the like. In the end she won out, and a whole crate of furniture and other items was shipped to Palestine, so that she was able to recreate in their house in Shekhunat Boruchov, where they moved, a semblance of their beautiful Budapest home.

Mother's letters from those concluding months in Budapest kept me informed of the developments in the position of the Jews of Hungary, or rather of its apparently irresistible deterioration. For instance, in the same letter excerpted above, she wrote (in Hungarian):

> Yesterday Ernő Munkácsi called to congratulate me on Father's lead article. He said he had never read anything as beautiful. Otherwise he was very depressed, for there is a chance the Jewish law will be eased for converts, and he thinks that this will create a new wave of conversions. He fears that at the end there will be nobody left for whom one can work as chief counselor. Thus do the great positions fall. Alas, the *round table conference* is not promising. What will happen to Palestine? That is the most burning question.

Father's lead article was published in the January 1939 issue of *Mult és Jövő*, under the title "Like a Flock without a Shepherd." It was a bitter denunciation of the leaders of the Israelite Congregation of Pest for their shortsighted conduct of affairs, their anti-Zionism, their stubborn insistence on isolating Hungarian Jewry from the rest of the Jewish people, and their closing of their eyes to the clear and present dangers and to the anti-Jewish plague that was spreading across frontiers and was about to engulf Hungary as it did its neighbors to the north. It was a voice crying in the wilderness, a prophetic warning that echoed the heartbreak of Jeremiah in besieged

Jerusalem. It was also—and this is unspeakably sad for me to recall—Father's swan song, his last utterance as a leader addressing his people, before he made his *'aliya* to Palestine, only to be reduced there to a drudge in the service of a small, petty, and contentious society.

The Jewish law Mother mentioned must refer to the first of such laws issued in 1938. It restricted the number of Jews, including those who had converted to Christianity after 1919 and those who were born of Jewish parents after that year, to twenty percent of the total in liberal professions, administrative positions, and commercial and industrial enterprises. The "round table" or "St. James Conference," which opened on February 7, 1939, was convened by the British government to discuss the problem of Palestine with Jewish and Arab leaders. Since the Arabs refused to attend joint meetings with the Jews, the British government conferred with each side separately. The proposal offered by Britain on March 15 was that an independent Palestine state should be established, possibly of a federal nature, in which the essential interests of both the Arab and the Jewish population would be safeguarded. Both the Jews and the Arabs rejected this proposal.

Mother addressed her next letter to Father in Palestine (probably February 15; in Hungarian):

> Today I am totally under the influence of the news about the London Conference. It is terrible that these Britishers, although they ceaselessly proclaim their humanism, should come with such proposals. How can it be that they have no feelings at all that it is not possible to rob the Jews of all their human rights in the only place where they can live a human life? But what does all that count next to imperialist interests? Though it seems that England is now in a much more favorable position, partly because of the progress in arming, and partly due to the active policy of America.

Passing on to personal problems, she asked Father whether she should sell the Nyúl Street apartment, for which one could get no more than 20,000 pengős. She also writes of the problem of her parents, who were supported mainly by Father, and offered the opinion that they could not live on what they were getting at the time:

> This problem, although the Patais do not want to become immersed in it, depresses me and weighs very much on me, since I do not share in the good fortune of having been born a Patai, and my role in world history is confined to having been a bridge between the two Patai generations. After all, we still live very well and comfortably, and it is not such a unique case that the younger ones should support the

old ones—one can see this in Palestine among very poor people, I see it here in my seamstress who supports her uncle and aunt from her earnings. If God helps one in these terrible times, one cannot dole out the money so tightly that they should just not starve to death, for the 100 pengős are just enough not to die, but too little to live . . .

This letter is unique among the hundreds of Patai family letters in that it reveals a disagreement between Father and Mother: she wanted Father to allocate a higher monthly subsidy to her parents than he felt he was able to do. The other son-in-law of Mother's parents, Dr. Ernő Molnár, was a teacher of Jewish religion in the Budapest high schools. His meager salary did not enable him to contribute to the living expenses of his parents-in-law. Thus, practically the entire burden of supporting Mother's parents, who had no other source of income, fell on Father, at a time when he also had to support Guszti, an undergraduate at the Hebrew University, and when his own income, derived from his monthly journal and his books, was rapidly diminishing. After both Father and Mother had left for Palestine, Uncle Ernő took over the editorship of *Mult és Jövő*, and kept it going for several more years. In 1944 he was deported by the Nazis and was never again heard of. My grandparents, Moritz (Moshe) and Teresa Ehrenfeld, died in the Budapest ghetto in 1945. Dóra and Juci Molnár survived and moved to Israel in 1950.

The fate of my mother's and father's families, who stayed behind in Hungary when they could still have left the country legally, exemplifies what happened to the great majority of Hungarian Jews. Until the outbreak of World War II, and for several months thereafter as well, as far as the Hungarian authorities were concerned the Jews were free to leave the country. But the problem was that extraordinary efforts had to be made in order to find a place of refuge, a country that was willing to admit them, for the possibilities of immigration to Palestine or to any other country were minimal, and only people with means, connections, and extraordinary willpower were able to secure the necessary immigration visas.

To this was added the inertia factor. As long as the frontiers of Hungary were open to emigrants, the conditions inside the country, although gradually worsening, had not yet reached the stage to produce the determination to get out. No sane person would, in those days, have imagined what was to come. What had already transpired until then seemed less of an evil than facing the unknown, the deprivations, the dangers, that emigration meant. Thus, only a few Hungarian Jews left while leaving was possible, finding refuge in Palestine, France, England, Cuba, or the United States.

In searching for an understanding of why most Hungarian Jews stayed behind, one more factor must be taken in consideration. Several times in their past Hungarian Jews had experienced outbreaks of anti-Semitism, most recently after the end of World War I. Waves of anti-Semitism had come and gone, and the Jewish community, even though it sustained wounds, had survived. Hence, although anti-Semitism was unquestionably on the increase in the 1930s, it was nothing new for Hungarian Jews, who were confident that "this too will pass." The position of the official Jewish leadership was that anti-Semitism in Hungary was, as it had been in the past, an irregularity, a passing phase of aberration, from which the nation would soon recover. Hence, relatively few of the 600,000 Hungarian Jews were pessimistic enough to conclude, by observing the German Jewish tragedy that was unfolding in front of their very eyes, that this time the outcome would be horribly different.

Thus it came about that, when the frontiers of Hungary were closed, the overwhelming majority of the Jews were trapped in the country and no longer had any choice but to wait impotently until the final blow fell: in March 1944 Germany occupied Hungary, and the *Endlösung*, orchestrated by Adolf Eichmann, began.

This was the background against which the fate of my father's and mother's families in Hungary must be viewed. They too stayed, because as long as they could have left they did not have a sufficient incentive even to try to do so. Incidentally, the letters preserved in my files make it clear that even my own parents, despite all the Zionist convictions of my father, would have stayed on in Hungary in 1939 had it not been for the weighty factor that all three of their children by that time lived in Palestine. Father had the possibility to enter Palestine legally and had a job, even though one that was not to his liking, waiting for him there. Yet he felt so strongly bound to Hungary, to the position he had built up in the course of three decades, that it took a truly desperate effort on the part of his children, carried out in a flood of letters and long-distance phone calls and greatly intensified after the outbreak of World War II, to get him to the point of leaving Budapest.

The next letter Mother wrote, addressed to Father in Jerusalem, is a unique document. She wrote it on the back of a petition addressed in rather faulty English to the Jewish Agency in Jerusalem and signed by some two dozen well-to-do Hungarian Jews, who were waiting, with evident impatience, for the approval of their visitor's visas to Palestine. The petition itself testifies to the mood in at least one sector of Hungarian Jews in the last few months before the outbreak of World War II, and I think it is significant enough to be published here in full. I reproduce it without any change, with all its spelling and grammatical errors.

Budapest, the 4. February 1939

To the Direction of the Jewish Agency

Jerusalem

We beg to apologize for taking the liberty of addressing to You in an important matter. We apply to the Direction to favour us with his aid to obtain an assent for the journey to Palestine.

The Undersigned all are distinguished, wealthy Hungarian gentlemen in high social position, who have the true intention to go on a journey as tourists—and not as immigrants—to the Holy Land to be acquainted with it, or to visit there relations and—in part—to cultive or to establish business relations. The financial standing of the cited gentlemen, his real properties and goods in Hungary are of a kind that gives a complete security, that, without exception, all the supplicants will return to Hungary again.

We apply to the Direction of the Jewish Agency to provide for the needful before the Department of Migration for that the English Consulate in Budapest should grant us the assent for the journey.

The declarations about their assets also quoted in the following list will proved by the cited gentlemen with verified documents personally.

Mr. Dr. Mór Moskovits, sollicitor, capitalist, and son Dr. László Moskovits

Mr. Dr. István Porzsolt, physician, owner of a house, Budapest

Mr. Farkas Lichtmann, Director of the firm Guttman Testvérek [brothers].

Mr. Dr. Ignác Holländer, landlord and owner of a house, and Mrs. Ignác Holländer, Kiskunhalas

Mr. Dr. Lajos Fodor, sollicitor, and son, landlords, Hatvan.

Mr. Ignác Sacher, owner of several houses, Budapest.

Mrs. Jakab Schnitzler, capitalist, Budapest.

Mr. Dezső Paunz, owner of a house and owner of several cheese-shops, Budapest.

Mr. Dr. Jenő Klein, sollicitor, Monor.

Mr. István Sugár, engineer, and Mrs. István Sugár, Szeged.

Mr. Mór Rauchwerger, and son, Jenő Rauchwerger, manufacturers, landowners, Salgótarján

Mrs. Fülöp Nadler and her two sons: György Nadler and Sándor Nadler, manufacturers and capitalists

Mr. Károly Deutsch, and Mrs. Károly Deutsch, owner of a house, Budapest

Mr. Miklós Faragó, and Mrs. Miklós Faragó, owner of the publishing house

The bottom of the page is lost, and thus the names of any additional petitioners who may have been on the list cannot be retrieved. Of all the names listed only that of Miklós Faragó is contained in the *Magyar Zsidó Lexikon* (Hungarian Jewish Lexicon) published in Budapest in 1929. The brief entry about him states that he was a journalist in Budapest, where he was engaged in newspaper and book publishing. Mór and László Moskovits are mentioned in Mother's February 2 letter. Lajos Fodor, whom we have already met, was a good friend of Father. Mrs. Nadler and her sons are mentioned several times in Mother's letters. All the others are unknown to me. What the petition as a whole shows is that professional people and owners of property were eager to get out of Hungary and settle in Palestine—that this was their intention cannot be doubted despite, or precisely because of, their assertion that they wanted to go there only as tourists and not as immigrants. Mother used the reverse of the page to write to Father:

Monday [probably Feb. 6, 1939; in Hungarian]

Yesterday I took this list of names to Krausz for signature, since he had told me that it has to be submitted to a meeting of the committee because he himself cannot take the responsibility. And also that he knows, e.g., that the Binetters want to leave the boy out there. And that, e.g., Victor Jordan wants to remain there (this is really true, I also mentioned it to you). In brief, he will tell me only tomorrow whose names he will submit, etc. Each person must put down 1,000 pengős, and thus the consulate will know exactly who does not return to ask for it back. So they will know that he remained there. Krausz is quite right—but thus the time has become shortened again, so that I don't know whether the tour can be realized until the 7th [of March]. On the other hand, for Passover they will not have enough money, and even if we don't undertake it, we shall still have to provide them with accommodation. Besides, the Adriatica will urge us just as it did last time, or even more. Already I regret very much that instead of postponing I did not cancel the tour altogether: it grates very much on my nerves. Moreover, e.g., Mrs. Schnitzer, the daughter of Mrs. Brüll, and Lulu Grossmann want to remain out there. On the other hand, Mrs. Brüll came with the demand that you should now reciprocate the service she had rendered to you. Difficult things. It would certainly have been wiser to occupy ourselves with our own affairs, such as the early sale of the apartment—Krausz will urge [that I get] a functionary's ticket, but I won't even consider going out alone. There is no reason for it, and anyhow it is difficult to leave the whole comedy here. And there is nobody to whom one could leave it.

In any event tell me now what is your opinion about the tour. True, you cannot know it from there, when I, even though I am here, don't know. In any case I shall ask Krausz whom he . . . so that I should know approximately on how many one can count. The main trouble is that the people do not move at all, even though all of them want to go. Look after the affair of Dr. László Schächter, he is in a desperate situation. Please send copy for the March issue. Perhaps Raphael too could write something. He has not written for a long time.

Many hugs to all three of you,
Mama

New development! Tickets can be reserved only for March 28. Write me therefore whether one can go there for the Passover, and what you think in general. Of course, we send no memorandum to the [Jewish] Agency. Today I got my passport. Hugs, Edith. For the time being do nothing about the visa!

Mr. Krausz, whose first name I cannot ascertain, was the head of the Palestine Office in Budapest. The task of that office was to represent the Jewish Agency for Palestine and especially to serve as liaison between it and the Hungarian Jews. Of the other names mentioned in the letter I know only that of Victor Jordan, who was a Zionist activist in Hungary. Adriatica was the Italian ship line used by Father for his tours to Palestine; it replaced the Lloyd Triestino.

It is nothing less than remarkable that with all the things Mother had to take care of for Father and her children, she still found time and energy to concern herself about the affairs of strangers who turned to her for help. She substituted for Father as editor of *Mult és Jövő*, took care of the liquidation of the Patai household, applied and fought for the permission of the Hungarian National Bank to transfer money for Saul's livelihood in Jerusalem, packed and mailed books to him and to me, supported her old parents both financially and morally, and settled many other personal affairs. But at the same time she helped people who were forced to or wanted to leave Hungary and go to Palestine. In many of her letters written to me in those first three months of 1939, she referred briefly to some person who had come to her and asked her help, which she unstintingly gave to the best of her ability, or else passed the request on to me and urged me to do my utmost in Jerusalem at the immigration department of the Jewish Agency, where I had become a well-known lobbyist for my Hungarian compatriots.

Since Mother had no time to write detailed letters (and her letters were always detailed) separately to the three members of her family who were in Palestine as well as to her daughter in Paris, she addressed her letters "Dear Yóshka, Gyurikám, Évikém, Gusztikám," typed them in an original and a carbon copy, and sent one to Jerusalem, the other to Paris. In one of these letters in duplicate, written a few days before she left Budapest for Palestine, she told us about a case that touched her more closely than the others:

Sunday, March 19, 1939 [in Hungarian]

Just now it has developed that I am forced to collect a sizable amount for the *'aliya* of a man named Davidovits. He has been shoved 18 times from one frontier to the other, now Betar is willing to take him out, but, of course, travel expenses are needed. Alas, that does not go easily in the present circumstances. So far Szőnyi gave 20 pengős, very pleasantly and easily, Margit Székely 10 pengős. Ella Friedmann also promised. It will pile up somehow . . . A public personage by the name of Markus Ernst called me—he heard that I am taking an interest in Davidovits, he knows him, he often visits the detention barracks where the two [Jewish] congregations jointly supply food for the detainees. The son-in-law of Károly Freudiger (whom I also called in this matter) gave him 20 pengős for D. At the same time Ernst also asked me to write to you concerning his son Fülöp, whose application has been submitted to the university. Please inquire about it when next you go there.

Next day Mother added on the reverse of the page:

Monday

Dear Yóshka:

Yesterday, in connection with the collection I went to the Kahan-Frankels, who received me very kindly and nicely gave 50 pengős in the name of the Bureau and 20 in their own name. At the same time they asked that you recommend their domestic tutor to be admitted to the university. They have already submitted an application to the Palestine Office where they were promised everything, but also were told that it would be good to have some patronage in Jerusalem. The data of the man: Jacob Müller, born May 4, 1906, in Sátoraljaujhely, finished *polgári* [junior high] school in Pest, spent ten years in a yeshiva, passed his high school exam in London in 1937. Is perfect in Hebrew, English. Do everything you can, they have always behaved very nicely, and now they simply went out of their way when they received me.

Apart from that, they told me that they had heard the London radio, Chamberlain spoke in very bellicose tones. I beg you, get there some foodstuffs, if God forbid there should be war, Palestine will have nothing to eat. Sugar, dry peas, beans, canned tomatoes, and good oil keep for a long time. These things can also be used later in peacetime. Otherwise the mood here is very depressed, I am glad that you are there. Try to arrange for my visa—it is a question of whether it will not be late. I phoned the British consulate: they said new instructions come all the time . . .

Hugs,
Edith

I think that the Kahan-Frankels are Mr. and Mrs. Adolf Frankl. He was president of the Orthodox Jewish National Bureau, the countrywide organization of the Orthodox Jewish congregations of Hungary. A few days later Mother returned to the subject and wrote that "Yesterday . . . I asked the Palestine Office for the telephone number of Betar regarding my protégé (in recent days quite a number of such have turned up) . . ."

As the day of Mother's own departure from Budapest drew closer, the fate of her parents worried her more and more. In one of her letters written at that time she says:

> If our plan is realized, I shall have an enormous number of things to do, but, of course, I shall be glad to do them. Only the fate of my parents weighs on me very, very heavily. Even if we assure them a minimum of livelihood, I don't know that I shall have the heart to leave them here in this uncertainty. Really, how hard is this otherwise wonderful life! And I have never as yet let down, not even in small matters, anyone who counted on me. This would totally destroy my tranquillity.

As it happened, Mother had only two options: either to stay behind with her parents and sister or to leave them behind and go with Father to Palestine to join her three children there. It was a difficult decision for her, but in the end she chose to go. She saw her parents once more when, in the summer of 1939, she and Father spent several weeks in Budapest. For years thereafter, until Father's illness required her total emotional concentration on him, Mother was agitated by remorse over having abandoned her old parents. She discussed with me repeatedly what she *could have* done to get them out of Budapest while it was still possible. It so happened that Grandfather and Grandmother survived the years of horror in the Budapest ghetto, in semistarvation, and died of sickness, exhaustion, malnutrition, and old age shortly before the liberation of Budapest in 1945. Both were in their eighties.

The Unfriendly "Friends"

An early reference to Father's interest in a position with the Palestinian Friends of the Hebrew University is contained in a long letter Évi wrote me from Paris on September 1, 1938, which she concluded with this incomplete sentence (I am giving it here in a literal translation from her Hungarian with all the emphases contained in the original): "If Papa gets the job (*write me express what could Goldmann do in that matter through Weizmann,* or through somebody else, he is very friendly with Weizmann and precisely during these weeks he will meet him frequently, and *he is willing to intervene on Papa's behalf*) write to me about this to my Paris address, I want to make use of this behind Papa's back. *Don't forget!!!!*"

That the job Évi refers to was with the "Friends" becomes clear from my response dated September 10, 1938 (in Hungarian):

> In Papa's affair Goldmann could do this: as you are probably informed, the matter under discussion is that Papa should be entrusted with the organization, primarily in the cultural field, of the Society of Friends of the Hebrew University. Members of the Society pay a membership fee of one pound annually, but for the time being there are only very few of them in the Palestinian cities (mainly in Tel Aviv, Jerusalem, and Haifa), and therefore they would entrust Papa with the organization of cultural propaganda in the country, and, in general, with leading and supervising the work of the Society. Schneursohn himself (the financial secretary of the university), who is the responsible authority in this matter, and "under" whom Papa would have to work, proposed it to Papa (of course, Ibn-Zahav's hand is in the background, but this must remain between us), and he, that is, Schneursohn, will certainly do everything he can to arrange it. For your information: we are talking about a monthly salary of ca. 20 pounds, which, of course, one should try to increase. When all is said and done, the realization of the plan depends not on Schneursohn, who can only suggest and recommend, but on the highest authorities of the university, that is, on Salman Schocken, who is nominally the chairman of the executive committee of the university, but in reality its practically omnipotent minister of finance, and on Weizmann, who is the chairman of the university's board of governors. If, therefore, Goldmann is really so friendly with Weizmann, he could tell him how great is the importance of developing cultural propaganda for the university precisely in Palestine, and how beneficial it would be to win for this work such an outstanding cultural organizational power, lecturer, and personality suffused with true Jewish spirit, etc., as Patai. I think Weizmann is the only one who has real influence on Schocken, so that if Gold. could win Weizmann the matter could be considered settled. On the other

hand, it is also possible that Weizmann would not even have to win over Schocken, but could settle the matter within his own sphere of authority. Of course I don't know this for certain; however, not this is the important thing, but that Gold. should really convince Weizmann that we must get Papa to work for the university. Together with this work, Papa should be entrusted with lecturing, two hours a week, on Hebrew poetry after the Spanish-Jewish Golden Age (this subject is so far not at all covered at the university), and he would have to be given, at least *ad personam*, the title professor, so that the required framework should be created for him. I want to add that in the decision on this issue also the following two have an input: Berl Katzenelson, editor-in-chief of *Davar*, Tel Aviv, 115 Allenby Road, and Justice Gad Frumkin, Jerusalem, Rehavia, who is president of the Palestinian Agudat Shohre haUniversita! [Society of Friends of the University]. If therefore Gold. has influence on these two, that too should be used.

For lack of documentation I am unable to say whether any further step was taken in connection with this plan in the fall of 1938. However, when Father arrived in Palestine in February 1939, following his visit to Paris and London (see above), it had become evident to him that none of the plans he had discussed in those two cities would come to fruition. Thus, he was forced back into the position of making efforts toward the realization of the one alternative he liked least, but which was the only one with serious chances to succeed: his appointment as director of the Palestinian Friends of the Hebrew University, a position that in effect was nothing but that of fund-raiser.

Although the purpose of the Palestinian Friends, like that of similar societies in other countries, was to drum up support for the university, there was one difference between them: the other societies were far away from and independent of the university administration, while the Palestinian Friends were to a considerable extent controlled, or at least influenced, by that administration. This being the case, the appointment of a director, officially in the jurisdiction of the Friends, was in effect also dependent on the people in charge of the administration of the university. Because of this somewhat murky situation, Father's appointment became a protracted process that involved a kind of power-play between the executive of the Friends and the university. Father in his letters kept Mother informed of the developments, and she, in a letter to Father, Saul, and me in March 1939, reflected the lack of enthusiasm they must have conveyed. She remarked, "Be careful, all of you, about your health. Especially you, Yóshka, in that oriental winter. I am afraid you undertook a difficult and strenuous task with that propaganda job. But let us hope it will be possible to exchange it for something better."

At the end of a letter Father wrote to Évi on March 3, 1939, in Hungarian, he said:

Concerning the position of the leadership of the Friends of the University, yesterday took place the meeting of the narrower executive committee, which resolved that they would entrust me with it. Next week will be the meeting of the larger committee at which they will probably confirm this. Of course, one can never know whether some intrigue won't interfere and bring it to naught. If I get the appointment I shall accept it and shall start working, which, however, will not prevent the carrying out of our "great plan." I want to add that Justice Frumkin, who is president of the Friends of the University, is of the opinion that our plan should be connected with the Friends, or, rather, that it should be realized within its framework . . .

The "great plan" Father refers to was the plan of establishing a "Jerusalem Academy" on which he, with my most active participation, had been working for quite a while (see chapter 7).

Although the "larger committee" approved the decision of the narrower executive, there was much additional quibbling concerning Father's salary. Even at the last minute, one day before Father was supposed to start working, they still had not fixed his remuneration and haggled with him about it. He touched upon this in one of the letters he wrote to Évi in Paris, which he dictated to Saul:

Jerusalem, March 22, 1939 [in Hungarian]

Dear Évikém:

A few days ago I wrote to Mama that she should pack up everything and come, even if she cannot settle all the affairs. After all, Grandpa is there, he could take care of either letting the apartment or its sale and of the delivery of the things to the forwarder if by then we have the permit from the National Bank. Mr. Dénes, the manager of the Schanker firm, happens to live in the house; he can certainly arrange that everything should be dispatched quickly from there. We too here think that it is best that Mama should be here as soon as possible, and at the utmost we shall go back in the summer to settle the things that have been left over. (This we shall permit under no condition— Raphael and Saul.) [. . .]

(I make use of the pause while Papa thinks over what to dictate next, to emphasize repeatedly on my part that Mama must come without delay with the first available ship. Enough of living apart. Saul.)

Yesterday there was a huge wedding at the Frumkins, *à la* Budapest, with hundreds of guests. Traffic policemen, British and Jewish, directed the cars that brought all Jerusalem to greet the young couple and their parents. We were there with Raphael, who was very elegant in his eight-year-old dinner jacket from Budapest. (I have always said that Raphael is a changeling, the son of a count. Saul.) We hope that in a few days it will be possible also to consult with Frumkin about the affairs of the University Friends, he needs a few days for thanking for the greetings and presents. [. . .]

The Patais of Jerusalem

Évi in her next letter again urged Mother to go to Palestine without delay and also to visit her in Paris. She sent the letter to us in Jerusalem, with a copy to Mother in Budapest.

Paris, March 21, 1939 [in German]

Dear Parents, Raphael, Saul:

A few days ago I spoke to Mama over the phone, for I wanted to tell her personally that she must take care of all her visas. My view is that it would, in any case, be good if she would obtain not only the transit visas she needs for Palestine, but would also apply for a French visa, on the basis that on her way to Palestine she must, or rather wants, to visit me and Tirzah, who are here alone. I hope Mama is not careless and will arrange all this.

I hear, thank God, optimistic utterances from all sides: there will be no war. But Mama's trip to Palestine becomes more and more urgent, for it can happen easily that later she would want to go and could no longer, in view of the fact that freedom of movement is not always and not everywhere accorded to Jews. I think this is clear. My view is that Mama should in any case join Papa—it is an unnatural situation, this being separated, and it can, if one hesitates long, drag out longer than one would like it . . .

Please, listen to me, my instinct that Papa should go to visit the boys was also correct, I am sure I am not mistaken this time either. One must not anger the gods. [. . .]

I don't know whether Papa and Mama have read in the papers that in Prague the Zionists, among them the wonderful one-armed Fritz Kahn, have been arrested. The poor people—it is terrible! And certificates will be available only in mid-April, so that until then nothing can be undertaken in order to bring them out. One should read such news carefully. Also women—Mme. Hannah Steiner, Mrs. Marie Schmolka—are detained. And these women, as far as I know, did nothing but work in charity . . .

Otherwise nothing new. [. . .]

A thousand kisses to all of you with great love,
Évi

All the three people Évi mentions were well-known public figures in the Jewish life of Czechoslovakia. Fritz (Franz) Kahn (1895–1944) was a Zionist leader who had lost his left arm in World War I. When the Nazis occupied Czechoslovakia he chose to stay on, was arrested, and was sent to Theresienstadt. In October 1944 he was taken, together with his wife and many other active Zionists, to Auschwitz to perish in the gas chambers. Hannah Steiner (1894–1944) was a founder of the Women's International Zionist Organization (WIZO) and a leader of the relief committee for refugees. On March 16, 1939, the day after the Nazi occupation of Prague, she was arrested but was released a few weeks later. Together with her husband, Ludwig Steiner (a high school teacher), she chose to remain in Prague with their oppressed co-religionists. Both were interned in Theresienstadt and in 1944 deported to Auschwitz, where she died in the gas chambers. Marie Schmolka (1890–1940) was a leader of the Jewish women's movement, and, together with Hannah Steiner, was the moving spirit of the relief committee. When Hannah Steiner was arrested by the Nazis, Marie Schmolka presented herself to the Gestapo and declared that she, and not Hannah Steiner, was responsible for the activities of the committee. She was imprisoned, but subsequently released and authorized by the Nazis to go to Paris and London to arrange for the emigration of Jews from Bohemia and Moravia. She died suddenly in London.

On March 26 Father repeated his instructions to Mother that she pack up and leave.

Jerusalem, March 26, 1939 [in Hungarian]

Dear Edith:

I thought that you had long ago received the letters in which not only Guszti but all the three of us wrote that you should pack up and come here with the first ship, whether or not it is possible to sell or let the apartment. Neither the letting of the apartment nor its sale can be decisive. Both can be arranged by your parents, who will need the rental income, and if possible they can send part of it here through the National Bank—the applications needed can be submitted by your father. The situation is the same with the journal and my pension, of which we can take care by mail, and if I am too busy you can do the work from here as well . . . And if the situation should clear up, then, after all, both you and I will have our tickets for the trip back, and we can go to Pest for the final settling of affairs. I repeat therefore: purchase a round trip ticket from the Adriatica (which owes us some money, and perhaps they will also give some discount, as I wrote to you previously), and pull some strings so that even if the ships are fully booked, you should be given space, if possible on the first ship.

Continuing his letter Father suggests that Mother should contact a forwarder and have him pack all the furniture, books, pictures, rugs, etc., and ship everything in a crate to Tel Aviv. "We have written to you that it is not worthwhile to make a selection now, but rather pack up and send everything. Likewise it is not worthwhile to select books either, but send all the books. Likewise all the papers, letters, notes, old newspapers . . ."

This letter did not reach Mother in Budapest, for she left the city on March 27 and the next day took the ship from Trieste to Haifa. She arrived about April 3 and took up residence with Father temporarily in the Shaf Hayam Hotel in Tel Aviv.

In the meantime Évi again wrote from Paris:

Paris, April 2, 1939 [in German]

Dear Parents, Raphael, and Saul:

[. . .] The day before yesterday I was invited to a little dinner party given by Professor Mawas (Tirzah's ophthalmologist) in my honor in order to be able to greet me in his home . . . Present were the widow of a French minister of state, the Aighion couple (enormously rich aristocratic Egyptians, Mawas too is of Egyptian origin), and Mawas's daughter. (Mawas is divorced, his ex-wife lives in Egypt, his twenty-year-old daughter, who is charming and conceived a great liking for me, lives with him: she has an apartment in his house, a separate chambermaid, etc., that is, everything in a highly feudal style.) It was very pleasant, they gave me the greatest possible *koved* [honor]. [. . .] Madame Aighion invited me, she and Mawas belong to the first circles of France; Leon Blum often dines in Mawas's house, also other ministers of state, barons, aristocrats, etc. So that it is very pleasant for me to move in this circle. Once Mawas has invited me I am *salonfähig* [fit for good society] in all France.

Of course Mawas is vehemently interested in me, but I have become friendly with his daughter, who intersts me more than her father—who, after all, even if a great authority as a physician and immensely rich, is fifty years old. He finds me "enchanting," and says I must get to know all his friends and his whole family. Thus—gradually I get into circles that are not open to everybody. Alas, mainly by being liked by men . . . but what should I do against it? I shall try to win this circle for the idea of the Academy. Eitingon too is good for it—are you so friendly with him? [. . .]

Évi

Leon Blum (1872–1950) was of course the famous French Jewish statesman, who was premier of France in 1936–1937 and again in 1938 and 1946.

A few days later Ibn-Zahav told me that the day before Schneursohn had met Frumkin in Tel Aviv, who took him to task: how was it possible that Father already knew what salary he would get, when this was, for the time being, a confidential matter? Schneursohn, on his part, took umbrage at Ibn-Zahav, because it was Ibn-Zahav who told Father about the 25 pounds monthly budget of the Friends. Now Ibn-Zahav asked me to write to Father that he should mention his salary to nobody, and that when he met Frumkin again he should tell him that on one occasion he had asked Ibn-Zahav what the budgetary allocation for his job would be, whereupon Ibn-Zahav answered that he did not know definitely but thought it would be 300 pounds annually, including all expenses. I duly reported this to Father in a letter dated April 14, 1939.

While this wrangling went on about Father's salary, he and Mother (who in those days relieved him of much of the editorial responsibilities) planned to publish an article in *Mult és Jövő* (which, edited by Uncle Ernő Molnár, continued to appear in Budapest) about the Frumkin family, especially about the father of the justice, who had been a pioneer of Hebrew journalism in Jerusalem, and his daughter, who was just about that time graduating as a lawyer from the government-sponsored law school in that city. Mother urged me in several letters, sent from Tel Aviv to Jerusalem, to obtain photographs from the Frumkins to accompany the article. I had to go to their house five times until I was finally able to get the photos, and it was only in May that I mailed them to my parents in Tel Aviv. The article on the Frumkins was published in the June 1939 issue.

Soon after Mother's arrival in Palestine I began to plan to visit my sister Évi in Paris. I had never in my life been farther west than Berlin and wanted to make use of her sojourn in Paris to pay a visit to that famous city of lights. At the same time my parents planned to return to Budapest in order to take care of the unfinished affairs they had left behind that winter. This plan was strongly opposed by Saul and me, and even more vehemently by Évi, who wrote to us from Paris:

May 4, 1939 [in German]

Dear Only Parents and Two Only Brothers:

I have as yet received no acknowledgment of my cable that Mama should give up her travel plans. Everything I wrote in that connection the day thereafter is and remains true, and I beg you to act accordingly. One cannot go to Hungary today, because it is and remains only a question of time until Hungary becomes officially a German protectorate and is forced to engage in an internal war against Poland.

In addition—I beg you to say nothing about this to anybody—but it is possible that the Gestapo already has the Hungarian police in its hands. [. . .]

It is almost certain by now that the [Zionist] Congress will open on Aug. 2 in Geneva. I am writing today to Franz Kahn, and G[oldmann] will write to Lauterbach. Has Gyuri got in touch with Lauterbach? His European trip is the only right thing, I am sooooo happy that he will come, it will be a recovery not only for him but also for me to have a Patai here . . .

In the next issue of *La Terre Retrouvée* a chapter of my novel will be published. [. . .]

In fact the 21st Zionist Congress was held in Geneva on August 16–26, 1939. *La Terre Retrouvée* was a French Zionist bimonthly published since 1928 in Paris.

In her next extant letter dated Paris, May 15, 1939, again addressed to the whole family in Palestine, Évi made yet another effort to dissuade our parents from going back to Budapest. She wrote [in German]:

Concerning the trip of Mama, resp. Papa, what I wrote about it is an unchanged fact, and I can only emphasize and repeat everything. Despite [Papa's] having been accepted into the Press Chamber. I repeat once more: I have political information from the source, and should the idea of a trip emerge, I beg you to consult first with me, and to decide only thereafter. One must not rush into misfortune. You have not the slightest idea of what is going on in Hungary behind the scenes.

On May 19, 1939, addressing herself this time to me alone, Évi expressed her fears about Saul and me having joined the Hagana, the defense organization of the *yishuv* [in German]:

Your Hagana work has cost me several sleepless nights. Fool that I am I was convinced that you had nothing to do with it. And yet, I recognize that it is almost impossible to steer clear of it. And I try to reconcile myself with it . . . At the same time I am glad that the two of you are at least in the same group. I would have done likewise in your place.

The Hagana-work consisted, to begin with, in training in firearms by a veteran member of the Hagana, the Jewish self-defense organization, which by that time enjoyed a semilegal status and was used by the Palestine police to augment its inadequate manpower. After the training, Saul and I were assigned to guard duty. Once a week in the evening we went to the Mahane Yehuda police station, where each of us was given a rifle, ammunition, and some sort of makeshift uniform, and then, thus equipped, marched to a house facing the Mamillah Cemetery, through which Arab attackers were known to have sneaked into the Jewish part of Jerusalem. We climbed up the stairs to the flat roof of the three-story building and stood, or rather sat, watch there until 2 o'clock in the morning, when we were replaced by another two men. We went back to the police station, returned our gear, and went home to sleep. Throughout the months we fulfilled this duty we never saw a suspicious movement, and, of course, never fired a single round.

About the same time Mother wrote from Jerusalem to Évi in Paris:

Wednesday [no date, probably May 1939; in Hungarian]

Dear Évikém:

Alas, this week no letter has come from you. As for last week, I barely remember it. In any case it seems to me that I haven't heard from you for a long time. According to Gyuri I am insatiable—possibly so. Papa is now in Haifa: he works there, I work here at the boys' as an *ozeret* [maid], which is not an easy job, but at least I have pleasure with it. I put the apartment in order, the kitchen functions splendidly, Gyuri has gained 2 1/2 kilos in 12 days! Of course, Muntner's injections also have a share in it. You can imagine how gladly I cook when finally Gyuri has an appetite for once. I have already got acquainted with all the butchers, and occasionally I get wonderful meat. Guszti has eaten until now mostly at the students' canteen, but I would like him too to eat at home. As a rule he comes down from the university only at 5. In my free time I study Hebrew, but, alas, my mind is not on it. I am awaiting impatiently what you will write about my trip to Pest. Everybody says I may go safely, only Papa shouldn't. But Papa wants to go under any circumstances, because there are many important matters he wants to settle. Thus: the transfer of his pension, the agreement with the employees, the securing of the continued permit for his journal for some time at least, the arrangements with the apartment and the furniture. If there is a real and serious reason, then of course everything is reduced to secondary importance, but if not—it is after all quite different if one can bring over one's furniture, and possibly can fit oneself out. The fact is that here the 18-pounds salary is not sufficient for this, especially since this month Guszti no longer received the transfer of 8 pounds (probably because we are not at home). But not this is what I should have mentioned in the first place, but rather the journal, which we want to maintain as long as there is any possibility, since one cannot know what will develop. In any case, one does not throw away one's life work, unless there are compelling reasons. Thus far there is complete quiet and order in Pest. Let me know if you have any *reliable* information about the situation there. People travel, come and go. Even those who have no important ties with Hungary as we do. On the other hand, one cannot count today on 100% safety anywhere. Of course the Palestine news of the papers is exaggerated, the Hungarian papers publish veritable chronicles of horror from here—but the 100% is not complete here either.

Gyuri is preparing for the trip. He is planning to leave on the 1st. His outfit is being readied. Lauterbach's letter of which Gyuri sent you a copy was sent to Geneva to the office of the Congress. See to it that they should arrange it positively as soon as possible. In addition Gyuri wants to know whether there is a Hebrew typewriter there. Is a dinner jacket necessary? I am glad that Gyuri is going, it will do him good to get out a little. If only the world situation should not be turned on its head in the meantime. What do people say about this there? Will there be an alliance with Russia?

[. . .] The Jewish people react to the White Paper with terror. It is possible that this is how it has to be, lest they say that the Jews acquiesce quietly in everything. In any case, this way the country again has no rest. Perhaps, if the European situation clears up the British will have a calmer head. But when will that be? Papa writes that in Haifa illegal immigrants are taken off the ship day after day. He does not write whether this is done with the consent of the British, but that is how it looks.

Gyuri went today to see Professor Fodor—he wants finally to print the stationery of the Academy—but did not find him at home. Tomorrow he goes up to the university.

Now that I am here with the boys I see how much they need somebody who takes care of their nourishment and comfort. Gyuri, rather than prepare food for himself, often did not eat. Guszti, it is true, liked to cook at home when he came home at night, but he was not this tired there. In any case I would very much like to live together with them, but I don't know whether it can be arranged that we should live in Jerusalem.

I conclude for today. I hope at last to have a letter from you tomorrow.

A thousand hugs to you and Tirzuli,

Mama

Dr. Sussmann Muntner (1897–1973) was a physician in Jerusalem and a very close friend of our family as well as our family doctor. He was also a medical historian and published important books on medieval Jewish medicine, including the medical works of Maimonides. In 1959 he became professor of medical history at the Hebrew University.

"The agreement with the employees" refers to agreements Father wanted to enter into with the employees of the editorial and administrative offices of his monthly who would be out of jobs once the journal folded. The "transfer of 8 pounds" refers to Father's monthly transfer of this amount from Budapest to Palestine through the Hungarian National Bank to provide a livelihood for Guszti.

The White Paper was the Malcolm MacDonald White Paper of May 1939, which stated, in part, that "His Majesty's Government now declares unequivocally that it is not part of their policy that Palestine should become a Jewish state." This was regarded by the Jews as a final betrayal of Britain's obligations under the Balfour Declaration and the Mandate and triggered the active struggle of the *yishuv* against the Mandatory regime in Palestine. The White Paper also restricted Jewish immigration to 10,000 per annum, whereupon the Zionist leadership retorted by declaring clandestine immigration a prime means in the struggle for Jewish independence.

Professor Andor Fodor was a friend of the Patai family. In the November 2, 1939, issue of the Jerusalem weekly *Ha'Olam* I published a detailed and very laudatory review of his slender book *Über das Wesen der Kulturwandlungen* (On the Essence of Cultural Changes), which dealt, not with chemistry, but with an anthropological subject. Of the plan for the Jerusalem Academy I shall tell in the next chapter.

One of the first tasks to which Father devoted himself after he finally got his appointment as director of the Friends was to organize a chapter for them in Haifa, where no such group had existed until then. He went several times to Haifa, met with influential people there, recruited them into the ranks of the Friends, and obtained contributions from them. In the home of Mrs. Rachel Goldberg, the widow of Yitzhaq Leib Goldberg, in Tel Aviv he met her daughter and son-in-law, Mr. and Mrs. Arno Hochfeld, who lived in Haifa in a luxurious villa on Mount Carmel. Hochfeld, a wealthy industrialist, promised to help Father in establishing a branch of the Friends in Haifa.

Father was so eager to produce quick results (or, perhaps, so afraid that in the absence of impressive results his job would be in jeopardy) that, as he wrote me in one of his letters, he "was working day and night." To which I responded (on April 30, 1939, in Hebrew):

I don't think it is right that you should work so much for the Society of Friends. Whether or not there are results, you must not overexert yourself. Under no conditions must you work more than seven hours a day. Especially in that Tel Aviv heat. Work beyond seven hours does not yield additional results, because one does it after having become exhausted, and, besides, it is known that the work invested is never proportionate with the results.

After the usual intensive family consultations we decided that Mother and I would sail from Haifa to Trieste on July 5, 1939, and Father would stay on in Palestine for a few more weeks to get into the stride of work for the Friends. I used the ticket that Father had for a Tel Aviv (or Haifa) to Trieste sailing of a ship of the Adriatica line, which was transferable. Mother, on her part, felt that the unfinished business she had left behind when she came from Budapest to Palestine in April demanded her presence, even if it meant again being separated from Father for a few weeks or even months. From Trieste Mother went on by train to Budapest, and I took another train to Paris. About my sojourn in Paris and subsequently in Geneva and my trip back from Trieste to Haifa after the war broke out I shall report in a later chapter.

As for Mother, in the last few weeks before she left Tel Aviv for Budapest she was ambivalent about the Palestine versus Budapest issue that confronted both her and Father. In this she undoubtedly reflected Father's own feelings and indecision. The attraction of Budapest for both of them lay in the fact that there Father's position, income, style of life, and activities would, for the time being, continue more or less unchanged, as against which there was of course the growing apprehension that under German influence Hungarian Jewry would have to face the same discrimination, deprivation of rights, and attacks as did the Jews of Germany—in 1939 this was as yet all they had to suffer: the unimaginable cataclysm came years later. On the other hand, to live in Palestine meant for Father the realization of his lifelong Zionist dream of 'aliya, relative safety under the British flag in case of war, even though the record of great, liberal England was tarnished by Britain's inability to quell the Arab riots and by its chiseling away—perfidiously, we all felt—on its undertaking to facilitate the establishment of a Jewish National Home in Palestine. And, of course, from the personal angle, the most serious negative aspect of Father's staying on in Palestine was the highly unsatisfactory nature of the only position he was able to obtain.

Even though Father's work in Haifa succeeded beyond expectations, his bosses in the Friends continued to behave toward him in a niggardly manner. In July 1939 he wrote from Tel Aviv to Mother, who by that time was again back in Budapest, in a rather discouraged, even dispirited, mood, and expressed his regret that he had not quit the whole caboodle and returned to Budapest. He devoted most of his letter to this issue, which was quite uncharacteristic.

Tel Aviv [no date, probably July 1939; in Hungarian]

Dear Edith:

I am here in Tel Aviv, I had my tooth taken care of, but they [the Friends] did not take care of the salary remittance, so that I must wait until tomorrow for those responsible to settle the matter. Thus, a whole week was lost. On the other hand they explained to me today that when I am on the road I can claim only an "additional allowance" and not all the expenses, for, after all, I have expenses at home as well. I told them we can talk about this as far as the future is concerned, but for now I have had the expenses, and at most I shall try in the future to travel as little as possible so as not to exceed the seven-pound limit. But it will not surely not help increase the income of the Society, if instead of helping me and discussing with me how to help in the work, they confer behind my back on what could be saved on me. Frankly, the matter annoyed me very much, and I regretted somewhat that Raphael used my ticket, for perhaps now I would have taken the ship right away. But then I thought it was not worthwhile to get annoyed over their robbing one of one's zest. [. . .]

I met Klausner—he sends you warm regards—he has already written the article about me, it will be published as the introduction. We made arrangements with *HaTzofe* that they will publish the Hebrew translation of *The Middle Gate* in installments and subsequently publish it in book form. Have a copy of *The Middle Gate* sent to Raphael to Paris. I mailed him from here the tractate of the Talmud so that he should be able to use it.

Today I met Mrs. Persitz: she invited me for Sunday, we shall see what if anything comes out of it. I shall try.

I cabled Mrs. Nadler. The matter of her son Gyuri is settled. It was necessary to speak from here on the phone with the [Budapest] Technical University; it was very difficult despite the scholarship.

I hope to have a letter from you tomorrow, and that you have written to Jerusalem about everything.

I visited Tchernichowsky: he will give a talk about me in the radio, and the local Pen Club will have a reception for me together with Max Brod. In a word—all is milk and honey.

Write about everything. Many regards to your parents and the Molnárs.

Hugs and kisses with great love,
Your Husband

The Middle Gate is the title of Father's memoirs of his childhood in the village of Pata, published originally in Hungarian in 1927. Since it contained many quotations from the tractate *Bava Metzi'a* (The Middle Gate) of the Babylonian Talmud (hence its title), Father felt that in translating the book into Hebrew I should have at my disposal the original of the tractate in question in order to be able to render those quotations in their original version. Max Brod (1884–1968) was a well-known Czech-German-Jewish writer.

On the back of this letter, which she forwarded to Paris, Mother wrote:

> One must not, from the distance, overestimate the quality of life in Jerusalem. There too there is much superficiality and incredible pettiness, as shown by Papa's letter on the reverse. (I can imagine how irritated Papa was. After the wonderful results in Haifa, this impertinence!) And probably Paris too is not as superficial as you think. What do the papers write about the chances of a war? Write about this! [. . .]

In another letter from about the same time written from Budapest to Évi in Paris Mother gave a picture of the difficulties she had with the Hungarian authorities:

> What you write about the things to be shipped, I can take into account only inasmuch as they are included in the list we submitted to the National Bank. It seems you have absolutely no idea how strict the control here is. Raphael's idea that I should simply send all the books in crates made us all smile here. Books are, first of all, subjected to expert review, then they are packed in the presence of customs officials. Of course, before that we must produce a certificate attesting that neither we nor the addressee owe taxes and that the things are my own consumer goods, a certificate from the Jerusalem university that Raphael teaches there, a certificate that Raphael has no property, an export license from the Museum of Fine Arts for the paintings, and one from the Museum of Industrial Arts for the rugs—only this. Yes, one more thing: a list of the books in four copies. Thank God, today the forwarder submitted all this, on behalf of all three of you, to the National Bank, where we also had to produce our tax books in which it was stated that Papa owns property valued at 36,000 pengő's, and thus is able to send his children items of such value. According to the forwarder everything will be in order. You cannot imagine how glad I was to hear this. The matter was several times in such a mess that it looked totally helpless. But I went again and again to the municipality, so that at the end I was quite well acquainted with all the premises.

In the same letter Mother informed Évi that Father had been appointed a delegate to the meeting of the Jewish Agency that was to take place on August 30–31 in Geneva, but that she did not think he would go because precisely at that time he wanted to come to Budapest. And that was what he actually did, although Mother did not know about his decision almost until the day he arrived.

A few days later Mother again wrote to Évi:

> The free hours of my last five or six days were spent in arranging the letters. It is incredible what emerged from the depths of wardrobes, drawers. I looked at almost everything, did not discard anything unseen, but even so we made veritable *autos da fé* in the kitchen. One must not, must not, hoard up things like this, especially we Jews under whom the earth constantly moves. And, interestingly, the apartment and the drawers are full even now—one cannot notice at all how much has been carried away, burned, recently.

It seems that in one of her letters Évi wrote to Mother that she felt it was not good for her daughter Tirzah to be an only child. Mother responded:

> What you write about the child—it is a great problem whether it is permitted to bring more children into the world, in this chaotic turbulence. As you know, I was always a partisan of many children, but this must absolutely be looked upon not from the point of view of the parents, but of the children. If we had a secure home in Palestine, and the possibility of a normal, human life, it would be something else again. But, of course, this, naturally, is not a matter of principle—everyone takes a position on it in accordance with his own feelings. It is true that the members of a bigger family stand more securely in life. At least, this is how it should be. But even this cannot be generalized.

Father became increasingly disillusioned with the attitude of both the Friends and the university administration, who wrangled about who should be in control of his work, and both of whom seemed intent on getting as much out of him for the smallest salary and least expenses they could get away with. For decades Father had been his own master in Hungary: he was used to undertaking whatever literary or public activity he chose, he was celebrated and feted wherever he appeared in public, his critical articles and speeches were read and listened to with a respect bordering on awe by one of the largest Jewish diasporas in the world, his words had an oracular quality for the Zionists and all those interested in Jewish culture in Hungary—and now he found himself in a position where he was dependent on and had to haggle with overweening and presumptuous men in charge of a small and insignificant society, who arrogated themselves the right to tell him what he should and should not do and how many pennies of expenses he could claim. It's no wonder that he found this situation intolerable and felt that the way out of it was for him to return to Budapest, despite the gathering clouds that cast their deepening shadow over Hungary.

It so happened that, soon after Mother's departure for Budapest, the university administration suggested to Father that he should fly to Riga, Latvia, together with Rabbi Simha Assaf, professor of Gaonic literature at the university, to raise funds for the university. In view of what happened in Europe a short while thereafter, this plan is eloquent testimony to the short-sightedness of the leaders of the *yishuv* or at least to the short-range view they took of the developments that were unfolding there. Within two years of the events described here, no less than ninety percent of Latvia's 40,000 Jews were slaughtered by the Germans. Of course, even in the summer of 1939, nobody could foresee the horrors of the Nazi Holocaust.

At first Father did not turn down the suggestion. In fact he thought that perhaps on the way back he could meet Mother in Paris and then return to Palestine together with her. Soon thereafter, however, he found the project definitely not to his liking and wrote to Évi and me in late July (in Hebrew):

> I have been so busy recently and also so exhausted and worn out by the "black labor" that I could write only to Budapest [to Mother]. In the meantime there were unpleasant negotiations in connection with the trip to Riga, Latvia, etc. Today finally I think I succeeded in getting out of that trip, which would involve all kinds of wanderings, peregrinations, without any advantage for me. If fate has imposed on me to be a "wandering agent" of the university in Eretz Israel, why should I add to it work abroad as well! At first they spoke of a visit of two weeks with Rav Assaf, then they spoke of six weeks, and wanted me to go there earlier to prepare the ground for him and then to stay on after his departure to organize the "practical action" of the fund-raising, and all this they decided in my absence and not in my presence, without consulting me. And they put my head between the "mountains" of the university and the Friends, with the well-known controversy between them. Finally I even got a "reprimand" from Frumkin that I was accepting instructions from the university, even though Berger had promised to settle the matter with the executive of the Society. However, without the express consent of the leadership of the Society I cannot stay away so long from my field of activity here, and the liquidation of the affairs in Budapest is now more important.
>
> Last week I met Hajdu, who was on his way to sail to Lebanon, and he too emphasized that it was very important that they should see

me in Budapest so that the journal should be able to go on appearing
and that they should not cancel my pension. As it is, there is still hope
of arranging things. Since a high official of the bank rented our apartment, perhaps it will be possible to arrange the transfer of the rental
here to Palestine. If I continue in my present work I shall not be able
to write even a line; it is my nature to devote myself fully to things,
and I cannot free myself and set aside times for contemplation or even
to breathe a little air. But we shall talk about this face to face. In any
case, I shall try to be back here early in October and to continue the
work. In Haifa I succeeded in recruiting 250 members, "and my hand
is still stretched out."

The success of Father's work in Haifa could not remain without recognition by the Friends. On July 17, 1939, Father was able to write to Évi (in
Hungarian): "Schneursohn considers my success in Haifa his personal affair.
He was so happy with it that it was touching. Now Frumkin already speaks
of plans for the winter and spring, about tours jointly with me, and lectures."

This temporary improvement in the attitude of the Friends toward him
was, however, not enough to deter Father from carrying out his plan of returning to Budapest at least for a sojourn of limited duration. He informed
the Friends that his affairs in Budapest demanded his presence there and obtained from them an unpaid leave of absence. On or about August 16, 1939,
he sailed from Haifa to Trieste. Both he and Mother were to remain in Budapest until a few weeks after the outbreak of World War II.

After their return from Budapest to Palestine in the fall of 1939 Father
resumed his work for the Society of Friends of the Hebrew University, but
the extant family letters contain no further reference to it. About a year later
Father's health deteriorated, and it soon became evident that he was no
longer able to go on with the rather strenuous activities demanded by his position. I do not recall and have no letters about the last phase of his work
and the circumstances of his resignation. But in a letter he sent me on January 19, 1941 (in Hebrew) he wrote: "It is good for me to rest up a little
from the evil of the 'Society'—I was a slave of slaves—and to devote myself
a little to literary work, which is 'the life of eternity,' instead of to 'the life of
the hour.'"

Literary work proved to be what sustained him in the remaining years
of his life. Although he was frequently bedridden, underwent several operations, was in and out of the hospital, and suffered recurrent fevers and infections, he kept up with his literary work, translated many of his writings
into Hebrew, arranged for the publication of his books, and was able to
enjoy being feted on the occasion of the thirtieth anniversary of the launch-

ing of his monthly, *Mult és Jövő*. In addition, he was kept going by the love and devotion of Mother for whom he was, and remained to the very end, the center of the universe. And he continued to be keenly concerned about the careers of his three children and to find delight in his grandchildren. The last, tragic phase of his life started in 1951, when he began to suffer from Alzheimer's disease, which turned him into a pathetic figure and caused untold heartache to his family. He died on February 21, 1953, at the age of seventy-one. Mother survived him by twenty-three years and died at the age of ninety in full control of her mental faculties.

7

Plans and Travels

The Jerusalem Academy

The "great plan" to which Father alluded so mysteriously in his letters from Paris (and about which he wrote more explicitly to Mother) turned out to be a great plan indeed: to found an institution in Jerusalem that would fulfill the functions of academies of science in European countries. Father was, of course, most familiar with the Hungarian Academy of Science, which had its seat in Budapest in an ornate nineteenth-century building facing the Danube. Membership in it was the highest accolade a Hungarian scientist or scholar could aspire to. Founded in 1830 by the great Hungarian statesman Count István Széchenyi following British, French, and German examples, by the 1920s and 1930s the Academy sponsored and stimulated scholarly work in many fields of the exact sciences, medicine, history, linguistics, archaeology, law, economics, etc. The lectures given in its great auditorium were also noted in academic circles beyond the borders of Hungary. Its membership was limited to 64 regular, 26 honorary, and 160 corresponding members. I still remember how proud I was to have known personally several Jewish members of the Academy, including Ignaz Goldziher (whom I met when I was ten years old), Bernát Munkácsi (who was a distant cousin on Mother's side), Henrik Marczali (who advised me in connection with my publication of a historical document), and Eduard Mahler (who was my professor at the Budapest University).

I don't know, of course, whether in conceiving the idea of a Jerusalem Academy (for which Father suggested the Hebrew name Aqademiya Yerushalmit, and Academia Hierosolymitana in Latin) he was influenced by the example of the Hungarian Academy, the Académie Francaise, or the British Academy (of whose work he must have learned during his brief sojourns in Paris and London). In any case, while he was in Paris he discussed the plan with Évi; needless to say, with her usual exuberance she undertook to do everything she could to help realize it. Father also discussed it with Évi's friend Dr. Dov Rivkind, and he too promised his help. When Father arrived in Palestine in February 1939 he informed me of the project, and he and I together began to take steps for its realization. A few days later Father reported to Évi about what we had done and intended to do.

Jerusalem, Febr. 12, 1939
Bezalel Str., Shiber Houe [in Hungarian]

Dear Évikém:

The plan has a positive response everywhere. We spoke about it to Professor Klein, Professor Fodor, Professor Fekete (who is now the dean of the faculty of sciences), and, of course, Ibn-Zahav. In general, the opinion is that the whole thing can have great significance and that it should not be tied to the university, but done with the help of the university's professors individually. Magnes is sick at present; in a few days we shall talk to him as well, also to Rector Fraenkel, and, this afternoon, to Yellin. They have no doubt that everybody will be willing to be a member of a committee that, with its work, will augment the prestige of the university and can render great service to the entire cause of Palestine. Hence, our plan is to form a small committee consisting of a few professors and other leading personalities, and a larger committee that could possibly comprise about one hundred of the country's most outstanding intellectual leaders. Then it will be established as the "Jerusalem Academy" or "Institute"—we shall have to consider the name—and a secretariat, led by Raphael, could immediately begin its work. Already for the coming summer we could invite Victor Basch and Bouglé, together with another two or three scholars, perhaps from England. One will have to appear on the very first occasion with great names; later we think of also inviting great writers, such as Thomas Mann, Tagore, etc., and shall award scholarships at French, English, and even Hungarian universities to bring here some of the most outstanding students.

Here we would arrange that the Jewish Agency and the Va'ad Leumi should receive the great personages in a proper manner, show them around the country, about which, upon their return home, they will give lectures—that will have great publicity value from the point of view of the upbuilding of Palestine, just as the sojourn here of youth representatives could have a great effect on contact with the Jews in their countries. For the lectures themselves not only will the university undoubtedly offer its auditoriums, but it will also furnish the proper framework.

According to Ibn-Zahav, the French consul here, with whom he is friendly, will invite the other consulates to the lectures, and Professor Fodor thinks that one can ask the High Commissioner to accept their patronage. Professor Fodor is a leading member of one of the high-ranking Freemasons' lodges here, together with Yellin, and according to him it will be possible to arrange through the lodge that the French Freemasons' lodge should help, and possibly cover the expenses of the lecturers to be sent here. The same could be done, he thinks, through the Swiss and American non-Jewish lodges. We shall ascertain the exact details concerning this.

In this connection, for example, one could invite the famous professor of the Zurich university, Köhler, whose article "Judaism's Three Gifts to Mankind" was some time ago published in *Mult és Jövő*. One can arrange, if one can take care of the expenses, that the universities abroad should invite, on the basis of reciprocity, some Palestinian scholars—this too will have great publicity value for the cause of Palestine and in general from the point of view of the Jewish cause. In brief, the perspective of the plan is constantly broadening, and now the most important thing is that we get, as soon as possible, the first budget item from Paris, through Ascher, Jefroykin, Naiditsch, etc., so that it should be possible thereafter to move on. With this one can, of course, turn only to people with whom one has a sufficiently close tie so that they should have complete confidence in the matter. Talk it over with Dr. Rivkind, to whom I send my best regards. In any case one must wait until we have our stationery with the names of the committee. I shall write to you about this again in a few days, but in the meantime I wanted to inform you.

The professors in general have confidence in the World Jewish Congress, and on the basis of my presentation they are of the opinion that it, or rather its youth department, could serve as the suitable background of the whole project. Its youth department could publicize it in youth circles, and by means of the WJC one could reach suitable American individuals and money sources. This could be a fine task for the WJC, and one should discuss it now with Goldmann and the others so that they should be informed.

I have not yet received the *Race et racisme* pamphlets that I left with you in the office. We need them here as prototypes, and, apart from that, they contain the list of the Paris committee, which you too should look at (on the inner side of the front cover), and you could discuss with Rivkind who on the list can be considered from our point of view. Those of the lectures that are suitable will be published here in Jerusalem in separate pamphlets in various languages, so that from

Zion will issue not only the teaching but also the defense of Jewish honor, from human and scholarly heights. The purpose therefore would be truly beautiful even if we were not connected with it.

I mentioned to Raphael that it is your opinion that one should organize real committees and representations of the WJC in Palestine, and even in Cairo, Alexandria, Beirut, and possibly even in Baghdad, which can be reached by plane in a short time. For this it would be necessary to have a commission, in fact, the covering of expenses, from the WJC, and I have no doubt that, just as in your case in Budapest, in the cities mentioned it would also be possible to raise enough money to cover the expenses. But the latter can be done only subsequently, one cannot start with it. After all, the WJC wants to give me a hundred dollars for a trip to America, so that it would not be a great thing for it to send here organizational expenses to Raphael, who subsequently would surely be able to raise that amount. But he must also get the appropriate instructions, announcements, and recommendations, as usual with the Congress, and he would have to know what has so far been done in those cities, with whom the Congress has connections, etc. Throughout March he is free from the university, and he could make use of those weeks.

As for Dr. Vardi, it is quite right that you should give him moral support and should write about the university in the papers there. Still, the connections should, in the first place, be utilized for the purposes of the institute to be founded, so that it should be possible to find financial backing for it. According to all opinions, this has to be developed independently of the university also in order that the Bergers and others like them should not be able to interfere. However, if the professors, headed by Magnes, are on the committee, and the lectures are held at the university, then there will be an external connection with the university anyhow. A close connection must also be avoided because the leadership of the university may get misgivings lest the matter acquire a political coloration, and the university cannot completely expose itself outwardly in this direction, because that could possibly lead to difficulties in countries with a Fascist tendency that have so far nevertheless made it possible for Jewish students to come to the Jerusalem university. This for your information only.

Schocken is ill now and went abroad for a few months to get treatment for his eyes. With Senator I have an appointment for Tuesday, likewise with Dr. Glicksohn. According to Fodor, there is not one professor at the university who would not like to see this done—one has only to realize it with full energy. He is willing to help. This is the opinion also of Fekete, who is skeptical only concerning the finances, since he does not know that the matter has such a splendid representation in Paris. Have a copy of *La Terre Retrouvée* sent here too.

Gyuri and Guszti are well and in good spirits. We are very glad that Tirzuli has struck roots in Parisian society; may she continue to develop beautifully and healthy with red cheeks like those of Bubie, to whom, together with the Marums, I send warm regards.

I wrote Mama that she should stop all activity about the tour. We have more important things to do. She can come here alone. As soon as we get copies of your book from Tel Aviv, we shall send the requisite number of copies.

Many kisses,
Papa

Célestin Bouglé (1870–1940) was a French philosopher and director of the Ecole Normal Supérieure, author of *Les Idées égalitaires* (1899), *La Crise du libéralisme* (1902), *Proudhon* (1923), etc. Victor Basch (1863–1944), born in Budapest, was a professor at the Sorbonne, a philosopher, defender of human rights, champion of Alfred Dreyfus, founder of the League for the Rights of Man, and leader of the Alliance Israélite Universelle. Wolfgang Köhler (1887–1967), the famous founder of Gestalt psychology, had by that time emigrated to America, a fact of which Father, it seems, was not aware. George Ascher (1884–1943) was a prominent Parisian artist who died in a Nazi extermination camp. Jules Jefroykin (b. 1911) was a French Zionist leader who from 1937 to 1940 was president of the Union Mondiale de la Jeunesse Juive. Isaac Asher Naiditsch (1868–1949) was a Russian-Jewish philanthropist and Zionist who emigrated to France in 1917 and became a founder and the first director of the Keren Hayesod. *Race et racisme* was the title of an important series of pamphlets published in Paris and dedicated to combating racism. Dr. Hayyim Vardi, an instructor of Italian, did public relations work in Paris for the Hebrew University. The Marums were the people who took care of Évi's daughter. As for the plan of the WJC to send Father to America, the brief reference in this letter is the only trace I can find.

In response to this letter, on February 21, 1939, Évi sent a letter from Paris to Father, me, and Guszti in Jerusalem, with a copy to Mother in Budapest. About the Academy she wrote briefly:

Tonight I shall meet M. Jefroykin in order to talk over with him everything relating to our great plan, of course the financial aspect in the first place. He has shown lively interest for the plan from the first moment. [. . .] How does the plan stand today? Who has already become a "partner"? I have so far received only one letter about it and am waiting for more details. To have stationery—very good, but should not also a few "great men" from Europe be listed on it? Or it may be better this way: first of all it should be called "initiative committee." And Dr. Rivkind says it must under no condition be called "Jewish Academy," but the name must unequivocally indicate what the matter is about. It should rather be a long name that can be used in an abridged form, but it must include that it wants to be an *Institute* for the fight against anti-Semitism, etc. Please discuss this with the people.

Part of the letter I wrote to Mother on February 26, 1939, was devoted to the Academy. I wrote (in Hungarian):

Ever since Papa's arrival he has been writing to you diligently so that I have scarcely anything to add. Until now we have paid four to five visits every day to local "great men," who, to be sure, are very small. But all of them are enthusiastic when hearing about the "great plan," so that, in all probability, it will be realized. In the meantime the intrigues around Papa's appointment as head of the University Friends are continuing, but probably that too will be decided in the next few days. As for the raise in my salary, there are no ardent hopes; at the utmost, in case of success, instead of the 4 1/4 pounds I shall get 6 pounds monthly. However, that too is better than nothing, and it too signifies an achievement for such young "professors" like us, the instructors in the Hebrew courses.

Two days later Father wrote again to Évi:

We are sending you enclosed the draft plan of the Jerusalem Academy in Hebrew and German. As you can see, we are working diligently together with Raphael, and those who have so far joined up actually constitute "the oil and fine flour" of the *yishuv*. This week we shall talk to Magnes, as well as to Professor Bergman, the former rector. Everybody attributes enormous significance to the idea; according to some it will have an unforeseeably great effect in the world, and it may yield immeasurably important results from the point of view of Palestine. And precisely now, when the political situation is deteriorating to such an extent, it has a manifold significance that spiritual currents should issue from Jerusalem far afield toward the diaspora, and should, on the one hand, strengthen the faith of the Jews and preserve their self-confidence from being shaken, and, on the other, create intellectual ties with those non-Jewish circles for which the spiritual treasures of Judaism, the ideas of the prophets, constitute immortal values even today.

Now the manner of execution is most important. On the basis of the enclosed text, which should be translated into French as well, one can undertake the first steps so that there should instantly be coverage for the initial expenses. The first budget would be roughly as follows:

Expenses: setting up an office in Jerusalem: rent, 5 pounds per month. Typist, 6 pounds monthly. Administrator (secretary), 12 pounds monthly. Managing president (director), 20 pounds monthly. Printed matter, telephone, postage, etc., 6 pounds monthly. Miscellaneous items, 1 pound monthly. Total—50 pounds monthly. That is, the administrative expenses of the first year would be 600 pounds.

For the first summer we could invite four world-famous intellectual leaders, the expenses of each of them, with first-class ship ticket, accommodation in the King David Hotel for two weeks, travel in the country, daily board 1 pound, total 80 pounds. That is, for all the four together 320 pounds. The invitation of twelve students from twelve different universities, each 25 pounds (including travel in tourist class, two weeks room and board, and sightseeing), or a total of 300 pounds. So that the total expenses of the first year will be 1,220 pounds.

All this, of course, would cover only the expenses of the initial activities confined to the narrowest framework, and with the development and growth of the Academy they too would grow. However, even in this narrow dimension there are possibilities on a larger scale:

1. The participation of intellectual forces of Jerusalem, or rather Palestine, that would not cost additional money, e.g., Professor Klausner, Buber, Sukenik, etc. One could even arrange for certain lectures on specialized subjects that will attract those who aspire to further education.

2. There will be professors, famous writers, and scholars, who wish in any case to visit Palestine and will willingly respond to an invitation of the Academy even without expenses paid.

3. There will also be students who will make use of the opportunity and will come together with their professors, at their own expense.

4. All guests will have friends and admirers who will accompany them. (When it was planned that Bishop Baltazár should come to Jerusalem at our invitation, the bank directors and leaders of Jewish communities indicated that they wanted to accompany him.)

5. One could prevail on individual institutions to award scholarships to students for this purpose or to send their leaders here. There are possibilities of having scholars of great renown sent here through

certain institutions and at their expense. (E.g., Professor Fodor thinks that at the initiative of the Palestinian [Freemasons'] lodge, the Zurich lodge could send Professor Köhler, who once gave a lecture here under the title "Die drei Geschenke des Judentums an die Kulturmenschheit" [Judaism's Three Gifts to Civilized Humanity], and that an enormous response to such a lecture could be created if it were given here on Mount Scopus and were to be translated into all the languages of the civilized world!)

Professor Yellin thinks that through the B'nai B'rith one could influence the Anti-Defamation League, which is active within the framework of the American B'nai B'rith, to send an American personality here at its own expense. This would also have to be supported by the American Jewish Congress, and Goldmann will probably be willing to mediate. Again, the task of the WJC youth department would be to organize the youth aspect of the plan; possibly it could also establish scholarships for a few young people for this purpose. One can imagine how great will be the propaganda power of notices posted in the *aulas* [halls] of various universities in the name of the "Academia Hierosolymitana." The expenditure of 25 pounds in relation to this is truly an insignificant trifle.

One can also count on the interest of publishing houses to publish the texts of the lectures, and there will always be those who, in the various countries, will want to distribute these pamphlets in large numbers. Neither must one forget the significance of the press campaign in connection with the Academy. It will be the task of the WJC youth department to invite the youth leaders after their return home to give lectures and to provide those lectures with as impressive a frame as possible. And as for the adult department of the WJC, it will help in the arrangements for suitable appearances for the returning celebrities, so that they should constitute great propaganda for Judaism and Palestine alike. We believe that the WJC must give financial support right at the outset to this institution, whose work will serve not merely Palestinian, but general Jewish, interests.

Now, on the basis of all this, the work should be launched in Paris, and those who have promised support should be persuaded to transmit to you the amounts, or parts of them, already now, or, possibly, we shall open here a bank account in the name of the "Academy of Jerusalem," of which the committee here will dispose, and the amounts can be deposited into that account. As soon as the first amounts arrive we shall set up the secretariat here, and the Jerusalem Academy can unfold its wings with full force.

Your idea that the Academy should subsequently elect people from abroad into its membership, respectively into its various committees, so that it should have a representation everywhere in a suitable form is a good one. For the time being we think that this name is the best, and we are not sure that the name should contain a reference to the fight against anti-Semitism. That would narrow the significance of the institution and the scope of its activity. This way, on the other hand, it will be the basis for the developing Jerusalem Academy of Sciences, whose palace, it is to be hoped, will some day stand on Mount Scopus, even if it will no longer be necessary to fight against anti-Semitism.

One would have to seek a way of finding suitable support also in London. At the time I was there the plan had not yet unfolded in this form. But I don't doubt that there too one can find people and win them over. I know, e.g., that Lord Rothschild gave a sizable amount to a Hungarian journalist to organize a pro-Jewish news service. Rothschild's wife, or rather the mother of the present young lord, is a woman of Hungarian descent, from Nagyvárad, her maiden name was Rózsika Wertheimstein. Perhaps Viscount Samuel too could be won over. According to Dr. Rosenfeld, the political department of the Jewish agency, and even the Keren Hayesod and the KKL [Keren Kayemeth L'Yisrael] should make major contributions for this purpose, since ultimately this will also be publicity on a grand scale for their work. Perhaps one could also influence Ascher in this direction.

Give my warmest thanks to Rivkind for his help, and discuss the matter further with him. About all other things next time.

I wrote about Bishop Dezső Baltazár (1871–1936) in my *Apprentice in Budapest*. Rózsika von Wertheimstein (1870–1940) was the scion of a distinguished Hungarian Jewish family, the wife of the Hon. Nathaniel Charles Rothschild (1877–1923). Their son, Nathaniel Mayer Victor (b. 1910), third Baron Rothschild, was a biologist, author of many scholarly studies, a Fellow of the Royal Society and supporter of the Weizmann Institute of Science and of the Hebrew University.

In a P.S. to her March 4, 1939, German letter to Mother, in which she reported in detail about her visit with Tirzah to the ophthalmologist Dr. Mawas, Évi added, in Hungarian: "Jefroykin has been away, I can talk to him only in another few days, but his son, the chairman of the youth department of the WJC, puts the whole movement at the service of this matter, which means a lot. That is to say, the thing is moving, of course, slowly as everything."

Even before receiving this note, Father sent off another long letter to Évi discussing the Jerusalem Academy in detail (in Hungarian):

March 6, 1939

Dear Évikém:

Mama writes that you have not yet received our last letter in which we wrote in detail about everything concerning the Jerusalem Academy. We also sent you the draft plan signed by most university professors. Since then I also spoke to Professor Bergman, the former rector of the university, who is also very enthusiastic about the plan and attributes great importance to its realization. He also called my attention to the following:

One must include the leaders of the local non-Jewish institutions, such as the École Biblique, as well as the learned heads of the Franciscans and the Dominicans, and other ecclesiastical institutions, and the leaders of the institutions engaged in archaeological work, such as the American School of Oriental Research, etc. Further, one must contact the French consul, who is a very enthusiastic pro-Palestinian. The French government maintains a chair at the university and has recently sent two Palestinian students from Jerusalem to a French university, and on that occasion the French consul said farewell to the two students in a very nice address, emphasizing the importance of French-Palestinian intellectual connections. In addition, Bergman mentioned that the French government every summer sends examining professors to the Near East; thus, recently Lévy-Bruhl too was here on a governmental mission, but, for lack of a suitable institution they were unable either to extend his one-day visit or to use it for arranging a lecture that would have been great propaganda. That is to say, in the future it will be possible to have the scholars sent by the French government also participate in the activities, almost without expenses.

Further, he called my attention to the existence in New York, 2 West 45th Street, of the Institute of International Education, which is interested in such activities, and when Bergman, as rector, was there in America, they discussed sending by the Institute American professors to the Near East, from Constantinople to Cairo. But, again, for lack of an institution in Jerusalem nothing came of it. That Institute of International Education is headed by Stephen Duggan, director, and Edgar J. Fisher, assistant director. Henry Morgenthau is a member of the Board of Trustees. The Institute publishes a news bulletin, which certainly is available there too. When Bergman was in Stockholm, the leaders of the university and the academy there broached the idea of closer intellectual ties with Palestine and rightly expected to get invitations from Jerusalem, but for lack of an institution and finances nothing came of that either.

The new plan, therefore, will fill a really palpable gap, and, according to Bergman, it must put an end to the total isolation of the intellectual life of Palestinian Jewry in which it finds itself today. Several years ago the idea of a summer course came up, and at that time they negotiated with the Palestine Lloyd (a shipping agency), which was very enthusiastic and thought that this would also give a lift to Palestinian tourism. They were ready to offer considerable discounts for this purpose, but since there was nobody to follow up the matter, nothing came of it either, even though it was suggested by Arthur Ruppin. That is to say, the success depends, apart from the fundamentals, on two things: 1. That there should be somebody who devotes himself to the matter seriously and with perseverance; and 2. that there should be people who understand, who give support, corresponding to the importance of the matter, to its launching and initial expenses. Thereafter, the institution will grow of itself, and later, no doubt, there will also be found those who, with major endowments, will lay the foundation for the construction of buildings, the founding of various departments, and the establishment of a veritable academy of sciences.

We also thought that one should already now draw into the committee a few Jewish and non-Jewish intellectual celebrities and Maecenases from various countries. It would be good to begin this in Paris too. I think Bouglé, Basch, Vermeil, and I believe Cardinal Verdier, and among the Maecenases those who would already now contribute larger amounts to setting up the Academy, should be brought in. I am sending you enclosed the list of the committee of *Race et racisme*—one can select some from it as well.

There in Paris you possibly know also who could be attracted from Belgium, Holland, Switzerland, and England. In England one should try to approach the Rothschilds, and those who come into consideration. Perhaps Goldmann can give advice in this connection. One should also write to Stephen Wise and a few American Jews who can be considered from this point of view, and one should write to somebody who would be at our disposal in giving advice and suggesting a list of names. I don't think that Goldmann can occupy himself in detail with these things, but he will surely be willing to sign a letter in this matter if he gets it all prepared.

For the time being it would not be advisable to ask for money in letters to America lest it be considered a drive competing with the university. That should be done only orally, with a few selected people, and one must not make of it a kind of popular campaign. Your thought that the WJC youth department should handle the question is correct. As soon as the small capital required for the launching is available one can start the public propaganda for the plan, and there is no doubt that the proper response will come. Then we can send the plan, in various languages, to the youth groups of the WJC, whose task will be to take care of the propagation of the whole matter in youth circles, to arouse interest in more and more young people in coming to Jerusalem on the occasion of these courses, to arrange in advance lectures with the participation of those who come into consideration for the trip, possibly to obtain the means of establishing scholarships for such purposes in the local groups, and later to distribute the lectures that were given and that will constitute a defense of freedom of thought and of Jewish rights, and will raise the prestige of Jewry everywhere. If the Congress office participates more intensively, it can be of great help, through its local groups, to this work that ultimately serves the cause of minority defense—this figured among the first tasks of the Congress from the very beginning, even in the days of Motzkin, with whom as far as I know, Jefroykin worked together in close friendship. So we are awaiting further news from Paris. Later, if it should so develop that it will be necessary, and there will be coverage for the expenses, I could perhaps again visit Paris and London.

[. . .] Let me add that Justice Frumkin, the president of the Friends of the University, is of the opinion that this plan should be realized within its framework. But I believe that this plan will fill much broader frames, as soon as it becomes known in wider circles. [. . .]

Many kisses,
Papa

Since Father never learned to type, he dictated all these detailed letters about the Academy to me (and occasionally to Saul). As for the term "Palestinian," which he used quite frequently, it must be understood that he used it, as we all used it in those days, in the sense of Palestinian Jewish. The usage of the term "Palestinian" in the sense of Palestinian Arab was to come into vogue only many decades later.

Most of the names mentioned in this letter can easily be identified. Lucien Lévy-Bruhl (1857–1939) was a famous French-Jewish sociologist and anthropologist. Henry Morgenthau, Jr. (1891–1967) was an American Jewish public official, who served as secretary of the treasury from 1934 to 1945. Arthur Ruppin (1876–1943) was a Zionist economist and sociologist who from 1933 headed the Jewish Agency's department for the settlement of German immigrants and later was professor of sociology at the Hebrew University. Edmond Vermeil (b. 1878) was professor of German history at the Sorbonne and the author of numerous books on political and literary subjects. Cardinal Jean Verdier (1864–1940) was archbishop of Paris, general supervisor of the Sulpiciens, and was entrusted with important diplomatic missions by the Vatican. Leo Motzkin (1867–1933) was a Zionist leader, had a leading part in establishing the Comité des Délégations Juives at the Paris Peace Conference, and served as permanent chairman of the Zionist General Council and of many Zionist Congresses.

This letter crossed Évi's addressed to the family as a whole:

Paris, March 6, 1939 [in German]

My Very, Very Dear Ones:

Today only quite briefly and factually: I got the letter with the news that Papa will probably get the position and am very happy about it. The exposé of the "Academy" is excellent, only it is difficult to pronounce the name, is there no other name? "Hierosolymitana" is terrible. The exposé is now being translated into French. Also the English will be done by somebody on an honorary basis. Tomorrow I shall see Jefroykin and others: I am invited to a big reception, 40 noble guests, in Naiditsch's house, in honor of Ussishkin. More details after the consultations. It will work. [. . .]

Three days later Évi again wrote to the whole family (in German):

Today I had lunch with Ussishkin, he had invited me, for he wanted to chat with me. I spoke about all kinds of things to him and then got to our "plan." To my greatest surprise I learned from him that something reminiscent of our plan is being planned in Eretz, namely, they want to organize a seminar to which students from abroad should also come, etc. I told him one would have to combine the two things. The plan he has would partly be financed by the KKL [Keren Kayemeth] and the KH [Keren Hayesod].

I got the agreement of Ussishkin that Papa, or Gyuri, should immediately get in touch with the people who are planning this thing there and mention that Ussishkin told me to inform them that he suggested it. The people dealing with it are Nathan Bistritzky, Yaari, and Gordon. So please, look them up, especially Bistritzky, immediately, and then let me know the gist of the conversation.

Under certain conditions this can prove very useful for the "Academy."

I am more and more of the opinion that the name "Academy H., etc.," is not a good one. First of all why Academy, and secondly why a name that is so difficult to pronounce? [. . .]

Nathan Bistritzky (later Agmon, 1896–1980) was a Hebrew dramatist and publicist who worked as an official of the Keren Kayemeth in Jerusalem. Yehuda Yaari (1900–1982) was a Hebrew writer and official at the head office of the Keren Hayesod in Jerusalem. Moshe Gordon was an official of the Jewish Agency in Jerusalem in charge of the Mossad Bialik (Bialik Foundation), its publishing arm.

A few days later Évi wrote again (in German):

> In great hurry a "factual letter."
> 1. Plan of the "Academy" to be translated into French—I will give it today to M. Jefroykin, and in the next few days to Naiditsch, etc., so that the raising of the first thousand pounds will probably take place shortly.
> 2. There are all kinds of misgivings about the name "Academy." It is thought that "Makhon Yerushalmi," that is, "Institute," is better. But this is not decisive.
> 3. The WJC youth organization is prepared to work for the thing in every way, to make publicity, etc., etc. The chairman is Jacques Jefroykin, the man who gives the money for it (for the work of the youth organization here, which is developing in a first-rate manner) is Israel Jefroykin.
> 4. Yesterday I heard from Goldmann, and indirectly from Weizmann, about the situation in London; both optimistic, thank God. [. . .]
> Everything you write about the "Academy" or "Institute," please write in German, I have translated everything noteworthy so that Rivkind should have an overview—he helps in everything 100%. [. . .]

Israel Jefroykin (1884–1954) was a Jewish communal leader, one of the founders of the World Jewish Congress in 1936, and the author of several historical books in Yiddish. I cannot identify Jacques Jefroykin.

Évi's March 9 letter was answered by Father:

Jerusalem, March 16, 1939 [in Hungarian]

Dear Évikém:
    It was very good that you spoke to Ussishkin. I shall get in touch with Bistritzky right away. I know that he, together with Yaari and Gordon, are engaged in a project for the education of young people, Vaʻad M'shutaf l'Iny'ne haNoʻar [Joint Committee for Youth Affairs], in which the Zionist Executive, the KKL, and the KH are participating.

When I spoke recently to Bistritzky he expounded on the aims of this committee concerned with youth education, and in that connection we spoke about promoting the Hungarian-language part of this activity and that we would devote one issue of *Mult és Jövő* to it. Bistritzky was interested in my book *Mai Héber Költők* [Hebrew Poets of Today] which is now being printed and which presents mainly the Palestinian poets of today, that is, has significance from an educational point of view as well, and we spoke about the purchase of a larger number of copies by that committee. We shall deal with this later. Bistritzky also wants to see youth courses in Palestine and other countries. Alas, the budget for that is likewise not big. In any case, I shall talk to him again in the next few days about what you have written.

I don't know whether you have had a chance to talk to Ussishkin about my placement. Did you mention to him the University Friends, etc.? As soon as he returns home I shall talk to him, because much depends on him. Actually, I also thought that this youth work could include the Hungarian-speaking territories, which include more than a million Jews.

As for the Academy, we shall consider another name. The designation of the French Academy is simply "l'Institut," so that in Hebrew it could be "Makhon," as we had thought originally. As I wrote to you, there is also talk about realizing the plan within the circle of the University Friends. About that later. It was planned that there should already be a final decision about me today, but what happened in the meantime was that Dr. Bar-Shira, the Tel Aviv attorney and leader of the Tel Aviv chapter, who has a big role in the whole organization, broke his leg while skiing in Lebanon, and thus he cannot come to Jerusalem for two weeks to attend meetings. But it is possible that they will decide without him.

Reading about the latest events I am terribly troubled that Mama is still not here, but, on the other hand, she takes care of important business in Budapest, and with God's help everything will be settled soon. [. . .]

Let us know whether there is any plan or initiative concerning the financial aspect of the matter, for I think that here it will be taken seriously only if we show some results from Paris. Here the plan is already at the stage where it is not possible to take further steps as long as there is no financial basis; therefore it would be necessary to provide a certain amount for the first steps. Write about this concretely. I kiss you with much love,

Papa

On March 26 Father wrote to Mother about the move from Budapest to Palestine, sent a copy to Évi, and added a few lines addressed to her (in Hungarian):

> This week I spoke to Dr. Eitingon, who is very enthusiastic about the idea and thinks that it can lead to the establishment of a real academy with various departments, even a library, etc. He said we should send him the plan, of which he would send one copy to Einstein (with whom he corresponds), and one to Freud. According to him it is necessary that foreigners, that is, intellectual giants from everywhere, should be members of this Academy, which should have regular and corresponding members. He will win the psychoanalysts, and hopes that they will be able to help financially as well. Accordingly, we rewrote the plan to some extent, and I am enclosing a corrected copy of it. Study it thoroughly. It would be good to obtain the first "organizing expenses" from somewhere now. The first founders will be engraved on a marble tablet on the wall of the future building of the Academy.
>
> As far as the name Academia Hierosolymitana is concerned, this Latin name will not be foreign to anybody. Moreover, this Latin name is international, and under it will appear the German, English, French, or Hebrew translation: Academy of Jerusalem, etc.
>
> Please add to the list you have in your hands: Dr. Max Eitingon, director of the Psychoanalytic Institute, Jerusalem; and Dr. Julius Guttmann, professor at the Hebrew University, dean of the Faculty of Humanities. It would be good to add even now the names of a few Parisian intellectual giants, of course, on the basis of their consent: Bouglé, Victor Basch, Cardinal Verdier, and some others who are of importance: Lévy-Bruhl. Perhaps you or Rivkind should slowly get in touch with the main people who still have to be won over. The time has come to find a trustworthy man in England who could win the local great ones there. Possibly also in Belgium, the Netherlands, Switzerland.
>
> It is now time to begin to assemble the first list of names who can be considered as members and lecturers, so that the Jerusalem Academy should be able to appear before the public instantly with great prestige.

While Évi was supposed to contact people in Paris, I did the best I could in Jerusalem. One of the people to whom I spoke was Dr. Magnes, president of the university. On April 18, 1939, I reported to my parents: "Yesterday we spoke to Dr. Magnes. He showed great understanding for our cause, and encouraged us to fight for it. But, according to Ibn-Zahav, Magnes is now in opposition and has no influence." By "in opposition" Ibn-Zahav meant that there was tension between Magnes and the top administration of the university, led by Schocken and Senator.

Encouraged by the sympathy Dr. Magnes manifested, as well as by letters I received from Dr. Eitingon in Jerusalem and Dr. Rivkind in Paris in which they expressed serious interest in the Academy, I suggested to Father that we convene a meeting in Jerusalem at which the planning committee would be formally constituted. I expressed my confidence that such a venture would be successful and tried to reassure Father that there was nothing incompatible between his work for the Palestinian Friends of the Hebrew University, which he had begun on a temporary basis, and his efforts to organize the Academy. For several weeks thereafter I continued with my efforts to win people for the planning committee and reported to Évi:

> Jerusalem, April 30, 1939
> Bezalel Str., Shiber House [in Hungarian]

Dear Évikém:

I hurry to reply to your letter, which arrived today and in which you enclosed Dr. Rivkind's letter.

Enclosed I send the draft of the stationery. Please substitute, on the left side, the requisite French text instead of the German. I think the German text is not necessary—French, English and Hebrew are sufficient. The list of the members of the Initiative Committee will be printed on the margins of the paper, in tasteful arrangement. If you have any comment, whether on the text or on the format, let me know, and we shall take it into account. Possibly the Hebrew list of names could be deleted, and we could be satisfied with the Hebrew masthead on the top. If you think it is right, we could add to the end of the list: Secretary Dr. R. Patai. I on my part attach no importance to this *koved* [honor].

By the time your answer arrives we shall have convened here those whose names are on the list, to obtain their consent to the printing of the stationery. After all, everything must be done most correctly. Then, as soon as we get from you the reply with the program and the circular, as Dr. Rivkind indicates in his letter, we shall proceed with the printing of the stationery and mail the circular to the addresses to be provided by you. Dr. Eitingon also promised that after the constituent meeting takes place, and the aims and programs of the "Institute" are better crystallized, he on his part will write to Einstein and Freud and will persuade them to join. So that there are also candidates for the honorary presidency in addition to Weizmann, but still I shall suggest to

Papa that he should go, perhaps together with Tolkowsky, to talk to Weizmann. From Tel Aviv they can easily reach Weizmann, who is at present in Rehovoth.

We also sent the plan to Ignac Friedmann, who is the attorney of the Paris and London Rothschilds—perhaps he will be willing and able to influence them.

Now for another matter. I gladly espouse the plan for a European trip. I spoke to Moshe Kleinmann, editor of *Ha'Olam*, who promised that he would recommend me in connection with *Ha'Olam*, resp. the *Kongresszeitung* [Congress News]. I do know Dr. Lauterbach, so that I think Dr. G's recommendation would be effective. [. . .]

> Many kisses, your loving brother,
> Gyuri

In order to be able to print the stationery for the Academy I visited all the people who had agreed to become members of the committee and obtained their signatures to have their formal consent. In June 1939 Mother reported to Évi:

> Raphael is happily making preparations for the trip. For 2 1/2 years he had bought no wearing apparel, now he is outfitting himself properly, and, thank God, looks very well. The stationery of the Academy has been signed by everybody except Eitingon, who wants to have some more detailed information. But the French text that you promised in your last letter nine days ago has not yet arrived, and so there will be only Hebrew and English text on the paper.

By June 1939 I definitely planned to go to Paris for a visit of several weeks, combining sightseeing, visiting my sister, whom I had not seen since the fall of 1937, and work in behalf of the Jerusalem Academy. After obtaining the consent of the persons concerned I was able to proceed with the printing of the stationery. By that juncture Father and I had agreed that the official name of the institution should be "Institute of Jerusalem for International Intellectual Cooperation." Of the stationery printed only one single copy has survived, due to a mere chance. I used a copy of it to write a letter to my sister in Paris, sent it to Mother in Haifa, and asked her to add whatever she wanted and then send it on to Évi. Today, more than half a century later, that stationery is something of a historical document, and I reproduce it here in facsimile. The translation of the Hungarian letters written on it is as follows:

Jerusalem, June 29, 1939

Dear Évikém:

I am sending to you the first letter I write on this showy stationery. Only briefly, because I want to send this letter at first to Haifa, and from there our parents will forward it to you.

I am glad that the child is well: I suspected some such reason for your scanty letters in recent times.

I shall board the ship on July 5 with Mother; she will go on from Trieste to Budapest, and I straight to Paris. I believe I shall steam in on the 12th—I shall cable you the exact date and hour so that you can make the required preparations for my festive reception. I am very glad that I shall be able to stay in the same house as you, but take the room for me only on a weekly basis because possibly we shall soon travel down to the Alps.

I spoke to Gravitzky about work in the press office of the [Zionist] Congress; for the time being he can say nothing definite. According to Lauterbach, this depends on a certain Mechner who sits in Geneva. Perhaps you have some connection with him, if so, let him know.

Until we meet, many kisses, your loving brother,

Gyuri

Dear Évikém:

I am writing here in Haifa: there is no news. I don't know whether Papa will go to the Congress. The whole European situation is like in some madhouse. I get reassuring news from Pest, but what will happen in Danzig? I hope God will help, and there will be no war. Dear Tirzuli even when sick is sweeter than any other child, that I know. Thank God that she is already well. A thousand hugs, kisses,

Mama

Since the scene of the last phase of our efforts to set up the Academy or Institute was Paris, I interrupt its story here to tell first about my first visit to that famous city, whose light was soon to be extinguished by the German occupation.

Paris

Paris had been a definite concept in my imagination ever since I was a teenager, due mainly to the poems of Endre Ady, the greatest modern Hungarian poet, about that great city of light, love, and song. Like many a Hun-

INSTITUTE of JERUSALEM
for International Intellectual Cooperation

המכון הירושלמי
מוסד אקדמי לשיתוף־פעולה רוחני בין־לאומי

Jerusalem
P. O. B. 734

1939.Junius 29.

ירושלים.
ת. ד. 734.

Drága Évikém,

Neked küldöm az első levelet,melyet a jelen diszes levélpapiron irok.Csak röviden,mert előbb Haifába akarom küldeni ezt a levelet és majd onnan továbbitják anyuék.

Örülök,hogy a gyerek jól van,gondoltam,hogy valami hasonló oka lehet annak,hogy az utóbbi időben olyan gyéren irtál.

Én julius 5.-én ülök hajóra Anyuval együtt,Anyu Triesztből Pestre utazik,én pedig Triesztből egyenesen Párisba.Azt hiszem tizenkettedikén fogon berobogni,a pontos dátumot és órát megsürgönyzöm,hogy megtehesd a kellő előkészületeket ünnepélyes fogadtatásomra.Nagyon örülök,hogy mód lesz rá,Veled egy házban lakni,de végy szobát nekem csak hétszámra,mert hátha nemsokára leutazunk majd az Alpokba.

Beszéltem Gravitzkyvel a kongresszusz sajtóirodájában való müködésről,egyelőre semmi bizonyosat nem tud mondani.Lauterbach szerint ez egy bizonyos Mechnertől függ,aki Genfben ül.Talán van valami összeköttetésed hozzá,ha igen,értékesitsd.

Viszontlátásig sokszor csókol szerető bátyád

[handwritten note follows]

garian adolescent, I was enchanted, nay, entranced, by Ady, and to this day I believe that, although he wrote in the genre of Charles Baudelaire, Stéphane Mallarmé, and Paul Verlaine, he was a greater poet. In school our classes in Hungarian literature never got as far as Ady and his times (he died in 1919), but at home I lapped up his poems thirstily, and I still remember many of his lines by heart.

Ady had lived for several years in Paris and wrote some of his greatest poems there, including some that reflected the life and atmosphere of the city itself as experienced by an impecunious foreigner. Thus, Paris for me was and remained until I first saw it with my own eyes Ady's Paris, a great, throbbing heart, full of pleasures and pains, of luxurious riches and abject poverty. Talking of riches and poverty, I remember something that may sound like a socialist criticism of Ady, but really is not: in one of his Parisian poems he contrasts his fantasy of being a king driving out with his queen at his side in a gilded carriage and distributing largesse to an admiring crowd with the misery of his real life, which he epitomizes in the refrain *Döcög, döcög, az ócska konflis és mi sápadtan reszketünk,* that is (in my inadequate literal translation), "The old fiacre bumps, bumps along, and we sit pale and shivering." Strange, I thought, that for Ady the contrast between a life of richness and poverty was symbolized by a luxurious ride in a gilded royal coach and bumping along in an old rickety cab, while for me a ride in any horse-drawn vehicle, even the poorest and shakiest one, represented a moment of luxury that I had tasted only very rarely in my life.

But Paris as painted by Ady—a city that "was singing, singing," and, whether it satisfied his longings or left them frustrated, always awakened new desires in his heart with its endless variety of lures and allures—was the city that had lived in my imagination for more than a dozen years before I first set eyes upon it. Once I did see it the imaginary images were, of course, quickly replaced by actual impressions, less romantic but no less fascinating.

Upon my arrival in Paris in July 1939 I found my sister hale and well, recovered from the trauma of her divorce, and busy working for the World Jewish Congress. She lived in a nicely furnished room in a stately building (*pierre de taille*), in a side street of the Avenue de la Grande Armée. It so happened that another room was vacant in the same apartment, and Évi reserved it for me. The first thing that struck me about the room was that its floor was covered with dark red velvety wall-to-wall carpeting. Up to that point I had not even known that such a thing as wall-to-wall floor covering existed. In my parents' home in Budapest there were fine Persian rugs, but all around them the parquet floor was always visible. In Jerusalem the tile floors of rooms were also covered only partially by area rugs, often of Arab tribal manufacture, even in the richest houses to which I had entry. Now in Paris the wall-to-wall *moquette*, together with the heavy drapes that prevented much of the outside light from penetrating the room, the heavy furniture, and the large and soft double bed made on me the impression of a world of luxury, pamperedness and softness, very different from the environments I had known before.

After helping me settle in, my sister informed me that Dov Rivkind, whose name was familiar to me from her letters, was her boyfriend and explained that the rule in sublets such as the one she lived in was that if the roomer had a friend she introduced him to the landlady, who thereafter had no objection to his occasionally staying overnight. The next day when I met Dov—I liked him at first sight—and he saw the stubble on my cheek, he gently advised me that in Paris it was customary for men to shave every day. In Jerusalem I shared with most other men the habit of shaving only once every two days.

My sister, Dov, and I met for lunch, and he took us to a small restaurant—I no longer remember where. But I do remember that the restaurant too made on me the impression of refinement with its small tables covered with white tablecloths, with two glasses at every table setting—I soon found out that one was for wine, the other for water—several forks, spoons, and knives, and a nicely folded napkin. Along the walls stood rows of wine racks, with all kinds of brass fittings, pictures, and I don't know what else. After we were shown to a table, a polite waiter handed us large menus listing a confusing abundance of choices, most of them with names I did not understand. All this reinforced my impression that I found myself in a world greatly differing from and on a much higher level of sophistication than that of Jerusalem. In a typical Jerusalem restaurant the usual menu listed two kinds of soups: "meat soup" and "vegetable soup," to which a third one was added in the summer: "fruit soup." As for meat, there were again two kinds: "beef" and "fowl" (that is, boiled chicken). The meal could be finished off either with *liftan* (compote) or with *'uga* (cake). If one preferred a milky repast, there was either "white cheese" or "yellow cheese." Since that is how far my familiarity with the culinary art went, I simply told Dov to order for me whatever he chose for himself.

What I ate on that first opportunity to enjoy French cuisine I no longer remember, but a sight I could observe at a neighboring table impressed me so deeply that I can recall it to this day. There sat a woman, alone, having lunch. She was somewhat beyond the middle years, with evidently dyed reddish-brown hair, rouged cheeks, carmine lips, and long eyelashes that, although it was the first time I saw such a thing, I immediately recognized as being artificial. However, what struck me most were her very long red fingernails, with which she delicately but determinedly picked apart the claws and legs of a big lobster—it was the first time I saw a person eating a boiled lobster. While she was working away at her lobster it seemed to me that her fingers were red with blood.

Since my sister had a full-time job, she could not act as my guide to the sights of Paris, and I had to find my way alone. This caused no problem; I "did" all the sights that visitors to Paris were (and still are) supposed to see: the Louvre, the Arc de Triomphe, the Invalides, the Panthéon, the Eiffel Tower, Notre Dame, the Sacré Coeur, the Place de la Concorde, the Tuileries, the Champs Elysées, the Quartier Latin, and so forth. Since then I have visited Paris many times and have seen those sights so often that I can no longer remember the first impression they made on me. The one thing I clearly remember from those first lone peregrinations is a scene that had nothing to do with the famous Parisian sights. As I was coming out of the Louvre, I noticed a group of young people in front of its entrance. They were tall, thin, well dressed, and clustered around a beautiful blonde girl. They chatted in an animated but restrained manner, and, as I passed by them, I heard that they were speaking English. At that moment I was seized with a feeling of envy and sadness: I felt that in relation to that group of young people, young aristocrats as they registered in my mind, I was an outsider, who caught by chance a fleeting glimpse of what it was to be children of an elite class: carefree, self-assured, rich, arrogant, and unquestionably destined to take their parents' places at the top of the world.

The need to hold down a full-time job made it impossible for Évi to keep her little daughter with her in the lodging that she had rented. So she did the next best thing and placed the child in a home where she was sure Tirzah would be taken good care of and would be in the company of other children of her age. The home Évi found for Tirzah was in Palaiseau, a pleasant suburban town, at a distance of some twenty minutes by the Ligne de Sceaux train from Paris. Tirzah remained in that place for more than a year, as long as Évi lived in Paris. Thus it came about that the first language Tirzah spoke was not Hungarian, the mother-tongue of her mother, or German, that of her father, or Hebrew, that of the society in which she was destined to live, but French, the language of the home in which she spent the crucial second year of her life, during which she learned to speak.

Every weekend my sister took the train to Palaiseau to spend a few hours with her daughter. In the course of the weeks I spent in Paris I went with her on several of these visits, and the child soon became quite familiar with me, calling me *oncle*. Once, I remember, my sister had to go to the police station near her lodgings to have her *permis de séjour* and work permit renewed, and she took Tirzah along. I accompanied her; as we sat across the desk from a very serious young police officer who asked my sister all sorts of questions, the child suddenly piped up and said in a ringing loud voice, *Oncle est méchant, oncle fait pipi au lit!* (Uncle is bad, uncle made pipi in the bed!) We all broke into laughter, and Tirzah's reputation as a little *mademoiselle sans gêne* was thenceforth firmly established in the family. The fact of the matter was that because of the unsettled circumstances in which Tirzah had lived almost from her birth she frequently experienced the mishap she so boldly attributed to her uncle.

Apart from seeing the great world and visiting my sister, my trip to Paris had the more serious purpose of obtaining support for the Institute of Jerusalem, to whose organization both Father and I devoted much effort in the weeks prior to my trip. We hoped that I could make use of my sojourn in Paris to enlist a number of leading academicians in the provisional executive of the Institute and also to find financial support for it.

The first person with whom I discussed the Institute plan was Évi's friend, Dr. Dov Rivkind. He worked for the World Jewish Congress, was very knowledgeable about the Jewish and non-Jewish academic circles in Paris, and was willing to help. He suggested that, as the first step, we ask a well-known French author to compose a letter describing the aims of the Institute. Dov would have the letter duplicated in the requisite number of copies and sent out to a selected list of French Jewish and non-Jewish intellectual leaders. The letter, we agree, should not only state clearly and succinctly the aims of the Institute, and the significance of its planned programs, but also ask the addressees for their consent to become members of its executive committee. Dov said that he knew precisely the right man to write such a letter: Henri Hertz (1875–1966), the well-known French poet, novelist, and critic, who was said to have influenced Guillaume Apollinaire and Jean Cocteau. Hertz was, Dov told me, a highly respected literary figure in France, the author of numerous acclaimed works, and since 1925 the secretary of France-Palestine, a French Zionist body. A few days later Évi, Dov, and I met Henri Hertz and explained to him the idea of the Institute; he kindly undertook not only to draft the letter we had in mind, but also to compile a list of names to whom it should be sent. When Dov got the text of the letter from Hertz, this I remember distinctly, he was greatly impressed by its elegant style and sophisticated manner of approach.

A few copies of M. Hertz's letter happened to survive due to a series of fortuitous circumstances. When I returned to Palestine I took along several copies of the letter and gave them to Father. In 1942, when there was a paper shortage in Palestine due to the war, my parents used the blank reverse of those sheets to write several of their letters to me. In this manner the copies of the letters addressed in the summer of 1939 to Madame Geneviève Tabouis (Paris), M. Georges Duhamel (Membre de l'Académie Française), M. Jean Picot (Ancien Député, Rédacteur en chef de "*l'Oeuvre*"), M. Roger Martin du Gard (Membre de l'Académie Française), and M. P. Langevin (Membre de l'Institut, Professeur au Collège de France) have been preserved in my family files. These copies are the only surviving testimony to the letters; I have no idea how many of them were actually sent out. Here is my literal translation:

Madame/ Maître/ etc.

We permit ourselves to invoke a memory as a preamble to our request: that of the celebration at the Sorbonne a few years ago of the tricentenary of the Institut de France.

On that day, we were proud to hear mentioned by name the Hebrew University of Jerusalem together with those of the oldest and most illustrious universities of the world, and it was a great French *savant* who spoke for it. We understood better, at that moment, what duties we, Palestinian Jews, have before us, and in what manner we shall have to fulfill them in accordance with the highest spirit of France.

Outside the university itself the young people of Palestine, for whom even the least work, the most modest task, is an act of faith, are moved by the feeling that its renaissance, again buffeted by so many vicissitudes, must not cease to obey the motives that confer upon it a particular consciousness that inspires its *raison d'être*, and constantly embellishes our public life.

Thus it appears to us that Jerusalem, in the new role that it has assumed in the last twenty years under the control of the League of Nations, where the freedom the Jews had lost elsewhere is guaranteed, must become the recognized representative, the house of resistance to racism so nobly undertaken in other countries. It seems to us natural that, if this struggle, so magnificently led in Paris, in London, in New York, in Geneva, and in all the free countries, in order to be effective must have a center in which will be found assembled its references, its instruments of work, its plans of action, that center should be in Jerusalem, the symbolic city, capital from now on of a great number of those who are the first victims of racism and are most implacably sacrificed by it.

It is from these points of view that we ask you, *Monsieur le Professeur*, to do us the honor to join the French Committee whose formation, with the participation of men like you, is indispensable so that the prestige of the Center for International Intellectual Cooperation that we are establishing, and the mission that will be incumbent on it, should acquire all the significance it must have.

We should be happy if M. R. Patai, lecturer at the University of Jerusalem, secretary of our initiative committee, sent by us to Europe, could discuss this subject with you in the next few days, and if you would be kind enough to make an appointment with him at 83 Av. de la Grande Armée, 16e.

Please accept, *Monsieur le Professeur*, the expression of our most sincere regards,

[Place for signature left blank]

The letter in which I reported to Father of our meeting with Hertz is lost, but on July 17, 1939, I was able to write to him (with a copy to Mother in Budapest):

I have begun steps for the "Institute." Of course, everything goes terribly slowly, one has to travel an hour until one reaches a person, and people don't have much time to be at the disposal of others. Thus, of course, one cannot know what will come out of the whole affair. What I do know is that I shall do all I can in the interest of the success of the matter.

A few days later I sent Father in Tel Aviv a detailed report of my work for the Institute:

Paris, July 26, 1939 [in Hebrew]

Dear Papa:

I cannot as yet mail out the letters I mentioned in my last letter, and it seems the preparations will take several more days, because Mr. Hertz has not yet compiled the list of personages to whom the letters should be sent. Only after we have the full list in our hands can we begin to copy the letters in the requisite number, and only then can we send them to you to obtain the signatures of the suitable people there. And since I am afraid we shall be late, for by the time the letters reach you most of the people will have left Palestine for the Congress, and you will have no chance to talk to them, and, on the other hand, I am afraid that even if I do reach them in Geneva, my words will not have the weight yours would in their eyes—I am writing to you again today, before the preparation and mailing of the letters, so that you should be able to talk to the people while they are still in the country.

As I wrote in my last letter, it is the opinion of Mr. Hertz (and his opinion is decisive concerning the situation in France) that only three persons of highest rank should sign the letters. That is to say: not people who are important only in their own field, but personages who, due to their high office and outstanding position, are important in the eyes of the world, including the eyes of the great men of France who don't know the people of Palestine. For instance: presidents, directors-general, rectors, mayors, and other leaders. After much consultation we found that we should have the letters signed by three or four of the following:

3. Mr. Daniel Auster, deputy mayor of Jerusalem

2. Mr. Israel Rokach, mayor of Tel Aviv } one of these three in order of the numbers

1. Mr. Isaac Ben-Zvi, president, Jewish National Council

1. Mr. M. M. Ussishkin, president of the KKL

2. Mr. Leib Jaffe, director of the Keren Hayesod

} one of these two in order of the numbers

1. Rabbi Herzog, chief rabbi of Eretz Israel

2. Rabbi Ouziel, chief rabbi of Eretz Israel

} one of these two in order of the numbers

2. Prof. Fraenkel, rector of the Hebrew Univ.

1. Dr. J. L. Magnes, president of the Hebrew Univ.

4. Prof. Bergman, former rector, if no other choice

3. Mr. Salman Schocken, chairman of the ex. com. of the Hebrew Univ.,

   would, of course, also be suitable

} one of these

I know it will not be easy to get these signatures, but *if we do have* them, then (and this again is the opinion of Mr. Henri Hertz) the success of the whole matter is almost assured. And for that it is worthwhile to make efforts. I think some of these people are still in the country, and you could talk to them now, and if they agree I can then get their signatures in Geneva. Mr. Auster should also be asked to take the position of honorary treasurer. This will not give him any work, only if I get (with God's help) donations, the donors will write the checks to his order, he will countersign them, and then we can get the money from a bank in Eretz Israel.

The letters referred to above will be typed on blank paper. That is, those signatories who are not yet members of the committee do not have to know at all that we have already printed stationery with the names of the committee members. To these letters I shall attach a letter on the stationery of the "Institute," in which I shall ask for an appointment. You should emphasize, when talking to the people whose signatures you want to obtain, that the text of the letter was composed by Mr. Henri Hertz, secretary-general of France-Palestine, which organization in general is enthusiastic about the idea of the Institute. Mr. Hertz will also write separate letters of introduction, which we shall also attach to each letter.

And now for another matter. I think that in connection with the Congress, a few days before or after it, the meeting of the Board of Governors of the university will take place in Geneva. Doubtless, it would be very useful if I could be present at that meeting. Perhaps you could arrange there at the university administration that, since I shall be in Geneva at that time anyhow, I should get some kind of work (e.g., secretarial work, or assistant to the secretary, taking care of the minutes, or journalistic work, or the preparation of translations) in connection with that meeting. I shall be satisfied with a minimal fee for my work. Please inform me also of the date and place of the meeting.

I was glad to read in your letter about the additional success of your work in Haifa. Would that your work also continue in the future under the sign of this successful beginning! Hava and I together read Tchernichowsky's article on "The Patai House" with great pleasure.

I am expecting your immediate answer both about the signatories and about the work for the Board of Trustees. Please continue to write, for the time being, to the address of the World Jewish Congress, and they will forward all the letters to our new address in the Alps, where Hava and I shall spend two weeks, from August 1 to 15. On the 15th we shall both proceed to Geneva, with the help of God, and if need be, in connection with some work, I can go there even before that date. Your son who sends greetings to you and Saul with love,

Raphael

In Geneva (from Aug. 14 to Sept. 1, 1939), we shall stay with Nelly Frank. The address is c/o Nelly Frank, 15 r. Athénée, Genève.

As indicated in this letter, as the month of July drew to a close we planned to conform to the time-honored French custom of going to the country for the vacation month of August. It was Dov who suggested that we go to Annecy, on the shores of the lake of the same name. On August 1 we took the train there and put up in a nice little hotel on the lakeshore. Two days later I wrote to Father (in Hebrew):

Dear Papa:

We have been here now for two days on the shores of Lac d'Annecy, a wonderful, quiet place—when I see the lush greenery and the fields covered with grass, my heart aches remembering the bald mountains of Eretz Israel. Évi and I are staying in a small hotel on the lakeshore and shall stay here until the 7th of August. Then we shall go to Chamonix, at the foot of Mont Blanc, at an elevation of 1,050 meters. We shall stay there until the 14th and then shall go on to Geneva, to the Congress. We shall use these days for nothing but rest and then, with renewed vigor, shall continue to work.

About the Institute: only one day before we left did we receive from Mr. Hertz the final text of the circular letter and the complete list of the people to whom we shall have to send it. Of course, we had no time to prepare the copies of the letter. The list contains the names of 50 leading French personalities, priests, journalists, lawyers, professors, former cabinet members, etc. All "mighty men and men of renown." Hertz compiled the list himself, but now we must find the first names, the titles, and the addresses for all of them. In this Mr. Rivkind will help us in Paris, and once we get from him the completed list we can have 50 copies of the letter made. We shall do this in the first few days after our arrival in Geneva.

I also thought that it would be futile for me to send the letters to you now, since the Palestinian great ones have undoubtedly already left for the Congress and are no longer in the country. Please let me know (address below) with whom you managed to talk or whom, in your opinion, I could approach in Geneva to have them sign the letters. (By the way: I think Professor Fraenkel, the rector of the Hebrew University, whose signature Mr. Hertz considers important, will also be in Geneva in connection with the meeting of the Board of Trustees of the university, and I think he will not object to signing the letters, since you have spoken to him once, and we have included him in the provisional list of members of the committee. In any case, it would be good if you could talk to him once more.) In general, I have the impression that if we succeed in getting the signatures of suitable people, therewith we shall have actually secured the success of the matter. Neither I nor Mr. Hertz have any doubt that the people to whom we shall send the letters will respond positively to our request that they become members of the French committee, and if there will be such weighty names in the committee, it is almost certain that it will be possible also to arrange the financial side of the matter. The only question is whether I shall be able to take care of everything, for it is not possible, according to all the *mevins* here, to begin fund-raising before we have the committee, and the recruiting of people into the committee will take a long time because of the slow tempo in which things are being done here. In any case, I shall do everything in my power.

Please let me know when the academic year begins at the university and when I have to be back in Jerusalem.

And when will you leave for Riga? Will you go at all? And if so, when will you come to Paris?

How is Saul? I want to ask him to let me know what he arranged about my monies. And, did Mizrahi and Dabbah pay the IOUs I gave them?

> Your son who greets you with love,
> Raphael

P.S. I have already started to translate the *Bava Metzi'a* book. After I get the *Bava Metzi'a* tractate, and can enter the quotes, I can send you the first chapter.

The only thing I remember from those vacation days is that we had de-

licious meals in the garden of the hotel facing the lake. Dov used to entertain us with anecdotes of French life, of which I remember one. Two professors of philosophy at the Sorbonne meet on the train returning from their
summer vacation. Both happen to be experts on Descartes. What do you
think they discuss to while away the hours on the train? No, not Descartes.
They discuss in detail the cuisine each of them enjoyed at the hotel where
he stayed.

Geneva

I have a vague recollection that in the event only I went on from Annecy to Chamonix, while Évi went directly to Geneva. In any case, our plan
was to stay in Geneva until September 1 and then return to Paris. The relatives who invited us to Geneva were Erwin Tauber and Nelly Frank, who, although not married, lived together as man and wife. Erwin was a second
cousin of Mother, an amateur author with great literary plans about which
he liked to hold forth to my sister and me at great length, but which, as far
as I know, never came to fruition. He took great pleasure in having a certain
facial resemblance to Bruno Walter, and he beamed whenever somebody
mistook him for the great conductor and stopped him in the streets of
Geneva asking for his autograph.

Nelly Frank was the widow of Gabriel Frank, a brother of my Uncle
Berti's widow Ruth, whom I mentioned in the first volume of these memoirs. Nelly was a big woman, very hearty, with a big nose, a big head, a big
body, and, what I think was equally important for Erwin, a big fortune. She
was a cousin of the composer Kurt Weill, and her ample finances were the
result of inheritance from both her father and her husband, who had been a
successful film producer in Berlin. The third member of the Tauber-Frank
household was Marion, the eighteen-year-old daughter of Nelly and the late
Gab Frank.

The Tauber-Frank apartment was not big enough to put up both Évi
and me, so Évi stayed as their house-guest while I rented a room nearby, of
which I reported to my parents:

> For the room and breakfast I pay 3.50 francs per day, which corre-
> sponds to 175 mils. Lunch and dinner I almost always have with the
> Franks. However, if it should turn out that I must stay for a longer
> time, I shall rent a room by the month, which costs, depending on the
> quality, from 30 to 50 francs, that is, about 1.50 to 2.50 pounds. At
> the moment the fortune in my pocket consists of 13.50 pounds. It is
> also possible to get full room and board for 5-6 francs, or 25-30 pi-
> asters, daily.

As one can see, my "fortune" was indeed very limited—it was the equivalent of ca. 1,350 U.S. dollars today, which would have sufficed to cover my expenses for some thirty days, if I wanted to have enough money left for the trainfare from Geneva to Paris and thence to Trieste. Fortunately, I did have my return ship ticket to Haifa.

Marion was at home from her school for the summer vacation, and we instantly took a liking to each other. She was a pretty girl, almost as tall as I was, that is, close to six feet, ample in build, though not exceedingly so. We had many pleasant outings: strolling along the lakefront, rowing in a canoe the family kept in a small boat basin near their home, and Marion showing me the sights of Geneva—the Palais des Nations, the monuments, and the surrounding mountains. It is again an example of the selectivity of memory that while I have a hazy recollection of these outings, I retained nothing at all of the meetings of the 21st Zionist Congress that took place in Geneva on August 16 to 26, which I am sure I attended conscientiously, and which was historical in the sense that its resolutions amounted to a *de facto* declaration of war on the part of the *yishuv* against the restrictions of the White Paper. Nor do I have any memory of any steps I may have taken to contact some of the Jewish leaders who were assembled in Geneva to try to win their help for the planned Institute, to which I had devoted so much effort in the preceding weeks. What I do remember instead is that in the course of those meetings with Marion my thoughts for the first time in my life began to incline toward the possibility of marriage. It was at that point that Marion told me that she had a boyfriend, some two years her senior, who wanted to marry her, but that she was still far from considering such a decisive step.

A few days later I met Marion's friend. He was a nice, intelligent boy, very young, or so it appeared to me from the superior perspective of my twenty-eight years, but I found that his medium stature made him look puny next to the Junoesque Marion. I suggested that he and I have a talk; soon thereafter we met and walked down to a park where we sat down on a bench and had a long and very serious conversation (in German). He told me that he loved Marion and wanted to marry her, but that she was undecided, and, in addition, her mother strenuously objected to any such plan because he was a struggling young businessman, and Mrs. Frank wanted Marion to marry well. I on my part told him that I had fallen in love with Marion, that if things continued to develop satisfactorily between us I would want to marry her, and that—and here I exaggerated somewhat—I was a university instructor and had good prospects of a fine academic career in Jerusalem. We agreed that we were rivals, but parted in the most friendly manner.

Although I was young and impetuous, I was neither young enough nor impetuous enough to ask Marion to marry me after a brief acquaintanceship of two or three weeks. Instead, since the day of my return to Paris and then to Palestine drew near, I tried to persuade her to come to Jerusalem for a year of study, which would give us time to get better acquainted and, I hoped, to get closer to each other. I don't know what would have been the outcome of these efforts at indirect wooing had I been able to stay in Geneva for another few weeks as I originally had planned. But at that point world history intervened and drew a line across the plans of mice and men, my own included.

I still remember the day on which it suddenly hit me that we all were but pawns in a game played out on the global stage. Marion and I were sitting in the living room of the Tauber-Frank apartment, when we heard distant drumming that rapidly grew louder. We rushed to the window and saw a Swiss army unit march down the broad avenue in front of the house. The drum beat sounded to my ear like the tattoo of fate that was tearing me away from Marion and from a chance of a common life with her. I hugged and kissed her, and as I pressed her body to mine, I knew that this was a gesture of parting.

In the second half of August, as the political cauldron stirred by Germany became more and more heated up, my sister felt that she could no longer stay in Geneva but had to go back to Paris to be near her daughter. She took the train to Paris, and on August 26—three days after the German-Russian nonaggression pact and one day after the announcement of the British-Polish full-fledged alliance—she wrote me (in German):

> The trip was absolutely smooth, we arrived without any delay. In Paris there is quiet, the French behave wonderfully. I am staying at the rue Monge. Dov is, as always, touching. I have rested, today we go out to Palaiseau for a few hours to talk to Mrs. Joachim. Her husband (a sports instructor, the poor man) has already been called up. We want to hear what will happen with the children. I am very anxious to hear what the Palestinians will do in Geneva. Have they found a ship? Or what is happening? Here the Lustigs have the intention of going to the provinces. *Perhaps* we too shall go for a few days—although I am against it and have for the time being not given my consent. In the provinces, cut off from the world, it must be dreadful.
>
> What are our parents doing? I shall wait until the evening, perhaps a letter will come from you with word about them—if not, I shall myself phone to Budapest. Such a situation! Ruth will possibly go to Geneva. "Be nice to her." . . .
>
> Don't worry about me. I shall scrape through with Dov's help, come what may. Only take care of yourself, Gyurikám. Everything that, heaven forfend, happens to you strikes us to the bone . . . Arrange things cautiously, not optimistically, and do consult knowledgeable people. I am writing today to some . . .

It is, after all, still not certain that war will break out. May God grant that it should not happen.

Please hand the enclosed letter to the Frank family.

Please write, even if only briefly, but frequently. Write also to Guszti, who now sits alone in Jerusalem. A thousand thoughts come into one's mind, but one cannot as yet make right decisions. Shall I come to Geneva with Tirzah? What do you think? In any case, *your French visa!* For should you get stuck in Europe we must of course be together, I shall come to you or vice versa. So: write!!!

The Lustigs were Emil and Friedl, relatives of ours: Friedl was the sister of Ruth Ehrenfeld, the widow of my Uncle Berti.

Within a few days after mailing this letter Évi had made up her mind that she would return to Palestine with Tirzah. On August 30 she wrote from Paris to Guszti in Jerusalem (in German):

I want to inform you quickly about the momentary situation of the family. Tirzah and I are in Paris, with the intention of going to Palestine as soon as possible. Gyuri is in Geneva, our parents are on their way there too—we want to go to Jerusalem, all of us together, if God helps.

Otherwise we all are occupied with waiting, calmly and cool-headedly, for developments, and in case of need naturally to seek safety following the instructions received by the population.

It pains me a lot that just now you are alone—but you are, after all, already grown up and clever, and, hopefully, *very* careful. Don't forget that you must take care of yourself not only for your sake but also for *ours . . .*

What is there to write now?—for the moment this is all. I always think of you and hope that God will help and that we shall be able to tell about these horrible times in joy. The child is in a safe place, and I too can go there should it become necessary.

Take care of yourself, *dråga szivem* [my dear heart], think of us and be reasonable . . . May God protect you a thousandfold.

The very next day Évi wrote to me again to Geneva [in German]:

I cannot understand your silence. Neither a letter nor a telegram . . . Have you completely forgotten me? Let me hear from you immediately. *I* have nothing to report, the child is, thank God, well, I too am healthy, and am constantly together with Dov.

It seems, however, that I shall leave here, since I want to be together with you. But I don't know *where* you are? No news from the parents either—this is bad. What could they be doing?

Please *write or cable* immediately, cable only in French, that is the rule. Marion can, after all, prepare the text.

Don't leave me like this without news!!! All the people get letters from Geneva constantly. A postcard every two days—that is, after all, the least. I cannot understand how you can do this, when I am waiting for news soooo much.

None of the letters I wrote to Évi in those days has survived. She either did not receive them (as it appears from the above letter), or, if she got any after she mailed this letter, she did not take them along when she left Paris for Geneva.

In any case, after she had left Geneva for Paris my feeling was that I should return to Palestine as soon as possible, and I am sure that I urged Évi to do the same. It so happened that in this resolve I was strengthened by the attitude of cousin Erwin who, apprehensive lest Évi and I get stuck in Geneva and become a burden on him and Nelly, explained to me, gently but with unmistakable clarity, that in the uncertainty that lay ahead the only right thing for us to do was to return to our home country, Palestine. So I laid siege to the Geneva office of the Adriatica to make reservations for us on the first ship that was to sail from Trieste to Haifa.

This, however, did not mean that I instantly ceased to be preoccupied with Marion. While I knew that at that juncture nothing definitive could develop between her and me, I still felt that I would like to have a chance to get better acquainted with her at a (hoped for) later date. It so happens that my encounter with Marion is the only one among my various relationships with women of which I have a detailed contemporary document in the form of a long and for me unusually frank letter I wrote my parents just a few days prior to the outbreak of World War II. I wrote in Hungarian:

> Geneva, August 30, 1939
> 15 rue de l'Athénée, chez Mme Frank

Dear Mama and Papa:

Although I don't have much hope that this letter will reach you soon, nevertheless I am sitting down to write, since yesterday was the first time in five days that we did not talk over the phone, and I want to make up for it, and to give you a detailed account of the "situation."

As for the political situation, actually I cannot say much about it. The trains are still running. Most of the Palestinians, ca. 300, sit in Marseilles and wait, a few, about 30, do the same here in Geneva. We are in touch, as far as possible, and as soon as the ships start to sail from Marseilles they will let us know by telegram, so that we reach the first ship out. The distance between Geneva and Marseilles is only eight hours by train. But, to be frank, I have not yet been able to decide whether, in that case, I should immediately leave with the others or should remain alone here in Geneva somewhat longer, until "the wrath subsides." Of course, all my feelings, as well as the sense of duty, pull me back home; the idleness and uncertainty here make one restless and nervous. If I visualize that in case of war I would have, *nolens volens*, to stay for a long time in this small lifeless nest where, by the way, I don't even have a livelihood and would not be able to return there where my place is—well, this thought in itself is enough to sweep one into rash travel attempts. On the other hand, I am held back by the logical consideration that it is in any case more sensible to await developments here, in this neutral country, where one enjoys relatively great safety, whatever happens. So, for the time being, I sit and wait, and when the possibility to travel actually arises I shall then see what to decide under the influence of the moment. When all is said and done, I can therefore write nothing definite in this respect.

Likewise I can write nothing definite about that private "situation," which, as a result of Évi's last letter, undoubtedly preoccupies Mama's thoughts as a subject second only to the war. What Évi wrote was partially true—we wrote it mainly in order to lure Mama and Papa here with this "bait." Alas, we did not succeed. Well then, I want to give now an account, sticking to the truth, about how the affair stands.

For there can be no longer any doubt that a certain "affair" does exist. In the last few days I have spoken with Marion frequently, and a mutual sympathy and interest have quickly developed between us. But the situation is, naturally, quite different from what Évi painted at the time in her letter addressed to Jerusalem, in which she referred to all the external and internal characteristics of Marion only in superlatives. If, as against that, we look at everything realistically and without prejudice, then, proceeding from the outside toward the inside, we get the following picture:

The most external circumstance is constituted by the finances. In this respect I don't have the impression that there is a considerable fortune here. True, they maintain a big house, the rent alone amounts to 13 pounds monthly, there are always guests, they travel a lot, go out, and since there is no breadwinner in the house all this they must cover from what is extant. On the other hand, Nelly several times has let drop remarks in connection with more distant plans such as "If we still have money then" and the like. Marion herself mentioned several times that her mother wants her to marry a millionaire. This point, therefore, would have to be clarified, if we think that the matter could become serious.

Within the sphere of *materia* is the physical sphere. This is 176 centimeters tall and weighs 70 kilos. That is, she is much taller and heavier than Évi. I myself am 182 cm. tall and weigh 73 kilos. In this respect the danger of obesity is disquieting. (I am smiling at myself: in today's atmosphere, laden with catastrophes, I call that a "danger"!) See: her mother. Some time ago Marion weighed 74 kilos. When she suddenly shot up, her heart was unable to supply the grown organism sufficiently, and for quite a while she had to refrain from all exertion. Even today she is not allowed to swim or to go in for other sports that involve an effort for the heart. Of course, she can still grow out of this (the kid was only eighteen this past April), but, on the other hand, her father, I believe, died of heart disease. Her figure is good, her head round and well shaped, the features of her face are pretty, her eyes very beautiful, the overall impression, already at first glance, also very good.

Within the physical sphere there is the mental sphere. Her culture and education are deficient. She was taught only so-called practical things. She knows German and French, typing and shorthand, she can cook, do all kind of housework, in a year she will complete a course of some kind of *soziale Fürsorge* [social work] or whatever, here at the university. She works ably and willingly, likes to help everywhere and everybody. As for her mentality in the narrower sense, it is difficult to say. In this respect she is still quite childish. But, as far as I can see, the psychological material is very good and still totally pure. For the time being the basic elements are interest and receptivity. The first signs of a developing individuality gain expression in a certain defiance and an instinctive resistance to strong influences. The overall psychological impression is also very good, but here too, just as with respect to the physical development, there is an open question: what will be later? On the other hand, much depends here on the further education and formation, which, of course, would have to take place in a different environment.

For the last half year she has been friendly with a young man, of Russian descent, Jewish, twenty years old, a merchant, likable. Some kind of childhood, or semichildhood, friendship, whose insignificance and lack of weight are clear to Marion herself. When about a week ago we strolled along the lakeshore, arm in arm, and reached the end of the pier, I succumbed to the mood of the situation and took her in my arms and kissed her; she timidly returned my embrace, but did not let me kiss her on the mouth. In response to my question she said that she would not consider herself decent if she would let herself be kissed by two men. This answer sheds light on her psyche: unspoiled, straight, and charming.

At present the situation is this: in the course of lengthy talks, in which, of course, I was the one who carried the conversation, and Marion rather the one who was carried by it, it became clear that we are interested in each other, and that we contain certain possibilities for each other. The few days, or even weeks, I can still stay here, are of course not enough to enable us to get thoroughly acquainted and to reach any kind of resolution. Even if we had fallen desperately in love in these days, I still could not have made up my mind to tear away such a kid from her accustomed environment, and to take her with me into a country totally strange for her, into an unknown world. And, of course, I don't know how she will develop, physically and mentally, in the coming times. To fix something now would involve too great a risk.

Why and how was I able to talk to her so openly, frankly, and without inhibition? This was brought about partly by the circumstance that I quickly discovered that it was *possible* to talk like this to this kid, and, more than that, that it was right to talk like that to her, and partly by the tense, nerve-racking situation, the uncertainty in which I have been living here for the last several days. We spoke about these things between two ominous radio announcements, in the meantime our voices were drowned by the roll of drums rising from the street when a contingent of the Swiss *Wehrmacht* [defense army] marched by under the window, any minute I was waiting for the phonecall telling us that within the hour we must set out for Marseilles . . . In such a frame of mind one is, of course, seized with the anxiety that perhaps one shall have to leave suddenly and will have no more opportunity to talk to her, and thus all the possibilities still hidden in the future will remain unknown. Therefore, quickly, promptly, to fix some points of reference, on which later one can possibly build further . . . Well, the end result was that early next summer Marion will come to Palestine, and then, if we still want it, we shall again take up the thread that will have to be cut in the next few days. Of course, all this will be realizable only if there will be peace until then!

We are at present living through times in which it is much more difficult to sit quietly, to wait, not to act, than to make a quick decision and act upon it. It was under the influence of this impulse that, a few hours after the first serious news came, Évi rushed off to Paris. To this day only one thing has become clear: that haste was unnecessary, for she could have gone to Paris even today. The same impulse to act drove most Palestinians to Marseilles, where they wait for the ship, in crowded hotels and constant excitement, exposed, in case of the outbreak of war, to the first attacks of the Italian fleet. And the same impulse goads me too to get out of here as soon as possible and impelled me, after but a few days of friendship with Marion, to talk to her in such a, for me unusually serious, tone. And, finally, it is this same activity-instinct that must be blamed for this letter being so frank, open, and detailed, likewise unusually, and probably surprisingly.

Of course, I would have liked very much if Mama would have come here to let me hear her maternal word and advice and to be with me *mit Rat und Tat* [with advice and deed]. Because, although, as it becomes evident from this letter as well, there is no lack of sober judgment and reflection in me, nevertheless Mama's counsel and opinion would weigh heavily. If, by any chance, the situation should improve in the next few days, then it would be possible for both Mama and Papa to come here, as we had originally planned. Please write about this as well, by return mail, if the mail will still return at all. After all, the best thing to do would be still for all of us to sail together from here to Eretz . . .

In the absence of other subjects, I conclude this exhaustive letter, and await your answer with concern. Many kisses to the whole family, your loving son,

Raphael

Rereading this long letter today, after more than fifty years, I cannot escape the impression that although I wrote in a tone quite unusually frank for me, basically I was embarrassed to talk to my parents about my feelings for Marion, and that is why I took refuge in an elaborate and somewhat pompous style that differed considerably from the manner in which I was wont to write to them. Still, I imagine that when I was debating with myself what to do about Marion, the considerations I put down in the letter were those that motivated me not to settle anything apart from the vague plan that she would, a year later, come to Palestine.

The War Breaks Out

The war, as is indelibly etched in the memory of all of us who lived through it, was triggered by the German attack on Poland on September 1, 1939. Two days later Great Britain and France declared war on Germany. What followed thereafter is a part of world history and too well known to require recapitulation here. Well known too is the staggering number of people killed—a slaughter of twenty million, never before even approximated in the long history of man's inhumanity to man. In those early days of September 1939 nobody could have imagined that carnage—nor that six million, almost one-third of all those who fell victim to the new Nazi version of the *furor teutonicus*, would be nonbelligerent Jewish civilians. Systematic genocide of innocent civilians, slaughtered not because of anything they did, but because of who they were—Jews—was totally beyond even the worst nightmares at the beginning of the war.

A few days after the outbreak of the war, to my great surprise, I got a postcard from my sister, mailed in Bellegarde, France, near the Swiss border, just a few miles from Geneva. She wrote (in French):

Sept. 8, 1939

Dear Raphael:

One cannot phone! Don't you know that? Speak to Mr. Goldmann and wire and write! One must do something fast. Speak to Dr. Goldmann and ask him to do what is necessary. When do you want to leave for Palestine? Write quickly and answer, Poste Restante, Bellegarde. I am, and the child too, in good health, but we are very, very tired. One must obtain the permit to enter Switzerland quickly. I cannot travel alone with the child! It is very difficult. I am staying in the Hotel de la Paix here. Write! Do *nothing* without Mr. Goldmann!

Yours,
Eva

Where is Mr. Lustig? Speak with him too, but Goldmann is the most important.

A day or so after I received this card my sister arrived in Geneva with Tirzah, exhausted and disheveled. The worst part of her trip from Paris to Geneva was that until the very moment when her train finally crossed the French-Swiss border she could not be sure that Swiss authorities would permit her to enter neutral Switzerland from belligerent France. After Évi's arrival I continued my daily visits to the Geneva office of the Adriatica, but each time all they could tell me was that they had as yet no definite information as to the sailing date of their next ship to Haifa. Finally—I no longer remember after how many days of tense waiting—we were told that a ship was definitely going to sail in another few days, that yes, we did have reservations on it, and that although the exact date of departure was still uncertain, we should forthwith proceed to Trieste and wait there, since after the date of sailing was set there might not be enough time left for the Geneva-Trieste train ride. So we said good-bye to Erwin, Nelly, and Marion and, not without some trepidation, proceeded to Trieste.

(After we left Geneva I neither saw Marion nor had any contact with her for forty years. Forty years! Then, one day, in New York, Aunt Ruth called to inform me that her brother Fred Frank had died. He must have been in his late seventies. The funeral, she said, was to take place next day in a funeral parlor on Queens Boulevard, not far from my Forest Hills home. I went to the funeral with my wife. Marion, whose father had been an older brother of Fred, was there. She was now close to sixty. Her hair was a mixture of gray and dark brown. Her face was rounder than I remembered it, her figure fuller. She was still a very attractive woman. When the obsequies were over, we walked together a few blocks down Queens Boulevard. We exchanged compliments, each assuring the other how well, how young we looked. We had nothing else to say to each other. When we parted I thought I saw a sad smile pass momentarily across her face. Perhaps she noticed the same on mine. Later I was told by Aunt Ruth that Marion and her wealthy husband had divorced years earlier and that she had a beautiful house in the Old City of Jerusalem, but spent most of her time in the immigrants' town of Kiryat Sh'mone in the Galilee.)

Normally the train ride from Geneva to Trieste took not more than some eight hours. But on that occasion I had an opportunity to see for myself that what my sister told me about the tribulations of her trip from Paris to Geneva was not at all exaggerated. It seemed to me that the whole journey was an unceasing stop-and-go affair, with much longer stops than goes, and an especially long halt on the Italian border. The examination of our passports by the Italian border police seemed unnecessarily thorough and time consuming, as was the search of our luggage.

When we finally reached Trieste we were faced, first of all, with the problem of finding a hotel. Our funds by that time were quite low and we knew of no way of drawing money through a Trieste bank from our accounts in Paris or in Jerusalem, and so we had to look for a cheap hotel. However, the war-scare had set many people in motion, and most hotels were fully booked. Finally we had to put up in a dismal *locanda*, which had a free room with two beds. I was to sleep in one, my sister with Tirzah in the other.

When the time came to put the child to bed she was in such an excited state that she could not fall asleep but went on crying for a long time. We had no choice but to let her cry herself to sleep, while Évi and I sat on a table (there were no chairs) in the narrow corridor outside the room. When, at long last, Tirzah ceased crying and my sister thought that she had fallen asleep, we very quietly entered the room, got undressed in the dark, and went to bed. However, this did not mean that we could fall asleep right away, exhausted though we were from the long train ride. The hotel proved to be a veritable fleabag, or rather bedbug bag, and it seemed to me that I was awake most of the night, scratching myself and waiting for the dawn. In the morning, when we got up, red bites all over our bodies testified to the feast the bloodthirsty little beasts had had on us.

The first thing we did was to go to the Adriatica again. Yes, they said, the ship was in the harbor, our reservations were confirmed, but no date for its sailing had as yet been set—please come back tomorrow morning.

I don't remember how we spent the day, and the next, and the one after that, except for our daily visit to the Adriatica office. But I do remember what we did in the evenings: we put through long-distance phone calls to Budapest to talk to our parents. By that time Father and Mother no longer lived in their Nyúl Street apartment. They had shipped most of their furniture and belongings, including Father's library, to Palestine, rented out the apartment, and moved into the Hotel Esplanade, a fine hotel on the Buda side of the Danube. Yet, despite these seemingly definitive steps, Father could still not bring himself to making the final move and book passage for Mother and himself for Palestine. He knew, or felt, that if he left Budapest this time, it would mean leaving behind and giving up for lost everything he had built up in the course of thirty years of work, creativity, and achievement. In addition, he still had a deep trust in Hungary and the Hungarians, built on a lifetime of experiences that in his case were largely favorable. To give up—to abandon—his journal, his position as the undisputed cultural leader of Hungarian Jewry, the prestige, the respect, the honor that were his, and beyond all that the task that he felt he could and should still fulfill, and move to Palestine where nothing attractive awaited him, where he had no prospect for any activity even remotely commensurate with what he would leave behind in Hungary—this was certainly no easy decision to make. As for retiring, even if his finances had allowed it, he was fifty-seven years of age, much too young and energetic to even think of such a step.

As for Mother, she shared, of course, all these considerations, but had one important additional one that almost tore her apart. While Father had only one brother left in Hungary, with whom his relationship was not particularly close, Mother had her parents and only sister in Budapest and was deeply attached especially to her mother. To leave her old parents behind in a situation from which she herself chose to escape seemed to her nothing short of desertion.

These were the feelings and considerations that my sister and I tried to overcome in our phone calls from Trieste, evening after evening. Fortunately we had just enough money left to make those calls from the shabby lobby of the hotel and to engage our parents in animated, excited, and on my sister's part often hysterically emotional conversation. We marshaled all the arguments we could think of, the most powerful among which was my premonition, to which I gave as forceful an expression as was possible over the phone, that before long Italy would enter the war on the side of Germany—then the only route out of Hungary to a country belonging to the opposing camp would be closed, and our parents would be trapped in Hungary for the duration of the war. And who knew what would happen to the Jews of Hungary, and to my parents in particular, if Hungary itself, already clearly under strong German influence, would enter the war as Germany's ally, as in World War I? The "final solution" was, of course, beyond the ken of any human mind at that time, but great hardships in a country at war with France and England could reasonably be foreseen. I painted as dismal a picture of the future that awaited the Jews of Hungary as I was able to at that juncture, when the true horrors of the genocide still lay hidden in the future.

I don't know whether it was my repeated and forceful argumentation or my sister's hysterical crying at never seeing her parents again that finally tipped the balance, but at the end of our last call, the night before we sailed, our parents finally gave up resisting and gave us their solemn promise that they would leave Budapest as soon as they could and catch the first ship out of Trieste.

The next morning the Adriatica finally told us that we could board the ship, which would sail a few hours later. The few hours stretched into a long day, but shortly after nightfall the ship did, in fact, steam out of Trieste harbor.

Of the voyage itself I remember nothing. It was the third time within a few years that I took the same Trieste-Haifa passage (the first was in May 1933, the second in January 1937), and, being something of an old Palestine hand, I was soon besieged by those for whom it was the first trip with many questions about the country, the *yishuv*, conditions of housing, employment, and the like.

Five days later we approached Haifa and could already see not only the outlines of Mount Carmel, but even the individual houses dotting its slopes, when we noticed that the ship slowed down, then turned around and sailed back in the direction of the open sea from whence it had come. When the passengers noticed this, a not unreasonable fear took hold of many of them, and the possible reasons for this unexpected navigational maneuver were discussed in a mood of near panic. Some said Italy must have entered the war on the side of Germany, and the British port authorities in Haifa would not permit what had become an enemy ship to enter the port. Others opined that due to war conditions the limited area inside the breakwater was probably overfilled with ships, and we had to wait until space was available for our ship to berth. Yet another opinion, offered by a self-appointed expert, was that because of the war the mouth of the harbor was surely blocked by mines to keep out enemy submarines, and we were ordered away so that the Italian seamen should not be able to observe how and from where the mines were being towed aside to enable the ship to enter the port. I never found out what was the real reason for our temporary retreat, but about half an hour later, to everybody's great relief, the ship again turned around and this time sailed straight into the harbor to a berthing place.

After we reached Jerusalem we waited anxiously for word from our parents. I no longer remember how long the wait was and precisely when they arrived. But, at long last, arrive they did. They took, or so I remember, the last Adriatica ship to sail from Trieste to Haifa, before war conditions made it impossible for Italian ships to enter British or British-controlled ports.

The parting present the Hungarian government gave Father was the order to change the subtitle of his monthly. Up to that time the subtitle, printed under the main title *Mult és Jövő* (Past and Future) had been "Jewish Literary and Critical Journal." Now, from October 1939, this had to be changed to "Jewish Paper." Still, even so, it was quite remarkable that the Hungarian authorities permitted the monthly to survive—albeit in a greatly reduced size—for almost five more years. Uncle Ernő Molnár functioned as its *de facto* editor, but Father's name remained printed on the cover and the masthead as the editor.

In the early years of the war we in Palestine were still able to maintain tenuous contact with relatives and friends in Hungary. In March 1944 came the German occupation that placed Eichmann in charge of the Hungarian Jews, but even then we did not know that it meant the beginning of the end for them. When the catastrophic significance of the German regime was first suspected and then confirmed, my sister and I had reason to become convinced that by "carrying on" over the phone from Trieste we actually saved our parents' lives. Today, half a century later, it still appears to me most probable that had my parents not left Budapest at that time, they, or at least Father, would have perished in 1944 in one of the "roundups" carried out by the German and Hungarian Nazis, as did my Uncle Ernő.

Thus it came about that while practically all our more distant relatives—uncles, aunts, cousins—perished in the Holocaust, our small immediate family—Father, Mother, Évi, Saul, and I, as well as Évi's little daughter Tirzah—was saved and united in the land where we, the Patai children, had wanted to live ever since we knew our minds.

As for Father, once he returned to Palestine, he had no choice but to bend his neck to the yoke of the Friends of the Hebrew University.

The Jerusalem Academy became one of the minor casualties of the war.

8

Marriage and Family

Marriage

Jean de la Bruyère, the seventeenth-century French writer and moralist, has much to say in his aphorisms about the relationship between friendship and love. I remember two of them: "Love and friendship exclude each other" and "Love begins as love; even the strongest friendship can change only to the feeblest of love." My own experience proves these categorical assertions utterly wrong.

The relationship between Naomi and me began with friendship, and not too strong at that, and changed to love, not a feeble one, but the most powerful and overwhelming love I had ever experienced. This chapter tells about that remarkable transformation.

As I described in an early chapter, I first met Naomi Tolkowsky in the spring of 1933, soon after I arrived in Palestine. She was fifteen and I twenty-two. For several years thereafter I saw her perhaps once or twice a year, when I happened to spend the weekend in Tel Aviv and dropped in at her parents' institutionalized "at home" on Friday afternoon. In 1935, by the time Naomi finished her high-school studies at the Gimnasiya Herzliya in Tel Aviv (which was located only two short blocks from the Tolkowsky residence), it was a foregone conclusion that with her pronounced intellectual bent she would go on to study at the Hebrew University of Jerusalem. But since she was not yet eighteen her parents thought her too young to leave home, so that she came to Jerusalem only a year later, in the fall of 1936. She registered for a variety of courses, including Archaeology, Prehistory, Hieroglyphics, Coptic, Greek, Greek History, and Ras Shamra Tablets. Hers was not a curriculum leading to a degree in a definite field, but rather an assortment of courses chosen to satisfy her eclectic interests wherever they led her.

I returned from Budapest to Jerusalem in January 1937 and soon thereafter I met Naomi by a mere chance. I went to visit my friend Dr. Stephen Krauss, a young physician, son of the famous Jewish scholar and head of the Viennese Jüdisch-Theologische Lehranstalt (Jewish Theological Institute), who had shortly before reviewed my Jerusalem doctoral dissertation very favorably (the review was published in the January 1937 issue of my father's monthly in Hungarian and then in my own Hebrew translation in the January 22, 1937, issue of the Tel Aviv daily *HaAretz*). In connection with that review I had some correspondence with Professor Krauss; when his son came to Jerusalem he asked me to concern myself with him, which I was glad to do. Upon entering the apartment in Rehavia in which Stephen Krauss occupied a furnished room, I noticed on a door leading to another room a card with the name "Naomi Tolkowsky" on it. After visiting with Stephen I knocked on Naomi's door, found her at home, and chatted with her a while. Thereafter I visited her occasionally and invited her when I entertained friends.

Thus it came about that a friendship gradually developed between Naomi and me, expressed for another two years or so in incidental meetings and confined to intellectual exchange. I found that despite her young age she was unusually well read in many fields and was interested in several of the scholarly areas to which I had devoted myself with increasing concentration. In addition to Hebrew—the language in which we conversed—she also knew English, French, and some German, and, in general, was a young lady with a keen intellect, with definite views and opinions, with a personality and individuality. But at the same time she was extremely reserved and reticent the moment our conversation touched on personal matters: in that case she would instantly withdraw into herself and become uncommunicative and even curt and tongue-tied. This, however, did not bother me at all since in the course of those two years I was amorously and sexually involved with several young women, seriatim, that is, and thus did not feel the erotic attraction to Naomi that for me has always been a prerequisite for falling in love. The last of my girlfriends was a self-assured, serious, pretty, and friendly German Jewish girl, tall and full of stature, with dark brown eyes, black hair, and very white skin, who made a good living as an independent dental technician. She had a small apartment in Ben-Yehuda Street in which one room served as her laboratory (or should one call it workshop?). We were not in love, but we certainly enjoyed and were at ease in each other's company. Now, as I became increasingly attracted to Naomi, I felt a growing inner constraint to put an end to my relationship with the German girl. I gradually reduced and within a few weeks altogether discontinued my meetings with her. (Subsequently I heard that she had married one of her dentists.)

How I won the love of Naomi is a chapter in our relationship that completely escapes me. However, given her utterly reticent and withdrawn nature, there must have been something overwhelming in the manifestations of my love for her that produced in her a response strong enough to overcome, within a short time, whatever inhibitions she had. I do remember that she underwent a profound change. She was no longer the flinching, wincing girl-child who shrank from the slightest emotional and physical contact, but instead a young woman, glowing, burning with love.

It is now more than fifty years since all this happened. Half a century is long enough in the mind to blur even the most memorable events, and much more so to cover with the dust of distance the thousand little acts and moments that mark the way of a man and a woman irresistibly pulled together by the power of love that the ancient Hebrews recognized as being as strong as death. Was there a precise moment when that mystical metamorphosis from friendship to love took place? I don't know. But whether it happened like sustaining a sudden wound from Cupid's bow, or was a blossoming-out like the one Heine experienced in his *wunderschön* month of May, I know that it must have happened between September 1939 when I returned with my sister and her little daughter from Europe and the spring of 1940.

As against the loss from the storehouse of my memory of the inner developments and their external manifestations that signaled this transformation, I still have a clear picture of Naomi as she was—or as I saw her—in those most crucial weeks of our lives. She was of medium height, somewhat on the small side, with a slim figure, narrow hips, beautiful full arms, and a slender neck upon which she carried proudly a head crowned with rich, dark-ashblonde hair that fell to her shoulders in large waves. She had a beautiful forehead about which I used to quote with loving humor (and with the required change of gender in the pronoun) what Heine said about Bertram de Born the troubadour: *auf ihrer Stirn Gedankenspur* (upon her forehead the spoor of thoughts). Under straight eyebrows her gray-blue eyes were deep-set, and although she had inherited nearsightedness from her mother, she had been trained from childhood to refrain from squinting, the giveaway of myopic people when trying to focus on something in a distance. I no longer remember whether she wore glasses for reading. She had a straight and shapely nose set under a slightly projecting brow, and a bow-shaped mouth arched somewhat downward, enclosing beautiful white teeth. The regular oval of her face rose from a strong jaw that lent her an air of determination, which, in actuality, did not frequently come into play. While I remember these features of my bride-to-be quite clearly, I remember even more clearly that I loved her because I found her altogether charming, because I was attracted to her personality, because she was interested and knowledgeable in those areas of scholarship to which by that time it was evident that I would devote my life, because I felt that she was my intellectual equal, and most of all because I knew that she fully reciprocated my love. I also remember that once we agreed that we would marry, my love of her became enriched with an additional quality, a new dimension that had been absent in all my earlier relationships with women.

Once we made that decision, the next thing to do was to obtain her parents' consent. Having no phone, I went to a neighbor who had one, put through a call to Naomi's father in Tel Aviv, and told him I would like to see him. He gave me an appointment in his office, and a day or two later, facing him across his desk, I told him that Naomi and I wanted to get married and asked for his consent. He inquired about my earnings, but had no visible reaction when I told him that they were just enough to cover my own living expenses as a bachelor. On the way down from Jerusalem to Tel Aviv, considering what I would say to Mr. Tolkowsky, I thought I would ask him to continue his support of Naomi for the time being, but in the event I was too embarrassed to come out with the request. When our meeting ended all he said was that he would have to talk the matter over with his wife. The same afternoon Naomi got a phone call from her mother: Mrs. Tolkowsky was delighted to learn of our plans, sent her warm regards to me, and asked both of us to have dinner with them next Friday.

Having thus given formal notice to Naomi's parents that we planned to get married, and having received their consent, we considered ourselves officially engaged, and felt—without saying a word about it—that we could not wait with the consummation of our love until the wedding that, we knew, would inevitably be several weeks if not months away. I lived at the time in a house owned by a certain Mrs. Rosenthal, in the centrally located Abyssinian Street in Jerusalem, in which I shared an apartment with my sister Évi. During the weeks that preceded my conversation with Mr. Tolkowsky Naomi visited me there frequently, and each evening after her visit I would take her back to her room in Rehavia. This time she agreed to stay for the night.

In the last minute before we fell into each other's arms, I removed from my finger the signet-ring I had received from a relative for my Bar Mitzva and put it on a finger of Naomi's right hand. At that moment, which I felt was our true wedding, the ancient hallowed words of the traditional Jewish marriage ceremony came to my mind: *Hare at m'quddeshet li b'taba'at zo* (Behold, thou art consecrated to me with this ring). But as a modern son of the *yishuv*, proud to have liberated myself from all formal observance of Jewish religious ritual, I was embarrassed to pronounce them aloud.

On Friday we took the bus down to Tel Aviv to have dinner with the Tolkowskys. Nobody else was present at that dinner, during which Mr. Tolkowsky was his usual formal and reserved self, while Mrs. Tolkowsky was all charm and friendliness. After dinner Naomi stayed with her parents, while I went to stay overnight at the Shaf Hayam hotel, my old standby in Tel Aviv. Since on Saturday there were no buses between Tel Aviv and Jerusalem, we stayed overnight for one more day and returned to Jerusalem on Sunday morning.

The public wedding was something of an anticlimax compared to our private one. It took place on July 11, 1940, in the garden of the Tolkowsky-Goldberg house. Rabbi Moshe Avigdor Amiel (1883–1946), the chief rabbi of Tel Aviv, officiated, wearing a silk top hat that neatly counterbalanced his long white beard. The *huppa* (wedding canopy), whose four staves were held up by my father and friends of the two families, was supplied for the occasion by the Tel Aviv Chief Rabbinate. It was embroidered with a big Star of David, surrounded by the words of the traditional Hebrew benediction, *Qol sason v'qol simha, qol hatan v'qol kalla* (The sound of joy and the sound of rejoicing—the voice of the bridegroom and the voice of the bride). The wedding itself was a one-hundred-percent Orthodox ceremony. The bride was led around the groom seven times, the rabbi recited the blessing over a cup of wine, which then was given to the groom and the bride to drink from; I placed the ring (another ring) on the forefinger of Naomi's right hand and recited, this time aloud, the *hare at* formula, then the rabbi read out the *ketubba* (marriage contract), following which he recited the traditional "Seven Benedictions." Then a glass, wrapped in a white handkerchief, was placed before me on the ground, and I crushed it with my right foot. All those present broke out into loud *mazal tov* (good luck!) cries, and therewith the ceremony was over. Now only the traditional *yihud* (union) was left, which was performed by leaving Naomi and me alone for a few minutes in a room of the house. For a while we mingled with the guests and partook of the refreshments served. One of those who went around serving hors d'oeuvres was Naomi's father—I still have a snapshot showing him bending over Rabbi Amiel with a tray in his hands. Then Naomi exchanged her wedding dress (which, to the considerable chagrin of my mother, was not white but made of light blue tulle with a flower pattern), for a simple everyday dress, and taking only a small valise, we sauntered down the length of Allenby Road to the Shaf Hayam hotel for an overnight stay.

Next morning when we left the hotel, its owner, my old red-bearded diminutive friend Mr. Yakubovich, congratulated us. He had seen an announcement of our marriage in that morning's *HaAretz*. We took the bus out to Shekhunat Boruchov, where my parents' house stood empty—that same morning they went up to Jerusalem, where they planned to spend the remaining weeks of the summer, and kindly put their apartment at our disposal. Thus, instead of setting out on a wedding trip we embarked on the very next day after our wedding on a practical course in housekeeping and living together.

The apartment on the second floor of the house was rented to a certain Mr. and Mrs. Bretschneider, who also worked the plot of land around the house growing vegetables and keeping a few animals. Some months later I had to involve myself in a lawsuit against him in order to get him out of the house and off the land, but at that time the relationship between us was still friendly. Funny the things one's memory retains: one morning we observed him trying in vain to induce a he-goat—he called it *tash* in his faulty Hebrew instead of *tayish*—to mount a she-goat. He tried to drag the male animal toward the rear end of the female, but the stubborn billy-goat just could not be bothered. Finally, cursing under his breath in his native Rumanian, the would-be breeder had to give up. Once my father had something to do in Tel Aviv and let us know that he wanted to stay overnight in the apartment, which had two bedrooms. I felt it was an intrusion into our privacy, but, of course, could not even let Father suspect it.

We stayed in Shekhunat Boruchov, I believe, about four or five weeks. Most of the time we remained indoors or lounged around on the spacious terrace. Shekhunat Boruchov at the time was still entirely rural, with a few small houses scattered among orange groves, vegetable gardens, and utility sheds. The rural atmosphere of the place contrasted strangely with my parents' apartment, furnished with the best pieces of furniture they had brought along with them from Budapest only a few months earlier—I remembered them well as the familiar and friendly environment of my childhood and youth. Those weeks were an important period for both Naomi and me. They were the time, first of all, for the process of adjustment to each other, of learning how to take account of the other's preferences in simple everyday matters such as when to get up in the morning and when to go to bed in the evening, when to eat and what to eat, how to take care of the daily household duties of shopping, cooking, and cleaning the house—we had no maid of course—when and where to go out, whom to visit and whom to invite, and even such very minor points as when and what to listen to on the radio. What I remember of all this are not the actual details—I have long forgotten those—but the very fact that there were two young people who prior to that time had for years lived alone, each in his/her own room where he/she could do absolutely and uninhibitedly whatever he/she wanted, and that the changed circumstances of having suddenly to share everything with one other person, twenty-four hours a day, day in and day out, did not cause even the slightest ripple of disagreement between us. We were either very similar in our tastes, preferences, and domestic habits, or, being young and flexible, we quickly adjusted to each other—or else love, which for the Romans conquered all, pulled us together so powerfully that disagreements simply had no chance to arise.

In another respect, too, those first weeks introduced something entirely new into my life. Prior to my marriage my life was composed of two totally separate and unconnected parts. There was my work, to which I devoted most of my days and most waking hours of each day, during which I was alone with my books, pen, and paper, busy reading and writing what I wanted when I chose. It was not a lonely but a solitary way of life, which I did not precisely enjoy, but the results certainly gave me satisfaction. And then there were my relationships with my women friends who, even though they showed polite interest in my work, knew so little about the whole world of Jewish cultural history to which I devoted so many hours every day that any meaningful conversation about it would have been impossible. This meant that, when I put down the pen and went to meet one of them, I entered a totally different world, which had nothing in common with the world of my scholarly work. Not that I had any acute sense of lacking something in those relationships—on the contrary, precisely because of it they provided me with a complete mental relaxation that made the satisfaction of my libido even more central. Still, there was always that sharp dichotomy between those two worlds that alternatingly absorbed me.

Now, in my relationship with Naomi, this whole situation underwent a profound change. First of all, instead of spending a few hours every week with her, as I had done with my women friends, she and I were together, at least during those first weeks of our stationary honeymoon, twenty-four hours a day. That new situation in itself had several novel and significant aspects for me: for the first time in my life I was not alone in the room in which I did my work; there was no longer a dividing line between my work and my love; and the woman I loved was also an intellectual partner with whom I was able to share my scholarly interests, concerns, and problems to the same extent to which I shared with her the joys of a love fulfilled. Thus, what I remember most clearly from those first weeks of married life in Shekhunat Boruchov is the feeling that I had found what subconsciously I had been looking for ever since reaching manhood—my 'ezer k'negdi, my helpmeet.

I also remember the work I did during those weeks—for our honeymoon did not mean for me cessation of work, of course. I put in order the notes based on interviews I had made in the preceding months on birth, marriage, and death customs among several Middle Eastern Jewish communities and wrote brief articles based on them for the Tel Aviv Hebrew daily *HaTzofe*—they were published in October and November of that year. More importantly, I worked out the plan of a major study on the relationship between man and earth in ancient Judaism, mainly in biblical and talmudic times, as it was expressed in custom, belief, and legend. I had carried in me the idea of such a work for several years, as a sequel to my 1936 doctoral dissertation, which dealt with water in the life of biblical and talmudic Israel, but it was only now, in the elated and yet tranquil atmosphere I enjoyed as a newly married man, that I was able to embark upon sketching out its outline and starting to draft its introduction, which set forth the research method. At that time I was still strongly under the influence of the Frazerian school of anthropology and devoted much of the introduction to outlining the concept of "cultural survivals" in biblical and talmudic Judaism—a rather touchy issue in those days in the conservative corridors of the Hebrew University. I planned a three-volume book, two of which were eventually published by the Hebrew University Press in 1942 and 1943, respectively, under the title *Adam vaAdama*. I dedicated the first volume to my mother, and the second to my wife.

Late in August we returned to Jerusalem. Our timing was fortunate, for on September 9 there was a heavy Italian air raid on Tel Aviv in which 119 persons (105 of them Jews, including 55 children) were killed, and another 124 were wounded.

In Jerusalem we at first rented a furnished room and set out to look for a suitable apartment. Before long we found one, by coincidence in the very house in which Professor Klein had lived until his death just a few months earlier and where his widow and her brother Judah Hershkovitch (who later changed his name to Elitzur, and became a professor at Bar Ilan University) were still living. The house was located in the Bukharan Quarter of Jerusalem at 34 David Street, a stately building of two stories, with a small garden at its back from which one could exit to a large, vacant, stony area gently sloping upward towards the Kerem Avraham Quarter. Number 34 was the last house in David Street, but the pavement in front of it extended somewhat beyond it to a small circle where a municipal bus had its last stop before it turned around to go back to the center of the city.

The house itself was faced with the typical pink Jerusalem stone. From the front a few steps led up to the central entrance of the ground floor apartment of the Kleins that occupied about half of that floor. In the other half Rabbi Akiva Barukh Posner (1890–1962), a scholar and librarian, lived with his family. Around the left of the house a paved path led to the back where an open stairway mounted to the second floor that was divided into three apartments. I no longer remember who lived in the right-wing apartment. In the left wing lived the owner of the house, a Meshhedi Jew, Ismailoff by name, with his wife. The Ismailoffs spent much of their time in London, and when discussing with them the rental of the central apartment I found it rather peculiar that they knew no Hebrew but only Persian and English. I signed a lease and gave Mr. Ismailoff the customary IOUs, one for each month of the rental's two-year duration. The Ismailoffs later moved to London permanently, and their apartment was taken by a Viennese family, Mr. and Mrs. Austerlitz, and their teenage daughter.

I possessed only a very few pieces of furniture, so that moving them into our new apartment presented no problem, although moving from one place to another in Jerusalem of those days had to follow a certain customary procedure. First one had to go to the Mahane Yehuda Quarter and seek out a mover with a horse-drawn cart (in most cases a Kurdish Jew) and ride with him on his vehicle to the apartment. There he would cast an expert eye over the furniture to be taken, and after some haggling one would agree with him on the price and the date—all this, of course, only orally. As a token of closing the deal a deposit was given, but not, as one would imagine, to the mover by the man who hired him, but the other way round, by the mover to the person who wanted to move. If the mover did not show up at the agreed-upon time, he forfeited his deposit; if he did, it was returned to him together with his fee. The reason for this arrangement was that, since practically all the moves into new lodgings took place at the beginning of the Muslim month of Muharram, the movers at that time were in great demand; often after agreeing to do a job they found another, more lucrative one and simply did not show up.

Incidentally, the movers who owned horse-drawn carts were the elite of the moving business of Jerusalem in those days. Many more had no vehicle at all, but carried everything on their backs. Most of these were again Kurdish Jews or else Arabs. All of them used only two pieces of equipment: a hard, straw-filled cushion strapped to their back around the waist and hanging down, upon which they balanced their load, and a heavy rope that went around whatever they carried and circled their forehead. The heavier the load, the more the porter had to bend forward and down to be able to carry it. In this manner he was able to carry astonishingly heavy objects. I remember having once seen a porter carry a piano; his whole upper body was bent into a horizontal position, and he held the hand of a helper who walked next to him and a little ahead of him. I have never seen two porters carrying one object between them.

But to return to 34 David Street: our apartment consisted of an entrance hall, from which the kitchen opened to the right and the bathroom to the left. The only equipment the kitchen had was a cold-water tap with a sink under it—this was the usual kitchen equipment in those days. The bathroom had a toilet, a basin, and a tub, and a water-heater that could be fired with wood but could also accommodate the small kerosene heater we installed into it. The door opposite the entrance led into the living room, which was surprisingly large: I believe it measured some twenty-five by sixteen feet and was fronted by a sizable terrace facing David Street and extending across the whole width of the room. From the right front part of this room a door led to a second room, perhaps eighteen by eighteen feet in size, which also had a small balcony facing David Street.

The apartment, we felt, was much superior to anything else we had seen, and its size made up for the drawback of being located somewhat away from the center of the city and at the opposite end to Rehavia, the fashionable new residential quarter with its pretty one-family houses. I was undoubtedly also influenced by the consideration that if the location was good enough for Professor Klein it was good enough for us. As it turned out, the location of the apartment in the Bukharan Quarter proved a great asset for my work for it put me at a short walking distance from a major concentration of Persian, Bukharan, and other Oriental Jewish communities whose study was to preoccupy me during the last five years of my sojourn in Jerusalem.

We set up the big room as a combination study, living room, and dining room. We got from Naomi's parents a nice sofa and two matching easy chairs with upholstered seats and backs and cane armrests, and a coffee table to go with them. In the opposite corner we placed my old bed, which consisted, as most beds did in those days, of an iron bedstead and a mattress—not an inner-spring mattress, but one stuffed with some kind of cotton batting. My old favorite bed cover, the one I myself had sewed together many years earlier from two Bedouin *'abā's* (white-and-brown striped cloaks made of heavy and rough camel hair), continued to serve in the same capacity. Before the window—actually a glass door that led out to the terrace with two windows flanking it—we placed a large table angled so that the light should fall on it from the left side. It was a cheap wooden table with three shallow drawers in the front, which I converted into a pedestal desk by building two low and deep shelves under it, leaving enough room in the middle to accommodate my long legs. To make the desk more attractive, I stained it with a mahogany stain. Also under the desk between the two pedestals went a small electric heater, much needed in the cold Jerusalem winter. Upon it I placed a lamp I myself constructed of an earthenware Arab water jug on top of which I fixed a domelike shade made of paper stretched over a four-sided wire frame, carefully sewn in place and made stiff and at the same time semi-transparent by coating it with some kind of lacquer.

For the long wall behind the desk I built bookshelves that reached to a height of about seven feet and left enough room on top for a medley of decorative objects, such as two glazed vases from an Armenian workshop in the Old City, a round Hungarian *kulacs* (flask) adorned with the coat-of-arms of Hungary, a small bronze amphora from Venice, an eighteenth-century heavy brass Hanukka-lamp from Poland (a valuable present from my parents), and one or two small figurines. For the corner behind the desk and next to the window I constructed a rectangular wooden pilaster to serve as the base for the plaster cast of the bust I had modeled from my own head when I was about sixteen, which my parents brought along in their crate together with their furniture when they moved from Budapest to Palestine.

The contents of the bookshelves were enriched by several multivolume sets the Tolkowskys gave me as a wedding gift. I remember the four big volumes of a fine old edition of Jacob ben Asher's *Arba'a Turim*, the ten volumes of Wilhelm Wundt's *Völkerkunde*, the full set of Lepsius's lavishly illustrated *Antiquities of Egypt*, and the complete Warsaw edition of the *Miqra'ot G'dolot* of the 1860s, which I put to good use while working on my *Adam vaAdama*, as well as later, and which I still have today in my library in New York.

On the walls of the big room there was enough space to hang the pictures I had received from my parents, including several oils by well-known Hungarian Jewish painters. And, I must not forget to mention, in the corner next to the sofa we placed a radio—a gift from Grandma Goldberg—our main source of news, since our limited budget did not allow us to subscribe to a daily paper or to buy one regularly at the corner store.

Over the sofa hung the old Arab lamp I had purchased several years before in the Old City with the help of my friend Ahmed. I still have that lamp—it hangs in the porch of my house in Forest Hills—and hence I don't have to rely on my memory in describing it. It consists of a dome-shaped upper part made of brass latticework from whose bottom hang down three udderlike glass tubes of various shades of red, each with a round knob at the bottom. The lamp was suspended in Jerusalem and is again in Forest Hills from the ceiling on three thin brass chains that meet pyramidally at the top. Originally lamps such as this used to burn oil: the glass tubes were filled with water to about four-fifths of their length, then about an inch or so of oil was used to top them off and to supply fuel to the wicks. When I bought the lamp I electrified it, putting a long tubular bulb (not easy to find in Jerusalem at the time) into each of the red glasses and a round white bulb on top of them under the brass dome. My little daughters used to enjoy greatly sitting in the evening, just before their bedtime, on the sofa to my right and left, and watching the spots of light and shadow the lamp cast on the ceiling. They liked it especially if I gave a little push to the lamp that made the flecks of light dance about mysteriously all over the white ceiling. It was under the spell of that lamp that I would tell them a "Puntzi story," one of the fantastic tales I invented for their delectation and for my pleasure in seeing their rapt attention, about the little boy who was only one foot tall but managed to acquit himself creditably in the most hazardous situations. There was much magic in that lamp for them—there was some even for me—and years later my daughter Daphne incorporated her memory of it into one of her short stories.

Later in the evening, after we put the children to bed, Naomi and I would sit next to the radio and listen, especially during the tense war years, to the news broadcast from Europe and America. Even more fascinating were the occasions when we could hear live transmissions of speeches made by the leaders of the nations engaged in that apocalyptic war of Gog and Magog. We would be glued to the radio listening to the high-pitched hysterical voice of Hitler addressing Nazi mass meetings, to the great war speeches of Churchill, or to the less distinct but still understandable voice of Roosevelt from Washington. It is difficult for people living today in America after the communication revolution to imagine what it meant for us at that time, in isolated Jerusalem, to have the voices of history in the making brought into our living room by that fragile little radio.

Our bedroom was very simply furnished. We bought two twin beds—the usual iron bedsteads with straw- and cotton-stuffed mattresses—and got two old but serviceable wardrobes from Naomi's grandmother Goldberg, one to hang our clothes, the other with shelves for our underwear and linen. In addition, we placed in that room the small fine mahogany desk with a glass top that Naomi had been using for some years. After Ofra was born we put a crib for her in the same room, and after the birth of Daphi there was still room in it for her crib as well.

The living room, as I mentioned above, opened onto a large balcony, protected on three sides by the walls of the house. On that balcony we kept a field-bed consisting of a collapsible wooden frame over which was stretched a heavy pale green canvas. It was characteristic of Jerusalem's climate that several times a year, especially in the spring, there was an inversion of the weather with the wind blowing from the east, from the desert, bringing with it a very fine dust and a dry heat that, in contrast to the usual cooling down in the evening, persisted throughout the night. This type of weather was called *khamsīn* (Arabic for fifty) by both the Jews and the Arabs. Folk-meteorology said that it was called this because there were fifty such days in the year—to which I must add that, throughout the fifteen springs and summers I spent in Jerusalem, I never counted more than twenty *khamsīn* days. In any case, when a *khamsīn* made the nights in our apartment uncomfortable, I would sleep on the balcony on that field-bed.

Once we settled down at 34 David Street, our lives quickly became routine. Naomi discontinued her attendance at the university, and, while taking charge of the household, spent most of her time doing what she liked best: reading books on history, archaeology, psychology, Jewish and Oriental studies, etc. When the fall 1940 term began I went back to teaching my Hebrew language classes that were given in the late afternoon or evening, not at the university campus on Mount Scopus but in a school building in midtown Jerusalem. About once a week I took the bus up to the university, often accompanied by Naomi, to return books, take out new ones, and look up things in encyclopedias and other sources that could not be removed from the reading room.

Our main meal was taken at lunchtime, followed by a lighter repast in the evening. Our social life consisted in the main of exchange of visits with the Patai and Tolkowsky families and with our friends, many of whom were on the faculty of the Hebrew University or were writers and artists. Several of them I have already mentioned in earlier chapters; of others I shall have more to say later. As for entertainment and amusement, there were the movies, less frequently the Hebrew theaters, concerts, lectures, and—either in the company of my friend Ahmed or only with Naomi—walks in the Old City, which never ceased to have its fascination for me.

During the first year of our married life Naomi and I frequently went down to Tel Aviv to visit her parents, who soon after our wedding moved from their house in Allenby Road to an apartment on the third floor of a house in a nearby street. One evening while we were having dinner, the air-raid sirens began their ear-piercing wail, and all of us hurried down to the makeshift shelter that was constructed on the ground floor of the house, I believe, after the first Italian air-raid on Tel Aviv in September 1940. The shelter consisted of nothing more than a few 4" by 4" studs and beams used to shore up the stairway, which was considered the structurally strongest part of houses in general. Of course, the blackout rules had to be observed, and we went down the stairs at the light of a weak flashlight carefully directed at our feet by Mr. Tolkowsky. Once we reached the shelter we groped our way along the benches and sat down in almost total darkness. By the time we got from the top floor to the ground floor the other tenants of the house who lived on the lower floors were all assembled and had to squeeze together to make room for us. I sat down on one of the places thus made available and found myself next to a corpulent gentleman. For a while we all sat in silence, straining our ears and trying to discern the sounds we knew we could expect: the droning of enemy planes, the ack-ack of the antiaircraft batteries, and the explosion of bombs. As the minutes passed and we heard nothing, we began to relax, and neighbors struck up conversations. I turned to the man who sat next to me and introduced myself. He responded by telling me his name: Rabbi David Prato. I had known that Rabbi Prato lived on the ground floor of the house but had never met him prior to that evening. I also knew that he was Italian and had been a rabbi in Italy and Egypt. Later I found out that he had served as rabbi in Alexandria, Egypt, from 1927 to 1936, when he became chief rabbi of Rome. In 1938, because of the increasing anti-Semitism in Fascist Italy, he left Rome and came to Palestine, where he filled some position at the Tel Aviv Chief Rabbinate. In 1945 he resumed his post in Rome.

We began to converse, and I told him about my work in Jewish folklore and my interest in the folk-life of the Jewish communities of east and west. It was about that time that I began to collect the Jewish customs and beliefs connected with birth, marriage, and death, and it occurred to me that Rabbi Prato could be a fine and reliable source of information on the Italian-Jewish and Egyptian-Jewish varieties of those customs. When the all-clear finally sounded (I don't remember whether we had heard any bombs falling in between) I asked the rabbi whether I could come to see him and talk to him about these matters. He readily agreed, and we made an appointment for next afternoon.

He received me in his study—the usual book-lined study of the Jewish scholar—and I spent about two hours asking him questions and taking notes. To my great regret, the notes did not survive. I happen to remember only one detail, probably because it struck me as most remarkable. While talking about circumcision he pointed to a fine polished wooden box that stood on top of a bookcase and said, "Do you see that box? It contains all the foreskins of the children I circumcised in the course of my many years as a rabbi in Alexandria. When I die they will string them up and tie them as a necklace around my neck to serve me as an entrance ticket to the World to Come; it is the greatest merit a man can acquire, to enter Jewish children into the Covenant of Abraham."

What I remember as the most important factor of my life in those years was that our marriage was blessed with great harmony. Naomi and I saw eye to eye on everything, from questions of my career and scholarly work, to contact with friends, and even down to minute issues of managing our household and economizing. In the course of time she told me about the inner workings of her family, and I was surprised to learn that, in contrast to my own paternal family in which harmony among the five Patais was a natural given, the relationship between Mrs. Tolkowsky and her widowed mother, Mrs. Rachel Goldberg, as well as between Naomi herself and her mother, was characterized by tension, discord, and antagonism. As soon as I got somewhat better acquainted with Mrs. Tolkowsky I recognized that the root cause of these intergenerational problems unquestionably lay in her. In fact, in the early years of our marriage Mrs. Tolkowsky's attitude toward Naomi and me became, at least on and off, a thorn and an irritant in our lives and forced us to close ranks against her. An early occasion for the outbreak of open disagreement between us and Naomi's mother was supplied by the Goldberg Fund affair.

The Goldberg Fund Affair: A Documentary Account

The "Goldberg Fund affair" provides a striking example of the mysterious selectivity of memory I discussed in the first volume of these memoirs. Not the slightest trace of it has been retained in my memory. Hence, it came as a total surprise for me to find, when going over the old family letters put at my disposal only recently by my Israeli nieces Tirzah and Mira, that for several months in 1941–1942 I made sustained efforts to obtain a position with the Fund, that Naomi's mother opposed and frustrated those efforts, and that in reaction to her mother's attitude Naomi severed all relations with her parents. The issue clearly was of vital importance to me—to us—at the time, it was a matter of livelihood, and yet it completely disappeared from my memory. Since it is solely on the basis of the family letters that I can nevertheless reconstruct the sequence of events, I call this section "a documentary account."

When Naomi's maternal grandfather, Yitzhaq Leib Goldberg, died in 1935, he left in his will one-half of his estate to be distributed among his children and grandchildren, while the other half he left as an endowment to the Jewish National Fund with the proviso that its income should be used for the promotion of Hebrew literature and culture in Palestine. Goldberg had accumulated a sizable fortune mainly in real estate and wine marketing, and his legacy was quite considerable, amounting to about 300,000 pounds, which at that time had the value of some 30 million U.S. dollars in 1990. The legal arrangements in connection with the setting up of the Isaac Leib and Rachel Goldberg Fund, as it was called officially, took many years, but in 1941 they finally reached the stage where the Fund could embark on its designated activities.

The members of the Board of Trustees were Mrs. Rachel Goldberg, the founder's widow; Mrs. Hanna Tolkowsky, his daughter (Naomi's mother); Dr. Judah L. Magnes, president of the Hebrew University; the poet Saul Tchernichowsky; and, representing the Jewish National Fund, its president, Menahem Ussishkin, who, upon his death in 1941, was replaced by Eliezer Welikowski (Vulkani), a professor at the Agricultural Research Institute of Rehovoth. The first activity the Fund engaged in was rather modest: it purchased books and distributed them to the schools in the country. However, it soon became evident to all those who had any knowledge of the way literary and scholarly foundations worked that a Fund that had at its disposal the yield of 150,000 pounds annually needed a secretary to take care of the various aspects of its activities that could be anticipated to grow rapidly in scope.

My own financial situation at the time was still rather precarious. I received what we half sadly and half humorously used to refer to as "starvation wages" from the Hebrew University, and my outlook for a better position was dim, to say the least. It was in this situation that, searching in every direction for a new source of income, I hit on the idea that, with ten years of work behind me in Jewish scholarship and Hebrew literature, I was well qualified to fill the post of secretary for the Fund. When Naomi and I discussed the idea with her *sabta* (Grandma) Goldberg, whom we both loved very much, we found her more than receptive. At the same time I also discussed the idea with my father, who in turn spoke about it to our good friend Ibn-Zahav, and also to Mrs. Goldberg herself. Ibn-Zahav at that time was involved in seeking financial aid for writers, as my father informed me:

Shekhunat Boruchov, March 20, 1941 [in Hebrew]

Dear Raphael:

The evening in honor of Ibn-Zahav was a great success: there was a large audience, many speakers. I at their head—it should not happen to you!—spoke and celebrated the *Ari* [Lion] of the company, almost until dawn, until the students of the university came and demanded that their secretary return to Jerusalem. Ibn-Zahav spoke with self-importance, as—between us— he is wont to do, on the miserable state of criticism, on the jealousy of writers, on the popularity of his own books, "despite everything," on the "boys" who write lightly about weighty works, on the *bahurliks* [youngsters] who shake their heads at serious authors, etc., etc., and at the end he came out with a very fine idea: that from this gathering should issue a great action, that the officials of all the institutions, headed by those of the university, should give a tithe of their salaries for the benefit of newly arrived veterans who in their home countries had helped the Jewish national endeavor with all their energy, etc.—an idea that certainly will find no response from Senator and Co. on Mount Scopus.

We spoke, of course, of our Raphael, and his connection with the Goldberg Fund, and today I visited Mrs. Rachel (I am always glad to have a chance to talk to her) and told her that, in the opinion of Ibn-Zahav, it would already be necessary now to undertake steps that Raphael should get the secretaryship of the Fund, that Ibn-Zahav thought that the amount that the Tolkowsky family allocated to the young couple should be given in the form of a minimal temporary salary for taking care of the Goldberg Fund, and that thus Raphael would already now become involved, and then, when the matter is settled, they would arrange for a suitable salary on the part of the Fund itself—otherwise it could happen that the Jewish National Fund would put in one of its trainees even before the official discussion of the matter. [. . .]

In the meantime Mrs. Tolkowsky arrived and expressed a somewhat negative opinion, saying that for the time being the Fund has no income and that the distribution of books can be done without a secretary. I explained that, "in the opinion of Ibn-Zahav," the tasks of the Fund also include other public activities that need to be taken care of; the secretary would prepare plans for them and carry them out with the help of the Board of Trustees. It would also be meet to devote attention to the memory of Yitzhaq Leib Goldberg, to set up a memorial for that saintly man: his study should be maintained for the perpetuation of his memory, and could serve as the office of the future secretariat, wherever it will be. [. . .]

This letter, the rest of which dealt with other family matters, was the first intimation for Naomi and me that her mother was opposed to my appointment as secretary of the Goldberg Fund. For several months thereafter none of the extant family letters touched upon this issue, until my father returned to it after another visit he paid to Mrs. Goldberg:

Tel Aviv, July 22, 1941 [in Hebrew]

Dear Raphael:

Just now I visited Grandma Goldberg—truly she is a "grand lady" who understands everything, even a hint, and her heart is open to the affairs of others, even if they are strangers, and much more so to the members of her family, her grandsons and granddaughters. I gave her your book *HaMayim*—she was very glad to get your present and asks you not to spend money on binding a copy for her, let the book remain as it is, as a memento for her. It is always a pleasure to talk to her. She mentioned that she had sent a letter to Magnes, and he answered that he did not yet know when he would be in Tel Aviv, and therefore she immediately also sent him the letter you left with her, and she thinks *it would be useful if you would immediately go to see Magnes,* talk to him, and explain to him the details. She has not yet written Magnes that he should send such letters to the members of the Board of Trustees, let him first peruse the letter, and then, when he answers her and gives her his opinon, she will ask that too of him. But you could already now explain it to Magnes in such a manner that he should begin an energetic action.

Sabta [Grandma] goes next week to Haifa. I invited her, also in the name of Mama, to be our guest for a few weeks in Shekhunat Boruchov, and we would really be happy to see her in our house and to enjoy the grandeur that hovers over her face. My God grant her a long and good and peaceful life. Many warm regards to our Naomi, also in the name of Mama,

Your father,
Yosef

I have no recollection at all of the letter I handed to Mrs. Goldberg for the purpose of forwarding it to Dr. Magnes. But from Father's reference to it it seems that it was a kind of work-plan for the secretary of the Fund. It also appears, from this and other letters, that Dr. Magnes functioned as the chairman of the Board of Trustees. Three weeks later, in a letter in which he discussed mostly his own literary plans, Father returned to the subject (in Hebrew):

I spoke to Mrs. Goldberg, and she told me that she had received a letter signed by Dr. Magnes and Hanna Tolkowsky stating that they were requesting Ussishkin to convene the members of the Board of Trustees as soon as possible to discuss important matters. She hoped that this would take place. In general, she is a grand lady. We spoke of the Tolkowskys, and she said, *Zwei gebildete aber harte Menschen, gebildet aber keine Herzensbildung* [Two educated but hard persons, educated but without the heart's education], and immediately she corrected herself, *Das Wort ist eigentlich nicht richtig, das Herz kann man nicht bilden, Gefühle werden nicht gebildet, sind etwas Gegebenes, ein Stück Natur* [Actually the word is not correct, one cannot educate the heart, feelings are not educated, they are something given, a piece of nature]. She loves you very much. She told me how they, she and her husband, supported their children and their sons-in-law, without exception, and with what amounts! And at every occasion, and especially in the beginning and in bad days always.

A few days later Mother described what Ibn-Zahav had done in my interest and gave some further details about Father's conversation with Grandma Goldberg:

> Just now a letter came from Ibn-Zahav in which he described his efforts with Yavneh in connection with Papa's book, and with Magnes in your affair. It is really quite exceptional that somebody should do this much and with such devotion for others, even if those others are his good friends. [. . .]
> He writes that after he has spoken at length with Magnes and won him over completely, that Magnes will now try to get Ussishkin to come here as soon as possible, etc., and now Papa should talk to Tchernichowsky. This Papa will do tomorrow. You cannot imagine how happy I am that this matter and that of the military chaplainship are going so well. Didn't I tell you that every child brings with it its material fate, and by the time it arrives everything will be in order?
> In the meantime Mrs. Goldberg, whom Papa visited yesterday, became quite indignant over your father-in-law's refusal to help, and she told Papa how much and to what extent her husband had helped your father-in-law. Once, e.g., he let him have a share in a big merchandise delivery deal of his (he still lived in Russia at the time), on which he, T., netted no less that 25 thousand pounds. As a result of his bungling, however, he lost this huge amount, whereupon she, Mrs. Goldberg, suggested to her husband to send them 2,000 pounds to help them out. This was done. Mrs. G. thought that they give you 10 pounds a

month, and when Papa told her about our exchange of letters and T.'s answer about the difference in worldview, she said, *Weltanschauung um den Piaster* [worldview about the piaster]. [. . .] I want you, and especially Naomi, to know this. Still, we heard that your mother-in-law, probably at the request of Magnes and Ibn-Zahav, signed the invitation to the meeting of the Board of Trustees. Perhaps it is not right, in the interest of the whole thing, to continue squabbling.

Évi passed through here: she looks very bad, I am disquieted about her. From Pest a Red Cross letter came—they are well, the affairs are in order. Thank God!

It seems that about this time Mother got involved in an exchange of letters with the Tolkowskys about our financial predicament. Only one letter by her and one by Father contains reference to that correspondence.

[undated; in Hungarian]

Dear Son:

Naturally, no such sentence was contained in my letter. *I changed nothing* in the text I sent you. The relevant sentence is [in German]: ". . . I don't want to mention at all how it would pain us all if circumstances were to divert him [Raphael] from his career. Nevertheless, if something only halfway suitable should offer itself to him, I am convinced that he would take it gladly, etc."

It is quite possible that Mr. T. read into my letter the sentence he quoted. It is possible that memories from twenty-five years ago came back to him, when he received help from the other generation. In any case it is peculiar that he so simply deviates from the truth and, in addition, attributes such a naive sentence to my pen. He considers me such a bad judge of human nature that I would expect from him such a supplement of income (this word does *not* appear in my letter in *any* context), or that I could suggest to him something like this. Not because in world history it has never happened that a father-in-law should help his son-in-law, but because it is precisely he who is the father-in-law.

Until now I believed that he was heartless, hard, but at least correct. But that he should simply falsify a letter! It is better that we completely leave them out of our lives. There are enough difficulties in any case. But let us hope that everything will turn out for the good. I am glad that Naomi feels better and looks better. Alas, I can't say that about Évi, she is thin and pale. By the way, neither does her mother-in-law excel. I don't know how we deserved this company!?

I want to quote a sentence from my letter [in German]: "This is why we have always supported Raphael in his way as far as we were able to." Perhaps T. saw an allusion in this. On the other hand, the concluding sentence [in German]: ". . . at least in a psychological respect it should become somewhat brighter" shows clearly that the letter in no way pertained to financial help. You can write to them that you called me to account, why did I ask something from them, whereupon I protested indignantly. But, please, don't forget the gentlemanly forms, for, alas, one becomes very much debased in this ugly strife. Write to them in a gentlemanly tone. Alas, as Naomi told Évi, the whole family consists of abnormal people, and thus in any case not much result can be expected from the whole exchange of letters.

May God grant you soon a situation in which you don't need anything from them. Write to them that, by chance, because of habit, we retained a copy of that letter. Perhaps this will arouse a little shame in them.

Here there is nothing new. The gardener did not appear before the Va'ad [Council of Shekhunat Boruchov], so that they gave him one more date, and if he does not keep it they will proceed against him with all the means at their disposal. So many little battles in the midst of the big battle! But the main thing is that one keep one's mental equilibrium in the midst of all this.

I am writing late in the evening in bad light, but I hope you can read it.

Many hugs to Naomi and you, with much love,

Mama

[undated; in Hebrew]

Dear Raphael:

In connection with Mama's letter I want to caution you that I have no right whatsoever to pass on things we discussed with Mrs. Rachel Goldberg, and you must under no conditions use her words in family affairs, in order not to cause a quarrel between mother and daughter. We spoke in an intimate manner, and she poured out all her heart to me. I was truly shocked. I too told her confidentially things that I was unable to withhold, about her two *Lieblinge* [beloveds], Naomi and Raphael. It is enough for us that she is so attached to you, and it is forbidden to cause her pain . . .

I tried to see Tchernichowsky twice today, in the morning and at noon. His apartment was closed. I stayed in the city to return to him at four; perhaps I shall find him. It is important to explain the matter to him, this is what Ibn-Zahav also thinks, lest others influence him for evil, since he is liable to be influenced. I shall talk to him in the name of Mrs. Rachel Goldberg, and it will be in order. [. . .]

With *shalom* wishes and love your father,

Yosef

In the ensuing weeks Father continued to make efforts in connection with the Goldberg Fund. In his letter of September 7, 1941 (of which I have but part, eaten away by mice or bugs) he informed me that he had spoken to Tchernichowsky about the Goldberg Fund and also asked me to obtain a drug the doctor had prescribed for Mrs. Goldberg for headaches that was not available in Tel Aviv. A few days later Father wrote again:

> I am writing here in the house of Mrs. Rachel Goldberg. She is very sorry that she had no chance to talk to you once more, and to express her opinion about your affair, and she asked me to write to you and call to your and our Ibn-Zahav's attention that Magnes should be warned that he should be cautious in his suggestion in connection with the plan we mentioned. She suspects that Ussishkin is apt to spoil the matter with a counter-suggestion, if it becomes known to him that the issue is your appointment now. Mrs. Rachel thinks that it is better that the Board of Trustees should decide now only in principle that she has the right to use the 200 pounds as she wishes, on the basis of her husband's will, as known to Ussishkin. In his letter that is in your hands he has agreed that that amount should be put at the disposal of Mrs. Goldberg, and he promised that he would bring this to the Board and would support it. And if the Board decides to place the 200 pounds annually at her disposal, she will be empowered right away to decide that she appoints a secretariat, and you as the secretary, etc., as discussed. Consult our friend Ibn-Zahav immediately, and he will talk to Magnes in the proper manner.
>
> Mrs. Rachel told me that Hanna T. was here and asked her whether Mrs. Rachel will go to Jerusalem to the meeting of the Board, and she answered that, of course, she will go. They did not talk more about anything, and Hanna said that Naomi looks bad in the last few days. I wish full health to Naomi, and good mood.

The 200 pounds was the annual revenue yielded by the Hartuv Estate (a part of the Goldberg legacy) that was earmarked for Mrs. Goldberg personally. A week later Father, who despite his by then almost chronic illness was indefatigable when it came to working in my interest, informed me of new developments:

Tel Aviv, Sept. 16, 1941 [in Hebrew]

Dear Raphael:

Since it is difficult to talk to Mrs. Goldberg over the phone, I came here to arrange the matter personally. I composed the following telegram and am sending it off to Magnes right away: "Since meeting postponed request send out circular letter about secretaryship Goldberg Fund in your name and name of all Board members. Thanks and Happy Near Year wishes. Rachel Goldberg."

Mrs. Goldberg told me that when Hanna was here to visit her on Monday, she, Mrs. Rachel, told her that she wanted to get the rights to the 200 pounds from Hartuv that was earmarked as her property, and that Hanna replied that that was impossible, and that it was just not possible to do such things. Mrs. Rachel assumes that Hanna said this because she knew nothing about the secretaryship, and she, Rachel, even at that point did not tell her anything about it. Therefore, she thinks the right thing to do for Magnes is to send the circular also to Hanna, perhaps accompanied by a letter that would state that this was also the wish of Magnes and that he values your scholarly work so highly that he is trying as best he can to arrange this possibility for you. If so, the letters should be sent out as soon as possible, and when they are sent out let me know right away, and I shall again try to see Tchernichowsky, who is not in Tel Aviv now, he will return early next week, for *Rosh haShana*. In the meantime Mrs. Rachel too tried to get in touch with him.

It made a tragic impression on me today when I found Jacques Tolkowsky here, and Mrs. Rachel asked him to find her some work in diamond polishing. He was surprised, but said that there was only one possibility—that she should engage in selling among her acquaintances. But, she replied, that is impossible because she cannot walk much and especially not climb the stairs in the Tel Aviv houses. I almost burst into tears when I heard this exchange between her and Jacques, who appeared as a protector and promised that "he would do everything he could" for our Rachel Goldberg! [. . .]

With love, your father,
Yosef

Why Mrs. Goldberg should have been in such straitened finances is a puzzle, since there can be no doubt that she was amply provided for in her husband's will. The only explanation I can think of is that the untangling of the legalities in connection with the Goldberg estate took an unduly long time, and while they were being processed Mrs. Goldberg's budget was tight.

I know for a fact that Naomi, who as a Goldberg granddaughter was one of his heirs, received the first installment of her share in the legacy, in the amount of 200 pounds, only on the last day of December 1941.

On October 5, 1941, Father reported additional steps he took in my interest, even though his illness partially incapacitated him: "I spent almost the whole day with the doctor in Tel Aviv, and before I left the city I went to see Mrs. Goldberg, who told me about the 'events' since last I saw her. I hope that your affair will be settled, and that they will not postpone the meeting to a much later date. Magnes and Ibn-Zahav will certainly find a way to speed up the matter."

In the event our hopes were not realized, and the meeting of the Board of Trustees was postponed again and again, despite the goodwill of Dr. Magnes and the help of our friend Ibn-Zahav. I reported to my father, who replied on October 25, 1941: "We were glad to hear that Magnes is doing everything in your affair. It is good to know and feel that there are also such people in the country. Let us hope that he will succeed in his efforts, and you will be elected 'chief secretary' and 'chief rabbi' as well."

While this was going on my employment front, my family, and I in particular, had yet another fight on our hands. One of our tenants in Shekhunat Boruchov, a Rumanian Jew named Bretschneider, who had rented an apartment from us and had entered into an agreement concerning the cultivation of the few dunams of land in front of the house in which he lived, claimed that we did not have the right to terminate his tenancy of the land that he had worked for two or three years. There was at the time a law in the country whose purpose was to protect tenant farmers, and although that law was intended to cover only rural land, and not urban land such as our few dunams in Boruchov, Bretschneider invoked it and based on it not only a claim of tenancy but also of ownership. I still remember one scene that took place between me and Bretschneider: I confronted him and demanded that he clear off of our land, while he yelled back at me shouting something to the effect that the land was his. I was then seized with such an uncontrollable rage that I would have hurled myself at him had it not been that Mother, who witnessed the encounter, restrained me. At that moment I suddenly understood how quarrels about land ownership can incite passions to the point of murder.

Since Father at the time was often bedridden and in and out of the hospital, the defense of the family fortune fell to me, to whom Father and his co-owner, Dr. Lajos Fodor, had given a power-of-attorney for managing their property. Thus, it was I who had to sue Bretschneider and to appear repeatedly in a Tel Aviv court of law, to testify, to argue, to be examined and cross-examined, to make depositions, etc. All that was time-consuming, most unpleasant, and involved several tense encounters. The case dragged out for months and months, even though the town council of Shekhunat Boruchov recognized the justice of our position and threatened to turn off the water that Bretschneider needed for the cultivation of his vegetable garden.

The issue was clouded and complicated by the fact that one of the two owners, Dr. Lajos Fodor, was a Hungarian citizen, lived in Hungary, and thus, when the war broke out, became an "enemy alien." That meant that the Boruchov land, as half enemy property, came under the control of the Custodian of Enemy Property and that the validity of my power-of-attorney, signed by Dr. Fodor before the outbreak of the war, was now in doubt. Father was greatly troubled by the issue, and many of his letters to me in those months discuss in detail what should be done about it. Finally, after protracted litigation, and after the Boruchov council actually turned off the water, Bretschneider asked for a period of grace, after which he finally moved out both from the land and from the apartment. Soon thereafter father started to sell parts of the land piecemeal, because he and Mother needed the money for their living expenses.

On December 8, 1941, I wrote to Mother (in Hungarian):

> You can imagine what a fright I had when this morning I got Évi's telegram that Papa is again in the Asuta [Hospital] and that Guszti should come immediately. I instantly phoned Guszti at the university, and half an hour later I saw him off on the bus. In the afternoon at a quarter to three I got Guszti's telegram that Papa is well and that I should not worry. Please write me immediately what the trouble was and why he had to go again to the hospital. [. . .]
>
> Naomi's mother wrote to her and invited her to visit them from now until six weeks after the birth. Naomi answered her that she would not accept the invitation, because, even though physically she would undoubtedly enjoy greater comfort there than here, as against that she would not be able to tolerate a situation in which I could not visit her in their house, and she would have to listen to the kind of opinions about me the like of which her mother writes in her letters. Thereupon her mother replied: what an idea, why should I not be able to visit her there whenever I wanted to, if I don't want to meet them they will avoid me, and in general it is only up to me that a friendly relationship with them be restored. They on their part promise in any case that they will not mention my name disparagingly. Naomi answered this letter by saying that for the time being she did not feel the need of being cared for more attentively than I do it here at home, but should her condition deteriorate, that is, should she feel weaker and need more rest, then perhaps she will go down to them.
>
> Magnes wrote to the Keren Kayemeth asking them whether they

want already now to delegate somebody to the Board of Trustees of the Goldberg Fund to replace Ussishkin. He asked for a reply within two weeks, of which one has passed already, because thereafter he wants to convene a meeting. Thus, in all probability the matter will be decided in about ten days.

I hope Mama is not too worried about the war—neither about Japan's declaration of war against America and England, nor about the cheek of England in daring to take the field against such a dangerous opponent as Hungary.

Please write in detail at the first opportunity. Naomi sends her regards to Mama and wishes speedy recovery to Papa, which I join with full heart.

On December 17 I was able to report to my parents about further developments in the Goldberg Fund affair, in particular about the decision of the Board of Trustees that Mrs. Goldberg had the right to use the 200 pounds in revenue from the Hartuv Estate for the publication of my book *Adam vaAdama* (Man and Earth). By the second half of 1941 I had more or less finished the manuscript of this multivolume book, which I considered a major step forward in my research on ancient Jewish folk culture. It dealt with the role of the earth in the mental life of the ancient Hebrews in biblical times and of the Jews in talmudic times. It uncovered a whole unknown world of popular custom, folk belief, and a web of legends connected with the relationship between man and earth, centering on the concept of "mother earth"—all subjects about which nothing had been written in a Jewish context prior to my study. On the basis of the highly favorable readers' reports by Professor Buber and Professor Klausner, the book was accepted for publication by the Hebrew University Press. Since, however, the Press had no budget to speak of, we agreed that I would take care of the printing of the book both financially and technically.

Jerusalem, December 17, 1941 [in Hungarian]

Dear Mama and Papa:

As Saul probably reported to you, last Thursday the meeting of the Board of Trustees of the Goldberg Fund took place, in which it was decided unanimously that Mrs. Goldberg could dispose of the annual 200 pounds from Hartuv, and could decide for what purpose it should be used, of course, with the consent of the Board of Trustees. They also voted that if Mrs. Goldberg should decide to cover the publishing costs of my book from this year's money, they consent to it in advance.

As I found out from Ibn-Zahav, what happened was that Mrs.

Tolkowsky went to see Magnes in his hotel prior to the meeting and in the course of a conversation of more than an hour argued that the Goldberg Fund needed no secretary, the secretary would have nothing to do, and that she stated all this not out of personal antipathy toward me, but because she was keeping the interests of the matter before her eyes, etc. It seems that she presented all this with such convincing force that Magnes felt it was better not to bring up the motion before the meeting.

Now, yesterday, I wrote to Mrs. Goldberg asking that she should decide to use those annual 200 pounds for the salary of a secretary, because she considers the appointment of a secretary absolutely necessary and pressing. I sent her a typed resolution to this effect, addressed to the members of the Board of Trustees, and suggested that she have it signed by Tchernichowsky and Professor Vulkani, who is the representative of the Jewish National Fund on the Board, replacing Ussishkin. Once these two have signed it, and I have arranged through Ibn-Zahav that Magnes too should sign it, the matter will have been approved despite the opposition of Mrs. T.

Simultaneously with this letter of mine Naomi wrote a short three-line letter to her mother, without any initial salutation: since her mother did everything to frustrate the plan of the Board of Trustees concerning the secretarial position, which would have meant her (i.e., Naomi's) *bread*, it was unnecessary that her mother should continue to send her again and again *butter* and the like, and nice letters full of hypocritical motherly feelings. I believe that this letter by Naomi means the complete rupture of the relationship between her and her parents that was anyhow rather strained. Naturally, in these circumstances Naomi does not even want to hear about going to her parents for the prenatal and postnatal weeks. But that is really not at all necessary, Naomi feels perfectly fine, and at the Tippat Halav [literally, drop of milk, that is, maternal care] station of Hadassah she gets excellent instruction that is worth more than an expensive *ahot* [nurse] and costs very little.

Recently I met Rubin Mass: he told me that the 2,000 copies of the first edition of the *Mivhar haSippur* [Anthology of Short Stories] have been sold out and that he now wants to issue a new edition. This, in any case, will mean some income. A few days ago another article of Naomi's was published in the *Palestine Post*. She has not received translations for quite a while. Now Dr. Muntner gave her some translation with which we shall be able to settle part of the bill we owe him, or perhaps all of it. [. . .]

And how is Papa? Guszti and Évi told me that only after several hours of hesitation did he go to the doctor, which is nothing less than criminal negligence. Muntner says that massage has a better and surer effect than injections—perhaps it would be worthwhile to tell this to Dr. Boss.

Since we finally have the paper, we can begin the printing of Papa's books. Please send me the manuscript of the first volume (appreciations and poems) so that I can give it to the press.

Many kisses,
Raphael

On the very next day Mother replied:

Shekhunat Boruchov, Dec. 18, 1941 [in Hungarian]

Dear Gyurikám:

Your letter mailed on Thursday arrived only today. This latest act of your mother-in-law surprised me even after all its predecessors. It has only one possible explanation: they don't want anybody from the family to gain an insight into what they did together with the KKL to the detriment of the other members of the family. Otherwise one cannot understand such inhumanity. The quotation of Naomi's letter has quite shaken me. It is terrible that a young woman, before the birth of her first child, is forced to write such a thing to her mother.

As for the practical aspect of the matter, Papa thinks that you must unfailingly come down to Tel Aviv to have the matter signed and to go out to Rehovoth to that professor. We absolutely don't see the matter settled, at the utmost estimate it 50-50. After the receipt of your letter I phoned Mrs. Goldberg, but did not find her in: I spoke only to Ada, who told me that they expected her perhaps by 6 o'clock. I shall call her again, and if I manage to talk to her I shall add it to this letter.

You see how slowly and bumpily things go, if it is possible in this manner to cause even Magnes to waver. I hope Ibn-Zahav will counterbalance it, and will give the required explanation of Mrs. T.'s behavior (i.e., what I wrote above). And it is really ridiculous to say that a secretary would have nothing to do at the Fund. That, of course, depends on the secretary. But even your mother-in-law herself said that her father's generation is slowly dying out, and now would be the time to collect the data pertaining to his life and times.

Papa, thank God, is well, but must be very careful not to catch cold: even if the room cools down it has a bad effect on him. If it were not so he would immediately go to see Mrs. G. and Tchernichowsky in Tel Aviv. We don't believe that it is possible to settle such a thing by correspondence, especially if it has an opponent like Mrs. T.

In the gardener [Bretschneider] affair there is no new development. He received the letter of the Va'ad about the three-day deadline for turning off the water. They said they would turn it off this evening (they do such things in the evening so as to avoid attention). I hope they won't postpone it again.

It is not necessary that the poems should be in the first volume of Papa's works. It could be the Kabbala, which is there in the hands of Ibn-Zahav. (This is what they decided.) Of course, one must go over it carefully. Should you come down to take care of your affairs you could go over those proofs with Papa in one day. [. . .] Put aside for me the issue of *Palestine Post* in which Naomi's article was published. In the meantime a huge storm has brewed up, so that I cannot go over to phone.

Many hugs and kisses to both of you,
Mama

I cannot phone. Perhaps you should call Mrs. G., and if you think it is necessary, come down. (If it is not yet definitely settled, something one must, alas, assume, come down unfailingly.)

In her next letter (dated December 21, 1941, in Hungarian) Mother tried gently to make Naomi change her mind about her mother's invitation:

Alas, in this winter we cannot move out of here, and I dare not hope that I can be of help to Naomi in the first few weeks after the great event. I feel very bad about this. I don't know whether it would not be better to accept the invitation to Tel Aviv—she would probably get better and more suitable care there, and I too could be with her often, since I can leave Papa for half a day or even a full day, if I prepare for him everything he needs. But, of course, if Naomi is averse to it, one cannot interfere. This is really not so very important—the main thing is that everything should go well, as, with the help of God, it will.

Two days later I was able to report further developments:

Jerusalem, Dec. 23, 1941 [in Hungarian]

Dear Mama and Papa:
[. . .] The secretaryship affair stands as follows: Mrs. Goldberg wrote to Dr. Magnes that in accordance with the resolution passed at the meeting she wishes that I should be employed right away as secretary; the book can wait. The day before yesterday Ibn-Zahav told me

that this letter was received by Magnes, whereupon I asked Magnes for an audience yesterday. Since he was very busy, I could talk to him only on the phone. He asked whether I want the matter to be settled in accordance with Mrs. Goldberg's letter or rather that my book be published. I said that the secretarial job was much more important for me. Thereupon he said fine, and it was unnecessary that I should talk to him personally. As I know Magnes, this means that he will settle the matter favorably . . . So it seems that the matter will, after all, be in order.

In response to Naomi's letter her parents answered in a long outburst: how can she imagine that, under whatever pressure, Mrs. T. would give her consent to the dishonest use of part of the money of the Fund, etc. Then, out of the blue, the loving father-in-law offers me a job: the police are signing up supplementary auxiliary policemen to control the roads against the smuggling of oranges. For eight hours daily of "waylaying" they pay 11 pounds monthly. It is characteristic that he wrote this only now, suddenly, when the police had already employed the full complement of people; if one of them should not appear at the swearing-in, and thus a place becomes vacant, he can put me in. This letter arrived Sunday afternoon, and if I had wanted the job, I would have had to go Monday, that is, yesterday, in the morning to the Café Vienna, where I would have found Mr. T. The "position" would have been for three to four months, for the duration of the orange season.

I responded in a short letter: "Dear Mr. T.: Thank you for having thought of me in connection with the *ghaffir* [watchman] job. However, regretfully, I cannot take that job because in that case I would have to give up my university classes, which I am obliged to continue to the end of the academic year. Respectfully yours, Raphael Patai." I don't know at all how to explain this asininity on T.'s part—after all he knows well that I teach in the afternoon hours, and that *ghaffir*-job would have demanded my presence every second day in the afternoon, and, as the old rule has it, one body cannot be in two places at the same time. [. . .] Please write more frequently,

Love,
Raphael

Mother replied:
[undated, probably Dec. 25, 1941; in Hungarian]

Dear Raphael:
Truly, your letter with the report about T. caused me much embitterment. As you well know, I value even the lowest type of work, after all, even now I myself do almost all the housework, but that somebody

should suggest to a scholarly man, who has neither gone in for sports
nor been physically hardened, that he should, in this terrible weather,
stand drenched and cold on the road where a serious rheumatism is
certain (even to equip oneself with boots, etc., would cost several
pounds)—this is really more than enough. Alas, one cannot answer
them as they would deserve. It would be a hundred times better for
you to become a chauffeur. George told us only recently how much
those who have their own car for hire earn (30 pounds). Regrettably, I
don't think the secretaryship is assured, because your mother-in-law
went to Magnes in the service of her holy cause, and the same way she
can go also to Rehovoth and to Tchernichowsky. I think you yourself
should make an effort in this matter. [. . .]

I was very saddened to learn that Naomi's leg hurts, although at
such times that is not unusual, this is why she should have worn high
boots. But I hope your mood is not bad, everything will be in order,
despite everything. Guszti does not dignify us even with a single line:
please ask him to write to us at least about what he is working on.

Many hugs and kisses to both of you,

Mama

As additional details about Mrs. Tolkowsky's machinations became
known to me from Ibn-Zahav, I reported to my parents:

Jerusalem, December 29, 1941 [in Hebrew]

Dear Papa and Mama:

There is no need for you to get upset about the secretaryship,
which, I am sure, will be in order despite everything. During the weekend Ibn-Zahav was in Tel Aviv and spoke to Tchernichowsky, who not
only agrees, but even demands most energetically that the matter of the
secretaryship be settled and also spoke very angrily about the behavior
of Mrs. Tolkowsky at the meeting. After Mrs. Goldberg moved that
those 200 pounds should be placed at her disposal, and after Magnes
moved that she should use that money this year for the publication of
my book, Mrs. Tolkowsky repeatedly asked if she [Mrs. Goldberg]
should decide not to use the money for that purpose, in that case for
what purpose does she intend to use it? Mrs. Goldberg, according to
Tchernichowsky, evaded giving a clear answer to this question, whose
damaging intent was palpable. In any case, Dr. Magnes had already
given his consent in writing to Mrs. Goldberg's motion, so that we can
consider this matter settled. And, in any case, for the time being it will

be decided, as Dr. Magnes wants it, only temporarily, but Ibn-Zahav thinks that that makes no difference at all, because once I start to work, permanence will come with time. And as for Mr. and Mrs. Tolkowsky, believe me, neither Naomi nor I care a damn about them, and we are totally indifferent to what they think or say about me. The secretaryship will be settled despite their wrath, and whatever they say about me, nobody cares. A few days ago Yobi [Joab Auerbach, the Tolkowsky's other son-in-law] was here and told us laughing and mocking that they showed him and Ada the letter Naomi wrote her parents (the last one) and told them about the whole affair and also that I don't want to accept work, and the like. All this, of course, made no impression on Yobi, who knows them well from his own experience.

Since Yitzhaq Abiqsis, to whom I had sold my share in the HaMa'arav Press, still owed me a considerable amount of money, he and I now agreed that he would print my book as partial repayment of his debt. So in the last week of 1941 I delivered my manuscript to Yitzhaq and he started to work on its typesetting, promising me to print one signature weekly.

A letter I wrote my parents on January 2, 1942, shows that at that juncture I was quite confident of getting the Goldberg Fund secretaryship:

Most confidentially I want to tell you that this week we began to print my book, and I have already received the proofs of the first signature. Until I get an official notification about my appointment as secretary of the Goldberg Fund this must be kept secret, lest Mrs. Tolkowsky use this fact and announce that by beginning to print my book I revealed my consent to its publication by the Goldberg Fund instead of appointing me as its secretary. By the way, we also got a letter today from Mrs. Goldberg in which she informs us that Magnes has written a circular letter to the members of the Board of Trustees, "all for our good," as she expresses herself, and she has already replied to him. Thus, one can hope that the matter now has been settled. As to the secrecy of the printing of my book, Ibn-Zahav too thinks that we must be careful that Magnes should not know about it for the time being, for it may not make a good impression on him that while he is doing his best for me in order to provide me with a livelihood, I am expending a large amount on the printing of a ca. 800-page book. Actually, the book will cost me very little, for I shall save most of the expenses by having Abiqsis pay me back his debt in the form of printing the book. [. . .]

I thank you in my name and in Naomi's name for the presents you are preparing for your second grandchild. Naomi feels very well; recently Muntner gave her several articles of his to translate into English, and in this manner we can repay him what we owe him for medical treatment. Yesterday we got from Naomi's inheritance 200 pounds, therewith we are free of worries for the near future, whatever happens with my income.

Saul was here yesterday for dinner. I told him that you are complaining that he does not write. He said that last week he thought every day that he would go to Boruchov, and that was why he did not write. For a whole week he worked all night in the lab and tired himself out, but earned 5 pounds that week. [. . .]

On January 6, at the end of a long letter dealing with Father's Boruchov property, I wrote:

In matters of the secretaryship Dr. Magnes asked a response by Jan. 8 to his circular letter sent to members of the Board of Trustees. Hence, I hope that a few days thereafter I shall get the secretarial appointment.

Naomi is well, eats well, sleeps well, and looks with confidence and joy toward the approaching event. I paid Hadassah 2.500 pounds—this is the total expense, including seven days in the hospital. Before they accepted her they made me sign a declaration that if it is a boy I agree that they should enter him into the covenant of Abraham! It seems there have been here too "assimilants" who did not let this be done.

Despite Magnes's letter, the Goldberg Fund affair continued to drag out. On January 22, 1942, I wrote my parents (in Hungarian) about an apartment I located for them in Jerusalem, since they wanted to move up from Shekhunat Borukhov. I concluded my letter:

Still no news about the Goldberg Fund. Today I wrote to Dr. Magnes and sent him a detailed plan concerning the work of the secretary, so that he should have something on which to base himself at the Jan. 30 meeting, prior to which, as I see, there will be no decision.

Naomi continues to be well and was very glad to learn about the aforementioned apartment for the parents.

I hope Évi will keep her promise . . . and will appear here on Saturday, and will really remain until the "family event," which, according to calculation, should take place in the course of next week. Thus, in all probability, I shall become a "papa" sooner than a "secretary." Upon my word, I would never have believed this!

One of the reasons why my parents wanted to move to Jerusalem was that Father was more and more frequently ill. He had to be taken to the hospital several times, and they felt too isolated in Shekhunat Borukhov, which at the time was still a remote suburb of Tel Aviv—in addition, they had no phone. Father suffered from bladder troubles, urinary infections, colds, flus, and fevers. His health had become so unstable that he had to resign from his job as director of the Palestinian Friends of the Hebrew University. For me it was most depressing to observe this, and to become aware that Father, although only sixty years old, was rapidly becoming a permanent invalid and his vital forces were visibly ebbing. However, his deteriorating health did not prevent Father from devoting much attention to the publication of several of his books in Hebrew translation, prepared by himself, by me, and by Zvi Bar-Meir, Mordecai Avi-Shaul, and Emil Feuerstein.

Peculiarly, none of the surviving family letters contains clear references to what was decided at the January 30, 1942, meeting of the Board of Trustees of the Goldberg Fund. What seems to have happened was that, instead of deciding on my permanent appointment as secretary of the Goldberg Fund, the Board of Trustees voted to entrust me with a temporary job for one year with an agenda of whose nature I have no recollection at all, but which appears to have had something to do with cataloging libraries under the aegis of the university. The temporary nature of the job is alluded to in a sentence in the letter Father wrote me on February 23, 1943, after the birth of our daughter Ofra: "To Magnes I wrote a letter of thanks for his congratulations on the birth of the granddaughter, and for his sympathy with our family in general. I hope he will arrange the matter of the 'permanence' of your work in a suitable manner."

Looking back, from a distance of almost fifty years, at the Goldberg Fund affair, as its story is presented in the contemporary letters, there is only one point that still strikes me as remarkable: that Mrs. Tolkowsky, by the sheer force of her personality, was able to bend the Board of Trustees to her will, even though three of its five members throughout much of the negotiations supported my appointment as secretary, and one of those three, Mrs. Rachel Goldberg, certainly remained steadfast in her support.

A different question is why Mrs. Tolkowsky took the position she took. I think that none of the surmises expressed in my parents' letters explains her unwavering determination to prevent my appointment, even though it meant depriving her own daughter (pregnant at the time) of what would have been relatively comfortable and secure financial circumstances. Her true motivations remain a puzzle to me to this day. One possible explanation, I believe, is that she felt apprehensive lest she be reproached (by whom?) with nepotism, if the secretarial position in the Fund set up by her father and controlled by a Board of Trustees of which she and her mother were members was given to her son-in-law. Beyond that, however, there must have been a personal, instinctive, and rationally inexplicable antipathy between her and me, as there was between her and her mother.

Likewise puzzling is the fact that nothing at all of the months-long tribulations and machinations survived in my memory. This obliteration from my memory of a long series of actual events and efforts, moves and countermoves, contrasts sharply with the retention in my memory of a few personal incidents and of the intense feelings they evoked in me. Once, I remember with uncanny clarity, the Tolkowskys came to visit us. They happened to arrive at a time when I was busy binding a copy of the first volume of my *Adam vaAdama* with interlaced blank pages, to serve as desk copy for the preparation of a possible future expanded edition. Mrs. Tolkowsky observed what I was doing and said, "Raphael, why don't you get a job as a bookbinder?" This, of course, enraged me, and only my upbringing prevented me from giving her a resounding answer. After this run-in with the proverbial hateful mother-in-law I indulged in fantasizing about how I could bring about her early demise. I knew that she was deathly afraid of snakes, and in my imagination I saw myself catching a snake, killing it, and mailing it in a box to Mrs. Tolkowsky. She would open the box, see the snake, and— before realizing that it was dead—suffer a heart attack induced by the fright and die. This snake-fantasy was probably triggered by my having killed, shortly before, a big snake I found coiled up in a corner of the bedroom of my sister and brother-in-law in Gedera while I was visiting them.

Another interesting difference between the contemporary record of these events and the traces they left in my memory is that while in the letters my parents seem to have had a worse opinion of Mr. than of Mrs. Tolkowsky, in my memory it is definitely she, and she only, who was the villain of the piece, while Mr. Tolkowsky I remember as a man who tried to be fatherly to Naomi and kind to me, but was prevented by his strong-willed and malevolent wife from relating to us as he would have liked. Where is the truth and what was it? Who knows? Perhaps there doesn't even exist such a thing as truth in human micro-relationships.

Even though it will disrupt the chronological order I am trying to follow in this book, I want to add here what I can reconstruct about our relationship with the Tolkowskys in the years following the conclusion of the Goldberg Fund affair with the victory of Mrs. Tolkowsky over the other members of the Board of Trustees. The story will remain very incomplete, because my memory concerning that relationship is, again, a total blank, and because for almost five full years (from early 1942 to the end of 1946) there is no trace at all in my files of any correspondence or other contact with Naomi's parents. Even in the letters exchanged between me and my parents there is only one more mention of the Goldberg Fund—my father refers to the victory of "evil." He wrote to me on May 17, 1942 (in Hebrew):

Of course, I know that the most suitable thing for you would be to do something in connection with the Goldberg Fund and to remain within the confines of scholarship, but what can we do if evil has gained the upper hand and is not, it would seem, "consumed like smoke." And "let my food be bitter like an olive leaf, but not be a gift from the hand of flesh and blood."

In these few lines Father again evinces his inclination to resort to a Musive style: he quotes, or alludes to, Psalm 102:4, "For my days are consumed like smoke," and to the Babylonian Talmud (tractate 'Eruvin 18b), which tells that the dove sent out by Noah from the ark said to God, "Lord of the Universe! Let my food be bitter like an olive leaf, but come from Your hand, rather than sweet like honey but come from the hand of a man of flesh and blood!"

After the birth of our two daughters my parents frequently wrote to Naomi, Father in Hebrew and Mother in German, letters full of concern and love for her and admiration for the little girls, but containing no mention of the Tolkowskys, until, finally, in January 1947, my mother once referred to them. Shortly before, because of Naomi's rundown state of health, we had placed the children with Mrs. Mamlok, who ran a small children's home next door to my parents' house in Shekhunat Boruchov. Thus, my parents could frequently see their little grandchildren. Mother wrote:

> This morning Ofra and Daphi were here, in excellent spirits, flourishing, and very sweet. After you two departed I went over to control their *matzav ruah* [mood], and I can tell you that they did not at all take to heart the absence of their parents. I wanted to take them along to the "city," i.e., to Joshua, but since the other grandparents were also there, I had to go alone to take care of the shopping. Ofra said, *Madu'a at raq rega?* [Why are you staying only a minute?]

The date can be concluded from the note (in Hebrew) Father appended saying that he had just received from Dr. Alexander Rosenfeld a copy of a Bombay Jewish paper with an article of mine in it. The only article I ever published in a Bombay paper was "Jewish Tree Lore," which appeared in the January 1947 issue of the *Jewish Advocate*. Since Mother mentions the presence of the Tolkowsky grandparents without any further comment, it can be taken to indicate that by that time our friendly relationship with them was nothing new. And, of course, it was only from Naomi that they could have known that Ofra and Daphi were in Shekhunat Boruchov.

As for Mrs. Tolkowsky's relationship with me and my scholarly enterprise, there is indirect documentary evidence to show that it had been reestablished early in 1945 at the latest. The first issue of *Edoth*, the quarterly of the Palestine Institute of Folklore and Ethnology, which I edited and which was published in October 1945, carries the acknowledgment: "This issue of *Edoth* was published with the support of the Yitzhaq Leib and Rachel Goldberg Fund." This proves that several months earlier the Board of Trustees of the Goldberg Fund must have discussed my application for a grant; evidently, Mrs. Tolkowsky did not oppose the allocation or perhaps even supported it. Volumes 2 and 3 of *Edoth* were also supported by the Goldberg Fund (along with other public institutions) and so were several other books of mine that I published under the aegis of the Institute.

All the extant letters exchanged between the Tolkowskys and the Patais date from the nine months of October 1947 to June 1948. The Tolkowskys' letters are friendly, even warm, and reading them one would not imagine that only five years earlier Naomi had felt compelled to break off all contact with her parents. Mrs. Tolkowsky signed her letters, even those addressed to me, "Imma" in Hebrew or "Mum" in English, and Mr. Tolkowsky signed "Dad," while I addressed them, both in Hebrew and in English, as "Dear Parents." No letters written by Naomi to her parents have been preserved in my files.

Mrs. Tolkowsky's letters show that she was interested in my work, reading with appreciation the books and papers I had sent her and even finding in them points on which she had concrete comments. After I left for New York (in October 1947) and Naomi remained alone with the children in Jerusalem, her parents manifested concern for her well-being and safety. In December 1947 Naomi placed the children with a family in Ramót Hashavim, a few miles north of Tel Aviv, in order to be able to join me in New York, and thereafter her parents occasionally visited their granddaughters there. In a word, all was well between them and us at that time. On December 6, 1947, Mrs. Tolkowsky wrote to me in New York (in Hebrew):

Dear Raphael:
    We received your letter of Nov. 20 and enjoyed reading it. At long last you are given the opportunity to address audiences of experts, and—if you succeed—it will be very important for your future here in the country.
    It is a pity that Naomi did not go with you. It is difficult to make arrangements for such a trip on short notice. Naomi is trying very hard to get the visa, and it seems that Dr. Magnes gave her the required recommendation. This is what she wrote to us on Dec. 2, and now she has to wait until they call her in a second time. The difficulty now is in transportation: it is dangerous to go out of the house in Jerusalem or to walk about in the city; the governmental offices don't function prop-

erly. Let's hope that "wrath will pass." Still, I doubt whether Naomi will manage to reach you before you leave for Albuquerque and Mexico. Also, there is no possibility at the moment to take the girls to Ramot Hashavim, because of the attacks on the roads, and in general all arrangements are frozen as long as the attacks in the country continue. We are in touch with Naomi with the help of an official of the *Palestine Post* in Jerusalem, who promised us to visit her every day. Yesterday we heard that everything was OK with her and that she does not lack food.

I copied your letter and sent it to your parents in Shekhunat Boruchov.

I imagine that you too celebrated together with all Israel the great day of the establishment of the Jewish state. Here the joy and the happiness rose to high heaven, but what was even more amazing was the change in the people themselves: their backs seemed straighter, some kind of special dignity enveloped each of them, even the smallest one in our circle of acquaintances, and it is clear that if only there will be peace we shall accomplish great things in the country.

And now I want to call your attention to the Goldberg Fund. Our annual meeting will take place on Jan. 27. I think you should submit an application for the continuation of the subsidy for *Edoth*. But to whom should it be paid out? If Naomi is here—and it is possible that she will not be able to leave until that time—the money could be paid to her as the secretary of the Institute. But if not? To whom should it be paid in her absence? What do you think?

I hope you had a chance to meet the members of the family: they certainly expect your visit.

Shalom to you, Raphael, and I wish you much success, and regards to the Aztecs in Mexico in whom I was very interested, and I even wrote an article about their theater.

Imma

I ordered from Naomi five copies of your *Introduction to Anthropology*, and 20 of the latest double issue of *Edoth*. By the way, many thanks for the beautiful copy of your *Introduction* and *Man and Temple*. I am looking forward to reading both. I am sure that the members of the Board are satisfied with the tempo of your work.

Mr. Tolkowsky added several lines in a similar friendly tone.

It so happened that on the very day the *Rossia*, on which I sailed from Haifa to New York, docked in Naples (October 9, 1947) two berths away lay the cargo-ship *Chioggia*, on which my parents-in-law sailed on their way to a vacation in Europe. At noon Mr. Tolkowsky sent me a note (in English) to tell me that later that day they would try to contact me, to which Mrs. Tolkowsky added in Hebrew: "Happy journey, dear Raphael, and many regards from Imma." Toward evening we met on the quay in front of my ship, and my father-in-law handed me a fine old gold pocketwatch that used to belong to his father and that his mother had asked him to give me as a present from her. I still remember the surreptitious manner in which he gave me the watch: he stepped very close to me, held the watch hidden in his clenched fist, and said, "Put this in your pocket!" Evidently, he wanted to make sure that nobody saw what he was giving me.

Some weeks later, when the question first arose whether I should stay on in America or return to Palestine, both my parents-in-law advised me not to return. On January 28, 1948, Mrs. Tolkowsky wrote (in Hebrew): "They are offering you to lecture in Philadelphia, and you hesitate . . . The future here in the country is very hazy, and who knows when our skies will clear up. In the meantime Jerusalem is under siege in every sense of the word, and those who leave it don't go back. If Naomi should return here she would certainly have to live in Shekhunat Boruchov with the girls. You must consider everything: what will you do here? If the situation continues, only enlistment will face you . . ."

Mrs. Tolkowsky's statement that Naomi would have to live in Shekhunat Boruchov with the girls indicates that despite the improvement of the relationship between her and Naomi she still continued to distance herself from her daughter. She did not suggest that Naomi could live with them, in their large Tel Aviv apartment, but postulated that she would have to live in Boruchov, that is, with *my* parents. Mr. Tolkowsky added to the letter (in English): "As to the new invitations to Raphael to stay on for some time in U.S.A., I agree with Mother's view; so long as you can stand the separation from the children, Raphael, it would be a great pity if you threw away these chances of strengthening the foundations of your career, of enhancing your reputation, of perfecting your professorial technique, of enriching your erudition and your intellect by continued contact and communion with masters in your science. Keep well, both of you . . ."

In her very next letter Mrs. Tolkowsky commented on my paper "Hebrew Installation Rites," of which I had sent her an offprint. Her comments show both her considerable erudition and her strong adherence to the theory of an early matriarchy. She wrote (in Hebrew):

Feb. 7, 1948

Dear Naomi and Raphael:

For lack of space I confine myself to a few notes on Raphael's paper about the coronation of kings in Israel.

a. If we assume that Saul was the first to be crowned in Israel in a legal manner, one must also assume that the entire procedure was taken as a whole from the custom common to the peoples of the Near East, including Israel, in contradiction to the biblical view that isolates the people of Yahweh from the other nations.

b. In the center of the coronation ritual of the peoples stood "the marriage" of the king and the queen, and one must not see in them only a fertility ritual, although that too had great importance at the time of the coronation, but also a legal procedure that gave the husband of the queen a share in the kingship. For according to the accepted historical development of ancient kingship the sovereignty was at first concentrated in the hands of the queen, and the crown passed from mother to daughter. This also explains the marriage between father and daughter and between brother and sister in ancient Egypt.

c. Are there any traces of this marriage ceremony left in the Bible? The authors of the Bible certainly erased their memory as far as was possible. Nevertheless, we see that David married Michal, the daughter of Saul. And perhaps thereby he aroused Saul and turned him against him. We also see that the new king marries the wife of the previous king, and perhaps there are allusions to this ritual in the Psalms and in the Song of Songs?

The paper is most interesting. Are you planning to publish it also in Hebrew?

With hearty regards,
Imma

The last communication I received from the Tolkowskys dates from July 3, 1948, several weeks after Naomi's return from New York to Israel, after she must have informed them of her decision to seek a divorce. They wrote in Hebrew, and Mrs. Tolkowsky mainly discussed the editing and translation into Hebrew of Dr. Erich Brauer's *Ethnologie der jemenitischen Juden*, for which purpose the Goldberg Fund had voted to give me a grant. It is a friendly letter, and the only sign of the changed relationship between us is that she signed it, no longer Imma, but with her initials, "H. T." Mr. Tolkowsky likewise signed his few lines "S. T." Thereafter I never had any contact with them. As for the Brauer book, my other scholarly projects kept me from it, and to this day it has remained untranslated either into Hebrew or into English.

A Child Is Born

Our first daughter was born on February 5, 1942, at the Hadassah Hospital on Mount Scopus in Jerusalem. I immediately sent a telegram to my parents in Shekhunat Boruchov, which they received that same evening. The next morning they sent a *mazal tov* telegram in response, and two days later Father wrote to us:

Shekhunat Boruchov, Feb. 8, 1942 [in Hebrew]

Dear Naomi, Dear Raphael, *mazal tov*!

On Thursday evening we got your telegram with the good news, and we were very very happy. Next day Mama went in to see Grandma Rachel Goldberg, to congratulate her, and when she returned to Boruchov she found here Hava, who told her about the details. The main thing is that everything went well. May God grant that you have joy in your daughter and bring her up in good health of body and soul! Hava told us that your daughter, our granddaughter, is not only healthy but also "weighty." Let us hope that she will remain thus also in the future, in spirit, in society, and in all aspects of her life.

The rest of Father's letter deals with several current affairs, including the Hebrew edition of some of his books that up to that time had been published only in Hungarian. It is puzzling to me why the letter my mother undoubtedly wrote to us at the same time has not been preserved. Incidentally, my sister Évi (Hava) had come to Jerusalem to be with us a few days before February 5 and remained there until February 8.

I no longer remember how and when, once Naomi's labor started, I took her from our home in the Bukharan Quarter to the Hadassah Hospital on Mount Scopus. More peculiarly, I don't remember where I spent the hours during which she suffered the pangs of childbirth that already in biblical times were considered so dire and at the same time so perplexing that they were attributed to a divine curse inflicted upon all womankind because of Eve's folly in listening to the Serpent. I can only guess that I must have spent them in an antechamber or a waiting room of the hospital. But I do remember with crystalline clarity the moment when I stood at Naomi's bedside, and a nurse brought in the new, small human being, all wrapped up in swaddling clothes, with only her round red face showing, her eyes closed, and her features barely discernible. The nurse gave the little bundle to me to hold while she arranged Naomi's pillows and covers, and in those few moments, before I placed the baby into her mother's arms, I was flooded by a wave of indescribable sensations whose nature was not clear to me, and which I certainly cannot recall today, half a century later, but whose intensity, this much I remember, was such that it forged then and there an unbreakable bond of love between me and my child. And because Naomi gave me this greatest of all gifts, and because she had to suffer long hours of pain in bringing my child into the world, my love of her became stronger, deeper, and richer. We gave the baby the double name of Ofra-Hayla—Ofra because that was the name we liked, and Hayla in memory of my father's mother in order to give him the satisfaction of having a grandchild bear the name of a beloved deceased parent.

Throughout the time Naomi spent in the hospital the nurses took care of the baby and brought her to Naomi's bed only when it was time for her to breastfeed the newborn, who was always bundled up from head to foot. Because of some complication Naomi had to stay in the hospital longer than the seven days of childbed customary in those days, and I took her home only on February 18, that is, thirteen days after Ofra was born. I do not remember the dates, but they are documented in letters my father wrote me on February 18 and 23.

Thus, it was only after mother and child arrived back home, and the nurse we had employed unwrapped the baby the first time to give her a bath, which, of course, both Naomi and I watched with awed fascination, that we noticed that the baby did not move her left arm. We were frightened, dismayed, and worried, and, as soon as we could, took Ofra to Dr. Weizmann, the pediatrician with whom we had arranged in advance that she would take care of our expected child. Dr. Weizmann found that the left arm of the baby had suffered a trauma, possibly prenatal, which, she assured us, was not infrequent and could be remedied by proper treatment, massage, and exercises, so that with time the arm would regain complete or almost complete mobility. This was confirmed by our family physician and friend, Dr. Muntner, whom we also consulted. To take care of this problem was to become a major concern and preoccupation for years to come for both Naomi and me, and to watch the slow but steady improvement of Ofra's arm was a source of deep gratification for both of us.

After her return home from the hospital with Ofra, Naomi wrote to my parents (the letter is no longer extant); from my mother's response it appears that she wrote in Hebrew and that my father translated it into Hungarian for Mother.

[undated, probably March 13, 1942; in German]

Dearest Naomi:

Just now "Opapa" translated your letter for me. Thank God he has much experience in translation, and thus it went well. Were it not so, I would regret it very much, because everything you write interests us. But it is quite natural that the few sentences about our new child touch our hearts—despite the miserable world in which we live, such a little being, such an open eye to which we can show light and color, is something quite wonderful. It is and remains an eternal mystery why we feel that a new human being is so sacred when humanity is so far removed from the sacred. Such a little child is a part of God, a piece from heaven, and endows the whole world with a new countenance. I know that you feel the same, and if I did not know it your letter in which you don't mention at all the sufferings you endured would show it to me very clearly. But I do believe that one must pay for everything in life, and precisely since you paid for little Ofra so dearly, now, with the help of God, what follows will go well and smoothly. Évi reported to me every detail, she was even after the event deeply touched; I know what a good, open-hearted person she is, and I am glad that you feel this too. We know that kinship and friendship are two totally different territories, and if they coincide by chance one cannot value it too highly.

You can imagine how gladly we would come to visit you, in fact I made an appointment with your grandmother to go together, but, alas, I cannot leave Papa alone now. Perhaps we shall succeed with the apartment in Jerusalem—it would be wonderful!

Write again soon, we were so happy with your letter. I embrace you and the little one with great love,

Mama

On March 18, 1942, Mother again wrote to Naomi (in German):

I was very happy with your two letters—everything you write about Ofra is very interesting for me and for the translator. It seems that she has already much of a routine and also knows how to behave vis-à-vis a serious university professor. He will probably attribute mystical meaning to her crying. You can imagine how much I would like to see her with my own eyes, precisely while she is still so small, so unconscious, so plantlike. Every age in a child has its beauty and interest, and one would not want to miss it. But who cares today about what the individual wants? I met Rina in the street in Tel Aviv; she saw a picture of Ofra at Grandma Goldberg's. Everybody says what a beautiful child she is. And it is really not nice of Professor Scholem that he did not lay his homage immediately at her feet. Yes, not everybody knows how one must behave with such a new little being. I am very glad that the nurse knows it, and that she does everything necessary for Ofra's well-being. The weather too has improved, so that she can enjoy the sun and the mountain air. And how are you? I hope that you are a smart, modern mama who knows that one must not . . . [the last few lines are missing]

The "serious university professor," Gershom Scholem (b. 1897), was professor of Jewish mysticism at the Hebrew University. He and his wife were our friends, and we occasionally exchanged visits. Rina Klebanov was Naomi's cousin.

As Ofra grew, so did our delight in her and my parents' love for her. Naomi kept them informed of the baby's development, I sent them snapshots, and they, in response, expressed their admiration for her many times in their letters. In June 1942 my parents planned to move to Jerusalem, where they rented a room in the apartment of Mrs. Yellin, the widow of the recently deceased David Yellin. At the same time they rented out their apartment in Shekhunat Boruchov to Mrs. Bialik, the widow of Hayyim Nahman Bialik. Early in June my mother wrote me: "I look forward very much to Jerusalem, and especially to you, for actually I don't know Ofra at all. By the time we arrive she will be quite a conscious being, at least that is what the pictures indicate."

As it turned out, the move from Shekhunat Boruchov to Jerusalem did not bring about the happy time my mother had hoped for. Father's prostate troubles increased to the point where he had to be catheterized several times, and he was in and out of the hospital. Once, I remember, I received a hand-delivered message from Mother saying that Father was seriously ill and had to be taken to the Hadassah Hospital; I should go as soon as I could to see him there. When I reached the hospital, I found him lying in bed, semiconscious, suffering, as the doctor in charge explained to me, from uremic poisoning brought about by kidney failure. I tried to speak to him, but he was unable to respond, and only a faint movement of his eyes toward me indicated that he was aware of my presence. I stood there next to his bed for quite a while, even though the doctor assured me that no change in his condition could be expected for several hours. When I left to go, I was so overwhelmed by anguish that right there in the corridor I leaned against the wall and cried. For the first time in my life I was forced to visualize that my father might die. However, the next day he was better, and a few days later he was able to leave the hospital.

During that summer in Jerusalem Father finally had to acquiesce in the necessity of surgical intervention. For some reason I did not quite understand, the urologists at Hadassah, the chief surgeon Dr. Joseph, and his first assistant Dr. Ehrlich, did not at once excise his entire prostate, but carried out what they termed "minor operations," no less than four times. Only when these proved insufficient did they, the fifth time, perform radical prostatectomy.

While I was thus forced to contemplate the inevitable passing of the parental generation, I also experienced a significant change in my own life due to the appearance, in the person of our daughter, of the next generation.

I don't know whether other men too experience the feeling I had when I brought Ofra and Naomi home from the hospital—here was a new human being for whom I, and I alone, was entirely responsible. Until her birth I had been totally ego-centered: my chief interest was to find gratification, whether intellectual or physical, and to forge ahead, to achieve, to succeed. True, members of my family were very dear to me; I loved them and was ready to go to great lengths to help them, to do things for them, but still they were peripheral to my own existence that filled out my day, my thinking, my sentience. Even Naomi, whom I loved deeply, and more so after the birth of our child than before, with whom I felt a great commonality, was nevertheless a person separate and different from me, carrying in her consciousness her own world that was not mine. But now, suddenly, here was my child, as much a part of me as my right arm, and as I watched her day after day, the consciousness grew in me that whatever I would do from now on, in doing it I would take into account how it would affect her now and in the future. Not that I would *have to* take it into account, but that I *couldn't* do otherwise. This, perhaps, is the truest meaning of fatherhood: the internalized and instinctualized sense of responsibility for the life and future of one's child, who is one's own most mysterious extension.

In the spring of 1942 I engaged in tutoring two private pupils, both of whom were referred to me by Dr. Magnes. One was Professor Jacob Isaacs (1896–1973), a scholar of English literature, who was the first professor of English at the Hebrew University from 1942 to 1945. When he arrived in Jerusalem he knew no Hebrew at all. Although he gave all his classes in English, a knowledge of Hebrew was necessary for him, if for no other reason then at least to enable him to follow the deliberations at departmental and faculty meetings. Dr. Magnes suggested me as tutor, and, until my departure for Haifa, Isaacs came twice a week to my apartment in the Bukharan Quarter for Hebrew lessons. Since he knew no Hebrew at all, while I had a passable facility in speaking English, our language of tuition was English, which meant that I learned at least as much English from him as he did Hebrew from me.

Professor Isaacs was a rather corpulent man, and he would always arrive at my second floor door somewhat huffing and puffing, but always exactly on time. As I once told him—I must have wanted to boast about my knowledge of English literature—he was as good as the sun in that famous English poem by Thomas Hood, which was never either a moment too soon or a moment too late. Since in Palestine we had all adopted a rather cavalier attitude to time—was it under Arab influence?—I was both surprised at and admired his unfailing punctuality and asked him how he managed it. "Quite simple," he said. "Wherever I have to go, I set out well in advance, so as to arrive in time." "And what do you do if you happen to arrive early?" I asked "I walk around the block," he said.

The same punctuality characterized his lectures. I remember one of the public lectures he gave at the Jerusalem YMCA. He spoke for precisely one hour, without any notes, and without even once glancing at his watch. At our next meeting I asked him how he was able to do it. His answer was "Practice." In 1945 Isaacs left Jerusalem to take up a post as professor of English at London University. I last saw him during one of my visits from America to London, when I ran into him on the steps leading to the entrance of the British Museum.

Of my other private pupil I remember much less. I cannot even recall his name, but I know that he was an American, an efficiency expert, who had come to Jerusalem to advise the administration of the Hebrew Unviersity. He was a Christian, even more corpulent than Isaacs, was accompanied by his wife, who was Jewish, and stayed in Jerusalem only for a few months in 1943 or 1944. He stayed at the Eden Hotel, near the center of the city, and I went there twice a week to tutor him in Hebrew. All I remember about the lessons I gave him was that, like many Americans, he had great difficulty in learning a foreign language and found it especially hard to pronounce the Hebrew words in a manner even remotely resembling the way they were pronounced in the *yishuv*.

In the fall of 1942 Naomi had to have her tonsils removed; while she was in the hospital I had a nurse take care of Ofra, some ten months old at the time. By that time I had started my work at the Technion, and on October 30, 1942, Naomi sent me a postcard to Haifa (in Hebrew): "*Shalom* to you, Raphael: I am minus tonsils—good riddance to them!—and feel well. I am very glad that you sent the nurse, perhaps we shall keep her for another week so that your mother should really have a chance to rest up . . ." On the reverse of the card Mother wrote:

Dear Raphael—I am sitting in here with Naomi who, thank God, *got over the operation very well* and is completely *well.* The *Schwester* [nurse] arrived yesterday afternoon, began her activities, and thus today I came from Papa directly to Naomi. She looks really surprisingly well and is happy that the operation is over. With Papa everything is all right, so that they plan the second operation early next week. Ofra is more charming than ever. [. . .]

Many hugs and love,
Mama

A few weeks later, when my parents stayed in my apartment in Jerusalem with Naomi, Father wrote to me:

Naomi is now feeding Ofra, and so I undertook to write to you in her stead, to send you regards from her and from Ofra, to you, to Grandma, to Auntie and Uncle, and to Tirzah. Ofra already knows all of them. When I entertained her today by clapping my hands, she almost cried aloud, "More! More!" At least this is how I understood it. She also expressed the same with her little feet, and Naomi says that now she understands that dancing is the first expression of feeling by human beings.

My parents' letters leave no doubt that they considered Ofra the sweetest, most beautiful, most intelligent, most charming child in the world. Of course, when our second daughter, Daphne, arrived twenty months later, Ofra had to share with her this position of global championship.

9

Final Years
in Palestine

Job Hunting, Man and Earth, Jerusalem Besieged

My attempts to find a better job than the part-time instructorship at the Hebrew University were by no means confined to the efforts I made in connection with the Goldberg Fund. In fact, a considerable part of my time and energy throughout 1941 and in the first half of 1942 went into job hunting. I know this not because I remember the steps I took to find a position, but because copies of many of the applications I wrote and the answers I received survived in my archives.

On March 11, 1941, I wrote to the director of education of the British Mandatory Government of Palestine asking for a position in their Department of Education, which supervised the Jewish school network in the country. A week later I got a negative response. In April I asked for a job from the Government's DOSFG (I no longer remember what these initials stood for) and sent the application to my friend Colin Malamet, who was at the time store's superintendent. In due course I received an answer from a captain stating that my application has been registered, and should a vacancy occur I would be "notified accordingly."

When we found out that Naomi was pregnant, and I became aware that I would soon be responsible for the livelihood of an additional soul, I redoubled my efforts to find a job that would yield more income than the measly few pounds I got from the university. I have in my files a brief note from the air commodore commanding the Royal Air Force, Palestine and Transjordan, acknowledging the receipt of my application of June 22 and regretting that there were "no vacancies" in which my services could be utilized. I have no recollection as to what job I had hoped to get. On June 29 I wrote to M. M. Ussishkin, president of the Keren Kayemeth (Jewish National Fund), offering my services for the three summer months and suggesting that, being an effective speaker, I could travel about in the country and give talks to arouse interest in the public in the "redemption of the Land," the central object of the Keren Kayemeth. Within a few days I had a negative answer.

On June 29 I also wrote to the assistant chaplain general of the British Forces in Palestine and Transjordan, submitting my candidacy as chaplain to the Jewish troops in Palestine. This was answered on July 8 by Rabbi Rabinowitz, the senior Jewish chaplain, from headquarters, Canal Area, to the effect that he would communicate with me "in due course." On July 20 Rabbi Rabinowitz wrote me again asking me to come to see him on July 30, at 10:00 A.M. "at the house of the Chief Rabbi, Dr. Herzog, Ibn Ezra Street, Jerusalem." I have no record or recollection of the meeting, but I know that I did not become an army chaplain.

On July 22 I wrote to Major H. G. Henman, DADPL (?), Baddour Building, Jerusalem, and an identical letter to the CORAF (Commanding Officer, Royal Air Force) Headquarters, Jerusalem, applying for a position, "such as, for instance, interpreter." The responses were negative. On July 30 I had an interview with Dr. Mossinson of the Department of Education of the Va'ad Leumi (National Council of the Jews of Palestine) in Jerusalem, concerning a teaching position in the Jewish school system. It yielded no results.

In July 1941 my friend Ibn-Zahav and I also got in touch with Moshe Tolkowsky, the father of my father-in-law, who had good connections in the United States. He declared himself willing to write to his friends in America concerning the establishment of a chair of Jewish and comparative folklore at the Hebrew University. In the event, nothing came of this initiative either.

On October 3 I submitted an application to the chief secretary of the Government of Palestine "for a position in the Civil Service." I enclosed a *vita*. In response I was sent on October 14 a form, "P. I. Application for appointment to the Colonial Service." I completed and returned it on October 16 with copies of all kinds of certificates, a list of my publications, etc. On October 31 this was acknowledged by somebody who signed for the chief secretary, stating that my application had been "noted by the Director of Education and will be considered on the occurrence of a suitable vacancy." No such occurrence materialized.

On October 25 I submitted a memorandum to the director of the Palestine Broadcasting Service, suggesting the establishment of a Hungarian news broadcast program over the Jerusalem radio and offering my services. I have neither documents nor recollections as to the reaction of the director.

On May 7, 1942, I applied to the director of education of the government for a position as assistant inspector of education. On May 11 the senior inspector of Jewish schools informed me that there was "at present no vacancy in this Department." On May 12 I suggested to Mr. A. Levinsohn, of the Cultural Center of the Histadrut (General Federation of Jewish Labor in Palestine) in Tel Aviv, that I give lectures on the painter Abel Pann in connection with exhibitions of his biblical paintings in the Jewish labor settlements in the country. Again, I have no recollection of what happened after this initiative.

In the early summer of 1942 I began my efforts to get the position of secretary at the Haifa Technion, which was crowned with success and of which I shall tell later. While that application was pending I continued to search for other jobs. I have in my files a letter I wrote on July 23, 1942, to a certain Mr. Jaffe, whom I cannot further identify, asking for his help in securing a position that required a knowledge of Hungarian. I cannot recall anything else about this attempt.

In addition to these steps, whose record happened to survive in my files, I must have undertaken many more in the course of my sustained efforts in those months to find a job. Still, my main preoccupation remained my scholarly work, and 1941 and 1942 were the years in which I did most of the work on my major study, *Man and Earth in Hebrew Custom, Belief, and Legend* (as its English title page reads), two volumes of which were published by the Hebrew University Press in 1942 and 1943, respectively. A planned third volume never appeared, but much of its material I subsequently published in Hebrew scholarly journals.

By late 1940 I felt I had enough research results on hand to warrant their presentation in a series of lectures at the university. How I went about it, to whom I suggested that I should be invited to give lectures at the university, what their reaction was—all this I have long since forgotten. But I have in my files a copy of a mimeographed invitation, issued by the Hebrew University, to three lectures I was to give on three consecutive Wednesdays, at 4:00 P.M., in the Rosenblum building of the university, under the general title "Man and Earth." The first lecture (February 19, 1941) was likewise titled "Man and Earth," the second (February 26) was "Man and Stone," and the third (March 5) "Man and Tree." The text of the lectures has not survived, but they were undoubtedly early formulations of chapters or parts of them that subsequently were incorporated into my book. Nor do I remember anything of the lectures themselves, whether they were well attended or not, but I do recall that the first of them was honored by the presence of Dr. Magnes, the president of the university, which gave me considerable satisfaction. Later I gave several lectures on "Man and Earth" or "The Earth in Jewish Folklore" in various places in the country. One poster announcing such a lecture is preserved in my files. It took place in Raanana, on April 19, 1942, under the joint auspices of the Friends of the Hebrew University and the Cultural Committee of the Raanana municipal council, and was introduced by the council's president, B. Ostrowsky.

While the printing of the first volume of *Man and Earth* was in progress (it was done at the HaMa'arav Press, of which I was ex-part-owner), I made arrangements with Mr. Yitzhaq Ornstein, owner of the Yavneh Publishing House of Tel Aviv, to undertake the distribution of the book. This, I believe, was necessary because the publisher of the book, the Hebrew University Press, had no sales or distribution capabilities. Although I was able to print only 400 copies of the book because of the wartime paper shortage in Palestine, Mr. Ornstein advertised it in the daily press. One of the ads, published in the April 23, 1942, issue of the Tel Aviv daily *Davar*, read (in Hebrew):

The Hebrew University Press Jerusalem

Just published:

MAN AND EARTH

A Study in Customs, Beliefs, and Legends in Israel and the Nations of the World, by Dr. Raphael Patai. In this new book of his, the well-known researcher of Jewish folklore gives a most interesting picture of the relationship of the people of Israel to the earth, the mother of all living, as it is reflected in customs, beliefs, and legends, against the general background of the relationship of man to nature in all ages. The book contains 304 pages in large format. The price is 620 mils in paper cover, 750 mils in luxurious cloth binding. Main sales: Yavneh Publishers, Tel Aviv, 80 Allenby Road. Telephone: 3134.

The cloth binding I chose, incidentally, was dark green, to resemble the books of Sir James George Frazer, of whom I was a great admirer.

The printing of the second volume of *Man and Earth* was carried on in the midst of curfews and siege conditions imposed by the British authorities on Jewish Jerusalem, and I remember a somewhat unusual arrangement I had to resort to in order to be able to continue with the printing despite the limitations of movement those edicts imposed on us. The reason for the British clamping down on us were the activities of the Etzel, the Irgun Tz'va'i Leumi (National Military Organization), and of the Lehi, the Lohame Herut Yisrael (Fighters for the Freedom of Israel), also known as the Stern Group, after its founder Avraham Stern. The philosophy of both of these radical Jewish organizations was that the only way the Jews would ever achieve the aims of Zionism—the establishment of a state of their own in Palestine—was to confront the British in the country with force and, if need be, with acts of terror. The clashes between the Stern Group and the British authorities reached their peak in January and February 1942, when the British, trying to impose or reassert their control over the Jewish population, introduced all kinds of restrictive or even oppressive measures. One of the steps they took was to seal off with barbed wire that part of Jerusalem in which, or so they suspected, were the nests of the Jewish resistance. The Bukharan

Quarter where we lived, as well as the neighboring Kerem Avraham and Geula Quarters, fell within the perimeter of the barbed wire fence, while the Mahane Yehuda Quarter, where the HaMa'arav Press was located, and the rest of the city south of Geula Street were outside it, as was the campus of the university on Mount Scopus. This made it impossible for me to go to the building where my Hebrew classes took place and almost impossible to send the proofs of my book back and forth between my house and the press.

I remember one day watching with my friend Pessah Bar-Adon, the writer and archaeologist, who also lived within the fenced-off area, as the British soldiers hammered in iron posts along the middle of Geula Street and stretched the big coils of barbed wire over them. "They are building the Land for us," Bar-Adon remarked with caustic humor. "To build the Land" (*livnot et haAretz*) was the old Zionist slogan descriptive of the entire Jewish enterprise in Palestine.

Inside the fenced-in area the British army conducted house-to-house searches, in the course of which, as rumor would have it, some of the soldiers acted rather brutally. When they knocked on our door, the two Tommies who came in behaved like perfect gentlemen. They looked around, but did not touch, let alone move, a single piece of furniture. Perhaps they were impressed by the many books that lined our walls and by our fluent English.

Telephone communication between the two parts of the city separated by the barbed wire fence was not interrupted, and thus I was able to maintain contact with Yitzhaq Abiqsis and to arrange that he meet me at a certain hour at a particular point along the fence and bring me whatever proofs of my book he had ready. When we met we found that the coils of the wire were much too wide to reach across them, but Yitzhaq overcame the obstacle by throwing the bundle of proofs over them. Two days later I returned to him the corrected proofs by the same method. Not far from us there stood a British soldier, but he did not seem to mind. In this manner we met regularly, and the printing of the second volume proceeded apace until the fence was removed (I don't remember how long it was in place). By the time I left for Haifa, in the late summer of 1942, 128 pages of the book had been printed, but at that point I felt it would be better to continue the printing in Haifa, where I had to stay six days a week.

Neither the ferment in the country nor the distant thunder of the great war deterred me from making efforts to find new outlets for my studies of Jewish folklore. In January 1942 I wrote to Gershom Schocken, editor-in-chief of *HaAretz*, the leading Tel Aviv daily, and suggested that he introduce a folklore column in the weekend (Friday) edition of the paper. I duly informed Father of this initiative, and he responded in his January 21, 1942, letter, expressing his hearty approval. However, it so happened that on the same day on which I got Father's letter I also got a negative answer from

HaAretz, of which I reported to him on January 22: "Today I got a reply from G. Schocken: he regrets, but there is no room in *HaAretz* for Jewish folklore." Undaunted, I thereupon contacted the editor of *HaTzofe*, another Tel Aviv daily, which was the official organ of the Mizrahi party, and he willingly accepted my suggestion. Beginning with the Friday, October 9, 1942, issue, and for several Fridays thereafter, *HaTzofe* published my column, titled "Min haFolqlor haYisr'eli" (From Jewish Folklore), each installment of which concluded with the footnote: "Those who know items of Jewish folklore (such as customs, beliefs, charms, incantations, etc.) that, as far as they know, have not yet been published are requested to send them to Dr. R. Patai (c/o *HaTzofe*, Tel Aviv). Every item will be published in the name of the one who sent it in." I have no recollection of whether or not I received any response to this request, but I did manage to publish a number of birth, marriage, and death customs that I collected from various informants, including the mother of Yitzhaq Abiqsis, who was very knowledgeable about Moroccan Jewish customs, Joseph Meyuhas of Jerusalem (deceased by that time), Ben-Zion Taragan of Alexandria, Egypt, and Rabbi David Prato of Tel Aviv (formerly of Rome).

The family letters also contain incidental information about the situation in Hungary up to the third year of the war. In a letter dated January 25, 1942, Father wrote to me (in Hebrew): "Did I mention to you that we got a letter from our relative Gyula Virág [the office manager of Father's monthly] that everything is in order there? It seems that the journal continues to be published, and provides a livelihood for them and for Grandpa and Grandma." Surprisingly, conditions in Hungary remained good enough for *Mult és Jövő* to publish until March 1944, under the *de facto* editorship of Uncle Ernő Molnár, with Father's name appearing on the cover page as editor and publisher.

After the birth of Ofra I redoubled my efforts to find a job satisfactory from the points of view of both salary and security. Once the barbed wire was removed—it certainly was removed prior to February 5, 1942, for otherwise I would not have been able to take Naomi to the Hadassah Hospital—and I could resume my university classes, it soon became evident that the life expectancy of those classes was extremely short and that, in all probability, they would not be renewed in the fall. The simple reason for this was that the war conditions cut off the flow of foreign students, who were the only ones required to take those Hebrew preparatory courses. Thus, I felt impelled to search far and wide for another job, as far as that was possible within the narrow confines of the *yishuv*. For a while I continued with my efforts to get the secretaryship of the Goldberg Fund, but at the same time I sent out feelers in other directions. My father and my good friend Ibn-Zahav were my two most steadfast helpers in these efforts, referred to in numerous extant family letters.

One of the possibilities I had already looked into (briefly mentioned above) was a position as chaplain in the Palestinian contingents of the British army. From 1940 on the Jews of Palestine were accepted as volunteers into the Jewish companies of the army, of which fifteen were formed, attached to the East Kent Regiment (the "Buffs"). Two years later these companies were to be formed into three infantry battalions of a "Palestine Regiment." It was not until September 1944 that the British government established a reinforced Jewish fighting brigade, some 5,000 men strong, under the command of Brigadier Ernest Frank Benjamin, a Canadian Jew. The brigade fought in Italy, Holland, and Belgium. In the summer of 1946, in the wake of increasing tension between Britain and the *yishuv*, the brigade was disbanded.

The relevance of this bit of military history to my own life revolved upon the appointment, in the summer of 1941, of several Jewish chaplains to take care of the spiritual requirements of the Jewish soldiers. The senior Jewish chaplain was Rabbi Rabinowitz, the son-in-law of Rabbi Moshe Avigdor Amiel, the chief rabbi of Tel Aviv, who only a year before had officiated at our wedding. Since I had a rabbinical diploma from the Budapest Rabbinical Seminary, I was fully qualified to serve as a chaplain. At my request Father went to see Rabbi Amiel to ask his help in securing one of the chaplaincy positions for me. Rabbi Amiel promised him that when his son-in-law returned to Tel Aviv—he was at the time in Egypt—he would talk to him about me. He knew that the army was, in fact, looking for two additional rabbis, and that the starting salary was 15 pounds (three times as much as I made at the university, but less than half of what I was to earn in 1942 as secretary of the Technion). But he had understood that the army was giving preference to British subjects. Still, the chief rabbi was of the opinion that if his son-in-law, who had considerable influence, were to recommend me my chances would be good. These details are based on two letters Father wrote me from Shekhunat Boruchov on August 16 and 17, 1941. I myself have absolutely no recollection of the whole affair, nor do I know what happened after my father's meeting with Rabbi Amiel. From a letter Father wrote me on October 25, 1941, it appears that the matter was still pending at that time, and on November 12, 1941, I was called in for an interview in connection with the chaplaincy, but I am sure that in the event no appointment materialized.

In January 1942 Father came up with yet another idea for me. He wrote (in Hebrew):

> Mama tells me that I should write to you about the following matter that may not be worse than being a *ghaffir* on the highway at midnight. For the time being, confidential! Back in the summer Mr. Pinkas, director of the Mizrahi Bank, wrote me about setting up a

"foundation" or "institute" for a lottery, and asked me to participate in its board or council as a representative of Hungarian Jews. Others who participate in the same way include Dr. Barth (of the Anglo-Palestine Bank) as a representative of German Jews, Dr. Meir Ebner as a Rumanian, Dr. Kugel as a Slovakian, etc. While I was bedridden in the hospital, the "chief founder," Mr. Duff, came to see me: he is from Budapest and there too dealt with this, being responsible for the government lottery of the country, which was similar to the Hungarian *osz-tálysorsjáték* [class lottery]. Mr. Duff is the father of the *docent* [lecturer] at the university whom we once met at the Ibn-Zahavs. I had met Duff the father before Rosh haShana [New Year] at Pinkas's, and at that time he came up with a complete plan in this matter, which, according to him, would bring an income of 40 pounds monthly to each member of the board. He also told me that in the meantime he had obtained the permit and wanted to start carrying out the plan. A few days ago he wrote me that he wanted to meet with me again in Tel Aviv. Mama went in my place, and he told her about great prospects, etc. He also wants to commission Hava to devise an emblem for the whole project. Mama thinks it would be good if you would visit him in Jerusalem— perhaps a source of livelihood for you will emerge out of this. Duff emphasized to Mama how much he loved and honored Patai, and that already people are coming to him with recommendations seeking work. Perhaps out of this will come the calf that you need, the real Golden Calf, and also in the holy city of Jerusalem they will build a palace like the one the government lottery had in Budapest on the bank of the Danube, in which the good Jew who headed it carried on his work in a splendid office. In any case, talk to him, and he will tell you what is what. He said that, apart from membership in the board, he wanted to entrust me with some special task. Perhaps it will be right that you mention this to him, and he will explain to you the nature of the work, and can also give it to you if the whole affair succeeds as he thinks it will. He already has an office in Tel Aviv, but he lives in Jerusalem, and you can get his address from his son at the university, without telling him anything about the whole matter.

I have absolutely no recollection of this matter, and thus I don't know whether or not I followed up Father's suggestion. Nor do I know whether Mr. Duff's idea of a lottery ever materialized.

From the extant family letters it appears that in 1941–1942, after my father retired from the Friends of the Hebrew University, he spent much of whatever energy his frequent illnesses left over on two areas of activity: preparing for the press a Hebrew edition of a series of his books, most of which had formerly been published only in Hungarian (a few also in German), and helping me to get a satisfactory position. The results of the former of his efforts are still extant in several Hebrew volumes constituting the "jubilee edition" of his writings; as for the latter, I have long forgotten almost everything he did, and it is only from the letters of those years that I know about them, as indicated in the foregoing pages. A few months after the last-quoted letter Father returned to the problem of finding a place for me:

Shekhunat Boruchov, May 17, 1942 [in Hebrew]

Dear Raphael:

[. . .] I met the teacher Spivak from Jerusalem, and inquired from him about teaching positions. He thought that precisely now there would be a possibility of getting such a job, since now they are opening parallel classes in almost all the secondary schools. He advised contacting Dinaburg, the principal of the Bet haKerem teachers' seminary, who, he thinks, has great influence. I think it would be good for you to see him and talk to him now, prior to the end of the school year. If you agree, I shall talk to Bograchov, the principal of the Herzliya high school, and also to the principals of other schools, and shall try also to approach Rokach, and go to all the places where there are any chances. Spivak advised that you talk in Jerusalem to Rieger, etc. In the meantime I wrote thank you notes to all the Haifa people.

Today I met Mrs. Emil Feuerstein; she told me that her husband has received an "invitation" to give twenty lectures in the *moshavot* [villages] under the auspices of the Histadrut. He has to give the lectures within six weeks. This too is an opportunity to show one's ability. And there are more and more such opportunities. Today I handed Dr. Rosenfeld a note about the memoirs of Etta [Itah] Yellin for *'Am v'Sefer*, to him too I spoke about a job, he thinks there are possibilities now. It is necessary, for instance, to go also to the education department of the Va'ad Leumi, to the executives of the KKL and the KH, they too are engaged in activities now, and possibly can use a man like you on a permanent basis. Also, the Agency employs many people, perhaps one should inquire there too, it won't do any harm. [. . .] Of course, one must not neglect the libraries, perhaps a decent thing will come out of it as well! I think one should put into the list the Schocken Library and the library of the seminary, whose principal is Dinaburg.

Mrs. Bialik said she would come tomorrow to have a look at our apartment, and perhaps to rent it.

Your father who greets you with love,
Yosef

Warmest regards to Naomi. It would be nice if she would give us a new report about Ofra.

Yitzhaq Spivak (1886–1977) was a prolific juvenile author and teacher. Ben-Zion Dinaburg (later Dinur), whom we have already met, was a historian, at the time head of the Jewish Teachers' Training College in Jerusalem, from 1936 lecturer, and later professor at the Hebrew University, and from 1951 to 1955 minister of education and culture in the government of Israel. Israel Rokach (1896–1959) was mayor of Tel Aviv. Eliezer Rieger (1896–1954) was professor of education at the Hebrew University. Emil Feuerstein (b. 1914), a nephew of Avigdor Hameiri, was a prolific popular author. Dr. Alexander Rosenfeld was the director of the B'rit 'Ivrit 'Olamit (World Hebrew Union) and editor of its monthly, the *'Am v'Sefer* (People and Book). Etta (Itah) Yellin (1868–1943), widow of Professor David Yellin, who died two years before her, was the author of a two-volume autobiography, published in 1938 and 1941.

On the reverse of Father's letter Mother wrote (in Hungarian):

Just this moment came your letter in which you write about Ibn-Zahav's trouble. Indeed, if one hears of such a thing one instantly feels that one must not take too tragically one's own small and passing worries. [. . .]

We would like to go up only on June 15 or July 1, because Papa must first finish the cure, and there is much to take care of here in the house and in Tel Aviv. [. . .] I think it would in all events be necessary to take steps about a teaching position in the *gymnasium* [high school] or another secondary school. After all, if in the meantime something else succeeds, one does not have to accept it. Papa also taught along with editing the monthly and weekly journals of *Mult és Jövő*; even János Arany was notary in Szalonta. I think anything is better than economic uncertainty. If I read about the life of any outstanding man, the conclusion is always the same: that which is a man's labor of love rarely serves as a basis for livelihood. I beg you, don't push away this matter because for the time being it is not urgent—if it is not needed, time can pass very quickly.

I am glad that Naomi and Ofra are well. Is it still necessary to massage the child's arm? With us nothing new. We are at the point of waiting in every respect and are glad if a day passes quietly. One discovers that this is not at all natural.

János Arany (1817–1882), whom Mother holds up as an example for me, was, next to Sándor Petőfi, the greatest Hungarian poet. Mrs. Bialik did rent my parents' apartment from June 23. She was one of many Tel Avivians who, because of the danger of Italian aerial bombardment of Tel Aviv, preferred to move out of the city, temporarily at least. At another time, when my parents did not live in their Shekhunat Boruchov house, the Tolkowskys moved in for a number of weeks. In May my parents went to Gedera to spend some time with Évi and her family—she was at the time pregnant with her second child. On June 23 they came to Jerusalem and settled in their room in the apartment of the late Professor Yellin, next to the Edison Cinema.

A letter Mother wrote me in June (undated, as usual) was again devoted mostly to my job problem (in Hungarian):

Papa is considering what steps he could take in your affairs. He could go to Rokach only indirectly, through somebody, but he thinks that one can get a job as a school inspector or a similar job only on the basis of merit. I understand that you are not enthusiastic about a teaching position, even though I know *from experience* that it has many advantages. First of all, as against the daily 8 hours at least of an officeholder, the working time is much shorter (which balances the work's more exhausting nature), in addition it has lots of undisturbed vacations as against the annual two, or maximum four, weeks' vacation of an official. But more decisive than all that is that this is the only thing for which there are serious prospects, for here there are not only one or two openings but, considering the great number of schools, many more. Of course, one has to do everything in other directions as well, and to consider this only as a reserve, but, as you see, there are twenty aspirants to the Haifa position.

Tonight will be Papa's induction into the [Freemasons'] lodge, and tomorrow he must go to the Petah Tikvah police station because we got a citation: our blackout was found unsatisfactory. Thus, almost the whole week passes without Papa being able to begin anything. Hoenig has paid. Yesterday Hameiri was here: he told us that Rachel Goldberg had published a leaflet in which she described how Hofien behaved toward her when she asked for 25 pounds—he insisted on giving it to her only if the KKL signed for it! Truly it is a very sad thing that such a noble woman as Mrs. Goldberg should have fallen on such days. Hameiri saw the leaflet but could not get a copy, he doesn't know how many of it were printed, etc. Have you done anything yet about the cataloging? I beg you, Gyurikám, don't neglect this matter, you should work on it at least to the extent as stated by the rector, lest they say that you draw that big salary for nothing.

Papa works diligently on the Herzl book, but there is always some interruption. What's new about the Herzl pictures? Ofra is really very sweet and even without words is very clever. Especially since the military situation has improved, probably in her honor. After all, she has better connections with the supernal powers than we. Write right away!

Eliezer Siegfried Hofien (1881–1957) was general manager of the Anglo-Palestine Bank with headquarters in Tel Aviv. I have no recollection whatsoever what kind of cataloging work I was supposed to do, but from other references in the family letters it appears that it had something to do with the Goldberg Fund and from the reference to "the rector" it seems that the Hebrew University also had some interest in it. The "big salary" is, of course, meant ironically. The "Herzl book" on which Father was working was published in 1943 under the title *Hezyon Herzl* (Herzl's Vision). It contains mainly analecta he collected about the life of Theodor Herzl, the founder of political Zionism, after the publication of his Hungarian Herzl biography in 1931.

Since Tel Aviv was the city with the largest Jewish population in the country, all efforts to find a teaching position had to be directed there. As early as in 1934 I tried to find a teaching position there, at the Gimnasiya Herzliya (see above) and now too the city's school system loomed large on our horizon. Father wrote to me about what he had found out:

Boruchov, June 16, 1942 [in Hebrew]

Dear Raphael:

Yesterday I went to the Tel Aviv Municipality and found out that they do not at all deal with educational matters, which are in the jurisdiction of the Department of Education of the Va'ad Leumi in Jerusalem. It is they who send all the candidates to Tel Aviv, whether in instruction or in supervision. Ben-Yishai told me you should apply to the Va'ad Leumi in Jerusalem, and find out there what positions are open and where. Of course, the best thing would be if you could get the job you mentioned, as lector in Hebrew, and together with it the setting up of the library, and thus maintain a relationship with the university. We shall talk about all this in Jerusalem. [. . .] We plan to go on Tuesday. Until we meet again!

Your father who greets you with love,
Yosef

Again, I have no recollection whatsoever of what Father could have meant by "lector in Hebrew" and by "the setting up of the library." Whatever they were, they came to naught. Aharon Zeev Ben-Yishai (1902–1977) was a translator, author, and editor, who from 1932 edited the publications of the Tel Aviv municipality.

In April 1942 I learned that the Technion, the Palestine (later Israel) Institute of Technology in Haifa, was looking for an academic secretary. Founded in 1912 by donations from the family of Kalonymus Wissotzky of Moscow and from Jacob Schiff of New York, the Technion began to function as a university-level engineering school in 1924, in the Hadar haCarmel Quarter of Haifa. Shlomo Kaplansky (1884–1950), appointed in 1931 as its "director" (this was his official title), developed the Technion into a technological university of the Central European type, well known to me from my abortive attempt to study engineering at the Budapest *müegyetem* (technical university) in 1928. As the only institution of higher technical education of Palestine, the Technion played a crucial role in the building of the Jewish homeland, which role it has retained to this day in Israel.

I submitted my application to Mr. Kaplansky on May 12, 1942; and, of course, notified Father that I had done so. It so happened that one of the professors at the Technion, Joseph Breuer (d. 1962), of Hungarian origin, was a friend of Father, who immediately wrote to him and asked him to support my candidacy. Breuer had been the man in charge in the 1920s of the draining of the Jezreel Valley that transformed that large marshy, malaria-infested lowland into the most fertile and most productive agricultural area of Palestine. I did not know Breuer personally, but I had known his charming daughter Piri in the early 1930s when she was a student in Jerusalem and roomed together with Hanna Kroch, about whom I spoke in an earlier chapter. Some time later Piri was killed by a bomb dropped by an Italian warplane on Haifa.

Father knew several other influential people in Haifa from the time he had worked with them in organizing the Haifa branch of the Friends of the Hebrew University. Among them was Shabbetai Levi (1876–1956), the mayor of Haifa, and Father also wrote to him in my behalf. In an undated letter to me, probably written in June 1942, Father reported: "I got an answer from Shabbetai Levi: he writes that he has no close connection with the Technion, but has forwarded my letter to Kaplansky and hopes that he will give due consideration to it. Have you heard anything?"

Father also wrote to J. Klebanoff, an influential lawyer in Haifa; to the graphic artist Hermann Struck, to whose work Father had devoted several articles in his monthly *Mult és Jövő* while Struck still lived in Germany; and to the Haifa magistrate Judge Shalom Kassan. Each of them was willing to support my candidacy. Although for several weeks my chances of getting the position at the Technion did not look too promising, at the end, among the twenty or so candidates, I was the one to whom the job was offered. What this meant for me, responsible as I was for wife and child, can easily be imagined.

A Year in Haifa

From June 1942 to March 1943 only a few family letters have been preserved, so I must rely mainly on my memory in trying to reconstruct the events that took place during that period.

My appointment to the Technion brought me the official title of *mazkir hahanhala* (administrative secretary), which meant that I was the second-ranking official of the institution, next to Shlomo Kaplansky, its *m'nahel* (director). My salary was 35 pounds monthly, a respectable amount in those days, sufficient to cover the expenses of my family in Jerusalem and mine in Haifa.

If I remember correctly, I moved to Haifa in August or September 1942, in advance of the beginning of the academic year, in order to have time to familiarize myself with my duties and with living conditions in Haifa in general. We decided that, for the time being, I would go to Haifa alone, while Naomi would stay in Jerusalem with Ofra, who was at the time seven or eight months old. I took a furnished room, at first in the Hadar haCarmel Quarter not far from the Technion itself, later on top of Mount Carmel, from which there was a rapid and frequent bus connection with the Technion campus, which consisted at the time basically of one large building—erected in 1912—and smaller surrounding auxiliary premises. My office was a long and narrow room with a window overlooking the broad square that the Technion fronted and that sloped gently downward toward the lower reaches of Hadar haCarmel, the central part of Haifa. From many of the streets in Hadar haCarmel and Mount Carmel there was a beautiful view of the downtown area, the port with its ships, and, beyond it, stretching far to the north, the great arc of Haifa Bay, at the time still clearly visible and not yet covered by the smog that later was to become its bane.

The work week in those days consisted of six days, with Saturday as the only day off. My work was from nine to five. Throughout the first term I took the bus from Haifa to Jerusalem Friday afternoon—on Friday we stopped working earlier than 5:00 P.M.—and arrived three and a half hours later in Jerusalem, where I took the local bus from the Egged bus terminal on Jaffa Road to our home. On Sunday morning I had to get up at 5:00 A.M. to catch the six o'clock bus that arrived in Haifa at 9:30—it was agreed that I could be a little late to work on that day.

For several weeks that fall and winter my parents, unable to find other accommodations in Jerusalem, stayed with Naomi in our apartment. Father was bedridden most of the time (we put in a second bed for him in the living room) with bladder and prostate troubles. My parents' presence meant that Naomi was practically confined to the bedroom with the baby. Mother shared Father's belief that cool air was harmful for him, so that she kept the windows shut all the time, and I still remember the smell of urine that hit me each time I entered the room upon returning from Haifa for the weekend. All that time Naomi never uttered a single word of complaint about the situation, although it could not have been easy for her.

The Technion in those days was a relatively small institution, ruled by Mr. Kaplansky like a benevolent tyrant. He did have to get the consent of the faculty for decisions of more than routine administrative nature, but I don't remember a single case in which the faculty meeting, which I attended in my capacity as administrative secretary, voted down anything he proposed. My duties included dealing with problems of students, corresponding with students who applied for admission by mail, drafting letters in Hebrew and English on the basis of Kaplansky's instructions, and occasionally taking dictation from him in those two languages. Once I drafted a letter, I gave it to my secretary to type in one original and three copies, proofread them, and then presented them to Kaplansky in a nice hard-cover folder. He usually read everything then and there; when he found an error he corrected it meticulously in all the copies and then signed and returned them to me for mailing.

Another part of my duties was to schedule the courses for the coming term. This was a rather complicated procedure because there were a considerable number of variables to take into account: first of all, there were the demands of the teachers, many of whom were architects, engineers, or chemists with private offices and practices of their own, who insisted on not having to come to teach more often than three, or at maximun four, times a week. Then there were the curricular requirements: each field (e.g., architecture) included a number of subjects in which the students had to take courses—therefore it was imperative not to schedule two or more such courses at the same time. A third consideration was the availability of classrooms and laboratories. There were other special requirements too, which I can no longer recall. What I do remember is that on one of the walls of my office there was a large board to which was pinned a chart that looked like a huge checkerboard with hundreds of small rectangular cards of various colors. On the top line were listed the names of the days, starting with Sunday on the right side and ending with Friday on the left. In two vertical columns on both left and right were listed the hours, from 8:00 A.M. to 6:00 P.M. Each of the 60 slots was subdivided into as many smaller squares as the number of rooms available. Into these squares had to be fitted pieces of cardboard on which the names of the teachers and their courses were written. I no longer remember the significance of the various colors in which these small cards came, but it was my job to tack them into the slots, taking into account all the limitations and requirements. The scheduling of the classes had to be prepared well in advance of the beginning of the term, to give the teachers a chance to ask for changes and adjustments. Once everything was finalized, the schedule had to be copied on typed pages, mimeographed in hundreds of copies, and made available to teachers and students alike. When I first faced that huge checkerboard and understood the task, I found it formidable and confusing. But, with patience and perseverance, and, equally importantly, with the help of H. S. Krupnik, the financial secretary of the Technion who had done it in preceding years, I was able to master it and had everything under control by the opening of the academic year.

Once this was done, most of my time was divided between working with Mr. Kaplansky—he soon got into the habit of discussing all his plans and problems with me—developing a publicity campaign for the school and dealing with faculty and students. The public relations aspect of my work included furnishing the American Friends of the Technion with informative material suitable for publicity and thus facilitating their activities. When the secretary of the Friends received my first articles and other publicity material I sent him, he responded with an enthusiastic letter saying that he thought my work would open a new era for the American Friends.

Among the faculty there was one professor whom I happened to know from 1934–1935 when both of us were teachers at the Talpioth school of Mrs. Nathan, of which I spoke in an early chapter. He was the electrical engineer Dr. Franz Ollendorf, with whom I had been friendly in Talpioth. After his year at the Talpioth school Ollendorf had returned to Germany to organize the transfer of Jewish children to Palestine. In 1937 he was expelled by the Gestapo, and in 1939 became professor of electrical engineering at the Technion. He was an outstanding scientist in the field of biomedical electronics, won numerous prizes, published important books (all in German), and became vice-president of the American Institute of Electrical Engineers. I no longer remember the stories he told me about his experiences in Germany, but I can still feel the sense of horrified fascination with which I listened to them.

I remember very well, of course, Professor Joseph Breuer, who, having initially recommended me to Kaplansky, took a kind of proprietary interest in my successful performance. He had a young assistant by the name of Irmay. Another of the professors whom I remember well was Yohanan Ratner (1891–1965), who was head of the department of architecture and one of the most successful architects in Palestine, having to his credit such major public buildings as the Jewish Agency complex and the Eden Hotel in Jerusalem and (after my time) the aeronautics buildings of the new Technion campus on Mount Carmel. A third activity of Ratner was soldiering. In 1938–1939 he was head of the territorial command of the Hagana and during the German advance on Egypt in 1941–1942 was one of those who worked out the so-called Carmel Plan for the concentration of the Jewish armed forces in the Haifa region in case of a German invasion from the south. In 1948, when the Israel Defense Forces were formed, Ratner became head of the general headquarters with the rank of *aluf* (brigadier general). From 1948 to 1951 he was military attaché of the Israeli embassy in Moscow. What I personally remember of Ratner is that he was a mild-mannered and soft-spoken man for whom I conceived a great liking as soon as I got acquainted with him. Several of the other professors caused me considerable trouble with their demands for specific arrangements of their teaching schedules, but never Ratner. Despite his many demanding extracurricular activities, he was modest, friendly, and accommodating.

One interesting thing I remember that was characteristic at the time, not only of the people connected with the Technion but also of the *yishuv* as a whole, was that private visits in each other's homes were very rare. Thus, while Kaplansky, the members of the faculty, and the staff were all most friendly to me, and in the course of incidental meetings we often talked about issues that had nothing to do with the school in the Technion building, none of them, as far as I can remember, ever invited me to his home, nor did I ever have a meal with any of them. I remember very clearly having visited the homes of only three people throughout the two terms of my stay in Haifa: the Hochfelds, Hermann Struck, and Mr. Foguelson.

Mrs. Hochfeld was a younger sister of Naomi's mother, a very friendly, grossly overweight woman, who lived with her husband (they had no children) in a large and luxurious villa on Mount Carmel. Arno Hochfeld was an industrialist, the owner of some kind of a factory in Haifa. He was an exceedingly handsome man, tall and dark haired, with a marked resemblance to Cary Grant, whom I greatly admired in *The Philadelphia Story* and *Suspicion*. During my stay in Haifa the Hochfelds always made me welcome in their beautiful home—but, again, as far as I remember, neither during the first term when I was alone nor during the second when Naomi stayed with me in Haifa did they ever invite me to a meal.

Hermann Struck was one of the most renowned Jewish graphic artists, many of whose pictures Father had published in his journal. Especially famous was his portrait of Herzl, showing the founder of Zionism in profile. After my arrival in Haifa I sought him out in his home on Hadar haCarmel; where he had a large studio. He remembered my father and received me in a friendly manner; thereafter I visited him from time to time.

Peculiarly, I don't remember the first name of Mr. Foguelson (this is how he spelled his family name; variant spellings of the same name are Fogelson, Fogelsohn, Vogelson, or Vogelsohn). Nor do I remember how I got to know him. He was a man in his fifties, a retired official, whose hobby was collecting antiques. We met quite frequently in his home, where he loved to show me his treasures. One of his acquaintances was the famous Yiddish novelist

Sholem Asch, and I remember that one day while I was there Asch appeared, stepped straight to the sofa in the living room, raised the cover, peeped under it, and asked, *vo zenen di gute zakhn?* (Where are the good things?). After Asch left, Foguelson explained to me that he would occasionally sell an object to him.

Once—this must have been after Naomi joined me in Haifa, so that I remained there over the weekend—Foguelson took me to Acco, on the northern end of Haifa Bay, and we visited several Arab antique dealers in the old city. Guided by him, I bought a small ancient Phoenician glass vase—it was cheap because part of its rim was broken off—and several ancient earthenware oil lamps. Another time I went with him to see the Jewish necropolis of Bet Sh'arim (Shaykh Abrek) to the southeast of Haifa, which had been partially excavated in 1935–1940 by my friend the archaeologist Binyamin Maisler (later Mazar).

While in Haifa I made the acquaintance of Dr. Yehezq'el Kaufmann (1889–1963), the biblical scholar and social historian. He was at the time teacher at the Reali school, whose building was next door to that of the Technion. He started to publish his multivolume magnum opus, *Toldot haEmuna haYisr'elit* (History of the Religion of Israel) in 1937; although it was generally acclaimed as a masterpiece and a milestone in the study of biblical religion, it was not until 1949, when he was sixty, that Kaufmann was finally appointed professor of Bible at the Hebrew University. Kaufmann's thesis in his book was that Israel's monotheism was not a gradual development out of early paganism, but an entirely new phenomenon *sui generis* in religious history. One of the very few voices raised in criticism was mine.

Since 1938 I had been one of the book reviewers of *Ha'Olam*, the official weekly of the Zionist Organization and, at the request of its editor, Moshe Kleinman, wrote two lengthy reviews of the first and second volumes of the Kaufmann book in the June 20, 1940, and the September 17, 1942, issues. My reviews were appreciative and respectful. I gave full recognition to the originality and value of the book as a counterweight to Julius Wellhausen's theory of the late origin of certain parts of the Pentateuch, generally accepted at the time by biblical scholarship. I emphasized that "nowhere, in no study, essay, or lecture, has until now existed such a clear and decisive, comprehensive and basic presentation of the contrasts that are as deep as the abyss" between paganism and biblical religion as there is in this book. But after these accolades I could not refrain from pointing out what I considered a "basic defect" in Kaufmann's approach: I faulted him for denying that there was any inner development in the biblical Hebrew God-concept, which, according to him, was unchanging and identical from the beginning to the end of the biblical period. I devoted a considerable part of my review to adducing examples from the biblical text that demonstrated, in my view, that the Hebrew God-concept evinces a constant development from an early primitive stage to the high ethical universal monotheism of Micha and Isaiah. I took Kaufmann to task for such erroneous statements as "the biblical legend does not know Israelite dream-interpreters in Eretz Israel (Joseph and Daniel functioned in foreign countries); from this we learn that also the popular belief did not know them." I pointed out that when Joseph told his brothers his dreams they unhesitatingly interpreted them as symbolic of his wish to rule over them (Gen. 37:5–11). This scene, I wrote, "is a clear testimony to a thorough knowledge of dream interpretation that was a familiar or even popular heritage." Likewise, I pointed out that Jacob dreamt of the ladder reaching into heaven and interpreted it himself in Beth-el, in Eretz Israel, adduced several other examples, and went on to show other similar errors in Kaufmann's book. For example, he wrote that the Hebrew people did not believe that "God entered the body of a prophet and spoke from this throat." I objected: what about the numerous biblical references to God's spirit having "clothed" itself in a prophet (Gideon, Amasai, Zechariah son of Jehoiada)? (The Hebrew expression *lavash* clearly shows that the divine spirit was believed to enter the body of the prophet and *put it on* like a garment.) In the conclusion of my review I stated that despite such errors, Dr. Kaufmann's book was of great value: it was a new foundation, a *Hebrew* foundation, of the study of the Bible and of the history of biblical religion. My review of Kaufmann's second volume was similar in tone and content, and since it was published just at the time I started my service at the Technion I was apprehensive lest a personal meeting with him turn out to be unpleasant.

I remember the antecedents of my first meeting with Dr. Kaufmann. I organized a series of lectures (I no longer know under what auspices; perhaps the Friends of the Hebrew University); although I was told that Dr. Kaufmann *never* lectured anywhere, I thought that I had to try to persuade him to make an exception. I went over to the building of the Reali school, and we had what turned out to be a very friendly chat. Neither of us referred to my reviews of his book. He turned down my invitation. Thereafter I met him another few times, but we never became friends.

Another place I visited a few times during my year in Haifa was the Carmelite monastery located at the tip of Mount Carmel, at the point where it jutted out to its extreme into the sea. The place was called, most appropriately, Stella Maris (Star of the Sea), and the monastery was built so that from it one could scan the sea, several hundreds of feet below, on three sides. I no longer remember precisely why I went to see the monastery the first time—it was quite out of the way in relationship to the Jewish quarters on Mount Carmel—I think it must have been simple curiosity to see the inside of the imposing building that I repeatedly admired from several points below it, from the port area, from the Bat Galim Quarter directly beneath it, and from the Khayyat Beach farther to the south. It so happened that the monk who opened the gate, to whom I explained in English that I would appreciate if he would allow me to have a look around, turned out to be a Hungarian—no sooner had he said a word or two when I recognized his unmistakable accent. Being able to converse in our mother tongue made it easy for us to become friendly, and thereafter I returned several times. My monk friend (his name has long escaped me) proved to be quite knowledgeable about the history of his order and was able to tell me interesting details about it and about the monastery itself. I learned that the Carmelite order was founded in the twelfth century, when much of the seashore of Palestine was under Crusader rule. A monastery was built at the time, on the very spot on which we stood, but it was destroyed by Baybars in 1291 and not rebuilt until several centuries later.

My memory has retained one detail from those visits that must have struck me as extraordinary. My friend showed me the library, whose open shelves contained a fair collection of traditional Catholic literature, including many beautifully printed large, vellum-bound volumes. In one corner of the library I noticed a small glass-enclosed bookcase, locked with a good-sized old iron lock. "What is in that bookcase?" I asked my host. "Books that we are allowed to read," he answered, "only by special permission from the abbot." I stepped closer to have a look at the restricted books through the glass door of the bookcase; to my great surprise, I noticed that many of its shelves were occupied by an old edition of the *Meyers Konversations Lexikon*, the standard German general encyclopedia that happened to be an old friend of mine from my childhood days. It was on my lips to ask my host why such a general encyclopedia should be accessible to the brothers only by special permission, but before I spoke I thought better of it and kept silent.

Speaking of books, I remember that I spent many a pleasurable hour in Haifa browsing in the secondhand book stalls that lined Herzl Street, the main thoroughfare of Hadar haCarmel. Enjoying an income that was slightly higher than my current expenses, I permitted myself—for the first time in my adult life—to buy books. Among the books I bought then and still have in my library were several anthropological classics: the three volumes of Baron Ferdinand Reitzenstein's edition of *Das Weib*, two of Oscar Hovorka and A. Kronfeld's *Vergleichende Volksmedizin*, and the two of S. Seligmann's *Der böse Blick*. They must have belonged to a German Jewish immigrant, perhaps a medical doctor, who found himself in straitened circumstances and was forced to sell them.

Despite my full-time work, I still found time to continue to do the last-minute polishing on the manuscript of the second half of the second volume of my *Adam vaAdama*. To be able to do this work, I had taken my Hebrew typewriter along to Haifa, and whenever I had a chance I worked on my book. Since the printing of the book had been interrupted in Jerusalem, I located a printer in Haifa to do the remaining part of the volume, which I estimated would run into ten to twelve signatures, or 160 to 192 pages. The printing press on which I settled was the Ot Cooperative Press, which had the same Hebrew and Latin type font as the HaMa'arav Press in Jerusalem and had the advantage over the latter of doing the typesetting by Linotype, which promised rapid progress. Prior to the Passover vacation that fell in that year on April 20–26, which I spent at home with Naomi and Ofra, I delivered the manuscript to the press. Once they started working on the book I had to take the bus about twice a week from the Technion to the port area where the press was located, to get the proofs, to return them, and, in general, to keep track of the printing. I used my lunch hour for the trip, and in most cases I did not have to stretch it beyond the usual one hour. On July 3, 1943, my brother Saul sent the paper for the book from Jerusalem to Haifa, and shortly thereafter the printing of the book was actually finished.

It was during that Passover vacation that Naomi informed me that she was pregnant again and that we could expect our second child to be born in October.

By the time the spring term of my work at the Technion began I had come to the conclusion that the technically oriented environment of the Technion was not a milieu in which a scholar like me, committed to folklore and ethnology, could thrive, or even survive. True, my external circumstances at the Technion were satisfactory, the work itself, although time consuming, was, exactly as Mother predicted, not onerous or exhausting, the attitude of Mr. Kaplansky and the faculty toward me was friendly, considerate, and appreciative, the salary was adequate and had I stayed on would certainly have increased. However, all these advantages were outweighed in my eyes by one overriding factor: I was a scholar who by that time had dedicated himself irrevocably to the study of Jewish cultural history (it was only a year or two later that the horizon of my interests expanded so as to embrace the non-Jewish Middle East as well), and the type of work done by the faculty and students to which the whole Technion was dedicated inevitably remained foreign to me. I felt like a fish out of water and was seized with the anxiety that if I continued my job, which was purely administrative, my intellectual abilities and whatever creative powers I possessed would wither and be doomed.

My parents, with whom, of course, I discussed the problem, were concerned in the first place about my material welfare and feared lest, as a young *pater familias*, I remain without a satisfactory livelihood, as I had been for years prior to my Technion appointment. They tried, both orally and in letters, to dissuade me from resigning. In one of the undated letters (probably from April 1943) Mother wrote:

I am very sorry that the work is so hard for you—I don't know what else I can say about it, except that which you know anyhow. It is a fact that most people earn their bread with the sweat of their brow. But—only be healthy, that is more important than everything else. Then you will certainly find suitable work, if not earlier, then after the war.

Tell Naomi that I was very glad to get her letter, and especially to hear that Ofra feels so well in the new environment. I am not writing to her separately because I have no time.

In one of the many serious discussions I had with my parents I tried to make them see my position by reminding them that only a year or two earlier Father was so unhappy about his administrative and fund-raising job with the Friends of the Hebrew University that he became quite embittered and considered himself a "slave of slaves," as he wrote me in one of his letters. In fact, if he gave up his job when he did, it was only partly because of his health: his unhappiness with his position had a major share in it. If he felt that way at the age of sixty, *after* a long and rich creative career, how much more understandable it must be that I wanted to get out of my administrative slavery at the age of thirty-two, *before* I had a chance to develop my capabilities. My argument did make an impression, more on Father, who had personally experienced what I was talking about, than on Mother, who was merely a bystander and whose worry about my livelihood overrode other considerations.

In my predicament I again spoke to Dr. Magnes, who again reacted to the presentation of my problem with great sympathy and understanding. In fact, he did more than that: he indicated that there were two possibilities that would enable me to return to Jerusalem and to the field of Jewish studies. One was that he himself might need a secretary and the other that he might soon have at his disposal a fund for the allocation of research fellowships in Jewish studies and would definitely consider me deserving of one. Allusions to that interview are contained in a letter Mother wrote to me on March 22, 1943 (in Hungarian):

> Today I have got over my fright with Papa's illness, and so I could think more quietly about your plan to leave your present job.
> Gyurikám, above all I beg you very much, don't act precipitously, and for the time being don't talk to the director. Weighing it with tranquil objectivity: Magnes has not promised anything, and besides, he himself is a private individual, a universally attacked politician, and even if he should give you some position connected with his person and activity, that, indeed, would be a very doubtful situation—in contrast to your

present job. After all, the housing shortage is not a permanent thing, nor is the value of the money, the time will come when your present salary will provide a full, proper livelihood. On the other hand, in the meantime it can also happen that the value of the 1,500 pounds will shrink so much that it will be insufficient to constitute the basis of your financial security. I don't even want to mention what a bad impression it would make if you suddenly left the job for which you had fought so hard, and how it could be a hindrance in finding a new position. You surely know how important your mental and spiritual harmony, your physical well-being are for me—but still I must say that you should not change the present situation unless something else is already assured.

In the meantime Ibn-Zahav was here, and even though he spoke mostly about his own things and Papa's books, in response to my question he reported in a few words about your affair and said that he was very angry and that the whole problem is Naomi's (I don't believe this, because I know how much you would like to stay with your real work, but in any case it shows how this astute friend judges the whole matter), etc., etc. He did not mention with a single word that there would be work with Magnes; in fact, he spoke as if you had asked for some fellowship. Although I accompanied him when he left, we were unable to talk the matter over to the end, but in any case I heard enough to see how dangerous it would be to be precipitate.

I know well, Gyurikám, that I am causing you annoyance with this letter, but that, naturally, cannot hold me back. Yesterday both Papa and I enjoyed your presence so much, we both became quite refreshed, for it was visible in what good spirits you were, and, of course, we know that the reason for it was mainly the hope that you can get back to Jerusalem. And still, I must say, especially thinking back on the times when worry about you hovered over us like a black cloud, at least think over the matter thoroughly and repeatedly and don't do anything until you have talked it over again with Ibn-Zahav and with us. Believe me, I know well what it is if one's work gives satisfaction—I always used to say to Papa what a privileged position he had to make a living by that which for him was a labor of love—I say not even a word to Guszti if he wants to live on 10 pounds in Jerusalem with suitable work rather than here on 25 (apropos: Guszti too will leave his present job only if the new position is assured), but in your case the situation is different. Why, I don't have to set forth, for I think it unworthy of you to live mainly on your wife's money.

What Mother writes about Dr. Magnes being "universally attacked" refers to the leadership position Magnes had in the small and highly unpopular Ihud (Unity) society, a successor of the practically defunct B'rit Shalom, both of which advocated the establishment in Palestine of a binational Jewish-Arab state. Ultimately both minuscule movements foundered, and even while they existed they never evoked any response whatsoever from the Arab side.

I am not sure of the background of Mother's reference to 1,500 pounds and to the indignity of living mainly on my wife's money, but I believe that at that time Naomi received a parcel of land as part of her share in her grandfather's estate, and we either planned to or actually did sell it. What I do remember is that Naomi saw eye to eye with me concerning my job problem and that she encouraged me to leave my position at the Technion and return to my own field of scholarship. Thus fortified, and hoping that a fellowship in Jewish ethnology at the Hebrew University would materialize, I made the decision to resign, and upon my return from my Passover vacation I so notified Mr. Kaplansky.

I remember the scene. I went into his office to see him and told him that I wished to resign effective after the end of the academic year. He was visibly taken aback, and his first response was to ask whether there was anything in particular with which I was unhappy in my job. I assured him that this was not the case and that my decision to leave was motivated solely by the desire to devote my life to scholarly work in Jewish folklore and ethnology, which desire had crystallized into an imperative, an irresistible force, in the course of the months I had spent at the Technion, working in a field far removed from those interests. Once Kaplansky saw that I was adamant, he suggested that I should stay on until he could find a replacement for me. I agreed and stayed until the end of August 1943. Throughout the remaining months Mr. Kaplansky, who was a real gentleman, continued to be as friendly and pleasant to me as he had been prior to my resignation.

During that Passover holiday Naomi and I decided that she would join me with Ofra in Haifa for the balance of my time at the Technion. Since our stay in Haifa was to be limited, we retained our apartment in Jerusalem and sublet it for the duration of our absence to a certain Dr. and Mrs. Soloveitchik. In Haifa we found a suitable furnished room on Mount Carmel, in which there was room enough for a crib for Ofra, who was fifteen months old. I do not remember where and how we took our meals while all three of us lived in that furnished room. Soon after Naomi arrived in Haifa with Ofra, the baby fell ill, which Mother attributed to the exigencies of the trip. She wrote (about May 1943), "I can imagine how unpleasant the first week was due to Ofra's illness. To be sure, travel in such a drafty bus is good neither for an adult nor for a baby. I hope Ofra has by now recovered from the difficulties of the trip and enjoys the seashore."

A few days later Mother wrote to Naomi (undated, in German): "I hope Ofra is by now completely recovered and lovely as ever. Whether she is a *gaon* [genius], as you write, I don't know, but one thing is certain: she is especially intelligent and well developed. In any case, a goodly portion of inventive spirit is needed for expressing herself so well and declaring her will to her slave and mother."

Mother continued to be unhappy about my resignation and lamented about it long after it was a *fait accompli.* In July 1943 she wrote to me from Jerusalem to Haifa (in Hungarian):

> Just now Ibn-Zahav was here and totally unsettled me, he spoke so pessimistically about your leaving the Technion. He says that with the peace rumors a crisis is already developing, and everybody clings to his job a hundredfold. He spoke to Magnes, who stated categorically that he did not need you now, that is to say, one can count on nothing there. And, according to Ibn-Zahav, if they come back from the war there will be 100 aspirants for every job. And as for folklore, there will be no chair for it even in twenty years, and if there will be, they will bring from afar somebody to occupy it. At the end he added that I must understand his indignation, for if he with his constitution, his insomnia, has carried the burdens of his position, why can't you carry it at least for a few years, etc., etc.
>
> He told me all this in Guszti's room, for, of course, one could not go in to Papa.
>
> My dear, dear son, you cannot imagine how every word I wrote hurts me, after all I know how you cleave to your work, etc., etc.—but I am so crushed by great fatigue, by Papa's illness, and by the pictures projected by Ibn-Zahav that I could not keep these things to myself.

While I was still in Haifa I not only finished the printing of the second volume of *Adam vaAdama,* but received reviews of the first. The reviews, of which I was able to preserve only a few, ranged from seriously appreciative to extravagantly enthusiastic. Among the most moderate in praise was that of Professor William F. Albright, widely recognized as dean of Palestinian archaeologists, who in his brief note published in the April 1943 issue of the *Bulletin of the American Schools of Oriental Research* said that "used critically the work is valuable." The following year, when he reviewed the second volume (in the October 1944 issue of the *BASOR*), he emended this by saying, "In view of the great wealth of material presented and the methodological arrangement, we should like to add a word to our previous characterization: used critically the work will be *very* valuable" (emphasis in the original).

Several of the reviews published in Palestine, in the *Palestine Post* and in the Hebrew dailies and periodicals, were lengthy analyses, in fact, review essays. They contained many favorable comments: "This new book by Dr. R. Patai, the well-known researcher of Jewish folklore, penetrates an entirely new territory in the area of Jewish historical folklore" (*Ha'Olam*, August 20, 1942, unsigned); "Perhaps the most interesting part of the book is the original and extremely suggestive theory on the different Jewish conceptions of the world which a careful study has revealed to the author" (*Palestine Post*, August 30, 1942, unsigned); "Congratulations to Dr. Raphael Patai, who has now enriched our scholarly literature with a seminal study . . ." (*HaBoqer*, September 25, 1942, Shalom Schwarz).

Of the second volume Moshe Kleinman, editor of *Ha'Olam*, wrote, "The studies of Dr. Patai signal important first steps in an entirely new field of Jewish studies: in Jewish folklore, in the historical-comparative study of the customs, beliefs, and legends of the Jewish people. This work—which is truly a pioneering work, a work of conquest in a scholarly field of research— is worthy of the greatest recognition by all those who hold dear the national-religious-popular treasures of the people of Israel" (*Ha'Olam*, December 2, 1943, signed Qore Vatiq, i.e., Moshe Kleinman).

On the bus back from Haifa to Jerusalem, Naomi (who held Ofra in her lap) and I discussed what I had achieved during my Haifa year and my plans for the future. Characteristically, neither one of us considered it of special value that as chief administrative officer of the second most important institution of higher learning in Palestine I had acquired a fund of experience that could stand me in good stead in the future. As it happened, as soon as two years later, when I founded and then headed the Palestine Institute of Folklore and Ethnology, my experience as the secretary of the Technion proved invaluable. Naomi and I were so totally convinced of the supreme value of scholarly research that we both felt that what I had achieved in that year in Haifa had to do only with my own research work in ancient Jewish custom, belief, and legend. In that field, I had seen through the press the second volume of *Man and Earth* and had begun to map out the outline of a new book I planned to write, in English this time. That new book was to carry forward my investigation of ancient Jewish myths and rituals, in particular those that centered on the role of the Jerusalem Temple and of the spiritual leaders of the nation in securing the proper functioning of nature and thereby assuring the well-being of the people. In the course of many lonely evenings I had spent in Haifa before Naomi joined me there I had entertained myself with thinking about this new scholarly venture; on the weekends in Jerusalem—and after she came to Haifa also on weekdays—I often discussed with Naomi what I was planning to do. This ultimately resulted in my first English book, *Man and Temple in Ancient Jewish Myth and Ritual*, about which I shall have more to say later.

It was also while I was in Haifa that my interest began to expand from the ancient world into the contemporary one. I no longer remember what gave me the immediate impetus, but I am sure it was during my stay in Haifa that I became aware of the importance, and the urgency, of studying the folklore, folk custom, and folk-life of the twentieth-century Jewish communities, many of which were by that time ingathered in Palestine. It was there that I decided that, as soon as the conditions of my life permitted it, I would devote as much of my attention as possible to collecting and publishing that type of highly perishable material and also to stimulating others to do the same. After I had been in Haifa for several months I began to publish a series of short notes on folk customs in connection with birth, marriage, and death that I had collected among the Moroccan, Egyptian, and Sephardi Jews, and I conceived the idea of writing what eventually became my first programmatic article on the imperative of preserving Jewish folklore.

By the time we arrived in Jerusalem I had described to Naomi in considerable detail what I wanted to do in the coming year and the years thereafter. What I did not know was whether the circumstances we would have to face would permit me to carry out those ambitious plans.

Family, Friends, and Work

After our return from Haifa to Jerusalem in the summer of 1943 there is a hiatus of almost a year in the flow of family letters due to the fact that during that time my parents also lived in Jerusalem, making the writing of letters redundant. As far as I can reconstruct from memory what developed after our return, for about a year I had no steady income, apart from my author's and lecturer's fees. What I thus earned was insufficient to cover our living expenses, and we had to draw on the capital we had from the sale of a plot of land Naomi had received as part of her share in her grandfather Goldberg's estate.

However, personal economic difficulties, the horrible news of the Holocaust that had reached Palestine by that time, the German war threat from across the Egyptian border, and even the growing tension between the British and the *yishuv* in Palestine itself could not stop me from immersing myself in the study of Jewish folklore. As soon as we were again settled in Jerusalem I drew up detailed questionnaires covering birth, marriage, and death customs and mailed them out to several dozens of rabbis, scholars, and other members of the various Jewish communities, because I knew they were knowledgeable about the traditions of the society in which they grew up. The first questionnaire dealt with the customs of birth and circumcision and contained no less than forty-two questions, covering all aspects of the subject and inevitably reflecting what I knew by that time about the customs and beliefs that surrounded that most important of events in the life of the Jewish family.

My questions touched upon the entire gamut of childbirth, beginning with the efforts made by childless couples to rid themselves of the curse of barrenness and ending with the elaborate ceremonies surrounding circumcision on the eighth day of the newborn boy's life. It included such issues as the protection of mother and child against demons, the position of the woman during parturition, the use of amulets and "names," the "salting" of the child, the treatment of the afterbirth and the umbilical cord, the meals, the visits, the prayers, the naming of the child, the circumcision, the disposal of the foreskin, etc. I treated in similar detail the customs and beliefs connected with marriage and death. It was my intention to use the data I hoped to gather in the projected third volume of my book *Man and Earth*, which, in the event, was never published. But I did publish a considerable part of the material I collected in articles that appeared in *Folk-Lore* (London) in 1944, in the *Hebrew Yearbook of American Jews* (New York) in 1949, and in the journal *Talpioth* (New York) in 1953, 1955, and 1965.

By mere chance a few of the responses to my questionnaires survived in my files. The most detailed answers were given by Hakham (the common designation for Sephardi rabbis) Shim'on Harus of Safed, who sent me on July 17, 1943, and on several subsequent dates no less than seventy-four tightly written pages on birth, marriage, and death customs among the Sephardi Jews of Safed and North Africa. In one of his letters Hakham Harus included a brief autobiography (I had asked for it), and from it I learned that he was born in Safed in 1893, studied in Safed *yeshivot*, married in 1913 Gracia, the daughter of R. Sh'lomo Hakim, the *hakham bashi* (chief rabbi) of Safed, and became a teacher in the Sephardi Tora school of the town. In 1915, the second year of World War I, the Turkish government of Palestine issued a decree to the effect that all the inhabitants of the country had to opt for Turkish citizenship or be expelled.

Hakham Harus writes:

> Since we did not want to give up our French citizenship, we left the country in Heshvan 5675 [October–November 1915] and went to Beirut (Lebanon) together with other French and English citizens from Safed and Tiberias. We got money for our livelihood every week from the American consul. Two months later an American ship came to Beirut and transported most of the French and British citizens, taking the British to the island of Cyprus, and the French to Corsica. There the French government received its citizens with courtesy and took care of their housing, for which purpose it took a big courtyard (*grand séminaire*) in which monks lived, and settled in it the citizens who had come from Eretz Israel. This caused quarrels between them and the people of the city, and they expelled all the monks who lived in that courtyard. The courtyard passed

from the hands of the monks and came under the control of the migrants. About one thousand souls lived in that courtyard on three floors. The government gave us a monthly allowance according to the number of souls, and we lived there in great affluence. In the month of Elul 5679 [September 1919] when there was peace and quiet in the Land [of Israel], the government sent back all the migrants to their places.

After his return to Safed Hakham Harus again took up teaching and a few years later became an emissary of the Sephardi Kolel (religious charity organization), in which capacity he spent the three years 1924–1927 traveling in Algiers, Oran, Tunis, and Tripoli. In 1929–1930 he undertook a second trip, and from 1932 to 1936 a third one, to the same places as an emissary of the Hebron Sephardi community. He succeeded in collecting enough money for the building of a large yeshiva in Hebron named after R. Amram ben Diwan. He himself, however, returned to Safed, where, as he wrote to me, circumstances forced him to engage in commerce (*manufaqtura*).

It was my friend Zvi Wohlmuth who "found" Hakham Harus for me. After the publication of our anthology of modern Palestinian short stories Zvi took a job as a teacher in Safed and got acquainted with the Hakham. At his suggestion I wrote to the Hakham, enclosed my questionnaires, and asked his help. His response to my questions was attached to a letter he wrote in the traditional Hebrew *maqāma*-style, that is, in rhymed prose, in a highly poetic, old-fashioned language. The rhyme of the entire first paragraph of his letter was the syllable -*ti*, which is the Hebrew first person verbal suffix in the past tense:

Very Honored Doctor:
    I heard your good and noble fame, but I have not met your precious countenance; I was honored by the letter of your holy scrolls, at the request of my friend Mr. Zvi Wohlmuth I respond most willingly, and I endeavored to answer your honored questions, and according to the poverty of my brain and the shortness of my understanding, I arranged the answers in brevity, I searched in books and in customs, and asked writers and elders, I finished the *mitzva* [commandment] of charity and truth, and added more customs and their reasons, I hope for the publication of your honored book . . .

In contrast to this poetaster's effluvium, the actual answers Hakham Harus gave to my questions were precise and scholarly. Let me give as an example his response to my very first question: "What remedies against barrenness do you know?" He started by saying that the true remedy was prayer and quoted several biblical passages to prove his point. Then he went on:
    And there is another charm: to swallow the foreskin of a child who

is circumcised. And I saw in the book *Yam haGadol* [The Great Sea], par. 53, p. 81, top, that the great Gaon, Rabbi Toledano, head of the rabbis of the Sephardi community in Tel Aviv, wrote, "I thought it right to consider the law about human flesh, whether its prohibition is a law of the Tora, and whether there is in it a prohibition of 'a part of a living being,' and flesh from the living. And this is relevant to the matter of women who swallow the foreskin of a child as a charm for pregnancy," and he quotes there the view of Maimonides that this is forbidden. But according to Nahmanides and Rashba [R. Sh'lomo ben Avraham Adret] it is permitted. Or this charm: when washing the body of a deceased they make small satchels and in them put *borit* [soap], and they wash the deceased with them. And what is left of those satchels, if the deceased was a kosher and decent man, they preserve it, and the woman washes her body with it when she takes the ritual immersion.

In response to another question the Hakham wrote that "they dry the foreskin and the umbilical cord, and put them in a little satchel, and put that satchel in the pillow on which the newborn lies . . . This is practiced here in the Sephardi community. The women believe that this will make the child quiet, but if they throw them away the child will become unruly."

My questionnaires brought in responses from some three dozen individuals, mostly elderly men from Oriental Jewish communities, including those of Adrianople, Gallipoli, Salonika, Syria, Iraq, Kurdistan, Iran, Yemen, Algeria, and Morocco. I also got some responses covering the Ashkenazi communities of the Ukraine, Poland, and Galicia—all three were supplied by women. Some of the informants attached Arabic and Ladino texts of songs sung at weddings in their communities. One of them included a list in Ladino (called *rol*) that was attached to a marriage contract dated 1905 and contained all the items the bride received as her dowry, with the monetary value of each item stated in piasters (*grush*). Most of the articles listed were clothes and bedding, but they included also a *ventador* (fan), *baul con su tafon* (box with its cover), *maqina de Singer* (Singer sewing machine), and gold earrings. The total value of all the items came to 8,420 *grush*, to which were added fictitious amounts "as customary" and "in honor of the family," so that the total reached 16,755 *grush*, and it was stated carefully that 109 *grush* equaled one Napoleon.

In addition to these direct responses I also got information from a few persons who themselves had collected data among various Jewish communities. I circulated another type of questionnaire whose purpose was to obtain data about the living conditions of members of various Jewish communities in Jerusalem. It contained questions about the birthplace of the respondent, his age, the community to which he belonged, his occupation (including salary if employed), the number of persons living in the dwelling unit, the numbers and ages of the members, the number of wives (in plural, since among the Yemenite Jews, e.g., polygyny was still legal), the sanitary-hygienic conditions in the dwelling unit, the number of persons per room, the lighting, furnishing, the kitchen, bath (if any), the water supply, toilet, etc., and also the educational level of each member of the family. It is my great regret that almost all the material thus collected was lost after my move from Jerusalem to New York.

By the fall of 1943 the German tide had receded so that the *yishuv* could breathe more freely; but, on the other hand, in Palestine itself the relationship between the Jews and the British Mandatory Government had grown worse. British sympathy for the Arab cause was expressed in successive government policy statements and in such moves as the encouragement of the creation of the Arab League (founded in March 1945). The Jewish demand that Britain enable the *yishuv* to participate in the war effort under the British flag was handled by Britain with such reluctance that it was not until the final phase of the war, in the spring of 1945, that Jewish service units recruited in Palestine could at last participate in battles on the Italian front.

The British also obstructed plans put forward by the Hagana to drop parachutists behind enemy lines in the occupied Central European countries for the purpose of organizing anti-Nazi resistance among the Jewish youth. Many volunteered but only thirty-two were able to reach their destination; of them, twelve were captured, and seven executed. Most of the latter were from Hungary and Hungarian-language areas (Slovakia, Transylvania), and it was there that they were dropped and apprehended and then put to death.

By 1943 the horrors of the Holocaust were known in the *yishuv,* and the effect of that knowledge was a combination of deep mourning, impotent rage, and the determination to rescue at least a remnant, "a brand plucked out of the conflagration." By 1944 an effort was under way to help the survivors leave ruined Europe and reach Palestine; the organization was called B'riha (Flight), and by the time Israel was established some 250,000 Jews, most of them from Poland, had left Eastern and Central Europe with its help.

As the battle line moved away from the Middle East, the British administration in Palestine hardened its position on the Hagana, and this, in turn, prodded the right-wing elements in the *yishuv* to greater resistance. While the Biltmore Program, adopted by the Extraordinary Conference of Zionists in New York in May 1942 and endorsed in November of that year by the Zionist Executive (the leadership of the World Zionist Organization), still envisaged the establishment of a "Jewish Commonwealth" in Palestine as achievable with the cooperation of Great Britain as the Mandatory power, by early 1944 the mood of the *yishuv* was definitely anti-British, and the violent attacks against British government institutions in Palestine, carried out by the Irgun and Lehi, were viewed with sympathy by a growing segment of the Jewish population.

One would imagine that the truculent atmosphere that enveloped Palestine in those months—comprised of such ingredients as gloom and despondency cast over us by the Holocaust, our embitterment at the anti-Zionist policies of the Mandatory power, and our ire against the Arabs, who were more and more vocal in their anti-Jewish attitude—would make it difficult if not impossible to immerse oneself in studies of an intellectual nature that had nothing to do with the issues that preoccupied the *yishuv*. But those were the days in which the saying was born, or in any case often heard, "The difficult things we do immediately, the impossible takes a little longer." Seriously speaking, and remarkably, the circumstances had on many of us, me included, precisely the opposite effect, one of energizing and invigorating. I felt it was my moral duty to exert the greatest efforts of which I was capable in my chosen field and thus to make the best contribution I could to the future of the *yishuv*, which I believed "with all my heart and with all my soul, and with all my being" was bound to come, to be great, and to lead to the development of a nation with a Hebrew culture built upon the millennial history of our ancestors in the land. How else, I asked myself, could I pull my weight? I had no military inclinations; in any case, as a married man with two children I would not have been accepted into any Jewish self-defense formations; I had even less interest in politics—what I observed of the working of the Zionist political parties in the country I found less than attractive; the only other types of activity for which I was qualified were teaching, which I found dull, and the rabbinate, against which I had an aversion going back to my Hungarian days—thus scholarly research had to be it. The muses may be silenced *inter arma*, but, I felt, the spirit of research must not, as it was not in the past, not even in the midst of the worst catastrophes that befell the Jewish people in its long and pain-studded history. I remembered the story of Rabbi Yohanan ben Zakkai, whom I had held up earlier as an example to an antagonistic audience in the Jerusalem Bet ha'Am, the great master who in the very midst of the siege of Jerusalem by the Romans was intent on one thing only: to secure the continuation of Tora-study by transferring his academy from Jerusalem to the little seaside town of Yavneh. And, closer to our own time, I thought of my great semilegendary ancestor Rashi (1040–1105—it was, of course, not he himself who was semilegendary, but the descent from him of my famous eighteenth-century rabbinical ancestors). In 1096 many of his relatives and friends fell victim to the Crusaders, who found it simpler to massacre Jews in the Rhineland than to fight Saracens in the Holy Land. But Rashi stayed on in his study in Troyes and continued to work on his great biblical and talmudic commentaries that were to secure him the position of one of the foremost, if not the foremost, medieval Jewish scholar. Not that I had the presumption of considering myself similar to Rashi in any way, but, having read several of the Rashi studies published from 1940 on in honor of the 900th anniversary of his birth and having even received a review copy from Rabbi Judah L. Fischman (later Maimon) of his *Sefer Rashi* (to my regret I never reviewed it), I was freshly aware of the greatness of the man and fancied myself following in his footsteps at least in the one respect of persevering in my studies in the midst of adversity.

Well then, what did I do during that academic year of 1943–1944, while I had no institutional affiliation? First of all, I had to shoulder many nonacademic duties. As Naomi's pregnancy with our second child advanced, I helped her in taking care of Ofra, who was an extremely alert and active child and demanded much attention. After the birth of Daphi, caring for two children placed a considerable strain on Naomi's limited physical strength; since we did not have enough money to employ a nursemaid, I had to pitch in and take over part of the parenting of our older child. I also took a share in the general household duties, such as cleaning our apartment and shopping for food, which, incidentally, helped me in getting better acquainted with members of the Oriental Jewish communities, and especially the Persian, Bukharan, and Kurdish Jews, who were our neighbors in the Bukharan Quarter and owned and ran its food stores. Although these activities did cut into the time I could have spent on my studies, compared to the full-time job I had in Haifa the work I did as a householder was negligible, and I felt happy and satisfied.

My other nonscholarly, but at least literary, activities in that year included the preparation of a new, expanded edition of the anthology of the Palestinian Hebrew short stories (originally published in 1938). Zvi Wohlmut and I got together again and selected another seventeen authors, thereby increasing the number of writers included by some sixty percent to a total of forty-four. The new edition, in two volumes, was published in 1944; since it sold well and was reprinted several times year after year, it also yielded some much-needed income. In the scholarly field I wrote two articles in English on "Jewish Folk-Cures for Barrenness" and submitted them to the London journal *Folk-Lore*, which published them in its September 1944 and December 1944–March 1945 issues. These two articles were reworkings of small parts of the material that was to go into the planned third volume of my *Man and Earth* that was never published. I also wrote an English paper on the meaning of the biblical word *'arisah* (dough or kneading trough); this was published in 1944 in the *Jewish Quarterly Review*.

I wrote an article in Hebrew titled "Naqim Yad l'Minhage Yisrael" (Let Us Erect a Memorial to Jewish Custom), which was published in the Tel Aviv daily *Hege*. (In the following year I published a different article under the same title in the Tel Aviv monthly *'Am v'Sefer.*) *Hege* was a paper intended for new immigrants whose Hebrew was rudimentary; hence, its text was vocalized, that is, the Hebrew vowel signs were added, and the less common words were followed by their German translation. In that article I explained briefly what folklore was, called the readers' attention to the rapid disappearance of folk customs and beliefs, and pointed out that the *yishuv*, and especially Jerusalem with its mosaic of Jewish communities from all over the world, was the most suitable place for doing research in that field. I wrote (the German translations in parentheses are exactly as they appeared in the paper):

> Collecting customs is one of the main tasks of the science (*Wissenschaft*) that is called, depending on the basic approach and the center of gravity (*Schwerpunkt*) of the research, folklore, ethnography, ethnology, or anthropology. (In Hebrew we can translate the first three terms as *y'di'at ha'am*, while for the fourth the Hebrew terms *y'di'at ha'adam* are suited (*passen*). These sciences . . . deal with folk-life, the life of people in a community in all its manifestations. Folk architecture, the traditional (*traditionell*) furnishings (*Möblierung*), the clothing (*Kleidung*), household utensils, work implements, musical instruments, the customs, the manners, the religious rites, the beliefs, the views (*Anschauung*), legends, proverbs (*Sprichwort*), folksongs, dances, games, charms and amulets— these constitute the multicolored (*vielfarbig*) treasures (*Schatz*) of the popular creativity called folklore. . . . The specificity of the communities is disappearing (*verschwinden*) with a disconcerting rapidity. . . . Because of the common general education, which is so valuable from the point of view of shaping (*Gestaltung*) the visage of the nation, the traditional characteristics of the various communities are becoming blurred, erased. Hence, one must not postpone until tomorrow the primary task of Jewish folklore research, the collecting of oral material. One must do this as long as there is still something to collect. . . . The Bet ha'Am in Jerusalem has begun the work of saving the last vestiges of Jewish tradition. . . . Now, for the systematic and thorough collecting of the rich storehouse of folk custom, what is required is an organized circle of researchers and interested persons who, *viribus unitis*, will carry out what individuals on their own cannot do: to save from oblivion the customs of the communities and diasporas of Israel.
>
> I first called for work in this field almost ten years ago, and from that time until today I have not ceased working on the study of Jewish folklore and trying to arouse public consciousness to become concerned with the urgency of work in this area. Hence I agreed willingly to the suggestion of the Jerusalem Bet ha'Am executive to undertake the organization of a "folklore circle" whose primary task will be to collect Jewish customs.
>
> The most urgent task is that of collecting the material. Here there are two possibilities: (a) to collect all the customs of individual communities, and to publish in separate volumes, e.g., all the customs of the Persian Jews, or all the customs of the Hungarian Jews, etc. Or (b) to collect the customs surrounding one particular event, such as, e.g., the Passover customs, of all the Jewish communities, or the marriage customs of all the Jewish communities, etc. Since the num-

ber of customs in any one community is almost unlimited, while the number of communities is limited to between ca. thirty and forty, it seems to me that the method that leads to results in the nearest future is the second one, that is, to collect one after the other groups of definite customs of all the communities. This method also seems convenient from the point of view of collecting and working up the material.

Our request to the representatives of the communities is that they help the future staff of our scientific workers to establish personal contact with individuals in their communities who are familiar with their traditions. And as for the scholars who already are working in similar fields, my request to them is: give us your help in this work with advice and deed, come and take the central places in this enterprize, criticize what there is to criticize, correct what there is to correct. Let us share our experiences, and thus clarify our ideas—in a word: let us cooperate for the sake of saving the traditional assets of the people of Israel!

My earlier call for work in folklore, mentioned in this article, was published in the March 15, 1935, issue of the Jerusalem daily *Doar haYom* under the title "HaFolqlor Mahu?" (What Is Folklore?). However, it was the 1944 article that was my first serious and concrete attempt to arouse interest in rescuing Jewish *customs* from oblivion and cooperating institutionally for that purpose.

In the spring of 1944 I got acquainted with the Hon. Edwin (later Viscount) Samuel (1898–1978), whose father, Viscount Herbert Samuel (1870–1963), had been the first British High Commissioner of Palestine from 1920 to 1925. Edwin Samuel had lived in Palestine since 1919, filled several positions in the British Mandatory Government, and published short stories and several books about governmental problems. In 1944 he became head of the governmental Palestine Broadcasting Service, and, being a connoisseur of English literature, gave a series of poetry readings on the English hour of the Jerusalem radio under the title "Voice of England." He read, in his beautiful, cultured Oxford English, poems by famous English poets and invited his listeners to enter a competition by writing him short letters indicating which of the poems they liked best and why. To listen to great English poetry was a most pleasant change and respite amidst the increasingly horrible news that reached us in those days about the fate of European Jewry, and I would tune in regularly to Samuel's program. Among all the poems he read I liked most Ernest Dowson's "Cynara," which, for some reason, struck a responsive chord in me. I responded to Samuel's invitation and wrote a letter telling him of what I felt about the poem—I have, of course, long since forgotten why I liked it and what I wrote about that highly sentimental and romantic poem, but to this day I remember its refrain line, "I have been faithful to thee, Cynara, in my fashion." To my pleasant surprise, when Samuel announced the names of the winners of his competition in the March 21, 1944, issue of the *Palestine Post*, I was listed as having won second prize. I dropped him a thank-you note and soon thereafter he invited me and Naomi to his home.

Samuel and his wife Hadassah lived on the ground floor of a house in Rashba Street in Rehavia. She was a tall and self-possessed woman, very attractive, a leader of the WIZO (Women's International Zionist Organization), a year or so older than he was. She was the daughter of Jehuda Grasovski (later Goor, 1862–1950), the Zionist pioneer and Hebrew linguist, author of important Hebrew dictionaries. Samuel himself was twelve years older than I was, in his middle forties when we met. He was a well-built, tall man, an inch or two taller than my own 6'1", with light brown hair and eyes, a ruddy complexion, a goodly nose, a wide mouth with narrow lips, and a strong chin. I still remember that we instantly took to each other. I was attracted by his friendly, matter-of-fact, restrained manner, and he, I believe, found me congenial, perhaps due to the fact that he had an interest in folk art and folklore and recognized in me the first Jewish scholar who was devoted to the study of these subjects.

In the course of that first visit Naomi and I paid to the Samuels, she mentioned that she and her sister Ada in their childhood had been the playmates of the two Samuel boys, who must have been a couple of years younger, and both Edwin and Hadassah recalled the circumstances of that early period in their children's lives.

There was at the time in Jerusalem a small folklore museum housed in part of the Citadel (the so-called David's Tower), one of the best-known landmarks in the Old City, just inside the Jaffa Gate. The museum's rather modest holdings consisted mostly of items of Palestinian Arab folk art—vessels, jars, implements, utensils, jewelry, clothes, rugs, lamps, amulets, etc. Samuel was one of the members, or possibly the chairman, of the museum's board of directors. Soon after we got acquainted, he suggested that I join the board, and I, of course, readily accepted. I am no longer quite sure about the identity of the other members of the board, but I believe that among them were Dr. Michael Avi-Yonah, who was at the time an officer of the Palestine Department of Antiquities (he was almost sixty in 1953 when, at last, he was appointed professor of classical archaeology and history of art at the Hebrew University); Professor L. A. Mayer, the historian of Muslim art at the Hebrew University; the Arab folklorist Dr. Tawfiq Canaan, whose book *Mohammedan Saints and Sanctuaries in Palestine* I greatly admired; and the British archaeologist Philip Langstaffe Ord Guy, who, until he joined the British Army in World War II, was director of the British School of Archaeology in Jerusalem.

(Let me digress here for a moment and mention that I remember Guy quite well, because, prior to my marriage, I had been an occasional guest in his house. He was married to a daughter of Eliezer Ben-Yehuda, the man who, more than anybody else, was responsible for the introduction of Hebrew as the colloquial of the *yishuv*. I found the Guys' daughter, Ruth, a charming, blue-eyed, blonde girl, very attractive. She spoke a beautiful, pure Hebrew, which was *de rigueur* in the families of Ben-Yehuda's offspring. I remember most clearly the spacious old Arab house not far from the Old City in which the Guys lived, in which the surprisingly large living room was furnished in a manner not unlike the *qāʿa* in well-to-do Arab homes, with low couches, cane-bottomed chairs, kilim rugs, beautiful large antique-brass jars, and other products of traditional Arab folk art. I liked that room very much and hoped that one day I would have such a room of my own.)

In the summer of 1945 Edwin Samuel organized a kind of informal college that he called Jerusalem Tutorial Classes. They consisted of courses intended primarily for British civil servants and other officials in Jerusalem, covering such subjects as the geography of Palestine, its history, the structure of the British administration in the country, its languages, and the like. At one of our meetings Edwin asked me whether I would be interested in giving a survey course on the ethnic groups in the population of Palestine. I was and said so, although my insufficient command of English made me somewhat apprehensive.

Preparation for that course was for me the best self-education I could have had at that time. It forced me to organize systematically information about the many subdivisions of both the Jewish and Arab sectors of the country, as well as about the many other groups that were neither Jewish nor Arab (e.g., Druze, Muslim Circassians, Christian Armenians, Ethiopians, etc.), and to present it in a coherent, logical sequence, and *in English* to boot. Although I could not know it at the time, it was this course that gave me the foundation for the classes I was to give at various universities in America on the "Peoples and Cultures of Israel" and similar courses on the Middle East as a whole.

The inaugural ceremony of the Jerusalem Tutorial Classes took place in a hall of the YMCA building, on September 25, 1945, with Mr. J. V. W. Shaw, chief secretary of the British Mandatory Government of Palestine, presiding. I sat on the dais among the other tutors. Shaw expressed his appreciation of the importance of the classes and announced that the government had allocated 100 pounds toward their expenses. After him, the Hon. Edwin Samuel, officially styled "registrar" of the classes, described their program. There were to be nine courses in the October–March term, each with ten to twelve sessions. The enrollment at that point stood at 110 students, most of them civil servants, the others British policemen, municipal officials, bank officials, Jewish Agency employees, and students. The tutors were drawn from the British, Jewish, and Arab communities. Each class was to have about 25 students.

I still remember that in my own introductory lecture I spoke in general terms about the three religious groups making up the Palestinian population and then discussed, in a preliminary fashion, the constituent elements of each, such as the various religious denominations among the Christian Arabs and non-Arabs, the townspeople, villagers (fellahin), and Bedouins among the Muslim Arabs, and the *'edoth* (communities) among the Jews.

My students were attentive and interested, and, although I must have committed atrocities in both English grammar and pronunciation and was more than occasionally hampered by searching for the proper word, all in all things went rather well. What I enjoyed most was that, for the first time in my dozen years in Palestine, I faced Englishmen not as a colonial of whom they were in charge, but as an equal, in fact, in a sense as a superior: after all I was the instructor and they the students.

In the 1948–1949 academic year Edwin Samuel became my colleague at the Dropsie College for Hebrew and Cognate Learning, since defunct but at the time a highly prestigious graduate school in Philadelphia, where we both served as visiting professors at its newly established Institute for Israel and the Middle East. In the following year Edwin returned to Jerusalem, and I, having been appointed full professor at Dropsie, stayed on. Thereafter Edwin and I remained in touch. We sent each other our books and met whenever I visited London, where he and his wife used to stay in the summer. The last time I saw him was in the House of Lords shortly before his death. He took me to the visitors' gallery, and when the session was over I had tea with him and Lady Samuel in the Lords' restaurant.

After the appearance of two volumes of my *Man and Earth* under the imprint of the Hebrew University Press and the critical acclaim they received, I felt that the time had come to launch a new attempt to obtain an academic position at the Hebrew University in Jewish folklore and ethnology. On November 4, 1943, I had an interview with the president of the university, Dr. Magnes, who had always been most friendly and helpful to me, and asked him to enable me to devote myself, as I put it, to the study of "the tribes of Israel." He declared himself willing to help, but at the same time emphasized that academic appointments depended on the rector and the senate of the university.

A few weeks later I asked for an appointment with the newly elected rector of the university, Dr. Leo Arye Mayer (1895–1959), who was professor of Near Eastern art and archaeology. Near Eastern art is to a large extent folk art—part of folk tradition and folklore—and I therefore had high hopes that Mayer would relate with sympathy to my aspiration to do research on Jewish folklore, folk custom, folk belief, and related subjects under the auspices of the university. The interview took place on January 6, 1944, and ended with Mayer's suggestion that I submit an application in writing asking for a position as a researcher of customs, beliefs, and legends current at present in the Jewish communities or preserved in the memory of their members. Three days later I submitted such an application, attaching to it an outline that amounted to a detailed research program, in fact, an inventory, of the Jewish customs, beliefs, and legends, and concluding with an appeal emphasizing the urgency of the work I planned to undertake. I wrote:

> In conclusion I wish to emphasize the importance and urgency of the work suggested above; its importance from the point of view of collecting the valuable national-popular treasure, which the universities of the world consider a task of the highest value; and its urgency due to the fact that the customs, beliefs, and legends are very rapidly disappearing in the Jewish communities. If the university responds to my proposal, this work will be carried out truly at the twelfth hour; if not, if the work is not done now, in a very few years it will no longer be possible to do it.

After submitting my proposal I had another interview with Mayer. He informed me that he had forwarded my memo to the Institute of Jewish Studies of the university, of which the various departments of Jewish studies were constituent parts. Mayer told me that the chairman of the Institute was of the opinion that before the Institute as a whole could discuss my proposal it should first obtain a recommendation from an *ad hoc* committee of three to be appointed for this purpose. However, no such committee had been appointed by September 1944. Hence, on September 25, I wrote again to Dr. Mayer, complained of the inactivity of the Institute, and repeated in writing what I had asked him orally: that he should recommend to the president of the university to act on my suggestion.

On the same day I also wrote to Dr. Magnes, informing him that, following up on his suggestion, I had submitted a memorandum to the rector in January 1944 and that in the seven months that had passed since nothing at all had been done in response. Now I repeated my suggestion and informed Dr. Magnes that Professor Buber and Professor Leon Roth (1896–1963), who was professor of philosophy at the university and had been its rector from 1940 to 1943, had in the meantime submitted their recommendations to the rector. I concluded by asking Dr. Magnes as emphatically as I felt was possible to act upon my memorandum.

It was about this time that the so-called Warburg Fellowships were established at the university for the purpose of enabling young scholars to devote themselves to the fields of their specialization. Professor Buber wrote a very warm recommendation for me and—typical of his kindness—gave me a copy, which survived in my files. The following is my literal translation of his Hebrew:

The Rector of the Hebrew University
Jerusalem

Dear Sir:

I the undersigned recommend herewith that one of the fellowships for the development of young scholars should be given to Dr. Raphael Patai.

Dr. Patai completed his studies at the University of Budapest and received in 1933 the doctoral diploma (*summa cum laude*), after examinations in Semitic languages, Persian language and literature, and the history of the Ancient Near East. In 1936 he was ordained as rabbi at the Rabbinical Seminary of Budapest. From 1933 he studied Palestinology at the Hebrew University, finished his studies in 1936, and received the doctorate (by the way: the first of the Hebrew University).

His doctoral thesis (*Water*) was largely devoted to ancient Jewish folklore. After the publication of this book (which was awarded the Bialik Prize of the Tel Aviv Municipality), Dr. Patai continued to devote himself to scholarly work and published several books and a considerable number of articles (in Hebrew and English), most of which are devoted to the customs, the beliefs, and the culture of the people of Israel.

His comprehensive book *Man and Earth*, chapters of which he gave as guest-lectures at the university and which was accepted for publication by the publishing house of the university (the undersigned was one of the readers), is a study of customs, beliefs, and legends among Israel and the nations. This study, of which so far two volumes have appeared, is the fruit of much labor. Its writing required the scholarly digestion of hundreds of books, both sources and research, and it not only shows knowledge, judgment, and scholarly method, but also gives hope of further development. Dr. Patai has excelled in a field which until now has been cultivated by almost no researcher in a scholarly and systematic manner, the field of Jewish folklore and ethnology. It seems to me that Dr. Patai is the first to use for this research the new methods that have been developed recently in the English-speaking countries and thereby he has established and enriched this new field and the science of Judaism.

Were his teacher, Professor Klein of blessed memory, still alive today, I am sure that he would find among his students no one who developed in the scholarly direction like Dr. Patai. And since the field in which he works is close to the sociology of culture (I think this is why I was asked to be a reader of his book), and since I know Dr. Patai's work intimately, I permit myself to be the one to recommend him for this fellowship. And since the direction of his work is connected with the need for thorough knowledge of the talmudic sources, I consulted with our colleague Professor Albeck, and his opinion is attested by signing together with me.

Martin Buber
Hanokh Albeck

Hanokh Albeck (1890–1972) was professor of Talmud at the Hebrew University.

On October 26, 1944, I was informed by Dr. Frederick Simon Bodenheimer (1897–1959), professor of zoology at the university and a personal friend of mine, that Dr. Magnes wanted me to submit to him a plan for the ethnological study of the Jews of Baghdad. In response, on October 29 I submitted a five-page plan to Magnes, discussing the ethnological study of Jewish communities in the Middle East in general. In it I presented a statement about the importance of ethnological research, the outline of an ethnological monograph of a Jewish community, a brief discussion of research methods, and a summation. I also sent Dr. Magnes my copy of Edward Westermarck's famous two-volume *Ritual and Belief in Morocco* and observed in my covering letter that an approach similar to the one used by Westermarck was suitable for a study of all aspects of the ethnology of the Jews of Baghdad or of any other Jewish community in the Middle East. I concluded with the remark:

To study the traditional folk-life of the Jewish communities is a most important and urgent scholarly task. An ethnological monograph covering a Jewish community must comprise both material and spiritual culture: the religious and secular life; social structure and public life; in brief: the entire way of life of the community. The study of the community must be carried out both in Eretz Israel and in its original location. The processing of the collected material and the writing of the monograph must be done in Jerusalem, where the library of the university is accessible to the researcher. The work on one community will take two to three years.

I have no record or recollection of any response from Dr. Magnes, nor of any follow-up by Professor Bodenheimer. But, at long last, in the fall of 1944, I was notified that I was awarded one of the three Warburg Fellowships. The other two recipients were Mordecai Margaliot, who from 1957 was to teach Gaonic Literature at the Jewish Theological Seminary of America in New York, and Eliahu Strauss (later Ashtor), who specialized in the history of the

Jews in Muslim lands and became professor at the Hebrew University. The stipend accompanying the fellowship was 25 pounds per month, the equivalent at the time of 75 U.S. dollars. Although this was 10 pounds less than my salary at the Technion, our expenses too were reduced since I did not have to spend money on traveling back and forth between Haifa and Jerusalem and on my food and lodging separately from my family.

Since the Warburg Fellowships were awarded and administered by the Hebrew University (it seems that Dr. Magnes was in some way directly involved with them), I was now again employed by the university in the capacity of a researcher. However, it is characteristic of the narrow-mindedness (or shall I be more charitable and say strict constructionism?) of the powers at the university that it was made clear to me and to the other two recipients of the fellowships that we were not entitled to identify ourselves as "research fellows" of the university, but only as "recipients of a research prize" (*ba'ale p'ras mehqar* in Hebrew). The distinction was a fine one, but since the university authorities insisted on making it, I felt that it indicated a withholding of the recognition warranted by my scholarly record—I had, after all, by that time no less than five books and two hundred articles to my credit. However, apart from this minor fly in the ointment, my new position was most satisfactory in every respect. I had no teaching duties, nor any other obligation, except for submitting an annual report on my work to the committee in charge of the Warburg Fellowships. As far as the work itself was concerned, I was totally my own master. I could engage in whatever research I wanted, when and how was entirely up to me, and there was nobody to tell me what to do or to control what I was doing. Had I wanted to, I could have done very little. In the event, I spent all my waking hours working hard on research tasks I set myself.

For the birth of our second child we made arrangements not in the Hadassah Hospital located on Mount Scopus—commuting was made unsafe by frequent Arab attacks—but in the Sha'are Tzedeq Hospital in midtown Jerusalem, not far from our home. The second birth, coming twenty months after the first, was much easier on Naomi. It took place on October 12, 1943. I still remember my keen sense of disappointment when I was told that the child was again a girl. Like most Jewish fathers, I wanted to have sons, at least one son, and since Naomi and I had agreed that we would have only two children, the birth of Daphne—as we called her—meant that I would have no sons to carry on the Patai name and the proud literary heritage of a long line of rabbinical, scholarly ancestors. Little did I know at that moment that within a few weeks Daphne would be as securely embedded in my heart as Ofra was, that my emotional attachment to both of them would become intense, and that many years later both my daughters would become respected authors of numerous books, and, in fact, carry on the literary heritage of the Patais.

The four years that were to pass from our return from Haifa to my leaving Jerusalem for New York were for me a time of happy family life, intellectual maturing, and intensive activity both in the scholarly fields of my choice and in promoting interest and research in the folklore, ethnology, and anthropology of the Jews. Whatever problems we had from the outside, Naomi and I faced together in complete internal harmony. Our two little daughters were a source of unending joy for both of us. The fact that I could spend most of my time working at home meant that I could actively participate in taking care of the children and also relieve Naomi of at least part of the burden of household duties.

I still remember the pleasure I had in seeing the development of Ofra and Daphi, the opening up of their intelligence, the burgeoning of their individual personalities, the growth of their charm and beauty, their gradual transformation from what my mother called plantlike beings into conscious little humans. I was, of course, convinced, in total harmony with Naomi and my parents, that they were the sweetest, most beautiful, most intelligent, and best children that had ever lived. In fact, my feelings for them were so strong that if today, after almost half a century, I think back on those days, my heart constricts with a bittersweet nostalgia. My relationship with Ofra and Daphi was to remain the best imaginable throughout the ensuing decades, but the intensity of my attachment to them in those first few years of their lives on this earth could never be duplicated in later years.

Between Naomi and me there continued to be love and harmony that in no way dimmed with the passage of years. She continued to be my faithful helpmeet who supported me in all my endeavors, decisions, plans, and projects. She followed closely with interest, appreciation, and understanding the studies I was engaged in and helped me with writing them. In addition to giving me the benefit of her wide reading and fine grasp of scholarly problems, she also assisted me in details of research. To mention only one example, traces of which still survive in my library, when I received my author's copies of the two volumes of my *Adam vaAdama*, I prepared a *Handexemplar* (a copy for my private use) of each by inserting and binding blank pages between each two of the printed pages, for the purpose of jotting down on them whatever additional material I found and thus preparing a possible future augmented edition. Many of those interlaced pages contain not notes written by me but excerpts and passages copied out from scholarly books in Naomi's hand—a surviving testimony to her reading in subjects related to my work and her active interest in it. No less important in those years of financial stringency was her full agreement with me about my decision to leave my job at the Technion and to return to Jerusalem, even though that step meant giving up what could have been a lifetime secure position and facing an uncertain future as a struggling, unemployed young scholar. And she stood by me resolutely in my disagreements with her parents, which, as far as I can recall, were renewed for some time after our return from Haifa.

I on my part tried to make Naomi's life as easy and full as possible. Her favorite occupation continued to be the same as it was in her student years: to read about the history and archaeology of the Near East and related subjects. I brought her books she wanted to read—as far as they were available in the library of the university—and tried to make sure that she should have as much time as possible for reading. When she had one of her migraine attacks—I no longer remember how frequent they were—I saw to it that she should be able to stay undisturbed for hours in our darkened bedroom (she could not tolerate light at those times), while I kept the children busy and quiet in the living room or outside the house.

It was late in 1944 or early in 1945 that we made the acquaintance of Mrs. Bath-Sheba Kesselman, which led to the only literary venture Naomi and I undertook jointly. Mrs. Kesselman was the widow of the American Zionist activist Robert Kesselman (1881–1942). Soon after she met us she asked us to write his biography and offered us a modest fee for the work. She also put at our disposal letters, notes, documents, and other material, and we spent many hours interviewing her and writing down the information she was able to give us based on her reminiscences. We actually completed the manuscript within a few months, and Naomi herself typed it. The title page of the only extant copy preserved in my files reads:

The Life and Letters of
Robert D. (Reuven David) Kesselman
By
Naomi and Raphael Patai
With the Collaboration of
Mrs. Bath-Sheba Kesselman

The 446-page typescript contains Kesselman's biography on 336 pages, followed by another 110 pages of letters exchanged between him and Justice Louis D. Brandeis and Dr. Harry Friedenwald. Mrs. Kesselman sent a copy of the finished manuscript to Dr. Magnes, and on February 12, 1946, he wrote her a beautiful letter of thanks and appreciation, of which I have a copy in my files. I made efforts to find a publisher for the book, as did Mrs. Kesselman, but we were unsuccessful, and the book was never published.

The only differences that ever emerged between Naomi and me—and they were slight ones, until, to my great surprise and dismay, she decided to leave me in the spring of 1948 in New York—were in connection with the upbringing of the children. Naomi had been brought up from her early childhood not by her mother but by English nannies, and when she herself became a mother she firmly believed that the same strictness with which those British nursemaids had treated her should be applied to our children as well. She certainly loved Ofra and Daphi as much as I did. She was, in fact, a totally devoted mother who could not do enough for the children, who incessantly sang their praises in the letters she wrote to my parents, but at the same time she felt strongly that the British-type discipline was imperative for their proper upbringing and that they must learn from the very beginning to live by definite rules. I, on the other hand, was brought up by a mother whose love for her children knew no bounds, who pampered me and let me have all the freedom I wanted, limited only by her concern about my health. Hence, this type of permissive upbringing had conditioned my own attitude to my children. Thus, I was softer than Naomi in treating Ofra and Daphi, and it was in this single area that occasional minor disagreements arose between us.

I was especially sensitive to the crying of the children. When they broke into tears my heart would bleed for them and I instantly would try everything to make them stop crying. I remember in particular one incident in which this led to an altercation between Naomi and me. Her rule, which she insisted on following, was that at a certain hour in the evening the children had to be put to bed and given a good-night kiss, the lights in their room (which was also our bedroom) were turned off, and we retired into the living room, closing the door between the two rooms. If the children went to sleep quietly—fine; if they cried before falling asleep—that, Naomi felt, was too bad but could not be helped; they just had to learn that it was an inviolable rule that they were left alone in the evening and had to go to sleep in a dark room.

Some nights the children fell asleep without crying, on others one or the other of them cried a little before going to sleep. On the latter occasions I would listen tensely to the crying, which was clearly audible through the closed door. I could easily distinguish between the voices of the two; it was in most cases the little one who cried. I had to exercise considerable self-control not to jump up, go into the dark room, and sweep up the crying baby into my arms, to hug and comfort her. I didn't do it because I recognized that Naomi's bedtime rule was correct in principle, and because the crying would stop after a few minutes.

One evening, however, when Daphne was less than a year old, she started crying after we put her to bed and just would not stop. When it had gone on for a while, I said to Naomi that I wanted to go in to see what was the matter with the child. She objected, and I stayed put. The crying continued, and it seemed to me that it grew louder and more desperate. Finally I could no longer listen to it and over Naomi's protests got up and went in to see what was wrong.

The furniture in the room that served as the bedroom for all four of us was so arranged that Daphi's crib stood right next to Naomi's desk. The crib was a high one, so that the surface of its mattress was not much lower than the top of the desk. Like all cribs, it had high sides and ends to keep the child from falling out, but the sides proved not high enough to prevent Daphi from climbing over them and up onto the desk top. When I entered the room I found her crouching at the outer corner of the desk, facing a precipice at whose bottom, far below, was the floor. She was clinging to the glass desk top for dear life and crying desperately. That time I did sweep her up into my arms, comforted her as best I could, then put her back into her crib and stayed with her until she fell asleep. Ofra had slept through the whole incident. In my anger I accused Naomi, totally unjustly, of heartlessness and I don't know what else. It was one of the very few heated altercations that took place between us. I don't remember whether or not Naomi relaxed her bedtime rules for the children after this incident.

Another of Naomi's disciplinary rules was that the children had to have a bowel movement at a certain hour every day. I suppose that this too was something demanded of her in her infancy by her English nanny. This was not a rule I had any objection to since it did not involve crying on the part of the children; it only meant that they had to sit on their potty, occasionally for quite a while, until they produced what was expected of them. At times— I remember this from the time when Ofra was a year or a year and a half old—while I was working at my desk in the living room Naomi would place the potty on a corner of the desk, seat Ofra on it, and leave her there for me to take care of the sequence. I would continue to work and, when the child was done, wipe her rosy little behind, lift her down from the desk, empty the pot, and return to my work. Thus, I can say that occasionally at least I worked on my studies with little Ofra quite literally overlooking what I wrote.

Another passing disagreement between Naomi and me about the children was that she wanted to give them a daily rubdown with cold water— again probably in memory of the treatment she had received as a child in England. Since the winter was quite severe in Jerusalem and our apartment was not very adequately heated, I objected to this. On our next visit to our pediatrician Dr. Weizmann we asked her for a ruling. She smiled and said to Naomi, "If your husband objects, don't do it." She was, evidently, not only a good physician, but also a wise person.

What else do I remember about the early childhood of Ofra and Daphi? One day, walking about in the Mahane Yehuda Quarter of Jerusalem, where the HaMa'arav Press was located, I noticed in front of a store a set of small children's furniture; it consisted of a small table and two tiny wickerwork arm chairs. They were just the size suitable for children between the ages of two and four. Although my finances were rather limited, I could not resist and on the spur of the moment bought the set, then had quite a task in lugging it home. The children were happy with it, and thereafter they often sat at the small table engaged in drawing with their colored crayons and later copying the letters of the Hebrew alphabet.

Twice in the course of those four years between 1943 and 1947 Naomi's health was so poor that, probably at the suggestion of our friend and family physician Dr. Muntner, we decided to send the children to a children's home for a few weeks. The first time we took them to Shekhunat Boruchov, where, in the immediate neighborhood of my parents' house, Mrs. Mamlok was taking in a few children. Her husband had a pharmacy in the same house in which they lived, and both of them were kind and good people under whose care the children felt fine. The place also had the advantage that my parents could go over there to see how the children were, and they in turn could visit my parents. In one of her undated letters Mother wrote me (in Hungarian):

> It is Friday morning, I am writing to you in a hurry, in Hungarian, to reassure Naomi that the children are very well, they behave well, are very sweet, Ofra is a beauty, Daphi a charmer. [Here Father added in Hebrew:] According to the testimony of the "management" of the kindergarten I obtained today, "they behave very well." Remark by Grandpa.

After his serial prostate operations Father was granted a grace period of some five or six years before the onset of the Alzheimer's disease that devastated him and Mother until his death in 1953. During those years he and Mother remained in Shekhunat Boruchov. Father devoted himself to literary work, wrote some poetry in Hebrew, and, in particular, translated some of his Hungarian books into Hebrew and saw to their publication. In his gradually weakening physical and mental condition he found solace in religion: he became religiously observant again, of which the most visible sign was that he started to wear a skullcap (*yarmulke*), something he had not done since, as a teenager, he had left his yeshiva and started studying in a Catholic high school in a Hungarian country town. He also resumed going to synagogue—there was one nearby—on Friday nights and Saturday mornings, and in his letters he began to use religious terminology and traditional pious abbreviations more and more frequently. As for Mother, her life came to be centered on Father's health and was filled with concern about her children and grandchildren. But she also took up writing again: in the mid-1940s she wrote, in German, a book-length account of Father's illness and of his experiences at the Hadassah Hospital, where he was such a frequent guest. This manuscript has remained unpublished to this day.

About the same time my parents vacated their five-room apartment in what the family referred to as "the big house" in Shekhunat Boruchov, to enable my sister and her architect husband, George (Mordecai) Koigen (they got married in 1941), and their two daughters to occupy it. They themselves moved over into the neighboring "small house," into one of its two three-room apartments. Mother found this arrangement ideal in every respect: she and Father now lived next to Évi and her family, and she was able to spend as much time as she wanted in the company of her beloved daughter and grandchildren. The proximity of Évi was a great moral and practical support for Mother in coping with what proved to be Father's final, tragic illness.

To what extent children can enrich the lives of parents I experienced from the very time of my daughters' births. A few years later, when they started to understand stories told to them, one of the greatest pleasures I had was to sit down with them and tell the kind of story they loved to hear. All four of us would have an early dinner (the main meal of the day was lunch), and after it was over I would switch on the dome-shaped brass "Arabian Nights" lamp that was suspended over the sofa. Usually, even before I could ask them what story they wanted to hear, they would say, almost in unison, *Abbatov, sapper lanu sippur Puntzi!* ("Gooddaddy, tell us a Puntzi story)—*Abbatov* (for *Abba tov*, good Daddy) was the way they always addressed me. Both Ofra and Daphi loved Puntzi dearly, and more than once I overheard them telling each other something they invented about him.

Those minutes I spent with them most evenings under the spell of the magic lamp were the high point of the day for the children and, unbeknownst to them, also for me. What tales I told them about Puntzi I have long forgotten, but the recurrent scene itself, although I was inside it, I can still see as if from the outside: I am sitting on the sofa with the two children at my sides, all of us basking in the red glow of the lamp, their little faces turned up toward me as they are listening with rapt attention.

On the last day I spent in Palestine, before I boarded the ship in Haifa (on October 5, 1947), I wrote a letter to Naomi and enclosed a Puntzi story for the children. I gave the letter to my friend Colin Malamet, who was with me in Haifa, to take back to Jerusalem. I don't remember what I wrote in that letter, but Naomi, in the first letter she addressed to me in America (it was written piecemeal, dated October 3, 4, 5, 6, 7, 8, and 9, 1947, and contained sixteen pages—one of the shorter letters she wrote to me in the two months after I left Jerusalem and before she joined me in New York), reported how the children reacted to receiving the story (I am translating from her Hebrew):

Oct. 5, 1947; 6 in the evening

Since I last wrote to you, my beloved boy, several hours have
passed. In the meantime . . . I went out with the children for a walk
. . . And, imagine, during the short time we were away somebody came
by our apartment (Malamet?) and left your letter under the door.
Thank you for the letter, it was so very good to see your writing and to
hear from you—it was as if you had been actually here. I read the letter
quietly, sitting on the sofa, and then went out to the kitchen where

Daphi was busy mashing bananas for the children's meal. I read out to her what you wrote about Puntzi. You should have seen her eyes! She listened with such a serious and sad expression in her eyes that I thought she would start to cry. But in the end she began to smile, slowly, slowly, and said nothing. You know, Raphael, that little one misses you very much. You loved her and played with her, and now she really misses it. I don't believe I can fill your place for her, not even a little bit. After all, I have always been here; but you, who showed her more love than to all the rest of the family, are away.

Then I went and read out the Puntzi story to Ofra—Daphi quickly came in to hear the story a second time. Ofra was very happy about Puntzi, about his trip to America, and about the lamp with which he lighted up the sea at night for himself! She laughed a lot and was so happy!

Now the two little ones are downstairs at the Kleins, it is the eve of Simhat Tora, and they went down with their little flags to enjoy the feast. I am lying on the couch and writing to you—my chief occupation for the time being . . . I see you in my mind's eye on the sea, on the nocturnal sea. And I dream—that I too stand there at the railing, on the deck, and watch the sea and the night. Do you feel well? How is your cabin? Are you warm enough? To think that I won't hear from you now for at least three weeks! (Somebody just rang the bell! Who can it be?)

8 in the evening

I continue my letter after a rather long interruption. It was Malamet at the door. I was glad to see him—he told me about you, about the hotel in which you and he stayed, the movie, the visit to the Hochfelds, what you ate, what you did, and the like. He promised to bring me soon the snapshots he took of you on Mount Carmel—what a pleasant surprise! The balloons you asked him to get for the girls he will buy and bring next time. You are sweet . . .

The girls returned happy and satisfied from the Simhat Tora dances. I bathed them, fed them, and put them to bed. Ofra behaves "really" like a mature person—it seems she feels that now that we three have remained alone, "without *Abbatov*," she must be a *Mensch* [human being]. Daphi, on the other hand, was so amusing. She told Ofra in the kitchen stories that she invented. They both laughed a lot, and in the end Ofra said, "But this is not true! There is no such thing!" Whereupon Daphi, the little jewel, said, literally, "Of course it is not true! If you look into my eyes you will see that I *really* am lying to you!" And she broke into her gurgling laughter.

The Palestine Institute of Folklore and Ethnology

My memory is so vague about the initial steps I undertook to found an institute for the study of Jewish folklore that I can tell the story of that phase of my activities only on the basis of those few news items that were published about it in the Palestinian press.

In February 1944 I must have suggested to my friends T. Ben Hefetz and David Avisar, the two active executives of the Jerusalem Bet ha'Am, that we establish a circle for the study of Jewish folk customs—this much I can conclude from the fact that in March of that year the Jerusalem weeklies *Ha'Olam* and *Hed Y'rushalayim* informed their readers that at the initiative of the Bet ha'Am such a circle was launched with two lectures given by me, that it would be directed by me, and that it was planned that scholars and researchers from all communities should participate in its work. The announcement also requested the cooperation of the executive committees of all the communities in Jerusalem, stated that the meetings of the circle would be held every Sunday at 7:00 P.M. at 3 Ben-Yehuda Street, room 3, and that the phone number of the circle was 4984. (I would love to know who put the room at our disposal.)

Three weeks later the papers repeated the announcement with a change: they now stated that the Jerusalem Bet ha'Am had organized a circle for the study of Jewish folklore (i.e., not only folk custom), that at the request of the Bet ha'Am I had agreed to serve as its scientific director, and that a meeting of community leaders would take place at 3 Ben-Yehuda Street on April 11, 1944. On April 16 the papers, including the Tel Aviv daily *HaZman*, reported that during the half-holiday of Passover a meeting of community leaders had taken place, with the participation of the Sephardi chief rabbi of Palestine, Ben-Zion Meir Hay Ouziel:

> After opening remarks by Mr. D. Avisar, his reverence Rabbi Ouziel greeted those assembled and reminisced about his time as chief rabbi of the Salonika community, of which only a few survivors have remained. He stressed that it was a duty and a *mitzva* to preserve the memory of the customs of the communities that are about to be forgotten in the wake of the great destruction. Dr. R. Patai gave an instructive lecture about the importance scholarly folkloristic work had among the nations of the world, and said: "We have the special duty to create a central institution whose task will be to collect the customs of Israel as long as there is still time to do it." It was resolved to establish an institute for the study of folk customs.

The Tel Aviv daily *HaBoqer* (April 17, 1944) gave somewhat more details. It stated that Moshe Attias, T. Ben Hefetz, Z. Kotler, Y. Molkho, Dr. Meizel, R. Kohen, and Dr. H. Schmetterling participated in the discussion and that it was resolved to publish an annual volume devoted to this study.

Of the other papers that reported about the meeting, only the Tel Aviv daily *HaTzofe* (of April 20, 1944) came to my attention.

The next clipping that has survived in my files is from May 12, 1944, issue of the Jerusalem weekly *Hed Y'rushalayim*. Under the title "Institute for Folklore in Jerusalem" it stated:

> We welcome the idea conceived by circles close to the Bet ha'Am in Jerusalem to found there a special institute for folklore. There is a society by this name in Tel Aviv, but it studies mainly written sources, while the Jerusalem Institute, which will be headed by the folklore expert Dr. Raphael Patai, will have as its task to research mainly the oral sources: customs, songs, proverbs, etc. All this is fast disappearing from among the tribes of Israel that had been so rich, each in its own particular folklore, and if we don't hurry to study and to record it we shall undoubtedly miss the opportunity. To our regret there is no interest in our midst in this matter: our lecturers and writers "please themselves in the brood of aliens" [this is a quote from Isaiah 2:6] and concentrate on the customs of fellahin and bedouin (see, for instance, the plan of summer courses in the Jerusalem seminar of workers); but until now we have not studied properly the customs of our brethren who came from various countries. Let us hope that the Jerusalem institute will make straight that which is crooked [reference to Ecclesiastes 1:15]. [Signed] Sh. Sh.

About the same time I sent out an invitation in the name of the "preparatory committee of the Institute of Jewish Folklore, affiliated with the Jerusalem Bet ha'Am," to a meeting that was to take place in May 23, 1944, in the Bet haHalutzot (Women Pioneers' Hostel) at 18 Ibn Gabirol Street in Jerusalem. Since this institution was headed by Rachel Yannait (Mrs. Yitzhaq Ben-Zvi), I must assume that I had requested her to put its premises at our disposal and that she agreed. In the program were opening remarks by Yitzhaq Ben-Zvi, chairman of the Va'ad Leumi; a lecture by me on "The Value of Folklore as a Scholarly Discipline"; a talk by David Avisar on folk life in Hebron; and a report on the work of the preparatory committee by Yitzhaq Molkho. It concluded with resolutions and elections. I no longer remember what transpired at the meeting, but the May 26 issue of *Hed Y'rushalayim* and the May 29 issue of the *Palestine Post*, as well as other papers, reported that Chief Rabbi Ouziel, Mr. Yitzhaq Ben-Zvi, and Dr. Max Grunwald, the veteran folklorist, were elected as honorary presidents; D. Avisar, Molkho, Tuvya Z. Miller, Dr. M. Zobel, Dr. Joseph J. Rivlin, Dr. Moshe Shulvas, and Mr. T. Ben Hefetz were elected to the executive committee; and Dr. R. Patai was elected director of research. The executive committee was entrusted with the task of setting up a council.

Of what followed next I happen to have retained some general recollection. None of those present at the meeting were either able or willing to undertake any work for the Institute, and hence it fell to me to do everything.

I sought out those who were designated (rather than actually elected) as officers and obtained their *ex post facto* acceptance. All of them were willing to lend their names but not to do any work. Thus it developed that, apart from the moral value represented by the use of the names of respected scholars and public figures, I got no actual help from anyone, and I alone organized and subsequently managed the affairs of the Institute, without receiving any remuneration.

Among the people thus involved in the "work" of the Institute and its journal (see below) I want to mention in particular Dr. Max Grunwald (1871–1953), one of the great figures in Jewish folklore studies, who not only readily agreed to be one of the honorary presidents, but also contributed more studies to its journal than anybody else except me. Grunwald had served as a rabbi in Hamburg and Vienna and settled in Jerusalem in 1938. He was a prolific and many-sided scholar, but his major interest was Jewish folklore. In 1897 he founded in Hamburg the Gesellschaft für jüdische Volkskunde and edited its *Mitteilungen* (1897–1922) and *Jahrbuch* (1923–1925). After he settled in Jerusalem the sixty-seven-year-old widower was a lonely figure in an intellectual environment in which his field of specialization —Jewish folklore, to which he had devoted his entire life—was totally neglected, and hence the contribution he had made to it was unappreciated. When I went to him (in 1944) to ask him to be one of the three honorary presidents of the Institute, the seventy-three-year-old Grunwald almost burst into tears, blessed me, and wished me all possible luck in my undertaking that, he said, brought back to him the memory of his own early years when, as a young rabbi, he founded his society of Jewish folklore. He promised to cooperate with me to the best of his ability, and, in fact, among all the honorary presidents, executives, and council members of the Institute (who numbered no less than 50 by 1946), he was the one who most generously contributed articles to its journal. His intensive participation in the work of the Institute was the occasion of numerous visits I paid to him, and I like to think that the attention he received from me made those late years in his life more zestful and more interesting than they would have been otherwise.

When Dr. Grunwald's seventy-fifth birthday approached, I told him that I wanted to make the forthcoming issue of *Edoth* a double one and dedicate it to his jubilee. He was visibly touched, and when I asked him to contribute a brief memoir he readily agreed. His reminiscences, titled "Folklore and Myself," were published in *Edoth* 2:1–2 (October 1946–January 1947). In them he recalls that his interest in Jewish folklore was awakened in 1895 by two old women who were his first neighbors in Hamburg: the widow of Berman Bernays, whose daughter Martha married Sigmund Freud, and Klärchen Hirsch, who was an inexhaustible source of Jewish proverbs and sayings. All in all, that brief article reads like a sketch of Jewish intellectual life in Germany at the turn of the century.

Dr. Grunwald's reminiscences are preceded by a two-page appreciation of the man and his work, in which I wrote: "In my conversations with him in the course of several years, and especially since the foundation of the Institute, I had occasion repeatedly to listen to his utterances and views on the place of folklore in the culture and national life of the Jewish people: 'Folklore research fosters the national spirit. . . . It is the customs that kept Judaism alive for thousands of years. . . . One must revive the customs. . . . Only by revitalizing the customs can the survival of Israel be assured. . . . '" Then I went on to show that this nationalistic approach to the study of folklore was in full keeping with the one that was prevalent until World War II among the European folklore scholars. And I concluded by saying that Dr. Grunwald could derive satisfaction from "seeing in Jewish Palestine a new generation of folklorists who look upon him as the founder of their discipline and are ready to face new challenges."

When I told Dr. Grunwald that I planned to dedicate a double issue of *Edoth* to him, he also offered to contribute to its increased publishing costs. What he had in mind was to enlist the help of his son, Dr. Kurt Grunwald, who was a banker, an economist, an author, and a public figure in Jerusalem. However, since by that time I had secured sufficient funds for the publication of *Edoth* from various public sources, I was in the fortunate position of being able to turn down his generous offer. Instead, I suggested to him that he might try to interest his son in establishing a Max Grunwald chair of Jewish folklore at the Hebrew University. I don't know whether Dr. Grunwald ever discussed this idea with his son, but in 1974 Kurt Grunwald endowed a chair at the Hebrew University, named the Max and Margaretta Grunwald Chair of Folklore.

Much of the recognition reaped by a new scholarly institution depends on the prestige of the people involved with it. Hence, to facilitate my undertaking I felt that it would be advantageous if I would enhance my own standing in the scholarly world outside Palestine and applied for fellowship in the Royal Anthropological Institute of Great Britain and Ireland. I was duly elected a Fellow on October 24, 1944, and thereafter, for a few years at least, I proudly added the letters "FRAI" after my name when it appeared in print.

In my capacity as director of research of the Institute, whose foundation was resolved by a small and rather informal meeting but which did not yet exist in reality, I was faced with two major tasks. One was to enlist more members in the executive committee and to set up a broad-based council; the other, to obtain funds so as to be able to embark on a publication program that, for lack of funds sufficient for the employment of paid re-

עדות

רבעון לפולקלור ואתנולוגיה

שנה א׳	תש״ה
חוברת א׳	תש״ו

התוכן:

הוצאת המכון הארצישראלי לפולקלור ואתנולוגיה ירושלים

E D O T H

(„C O M M U N I T I E S")
A QUARTERLY FOR FOLKLORE AND ETHNOLOGY

VOLUME I
NUMBER I

OCTOBER
1 9 4 5

CONTENTS

PUBLISHED BY THE PALESTINE INSTITUTE OF FOLKLORE
AND ETHNOLOGY JERUSALEM

searchers, was the only way I could envisage to stimulate research. Since I did all the work for the Institute, I felt I could take it upon myself to make all the decisions in connection with it on my own. Thus, when I came to the conclusion that, in addition to the three members of the "presidium," Rabbi Ouziel, Mr. Yitzhaq Ben-Zvi, and Dr. Max Grunwald, it would be useful also to have Rabbi Judah L. Zlotnick of Johannesburg, South Africa, as an honorary president, I offered him the honor without consulting anybody. He accepted and in the event not only contributed to the publications of the Institute, but was most helpful in obtaining funds for it from South African Jewish institutions. Rabbi Zlotnick (1887–1962) had been the director of the South African Board of Jewish Education since 1938 and was a folklorist of renown. On the occasion of his sixtieth birthday I dedicated a double issue of *Edoth* to him (April–July 1947). In 1949 Rabbi Zlotnick made his *'aliya* to Israel and changed his name to Avida. He contributed several articles to *Edoth* and a volume to the Studies in Folklore and Ethnology series of the Institute.

The foundation of the Institute did not proceed without internal crises and difficulties. The two leaders of the Jerusalem Bet ha'Am who had lent me a hand in the first steps, David Avisar and T. Ben Hefetz, resigned from its committee—I no longer remember for what reason. A few more members of the originally elected committee also resigned. Their places were taken by others, and in the third issue of *Edoth* (July 1946) I was able to list more than forty members of its council who resided in Jerusalem, Tel Aviv, Haifa, Rehovoth, London, Johannesburg, and Chicago, and later members residing in Pittsburgh, New York, Leeds, Oxford, and Melbourne.

The first item I wanted to realize in the agenda of the Institute, whose final name I decided should be Makhon AtziYisr'eli l'Folqlor v'Etnologiya in Hebrew and Palestine Institute of Folklore and Ethnology in English, was the launching of a journal. To be able to do so, I felt I needed the cooperation of a scholar who had greater seniority than I and was a respected figure in the Jerusalem community. Dr. Joseph J. Rivlin, whom we have met earlier, filled the bill perfectly. I suggested to him that he and I jointly should be co-editors of the Institute's journal: when I assured him that I would do all the work and would only consult him when it came to the acceptance of items to be published in the journal, he agreed. Typical of his modesty and decency was that he stipulated that my name should be listed first and his second as co-editors.

Next there was the question of the title of the journal. I suggested *Edoth* *("Communities"): A Quarterly for Folklore and Ethnology*, and Dr. Rivlin agreed—this was the first thing about which I consulted him. Once this was settled, I cast around for an emblem or logo that would express in the shorthand of a simple image what the journal (and the Institute) was about. I had by that time begun to collect Jewish amulets; taking as the basis the shape of the well-known *khamse* I designed an emblem consisting of the stylized outline of a hand with the Star of David in its middle, which subsequently appeared on all issues of *Edoth*, as well as on all the other publications of the Institute. Incidentally, the word *khamse* literally means "five" in Arabic (it would be *hamesh* in Hebrew), but the term has been preempted for the designation of a hand-shaped amulet with five fingers by both the Arabs and the Jews in Arab lands.

Once the decision was made to publish a quarterly I began to approach scholars as well as laymen, both in Palestine and abroad, requesting articles for publication. The response was immediately most satisfactory and remained so throughout the three years of the journal's existence. I was never in a position to have to worry about lack of material; on the contrary, after the first issue saw the light of day I always had more contributions than I could accommodate. This was, to a considerable extent, due to the editorial policy I adopted from the very outset: I wanted to publish in *Edoth* not only contributions by scholars—many of whom, even if not folklorists, were able and willing to supply articles of folkloristic interest—but also by nonscholars who had some knowledge of customs and beliefs in a certain Jewish community for the simple reason that they belonged to it or happened to have acquaintance with it. This, of course, meant that I had to work with them closely, and in many cases also to help them with writing their articles, something that I always enjoyed doing.

As for the second major task I was faced with, securing the finances for the publications program, I found it difficult but not insurmountable. First of all, the expenses in connection with the publications were minimal. They consisted of nothing but printing costs and mailing. All the work, from soliciting articles and editing to addressing and mailing out the copies to the subscribers, was done by me with Naomi's help and, of course, without any remuneration. As for institutional support, the inside cover of the first issue (October 1945) of *Edoth* carries this note: "This issue of *Edoth* was printed with the help of the Yitzhaq Leib and Rachel Goldberg Fund." I no longer remember anything about how I managed to obtain financial aid from the Goldberg Fund for this purpose—by that time Mrs. Tolkowsky must have ceased her opposition to the allocation of a modest amount to a scholarly venture headed by her son-in-law. From the July 1946 issue on the name of my father-in-law, S. Tolkowsky, appeared among the Tel Aviv members of the Institute's council. From the January 1946 issue *Edoth* was published with the support of the Rabbi Kook Foundation of the Mizrahi Organization. In the course of its short lifespan the journal also enjoyed the support of the Hebrew Association of South Africa and the American Fund for Palestine Institutions.

However, the sum total of the grants received from all these funds was still not quite enough to cover the expenses of printing *Edoth*. In order to supplement our financial base, I obtained ads from a few publishing houses and bookstores, as well as from a few commercial companies. All the advertisements together took up two pages in each issue of *Edoth*, placed between the Hebrew text of the articles and their English summary.

The lead article of the first issue of *Edoth* was titled "Jewish Folklore and Ethnology: Problems and Tasks." In it I made a programmatic statement of what at the time I considered the main agenda of research in those two fields. I cast my net far afield and included not only customs, beliefs, and folk literature, but also dialect studies and even physical anthropology. Half a year later I published an English translation of that article in the January–March 1946 issue of the *Journal of American Folklore*.

While working as editor of *Edoth* and factotum of the Institute, I was still able to engage in anthropological fieldwork. The community I studied was that of the Jews of Meshhed in Jerusalem. Meshhed, the holy city of Shī'ite Islam, is the capital of Khorasan, the easternmost province of Iran. The history of its Jewish community dates back to 1740, when Nadir Shah settled forty Jewish families in the city. The community grew rapidly, until, in 1839, it was attacked by a fanatical mob and given the choice between explusion and conversion to Islam. Many chose to leave, and a considerable number of them settled in several cities of neighboring Afghanistan, where they materially contributed to the revival of Jewish life. Those who remained converted to Islam, and from that time on became known as Jadīd al-Islām (New Muslims). Outwardly they scrupulously observed, as they had to, all the tenets of Islam, but in secret they continued to adhere to their Judaism. How they managed to maintain themselves as a separate community, to organize a secret school for their children in which they taught them Hebrew, to conduct secret synagogue services, and to observe all the commandments of Judaism is one of the most fascinating chapters in the history of the Jewish people, matched only by the story of the Marranos of Spain. Before the end of the nineteenth century many Jews from Meshhed settled in Jerusalem, where they soon came to form the large Meshhedi community, with two impressive synagogues in the Bukharan Quarter, where I lived from 1940 to 1947.

Mr. Ismailoff (because of their commercial contact with Russia many Meshhedi Jews adopted surnames ending in *-off*), in whose house I rented an apartment, was himself a Meshhedi Jew, and I think he was the first to call my attention to his community. Subsequently, in the course of my exploratory visits to the synagogues in the Bukharan Quarter, I went several times to the two Meshhedi synagogues and there made the acquaintance of the head of the community, Farajullah Nasrullayoff. Like many Meshhedi Jews, Farajullah was a rug merchant and spent much of his time sitting in his store in Geulah Street. His Hebrew was good as far as reading and comprehension were concerned, but he had difficulty in speaking it. He was willing to spend time with me in his store, where customers were few and far between, and with the help of his eldest son (who had changed his family name to Levian) I managed to obtain from him a considerable amount of information about the history and way of life of the Meshhedi Jews. Mr. Levian translated my Hebrew questions into Persian for his father and then translated his Persian answers into Hebrew for me. I wrote up much of what I thus learned from Mr. Nasrullayoff in several articles published in *Edoth*, covering such subjects as the Jewish education of the Meshhed Jadīdim, their marriage customs, and their folktales. In addition, in 1945, another leading Meshhedi family, the Aharonoffs, planned to publish a booklet to commemorate one of its sons, Raphael, who had died in 1943 in a traffic accident at the young age of twenty-five, and asked me to write a study about the Meshhed Jews that would be suitable for the memorial booklet. I wrote a paper entitled "Historical Traditions and Mortuary Customs of the Jews of Meshhed," which was published as a booklet that very year. The information on which I based that article was supplied by Mr. Nasrullayoff, Mr. Yitzhaq Gohari, and other members of the community.

In 1946, after I had studied the Jews of Meshhed in Jerusalem for well over a year, I wanted to visit Meshhed in order to find out how the remnants of the community lived in their old hometown. My Meshhedi informants in Jerusalem did have contact with their relatives back in Meshhed, and from them I gathered that, after the end of World War II, the situation of the Jadīdim had considerably improved, in the sense that they came to occupy a kind of intermediary position between the strict Marranism of the past and open adherence to Judaism. What this precisely meant was difficult to establish on the basis of what my Meshhedi informants in Jerusalem knew from letters from Meshhed. Hence, I felt that a study-trip to Meshhed was in order. The problem was that I had no money for the expenses of such a trip and therefore thought that I would apply to the World Jewish Congress for funding. Before writing to Dr. Stephen Wise, president of the WJC, I asked Yitzhaq Ben-Zvi, president of the Va'ad Leumi, who was one of the patrons of the Institute, for a recommendation. He instantly complied with my request and answered (in Hebrew):

October 23, 1946

Dear Dr. Patai:

Enclosed I am sending you the promised letter which you can attach to your letter to Dr. Wise, president of the World Jewish Congress.

Also, I can inform you that the day before yesterday I received a visit from Dr. Arye Tartakower from America, who, as you know, is a member of the presidium or executive of the World Jewish Congress.

Perhaps you should see him, and talk to him about your trip to Persia.

Yours sincerely,
Y. Ben-Zvi

The attached letter read as follows:

25th October, 1946

Dr. Stephen Wise, President,
World Jewish Congress,
1834 Broadway,
New York.

Dear Dr. Wise,

In compliance with the request of my friend Dr. Raphael Pattay [sic], Director of the Palestine Institution of Folklore and Chemography [sic], I wish to say a few words of personal appreciation of Dr. Pattay's personality and his scheme.

I am deeply interested in the conditions and fate of remote Jewish communities, and especially in those of the community of Marranos who have secretly upheld their faith for over a century. A great many members of this community—no less than one thousand—have overcome all obstacles and come to Palestine to live here openly as Jews. However, some thousands had to remain in their native town of Mashhad. They practice their usual way of living, but are all firm in their resolve to return to their people and its national homeland. This phenomenon calls for research. Moreover, it is imperative to strengthen the bonds between them and the Yishuv and to help them in their struggle for an openly Jewish existence and mode of living.

I do not doubt that Dr. Pattay is the very person competent to carry out such research work, and I believe that he will succeed in finding the most suitable way of linking these Marranos with the Yishuv and the entire nation, in order to strengthen their spirit toward the organisation of their spiritual life as Jews and as an integral part of the people of Israel.

I should be very glad if the World Jewish Congress Executive would enable Dr. Pattay to carry out his mission. Naturally there still remains the question whether this is just the suitable time, considering events in

Iran; but before all, it would be necessary to hear from you whether the World Jewish Congress endorses this scheme. The problem of *the time* suitable for Dr. Pattay's journey could be discussed as a secondary issue.

Yours sincerely,
I. Ben-Zevie,
President

To my regret no letters exchanged between me and Stephen Wise have survived in my files, nor do I have any recollection of the steps I undertook in connection with my scheme to visit Meshhed. In the extant family letters there is only one single reference to it. In an undated letter Mother wrote to Naomi and me (in German), probably in the fall of 1946, she asks, "What is the situation with your so-called stipend, Gyurikám? And the trip to Meshhed? The events in Hungary show how confused the situation is there." For reasons I can no longer recall my plan to visit Meshhed never materialized.

Yitzhaq Ben-Zvi, let me add here, was always ready to help the work of the Institute. On January 3, 1947, I wrote to him and asked him to recommend the Institute to the American Fund for Palestinian Institutions. He answered by return mail (in Hebrew):

Jan. 5, 1947

Dear Dr. Patai:

This is to acknowledge receipt of your letter of Jan. 3 concerning the American Fund for Palestinian Institutions. I think you should apply directly to the Palestinian advisory committee of the Fund, in the name of the Palestine Institute of Folklore and Ethnology, and state the amount needed. When I have a copy of your letter in my hands, I can turn privately to Messrs. Soloveitchik, Simon, and Passman.

Yours sincerely,
Y. Ben-Zvi

I must have followed up Ben-Zvi's advice. I don't remember doing it, but in the April–July 1948 issue of *Edoth* brief notices were published to the effect that the American Fund for Palestinian Institutions had allocated a grant of $2,400 to the Institute for the year 1948, donated a wire recorder, and organized a series of lectures for me in various American cities to discuss the importance of ethnological research among the Jewish communities. Correspondence preserved in my files indicates that the Fund allocated to the Institute $400 for 1947, and $2,000 for 1948, and, in addition, covered the expenses of lectures I gave about "Palestine—the Jewish Melting Pot" and "The Culture of New Palestine" in several American cities. In February and March 1948 I sent material for *Edoth* from New York directly to the Azriel Press in Jerusalem, and that last issue was seen through the press by Dr. Rivlin, Saul Angel, and Colin Malamet. Until the end of 1948 I still made sustained efforts to continue the publication of *Edoth*, which, with the assistance of the American Fund for Palestinian Institutions, would have been financially feasible. But my academic commitments made it impossible for me to return to Jerusalem, and in my absence there was nobody there who would have been able and willing to take over the editorial responsibilities from me. Thus, the quarterly, and with it the Institute itself, quietly expired.

The year 1947 was a watershed in my academic career. It was the year in which I moved from Jerusalem to New York, and in which, in addition to my books and articles in Hebrew, my first English book saw the light of day. I had completed its manuscript, titled *Man and Temple in Ancient Jewish Myth and Ritual* in 1946, and sent it to Dr. Harold H. Rowley, who at the time was professor of Semitic languages and literature at the University of Manchester, a foremost biblical scholar, and adherent of the British Myth and Ritual school. My acquaintance with Rowley dated from the first issue of *Edoth* (October 1945): he sent me some interesting comments on one of the articles. Rowley liked my manuscript and sent it on to the Edinburgh publisher Thomas Nelson, who immediately accepted it and brought it out in the summer of 1947. That slight book was hailed by scholarly critics in Europe and America as an important contribution to our understanding of the religious world of Judaism in the Second Temple period, and, among other things, brought me the friendship of Robert Graves and thus ultimately led to the writing of our joint book, *Hebrew Myths*. As to what I set out to demonstrate in that book, it is best described in the words of a summary I appended as part of a postscript to its second edition, published by Ktav in New York, in 1967:

> At various levels of cultural and religious sophistication, man has developed sets of rituals performed with a view to influencing nature or natural forces and elements in his favor, by showing them what he expected them to do, or by cajoling them into fulfilling his wishes. The mythical correlate of this type of ritual is the attribution of human-like qualities, acts, and behavior to the forces and elements of nature (Chapter I).
>
> The greatest and most popular annual feast performed in the Second Temple of Jerusalem, the so-called "Joy of the House of Water Drawing," was a fine example of such a ritual. All the acts performed, and first and foremost the ceremony of water libation, had one central purpose: to bring about the onset of the autumnal rains on which depended the welfare and the very existence of the people. This purpose was subserved by the performance of a rich array of rites which symbolically but unmistakably indicated the natural phenomena they were

supposed to bring about: favorable winds, thunder and lightning, and, most importantly, rain—good, rich and soft rain. One of the many rites performed was that of "lightheadedness," i.e. the indulgence in sexual licence, whose ritual purpose was to induce the rain to copulate with the earth (Chapter II).

The mythological counterpart of these rituals was twofold: one type of myths told about the creation of the world, about the primal separation by God of the Upper Male Waters from the Lower Female Waters, and the ceaseless yearning of these two lustful elements to reunite: when it rained, their desire was actually achieved. The other told about the place and role of the Temple in the great divine cosmogonical and cosmological scheme: the Temple was the center of the whole universe, the navel of the earth; its foundations pressed down upon the Female Waters of Tehom, the primeval abyss, and its underground shafts reached down into its very depths. Also, the Temple was located on the highest peak on earth, very near heaven and facing its heavenly counterpart, the Sanctuary on High. Therefore, the ritual performed in the Temple, not only the ritual of Water Libation and its attendant ceremonies, but any ritual, had an unfailing, direct, and immediate effect on the world, on the order and functioning of nature (Chapter III).

Moreover, the Temple symbolically represented the entire universe, and each and every rite performed in it affected that part or aspect of nature of which the rite itself was reminiscent. In fact, the function of the Temple was of such basic importance that the very existence of the entire world depended on it. According to the Talmud, the destruction of the Second Temple (70 C.E.) resulted in the gravest disturbance in the natural order, and thereafter the fertility of Palestine was reduced to a mere fraction of its former riches (Chapter IV).

However, the functioning of the natural order was believed to have depended not solely on the regular and precise performance of the Temple ritual but also on the conduct of the people, particularly of its leaders, outside the sacred precincts. There existed, it was believed, an inner, a sympathetic connection between human conduct and the behavior of the natural forces. Sins, i.e. improper or illicit human acts, brought about improper or illicit occurrences in nature—it was in this view that the original, basic sanctions that made for religious conformity were anchored. In the earliest form of this religious imperative, the assumption was that the greatest of all sins was fornication, that is to say any form of illicit sexual intercourse, because by the inexorable laws of sympathy such transgressions caused similar irregular interactions between the male and female elements of nature: droughts, floods, or other natural calamities, which can, and in the days of the Flood actually did, destroy the world (Chapter V).

The other side of the coin was the complementary notion that a central personality, such as a patriarch, a king, or a pious and saintly man, had it in his power to influence the weather and thereby insure the well-being of his people, either directly, through the working of the same laws of sympathy, or indirectly, through the intermediacy of God. Either way, the merit possessed especially by the pious and righteous men was of such force that what they ordained had to come to pass. The culmination of this trend of thought was the idea that the coming of the Messiah would usher in a period of great fertility in the vegetable and animal kingdoms, and an era of peace and general welfare for mankind. Once this type of thinking was achieved, man was assumed to influence nature no longer through ties of magical sympathy, but through a spiritual and moral sympathy in which God served as the supreme catalyst between man and nature (Chapter VI).

I have mentioned that *Man and Temple* was extremely well received by the scholarly community. Laudatory reviews of it appeared in scholarly journals all over the world, but only one of them reached me while I was still in Jerusalem. It was written by Professor S. H. Hooke, the famed founder of the British Myth and Ritual school, which sought to show how pervasive the central rituals of ancient societies were, especially those of the ancient Near East, where they focused on the celebration of the New Year and the place of the king in it, and how inseparable from them was the recital of myths. My *Man and Temple* was grist to the mill of the Myth and Ritual school, and Hooke heaped lavish praise on it in his review, which was published in the August 22, 1947, issue of the *Jewish Chronicle* of London:

> It is very welcome that [Dr. Patai's] valuable work, which has hitherto only been available to those who read modern Hebrew, should now appear in English. . . . Dr. Patai has provided us with what we hope may be only the first of similar studies from his pen for English readers. . . . He discusses in a most interesting and illuminating way the anthropological significance of certain ancient Jewish Temple rites. . . . The special value of the book begins to appear in the 2nd chapter with its most valuable description of the ritual of Water Libation, and its well-documented use of parallels from many sources. . . . The third chapter contains a mass of what will be to many readers new and most interesting material concerning Hebrew and Jewish legends of the Deluge and Creation. . . . There is a valuable chapter on "Symbolism and Function," and one on "Sins and Calamities," both of which illustrate the peculiar way in which the Jewish religious genius transformed myth and legend into stories with symbolic and moral purpose. . . .

Of the many other studies in which I was engaged in those last few years in Jerusalem let me mention only one more because it again struck out into an entirely new territory of research. It was a long paper titled "Hebrew Installation Rites: A Contribution to the Study of Ancient Near Eastern–African Culture Contact" and was published in volume 20 (1947, pp. 143–225) of the *Hebrew Union College Annual.* In it I tried to reconstruct the complex biblical royal installation ritual by adducing features from the royal installation rituals of Sudanese peoples and thus shed light on, and explain, the often obscure references to such rites contained in the Bible. I still remember the difficulties I had in trying to obtain books I needed in order to be able to write this study. Some of the books I found in the private library of Professor Buber, who put them at my disposal with the greatest courtesy, including proofs of a book of his own titled *Das Kommende,* which was partly typeset in Germany in 1937 but could no longer be printed. Another book that was truly indispensable for my study was Professor Melville J. Herskovits's two-volume *Dahomey*, which was published in New York in 1938 and by 1946 was available neither in Palestine nor in America—he kindly lent me his own spare copy and mailed it to me to Jerusalem. In the end I had to resign myself to spend what at the time was an inordinate sum on purchasing books from Probsthain in London. My "Installation Rites" created quite some interest, and even controversy, in scholarly circles and even years later was discussed in a scholarly meeting organized in New York by the Conference on Jewish Social Studies.

Those last years in Jerusalem were a time of intensive work and considerable productivity for me. The bibliography of my published writings, compiled by Gertrude Hirschler and published in the *Fields of Offerings: Studies in Honor of Raphael Patai* (edited by Victor D. Sanua, New York, 1983) lists for the three years 1945–1947 eighty items I published (including fifteen book reviews), of which fifty-eight were in Hebrew, twenty-one in English, and one in German.

But to return once more to *Edoth*, while preparing for publication its April–July 1947 issue, I decided (with the concurrence of Dr. Rivlin) that from that issue on our journal should contain not merely summaries, but full translations in English of the major articles. Accordingly, I inserted an announcement reading:

Announcement for 1947/48
EDOTH
A Quarterly for Folklore and Ethnology Vol. III

In the course of the two years since *EDOTH* first began to appear, many readers and researchers from different countries have expressed their wish to have a full English translation of various articles published in *EDOTH*. In order to comply with these wishes, and to enable also researchers who cannot read Hebrew fully to utilize the studies and articles appearing in our journal, it has been decided to publish *the full English translation of the main articles* in each copy of *EDOTH* as from vol. III, no. 1 (October 1947). Although the size of each issue will thus be greatly increased, the subscription fee remains unchanged, abroad $6.00 or £1/8/- per annum.

As it happened, only one volume of *Edoth* appeared after this announcement, and its size was only modestly increased: instead of the 320 pages contained in the second volume, it had 372 pages, of which 226 were in Hebrew and 146 in English.

The last issue of *Edoth* (vol. 3, nos. 3–4) was published in the summer of 1948. Before I left for America in October 1947 I asked my friends Saul Angel and Colin Malamet to see that issue through the press. Into it, under the column "News of the Institute," Saul Angel inserted a brief note (in Hebrew):

To Our Honored Readers

With the publication of this issue of *Edoth*, I consider it my duty to ask forgiveness from our readers for errors, if such have remained in the texts.

In this time of emergency, in the midst of unceasing bombings, disruption of the services, and mortal danger, the workers and the management of the Azriel Printing Works put their heart and soul into efforts to bring the printing of *Edoth* to a conclusion, for which the editors are grateful to them.

In the absence of Dr. Raphael Patai, who is at present in America on a mission in behalf of the Institute, I was entrusted with bringing the articles to the press, to correct and proofread them, and I did it with the best of my ability. Dr. J. J. Rivlin, a member of the editorial board, went over the last proofs.

Shavu'ot Eve, 5708, in the days of the siege of Jerusalem

Saul Angel

This brief note was also the epitaph of *Edoth*.

But let me go back to other activities I carried out under the aegis of the Institute in the last two years prior to my departure for America. In 1946 I lectured in several places in Palestine, always with one purpose in mind: to awaken interest in Jewish folklore and ethnology and to obtain support for their study. One of the few appearances of which documentation survived in my files was an interview I gave over the Jerusalem radio. My interviewer was Mr. Turoblin of the Hebrew Academic Departure of the radio, and the subject was, of course, the work of the Palestine Institute of Folklore and Ethnology. The typescript of the interview I still have in my possession allows an insight into the manner such interviews were handled at the time. The typescript makes it clear that I had to prepare in advance, in writing, the whole interview, including Turoblin's introductory statement and the questions he asked. This meant some work for me, but it had the advantage that I could put precisely those questions in his mouth that gave me the opening to tell whatever I wanted about the work of the Institute. As a result that interview gives a complete picture of the work the Institute had accomplished by that time and the plans it had (or, rather, I had) for the future. The last question I had prepared for Turoblin was "What are your plans for the future?" I answered:

> We plan to open a course of instruction for the training of young researchers in collecting material, and then to award research-fellowships for the study of Jewish folk-life, etc. We have established a ranking order of urgency in our activities, and the first place in it is occupied by the collecting of material. Jewish folk-life is disappearing in all the Jewish communities. The Nazi Holocaust and the war on the one hand and the proclivity to assimilation on the other already have destroyed, and continue to destroy, much of the specific aspect of our communities. In this manner priceless treasures of Jewish folk-life are becoming forgotten, and every day that we don't use for noting them down and collecting

represents an irrevocable loss. Therefore, if I want to sum up in a short sentence the basic purpose of our Institute, I will say that it is the saving of Jewish folk-life.

Also in 1946 I launched a Hebrew book series titled "Studies in Folklore and Ethnology," of which again Dr. Rivlin was my nominal co-editor. All in all five volumes were published in this series. The first, published in 1946, was a scholarly annotated edition of the old Hebrew and Arabic manuscripts of the medieval Jewish folk-novel *Ma'ase Y'rushalmi* (The Story of the Jerusalemite), attributed to Abraham ben Maimon, the son of Maimonides. It was a fine example of cooperation among no less than seven scholars: I wrote the preface and added numerous notes to the body of the book, which consisted of an annotated edition by Rabbi J. L. Zlotnick of two Hebrew manuscripts of the story, one of which he himself owned. That was followed by the Arabic version of the story, edited and annotated by Nehemia Alloni, and checked and commented upon by Dr. Joseph J. Rivlin and Mr. L. Kopf. Professor Simha Assaf added a special note on the question of "suspension of prayers" that plays an important role in the story. Dr. Max Grunwald gave several possible explanations of the puzzling name "Dihon," the name of the hero of the story. I could not refrain from stating in the preface:

> The study of folklore, pursued among the peoples of Europe and America for a hundred years, and recognized by them as a scholarly subject of no less importance than others in the humanities, has yet to attain similar recognition from Jewish scholarship. Among all the Jewish institutions of higher learning, whether in Palestine or abroad, not one has included among its offerings the field of Jewish folklore, or its sister-science, Jewish ethnology. It was in order to fill this vacuum that we founded the Palestine Institute of Folklore and Ethnology, and the present book, which is the first in the series of our publications and which shows that research methods and viewpoints developed in the study of other peoples' folklore can be applied to Jewish folklore as well, will be, we hope, a further step in the penetration of the recognition that the scholarly study of the folk-life of our people in its communities and tribes must take its place side by side with the study of its history, literature, and other aspects of its spiritual and material existence.

The second volume in the series was the late Dr. Erich Brauer's *The Jews of Kurdistan: An Ethnological Study*, which I completed and translated into Hebrew. This was the first ethnological monograph of any Jewish community to be published in Hebrew. Its English original has remained unpublished to this day.

The third and fourth volumes were my own *The Science of Man: An Introduction to Anthropology* (published in 1947–1948 by Yavneh Publishing House for the Palestine Institute of Folklore and Ethnology). This book, incidentally, remains to this day the only introduction to anthropology in Hebrew.

The fifth and last was Dr. Michael Ish-Shalom's *Holy Tombs: A Study of Traditions concerning Holy Tombs in Palestine.* It was published jointly by our Institute and the Rabbi Kook Foundation, in 1948.

In 1947 I launched yet another series, titled "Social Studies," under the joint editorship of Professor Roberto Bachi, the demographer of the Hebrew University, and myself. Two volumes were published, both with prefaces by Bachi: one by Sarah Bergner-Rabinowitz on *Hygiene, Education and Nutrition among Kurdish, Persian, and Ashkenazi Jews in Jerusalem* (published in 1948 with the support of an award from the Bank Quppat 'Am); the second in 1949 by Abraham A. Weinberg, M.D., titled *Psychosociology of the Immigrant.* By the time this book was processed through the press I was in America, but despite my very busy schedule in my new environment I read and corrected the manuscript. This was to be the first and last publication of our Institute under its new name, the Israel Institute of Folklore and Ethnology.

My three years of editorship of *Edoth* and of the two book series brought me many useful and important new experiences. First of all, my scholarly interest expanded from being focused on ancient Jewish (biblical and talmudic) folklore, folk religion, and folk culture, to the more timely provinces of the folklore and the ethnology of the nineteenth- and twentieth-century Jewish communities, as well as of Arab Palestine and the Muslim world in general. In the October 1946–January 1947 issue of *Edoth* I published a study titled "On Culture Contact and Its Working in Modern Palestine," which dealt with the mutual influences Arab and Jewish cultures exerted on each other in the country and analyzed them in the light of modern anthropological theories of acculturation. At the time I prepared its English summary for *Edoth* Naomi and I were not sufficiently at home in English to recognize that the proper phrasing in English of the Hebrew title of the paper was "On Culture Contact" and not "To Culture Contact" as we put it. I remember that I presented a copy of that issue to Dr. Magnes, and when he saw that faulty title he pointed out to me, with some irritation, that it was wrong and told me how it should have been phrased. Subsequently I translated the study into English and mailed it to Dr. J. Alden Mason, editor of the Memoir Series of the American Anthropological Association (of which I was by that time a member), who promptly published it in October 1947, as no. 67 of the titles in the series. Needless to say, I had corrected the title. When Professor Melville J. Herskovits, one of the leading American anthropologists, read the paper, he was so impressed by it that he quoted it *in extenso* in his *Man and His Works,* one of the finest introductions to anthropology, published in 1948 by Knopf in New York. He summarized my findings and used them as examples validating his theory of cultural focus and reinterpretation.

The editorship of *Edoth* also gave me the opportunity to get in touch with folklorists and anthropologists in the Western world and to learn what was going on in these fields, especially in America, England, and Scandinavia. From the first issue on I introduced a section devoted to book reviews, and as a result I began to receive many books from both Palestine and abroad, most of which I reviewed myself. Thus, I established contacts with the scholarly world, with the result that when I arrived in America, in the fall of 1947, I found there a friendly reception by quite a number of scholars who knew about my work.

The reception of *Edoth* was without exception very favorable both inside and outside Palestine. As early as in the second issue I started a column entitled "News of the Institute," in which I quoted comments I received on the first issue. Among those who wrote congratulatory notes was Stephen S. Wise, president of the Jewish Institute of Religion in New York, who characterized *Edoth* as "the only Jewish quarterly of its kind in the world" and informed me that several scholars had expressed their intention to send contributions to it. Professor Salo W. Baron (of Columbia University), Professor A. Marmorstein (of the London Jews' College), Professor Erminie W. Voegelin (editor of the *Journal of American Folklore*), Professor Melville J. Herskovits (of Northwestern University), Professor Leslie Spier (editor of the *Southwestern Journal of Anthropology*), Professor Robert H. Lowie (of the University of California), Dr. Abraham A. Neuman (president of Dropsie College), Professor R. S. Boggs (editor of *Folklore Americas*), Professor J. Alden Mason (editor of the *American Anthropologist*), and many other scholars from Europe, Africa (both North and South), and Australia also sent me expressions of welcome.

At the same time I tried to make the most of what little work had been done up to that time in Palestine in the various fields of anthropology in my response to a request I received from the chairman of the Committee on International Cooperation in Anthropology of the National Research Council of the United States to furnish him with a report on Anthropology in Palestine during World War II. I prepared the report with the help of the archaeologist Professor Eliezer L. Sukenik, the musicologist Dr. Edith Gerson-Kiwi, and others, and it was subsequently published by Professor Herskovits as part of his annual report on anthropology in the July–September 1946 issue of the *American Anthropologist*. I, for my part, translated into Hebrew and published in *Edoth* the reports on anthropology in 1943, 1944, and 1945, which I received from Herskovits, which for the first time gave Palestinian Jewish scholars an idea of the extent of the work done in this field all over the world. Thus, while living in Palestine, where the only university of the country would not recognize either folklore or anthropology as academic disciplines that had their places among the departments or course offerings, I nevertheless became the spokesman of these fields of scholarship and their connecting link between Palestine and the "great world."

While *Edoth* and the Institute existed, dozens of Palestinian Jewish scholars became associated with them either actively, by contributing articles, or at least nominally, by having their names listed among the members of the governing bodies. Many of them were men of renown in various fields of scholarly endeavor, who taught at the Hebrew University or were recognized as scholars and researchers. Thus, I believe that even though the seeds I sowed took many years to germinate in the form of the incorporation of Jewish folklore and anthropology into the academic framework of the Israeli institutions of higher learning the work I invested into *Edoth* and the Institute had a historical role in preparing the ground for that development. In addition, *Edoth* was the only forum in Palestine in which young scholars interested in the subjects to which it was dedicated could publish their early, and in some case their first, articles. Several of them subsequently went on to distinguished academic careers in Israel and abroad. The three volumes of *Edoth*, published from October 1945 to April–July 1948, contain (as a glance at their tables of contents shows) a variety of valuable articles, delineate the areas of research in Jewish folklore and ethnology, and constitute a pioneering effort in a formerly neglected field of study.

As can be seen from the foregoing account, in the three years from 1944 to 1947 my attention was focused on my own folkloristic-anthropological research on the one hand and on managing the affairs of the Palestine Institute of Folklore and Ethnology on the other. This did not mean, however, that I had given up hope to be appointed to the faculty of the Hebrew University in a teaching capacity. In the last few weeks of 1946 I learned that the university was planning to set up a department of social sciences. I felt that this was the opportune moment to push for the introduction of anthropology (or ethnology—we were not very strict about terminology) as one of the fields to be taught within that department and immediately sat down and composed a memorandum to Dr. Magnes on "the place of anthropology in university offerings in the social sciences." I did not refer to my desire to be appointed as an instructor of the subject but confined myself to discussing the issue in general terms. I handed the memorandum to the secretary of Dr. Magnes on December 22. In its first part I stated:

> The purpose of this memorandum is to call the attention of the academic and administrative authorities of the Hebrew University to the necessity of introducing instruction in anthropology at the very outset of instructional activity in the department of social sciences. I shall first devote a few words to the place of anthropology in the structure of instruction in the social sciences in the universities of the English-speaking world.

The universities whose anthropology offerings I discussed were Harvard, Columbia, Northwestern, and Pennsylvania in the United States and London and Oxford in England. I concluded with concrete suggestions:

> The conclusion from the foregoing is self-evident: anthropology is a subject of study equal in value to the other subjects comprised in the social sciences. In the universities discussed anthropology constitutes one of the important and basic disciplines in the departments of social sciences. When the Hebrew University is about to organize a department of social sciences, it must also include in the program of that department anthropology if it wishes the course offerings in the new department to be complete from the methodological point of view and not be inferior in value and level to the program of instruction offered in parallel departments of other universities.
>
> The same holds good with regard to the course offerings that are represented only in the Hebrew University among all institutions of higher learning in the world: Jewish sociology. Methodical instruction in Jewish sociology demands courses in *Jewish ethnology* both as a preparation for it and as a complementary offering.
>
> Since the purpose of this memorandum is only to induce the university authorities to consider in principle the inclusion of ethnology in the department of social sciences, this is not the place for practical and concrete suggestions concerning the organization of the courses themselves. I want to remark only in general terms that the anthropological studies can be introduced gradually. As a beginning it should be possible to offer only an introductory course in anthropology, of one or two hours weekly, and a similar introductory course in Jewish ethnology.

Three days later Dr. Magnes's secretary informed me that he wanted to see me the following day. In the course of the interview Dr. Magnes expressed serious interest in my ideas and asked me whether I had received any information from Professor Robert H. Lowie, the famous anthropologist of the University of California at Berkeley, with whose work Magnes was acquainted. I had not at that point, but was able to tell Magnes that I had written to Lowie and hoped to get a reply from him soon. When I returned home from the university that day I found a letter from Lowie waiting for me, and a few days later I also received the bulletin of the University of California from him. On January 6, 1947, I forwarded Lowie's letter and the bulletin to Dr. Magnes and summarized for him the information they contained: that anthropology was a part of the social sciences at the University of California, that in addition to Lowie himself (who was the chairman of the Department of Anthropology) ten other professors taught in that department, and that anthropology was both a separate field of study and a preparatory subject for those students who majored in sociology. I sent a copy of my letter to Professor Buber and also a copy of my December 22, 1946, memorandum as suggested by Magnes. On that occasion I reiterated my request to Buber that he present my memorandum to the competent academic bodies of the university so that a discussion in principle could take place on the inclusion of anthropology in the program of the social science department.

I have no record or recollection of what response if any was given by the university to my memorandum. However, I do remember that, when the department of social sciences was organized, anthropology was not included. It is a matter of record that some fifteen or twenty years passed before the first course in "social anthropology" was offered by the Hebrew University.

The Viking Fund Fellowship

My move from Jerusalem to New York came about entirely fortuitously. I never planned to leave Palestine. I remember that after I got my doctorate from the Hebrew University Dr. Magnes suggested to me that I take a rabbinical post in Hungary, where, he said, I would be in a position to do a lot for Zionism and the Land of Israel. My response was that there was somewhere in the Talmud a saying to the effect that it was better to live in the deserts of the Land of Israel than in palaces abroad and that I considered that the leitmotif of my life. But the force of destiny willed it otherwise.

After the end of the 1947 spring term Professor Michael Fekete, at the time rector of the university, left for a visit to America. He was of Hungarian origin, had accepted the invitation of the Hebrew University in 1928 to be lecturer in mathematics after my father advised him to do so, and was soon thereafter raised to the rank of professor. Since I am totally ignorant in mathematics I cannot even try to understand the significance of Fekete's contributions to the theory of numbers and theory of functions and his discovery of the transfinite diameter listed in the *Encyclopaedia Judaica* as his major achievements. What I do remember very clearly is that throughout my Jerusalem years Fekete was one of the most friendly people I knew and that I occasionally visited his home in Rehavia, where his niece kept house for him. He was a small, slightly built man with a sensitive face and the long hair that was in those days greatly favored by violinists and mathematicians.

Upon his return from his visit to America Fekete asked me to come to see him. He told me that while he was in New York he met a fellow-Hungarian, Dr. Paul Fejos, who was director of research of the Viking Fund, a foundation for anthropological research. (It later changed its name to Wenner-Gren Foundation for Anthropological Research.) Dr. Fejos asked him whether there was in Palestine a young anthropologist who would be interested in coming for a year to the United States on a Viking Fund fellowship. Fekete instantly responded that indeed there was and gave him my name. Dr. Fejos thereupon asked him to tell me about the Viking Fund and to suggest to me that if I was interested I should submit to him an application. He added that the emolument offered by the fellowship would be $2,500.

Needless to say, I was more than delighted with the opportunity to go to America, at the time the undisputed center of anthropological research, with several of whose most outstanding representatives I had shortly before established contact through *Edoth*. Nor could I be indifferent to the stipend, which appeared to me a lavish sum. The fellowship I had from the Hebrew University yielded, as I mentioned earlier, 25 pounds a month, corresponding to $75, and now I had a chance to get—I made a quick calculation— the equivalent of some 66 pounds a month!

I sent off my application without delay and *mirabile dictu!* late in July received a letter, dated July 18, 1947, from Dr. Fejos, in which he informed me that my application had been approved and that I could come to New York as soon as convenient.

After taking care of the visa formalities—to get a visitor's visa to the United States was in itself considered a major achievement in those days—I booked passage on the liner *Rossia*, which, I was told, the Russians had acquired from Germany as part of the war damages. In keeping with my new status as a well-endowed Fellow of an American research institution, I took a second-class berth. There was some delay in the sailing date of the ship, but finally it did arrive from Odessa in Haifa on October 5 and was to leave the same day for New York, with several stops on the way. The whole voyage from Haifa to New York was to take two weeks.

On the way from Jerusalem to Haifa I stopped over in Shekhunat Boruchov to say good-bye to my parents, who were greatly gratified at what they considered my first scholarly recognition from overseas. In Haifa, two days before boarding the ship, I had to get a bubonic plague and smallpox vaccination, as required by the American immigration authorities. I also met my friend Colin Malamet there and had a long conference with him about what to do about the various unfinished businesses of the Palestine Institute of Folklore and Ethnology, especially the printing of the next issue of *Edoth*, which was due to be published in the spring of 1948. I told him I would send him from New York material to fill a double issue, and Colin volunteered his help in seeing the issue through the press in collaboration with Saul Angel and taking care of the other affairs of the Institute. His friendship and help, and those of Saul Angel, were of the greatest value for me and made me feel that the work of the Institute I had built up in the preceding three years would continue during my absence in America.

As I stood on the deck of the *Rossia* and watched the outline of Mount Carmel recede in the background, I remembered the moment, almost fifteen years earlier, when I stood on the deck of the *Vulcania* and watched the same mountain range loom up as the ship approached the shore. Although I did not know at the time that I would remain in America for the rest of my life, I had the feeling that an important chapter in my life was closing and that the years of my being a journeyman in Jerusalem had come to an end.

Raphael Patai

Books by Raphael Patai

Shire Yisrael Berekhya Fontanella (in Hebrew: *The Poems of Yisrael Berekhya Fontanella*)

HaMayim (in Hebrew: *Water: A Study in Palestinology and Palestinian Folklore*)

HaSappanut ha'Ivrith bIme Qedem (in Hebrew: *Jewish Seafaring in Ancient Times*)

Adam vaAdama (2 vols., in Hebrew: *Man and Earth in Hebrew Custom, Belief, and Legend*)

Mada' ha Adam (2 vols., in Hebrew: *The Science of Man: An Introduction to Anthropology*)

On Culture Contact and Its Working in Modern Palestine

Israel between East and West: A Study in Human Relations (2 editions)

Syria, Lebanon and Jordan: An Annotated Bibliography

The Kingdom of Jordan

Current Jewish Social Research: A Bibliography

Cultures in Conflict (2 editions)

Sex and Family in the Bible and the Middle East

Golden River to Golden Road: Society, Culture and Change in the Middle East (3 editions)

Hebrew Myths (with Robert Graves)

Society, Culture and Change in the Middle East

Tents of Jacob: The Diaspora Yesterday and Today

The Hebrew Goddess (3 editions)

Myth and Modern Man

The Arab Mind (2 editions)

The Myth of the Jewish Race (with Jennifer Patai, 2 editions)

The Messiah Texts

Gates to the Old City

The Vanished Worlds of Jewry

On Jewish Folklore

The Seed of Abraham: Jews and Arabs in Contact and Conflict

Ignaz Goldziher and His Oriental Diary
Nahum Goldmann: His Missions to the Gentiles
Apprentice in Budapest: Memories of a World That Is No More
Robert Graves and the Hebrew Myths
Between Budapest and Jerusalem: The Patai Letters, 1933–1938

Works Edited by Raphael Patai

Mivhar haSippur haArtziYisr'eli (2 vols., with Zvi Wohlmut, in Hebrew: *Anthology of Palestinian Short Stories*, 5 editions)

Edoth (Communities): A Quarterly for Folklore and Ethnology (3 vols., with Joseph J. Rivlin, in Hebrew and English)

Sifriya l'Folqlor v'Etnologia (5 vols., with Joseph J. Rivlin, in Hebrew: *Studies in Folklore and Ethnology*)

Mehqarim Hevrutiyyim (2 vols., with Roberto Bachi, in Hebrew and English: *Jewish Social Studies*)

Erich Brauer's The Jews of Kurdistan (in Hebrew; translated and completed by R. P.)

The Hashemite Kingdom of Jordan

The Republic of Syria (2 vols.)

The Republic of Lebanon (2 vols.)

Herzl Year Book (7 vols.)

The Complete Diaries of Theodor Herzl (5 vols.)

Angelo S. Rappoport's Myth and Legend of Ancient Israel (3 vols.)

Women in the Modern World

Encyclopaedia of Zionism and Israel (2 vols.)

Index

Abbreviations: JP - Joseph Patai; R. - Rabbi; RP - Raphael Patai.
Arabic names beginning with the article *al-* are listed under the letter following it.